Anonymous

The World's Columbian Catholic Congresses and Educational Exhibit

Containing two Volumes in one

Anonymous

The World's Columbian Catholic Congresses and Educational Exhibit
Containing two Volumes in one

ISBN/EAN: 9783744653343

Printed in Europe, USA, Canada, Australia, Japan

Cover: Foto ©ninafisch / pixelio.de

More available books at **www.hansebooks.com**

Most Holy Father
LEO XIII.

...THE...

World's Columbian Catholic Congresses

AND

EDUCATIONAL EXHIBIT

Containing Two Volumes in One

EMBRACING

Official Proceedings of all the Chicago Catholic Congresses of 1893, giving in full the Addresses delivered by Monsignor Satolli, Apostolic Delegate; His Eminence, Cardinal Gibbons; Archbishop Ireland; Archbishop Corrigan; Archbishop Redwood of New Zealand; Bishop Keane of the Catholic University, Washington, D. C.; Monsignor Nugent of Liverpool; Reverend P. J. Muldoon, and Honorable C. C. Bonney of Chicago;

Catholic Education Day at.... World's Columbian Exposition

WITH

Addresses by Most Reverend P. A. Feehan; Most Reverend John J. Hennessy; Most Reverend P. J. Ryan; Right Reverend J. L. Spalding, D. D.; Brother Maurelian, F. S. C.; Honorable Morgan J. O'Brien of New York; Honorable Thos. J. Gargan of Boston, and others.

Embellished with Numerous Engravings.

Published with the approbation of His Grace The Most Reverend Archbishop of Chicago. Preface by Rev. P. J. Muldoon.

CHICAGO:
J. S. HYLAND & COMPANY.

IMPRIMATUR:

✠ Patrick A. Feehan,
Archbishop of Chicago.

Copyright, 1893, by
J. S. HYLAND & CO.

ROKKER-O'DONNELL PRINTING CO.,
PRINTERS AND BINDERS,
CHICAGO.

PREFACE...

THE period of the World's Columbian Exposition has been one of pleasure and education. Shortly, according to present indications, not only the exhibits will be returned, but also the magnificent palaces on the shore of the great lake will be destroyed. Those who have enjoyed the privilege of a visit to the wonders of Jackson Park will bear with them a life-long blessing. The millions of our countrymen who have been unable to avail themselves of this great educational exhibition must enrich themselves by such printed accounts as American enterprise may place within their reach.

In the name of these many millions we hail with gratitude, not only the volumes descriptive of the Fair in its exhibits, its architecture, and its landscape features, but also the works bearing upon the congresses, and special days at the Fair, for these latter contain the ripest erudition of the Old and New World.

The present volume has the worthy aim of giving a wider audience to the Catholic Congress held during the past summer, and of affording sound instruction on that most important subject, Catholic education, through the speeches of Education Day. The guides upon mountains have spoken wisely and well, but save through the instrumentality of such a volume how narrow the audience!

The various congresses were watched with interest, attended in large numbers, and reported in a princely manner, but none received such marked attention from people and press as the Catholic Congress. From the opening prayer to the last word of the strong resolutions, the halls were filled, and seeds were sown that no doubt will one day bear rich fruit. Notwithstanding all this, a feeling of sadness steals in the heart, when we consider that the congress convenes after many trials, difficulties, and expense; listens (without discussion) to admirable papers, and adjourns, trusting to the enterprise of publishers to continue the work of the congress by placing the essays before the people. In its sessions, all is vitality, but after adjournment, there is no organization to spread abroad that vitality and render practical the suggestions that have been wisely made in various channels of charity and education. We reflect, how justly we leave others to decide, would it not be practical and extremely beneficial to have as an adjunct of every such congress a permanent committee or organization to nurture the good seeds, and make daily more manifest the glory of the spouse of Christ in her charity, strength, intelligence, organization, and unity.

This volume will, in a small way, supply such a need, hence we most affectionately wish it a godspeed on its apostolate, for if God blesses good books, how fruitful must be the benediction bestowed upon a work avowedly Catholic.

Besides the work of the Catholic Congress, this volume presents the admirable speeches on Catholic education delivered in Festival Hall on Catholic Education Day. The educational question is one of the questions of the day. It can not be thrust aside. There is a necessity for sound doctrine on this important topic. In these speeches the Catholic will more clearly understand the true reason for the Catholic school, and non-Catholic will readily perceive that conscience and not bigotry prompts Catholic parents, who value the souls of their children above their bodies, to eagerly make every sacrifice to enrich their offspring with the choicest of legacies, the faith of Jesus Christ. After perusing these strong and sound speeches, Catholics will more cheerfully bear the double burden, and the opponents may pause and question, " Well, after all, is not the position of the Catholic Church logical ?" To Catholics and dissenters these burning words must have more than transient effect.

The Columbian Exposition gloriously surpassed all former efforts in the same line, and unmistakably the Catholic Church never worked so energetically or displayed herself so conspicuously to engage the respect, admiration, and love of the world as in this Exposition. All classes and creeds, some in praise, others in criticism, announced that the Catholic Church had caught every inspiration, and had taken advantage of every opportunity. We feel that this was nowhere more conspicuously patent than in the Catholic Educational Exhibit. Catholics visited the section, and beheld in astonishment the abundance, variety, and general perfection of the exhibit. They departed proud that they were of the fold, and silently promised to be more generous in the future in aid of the good cause. Non-Catholics found their way to the Catholic exhibit, and some willingly, others spitefully, pronounced it a revelation, a lesson, and a herculean task wonderfully well accomplished. The Catholic educational display has advanced among Catholics at one bold stroke the cause of Catholic education a quarter of a century, and among non-Catholics it has undoubtedly dissipated prejudices that in the usual flow of events would not have been obliterated in fifty years.

PREFACE.

Listen to the statement of the *Popular Educator*, published in New York. "The parochial-school system has scored a point at the Fair, giving much good reason for the erasure of the past criticism that parochial schools teach sewing and catechism., Sewing and beautiful embroideries and water-color drawings are there, to be sure, making the aisle rich with tints, but there is also plenty of good work in the line and apparently according to the methods of the public schools." (Nov., 1893.)

The Chicago Herald of June 5, 1893, says: "In the southeastern section of the Manufactures Building, on the gallery floor, is an exhibit which should attract the attention and excite the admiration of all good people, be they Presbyterians, Methodists, Baptists, or the people who are responsible for the show. The Catholic Educational Exhibit is the feature referred to. It is not intended as a religious propaganda; it is simply a material exposition of what the people of one great faith can do in the way of promoting humanity and the world's progress. All together, when fully installed, the Catholic Educational Exhibit will be one of the most interesting features of the great Fair." We might quote indefinitely from non-Catholic sources the highest encomiums passed upon the exhibit, but we refrain, and beg to place before you the kind and strong commendation of Dr. Selim H. Peabody, the Chief of the Liberal Arts Department. From his official capacity and his intimate knowledge with the various exhibits in his department, his judgment implies far more than that of any other.

In his speech of reception of the exhibit from Right Rev. John L. Spalding, D. D., as president of the Catholic Exhibit, Dr. Peabody was frank and generous to state that he considered the Catholic Educational Exhibit not only one of the choicest of his department, and a revelation to the American public, but also one of the great features of the Exposition. At another date, in response to Most Rev. P. A. Feehan, D. D., who presented the Educational Exhibit of the Archdiocese of Chicago, he said: "It affords me much pleasure to be present to-day, as I stand before you, the Chief of the Liberal Arts Department, to receive in the name of the great Columbian Exposition the Chicago Educational Exhibit. None save those who have labored in this field can value the vast amount of labor of such an exhibit, and one so neat, and so tastefully arranged. Without flattery, I can honestly say and feel that the compliment is justly given that the Chicago Exhibit is the gem of my department. We may have different views in school policy, still I feel that all true educators will be greatly benefited by our entire Educational Exhibit. You may see what we are accomplishing and we may examine the result of your school system. The result of such intercourse in the Exposition will be a broader conception of education and a larger love for all who are tending to one end, namely, to make our youth holier, truer scholars, and better citizens."

PREFACE.

We feel it incumbent upon us to record the written testimony of the Apostolic Delegate, Most Rev. Francis Satolli, D.D., made after a careful scrutiny of the exhibit. It is as follows: "I admire the evidences of good methods of teaching in so many branches of instruction, but most particularly do I admire the perfection of all the work exhibited. I regard the Catholic Educational Exhibit as the glory of the church and Catholic institutions. The whole American country will appreciate it."

These encomiums from such eminent educators crown the Catholic Educational Exhibit with laurels that years will render more beautiful and significant. The year 1893 will be the turning point in educational life. The difficulties of the past for Catholics have been many and severe. Thank God, as the country has prospered, we, one-sixth of its population, have shared in its prosperity, and our opportunities were never better, or our difficulties fewer than at present, and hence we may consistently hold fast to the safe-teaching "Catholic education for Catholic children." Since we have accomplished so much in our infancy and with limited means, may we not justly cherish brighter hopes for our Catholic schools in the near future, even if totally deprived of state aid, justly ours but unjustly withheld? We consider that such hopes are well founded, because our people are richer and better educated, our churches at least partly built, and our schools throughout the country partially in operation. Let us then cherish the fond hope that no very distant day will behold free Catholic schools, thoroughly and consistently Catholic, open to every Catholic child in America. It will be accomplished though, only through the faith that prompts to works. That faith which teaches the wealthy to give generously of their abundance, and inspires the poor to make sacrifices to put their children within the influence of the best of all knowledge, the knowledge of God.

We trust that this volume may aid in the movement to render our schools more numerous and more finished, by imparting the true meaning of education to those who should assist in the good work.

CHICAGO, November 16, 1893.

P. J. MULDOON,
Holy Name Cathedral.

"THE WORLD'S COLUMBIAN CATHOLIC CONGRESSES."

LETTERS OF COMMENDATION.

CATHOLIC UNIVERSITY, WASHINGTON, D. C.

Messrs. J. S. Hyland & Co.
DEAR SIRS: Allow me to express my thanks for the copy of the "Catholic Congress" edition of the "Columbian Jubilee" you so kindly sent me. As you have received so many other congratulatory letters from so many distinguished prelates, I can do nothing better than to adopt their sentiments, and, in conclusion, express my deep appreciation for your work, and my sincere hope for its deserving success.

Believe me, yours truly,

FRANCIS ARCHBISHOP SATOLLI, Delegate Apostolic.

Messrs. J. S. Hyland & Co.
GENTLEMEN: In compliance with your request, I have this day dictated to a stenographer my address made at the Columbian Catholic Congress recently held in Chicago, and have expunged redundance from the proof submitted by you. Please send me a copy of the new edition of the "World's Columbian Catholic Congresses," and oblige,

Yours respectfully,

M. A. CORRIGAN, Archbishop of New York.

Messrs. J. S. Hyland & Co.
DEAR SIRS: I herewith acknowledge receipt of your favor of December 12th with volume, "The World's Columbian Catholic Congresses," as a contribution to the Columbian Library of Catholic Authors. This volume, containing the addresses of the Catholic Congress, and of Catholic Education Day, as well as other very interesting matter, is worthy a place in every library, educational institution, and intelligent family in the country. It will undoubtedly receive the patronage that such a rare literary production deserves. I remain,

Very sincerely yours,

BROTHER MAURELIAN, Sec. and Man. Catholic Educational Exhibit.

Messrs. J. S. Hyland & Co.
GENTLEMEN: I am in receipt of the beautifully illustrated book, "The World's Columbian Catholic Congresses." The work is so timely and instructive, attractive in style, and admirable in arrangement and appearance, that I would prove my appreciation of your quadri-centennial enterprise, by requesting that you also send me the "Columbian Jubilee."

REV. JOHN F. HYLAND, Ilion, New York.

DE LA SALLE INSTITUTE, CHICAGO.

Messrs. J. S. Hyland & Co.
DEAR SIRS: Accept my sincere thanks for the elegant volume containing the papers of the Catholic Congress you so kindly sent me. I trust a copy will be found in every family. The importance of the matter it contains gives it a claim to be in every Catholic household.

Very sincerely yours,

BROTHER AMBROSE.

Messrs. J. S. Hyland & Co.
MY DEAR SIRS: The very interesting and valuable work entitled, "The World's Columbian Catholic Congresses," came safely to hand. From a cursory view of the work I am convinced that you have succeeded in producing a book written in an elegance worthy of its great subject.

Yours truly in Christ,

WM. H. GROSS, Archbishop of Oregon.

Messrs. J. S. Hyland & Co.
GENTLEMEN: I beg to acknowledge the receipt of your new publication, "The World's Columbian Catholic Congresses," and tender you my thanks for the beautiful work.

WM. H. ELDER, Archbishop of Cincinnati.

AMERICAN COLLEGE,
ROME.

Messrs. J. S. *Hyland & Co.,*
　　　　Chicago, Ill., U. S.

DEAR SIRS:—I beg to return you my sincere thanks for the beautiful volume you sent me of the "World's Columbian Catholic Congress," and at the same time to offer you well-merited congratulations on the handsome contribution you have thereby made to Catholic literature in America.

I had also the honor of placing in the hands of the Holy Father, the rich copy you destined for him, and I know that you will learn with pleasure that His Holiness accepted your offering with great satisfaction, and bade me write you to say that he sends you a special blessing.

With sentiments of great regard and best wishes for your success, I remain,

Very Sincerely yours,

D. J. O'Connell,
　　　　Rector.

Catholic University of America,
WASHINGTON, D. C.

Messrs. J. S. *Hyland & Co.,*
　　　　Chicago, Ill.

GENTLEMEN:—I return thanks for the beautiful copy of "The World's Columbian Catholic Congresses" which you so kindly sent me.

You have done good service to religion by publishing so creditable an exhibit of this most noteworthy Catholic assemblage.

Very truly yours,

John J. Keane,
　　　　Rector.

THE WORLD'S CONGRESS AUXILIARY

OF THE

WORLD'S COLUMBIAN EXPOSITION

▰CHICAGO 1893.

GENERAL OFFICERS:
President—Charles C. Bonney.
Vice-President—Thomas B. Bryan.
Treasurer—Lyman J. Gage
Secretaries— { Benj. Butterworth.
{ Clarence E. Young.

Chicago, June 8, 1894.

MESSRS. J. S. HYLAND & Co., Publishers, Etc.,
  323 Dearborn Street, City.

Gentlemen:

I have examined with much interest the large and handsome volume recently issued from the press under the title of "The World's Columbian Catholic Congresses and Educational Exhibit," with the Imprimatur of the Most Rev. Archbishop Feehan, and a preface by the Rev. P. J. Muldoon, Chancellor of the Archdiocese of Chicago. You have by this publication rendered an important service, not only to the Catholic Church, but to the general American public which manifested so deep an interest in the proceedings of the Catholic Congress. You have thus made easily accessible the addresses delivered and the papers read before the Congress, many of which were characterized by remarkable eloquence, liberality and learning It is universally admitted that the Catholic Congress held at Chicago last year, was one of the most important and commanding of the great series of World's Congresses which will make the year 1893 illustrious in human history.

Containing as it does the very Cream of Catholic thought it will be of even greater interest to the Protestant public than to Catholics, for it will show to the former the hardships and persecutions through which the Catholic Church of America has come into the perfect, civil and religious liberty which is now enjoyed under the Constitution of the United States, alike by Catholic and Protestant, by Jew and Gentile.

The full account of the Catholic Educational Exhibit at the World's Columbian Exposition, adds much to the interest and completeness of the work.

Wishing you a large and satisfactory circulation of your publication, I am, with much respect,

  Very sincerely yours,

  Charles C. Bonney,

  President of World's Congresses, 1893.

CONTENTS

FIRST VOLUME.

The World's Columbian Catholic Congresses.

FIRST DAY'S PROCEEDINGS.
Opening of the Congress.
Rev. P. J. Muldoon's Welcome.
Archbishop Feehan's Welcome.
Hon. C. C. Bonney's Address.
Address by Cardinal Gibbons.
Greeting from Pope Leo.
Chairman O'Brien's Address.
Archbishop Redwood's Address. (New Zealand).
Message from Cardinal Vaughan.
Paper by Dr. R. A. Clark, LL. D.
Paper by Miss Mary J. Onahan.
Paper by Mr. E. H. Gans.
Archbishop Ryan's Address. 41

SECOND DAY.
List of Delegates.
Bishop Watterson's Address.
Monsignor Satolli's Address.
Paper by E. O. Brown, Chicago.
Paper by John Gibbons, LL. D.
George Parson Lathrop's Address. 66

THIRD DAY.
Archbishop Corrigan's Address.
Woman's Good Work.
Archbishop Ireland's Address.
Rev. Patrick Cronin's Address.
Paper by Rev. James M. Cleary. 78

FOURTH DAY.
Bishop Burke's Address.
Paper by Eliza Allen Starr.
Paper by Eleanor C. Donnelly.
Work of St. Vincent De Paul.
Bishop McGoldrick's Address.
C. Y. M. U. Resolutions. 94

FIFTH DAY.
Bishop Keane's Address.
Paper by Brother Ambrose.
Paper by H. L. Spaunhorst.
Paper by Dr. M. F. Egan.
Paper by Katherine E. Conway.
Address by Rev. J. T. Murphy, S. J.
Paper by W. E. Mosher.
Paper by Rev. F. J. Maguire.
Brother Azarias' Paper.
Future of the Negro Race (C. H. Butler).
Paper by William F. Markoe.
Paper by Richard R. Elliott.
Paper by Thomas Dwight, M. D.
Pope Leo on Labor (H. C. Semple).
Paper by Dr. A. Kaiser.
Rev. M. Callaghan's Address.
Paper by Martin F. Morris.
Trade Combinations and Strikes (R. M. Douglas).
Paper by Rev. J. R. Slattery.
"Prayer for America" (Rev. F. G. Lentz).
Paper by Frank J. Sheridan.
Paper by Anna T. Sadlier.
Paper by J. P. Lauth.
Paper by E. M. Sharon.
Essay by Rev. J. L. Andreis.
"Pauperism, Cause and Remedy" (M. J. Elder).
Paper by Elizabeth A. Cronyn.
Address by W. G. Smith.
"Duties of Capital" (Rev. Dr. Barry, England).
Paper by Dr. C. A. Wingerter.
Paper by Thomas F. Ring. 196

SIXTH DAY.
Resolutions of the Congress.
The Cardinal's Closing Address.
Peace Memorial to All Nations. 202

VOLUME II.

CONTENTS

CATHOLIC EDUCATION DAY.

Title Page	1
Letter from Pope Leo XIII	2
Catholic Education—Order of Exercises	3
Archbishop Feehan's Address	3
Dr. Selim H. Peabody's Address	5
Archbishop Hennessy's Address	6
Archbishop Ryan's Address	16
Hon. Morgan J. O'Brien's Address	21
"Catholicity and Patriotism"—Hon. Thos. J. Gargan	28
Bishop Spalding's Address	32
Mrs. Elizabeth Hooker's Address	33
Bishop Spalding's Plea for Pure Morals at World's Fair	34
Bishop Spalding's Protest Against Exhibiting Indecent Pictures	37
Columbian Library of Catholic Authors	38
Appreciation of Exhibits	39
Letter from Director-General Geo. R. Davis	39
Letter from Rt. Rev. J. L. Spalding	40
Visitors on Catholic Education Day	42
Press Notes on Education Day	45
An Authoritative Expression	46
Letter Expressing Thanks by Brother Maurelian	47

ILLUSTRATIONS.

	PAGE
LEO XIII	Frontispiece
CATHOLIC CONGRESS	12-13

GROUP I 20-21
    Cardinal Gibbons, Baltimore.
    Archbishop Feehan, Chicago.
        "   Ireland, St. Paul.
        "   Corrigan, New York.
        "   Ryan, Philadelphia.

GROUP II 30-31
    Mary J. Onahan, Chicago.
    Anna T. Sadlier, New York.
    Eliza Allen Starr, Chicago.
    Louise Imogen Guiney, Boston.

GROUP III 36-37
    Archbishop Satolli, Washington.
        "   Riordan, San Francisco.
        "   Katzer, Milwaukee.
        "   Hennessy, Dubuque.
        "   Janssen, New Orleans.

GROUP IV 52-53
    Cardinal Taschereau, Quebec.
    Archbishop Kain, St. Louis.
        "   Walsh, Toronto.
        "   Elder, Cincinnati.
        "   Williams, Boston.
        "   Gross, Oregon.
        "   Kenrick, St. Louis.

GROUP V 68-69
    Bishop Spalding, Peoria.
        "   Cosgrove, Davenport.
        "   Gabriels, Ogdensburg.
        "   Matz, Denver.
        "   Jensen, Belliville.
        "   Bradley, Manchester.
        "   McClousky, Louisville.
        "   Ryan, Alton.

GROUP VI 84-85
    Chancellor Muldoon, Chicago.
    Brother Ambrose, Chicago.
    Brother Maurelian, Chicago.
    Rev. Patrick Cronin, Buffalo.
    Rev. J. M. Cleary, Minneapolis.
    Rev. F. G. Lentz, Bement, Ill.
    Rev. Walter Elliott, C. S. P., New York.
    Rev. F. J. Maguire, Albany.
    Rev. Jos. L. Andreis, Baltimore.

GROUP VII 100-101
    Bishop Radsmacher, Ft. Wayne.
        "   Keane, Washington.
        "   Foley, Detroit.
        "   Healy, Portland.
        "   Scannell, Omaha.
        "   Burke, St. Joseph.
        "   McGolrick, Duluth.
        "   Messmer, Green Bay.

GROUP VIII 116-117
    Maurice F. Egan, LL. D., Notre Dame, Ind.
    Dr. August Kaiser, Detroit.
    Hon. C. C. Bonney, Chicago.
    John Gibbons, LL. D., Chicago.
    Thomas F. Ring, Boston.
    Col. R. M. Douglas, LL. D., Greenboro.
    Henry C. Semple, Montgomery.
    E. O. Brown, Chicago.

GROUP IX 132-133
    Hon. Morgan J. O'Brien, Chairman, N. Y.
    Thomas Lawler, Sec'y, Prairie du Chien.
    James F. O'Connor, Sec'y, Chicago.
    Thomas Dwight, M. D., Boston.
    John M. Duffy, Sec'y, Chicago.
    Richard H. Clarke, LL. D., New York.

VOL. II.

GROUP X	Frontispiece
Satolli, Maurelian, and O'Connell.	
Archbishop Feehan's Statue	6-7
Notre Dame Exhibit	10-11
Chapel Scene	26-27

WORLD'S COLUMBIAN CATHOLIC CONGRESSES.

A Landmark in Catholic Progress.—Motive of the Columbian Congress.—Sermon of Welcome.—Greeting of the Chicago Archbishop.—Cardinal Gibbons' Address.—The Official Welcome.—Judge Morgan J. O'Brien's Address.—Voices from Foreign Lands.—Mission and Character of Columbus.—"Isabella the Catholic."—The Angel of Philadelphia.—Bishop Watterson Sounds a Keynote.—Rousing Words from Mgr. Satolli.—The Rights of Labor.—The Duties of Capital.—Address of a Gifted Convert.—Religious Orders of Women.—Charities of the Church.—Missionary Work in the United States.—The Curse of Intemperance.—Women in Art, Literature, and Society.—The Work of St. Vincent de Paul.—Catholic Higher Education.—Welcome to the Archbishop of New York.—The Catholic Educational Exhibit.—Other Addresses from the Bishops.—Piercing into the Future.—Ringing Resolutions of the Congress.—The Cardinal's Touching Valedictory.

THE second Catholic Congress of the United States was held in the great and prosperous city of Chicago, Ills., September 4-9, 1893, and offers a noble landmark in these outlines of the career of Holy Church on American soil.

The busy Western metropolis had been the theater, during the summer months, of a stupendous "World's Fair" of arts and industries, held under Government auspices in honor of the quarto-centenary of the discovery by Christopher Columbus. Visitors from all nations thronged to this Columbian Jubilee—an appropriate title for such a grand Catholic assembly—and advantage was taken of the occasion to hold a series of congresses of more than national interest, the beautiful Art Palace provided by the Exposition authorities being devoted to their sessions. Here, accordingly, was held the Catholic Congress, which was the Mecca, from day to day, of vast crowds of the faithful, and was honored by such an attendance of our prelates and clergy as were never before present at an assembly of the kind. In many respects, indeed, the gathering was unique even in the history of the Church of God, and in the addresses and papers delivered on the occasion, the more relevant of which are here presented, may best be learned the inspiration, the aims, and the glorious work of the Columbian Catholic Congress, as it was officially styled

On the morning of September 4th, the first day of the assembly, the Holy Sacrifice was offered in its behalf at St. Mary's church—the oldest and formerly the cathedral parish of Chicago—in the presence of H. E. Cardinal Gibbons, the most Reverend Archbishop of the diocese, and many illustrious prelates and priests, besides the body of the delegates who were to participate in the Congress. The solemn High Mass was celebrated by Rev. E. J. Dunne of Chicago, with Rev. J. Ballman of Sag Bridge as deacon, and Rev. J. P. Dore as sub-deacon. The discourse of the occasion was made by Rev. P. J. Muldoon, Chancellor of the Chicago archdiocese. as follows:

SERMON OF WELCOME.

Your Eminence, Most Reverend Archbishops, Right Reverend Bishops, Very Reverend and Reverend Brethren of the Clergy, Brethren of the Laity: Through the graciousness of my superior, the greatest pleasure of my life, and an honor never to be forgotten, has been placed within my keeping. It surpasses me to rise to the full dignity of this occasion, and to welcome, in terms appropriately tender and sufficiently strong, this vast congregation of the priests of the Most High and brethren of the laity assembled together, not for self-glorification, but to seriously discuss weighty and pregnant subjects, and to solve, as far as possible, vexatious questions crying aloud for a solution. To your Eminence, to Archbishops, Bishops from home and abroad, to the very reverend and reverend brethren of the clergy, and a host of brethren of the laity, in the name of our most worthy Archbishop, I can declare no more than, brethren of the Faith, accept and share our good will and our hospitality; accept and share the hospitality of Chicago, justly termed, by her progress and generosity, the "Queen of the North and the West."

Genuine and broad as this expression is, permit me to briefly place before you other reasons why you should recognize that you are at home here and with your own in numbers, in thought, and in works.

Chicago, my friends, stands unique in city building and challenges the world in the progress with which God has blessed her. Sixty years ago Chicago meant a lonely fort upon the banks of a muddy stream; to-day she is the admiration of two hemispheres. And forget not that Catholic hearts and Catholic hands have not been inactive during these three-score years, and as proof over one hundred churches within the boundaries of our city open wide their portals and beg you, during your stay, to make them your own, and one-third of the population of this mammoth city joins in one profound chord of proud welcome, and extends to you the hand of fellowship, saying: "We are one in faith, in motives, and in interests."

Yet more: Not alone does Catholic Chicago greet you, but the entire commonwealth speaks in no uncertain terms to this as to every other Congress to the World's Fair city, for this is our year of jubilee, this our day of joy, this our time of reception. But to whom more appropriately than to Catholics could the word of good cheer, "Hasten and partake," be extended, for Catholics, and Catholics alone, are the only representatives of that Church which had being when he who to-day is revered with unheard-of praise set forth to discover the Western world. Catholics listened to his projects, strengthened his hands, and made possible by their aid and encouragement our meeting in Chicago to-day.

Besides, it seems you enter upon a soil permanently your own, for hear you not the feeble voice of the humble Jesuit missionary lying upon a rude couch in a ruder dark hut? He appears to say in dulcet tones: "Thank God! you follow where I have led. Chicago should be the home of Catholicity before aught else, for I was the first white man who looked upon its foundations, first blessed its soil, and from my heavenly home I to-day bless and welcome you, and pray God that your deliberations may be fruitful in the extension of that Faith which two hundred years ago I preached on this very spot to the red men who were sitting in darkness and the shadow of death." Again, sixty years ago, through the exertions of our Father St. Cyr, the first church whose spire received the kiss of the sun, rising out of the bosom of Lake Michigan, was Catholic and dedicated as St. Mary's of the Lake.

Yet more, the spirit of kinship entices you nearer and forbids a halt in any exterior sanctuary, for the White City waves its flags in joy, and Columbus, the saintly Catholic mariner, in triumphal chariot comes to greet you, and the mighty Exposition proclaims in power beyond ten thousand tongues the glorious works of Catholic peoples and individuals. The aroma of Catholic life is so clearly discernible in this greatest undertaking of the 19th century that every nook and corner voices the sentiment: "Rejoice and be glad, all Catholics who enter here; rejoice and be glad, for the same genius that made the Church the mother of art, the fosterer of education, the protector of the poor and defenseless, reigns triumphant here." From the Catholic chapel on the south, a picture of Catholic times, redolent of Catholic life and art, and surrounded by the famous caravels with the Immaculate Virgin upon the prow of the Santa Maria, as if now keeping vigil over the destinies of the New World as when guiding Columbus on his first voyage, away to the villages on the north, and from the Liberal Arts Building on the east to the Woman's Building on the west, all manifest in grand unison by the works they contain the broadness, the liberality, and the genuineness of Catholic teaching, and proclaim anew the Church to be the salvation of all that is best for man.

This unsurpassed Columbian Exposition places a new gem in the crown of Mother Church, for no object lesson of the greatness and universality of the Church has within modern times been placed so impartially and publicly before just and inquiring minds.

Above all this, my friends, another sturdier reception awaits you from the truth-seekers throughout the world. Assembling for the amicable discussion of important and pertinent subjects, and especially at this time, when all avenues lead to Chicago, and when the wires radiate every item of interest to the extremes of the earth, you hold the attention of the entire truth-seeking world. And no matter how bitterly at times the Church may be or may have been assailed, she has at all times commanded and does at present command the respect of the majority of intelligent mankind. This vast audience, seeking something higher and more permanent than is at present within its grasp, wishes you Godspeed, for it comprehends that your aim is to better and assist humanity. The poor, the rich, the educators, the American citizens, all appear with upturned faces, hoping from you for some new inspiration, appealing to you for some potent consolation, awaiting patiently the portrayal by you of the richest ideas for the man and the citizen. They greet you with the heartiness of those who have long gazed wistfully for the white sails upon the ocean's bosom, and they pray with the fervor of the interested that God may direct your thoughts and keep your words strong for righteousness, clean from personalities, healthful to the wounded, and inspiring to the negligent.

What a pulpit to preach from, and what an intelligent, numerous audience to listen! This is surely an opportunity of a century! Beg, then, the Holy Ghost to enlighten your minds and strengthen your hearts during the Holy Sacrifice, that the pure and undefiled teaching of the Church, in statement and in application, may worthily proceed from your lips. None save God can possibly count the vast influence this representative body must necessarily and naturally exert, not upon Catholics alone, but especially upon our non-Catholic brethren. Leaders of one-sixth of the entire population of America, spokesmen of ten millions of free people, assisted by worthy representatives from other nations, surely the outcome of your deliberations will be something extraordinary in the religious world.

Purblind indeed would we be did we not interpret the signs of the age aright.

A magnificent, a wonder-working century. Old ideas have been torn asunder, theories made principles or cast to the winds. Every fiber of American life speaks of energy and perseverance, and if not at all times progress, at least mutation, generally indicative of at least the desire of progress. So much for the material side, but can we predicate the same general onward movement in the social and moral life? We fear not. The same unrest prevails—the same mutation is under way, but alas, how frequently does it remain a pure mutation without progress. The materialism and humanitarianism have impregnated the spiritual, and the cry for light which we hear on all sides is all the more poignant and its echo resounds more sadly mournful, because we detect in it so much of materialism and pure humanity, unregenerated by the grace which makes the human at least in part divine.

We hear this mournful cry in various forms. One blinded to higher things boldly announces that no provident eye watches over the poor and that the poor man must be a providence to himself. Another asks what is religion, or is there any religion? Again we hear an unfortunate shipwrecked mariner proclaim that we should wipe out entirely the idea that man can be saved by dogma, and in its place preach the eternal truth that man is saved by his character and that creed and dogma dwindle into insignificance in comparison with character. Who shall pour oil upon these troubled waters? Quis medicabit? Who except the sons of that Church founded by Christ to heal the wandering, wounded nations until the consummation of the ages? New dogmas are not necessary. Within the dispensary of the Church are medicines potent enough to heal the ills of those unfortunates, but oh, how tender, how delicate, must be the hand that will apply them.

The Church of saints and martyrs is more than equal to the delicate task, but only through her devoted children in the practical, everyday exercise of two virtues, always a part of sanctity—namely, self-sacrifice and activity. Yes, my friends, self-sacrifice, which signifies more than leading Christian lives and strict adherence to the dogmas of the Church. This is stationary Christianity. The monks of old and the confessors of the Faith went forth and brilliantly illustrated the beauty of Christianity by their teachings, and the people converted their neighbors by their heroic acts of charity. Our heart rejoices at the outlook, for self-sacrifice opens up an expansive field to the missionary in the United States, but oh, how narrow and how galling to human pride and sloth is the path that leads thereto and the paths that intersect this field of gold in an infinity of directions! To curb our own passions is only elementary; we must cut deeper, bring purer blood; aye, we must penetrate to the very center of our life and give a portion of this life to the stricken and needy, and then, and then only, will the hungering, inquiring multitude turn to us as guides and leaders in a noble cause, and petition us to know the Spirit that moves us into such arduous fields, and, knowing, they will kneel and adore.

Such abnegation implies activity. No sluggard can be found within the ranks. The watchwords of the age are "to do and dare," and since ours is the merchandise of Heaven, shall we falter in the competition? The words of the Spanish philosopher may be justly here applied:

"The little minds which do not carry their views beyond a limited horizon; bad hearts which nourish only hatred and delight only in exciting rancor and in calling forth the evil passions; the fanatics of a mechanical civilization, who see no other agent than steam, no other power than gold and silver, no other object than production, no other end than pleasure; all these men, assuredly, will attach but little importance to the observations which I have made; for them the moral development of individuals and society is of little importance; they do not even perceive what passes under their eyes; for them history is mute, experience barren, and the future a mere nothing. Happily, there is a great number of men who believe that their minds are nobler than metal, more powerful than steam, and too grand and too sublime to be satisfied with momentary pleasure."

Far be it from me to criticise the noble efforts of contemporaries in spreading Faith or to reflect upon the past. Their works are their monuments. The past century of Church work is a wonderful foundation; but the future, what possibilities! The superb magnificence of the opportunity turns the head, and must set ablaze the heart of every Catholic. We can not live on the glory of the past; ours it is to raise the walls upon the foundations and leave to another generation the ornamentation of the edifice. When souls are to be saved and when generous, honest souls are hurrying hither and thither in the shadow of death, following foolishly phantom lights, who will rest, who will spare the sacrifice and sit with hands piously folded pronouncing the idle word, "enough"? None; for we expect the reward of the Master who acted so generously

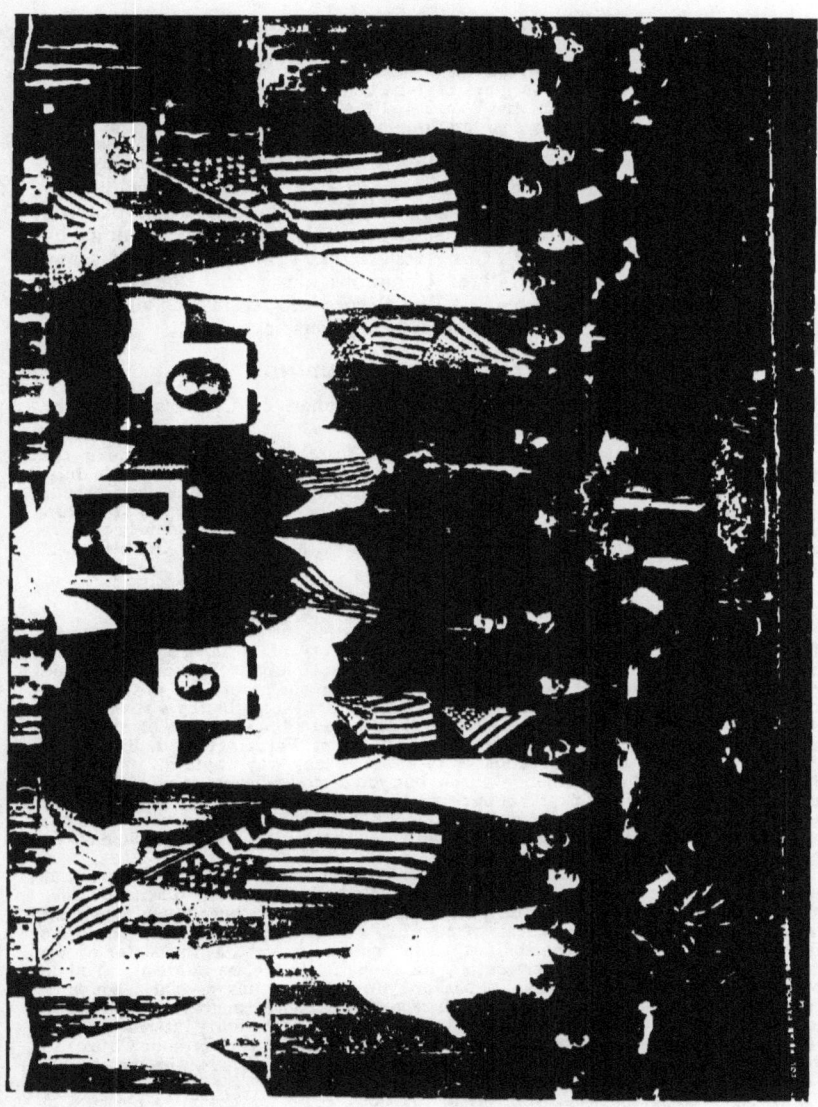

SCENE AT THE ART PALACE, CHICAGO.
THE WORLD'S COLUMBIAN CATHOLIC CONGRESSES IN SESSION.

toward the one who had not folded the talent in the napkin. We must labor valiantly, that those following the deceptive glare of false teaching may be brought within the vivifying influence of the Light of the World, and their gain will be our reward.

For these various reasons, my dear brethren, we welcome you; the needy in moral and intellectual life we welcome, and Christ, who promised reward for the smallest act in His name, draws you nearer to His Sacred Heart and blesses and welcomes you.

On the conclusion of the sacred services the delegates marched in procession to the Art Palace, the Cardinal and other dignitaries accompanying in carriages. These were welcomed at the door of the beautiful edifice by President Bonney of the World's Congress Auxiliary, and other officials, and in a very few moments the Hall of Columbus, designated for the larger assemblies, was filled in every part. The decorations were rich and appropriate, the colors of the Sovereign Pontiff being conspicuous.

THE FIRST DAY'S PROCEEDINGS

Were promptly inaugurated by Hon. W. J. Onahan of Chicago, Secretary of the Committee on Organization, who said:

Gentlemen, and I am happy to add, *Ladies*—for there are ladies among the appointed delegates to the Catholic Congress: It is my pleasant and honorable duty, representing the committee on organization, to call to order the Columbian Catholic Congress, which I now cordially do. The first words to be addressed to you are naturally words of hearty welcome. By no one may those words be more graciously or more appropriately spoken than by the venerable and Most Reverend Archbishop of Chicago.

ARCHBISHOP FEEHAN'S WELCOME.

Members of the Catholic Congress—both the ladies and the gentlemen composing it: It is for me a most happy occasion that it becomes my duty, in the name of the Catholic body of this city, and also in my own, to welcome you to Chicago. You are assembled here from various portions of our country, not only from the parts that are near but also from the most remote. You must have been brought together by a strong, high motive, as you are bound together when you come here by the strongest of all bonds, that of a common Faith. You come in the spirit of our Faith, actuated, directed by our Faith. You come not to question or to affect, in any way whatever, the ancient Faith and discipline of the Catholic Church, but you come to discuss some of the great questions and problems of life and of our time that are intimately connected with, and that spring from, the teachings of our Catholic Faith. There are no questions of our time more interesting or more important than those that are on the programme of the Catholic Congress.

We have that great question of the independence of the Holy See; you have that great question—one of the greatest of all—that of Catholic education. Then you have the great social questions of the day, the ideas of which have been taken, in a great measure, at least, from the encyclicals of our Holy Father, Pope Leo XIII. You come here then with very grave responsibilities. You come, as it were, as the center of the Catholic Church. You come representing its thought, its life, its interests. You do not represent yourselves individually, nor do you represent any special theories or fancies of individuals of our times; but you represent parishes, congregations, bishops, whole dioceses, great States—you represent all these vast and mighty interests, and as a vast body you represent at least the ten million members of the Catholic Church, if not more. You come then as if to a great center. You come as brave, wise men to discuss great questions for the interests of those millions.

You don't come to please yourselves; you don't come for the mere pleasure of coming, nor for recreation, as so many multitudes are coming just now to our city, though these need not be excluded; but you come principally for that grand, high work that has been placed in your hands of looking after the interests that are involved in some of the great questions that will be discussed and spoken of in this assembly. You assemble here to-day in a high spirit of loyalty to the Catholic Church, of loyalty to its supreme pastor, Pope Leo XIII. You come together as sons of the great head of the Faith. You come mindful that God's Church is your great mother, and, as the loyal sons in a family will always uphold the dignity and honor of the family, so will this vast assembly uphold before the whole world the honor, the nobility, and the dignity of the Catholic Church. Not less are you concerned for the interests of our common country. The men of other lands are to-day, and to-morrow will be, looking to the results of this Catholic Congress in Chicago. The world is full of agitation. Men's minds are everywhere active, and men in every civilized land to-day and to-morrow will be looking forward to know and to see what free men in a free land can feel and think about the great questions that are agitating our times, and that are everywhere pressing for a solution. You have then at heart the honor and the dignity of the Church and of the whole Catholic Faith. You will watch over them carefully in your addresses and in your deliberations. We know and believe, all of us, earnestly and firmly, that no word will go out to the world from this Catholic Congress that will wound or offend in the slightest degree the Catholic conscience or Catholic feeling of our people throughout the United States.

We know that all your deliberations will be guided by that Spirit under which you have sat to-day. Within an hour or so you have been in God's presence and in his temple, and you have asked the Spirit of God to come down to your souls and guide your deliberations. We all hope that the Spirit of God and the Spirit of light will be with you, and that everything you say or do will be guided by that high, strong fidelity of Catholic sons to our Catholic Faith, and that everything you say or do will be distinguished by the dignity and the harmony that we have the right, as we have every reason, to expect from this great representative body of the Catholic Faith and the Catholic people. You will have the pleasure now of hearing from Mr. Bonney, the gentleman who has been the life and soul of all these organizations and congresses, except the Catholic Congress, connected with the great Exposition.

Hon. Chas. C. Bonney, who is a non-Catholic lawyer, then delivered what may be termed the "official" welcome:

PRESIDENT BONNEY'S ADDRESS.

Officers and Members of the Columbian Catholic Congress: In the name of the World's Congress Auxiliary, organized to conduct the moral and intellectual part of the World's Columbian Exposition of 1893; and in the name of the Government of the United States, which invited all nations to participate in the congresses to be held under the auspices of the Auxiliary; and in the name of fifty millions of non-Catholics who love justice and believe in equal religious liberty for all men, I salute you and bid you welcome. This memorial building, and every facility which the World's Congress Auxiliary can command, is most cordially offered for the purpose of your Congress.

That a great change has come in the relations of the Catholic Church and the Protestant churches with each other is known throughout the world. That this change has largely increased human happiness and has in many ways promoted the cause of peace and progress is also widely acknowledged. A brief reference to some of the leading causes of this change seems, however, especially appropriate to this occasion, and may serve to strengthen the gracious bonds of charity and affection which are now gently drawing nearer and nearer to each other all the various branches of the great family of mankind. Of those causes the benign spirit of the new age should first be named.

Descending from the sun of righteousness this spirit of progress is filling the whole earth with its splendor and beauty, its warmth and vivifying power, and making the old things of truth and justice new in meaning, strength, and energy to execute God's will for the welfare of man.

Among the secondary causes of the change to which reference has been made there are several which it seems a duty as well as a pleasure to recall on this occasion. The noble and successful work of the Catholic Church, in the field of practical temperance reform, first attracted the attention and won the sympathy of the Protestant people of America.

The new Catholic movement for the relief and elevation of the toiling masses, which culminated in the great Papal encyclical on the condition of labor, deepened the interest of the Protestant world in the work of the Catholic Church and excited the love and admiration of many non-Catholics. The new Catholic activity in the extension of higher education is another cause of the better relations which have recently been established. For science and art and literature are of no sect or creed. They belong to man, whatever may be his political or religious views, and are bonds of fraternity everywhere. Over the grave in which was buried the dead strife of former generations the apostles of the new age have clasped hands in a new pledge of fidelity in the pursuit of learning and virtue, and the life that is called charity.

There is one important particular in which the ideas of Catholic educational leaders are in peculiar accord with the original American doctrine of popular education. The third article of the great ordinance of 1787, for the government of the territory of which Chicago is the metropolis, declared that "religion, morality, and knowledge being necessary to good government and the happiness of mankind, schools and the means of education shall forever be encouraged."

Not knowledge only; not knowledge and morality merely, but religion, morality, and knowledge, sacred trinity of the powers of human progress, are essential to the proper education of the people.

The new apostles of Catholic progress have become especially endeared to enlightened Protestants. Henry Edward Manning, Cardinal Archbishop of Westminster, can hardly be more beloved nor his loss more sincerely mourned within the Catholic Church than without its fold. His gracious and earnest words on "Protestant Dissenters," "Disinherited Christians," "Blameless Ignorance," and "Unconscious Catholics" won for him and the Catholic Church hosts of friends outside of his own communion.

In America the work of his brother cardinal, His Eminence James, Cardinal Gibbons, honorary President of this Congress, has been equally auspicious. His book on "Our Christian Heritage," in which he gladly holds out to Protestants the right hand of fellowship for union against the common foe, commends him eloquently to them as well as to his own brethren.

The burning words of His Grace Archbishop Ireland in the advocacy of temperance, education, social purity, and every moral virtue have made his name and Church household words in many Protestant homes.

When a Catholic bishop like Bishop Spalding of Peoria, speaking for Catholics, says, "We love liberty, we love knowledge, we love truth, we love opportunity; and forgetting nationality, forgetting sects, forgetting all save God's image in every human being, we would uplift men by uplifting humanity," millions of Protestant hearts respond, Amen! Amen!

But a greater agency of union and progress still remains to be named—the illustrious head of the Catholic Church, Pope Leo XIII., than whom no more able, enlightened, and benign pontiff has borne the name of Holy Father in a thousand years. Like the morning bell of a new age, his earnest words, in speaking of the American people, are: "I love them and I love their country. I have a great tenderness for those who live in that land, Protestants and all. Under the constitution, religion has perfect liberty, and is a growing power. Where the Church is free, it will increase; and I bless, I love Americans for their frank, open, unaffected character, and for the respect which they pay to Christianity and Christian morals. My only desire is to use my power for the good of the whole people—Protestants and Catholics alike. I want the Protestants as well as the Catholics to esteem me." Is it any wonder that Pope Leo XIII. is respected and beloved by the Protestants to whom these words were addressed?

On the Protestant side similar causes have been at work, producing similar results. The time now at command will not permit a presentation of these results, but it may suffice to say that it has culminated in the arrangements for the World's Religious Congresses of 1893.

Blind, indeed, must be the eyes that can not see, in these events, the quickened march of the ages of human progress toward the fulfillment of the divine prophecy of "one fold and one shepherd," when all forms of government shall be one in liberty and justice, and all forms of faith and worship one in charity and human service.

With these sentiments I greet and welcome the Catholic Congress of 1893.

The most generous applause, which only needs mention here, had accented the various addresses so far, being raised to the point of enthusiasm by the following beautiful

ADDRESS OF H. E. CARDINAL GIBBONS.

What an inspiring and consoling spectacle is this! Whether I consider the magnitude of your numbers or your representative character—for you represent almost every State and diocese and city of the Union—or whether I contemplate the intelligence that beams on your faces, I can not but exclaim: This is a sight well calculated to bring joy and gladness to the heart of American Catholics.

During the past four months millions of visitors have come from all parts of the United States, nay, from every quarter of the globe, to contemplate on the Exposition grounds the wonderful works of man. They knew not which to admire more—the colossal dimensions of the buildings, or their architectural beauty, or the treasures of art which they contained. The caskets and the gems were well worthy of the 19th century, worthy of the nations that brought them, worthy of the indomitable spirit of Chicago. Let us no longer call Chicago the windy city, but the city of lofty aspirations. Let me christen her with another name—let me call her Thaumatopolis, the city of wonders, the city of miracles. And the director-general, with his associates, deserves to be called the Thaumaturgus of the enterprise.

But while other visitors have come to contemplate with admiration the wonderful works of man, with the image of man stamped upon them, you have come here to contemplate man himself—the most wonderful work of God, with the image of God stamped upon him. Others are studying what man has accomplished in the material world. You are to consider what man can accomplish in the almost boundless possibilities of his spiritual and intellectual nature. You will take counsel together to consider the best means for promoting the religious and moral, the social and economic well-being of your fellow-citizens.

It is true, indeed, that your deliberations will not be stamped with the authority of legislative enactments, like the proceedings of Congress and the decrees of a national council. Nevertheless they will go far toward enlightening public opinion and molding and shaping public thought on the great religious, moral, and social questions of the day.

When I look into your earnest and intelligent faces I am almost deterred from imparting to you my words of admonition. But you know well that we clergymen are in the habit of drifting unconsciously into the region of exhortation, just as financiers drift into the region of dollars and cents and figures. I may be pardoned, therefore, for giving you a word of advice. In all your discussions be ever mindful of the golden saying of St. Vincent Lerins: "In necessariis unitas, in dubiis libertas, in omnibus caritas: In essentials, unity; in doubtful things, liberty; in all things, charity." Happily for you, children of the Church, you have nothing to discuss in matters of faith, for your faith is fixed and determined by the divine Legislator, and we can not improve on the creed of Him who is "the way, the truth, and the life."

But between the calm and luminous region of faith and the dark and chaotic region of error there lies a vast field for free discussion. I should be very sorry that any member of this Congress should attempt to circumscribe this free space by erecting his little fence of ipse dixits, and saying to all others: "I am Sir Oracle; thus far you shall come and no farther." Let all your proceedings be marked by courtesy and charity, and by a spirit of Christian forbearance toward each other. Never descend to personalities. Many a delicious speech has lost its savor and been turned into gall, because a few drops of vituperation had been injected into it. The edifice of moral and social improvement which you aim to build, can never be erected on the ruins of charity.

Perhaps the best model of courtly dignity and courtesy that I could set before you is W. E. Gladstone, the Grand Old Man. I happened to be in the House of Commons in 1880, when Mr. Gladstone was Prime Minister, as he is to-day. A very long debate was going on regarding taxation. The ministry were in favor of transferring a tax from the grain to the malt and of relieving the farmer at the expense of the brewer. It was a measure that would bring joy to the heart of the Archbishop of St. Paul. A young lord on the opposition side was making a dreary speech to the effect that it was better to let well enough alone, and that the relations between the tax collector and the tax payer were of an amicable character and should not be disturbed. As soon as it was announced that Mr. Gladstone was going to speak, the house was suddenly aroused from its lethargy and was inflamed with enthusiasm. He was greeted with cheers. He had spoken but a few words when he was rudely interrupted by the young lord. Mr. Gladstone gracefully bowed to his opponent, receded a step, and sat down. When his lordship had finished he resumed his speech; he dissected his opponent with his Damascus blade; his lordship cheerfully submitted to the operation because the blade was pointed not with poison, but with honey.

"I have studied the subject of finance," said Mr. Gladstone, "under Sir Robert Peel. I have sat at his feet like Saul at the feet of Gamaliel. I am an old man and have not the sanguine temperament of my honorable young friend. And as for me, I never expect to see the day when the tax collector and the tax payer will rush into one another's arms and embrace one another."

God grant that our fondest anticipations of your labors may be realized, and that the invocation to-day of the divine blessing, which is so full of hope, may be crowned at the end of your sessions by a Te Deum full of joy and gratitude for the success of this convention. As an earnest of this result I hold in my hand a letter which I had the honor to receive the other day from him who has been so beautifully and justly extolled by the preceding speakers. I hold in my hand a letter from His Holiness Leo XIII., and in this letter he pours out upon you all his apostolic paternal benediction. May the blessing of the Holy Father, may the blessing of Almighty God—his God and our God, his Father and our Father—descend upon you all and upon your deliberations. May his blessing enlighten your minds and inflame your hearts and be a happy earnest of the harmony and union that will dominate all your proceedings.

Following is the translation of the letter of the Holy Father referred to in His Eminence's address, and which was then read to the Congress by Hon W. J. Onahan:

POPE LEO'S GREETING AND BLESSING.

Leo XIII., Pope: To our Beloved Son James Gibbons by the Title of Santa Maria in Trastevere Cardinal Priest of the Holy Roman Church, Archbishop of Baltimore, Beloved Son: Health and apostolic benediction. It has afforded us much satisfaction to be informed by you that in the coming month of September a large assembly of Catholic gentlemen will meet at Chicago, there to discuss matters of great interest and importance.

Furthermore, we have been specially gratified by your devotion and regard for us in desiring, as an auspicious beginning for such Congress, our blessing and our prayers. This filial request we do indeed most readily grant, and beseech Almighty God that by his aid and the light of his wisdom he may graciously be pleased to assist and illume all who are about to assemble with you, and that He may enrich with the treasures of his choicest gifts your deliberations and conclusions.

To you, therefore, our beloved son, and to all who take part in the Congress aforesaid and to the clergy and faithful committed to your care, we lovingly in the Lord impart our apostolic benediction.

Given at Rome, at St. Peter's, the 7th day of August, in the year of our Lord eighteen hundred and ninety-three and of our pontificate the sixteenth.

LEO XIII., *Pope.*

The temporary organization of the Congress was then announced by Mr. Onahan, as follows:

Temporary chairman, Hon. Morgan J. O'Brien of New York.
Secretaries, James C. Lawler, Prairie du Chien; Professor James F. Edwards, University of Notre Dame, Indiana, and James F. O'Connor and John M. Duffy of Chicago.

This was speedily followed by

JUDGE O'BRIEN'S ADDRESS AS CHAIRMAN.

Gentlemen: The official call issued by the committee on organization, which has been printed and is now in the possession of all the members present, relieves me from the necessity of stating the objects of this Congress. That call defines and limits its scope to the consideration of the social question, to which has been added that of Catholic education and the independence of the Holy See. As stated in that call, "permanent and effective results and enduring benefits are looked for at our hands as a fitting outcome of this memorable assemblage of Catholic intelligence and Catholic earnestness." No more fitting time or place could have been selected than the present to give expression to those sentiments which, as Catholics, we hold in common, and for the purpose of consulting upon those measures which are of most importance to our Church and country. This city has been selected by the Nation as the place to celebrate by a Fair which, in its proportions and beauty, surpasses all that the creative genius of man has attempted or accomplished, and the event thus celebrated has been fraught with such momentous results and happiness to man as to make it the most memorable in the history of civilization. Naturally our minds go back to that event through the vista of years; we see the march of progress, the development of material and mechanical triumphs, and above all the struggle for emancipation and freedom, which has finally culminated in the freest government the world has ever seen. When we remember how, over the trackless ocean, Columbus and his little band of followers came, soon to be succeeded by others who, penetrating impenetrable forests, removed the physical obstacles to development; how they established, through their religion, zeal, and courage, society and government and laws, and how they finally threw off a foreign yoke and established an independent Government upon a foundation which guarantees the fullest and greatest freedom to the individual, and how to these were added commerce and art, poetry, eloquence, and song, it becomes a just subject for pride to all those who had any hand in producing such magnificent results.

If any justification were needed for our assemblage here to-day it is furnished by the recollection that it was a Catholic monk who inspired Columbus with hope; it was Columbus and a Catholic crew that first crossed the trackless main; that it was a Catholic queen who rendered the expedition possible, and that it was a Catholic whose name has been given to the entire continent. Ay! more than this, the early history of our country is the history of its Catholicity. And the Catholic names given to the early discoveries in the four quarters of our country attest the fact that Catholics were the discoverers. And it is impossible to read the history of our country without recalling the exploits of Ponce de Leon, Cartier, Balboa, Marquette, De Soto, Melendez, La Salle, Champlain, and others whose names can never be obliterated, because molded in enduring brass upon the massive gates of the capitol at Washington; nay, more, the very soil on which this city stands was sanctified by the great missionary, Marquette, who was here in 1674 to 1675, and whose body even now rests on the opposite shores of Lake Michigan. How fruitful of good results his works were, may be known by recalling a single fact that to-day, in Chicago, the spires of more than a hundred Catholic churches glisten in the morning sun. We can, moreover, truthfully say that not a land was found, not a mountain crossed, not a valley entered, or a stream forded, but Catholic missionaries led the way. And wherever from the depths of primeval forests cities, towns, and States sprang up; where, instead of the savage, there appeared men longing for freedom, there will we find the mark of the missionary's footsteps. And from that time down to the present, whether groaning under the iron heel of despotic rulers, whether amidst the trials of our revolutionary struggle, whether amidst the wars that succeeded wherein the autonomy of our nation was threatened, there, sharing with their fellow-countrymen in the trials and tribulations and in the subsequent triumphs, were to be found the Catholics.

Our country, therefore, is doubly dear to us. We were here at its first discovery, we participated in its struggle for civil and religious liberty, and in turn have participated in its glories and enjoyed peace, security, and happiness. It is more dear to us, because in this land above all others the old Faith has fair play. Its schools, its churches, and its cathedrals are not the result of the contributions of unstable governments, but are the gratuitous offerings of more than ten million of freedmen.

We fully realize, however, what has been said by a great writer, that a nation, like a man, may live to the fullness of its time or perish prematurely by violence or internal disorders.

The world knows of but two principles of government. One, the power of the sword sustained by the hand that wields it; the other, the power of the law sustained by a virtuous people. Or, differently expressed, there is the principle of force and the principle of love. Our form of government being a republic is essentially founded upon the virtue of its citizens, and this foundation can neither be weakened nor destroyed without threatening the entire social structure. The early discoverers of America, as well as our revolutionary forefathers, were imbued with strong religious principles upon which alone virtue can be grounded, and this, added to their hardy and physical natures, laid the foundations and gave the impetus to that splendid civilization which is now the heritage of all.

While, therefore, glorying in our triumphs and proud of our wonderful development, we could not, if we would, fail to discover those dark and ominous clouds which hover over our national firmament and which are the inevitable forerunners of a violent storm. The presence of these clouds is not difficult to account for. The hardy and rugged virtue of our forefathers no longer exists; for the history of our country will show that the moral decadence of our people has kept rapid pace with the augmentation of our material prosperity. That we have steadily advanced materially is unquestioned; our towns, cities, and States have multiplied, our citizens have amassed wealth running into the millions and hundreds of millions; our corporations are striding a continent; but under the shadow of this magnificent prosperity we find incipient pauperism and discontent; men, women, and children without the necessaries of life, deprived of religion and education, and who are prevented from participating in those blessings which God seemingly intended for all.

The thoughtful statesman of America, the hopeful patriot, and the virtuous citizen knows and feels that the evils that menace our national prosperity—that the apparent social inequalities and the rights of capital and labor—can be reconciled in some way consistent with the preservation of law and order; in some way consistent with the preservation of the rights of all, so as to prevent the outbreak of a class of men who are prepared to seize upon any occasion, and are seemingly mad enough in their fury to tear down the very constitution upon which our peace, our happiness, and our security depend.

We think the remedy is to be found alone in a return to those principles of virtue and religion with which our forefathers were imbued, and upon which our Government was founded, and which we think is alone needed to restore the original vigor of the nation. It must be remembered that materialism, infidelity, agnosticism, and other forms of irreligion have never been fruitful either in forming or perpetuating a state. Like all negative principles, there is included within them a principle of destruction; they are powerful in the direction of pulling down, but never of building up. And against irreligion, the implacable foe to our present civilization—whatever form it may assume—all those, whether Protestant or Catholic, who believe in the vital force of religion have a common ground upon which they can stand. Not only in this have we a bond of union with our Protestant countrymen, when in good faith these are engaged in disseminating virtue and religion, but also in general charities, which look to the amelioration of the condition of the poor, the sick, and the aged, as well as measures designed to suppress intemperance and gambling, and prevent the desecration of the Sunday. These are among the subjects which will receive consideration by this Congress, and it is in a spirit of generous rivalry—according to all the same religious freedom which we claim for ourselves—that we endeavor to discharge that duty which we owe to our Church and to our country. As stated in our call: "All men feel and admit that the present relations of labor and capital are strained and unreasonable; that civil and social order are seriously menaced, trade and business hampered."

Under such conditions, if but true to the principles which have animated our past and secured our present, we Catholics can render a signal service at this time to our country by suggesting the remedies for these evils which threaten our national existence, and which can be applied in a way consistent with vested rights and prevent outbreaks which would menace those blessings of life, liberty, and property which our constitution guarantees; thus again emphasizing our loyalty and devotion to that country whose interests are linked with every fiber of our hearts.

The deliberations of this Congress, therefore, are pregnant with important consequences to our Church and our country, and our proceedings will be watched with interest by all.

That the solution of the present social difficulties is to be found in the Catholic Church we know, for, as has been well said, "that Church is the friend of the poor, the champion of the oppressed and the downtrodden, the inflexible enemy to injustice of whatever kind wherever found, and is recognized as the synonym of authority, the foe to lawlessness, and the champion of law and order." Over the halls of this Congress, therefore, we will write the poet's words, so that all the ends we aim at shall be "our God's, our country's, and truth's."

Opportunity was given at this point to hear some of the distinguished prelates from foreign lands, the first of these who spoke being the Most Rev. Archbishop Redwood of New Zealand. He said:

A VOICE FROM NEW ZEALAND.

I shall ever consider this day as one of the happiest and most privileged of my life. Some months ago while I was in my diocese in New Zealand, I learned through the newspapers and through the very modest advertisements from this great city of Chicago, of the wonderful Columbian Exposition about to be held. I said to myself it would be a great pleasure, a great intellectual enjoyment, to be present at that great event, to see the marvelous productions of the human mind, to see the variety that has come forth from the genius of man; but I further said to myself that I have seen the greatest expositions of Paris and of London, and other parts of Europe, and that while no doubt this might be on a grander scale, still after all it is chiefly a manifestation of man's progress in the material world. Looking upon it in that light I made up my mind not to come.

But afterward I happened to hear that this Exposition was to be suddenly raised far above any other exposition ever known in the annals of mankind. I learned of the Auxiliary Congresses to be attached to this Exposition, and that other works of man were to be considered—that he was to be viewed in his mind, in his heart, in his soul; that man was to be viewed as a social being; and that in the Auxiliary Congresses all the most burning problems of the day were to be discussed by the most distinguished members of the laity of the United States. They were to be brought together as one grand focus, whose light was to be turned upon the most burning and actual questions of the times. When I heard this I made up my mind that I should come. I said to myself that it was like going to school again. I told my people I was coming to Chicago to meet, as it were, the very élite of the human mind, in the very center of the most intellectual life of the great Republic, of the great Union of man, governed by a vast democracy that is now wielding, you may say, the scepter of progress and of the world. But I never thought I would have the honor and the privilege of addressing this attendance. I intended to come as a listener. I wanted to hear what was said upon all the great questions of the day. I wanted to be abreast of the times, for I think every bishop and archbishop should be abreast of the times, or rather that he ought to be before the times.

Perhaps some of you may think New Zealand is still a land of cannibalism—a land in which you expect to find in every house good provision of roast missionary. But we are a progressive people in that far-off land; there we venture on experiments and try issues very quickly. We are, in fact, the world's experimental country. Some of those things which you are discussing here—for instance the eight hours' day—has been in existence in New Zealand for some years. I said to myself no doubt in that wonderful American country, where there is so much freedom and such determination for progress, where the characteristic of the people is a horror of routine, I must naturally hear suggestions and see new lines of thought open before me—new solutions of grave questions, and therefore, if I have to keep myself abreast of the times and *a fortiori*, if I have to go before the times, there is no place I can visit so appropriate to obtain correct information on burning subjects of the hour as at the Columbian Exposition of Chicago and the World's Congress Auxiliary. Then another thought struck me—that such a meeting of the élite of the Catholic intellect, both ecclesiastical and lay, must prove a great instrument for the progress of our holy religion which every missionary and every bishop has so deeply at heart. I said what we want in the 19th century is to see the Catholic Church everywhere, to see her penetrate into all kinds of assemblies, to see her make herself known; for if she were only known the whole world would be at her feet—that is, the world worthy of our consideration. It is because she is not known that she is often maligned in good faith. Well, we have to make her known, and where is it more possible to make her known better, to bring her focus of light into the most progressive country in the world? Here we meet to discuss the different problems of the day. We will show her influence in the great questions of education and labor and finance. I say the Church should be heard in every kind of public assembly. When the shackles of prejudice are passed from the human mind she must stand forth in her innate beauty. I have come nine thousand miles to assist in this assembly, and it is one of the proudest privileges in my life to take part in it.

Following this Archbishop from Britain's remotest colony came the words of him who is pastor in her mighty capital of London. Monsignor Nugent of Liverpool was present to act as spokesman for the Cardinal Archbishop of Westminster, and thus delivered the message entrusted to him:

FROM THE SEE OF WESTMINSTER.

My Lord Cardinal and Ladies and Gentlemen: I stand here as the messenger of congratulation and of the deepest interest of Cardinal Vaughan in the great Catholic work which will take place in this city during this week; but before I read his letter I wish to express how much I have felt those tender and affectionate references that have been made during the last two days to the illustrious and late lamented Cardinal Manning. When it was conceived of having a Congress of English-speaking people he was one of the first who was consulted upon the matter. The first proposition was that it should be held in London, but he, with his wonderful grasp of character, knew that with our crippled ideas and habits this was the true field for the expression of the Catholic mind upon all those great social questions which are the very root, not only of religion but of the stability of society. It has been my lot to have worked with Cardinal Manning, closely and intimately, and to have shared his confidence since the year 1853; and when I go back I shall be able, I trust, to place an immortelle upon his grave of the expression, the Catholic expression, aye, the universal expression, of honor for the deep interest which he took in the people, irrespective of creed or nationality. Cardinal Vaughan has been brought up, I may say, under his wing, and he has commissioned me thus to convey his sympathy.

ARCHBISHOP FEEHAN, CHICAGO.
ARCHBISHOP CORRIGAN, NEW YORK.
ARCHBISHOP IRELAND, ST. PAUL.
CARDINAL GIBBONS, BALTIMORE.
ARCHBISHOP RYAN, PHILADELPHIA.

Mgr. Nugent then read the following letter:

ARCHBISHOP'S HOUSE, WESTMINSTER, S. W., Aug. 15, 1893. *My Dear Mgr. Nugent:*—As Mgr. Gadd is not going to the States, I shall be much obliged if you will kindly represent me at the Columbian Catholic Congress. Kindly express as publicly and as heartily as you can the deep interest with which I follow the life and conduct of the Catholic Church in the United States. The interest is quickened by the personal relations of friendship which I have long since been happy enough to establish for myself among many of the clergy and laity in America. I rejoice to witness the Catholic Church entering thus deeply into the foundation and structure of the great civilization, which is covering so vast an area of the world's surface. The great social problem, which is the problem of our day, can only be solved by the action of Christianity. The American Church knows this, and the efforts which its cardinals and archbishops and bishops are making in this direction are most instructive to us here in England, who pursue our way, perhaps, rather more slowly, though traversing the same path, amid similar difficulties. Pray, therefore, express my own admiration and appreciation of the noble Catholic efforts which are being made at the present moment in Chicago. The Church has only to be known in order to be esteemed. A great service to religion and to the American people and to the advance guard of modern civilization is rendered by the determination of the American hierarchy to present the Catholic Church as distinctively modern in character, as she is venerable and ancient—to present her to the people as "of yesterday, to-day, and forever." Believe me, dear Mgr. Nugent, your faithful and devoted servant,

HERBERT CARDINAL VAUGHAN,
Archbishop of Westminster.

Continuing, Mgr. Nugent said:

My Lord Cardinal, I have been asked to say a few words, but this is not the time, when that clock already tells me it is ten minutes after one; but if I might express my feelings briefly I would say: Gentlemen, you have come from the different parts of this country and have before you a high mission. All over the world the struggle at present is how to lift up our people and to make them take their social position, and, just as they rise in the social scale, to remember they have duties to perform. If we have to build up our people and to save them from the terrible dangers that surround them in modern life, it must be by successful laymen remembering their social duties, and that after success comes terrible responsibilities, and that the more we succeed in the world the heavier and deeper are those responsibilities.

This ended the introductory exercises, when the following committee was appointed on organization:

D. B. Bremner, Ill.; William P. Breen, Ind.; Francis T. Furey, Pa.; Jeremiah Fennessy, Mass.; M. Smith Brennan, Del.; L. V. O'Donoghue, N. Y,; Michael Brennan, Mich.; P. P. Connor, Mo., and John B. McGorick, N. Y.

From the many able papers read in the Congress during this first day, the place is given to that of Dr. R. A. Clarke of New York, on

COLUMBUS; HIS MISSION AND CHARACTER.

Because of his exalted mission and character, America and the world honor Columbus. Not the least of these honors is this assembly of the second Catholic Congress of the United States at this fair city of Chicago.

That Columbus had a high and mighty mission is proved by four grand and salient facts in his wonderful career. First, he foresaw and foretold his mission; secondly, he trained himself especially for it throughout his life; thirdly, he undertook it—the most startling of human enterprises; fourthly, he achieved it.

The mission and character of Columbus are so thoroughly blended and interwoven, yet so admirably composed of varied and divergent forces, all united in a grand entirety, that it is impossible to view them separately—I shall treat them as an unique and majestic unit. They are one in origin, nature, kind, and caste, and mutually dependent in their harmonious action and great results. They are like a vast and graceful celestial rainbow, spanning the heavens, resting upon hemispheres, analyzing yet blending the beautiful rays of the sun, and sustained by the moisture from land and ocean. Such a phenomenon is not so beautiful in its parts, as grand and majestic in its whole. Such are the mission and character of Columbus, containing like the seven radiant prismatic colors, seven transcendent features: First, the inspiration; second, the preparation;

third, the faith; fourth, the apostolate or mission; fifth, religious zeal; sixth, the undertaking; seventh, the accomplishment.

Systems of worlds and universes, moving and harmonizing in boundless space, are grand and majestic evidence of creative and almighty power and glory. But what is the physical universe, what are countless centers and systems of universes, to that incomparable creation, that moral and intellectual being, superior to all matter—man? What are they to man, the lord of planets, worlds, and systems, and under whose dominion and for whose use they have been created by the Omnipotent? Regent of the King of Kings? Viceroy of the kingdom of heaven? Minister of the supernatural? United to the Godhead by a Savior becoming man; the price of a Savior's blood; himself both patriarch and prophet, priest and crusader!

Human history shows how man's genius, courage, intellect, ambition, powers of conquest, have explored, discovered the earth, and adorned with every culture this planet-inheritance he received from his heavenly Father. But what would mankind have been without that heroic caste of character and achievement, which the leaders and heroes of the race have exerted to best and greatest results? What, without those venerable patriarchs of old who, standing midway between heaven and earth, have been the law-givers of the soul—a Noah, to rescue the race; a Moses, to lead it to the promised land; a Solomon, to guide it by his wisdom; a David, to teach the royal road of penance; a Peter, laying the foundation of the Papacy; a Paul, to convert the nations; a Thomas Aquinas, to expound the mysteries of Christian theology; a Patrick, to convert a nation of saints and scholars; a Thomas-a-Becket, to uphold the law and die for it; an Ignatius, to create the link between the old monasticism and the modern religious; a Leo XIII., to expound the higher and the social law to men? And what without a Constantine, to see the cross and believe; an Alfred the Great, to found the Christian commonwealth on the unwritten law; a St. Louis, to show how a ruler can be a saint; a Washington, to emancipate his country?

The heroes of the race ennobled it by their works until a world seemed explored and conquered in its vast proportions. Mankind, in the midst of such achievements and conquests and in the fulness of time, produced a type of the race, a hero, a leader, a true Christian gentleman; a link between the middle ages and the new epoch which he himself inaugurated; the blended representative of ages mediæval and modern; science and faith, united in him, harmonized; child of the Church; antagonist of every popular superstition; crusader, ambitious to redeem the holy sepulcher; a sailor who voyaged to every corner of the known earth and, with true genius, declared that there was more to know and more to discover. So vast had been his travels and voyages that I might apply to him the verses of those English poets, Beaumont and Fletcher:

> There is a traveler, sir; knows men,
> Mariners, and has plowed the sea so far
> Till both the poles have knocked; he has seen the sun
> Take coach, and can distinguish the color
> Of his horses, and their kinds.

He was a man almost without scholastic or scientific learning, grasping the profoundest knowledge and revealing the most hidden truths to the incredulous learned; a man who united in himself the prophet and the explorer; a man who bravely lived down an ocean of reproach, ridicule, denial, and calumny; a man, from his boyhood, with a marked mission, which he religiously embraced, with an inevitable destiny, for which he sedulously trained himself; a man who believed in his destiny, who announced his mission and rested not, amid appalling obstacles, until he had fulfilled them both—Christopher Columbus!

Had he a mission? Yes, a mission of unequaled grandeur and beneficence. Every fact I am about to mention has a direct bearing on the mission and character of Columbus. Was he not born and reared in poverty, obscurity, and labor? A sailor from boyhood, the child of the seas for over twenty years, tempest-tossed, battle-scarred, shipwrecked, a voyager over the earth and encompassed by every temptation to crime—he emerged from such a life with his faith undimmed, his soul unsullied, his piety as tender as a mother's love, his filial affection and sense of duty unbroken, his whole character enriched with grace. Twenty-one years of utmost exposure to prevailing sin and profanity failed to tarnish the purity of his soul, and it was never known during his entire life that a profane or immodest word ever passed his lips. Father Arthur George Knight, the English Jesuit, said of him: "Few men indeed, perhaps only saints, have escaped like Columbus, with unwounded conscience from such turbulent scenes." When he arrived at Lisbon to commence his mission, a man of thirty years, his hair was gray with toil, hardship, danger, contact with peril and death, with sudden reverses and personal escapes; but his heart was young and tender; his cheeks bore the blush of youth and modesty; his voice and speech, eloquent and melodious; his carriage, manly and graceful; his eye, vivacious; his stature, robust; his manners, dignified; his presence, engaging; his conversation, grave yet attractive; his presence inspired interest, inquiry, respect, sympathy, veneration, awe. Did he acquire these graces from a sailor's life on the Mediterranean in the 15th century, when a sailor's life was spent in strife with pirate, corsair, Mohammedan? This man of the sea, deprived of chapel, priest, sacrament at Lisbon, was early and late before the altar and the tabernacle; his form devoutly bent in prayer became familiar to the worshipers at the Lisbon Cathedral and the chapel of the Convent of All Saints. Was this the training he received amid the struggles and exposures of naval warfare and adventure on the seas? Did he arrive at Lisbon, after twenty years of seafaring, laden with the booty of captured pirates or of the merchant marine? No, he was poor and friendless. He met at Lisbon not a friend or acquaintance, except his younger brother Bartholomew, who, poor and friendless as himself, like him gained a precarious livelihood by the art of drawing maps and charts.

But there was something marvelous in Columbus, which proved his mission. This stranger, sailor, dreamer, without an introduction received a welcome into the good old social circles of the capital ; in centers of nautical and maritime experience, science and distinction, he was welcomed and listened to; he became allied by marriage with three ancient and distinguished families—the Perestrellos, the Monizes, and the Aranas. But, stranger than all, this obscure mariner associated with the learned and the scientific men of his age, corresponded with scholars and scientists in different lands and harangued universities, prelates, ministers, and cabinets The palaces of capitals opened to him; he appeared at court and was the equal of kings and princes. He dictated terms to kings, and, with sybilline mysticism, repulses only enhanced the value of his secrets. There was a nobility, a royalty in his presence, in his associations, aspiration, and purposes of which history gives us no parallel in the lives of men. What is the mystery? What the secret of this interesting and progressive stranger ?

Everything about Columbus, his striking personal appearance, which was imposing; his poverty, which never detracted from his dignity; his acquired and practical learning, which never affected him with the pretentions of pedantry; his affability, which never impaired a reserve that was ever remarkable and pleasing in his intercourse; his social qualities, which harmonized with his characteristic gravity; his thoughtfulness, which never disappeared in the busy intercourse of the world; his marked purpose, which gave to his movements the energy of immediate undertakings ; a physiognomy, which seemed to reveal and yet conceal the inner movements of an ever active yet meditative mind ; a profound and mediæval cast of religious devotion and contemplativeness, which inspired veneration and won for him the friendship of pious laymen, of dignified prelates, of secluded monks, and of sovereign pontiffs.

In him also, according to a tradition recorded by the Count de Lorgues, the five senses were trained to acuteness in a fine degree, as witnessed by the most acute hearing which enabled him to catch the first sounds of danger on the sea and of approaching storms. By the keenness of his sight, which enabled him to meet many a direful crisis on sea and land and to discern the minutest shades and differences and to measure distances in his pursuit of continents and worlds; by the refinement of his taste, which enabled him to study the qualities and properties of nature; by the delicacy of his sense of smell, which enabled him to scent in advance the odors of continents he was seeking, the perfume of their flowers, fruits, and forests, and the ozone of their atmosphere; by the nicety of his touch, which aided his studies in physics, and at night in sleep protected him from sudden personal danger, and enabled him to know of perils at sea from every movement of his ship. Of him it has been said: "Columbus possessed visibly the three theological virtues; he practiced constantly the four cardinal virtues: the seven gifts of the Holy Ghost were apparent in his life, and we find God admirable in him as he is always in his saints." Frugality, abstemiousness, neatness, purity of language, utter subjection of a temper naturally violent, charity in word and deed, and profound piety were among the qualities which marked him as a man with a high mission and which fitted him for its accomplishment. Such was his religious character and life that he spent much time in prayer, studied the Scriptures and the fathers with profound astuteness, observed the fasts and vigils of the Church, attended mass on shore every day, practiced vows, pilgrimages, and votive offerings, recited daily to the entire canonical office of the cloister, and wore, sometimes publicly and at others under the gaudy insignia of office, the coarse habit and girdle of St. Francis, and he was versed in theological, patristic, and ecclesiastical lore. He was subject to violent and excruciating attacks of illness, to a profound lethargy, and to visions occurring at periods and in times of extraordinary disaster, misfortune, and illness—caused by excessive vigils, labors, and exhaustions of mind and body—occurring, as they did, in many of the most critical crises of his eventful life and career, and during these mental and physical prostrations, from his couch of illness and apparent death, he directed and navigated fleets in unknown seas, prosecuted voyages of momentous consequences, made and recorded observations and thoughts on the most new and startling phenomena of nature, and conducted enterprises of the utmost importance to mankind. He arose from such crises of health and approaches of death with a marvelous recuperation, which he and some of his biographers have regarded as miraculous.

The mission of Columbus was manifold, as is shown by his many transcendent achievements and services; by the services he rendered to religion, to science, and to humanity. His mission is proved by the absence of chance and by the manifest assumption by him of a great task; by his preparation and fitness for it; by its achievement. Strike from the history of mankind and from the present development of human affairs what Columbus undertook and achieved, the world will go back four hundred years; four hundred years of unprecedented progress in human culture, in civilization, in the humanities, in the arts and sciences, in the Christian missions and apostolate, in the practical application of the great principles of government and liberty, in commerce; in the arts of war and peace, in the efforts and approaches to the benign substitution of peaceful arbitration for human warfare, of progress in testing the inherent power of religion and of Christianity. As types only of all this, compare a caravan of camels loaded with Oriental products crossing the deserts for twelve months—compare it with the voyage of the modern steamship around the world, accomplished now in sixty-five days. Compare the slowly pacing camel itself with our modern steamship, now called the camel of the seas! Compare the first voyage of Columbus—three months and eight days in crossing the Atlantic—compare it with the same voyage accomplished now in five days, nineteen hours, and twenty-five minutes! From these pass to the comparison of higher and holier things; to the progress of mind, and soul, and humanity. It was Columbus who brought together those two great currents of human life which had run in different hemispheres, had never known each other, had never worshiped at the same altar. To achieve all this he had to discover a new world. Such was his mission. Such was his fulfillment.

Not only had Columbus such a mission in the design of Providence, but he was himself a firm and unswerving believer in that mission; that his mission came from God; that he was commissioned to do the work of heaven on earth. He announced his mission to the world, and he offered himself an ardent missionary to the apostolate of Christendom in bringing new and boundless realms, buried in ignorance of Christ and in heathenism, into the Christian fold. He announced a further, and what he esteemed a paramount purpose, of devoting his expected immense revenues from the Indies to the recovery of the Holy Sepulcher and the Holy Land and restoring them to the Christian world. These great objects he never lost sight of and he never ceased to aim at their accomplishment. In that solemn and characteristic act of his life, his last will, he commences with these self-dedicatory words: " In the name of the Most Holy Trinity, who inspired me with the idea and afterward made it perfectly clear to me that I should navigate and go to the Indies from Spain, by traversing the ocean westwardly."

This avowal of his mission is repeated in many letters and writings of the illustrious admiral. The most solemn and sublime self-dedication to God and his work and to the Christian apostolate that a Christian layman could possibly make was that which Columbus prepared and addressed to the Spanish sovereigns before sailing on his fourth voyage, which was based upon a profound study of the Scriptures, and whose remarkable title was in itself a self-ordination: " Collection of Prophecies Concerning the Recovery of Jerusalem and the Discovery of the Indies." Therein he solemnly announced himself as one chosen of God from his earliest years for the discovery of the New World and the redemption of the Savior's tomb; that Providence had inspired him with study that educated himself for this work by leading him to embrace a sailor's life from the age of fourteen, to observe and ponder over the phenomena and secrets of nature and of the earth, and to study with eagerness the greatest work and chronicles in geography, cosmography, navigation, astronomy, and philosophy. He said that by those studies God had opened his mind " as by a hand," an invisible hand, and that he was thus inspired and consumed with the idea of discovering the New World and of opening the way to all Christendom. He reminds Ferdinand and Isabella: " I spent ten years at your august court in discussions with persons of great merit and profound learning, who, after much argument, ended by declaring my projects to be chimerical. Your Majesties alone had faith and constancy. Who can doubt that it was the light derived from the Sacred Scriptures that enlightened your minds with the same rays as mine?" In this remarkable letter he extols the wondrous methods of the Holy Ghost, guiding the chosen instruments of Providence and educating them for their vocation and its accomplishment. He displays great learning in setting forth definite canons for scriptural interpretation, based upon St. Augustine, St. Thomas, St. Isidore, and Gerson.

He claims that his mission to discover a new world and its fulfilment was predicted by the inspired prophets; quotes the prophecies themselves, and then follows them up with cogent arguments, interpretations, and citations from the Fathers of the Church. This "ambassador of God," as the Count de Lorgues calls Columbus, self-dedicated by the very prayer with which he commenced every act of his life, and every writing of his pen, "Jesu cum Maria, sit nobis via," proves that he was always on the way, forever journeying toward a goal, an end, an achievement, perpetually laboring in his great mission. He chose for the companions of his sublime mission the immaculate Mother and divine Son; Jesu cum Maria!

Columbus, in the benign economies of Providence, and of Christian policy, and in the profound studies of philosophic history, has been likened to the patriarchs and prophets of old and the founders of states and nations. It is thus that he has been compared with Moses and David and with other patriarchs. The extraordinary and symbolical names he received in baptism and significantly bore and cherished, were both emblematic of his mission and prophetic of his vocation. Columbo, which means a dove, indicated his mission of peace, good-will, and salvation between the old Christian world and the new heathen world, which he discovered and went to convert. And Christopher means Christ-Bearer—not the ordained eucharistic priest, but, in another and exceptional sense, one who carries the living and teaching Christ, the brother, Redeemer, and Savior of man in his human, divine, and missionary personality, across continents and over oceans to other continents and oceans to the utmost boundaries of the earth. There was an ancient legend in Christian hagiography which, whether a reality or an ideality, derives its chief significance and value from its being prophetic of Christopher Columbus—the legend of St. Christopher, the patronal saint of Columbus, whose pagan name was Opheus.

Tradition, including Dr. Alban Butler's "Lives," makes St. Christopher a Syrian by nationality, a giant in stature, strength, and in prayer, miraculously converted from paganism and choosing the name of Christopher or Christ-Bearer, and after bearing Christ, symbolized in the Christian Faith, through Palestine, Asia Minor, and crossing oceans, with Christ upon his shoulders, he finally won the crown of martyrdom under the Emperor Decius. So truly prophetic was this legend of Columbus that after the latter had carried Christ across the Atlantic to unknown countries he had discovered, the legend seemed to loom up in sacred literature on account of the achievement of the great Christopher and then became merged in the reality. Even the image of the saint thenceforth bore the features of Christopher Columbus instead of the legendary saint, as was the case in the celebrated vignette in the map of Juan de la Cosa, in which also the literal name of Columbus was omitted, because it was rather represented by the image of the saint crossing the ocean with the Christ upon his shoulders, the features being those of Christopher Columbus, for it was he who carried the Redeemer's name across the ocean, as divinely expressed, "to them that have not heard of Me and not seen my glory."

The parallel between Columbus and Moses is equally or more striking. Both were living patriarchs of living races of men believing in the true God. Fifteen hundred years before the coming of Christ, Moses delivered the law of God to his people; fifteen hundred years after the birth of Christ, Columbus delivered the law of Christ to other worlds and continents which he discovered. Moses and Columbus were each forty years of age when they began the active missions they received from the same God. Both Moses and Columbus left wife and family heroically to perform the will of God. While the sea opened a passage for Moses to pass over, the ocean of darkness and storms, the then dread Atlantic, gave Columbus a first, a safe and gentle passage over its bosom. Moses gave the law of the covenant; Columbus announced the law of the New Testament. Moses appealed prophetically to the cross in the Greek Tau on the gateposts of the chosen people; Columbus carried the cross of Christ with him, saluted it, and planted it in the virgin soil, the cross made of mighty trees cut from primeval forests. Moses received repulses and even violence from his own people; Columbus endured the mockery and ingratitude of those he served. Both died in poverty—outcasts. Both reached the promised land and saw it. Moses was never permitted to enter it; Columbus never reached and never saw or entered the Indies which he sought, but, unlike Moses, he raised up new kingdoms and empires to Christ, planted the seeds of Faith over continents, and in his tracks have followed knowledge, Faith, civilization, free republics, and human liberty. Unlike Moses, he entered the promised land. Columbus felt an inward resemblance to Moses and to David, for, after likening himself to Moses, he said: "Let them give me what name they will, for, in fine, David, the wise king, was a shepherd, and he became king of Jerusalem, and I serve the same Lord who raised him to such high estate."

He was compared to St. Thomas the Apostle, who carried the Faith of Christ to the same peoples of the East, whom Columbus sought to visit and evangelize, and whom he believed he had discovered. According to traditions, St. Thomas, under sacred Indian names, evangelized the Indian tribes of America. Scholars point to distinct traditions and fragmentary creeds of Christian origin, and the Spanish missionaries of the 16th and 17th centuries were amazed at finding among the Indians of North and South America the prevalence of cruciculus and the attribution of miraculous qualities to ancient crosses, preserved and venerated from remote antiquity by the American Indians.

Christian scholars of four hundred years have found nine different passages in the Old Testament which they recognize as prophetic of Columbus, his mission, and his discovery. Some have traced in sacred verses descriptions of his ships, the very caravels he commanded and reproductions of which even here you have seen, and allusions to his armorial ensigns. Illustrious contemporaries of Columbus recognized his divine mission. The great Cardinal Ximenes and the learned Archbishop Diego de Deza of Seville, openly favored or advocated the project and mission of Columbus at the very time he was claiming to be the chosen missionary of heaven. And the great scientist of Spain, Jayme Ferrer, said of Columbus to Isabella: "I believe that in its deep mysterious designs divine Providence selected him as its agent in this work, which I look upon as the introduction and preparation of things which the same divine Providence has determined to make known to us for its own glory and the salvation and happiness of the world." And again: "I behold in this a great mystery." And addressing Columbus himself, he says: "In your mission, senor, you seem an apostle, a messenger of God, to spread his name in unknown lands."

The Count de Lorgues, in presenting the cause of Columbus to Rome for canonization, exclaims: "Evidently God chose Christopher Columbus as a messenger of salvation." And while our own Washington Irving says that he was led to know how much of the world remained unknown and was led to meditate on the means of exploring it, says that "The enthusiastic nature of his conception gave an elevation to his spirit and a dignity and loftiness to his whole demeanor," and that "his views were princely and unbounded," I can not pass over the high tribute of the English Jesuit, Father Arthur George Knight, to his genius, his learning, and his zeal for the conversion of the heathen and for bringing "the nations in willing homage to the feet of Jesus Christ, reigning once more in the Jerusalem of the Christians."

Typified by his symbolical names, foretold in ancient prophecy and sacred song, believed in and announced by himself, the mission of Columbus was providential. Even from the standpoints of skepticism, of the utter denial of the supernatural, and of agnosticism, Columbus, in fact, by his aspirations, his self-preparation, and his very enterprise, in the natural order, as a man, he made a mission for himself. His contemporaries also, men of learning, intellect, and religion, acknowledged his mighty vocation to great and stupendous achievements. Such men in every age, down to our own time and country, have paid homage to his recognized and acknowledged mission. There was something that marked Columbus out from other men—there was in him not only those traits of character which I have mentioned, that learning, that zeal, that courage, that faith, that unbounded zeal—but there was in his whole mental and moral structure, in his profound studies and deep reflection, his familiarity with sciences, and his quick seizure of the mysteries and secrets of nature, and of the physical world, in his very visions and dreams, his constant intercourse with the supernatural—such a combination of qualifications as placed him on a higher plane than ordinary men. There is in revealed and supernatural religion a spirituality, a religious mysticism in which the saints alone seemed to move and soar.

In this sense Columbus was a true mystic—one who saw in the fall of the sparrow, in the raiment of the lily and the rose, the mystic and ever-provident hand of God, and in every turn in his own eventful and dramatic career he recognized his own immediate touch with the ever-present Deity. He was a pilgrim, staff in hand, of religion and science, recognizing perfect union and accord between them. He was a pilgrim in the flesh, staff in hand, wending his way to shrine and altar, to fulfill a vow made at sea or to take a votive offering in return for many a deliverance from the perils of the sea

He was a crusader, and he bequeathed a crusader's injunction upon his heirs, never to rest until the Holy Sepulcher was redeemed and restored to Christendom. He was a rigid observer on land and sea of the fasts, vigils, and feasts of the Church. With all this, he was a man among men. Conceiving a high estimate of his services, insisting on providing title, offices, and estates for himself, and his posterity and successors; worthy of his position as the discoverer of the New World, he was a man in touch with earth and heaven.

The part he took in that momentous act, when the Sovereign Pontiff in 1493, just after the discovery of America, was called upon to arbitrate, for the preservation of the peace of the world, between the two leading maritime powers of the world, Spain and Portugal, then struggling for the supremacy of the unknown half of the earth, was such participation in the crucial events in the history of mankind as no man was ever before or since called upon to perform, second only to his own discovery of the New World. Then there was but one known hemisphere, and even its hemispherical form was not then known, Columbus, Dr. Toscanelli, and, perhaps, a few other learned ones being the sole expounders of the sphericity of the earth. Portugal was claiming distant lands, discovered by a southern and eastern route, and Spain was claiming distant lands, discovered by Columbus by a western route. No line had been drawn to mark off the east or the west. The character of a crusade had been bestowed upon these explorations and discoveries by the bestowal of papal blessings and indulgences. The nations appealed to Pope Alexander VI. In the then confused condition of geographical knowledge, where and how could a line be drawn? It was Columbus that gave this mystic line that preserved the peace of nations.

On his first voyage, on September 13th, just a month before land was discovered, Columbus, who had watched incessantly the magnetic needle and its variations in those unknown seas, and to whom the mysteries of heaven and earth then centered in that little magnet, observed that the needle ceased for a moment to vibrate, and pointed to the true north. This mysterious meridian was west of the Island of Flores. Immediately the mystery was solved. The east and the west were separated by a mystic line. When the Sovereign Pontiff came to divide the unknown world between the maritime nations, after the return of Columbus to Europe in the following year, the critical embarrassment of the situation was relieved through the remarkable discovery by Columbus of the line of no variation of the needle, and this line, by a singular coincidence, passed from pole to pole without touching the land, and without dividing an island. From these facts resulted the celebrated bull of demarkation, issued by Pope Alexander VI., on May 3, 1493. Now for the first time an east and a west were recognized and demarkated. The line was accepted. Afterward diplomacy of jealous nations effected a change of the papal line farther to the west. Under this change Portugal acquired the immense empire of Brazil; but for this change Spain would have preserved her claim to the New World entire. The bull of demarkation served the great purpose of preserving peace. Neither the Pope nor Columbus would ever consent to change it. Columbus, on his death-bed, inserted a clause in his will repudiating the new line, which had cost Spain the loss of more territory than she now owns on the earth, and she then solemnly reaffirmed the original line of no variations of the magnetic needle as the true line which God had established to separate the eastern and the western hemispheres.

The mission and character of a man who achieved so much, relying solely on his genius and on heaven, are marked out and sustained by every word I have said of his humble origin, his poverty, his maritime education, his studies, his correspondence with learned men, his personal bearing, appearance, and magnetism, his profound sense and practice of religion, the broaching of his new theory of the earth, his appeals to nations, his inflexible maintenance of it, his prophecy of the result, the prophecies of sacred Scripture, the apostolic character which he infused in the enterprise, his dedication of all to the conversion of heathens, and the redemption of Jerusalem, his poverty in the midst of grandeur, his wrongs and his sorrows, the bestowal of another's name upon the world he had discovered, the ingratitude of his king, and now, the contrast, the reverse current of honor and praise, which the world unites in bestowing upon his memory.

Columbus foresaw and predicted much; and much that he predicted was fulfilled. Errors of detail in so vast a field of new ideas, undertakings, and results, in which he was the pioneer, enhance the grandeur of his real achievement. His promise to lead Christian Europe with its missionaries to the boundless empires of Oriental potentates, which would embrace the Faith, has been more than realized by the rise and growth of Christian empires and republics in the world which he discovered. His offer to carry missionaries to the mythical Christian prince of the Orient, the Prester John, who tradition said had sent ambassadors to Rome in the middle ages to ask Christian missionaries, has been realized in the many delegations of the red men sent to ask that Catholic priests be sent among them, and by the acceptance of the Faith of the black gowns, by the Indian tribes of North and South America.

Let us recall the first visit of the Catholic missionary to the Indians of this State, in whose great and justly proud metropolis we are assembled this day to honor Columbus. It was the famous Jesuit black gown, Father Marquette. When he saluted the chief and his tribe they called out the word Illinois. The meaning of the Indian name Illinois is, "We are men." Well does this name describe the present men of Illinois, and of Chicago, our hosts, who have given us such a welcome to this Catholic Congress.

When Father Marquette, with the mute but appealing symbol of the cross, announced his mission to the Illinois Indians, Hiawatha, in the language of our poet Longfellow, said:

> Beautiful is the sun, oh strangers,
> When you come so far to see us;
> Never bloomed the earth so gayly,
> Never shone the sun so brightly
> As to-day they shine and blossom
> When you came so far to see us!

Then Father Marquette made answer to the chief:

> Peace be with you, Hiawatha,
> Peace be with you and your people,
> Peace of prayer, and peace of pardon,
> Peace of Christ and joy of Mary.

So, too, was the prophecy of Columbus answered and fulfilled by the touching appeal, which, after the establishment of our independence as a nation, the Catholics of this country made to Rome for the appointment of a bishop and for missionaries to be sent to the infant Republic, and, by the action of Rome, in appointing to the exalted position of first bishop an American priest in the person of John Carroll, the patriarch of Catholicism in America, and by the growth of that august hierarchy which he founded, and which is now composed of seventeen archbishops, in one of whom we recognize with pride the worthy bearer of the princely honors of the Roman cardinalate, whose august body is completed by an eighteenth archbishop in the person of the distinguished papal delegate; of seventy-five bishops, two archabbots, and ten abbots, and of nearly ten thousand priests, all carrying before them the very cross which Columbus was the first to plant in American soil. He promised popes and kings that his discoveries would lead to the spread of the Catholic Faith among millions of human beings; look around you and see the fulfillment of this promise in nearly one hundred millions of Catholics in North and South America. If the southward flight of birds had not induced Columbus to change his course to the south, he would have landed, first of all, on the soil of our own Republic, where there now worship before the cross which he brought over the Atlantic fourteen millions of Catholics, true and loyal sons of the Church; yes, fourteen millions of Catholics, represented here and now in this hall by their appointed delegates, assembled in the second Catholic Congress of America, in honor of the name, the virtues, the achievements, in recognition of the exalted character and mission of Christopher Columbus.

As a fitting pendant to Dr. Clarke's beautiful paper, and also as being in line with the subject matter of "The Columbian Jubilee," may well appear here a paper by Miss Mary J. Onahan of Chicago, on

"ISABELLA THE CATHOLIC."

Ideals are the great exemplars of the world. Inasmuch as men and women have high ideals, inasmuch as they have lived up to them, insomuch have they been great, insomuch have they been good, insomuch have they been glorious.

That the ideal of womanhood which called to Isabella in the 15th century was a great and a high one, and her life with but few, if any, missteps, gradually evolved toward it, this many biographers have shown, but it remains for the Catholic biographer to prove that this ideal, inasmuch as it was great and good and glorious, was the logical outcome of the Catholic Faith, which was her heritage. If she was pure in an age of impurity, if she was brave in an age of cowardice and oppression, if she was womanly when the type of womanhood was Queen Elizabeth of England, she was all of these things because of the Faith that was in her, for by it she patterned her life, by it she must be judged now.

The 19th century hugs to itself many delusions, none greater than the claim that it has discovered woman—woman that has come down to us from Adam all the way!

Æsop's fly, perched upon the axle of the chariot wheel, and exclaiming exultingly, "What a dust I do raise!" is but the symbol of a universal weakness. The present age always seems the most glorious age, its progress the most wonderful progress, and its importance far greater than the importance of any that has preceded it. So in the glamor of this delusion we almost forget that woman was a power, morally, socially, and intellectually, in the 15th century as in the 19th; that the doors of universities were open to her, that she not only studied but actually taught within their sacred precincts. In the University of Salamanca she had a place, and when Isabella, on ascending the throne, set about the acquisition of the Latin tongue it was to a woman that she turned to be her tutor. Nay, we can go further back than the 15th century, and to other parts of the world than Spain. In Italy, in the 13th century, a noble Florentine lady contended for and won the palm of oratory in a public contest in that city with learned doctors from all over the world. Further back still, in the 4th century, St. Catherine, of Alexandria, standing in the great hall of the royal palace, in the presence of the emperor and the assembled notables of his kingdom, converted by her learning and her wisdom the forty venerable philosophers arrayed against her. Plato and Socrates this modest Christian maiden could quote, and she knew by heart the books of the Sibyls.

The age of woman dates not from the 19th century, but from the 1st; is due not to modern civilization, not to modern progress, but to something grander than either—the mainspring of both—the religion of Christ and of his Church.

The greatness of Isabella need not, therefore, be looked upon as something extraordinary and unaccountable. She was merely the logical outcome of the country in which she was born and the religion in which she was bred—Catholic Spain of the 15th century. To understand the character of Isabella it is necessary to at least outline the political condition of the country in which she lived. Spain in the 15th century was not, as it afterward became, one of the greatest powers of Europe. It was divided into petty states, of which Navarre, Aragon, and Castile were the most important. Overrun by the Moors and tyrannized by numerous factions of the nobility, no wonder that Spain seemed to many a desolated country. And yet there was a spirit of freedom and of that modern shibboleth—democracy—among its people which no other country of Europe could match. "We, who are each of us as good as you," ran the oath of allegiance taken by the Spanish Cortes to a new king, "and who are all together more powerful than you, promise obedience to your government if you maintain our rights and liberties, but not otherwise."

It was over this people that Isabella was to reign. The court of her brother, King Henry of Castile, was a debauched one, the king himself a coward and worse, who drained the already meager royal treasury by his luxury and extravagance. Fortunately for Isabella her youth was not destined to be spent amid the glitter and frivolity of the court. Like the great majority who in after life have attained distinction, her youth was almost a solitary one—for solitude vivifies the powers of the soul. Until the age of sixteen she lived in retirement in the little town of Arevalo, under the care of her mother. Here this young Castilian girl came to understand the great heritage of her Faith and the responsibilities which were involved in her future.

The Church in the 15th century was indeed in the shadow of desolation, though here and there were wondrous bursts of light. The See of Rome was in continual turmoil, sometimes usurped by men whose lives only proved the gospel saying that the "gates of hell could not prevail against it." But however weak and unworthy her rulers, the Church of Christ was still there unfolding the wisdom of her Founder. Her great sacraments were being administered, sacraments which change the whole meaning of life. Isabella, too, received them; her young soul pondered over them; her young heart grew richer and sweeter in their graces. Baptism, marking with its chrism the child of a king and the child of a peasant as equal before God, inheritors of the Most High; penance, teaching that, no matter how great the sin, how despairing the sinner, the mercy of God is greater; confirmation, making of him a soldier valiant and true; the Holy Eucharist outrivaling in the estimate it puts upon man all the theories of the most ultra of optimists, outshining their wildest dreams. These and the other great sacraments of the Church were the heritage of this young Spanish princess in the 15th century, as they are the heritage of so many other young souls here and now in America, and all over the world in the 19th.

Religion is the atmosphere of the soul. It vivifies, colors, gives strength and light and beauty. (The inner spirit of religion is more than an intellectual question—it is a question of conduct, of self-government.) This inner spirit of religion, of law, permeated the whole life and character of Isabella. The Faith that had been handed down to her from ages, the faith for which saints had lived, and martyrs had died—it was her faith, too. It filled her soul with radiance, it made life great, full of meaning, sublime. When the girl became a woman her hand was sought in marriage by numerous suitors. She was present with her brother at an interview with King Alphonso of Portugal, who sought her hand, but neither threats nor entreaties could induce her to accede to a union so unsuitable from the disparity of their years. The Marquis of Calatrava, a fierce and licentious nobleman, next pressed his claim, whereupon Isabella shut herself up in her room and, abstaining from food and sleep, implored heaven to save her from the dishonor of such a union. Among her other suitors were the Duke of Gloucester, infamous forever under the title of Richard III., and the Duke of Guienne, brother of Louis XI., of France. They were all of them unsuccessful. For once old heads and young hearts were in unison. Statecraft, as well as youthful preference, pointed to Ferdinand of Aragon. The superior advantages of a connection, which should be the means of uniting the people of Aragon and Castile, were indeed manifest. Yet Isabella was too true a woman to be moved to so important a step by purely political reasons. She dispatched her chaplain to the courts of France and Aragon, and when he returned with the report that the Duke of Guienne was a feeble, effeminate, watery-eyed prince and that Ferdinand on the other hand was possessed of a comely figure, a graceful demeanor, and a spirit that was up to everything, Isabella was not slow to decide. She resolved to give her hand where she felt that she could give her heart. Owing to the intrigues of King Henry and his persistent efforts to thwart the marriage, the lovers were obliged to resort to subterfuge. Disguised as a mule driver, Ferdinand set out at the dead of night from the court of Aragon accompanied by a half-dozen of his followers, supposed to be merchants, while, to divert the attention of the Castilians, another cavalcade proceeded in a different direction with all the ostentation of a public embassy, from the court of Aragon to King Henry. Ferdinand waited on the table, took care of the mules, and in every way acted as servant to his companions. In this guise, with no other disaster save that of leaving at an inn the purse which contained the funds for the expedition, Ferdinand arrived late at night at one of Isabella's strongholds, cold, faint, and exhausted.

On knocking at the gates the travelers were saluted with a large stone rolled down from the battlements, which came within a few inches of Ferdinand's head, and would doubtless have put an end once and for all to his romantic enterprise. Expostulations were followed by explanations; when the voice of the prince was recognized by friends within great was the rejoicing, and trumpets proclaimed the arrival of the adventurous bridegroom. Arrangements were at once made for a meeting between the royal pair Ferdinand, accompanied by only four of his attendants, was admitted to the neighboring city of Valladolid, where he was received by the Archbishop of Toledo, and conducted to the apartment of his mistress. Courtly parasites had urged Isabella to require some act of homage from Ferdinand in token of the inferiority of the crown of Aragon to that of Castile, but with true womanly dignity she refused to do so. She never forgot that she was a woman even though a queen, and would not allow a sign of inferiority from one who was to be her husband. The interview lasted two hours. Ferdinand was at this time eighteen years of age, Isabella a little older. His complexion was fair though bronzed by constant exposure to the sun; his eye quick and bright. He was active of frame, vigorous of muscle, invigorated by the toils of war and the exercises of chivalry, and one of the best horsemen in the kingdom. His voice was sharp and decisive, save when he wished to carry a point. Then his manners were courteous, even insinuating. Isabella was a little above the middle size, her blue eyes beamed with intelligence, her hair was light, inclining to red, her manners dignified and modest.

When the preliminaries of the marriage were adjusted, so great was the poverty of the parties that they had to borrow money to defray the expenses of the ceremony. But in spite of all opposition, in spite of such humiliating obstacles, Ferdinand and Isabella were married on October 19, 1469, in the presence of the Archbishop of Toledo, the Admiral of Castile, and all of the nobility that espoused the cause of the youthful pair.

The first few years of married life were uneventful, but on the death of the king, in 1474, and the accession of Ferdinand and Isabella, the country was plunged into the war of the succession. The royal pair had refused from the beginning to be put in leading-strings by the Archbishop of Toledo, and the haughty prelate, disgusted with treatment to which he had not been accustomed, withdrew from their court and espoused the cause of the unfortunate Joanna, boasting that "he had raised Isabella from the distaff and he would send her back to it again." The death of the King of Aragon at this time called Ferdinand to the throne, thus uniting the two crowns. It would be

MARY J. ONAHAN,
CHICAGO.

ANNA T. SADLIER,
NEW YORK.

ELIZA ALLEN STARR,
CHICAGO.

LOUISE IMOGEN GUINEY,
BOSTON.

useless to dwell upon this long and stormy period. At one time, indeed, all parties were so worn out by the war that the King of Portugal, who had been affianced to Joanna, offered to resign all claims to the throne of Castile upon the cession of certain provinces. Ferdinand and his ministers were willing to accede to his proposal, but Isabella proudly replied that "she would not consent to the dismemberment of a single inch of Castile." After a struggle of nearly five years, a treaty was at last arranged, the King of Portugal resigned his pretentions to the throne, Joanna entered a convent, and Ferdinand and Isabella, relieved from the pretentions of ambitious rivals, were allowed to turn their attention to the internal welfare of their kingdom.

One of their first acts was to reform the laws, to prohibit the adulteration of money, and to gradually lessen the overbearing power of the nobility by the elevation of the Cortes. On certain days of the week the king and queen presided personally at the court of justice, and so prompt and so just were their decisions, that it came to be said that it was more difficult and more costly to transact business with a stripling of a secretary than with the queen and all her ministers.

There are many stories told of Isabella's promptness and heroism in the presence of danger. When news was brought to her of the revolt of the city of Segovia, she at once mounted her horse and, accompanied by a band of her followers, effected an entrance through one of the gates. Riding direct to the citadel, where the tumult was at its height, she demanded of the enraged populace the cause of the insurrection.

"Tell me what are your grievances," said she, "and I will do all in my power to redress them, for I am sure what is for your interest must also be for mine and for that of the whole city."

Such conduct won the respect, admiration, and love of her subjects. The insurrection was put down and the mob dispersed, shouting "Long live the queen."

One of the stumbling-blocks of the biographer in the reign of Ferdinand and Isabella is the inquisition. Volumes have been written about it—they need scarcely be added to. Primarily a political rather than a religious institution, as Prescott, a Protestant authority, says, it had origin partly, it is true, in a misguided zeal, but far more largely in avarice and greed. It was aimed at the Jews, whose position in Spain had long been a humiliating one, the outcasts of society, but whose wealth excited the cupidity of the nobles. To hold Isabella responsible for the injustices of the inquisition would be as absurd as to blame Washington for the evil of slavery, as absurd as to expect in the 15th century the enlightenment of the 19th. All history is a record of progress from ignorance to knowledge, from weakness to strength, from bondage to freedom. The history of the Moors in Spain, the recital of the splendors of their stately capital of Grenada and of its gradual overthrow, and of the subversion of the Arabian empire in Europe is a more alluring subject. Irving has dwelt upon it in his own picturesque and fascinating style. The Moors were as fierce and terrible in battle as they were luxurious and effeminate in peace. Cordova, with its narrow streets that seemed to whisper nightly of strange adventures, its lofty houses with turrets of curiously wrought larch or stone, its marble fountains and white columned mosques, its airy halls fragrant with the perfume of the orange, the olive, and the pomegranate— all this has a peculiar fascination for the student and the traveler.

In these wars with the Moors, as in all other wars, Ferdinand assumed the command of the army, while Isabella directed the internal arrangements of the kingdom, and supplied the sinews of battle. She held herself, indeed, ever in readiness to go to the front, and in some cases was called by her husband to do so when the spirits of the soldiers were flagging, and he wished to infuse new ardor into the struggle. She always responded with the greatest alacrity, and it was due to her wisdom that many reforms in camp life were instituted. She was the first to establish what were then known as "queen's hospitals"—tents for the sick and wounded. She was, in the words of Prescott, "the soul of this war," and her ever-present motive was zeal for religion. When the army lay encamped before Grenada, she appeared on the field superbly mounted and dressed in complete armor; she visited the different quarters and reviewed the troops. Everywhere she aided the king by her wise counsel, her consummate management, and her inalienable purpose. In 1492 Grenada fell, and with it the Moslem empire of Spain.

The traveler can still see the rocky eminence in the Alpuxarras from which the Moorish king took his last farewell of the scenes of his departed greatness, as the gleaming turrets of Grenada, crowned with the victorious ensigns of Spain, faded in the distance. The spot is called to this day the "Last Sign of the Moor."

1492 brings us the most important event in the reign of Isabella, the discovery of America. How Columbus had vainly importuned his native city of Genoa, had sought the aid of the King of Portugal, all the weary, fruitless years that passed waiting at the court of Spain, and how finally, in direst poverty and despair, he sought at the convent of La Rabida for food and drink for himself and his little son—all this there is no need to tell. The first astronomer who advanced the theory that the stars were worlds like our own was probably met with no more incredulity than the Genoese visionary, who, standing in the midst of the Spanish court, pleaded for this land of the Western sphere.

His learning, we are told, took all by surprise, but it convinced few. Isabella alone, who from the first seems to have been favorable to him, was won by his enthusiasm, and when there was some question of the means necessary to equip the ships, royalty declared that she assumed the undertaking for her own crown of Castile, and was ready to pawn her jewels if the funds in the treasury were found inadequate. Thus did the belief of a Franciscan monk and the unfaltering enthusiasm of a woman prevail over the arguments of men of science and the incredulity of statesmen. No need to tell of that voyage, the three small ships setting out so dauntlessly, guided by one who had a dauntless heart—

> Over the wide unknown
> Far to the shores of Ind.
> On through the dark alone,
> Like a feather blown by the wind;
> Into the West away,
> Sped by the breath of God,
> Seeking the clearer day
> Where only his feet have trod.

Beautiful as are those lines they scarce equal in grandeur and simplicity that sentence of Columbus, written in his log-book: "To-day we sailed westward, which was our course."

Woman's faith, called, until proved, woman's credulity, once more rose triumphant, and Isabella has no fairer crown than that woven by her trusted and valiant admiral. "In the midst of the general incredulity," wrote Columbus, "the Almighty infused into the queen, my lady, the spirit of intelligence and energy, and whilst everyone else was expatiating only on the inconvenience and cost, her highness, on the contrary, approved it, and gave it all the support in her power."

Religious zeal had dictated the war against the Moors; religious zeal urged Isabella to sanction the seemingly hopeless voyage of Columbus, and when these voyages were crowned with success her first solicitude was the welfare of the benighted and helpless natives. In view of Isabella's known principles and her many stringent measures, it is a little singular that her attitude on the subject of slavery of the Indians should ever be questioned. When the most pious churchmen and enlightened statesmen of her time could not determine whether it was or was not lawful and according to the Christian religion to enslave the Indians; when Columbus himself pressed the measure as a political necessity, and condemned to slavery those who offered the slightest opposition to the Spanish Invaders, Isabella settled the matter according to the dictates of her own merciful and upright mind. She ordered that all the Indians should be conveyed back to their respective homes, and forbade, absolutely, all harsh measures toward them on any pretense. Her treatment of Columbus was equally generous. When, owing to various mistakes and misunderstandings, the reaction set in against him, and he was sent to Spain in irons, Isabella indignantly ordered that he be set free at once, and herself sent him the money to come in state and honor to her court. He came accordingly, "not as one in disgrace, but richly dressed, and with all the marks of rank and distinction. Isabella received him in the Alhambra, and when he entered her apartment she was so overpowered that she burst into tears and could only extend her hand to him. Columbus himself, who had borne up firmly against the stern conflicts of the world and had endured the injuries and insults of ignoble men, when he beheld the queen's emotion could no longer suppress his own; he threw himself at her feet and for some time was unable to utter a word for the violence of his tears and sobbings."

It was under her special protection that he set sail on his fourth voyage, from which Isabella did not live to see him return.

The uses of suffering! They have often been dwelt upon; possibly they can never be learned by hearsay. As a queen, Isabella attained the greatest glory; as a mother she was called upon to endure the deepest sorrow. The anguish of a father's or mother's heart at the loss, the ruin of a loved child—that, indeed, must be something that only they who have felt in all its anguish and all its bitterness can ever fathom. While her husband was engaged in his brilliant wars in Italy, and the great captian, Gonsalvo de Cordova, was daily adding new glories to the crown of Spain; while the fame of that great prince of the church, Cardinal Ximenes, was spreading throughout Europe, Isabella's life, clouded by domestic misfortune, began gradually to decline. One after another her children had been taken from her by death and by misfortune worse than death. Her only son, Don John, died three months after his marriage. Her favorite daughter and namesake lived but a year after her nuptials with the King of Portugal, and their infant son, on whom were founded all the hopes of the succession, survived her but a few months. Isabella's second daughter, Joanna, married to Philip, Prince of the Netherlands, became insane, and there can be no sadder history than that of her youngest child, Donna Catalina, memorable in history as Catherine of Aragon.

These and other misfortunes clouded Isabella's years. When she felt the end to be not far distant she made deliberate and careful disposition of her affairs. Even on a bed of sickness she followed with interest the affairs of her kingdom, received distinguished foreigners, and took part in the direction of affairs.

"I have come to Castile," said Prosper Colonna on being presented to King Ferdinand, "to behold the woman who from her sick-bed rules the world."

There was no interest in her kingdom, her colonies, or her household that she neglected. In her celebrated testament she provided munificently for charities, for marriage portions to poor girls, for the redemption of Christian captives in Barbary. Patriotism and humanity breathed in its very line—she warned her successor to treat with gentleness and consideration the natives of the New World added to Spain; warned them also never to surrender the fortress of Gibraltar.

"By her dying words," says Prescott, "she displayed the same respect for the rights and liberties of the nation that she had shown through life, striving to secure the blessings of her benign administration to the most distant and barbarous regions under her sway."

The woman whom life had not daunted, death could not dismay. On the 26th of November, 1504, Isabella the Catholic breathed her last, in the fifty-fourth year of her age, and thirteenth of her reign. She had ordered that her funeral be of the simplest, and the sum saved by this economy be distributed in alms among the poor; that her remains be buried in the Franciscan Monastery in the Alhambra of Grenada, in a grave level with the ground and trodden down, and that her name be engraved on a flat tombstone. "But," she added, "should the king, my lord, prefer a sepulcher in some other place, then my will is that my body be transported and laid by his side, that the union we have enjoyed in this world, and through the mercy of God may hope again for our souls in heaven, may be represented by our bodies in the earth."

True queen and true woman she had proved herself through life, true queen and true woman she proved herself in death. The Catholic Church is not ashamed of the ideal in womanhood that it presents—an ideal that it has upheld for centuries, an ideal that is still shining as a new-risen star serene and beautiful in the summer sky. The queenly scepter of Isabella was laid aside, the womanly frame had long since crumbled into dust, but the Church of which she was so valiant a daughter, the Church that crowns her with that fairest of her titles, is not dead. It lives. The light of the eternal is in its eyes, life-blood courses in its veins, its strong arm reaches out now as it did in old Castile to the peasant in his hut, to the queen upon her throne. It stands to-day as it stood nineteen hundred years ago—logical, strong, consistent, serene. It is all of these things and more. It is dowered with immortality.

Therefore we hail not merely one of the many myriad of its daughters, but we hail the religion that made Isabella possible—the religion of the future, the religion that was taught by Christ himself in the purple-crowned hills of Galilee.

One more paper from the first day's proceedings is so important to the American Catholic as to demand admission to these pages. Its full title is: "The Relations of the Catholic Church to the Social, Civil, and Political life of the United States." It was furnished and read by a distinguished Maryland lawyer and soldier, Mr. E. H. Gans of Baltimore. Let us condense the title into

CATHOLICITY AND THE STARS AND STRIPES.

In this Columbian year all Americans are meeting together to celebrate the glories of the Republic. Within a domain, continental in its vast expanse, has been worked out on a stupendous scale the experiment of popular government, and now, after a century of trial, we assemble together to show the world how successful that experiment has been.

The palpable evidences of our material prosperity lie all about us. Would you have a portrayal of our boundless wealth, our diversified and inexhaustible resources, the marvelous results of our inventive skill, our triumphs over matter, go to yonder White City. Within its walls will be received impressions more vivid than those which any tongue, however eloquent, can create.

Material prosperity, however, does not make a nation truly great, nor is it the true measure of its success. There are many things in a nation's life more important than its wealth and power. It is, therefore, meet and proper that the spiritual and moral forces, which move and control this great confederation of States, should receive attention, and of these forces none is more deserving of examination than the gentle, benign, all-prevailing influence of the Catholic Church.

We Catholics, sons of the republic, come to her in her hour of triumph to say, All hail! to recall with pride the share which our forefathers had in establishing her institutions, and the equally important share we have in maintaining them in their integrity, and making them permanent. Yet 'tis passing strange that though we yield to no set, or class of men in our loyalty to free government, there are those, and the number is not inconsiderable, who would fain make it appear that we are not true and loyal citizens; that there is something in our belief inimical to the spirit of American institutions; that we are a transplanted foreign growth not indigenous to the American soil. The Catholic Church, they say, is a powerful, compact organization, the most wonderful the world has ever seen, through which its absolute ruler, sitting upon his throne by the banks of the Tiber, exerts an influence, which, if unchecked, will change the ordinary channels of our national life and subvert our liberties. These false notions, often boldly proclaimed, but more frequently insidiously disseminated through the community, are gradually melting away under the sunlight of the truth. They broke out into overt acts of violence during the feverish malignity of knownothingism, and even at this time hold potent sway over a large number of our fellow-citizens. There is an abundance of arrogance in these pretensions. They are born and nourished by an ignorance of the nature of the Church, and by false conceptions of the true spirit of our American institutions. Their pet theories are, forsooth, the only American theories, and their methods the exclusive American methods. All who oppose them are un-American. America, how many crimes are committed in thy name! It is time to strip the mask from these pretenders, and here in the full brightness of this centennial celebration to show the true relations between the Catholic Church, and the political, civil, and social institutions of the United States.

We come in no apologetic attitude. It was to the genius and bold intrepidity of a Catholic navigator that we owe the discovery of this continent. The bones of Catholic Americans whitened every battlefield of the Revolutionary War; Catholic Americans bore a prominent part in the establishment of our institutions, and the names of noble Catholics have from that time to the present been woven in our national traditions. We stand not upon the defensive. We claim that a man may not only be a Catholic and a true American citizen, but that if he is a good Catholic he is the best and most loyal of citizens.

The Church has no direct relations with any special form of civil government. Forms of government are the creations of man. The organization of the Church comes from God himself. Her empire is over the soul and the conscience; her power a moral not a physical power. Her kingdom is a spiritual kingdom and not of this world. Her mission of saving souls is a mission to the whole of humanity, and wonderfully is her organization adapted to accomplish the purpose of her Divine Founder. Being for the whole race, she is Catholic in space. She takes to her bosom the duskiest inhabitants of wildest Africa, the dwellers on Asiatic plains, the Siberian exile, the people of cultivated Europe, as well as the free American citizen. Under no form of government is she a stranger. The Church is the direct representative of God himself, and she is at home wherever she finds a beating human heart.

Being for the whole race, she is Catholic in point of time. She has seen the beginnings of all the modern civilized governments of the world, has witnessed their rise, their various mutations, and their development to the present time. She alone stands immutable, unchangeable. The empire of to-day may be the republic of to-morrow. The Church lives among them all, always the same and the same to all men. She speaks to prince, emperor, and king, as well as to the people, and with the same voice. Before her altars there is no recognition of nationalities. A man becomes subject to her ministrations not as an Englishman, Russian, or American, but as a man, a member of the whole human race. Of other church organizations, some ally themselves to the State and become part and parcel of the civil power, as in England and Russia; others finding their home among the people of certain countries. All, however, receive their special tendencies from their environment, are of necessity local and national, and change in character from time to time with the changes in their surroundings. The Catholic Church alone embraces the entire world and works out her mission irrespective of the special forms of civil government under which her members may live.

Such being the nature and such being the mission of the Church, it is idle to talk of her being foreign, or un-American. These terms can be properly applied to those organizations which have for their subject a participation in the civil government of the world.

What, then, are the relations of the Church to our free institutions? How does she exert her influence? In what way and by what means does she affect our national life?

The fundamental idea of the American system of government is the sovereignty of the people. It is a government by the people and for the people. The halls of Congress and of the State legislatures are filled, not with rulers, but with representatives of the people, elected to carry out their ideas. Many political problems are of necessity solved by the independent judgment of our legislators, but the voice of public opinion is very potent, and the decisions of all great questions are ultimately referred, by means of frequent elections, to the people themselves. They make and unmake administrations. Their policy ultimately becomes the policy of the Government. They are in reality the rulers; the true sovereigns. They govern themselves.

This, however, is true of every democracy. There are found in the American system other principles almost as fundamental as the one we have been considering. We have a number of independent sovereign States and one sovereign nation. The powers which may be exercised by the States and those vested in the general Government of the United States are carefully defined by written constitutions. To each government the people have surrendered only so much of their sovereign power as in their judgment is necessary for the preservation of law and order, and the promotion of the general welfare; and against the abuse of power they have protected themselves by constitutional restrictions. No one can be deprived of life or liberty except by the judgment of his peers, nor can his property be taken from him except by due process of law. Freedom of speech and of the press, the right of peaceable assemblage to petition government for a redress of grievances are all fully secured.

Above all, the Government can not pass any law respecting the establishment of religion, nor interfere, in any way, with the liberty of every man to worship God in such manner as his conscience may dictate. The powers of Government are divided. The legislative, executive, and judicial departments are made, as far as possible, independent of each other, and a number of other checks and balances are provided, to the end that power shall not be abused. Not only is provision made against the abuse of power on the part of the Government but the people are protected aginst themselves. No sudden gusts of folly or passion, even on the part of the sovereign people can, except by revolution, make an absolute change in the Government. Under constitutional methods, such a change can only be worked out in such a length of time as will necessarily bring with it reflection, and the sober second-thought.

The American people secure to themselves their rights of life, liberty, and the pursuit of happiness by creating their own governments, managing them by their own representatives, and limiting their powers by fundamental constitutions. Their liberties are secured by law, the law is framed and executed by the Government, and the Government is controlled by the people. Each man is the equal of his fellows, and has an equal voice in the conduct of affairs.

This is the American system. The relations of the Church are therefore discerned in her relations to the sovereign people; the influence she exerts is over their minds and hearts, and she affects our national life by fashioning and directing their lives and conduct.

Instead of finding in the potent moral influence which the Church exerts over the people, anything hostile to American institutions, the candid inquirer will discover in her teaching and tendencies, the strongest safeguards for their permanence and stability.

Government, according to the Catholic Church, is ordained by God. Man is by nature social and must live with his fellows. This is impossible without government, and, therefore, Government is a necessity found in the nature of man as created by God himself. We further believe that no man has any inherent right to rule over other men, but every nation, taken as a collective moral unit, is, by the very fact that it is a nation, sovereign. This sovereign nation has the right to establish any form of civil government which in its judgment is best suited to its character, and the form of government it adopts is sacred by the ordinance of God. "Let every soul be subject to the higher powers, for there is no power but from God, and the powers that be are ordained of God. Therefore he that resisteth the power resisteth the ordinance of God, and they that resist purchase damnation to themselves."

The Catholic is loyal to the American Government as the legitimately established Government of this country, not because it is stronger than he. His principle of submission is not founded upon the idea of physical force, nor yet entirely upon his strong affection and patriotic predilection for its great principles. He is of necessity loyal because it is his conscientious duty. Patriotism is sublimated and becomes a religious obligation. Is there anything un-American in this? Does this teaching not tend to make good citizens?

If, now, instead of viewing the citizen distributively as a subject of the Government, bound by the virtue of obedience, we examine his relations to the Government as one of the sovereign people, we will perceive the influence of the Church to be equally salutary.

Among the many evils that afflict the body politic, none is more deplorable than the frequency with which the will of the people is frustrated by frauds in elections. This has been the theme of statesmen and political moralists for years. All recognize it as the cancer which has been insidiously attacking the very life of the nation, which must be eradicated and destroyed if we are to preserve our institutions in their integrity. Not only in the less important elections held in the various States has this malign influence been felt but upon the larger field of our national elections it succeeded, at one time, in placing the title of an American President in doubt, and in bringing the whole country to the verge of civil war.

Here, again, the Church intervenes. According to the teachings of our learned doctors, the political sovereignty which is vested in a nation, under the ordinance of God, is vested so that it may be used for the public good. When the people exercise sovereign political power, they exercise a power given to them by the Great Sovereign, in trust, and they are bound, in conscience, to perform the trust honestly and with fidelity.

Thus another fundamental political duty is transformed into a conscientious obligation. As no man can be disloyal to his Government and be a good Catholic, so no man can be a good Catholic and pollute the ballot-box, or in any other way fraudulently frustrate the electoral of the people. Is this teaching un-American?

But our American liberty, our freedom, the theme of our song—

> My country, 'tis of thee,
> Sweet land of liberty,
> Of thee I sing—

How can an organization so despotic as the Church of Rome be anything but hostile to this, the very essence and spirit of our institutions? To what lengths do not prejudice and ignorance go in binding the eyes of men!

All the hostile criticism of the Church in this connection rests upon an ignorance of the real nature of liberty. To many unreflecting persons the word liberty conveys no meaning except the absence of restraint, the absence of any external power controlling the will. For them liberty means the right to follow their own wills and inclinations without let or hindrance. This, however, is the liberty of anarchy; it is not American liberty. We are free American citizens, but may we do as we like? May a man make a contract with me and break it with impunity? May he injure my property, infringe my rights or personal security, obstruct the conduct of my legitimate business, steal my goods, put a bullet through my brains, without becoming a subject for the coercive discipline of the law of the land?

Men can not live together without government, and government implies the restraining influence of law.

These ideas are not only obvious but they are very American. We find them incorporated in the fundamental charters of our liberties.

In the Declaration of Independence we read: "We hold these truths to be self-evident: That all men are created equal; that they are endowed by their Creator with certain inalienable rights; that among these are life, liberty, and the pursuit of happiness. That to secure these rights governments are established among men." The Constitution of the United States declares in its preamble: "We, the people of the United States, in order to secure the blessings of liberty to ourselves and our posterity, do ordain and establish this Constitution for the United States of America."

Therefore, by the highest American authority, for the security of liberty, governments are instituted and constitutions ordained and established. Liberty can not exist without the authority of government exercised under the forms of law.

ARCHBISHOP RIORDAN, SAN FRANCISCO. ARCHBISHOP HENNESSY, DUBUQUE.
ARCHBISHOP KATZER, MILWAUKEE. ARCHBISHOP SATOLLI, WASHINGTON. ARCHBISHOP JANSSEN, NEW ORLEANS.

But in order that the citizen may possess true civil liberty it is not only necessary that he should be subject to government but that government itself be restrained within proper limits; it must be just, and its sole end must be the public good. Any other governmental control would be despotic and tyrannical. It was to secure this kind of government that all the efforts of our forefathers were directed. Therefore it was that they insisted upon a government by the people themselves through their own representatives; for this reason the government agencies which they created were limited in their powers by written constitutions and fundamental rights reserved to the people; to secure this end the powers were divided into independent departments—the legislative, executive, and judicial. In a word, all the checks, balances, and guarantees devised by the framers of our Government were intended to secure to the people subjection to no laws except those which were necessary for the peace, good order, and prosperity of society.

This is the true spirit of our American freedom, and by no one has it been more aptly and eloquently portrayed than by Daniel Webster, the great expounder of the constitution. "All governments of law," he says, "must impose numerous limitations and qualifications of authority, and give many positive and qualified rights. In other words, they must be subject to rule and regulation. This is the very essence of free political institutions. The spirit of liberty is indeed a bold and fearless spirit, but it is also a sharp-sighted spirit; it is a cautious, sagacious, discriminating intelligence. It is jealous of encroachment, jealous of power, jealous of man. It demands checks; it seeks for guards; it insists upon securities; it entrenches itself behind strong defenses and fortifies itself with all possible care against the assaults of ambition and passion. It does not trust the amiable weakness of human nature, * * * and therefore it will not permit power to overstep its prescribed limits. Neither does it satisfy itself with flashy, illegal resistance to illegal authority. Far otherwise. It seeks for duration and permanence. This is the nature of constitutional liberty, and this is our liberty if we will understand and preserve it."

The Catholic Church welcomes this bright and beautiful spirit and takes it to her bosom, for she is its foster-mother. With tender devotion she nourished it through the ages. Time and again she has rescued it from the bold and impious hands of despots, whether they be kings, emperors, or a popular majority enthroned.

With the Church God is the only true sovereign and the source of all power. The sovereignty of the people comes from him as a sacred trust, and they must use this trust for the common weal. The Government called into being by them, in framing and executing laws, is but echoing the voice of the King of Kings, and obedience to it is obedience to God himself. Here is the ultimate sanction for human liberty. Subjection to no power except the power of the ruler of the universe—this is true liberty. Therefore, a government executing laws dictated by passion, personal ambition, greed of power, working injustice, is acting beyond the scope of its delegated power, and has not the sanction of God for its acts. It is tyrannical. And the Church condemns it and its authorized acts. Power without justice she will not recognize; and authority without right she deems usurpation.

Our American institutions are justly deemed the masterpiece of human contrivance for securing government which will rule only for the general good. It is in accomplishing precisely this result that the Church uplifts and sustains the weak hands of men by her potent spiritual power.

The Catholic Church has been the only consistent teacher and supporter of true liberty. In her spiritual empire over the souls of men, she is a government instituted and established not by the people, but by God himself. She administers laws; but they are divine, not human laws. Her children are protected from spiritual despotism, not by checks and balances of human contrivance, but by the sacred guarantee of the divine promise.

"Thou art Peter, and upon this rock I will build my Church, and the gates of hell shall not prevail against it."

The Catholic Church has been divinely commissioned to teach the truth; and in the possession of the truth her children alone have true liberty. "You shall know the truth and the truth shall make you free." With the Church spiritual freedom, as well as civil liberty, is possible only with law and government.

Is there anything un-American in this? Is it un-American to say that there is a sovereignty higher than the sovereignty of the people? Is it un-American to acknowledge subjection to God and his government? The American people are not, we think, prepared to admit that atheism, infidelity, and irreligion are part and parcel of their institutions.

Would that our countrymen should cease to view the Church through the dark mists of prejudice. If they observed her in the bright sunlight of truth they would see her sitting at the very fountains of their liberties, as their guardian spirit, preserving those bright and sparkling waters from pollution as they flow in copious and salutary streams over the green fields of our national life.

But from whatever point of view we examine our American institutions, we find them supported and sustained by the Church. The Declaration of Independence declares that "All men are created equal," and we have endeavored to follow the spirit of this truth in the practical workings of our Government, by giving each man an equal voice in the conduct of affairs, by discouraging ranks and classes, and by insisting upon perfect equality before the laws of the land.

But this democratic equality pales into insignificance before that taught and practiced by the Church. In her eyes all men are equal because they are sons of the same father and joint heirs of the heavenly treasure. Before her altars there is no precedence. The laborer on our streets has for companion the financial magnate; the lowly negro, once a slave in our Southern clime, bows with reverential awe side by side with the refined chivalric scholar, once his master, and the magdalen mingles her penitential tears with the chaste aspirations of the white-souled nun. No such real democracy can be found outside the Catholic Church.

And finally let us consider another striking characteristic of our American life. We boast with proper pride of the equal opportunity which every citizen has of rising, by his own merit, to the highest position of political honor. Any poor boy in the land has the right to aspire to a seat in Congress, to be vested with the judicial ermine, or, supreme honor, to occupy the chair once filled by Washington. There is nothing in the nature of our institutions which will make the fulfillment of his ambitious hopes impracticable. The brightest names in our history are the names of men who have sprung from an origin as lowly as his own.

Do you find this characteristic in Holy Church? Listen to the language of an eloquent Spaniard, a priest, one who lived in a monarchy and whose only practical acquaintance with democracy was with the democracy of the Church.

"In the Church, birth and riches are of no importance. If you are a man of high merit, untarnished by misconduct, and at the same time conspicuous by your abilities, your knowledge—that is enough—she will look upon you as a great man; will always show you extreme consideration, and treat you with respect, and listen to you with deference. And since your brow, though sprung from obscurity, is radiant with fame, it will be held worthy to bear the mitre, the cardinal's hat, or the tiara."

The history of the Church justifies this beautiful tribute. Many of our most famous pontiffs have been taken from the lowly walks of life, whilst the college of cardinals have received their honors, as a rule, solely as the award of merit and learning.

Have we not in this beautiful land of ours a most notable illustration of this truth? An humble American citizen is an august prince of the Church. In him, we have a living proof of all the principles for which we have been contending. He is a prince of the Church; and yet, is he hostile to democracy? He is infused with the very quintessence of the Catholic spirit; and yet, is he not the very incarnation of true Americanism? He knows full well the plenitude of his spiritual power, its high dignity, its wonderful authority; and yet, is he an enemy of American liberty? The whole country knows and acknowledges, that within the entire confines of the Republic there is no more ardent patriot, no more enthusiastic supporter of our American institutions than the gentle, modest, illustrious James Gibbons, Cardinal Archbishop of Baltimore.

As the various special relations of the Church to the social institutions of the United States have been selected as the themes of other papers to be read at this Congress, I have deemed it best to make them the subject of no special comment. In her relations to them the constant aim of the Church, in addition to the benevolent work of alleviating distress, is to constantly augment the virtue and intelligence of the people. To this end she sanctifies the home, inculcates the principles of justice, and educates not only the intellectual but also the moral and religious faculties of the soul.

An acute and profound critic of our American institutions has recently said: "It may be thought that a nation which uses freedom well can hardly have too much freedom; yet even such a nation may be too much inclined to think freedom an absolute and all-sufficient good—to seek truth only in the voice of the majority, to mistake prosperity for greatness. Such a nation, seeing nothing but its own triumphs, and hearing nothing but its own praises, seems to need a succession of men like the prophets of Israel to rouse the people out of their self-complacency, to refresh their moral ideas, to remind them that the life is much more than meat and the body more than raiment, and that to whom much is given, of them shall much also be required."

We have among us our prophets of Israel, divinely commissioned, as were the holy men of old, to guide, instruct, ennoble, and elevate the nation; and the American people will have achieved their highest glory when they seek the words of wisdom and truth from their lips—when they voluntarily submit to the gentle ministrations of the priests and bishops of the Holy Catholic Church.

The evening session of this opening day resolved itself into something like a grand jubilation, so eager were the faithful to honor and to listen informally to their illustrious Pastors. The occasion was marked by the following:

ADDRESS BY ARCHBISHOP P. J. RYAN OF PHILADELPHIA.

When the secretary of the Columbian Congress informed me this morning that I was expected to speak to you this evening, I should not have dared to slight you by coming before you with a few thoughts jotted down, if he had not assured me that these addresses were to be informal—that they were not expected to be prepared like the papers of the morning; they were to be addresses encouraging you, doing all that would be in our power to explain to you, perhaps more in detail, the objects of this great Congress. Therefore I come this evening to speak to you in an informal manner, possibly in a very desultory manner, but I hope the words I have to say to you will not be entirely without fruit. I feel that I am in my place when speaking at this Columbian celebration, because I feel, as a Christian bishop, that the discovery of Columbus was a triumph of Christianity, because whoever will examine the philosophy of his life, his motives for action, will find that the inspiration to spread Christian truth and with it Christian civilization, the civilization of our day, the charity, the tenderness, the advances in every direction, on the civilization of the past—that all these came from the deep religious principle within his nature; and as a Catholic I feel a just pride in the fact that the origin of this great country, which is to be in the future so marvelous in its effects upon human happiness, upon human progress, upon the intellect and the heart of man. And I remember that, warmed by Catholic feeling, illumined by Catholic faith, and clothed by Catholic love for our Lord, he came here to plant this civilization, and that he, the navigator of Genoa, came before the pilgrims from England, and the Santa Maria arrived long before the Mayflower.

I speak not this in boasting. It would not be his spirit, and on a great occasion like this, when all party lines should disappear, when in that magnificent and universal Christianity we meet to commemorate this great event, it is not a sectarian feeling, but it is in a Catholic and universal feeling in which I would find sympathy even in the non-Catholic descendants of these great pilgrim fathers. If we could imagine him as the patriarch Jacob when he fell asleep, and between earth and heaven there was the luminous avenue with angels ascending and descending; if Columbus, in his weary journeys looking for the means to prosecute his great discovery, should sleep and an angel of the Lord would point out to him the luminous pathway between the Old and the New World—point out the great future to him, the conversion to Christianity and civilization of the people of the New World; the cities that should rise in the future, the marvelous progress, the home for the exile and the persecuted—how his heart would throb with gratitude! Some of the things of which he may have dreamed were realized in his day. You remember that he returned to Spain, and when, with some of the docile Indians, he appeared at the court of Isabella the Catholic, and when he stooped—he, with the royalty of intellect before earthly royalty—with uplifted heart, and trusting not in the splendor of that intellect, but in Him, the "light of light" that had illumined it; when he spoke of the New World and its possibilities, physical and moral, and his heart glowed and his eyes glistened as in inspiration, and the heart of Isabella the Catholic went out to the glorious navigator, and the assembled court heard the words from the distant land, they all prostrated themselves, and from the palace chapel came the song of the Te Deum, "We Give Thanks." As they praised God in that Te Deum, it rang upon the soul of the navigator with a deeper significance than even upon the soul of Ambrose and Augustine, when they sang it a thousand years before. Now they could sing: "Thee Father Everlasting *all* the earth doth worship, Thee the Holy Church throughout *all* the world doth acknowledge." This was the beginning of his consolation, and as he looks down from glory—for we believe, as Catholics, that the dead take cognizance of the things that occur upon the earth—he sees this country advancing year after year in physical advancement, intellectual advancement, religious advancement. And now, ladies and gentlemen, particularly you members of the Columbian Catholic Congress, the Congress called after him, you have to continue his work, and continue it in that high order that should most of all please his spirit.

Before his time there were two worlds—separated. Between them rolled the dark ocean, and storms, terrible storms, agitated its ways. Monsters of the deep were beneath these waters. Columbus united these worlds. In this land, and for many years, there have been two moral worlds, separated by the ocean of prejudice, on which there have been storms of bigotry and hatred, and down among the coral rocks, down in the depths of the ocean, there have been deep animosities, wild spirits, that would separate these two worlds. There is the Catholic world and the non-Catholic world. Between them has rolled the ocean of prejudice—a dark ocean. Hearts that ought to have come nearer to each other, hearts that God made like each other, eyes that if they only looked into each other, He would have brought them together. It is the mission of the Catholic Congress to bring these two worlds nearer—to make men understand each other more fully, and this mission you have to act out, first of all by appreciating the great truth that the non-Catholic world is not opposed to the Catholic world at all, but to something which it thinks is the Catholic world. The very doctrines on which this animosity is formed are doctrines that we reject as emphatically, as constantly, as indignantly as the non-Catholic world could reject them. Therefore, we only ask to be known.

The anti-Catholic people had a cry, and they have it yet, of "No Popery." We join in it and say, "Know Popery," but we spell the word "k-n-o-w" popery. This morning, I confess, I was charmed and won over by the admirable address of Mr. Bonney. I know no interest he could have in flattering us; I know from his position and his evident honesty that he felt what he said. Seeing the initials of his Christian name, when I asked him, I had something like a premonition of what it might be, when he told me that his name was Charles Carroll, and that he was called after Charles Carroll of Carrollton.

For over forty years I have associated with non-Catholics. I know them, and I know that many of those that are called bigots hate the Church simply because they hate tyranny, because they hate hypocrisy, because they hate a number of things which they imagine are in the Catholic Church, and if they could love such a church, with such a view of it, they never would be worthy of receiving the True Faith. About a year ago I was invited to attend the annual dinner of the descendants of the pilgrim fathers in Scranton, Pa. All there, except the gentleman who accompanied me, and myself, were non-Catholics. I was surprised at the invitation. I promised, however, as I had to be in the city for a ceremony the next day, to attend the banquet. I declined saying anything however, until one proposed my health, and when I rose to speak I assure you that not even the Columbian Congress received me as enthusiastically as these children of the pilgrim fathers. There is a world full of principle, full of honesty, full of progress, full of intelligence, as we look across the water, separated from us, and we should be united with it. And because the members of the Catholic Congress are almost all laymen, it is their place so to speak and act, to bring us into contact more perfectly with that world. They will hear a layman when they will not hear a priest. They have to meet the laymen in daily life, in business, on many occasions when it is impossible they should meet the clergy, and they will have less suspicion of the layman, whom they know to be thoroughly honest, open, and frank, than of the priest, of whom they know so very little. Therefore, gentlemen and ladies of this Congress, it is your great privilege to do all that you can to explain to honest, open-hearted, fair-play-loving Protestant Americans that we do not believe but we anathematize and condemn many of the things that are laid to our charge, as articles of our Faith or as practices within the Church of God. And to do this effectually, through the action of the Congress, it must be clearly understood that the Catholic men of this Congress are left free by the clergy. There are articles of faith, there are essential practices of discipline, which can not be changed, but in the domain of free opinion, declared as such, no angel stands at the confines and says "thus far and no farther." This domain is immense, and to affect American people the Catholic layman must be understood to speak, not as our mouthpieces, but as free, intelligent Catholic American laymen.

It seems to me that the great unitive power to bring Catholics and non-Catholics together is that personal love for our Lord and charity toward his suffering children, on which both so perfectly agree. It is remarkable that when Christ sought a model of charity he selected not the orthodox Jew, but an heretical Samaritan, and made him the model for Jew and Christian for all time. Let us all meet in admiration and love for the great Founder of Christianity—the God of Columbus, and the inspirer and sustainer of our common Christian civilization. Let us bear in mind that our greatest enemies are sin, that corrupts the heart, and ignorance that obscures the intellect; and hence, that only the church bell and the school bell can prolong the echoes of the "Liberty Bell." United in love to Christ and to our suffering brethren for his sake, and zealous for the Christian civilization and true liberty which this zeal must produce, our perfect union is only a question of time.

SECOND DAY.

Tuesday's proceedings were of absorbing interest, and began by calling the roll of delegates to the Congress, their officers for the various dioceses reporting as follows:

LIST OF DELEGATES.

Kansas City—Chairman, S. A. Hegg; Vice-President, Judge Philip J. Henn; Committeeman, John H. Walsh.

Cleveland—Chairman, W. A. Lynch; Vice-President, F. J. Giebel, Jr.; Committeeman, C. X. Schlaudecker.

Fort Wayne—Chairman, John T. Meig; Vice-President, James Murdock; Committeeman, J. Ewing.

Vincennes—Chairman, John Breen; Vice-President, Charles A. Kolby; Committeeman, H. Canthorn.

Alton—Chairman, J. J. McInerney; Vice-President, Anton Binkert; Committeeman, Charles F. Degenhardt.

Portland, Maine—Chairman, M. R. Harrigan; Vice-President, D. J. Calahan; Committeeman, T. F. Donahoe.

Philadelphia—Vice-President, William F. Harrity; Committee on Resolutions, Martin Malony; Committee on Organization, Charles St Claire.

New York—Chairman, John D. Crimmins; Vice-President, John B. Manning; Committeeman, Victor B. Dowling.

Ogdensburg—Chairman, John B. Riley; Vice-President, Very Rev. T. E. Walsh; Committeeman, E. Villers.

Nashville—Chairman, William Hogan; Vice-President, Martin Kelly; Committeeman, Louis Kittman.

Denver—Chairman, E. L. Johnson; Vice-President, A. G. Gillis; Committeeman, R. S. Morrison.

Mobile—Chairman, Daniel S. Troy; Vice-President, Felix McGill; Committeeman, James G. Terry.

La Crosse—Chairman, J. J. Cavanaugh; Vice-President, Joseph Boshert; Committeeman, Dr. Edward Evans.

Brooklyn—Chairman, John McCarty; Vice-President, W. Hynes; Committeeman, B. J. York.

Lincoln—Chairman, J. J. Butler; Vice-President, F. J. Redamacher; Committeeman, Aug. Essen.

Little Rock—Chairman, Judge Murphy; Vice-President, John M. Gracie; Committeeman, James A. Gray.

Kansas City—Chairman, John Risse; Vice-President, Edward Carroll; Committeeman, John O'Flanigan.

Harrisburg—Chairman, Peter A. Mahon; Vice-President, James Monaghan; Committeeman, Andrew Mayer.

Hartford—Chairman, J. J. Phelan; Vice-President, P. Harvan; Committeeman, C. T. Driscoll.

Galveston—Chairman, W. L. Foley; Vice-President, Joseph Engelke; Committeeman, John T. Brown.

Erie—Chairman, Major J. B. Reid; Vice-President, James R. Burns; Committeeman, P. C. Boyle.

Chicago—Chairman, Charles Mair; Vice-President, General George Smith; Committeeman, Thomas Moran.

Davenport, Iowa—Chairman, Fred B. Sharon; Vice-President, J. M. Galvin; Committeeman, J. J. Smith.

Dubuque—Chairman, P. H. Donlin; Vice-President, Thomas Connolly; Committeeman, J. H. McConlogue.

Concordia—Chairman, W. R. Geis; Vice-President, Charles L. Schwartz; Committeeman, Leon Werry.

Columbus, Ohio—Chairman, Luke G. Byrne; Vice-President, John A. Kuster; Committeeman, John C. Finerman.

Salt Lake City—Dominick McGuire.
Idaho—Chairman, Christopher Faby; Vice-President, James F. Kane.
Milwaukee—Chairman, John Black; Vice-President, P. V. Druster; Committeeman, David Geraghty.
Wheeling—Chairman, Thomas Killeen; Vice-President, Charles A. Wingerter; Committeeman, W. S. Foose.
Indian Territory—Rev. D. I. Lanslots.
Arizona—Chairman, D. J. Brannen; Committeeman, M. J. Riordan.
Wilmington—Chairman. William Michael Byrne; Vice-President, J. Smith Brennan; Committeeman, Peter A. Harty.
St. Joseph—Chairman, Francis Browne; Vice-President, Thomas F. Ryan; Committeeman, James Hogan.
Syracuse—Chairman, Rev. Father Mullaney; Vice-President, Francis Baumer.
San Antonio, Texas—Chairman, J. C. Diemlann; Vice-President, H. P. Drought; Committeeman, Edward Braden.
St. Louis—Chairman, John J. Ganahl; Vice-President, Richard C. Kerns.
Omaha—Chairman, Thomas H. Dailey; Vice-President, John McCreery; Committeeman, J. C. Kinster.
Providence—Chairman, M. J. Harsen; Vice-President, M. Kelly, M.D.; Committeeman, T. E. Maloney.
Cincinnati—Chairman, John Rull; Vice-President, J. H. Kohmescher; Committeeman, Joseph P. Kealy.
Pittsburg—Chairman, C. F. McKenna; Vice-President, W. S. Head; Committeeman, T. J. Connor.
Ways and Means Committee—D. F. Bremner, Chicago; John B. Manning, New York; James Murdock, Indiana; James Black, Wisconsin; Anthony Kelly, Minnesota; Thomas C. Lawler, Wisconsin; Martin Maloney, Philadelphia.
Resolutions—T. A. Moran, Chicago; W. G. Smith, Philadelphia; O'Brien K. Atkinson, Michigan; Thomas J. Gargan, Boston; H. C. Semple, Alabama; Edgar H. Gans, Baltimore; C. A. Wingerter, Wheeling, W. Va.; Dr. J. A. Outherlong, Louisville; Victor J. Dowling, New York; Bishop Ryan, Buffalo, and Bishop Watterson of Columbus.

BISHOP WATTERSON'S ADDRESS.

It is not my purpose to do more this morning than to sound the keynote for the discussion of the social questions involved in the comprehensive programme of this Congress. That note is found in the encyclicals of our Holy Father, Leo XIII., and I am glad that his illustrious representative, the most reverend apostolic delegate, is here to bless and encourage the discussion by his distinguished presence. He is the precious hostage of the Sovereign Pontiff's love for America and the pledge of his fraternal solicitude for our beloved country and its institutions. The Pope must teach the truth to the world, for the world has need of truth to live and prosper. The lives of Leo the Great, Gregory the Great, Gregory VII., Innocent III., Pius V., and Pius IX. illustrate the marvelous correspondence between the qualities of these men and the needs of their peculiar times.

Our present great and glorious Pontiff, Leo XIII., continues this wonderful harmony. He guards the truth, natural and revealed, in all its integrity, as did his glorious predecessors; and with exquisite tact and providential kindness he draws from the treasury of truth the teachings suited to the present hour. In these times, when men are calling into question the very principles on which not only the Church but society itself—individuals, families, and states—depends, the special mission of Leo XIII. seems to be to strengthen the foundations of the whole social fabric. By his personal dignity and goodness, the practical wisdom of his teachings and the firmness of his acts, he is giving the world to understand that the Pope is a great thing in the world and for the world; and intellects heretofore rebellious are accustoming themselves to think that, if society is to be saved from a condition worse in some respects than that of pagan times, it is from the Vatican the savior is to come. Truth is the generous blood which, coursing through the social body, gives it light and energy, health and beauty, unto all the ends for which it was established by the providence of God. Wherever truth is abandoned or disregarded, society must suffer, and society is suffering to-day because, to a large extent, it has practically rejected the great fundamental principles of Christianity, and substituted mere material and selfish interests as the moving force in the life of individuals and nations.

Behold, then, why Leo XIII. is recalling to the minds of men those great bed-rock truths, on which the health and life of nations and society depend—those truths that made firm men of conviction and steadfast principles, and through principle and conviction, men of strong and sturdy natural and Christian character. It is such men that are always needed; it is such men that are specially needed to-day. Vigorous in all the fullness of harmoniously developed powers, devoted to higher than mere natural ends, alive to their duties as well as their rights, and ennobled by the love and faithful practice of those great principles of natural and Christian ethics which must underlie any safe system of social and political economy.

Leo XIII., like many of his illustrious predecessors in similar conditions of society, is fulfilling his special mission by defending the cause of the people against the encroachments of avarice and injustice, espousing the interests of the masses against the ruthless Moloch of misused wealth and power, and showing the shallowness of the social theories and mere philosophisms of the day, while upholding at the same time the rights of legitimate authority. The rationalists, materialists, socialists, and other mere humanitarians have been delivering natural reason itself to uncertainties the most poignant, the human heart to irregularities, and society to disorders, the inevitable consequence of a teaching without sound principles, and, therefore, without true morality. By awakening the love of strong and wholesome principles in the hearts of men capable of understanding, and inviting attention to the duties as well as the rights of men, in calling a return to those simple Christian truths on which society was reformed by our blessed Lord, Leo XIII. has been doing a grand work, not only for the present but for every future generation. There is not a question vital to modern society that he has not touched and solved in his great encyclicals on human liberty, political power, the Christian constitution of states, and the condition of labor.

The whole world listens with respect to his grand words, which excite our apprehension by revealing the mysteries of society and reassure us by pointing out their remedies. Brought into close and intimate relation with all conditions of mankind, he suggests the cure for the evils of our times and exhorts bishops, priests, and people, legislatures, and other departments of civil government to co-operate with him in the application of the remedies. He shows to-day what the history of the past can not but show to the sincere and candid student—that, as every single family, which is society in its germ, and every organized aggregate of families, called a state or nation, has its visible head for the preservation of union and the attainment of the ends of civil life, so, to promote order in society at large, the very unity of the human family supposes, under the providence of God, some visible and general authority superior to every other social power that will raise its voice, from pure and disinterested love of truth and justice, against the attacks of force and the encroachments of error and passion. He shows that the Papacy is this great necessity, this universal moral power in the world, the bond of union, and the principle of order in the human race, fixed by the hand of God in the midst of all society for the good of all society, revindicating, wherever its authority is recognized, the natural as well as the Christian dignity of man, and maintaining the rights and duties of individuals and nations in their integrity and just and even balance

Nor is the Catholic Church to be ignored in this great work. On the contrary, she is to be the most potent factor in reaching the consummation devoutly to be wished by all the lovers of their kind. And you, Catholic laymen and women, are to have an intelligent and active part in bringing about the improvement of the social system. You are to do it by your good example; you are to help it in various other ways. You are to spread the encyclicals of our Holy Father Leo XIII., not only among those of the household of Faith but also among your brethren outside the pale. You are to scatter them everywhere; you are to make them known to the people with whom you are brought into companionship in social and business life, and the seeds thus sown will bear speedy and happy fruitage. You are to organize Catholic workmen into associations; and, whether it is better to band them into Catholic associations under Catholic direction, or to try to desecularize already existing associations and infuse into them more of the spirit of Christianity, is a question that I leave to the deliberations of this Congress.

There is another thing that you all must take an active and interested part in. Intemperance is one of the great evils of society to-day. The annual drink-bill of the United States is said to be $900,000,000, and it is incurred for the most part by the working people. And let me say plainly here to-day that the very first encouragement of this work should be given by our bishops and our priests. For without their active interest and co-operation, nothing will be accomplished, even if you hold Catholic Congresses from now until the crack of doom.

Modern philanthropists have been trying to work out a social combination by which men are to league together everywhere and thus contribute to the general good of all humanity; but, well meaning as they may be, they must be blind not to recognize in the Catholic Church a society, ever ancient and ever new, independent and always devoted to the general good, true to the spirit of patriotism by which we love and serve our country, and show ourselves ready to devote our fortunes and our very lives to its defense, and answering in every point to the needs of universal peace and harmonious prosperity.

While conceding to material progress an important share in the happiness of nations, she gives the world to understand that temporal prosperity is, after all, but a secondary element. She has developed the moral and religious nature in man by inspiring him with self-respect, charity for his brethren, reverence for the truth, love for the beautiful and the good, and a childlike submission to Almighty God and every authority that represents him here on earth. Such a doctrine does more for the solid happiness of society than all the efforts of mere political economists and humanitarian philosophers. Any plan that leaves out these things, be it otherwise ever so plausible for the improvement of society, will be but a temporary makeshift. Far from reaching the root of the evil, it will only postpone the social catastrophe that is threatening the world.

In our own beloved country, one of the richest on the globe, evils are growing to an alarming extent. Class is arrayed against class, labor against capital, and capital against labor. The spirit of unrest and discontent is stirring the masses. There is a great and crying injustice somewhere. The true relation of rights and duties, extending all through the complicated elements of society, is disregarded or not understood. The social machine has lost its equilibrium. How can it be restored? For my part knowing that whatever social improvement has taken place in the whole human race has been wrought out by the principles of true Christianity in its action on the human heart, I have little confidence in any other power. Civil legislation has done something, and it may do something yet, but only when in harmony with the Gospel of Christian love.

Bring, then, from the religion of Christ, those saving lessons of divine wisdom and goodness with which it abounds. Infuse its spirit into the hearts of men until, by its sweet influence, it overmasters the avarice and selfishness that have made them obdurate and insensible. Teach the rich to love money less, and men more, individual employers and corporations to look upon their employes not as soulless machines or mere material instruments of production and consumption, but to take reverend cognizance of their intellectual, moral, and religious natures; unite men into great trusts of mutual Christian love.

Teach the poor that while inequalities of condition and class must exist, they are to be filled with the love of their fellowmen; they are to be sensible of their responsibilities, as well as their rights, and are not to regard wealth as a good in itself, but bear patiently the ills of life. And if all will learn the lesson in practice as well as in theory, Christianity shall again have occasion to exult in the triumph of her principles, and the world to exclaim, as in ancient days, "Behold how they love one another!" Evils will be remedied to a great extent, and society will bear again moral and religious fruits, and upon this triumph of the future, Leo XIII. will have his powerful influence.

Just as Bishop Watterson had finished his noble address the Most Rev. Apostolic Delegate, Mgr. Satolli, entered the hall, accompanied by His Grace the Archbishop of St. Paul. He was received with vociferous and prolonged cheering, in response to which the eminent prelate addressed the Congress in the Italian tongue, his remarks being thus interpreted immediately following, by Archbishop Ireland:

MGR. SATOLLI'S ADDRESS.

I beg leave to repeat, in unmusical tones, a few of the thoughts that his excellency, the Most Reverend Apostolic Delegate, has presented to you in his own beautiful and musical Italian language. The Delegate expresses his great delight to be, this morning, in the presence of the Catholic Columbian Congress. He begs leave to offer you the salutation of the great Pontiff, Leo XIII. In the name of Leo he salutes the spiritual children of the Church on this American Continent; in the name of Leo he salutes the great American Republic herself.

It is, he says, a magnificent spectacle to see laymen, priests, and bishops assembled here together to discuss the vital social problems which the modern conditions of humanity bring up before us. The advocates of error have their congresses, why should not the friends and advocates of truth have their congresses? This Congress assembled here to-day will, no doubt, be productive of rich and magnificent results. You have met to show that the Church, while opening to men the treasures of heaven, offers, also, felicity on earth. As St. Paul has said: "She is made for earth and heaven; she is the promise of the future life and the life that is." All congresses are, so to speak, concentrations of great forces. Your object is to consider the social forces that God has provided, and to apply, as far as you can, to the special circumstances of your own time and country these great principles.

The great social forces are thought, will, and action. In a congress you bring before you these three great forces. Thought finds its food in truth; so in all that you do, in all the practical conclusions that you formulate, you must bear in mind that they must all rest upon the eternal principles of truth. Will is the rectitude of the human heart, and until the human heart is voluntarily subjected to truth and virtue, all social reforms are impossible. Then comes action, which aims at the acquisition of the good needed for the satisfaction of mankind; and this again must be regulated by truth in thought and by virtue in the human will. The well-being of society consists in the perfect order of the different elements toward the great scope of society. Order is the system of the different relations of the different elements, one to the other, and these relations to which men are subject are summarized in three words—God, man, and nature.

Man has first of all his great duties to God, which never must be forgotten. He then has his duties to himself and to his fellowmen; and, finally, he has relations with the great world of nature over which his action is exercised. From the several considerations of these different relations spring up the great problems which at all times have vexed man's mind—the great problems which to-day are before us in view of the different evolutions, social and otherwise, which mark our modern needs. Your Social Congress has convened to-day. Bear in mind that there was a first great Social Congress, which is to be the model of yours, which gave out the principles which must underlie your deliberations. The great Social Congress, the ideal and model of all others, was held when Christ, surrounded by the thousands of the children of Israel, delivered his great discourse on the mountain.

There the solution was given to human problems; there were laid down the vital principles. "Seek first the kingdom of God and its justice and all other things shall be added unto you," says the good book. "Seek first the kingdom of God." Look up to the divinity without which man is absolutely at sea. Fill out first your duties to God, without the observance of which other duties are a name. Seek God's justice in your relations one with another. Be guided by the eternal law of the Most High, and then all things shall be added unto you. Know God's truth and live by God's justice, and the peace and the felicity of earth shall be yours. The same great voice said, "Blessed are the poor in spirit; blessed are they who thirst after justice; blessed are the merciful."

Men should not devote their whole being and all their energies to the seeking out of mere matter. "Blessed are the poor in spirit"—that is free and independent of the shackles of mere matter. "Blessed are they who hunger and thirst after justice"—justice first before self-satisfaction, before all attention to one's personal wants. And "blessed are the merciful." Blessed are they who know and feel that they don't live for themselves, whose hearts go out in sweetest mercy to all their fellows. History has proven that human reason alone does not solve the great social problems. These problems were spoken of in the pre-Christian times, and Aristotle and Plato discussed them. But pre-Christian times gave us a world of slavery when a multitude lived only for the benefit of the few.

There is authority throughout the story of man of a divine providential design. Blind is he who sees it not, and he who studies it not courts disaster. It was when Christ brought down upon earth the great truths from the bosom of his Father, that humanity was lifted up and entered upon a new road to happiness and felicity. Christ brought to nature the additional gift of the supernatural. Both are needed, and he who would have one without the other fails. The supernatural comes not to destroy or eliminate the natural, but to purify it, to elevate it, to build it up, and hence, since the coming of Christ, science, art, philosophy, social economy, all studies partake of the natural as well as the supernatural—the natural coming from man's own thoughts and man's own actions, and the supernatural pouring down upon those thoughts and actions direction, richness, and grace.

To-day it is the duty of Catholics to bring into the world the fullness of supernatural truth and supernatural life. This is especially the duty of a Catholic

Congress. There are nations who are never separated from the Church, but which have neglected often to apply in full degree the lessons of the gospel. There are nations who have gone out from the Church, bringing with them many of her treasures, and because of what they have brought yet show virgin light; but, cut from the source, unless that source is brought into close contact with them, there is danger for them. Bring them in contact with these divine forces by your action and your teachings. Bring your fellow-countrymen back; bring your country into immediate connection with the great source of truth and light, and the blessed influence of Christ and Christ's Church. And in this manner shall it come to pass that the words of the psalmist shall be fulfilled: "Mercy and justice have you one with another; justice and peace prevail."

Let us restore among men justice and charity. Let us teach men to be prompt ever to make sacrifice of self for the common good. This is the foundation of all social elevating movements; it is the foundation of your own Congress. Now, all these great principles have been marked out in the most luminous lines in the encyclicals of the great Pontiff, Leo XIII. We then study those encyclicals; hold fast to them as the safest anchorage. The social questions are being studied the world over. It is well they should be studied in America, for here do we have more than elsewhere the keys to the future. Here in America you have a country blessed specially by Providence, in the fertility of its fields and the liberty of its institutions. Here you have a country which will pay back all efforts, not merely tenfold, but a hundredfold; and this no one understands better than the immortal Leo, and he charges his Delegate to speak out to America words of hope and blessing.

Then, in conclusion, the Delegate begs of you American Catholics to be fully loyal to your great mission and the duties which your circumstances impose upon you. Here are golden words spoken by the Delegate in concluding his discourse: "Go forward! in one hand bearing the Book of Christian truth and in the other the Constitution of the United States."

Christian truth and American liberty will make you free, happy, and prosperous. They will put you on the road to progress. May your steps ever persevere on that road. Again he salutes you with all his heart. Again he expresses his delight to be with you, and again speaks forth to you in strongest and sweetest tones the love of your Holy Father, Leo XIII.

A pleasing incident of this session was an invitation extended to the colored Catholics, who had begun holding their meetings in one of the lesser halls, to come in and participate in the general Congress. An original and philosophical presentation of the current topic was then made by Hon. E. O. Browne of Chicago, in the following terms:

LABOR AND CAPITAL.

In common speech, as in the scheme for this Congress, labor and capital are used as contra-distinguished terms—things set off against each other—the rights of the one and the duties of the other being the matters especially to be insisted on, and reconciled, if reconciliation may in any way be between things assumed thus to be so antagonistic and engaged in such an irreconcilable conflict. That there is such a conflict in appearance, is as evident as it is in appearance that the sun circles about the earth. But I hold it to be no more a real phenomenon of our social life and organization than the motion of the sun is of the natural world.

It is because I utterly dispute the thesis that capital and labor are antagonistic, that they have separate interests, that there are duties incumbent upon one which are not duties of the other, or rights belonging to the one which are not equally the rights of the other, that I have accepted the compliment conveyed to me by the request that I should read a paper at this Congress, provided that I could take for its text but one member of the announced subject of discussion. "The Rights of Labor," simply, is my thesis, and I hold that this includes both the rights and duties of capital, for capital is but crystallized, accumulated labor, having no possible interests, economically speaking, diverse from those of labor. In one view it is but a subdivision of labor; in another, but a tool which labor has itself fashioned by its own hands, which is used solely in its own hands, and which is entitled, therefore, in and by itself, to that protection and consideration only which its creator, owner, and user demands for it, as one of its valuable adjuncts and belongings.

Briefly, my argument is to be that capitalist and laborer, economically speaking, are the same, entitled to one transcendent, all-important right, the right to liberty, and subject to one controlling obligation or duty, so to use that liberty as not to violate the freedom of any other. Carried to their only possible, rational, and logical conclusion, I shall contend that these propositions lead to the demonstration that the present lamentable condition of labor, or more properly and accurately speaking, of the laborer, is due not to encroachments, invasions, or injustice by capital or the capitalists, but by their common antagonist, monopoly and the monopolists, against whom it is indeed most necessary and wholesome that the rights of the laborer should be most strenuously asserted and defended. Not too loudly can the note of alarm be struck, nor the call to arms sounded.

To sustain my argument I need first to state clearly the sense in which I use, and as I submit accurately, use, the terms with which I am dealing. What is labor, what is capital, what is monopoly? To define labor in economics is easy. It is the employment of energy, physical or mental, toward the production of wealth in the largest sense—of goods, of those things, that is, which make for the health, comfort, instruction, and pleasure of men. But the words "production of wealth" are to be taken in no narrow sense. All will admit doubtless that wealth, for example, is as much produced by the excavation of a tunnel through the Alps, as in the rolling of the railroad iron which is laid through it after it is excavated, but the equally salient facts are not so well understood and plainly admitted, perhaps, that equally with him who fashions it, that man produces wealth who transports a thing from a place where it is not desired, or desired but slightly, to another where it is strongly desired, or who as a shopkeeper keeps it in store until the consumer at that point needs it. And it is even less apparent, perhaps, that the priest, the poet, or the minstrel, who by his exertion encourages and increases the potential energy of the manual laborer, is economically, under our description, a laborer, too. But these propositions are after all the commonplaces of political economy, and I must assume, not argue them, and ask you to think of labor in this large and comprehensive sense whenever I use the term in this paper.

Of capital it is a less simple task to make a definition which may be denominated both accurate and economically orthodox. But this springs not from any inherent difficulty or vagueness in the conception, but solely from the loose, unprecise way in which writers on political economy, accounted orthodox, have used the word. But the general idea, which has always, although with more or less vagueness and want of precision, been attached to the word in economic discussion, and which may therefore be properly presumed to be the meaning which belongs to it in the scheme of subjects chosen for the consideration of this Congress, has been expressed by late economic writers with substantial accuracy as "Wealth in process of exchange."

This, it will be seen, excludes what some political economists have inconsiderately included in the term capital—wealth reserved by its owner for consumption in his own physical and personal necessities—comforts and pleasures, and limits it to wealth used in the assistance of labor in the production of other wealth, in the course of which assistance to labor this wealth is changing form or use. For exchange in the sense in which it is here used does not mean the mere passing from hand to hand, but also such transmutations as occur when the reproductive forces of nature are utilized for the increase of wealth.

It is not necessary to allude to the vulgar and absurd conception of capital as money, and of the capitalist as the man who has stores of currency, for there is no one here, I am sure, who does not realize that money itself is but a labor-saving tool of trade to facilitate exchange, useful in the highest degree, but not even indispensable to life, civilization, and forming in its aggregate amount but a very small and insignificant part of that stored-up result of labor properly called wealth. The capitalist is not the man who has money necessarily. He may have no considerable amount of it, and yet in other forms of wealth—useful in production—be rich beyond the dreams of avarice. Of course, under any usual or ordinary conditions, money being the commonest medium of exchange, this possession of exchangeable wealth will give him great power of obtaining quantities of money should he prefer, as he very seldom will do, to have his wealth in that particular form. But it may be necessary to call particular attention to the fact that this definition of capital excludes many things which are carelessly and incorrectly called capital which are not wealth at all, for wealth consists economically only of goods, good things adapted by the energy, mental or physical, of man to the use of man. It is, therefore, the result of labor applied to natural opportunities, or, as we call them generically, land. Labor and land, therefore, are the primary and only essential factors of the production of wealth, but a portion of the stored-up wealth which labor applied to land has produced assists and increases the power of labor under the name of capital.

But it is evident that there are powers and privileges belonging to certain classes in every existing social organization, which, although not capital and not wealth in any sense whatever, give the persons and classes enjoying them the advantages which belong to capital and to the possession of true wealth. I am not here denying the necessity, the justice, or the propriety of the arrangements which give those powers and privileges, but merely calling attention to their existence. The people with these privileges and powers have the ability to control the labor of others, and to obtain the use of others' capital upon terms dictated not by free contract, but in a greater or less degree by their own choice. If you can for a moment eliminate from it any opprobrious signification, it would be most convenient to call this class in economic organization monopolists, as distinguished from laborers and capitalists, and, abstractly to speak, of labor, capital, and monopoly as three contradistinguished things. But it is to be borne in mind that monopoly is not like capital, the product of labor, at all. Wealth, of which capital is a part, is the natural product of the combination of labor and land, the natural result of the one applied to the other. Monopoly is the result of artificial, man-made conventions, agreements, institutions, and laws. To it belong all such things as franchises or rights, so-called, guaranteed to some people by some social convention or institution which others are not allowed to enjoy or compete for, all patent privileges, by which a portion of the labor of others goes to the original inventor or designer of some product of labor, and, infinitely more important than anything else falling under this classification, the guaranteed exclusive possession of purely natural opportunities, or land, in the economic sense, by which must be understood to be meant land in the narrower sense, without consideration of improvements—water powers, air, harbor facilities, and the use of natural bodies of water of whatever form or nature. For such guaranteed exclusive possession makes of the class of land-owners necessarily a class of monopolists. The land is not the result of their labor, or of any other human being's. It does not fall under the accurate definition of wealth, much less of capital. But the right to its exclusive possession gives, and gives with more certainty than any other thing, the advantages of the possession of wealth and the means of procuring it by the control and utilization for one's self of the labor of others.

As the oriental aphorism well puts it, "To whomsoever the soil at any time belongs, to him belong the fruits of it." White parasols and elephants made with pride are the flowers of a grant of land, or, as Carlyle has it, "From a widow gathering nettles for her children's dinner, the perfumed land-holding seigneur can by a subtle alchemy extract every third nettle and call it rent." I am not intending by this assertion of its character as monopoly to attack land-ownership, even in its present form, or under its present unrestrained and unlimited conditions. I have an abiding conviction that that form and those conditions ought to be changed, an unwavering faith that they must and soon will be so changed, but even the suggestion of this obligation and necessity I leave for the conclusion of my paper, while that in a changed and modified form such ownership as is involved in the private individual, guaranteed continuous and permanent possession of land, is right, proper, and necessary, I propose distinctly hereafter to point out. But I wish to insist here upon the essential nature of land-ownership. If it be a proper and necessary monopoly, it is none the less monopoly, as we have used that word in contradistinction from labor and capital.

When James I. granted to Buckingham the exclusive privilege of making gold and silver thread and prohibited under severe penalties all manufacture of it save under Buckingham's license or control, the income which flowed into the favorite's coffers was not a return to capital,—it was the profit of monopoly, taken as a toll or tax from the labor and capital of others, enslaving the first and confiscating the second. And when the iron mine operator pays to the holder of the title of the land on which that mine was found, but who has had nothing to do with its development or its working, a royalty on each ton of ore taken from it, that income of the mine owner is equally with Buckingham's, simply the profit of monopoly, a tax or toll upon the production of laborers therein employed and the capital by which that labor is assisted. The one may have been iniquitous and unnecessary, the other praiseworthy and necessary, monopoly. Be that as it may, they are both monopolies.

And now that I have endeavored to make clear the distinction between labor, capital, and monopoly, I wish to postpone suggestion of the rights of labor as against monopoly and to address myself to the immediate question: What are the rights of labor as against capital?

Is not the answer obvious from the statement of their nature which has been made? The rights of a laborer against a capitalist (labor against capital is but a vague way of expressing this concrete idea) are his rights as against another laborer, no more and no less. They do not belong to contradistinguished classes at all. At the very utmost, assuming the natural opportunity on which labor can act to be freely obtainable, the capitalist can be but the assistant of the laborer, who is willing to use the tools and assistance he offers for a part of the product of the more efficient labor which can thus be performed. Nothing has been more successfully disproved than the proposition that it is capital which employs labor. It is labor which employs capital as its tool. But we must keep in mind ever in considering this statement the distinction that has been made between capital and monopoly. Capital does not only employ labor, it is labor that employs capital. But monopoly does employ both labor and capital and at its own terms—in other words, in a sense it enslaves them.

To return. I have said that at the utmost the capitalists can be nothing but the assistants of laborers, but as a matter of fact they are very largely the laborers themselves. Not only are they clearly distinguished and antagonistic classes, they are not even separate classes at all. Every street laborer with his own pickax is a capitalist as well as a laborer, he can only be a laborer without being a capitalist if he is utterly without tools and is furnished them by others. And even then he may not be, for the capital which is used by labor as an assistance in all great works is generally, through the agency of a complex system of credits, a part of the wealth which the banks and various financial institutions of a country concentrate, manage, and control, but are far from owning. That wealth is very largely the property of laborers of all sorts and kinds. Every workman who has a savings deposit, or a share of building company stock, is furnishing capital to assist labor and of course is a laborer as well as a capitalist. And who should be the capitalist but the laborer? There were in any primitive state of society but two factors in production, the laborer and the natural opportunities he worked on.

Assuming the natural opportunities for work to be free, the laborers must have had all the results of production which are their natural wages. Nor under such a condition of freedom of natural opportunities could a class of capitalists distinct from laborers ever grow up even, for while undoubtedly in time some more provident than others would store up more of the products of labor to assist their own labor in future production and to the others it would be worth, and they would bid for it, a portion of the product of their labor, as thus assisted by it, yet the opportunity and ability to labor being always existent, capital would no more than in the beginning of the community life be indispensable to the life or production of the laborer, and it could and would demand and receive no more than its value as a tool increasing the efficiency of his labor. In such a state of freedom for labor, we may well be sure that no such idea as that of a wage fund would take root, nor capital become concentrated in the hands of a small class. But if, by some man-made law, some institution or convention of society, be it praiseworthy or blameworthy, such a position of advantage is granted or guaranteed to either capitalist or laborer, as places the other in a position where his freedom in the contract is gone—for example, if the social organization is so arranged that the capitalist can, with much greater ease than the laborer, become the monopolist, and either pass from the class which loans to labor its efficient tools to the one which controls the only opportunities for the use of either labor or tools, or, as generally happens, conjoin in his own person the two characters, there arises naturally, and at once, an apparent contest between the capitalist and laborer, such as at present exists. But it is not between the capitalist and the laborer as capitalist and laborer. It is between the monopolist and the man seeking an opportunity to labor. On the one side, theoretically, are the persons holding the natural opportunities on which alone labor is of any utility or effect, and who demand for the use of them as rent—toll, the profits of monopoly—as large a portion of the product of such labor as they can get. On the other are ranged together both capitalists and laborers, demanding only the chance to labor in and on those natural opportunities, but willing to give up for the use of them only the smallest part of the product of their labor for which they can obtain it. Natural opportunities, immense in quantity and number as they are, are limited by definite and measurable bounds, unlike the amount of capital (for the possibilities of the production of wealth are practically illimitable). Here the pinch begins. Here the contest must rage.

The laborer may make such terms, and come to such agreement with the capitalist, or the capitalist with the laborer, as they may choose. By themselves they will be futile, for labor, with or without the tool called capital, can find no employment except by application to monopoly. On the other hand, if monopoly gives its permission, labor can make its own way and sustain itself without the assistance of capital at all. It need never do so, however, for whenever the ability and opportunity for profitable work exist in the same control, capital flows and asks investment as naturally as water rolls down hill.

The correlative rights and duties of the laborer, then, I repeat, as against the capitalist, and of the capitalist against the laborer are the same. They are the rights and duties, too, of each laborer as against every other laborer, and of each capitalist as against every other capitalist.

The right is the right to liberty; that is, the right to one's own self, and the product of one's own labor, which involves entire freedom of contract. The duty is the duty of so using and limiting that liberty as to preserve the equal freedom of all others. Viewed from such a standpoint, of course the wrong theoretically involved in the intimidation of men willing and anxious to work, which frequently accompanies labor agitations and strikes, and the interference which then frequently takes place with their freedom of contract, becomes clear, and so, it seems to me, does the similar wrong which interferes with the freedom of contract in relation to the interest which the capitalist may ask for the use of the tool which he proffers to the laborer.

It is not due to anything in the inherent relations of capital and labor at all, that these views of rights and wrongs are not universally recognized under present conditions. It is because these relations are complicated by the antagonism that I have indicated heretofore. Capital and labor on the one side must meet monopoly on the other. And because of the great ease with which the capitalist can become the monopolist, or, perhaps, more properly speaking, the certainty with which the monopolist becomes also to some extent the capitalist, a general looseness and vagueness of thinking has placed on the words "capitalist" and "capital" an economical and social meaning which belongs not to them, but to "monopolist" and "monopoly" alone.

In a scheme like that of this Congress I would have named as the subject of discussion not "The Rights of Labor and the Duties of Capital," but "The Rights of Labor and Capital and the Duties of Monopoly." Capital, as I have shown, is, after all, but a subdivision of labor, and the terms might well be shortened to the contradistinguished ones, labor and monopoly. It is to the maladjustment between these two that I believe the economic misery of the world to-day is due, that misery for which the Holy Father so truly says some remedy must be quickly found. This it is that calls so loudly for the vindication of the rights of labor. For what is the result of the present conditions? Are not the material wants and desires of men everywhere those which the physical resources of this wonderful earth on which we have been put are able on the expenditure of labor to supply? Are not those physical resources lying in great proportion unworked and idle all over the globe? We have but scratched the surface of the earth, the treasures of its deeps have been but barely uncovered. On the other hand, are the skill and industry wanting in mankind to develop those resources? Look about you at the great exhibition and reply. But notwithstanding the co-existence of the wants, the resources, and the skill and industry, millions of willing men stand unemployed, while coal mines are unworked, and wheat fields untilled, and women and children in our great cities die of cold and starvation.

It has become fashionable in our day to deny the existence of natural human rights, to declare that civilization knows no general law but that of natural selection and the survival of the fittest, to hold that there is no remedy for human wretchedness but to limit population, that nature is niggardly and the economic problem lies in production and not in distribution. This is atheism, not Christianity. As men and women who believe in our holy religion which teaches the fatherhood of God and the brotherhood of man we can have none of it. For us God is no niggard and no bungler. He has not brought into the world more men than the world can abundantly supply with the means of a healthy, natural, developing life, nor men without the ability to turn these means to account. It is not the problem of production that confronts us, it is the problem of distribution, and our errors and mistakes in its solution must result from ignorance or denial of the law, in accordance with which he would have us act.

I say that maladjustments of the relations of monopoly and labor are the cause of the economic misery of men. Let me give you, as it were, a glimpse of what I mean by a concrete example. Such an illustration sometimes lights up an argument better than explanation can do. In the coal-mining region of Pennsylvania the coal miners suffer much discomfort from the heat in the summer time. Ice is a comfort or luxury which their wages do not permit them to purchase. In the winter there are frequently seasons of enforced idleness for them. During one of these seasons some years ago, it occurred to some of them to cut and store for future use and the increase of their comfort during the coming summer, ice that formed in the numerous sink holes on the mining corporation's land, and which in all previous years had melted unutilized in the spring. The ice-cutting commenced, the telegraph bore from the resident agent to the company's offices in Philadelphia the news of it, and bore back again the laconic message: "Permit no ice to be cut except on payment of rent." Then the ice-cutting ceased, and the ice as usual melted in natural course.

Do not misunderstand me. I have not said—I am not now saying—that monopoly and privilege are in themselves wrong. I assert, indeed, the very reverse. Some monopolies are necessary and as natural in the order of things as is the sunshine. Others, though not necessary, are undoubtedly expedient. The guaranteed private possession of land is of the former kind; patent rights and franchises examples of the second. But undeniable monopolies though they be, it is no wrong in itself to society that patentees' rights should exist. The inventors that profit by them have given a return to society in the new and useful ideas they have furnished to mankind. Nor is a franchise, a law granting to one man or a collection of men, privileges or rights withheld from others, necessarily a wrong. It and all other monopolies, however, become so whenever their beneficiary fails in that return to society which is a full and fair equivalent for the right of monopoly which has been conferred upon him.

And it is so with the greatest of all monopolies, the right of individuals to the exclusive and guaranteed possession of the earth's surface. The monopoly of individual possession of land is as necessary to the civilized life of man as the existence of the natural opportunities themselves; civilization of necessity evolves it. Without it no people can rise above the grade of a pastoral tribe. And as continuity and permanency of tenure is necessary, and as land differs in desirability and the difference is constantly varying in amount, the law of rent arises. As stated by all political economists worthy the name, it is that the rent of land is determined by the excess of its produce over that which the same application can secure from the least productive land in use, or, to put it in another form, less liable to the misapprehension that it applies to agricultural land alone, "the ownership, *i. e.*, the exclusive possession and control of a natural agent of production will give the power of appropriating so much of the wealth produced by the exertion of labor and capital upon it as exceeds the return which the same application of labor and capital would secure in the least productive occupation in which they freely engage."

This law of rent is as fixed a factor in economic science as is the law of gravitation in physics. The exclusive possession and control is necessary, the power of appropriation goes with it. What is the duty of the holder of the monopoly to the society which invests him with it? This is the question which confronts us, and which must be answered if the rights of labor and capital are to be protected, and the duties of monopoly enforced, for it is clear that what goes to monopoly and is not returned to society in some adequate form and amount, is so much taken from labor and capital of the product of their exertions.

Economically, I believe that liberty, the right of each man in himself to the whole product of his labor, is the ideal to be reached, and that when the product of labor constitutes the wages of labor, as Adam Smith a century ago declared was natural, and not until then, will the so-called labor problem be solved. Centuries ago, before the beginning of this marvelous era, with its prodigious increase in the effectiveness of labor by the mastery which man has obtained over the powers of nature, this question of the duty of the "lords of the land" was one with which the Church had often to deal.

Every element of the feudal system not formed by was influenced and modified by the Church, and in the feudal system, peculiar obligations, strenuously maintained, were imposed in return for the privilege of receiving rent. Among them were the support of the civil list, the public defense, the cost of public worship and instruction, and the care of the sick and destitute. What other are the purposes of taxation to-day? Against the protest of a priest who told them that they were remitting to the proprietors a tax which was one of the conditions on which they held their land, and reimposing it on the labor of the nation, the French Constituent Assembly, in 1789, abolished tithes and turned over the support of the clergy to general taxation.

The Long Parliament in the abolition of military tenures took from monopoly the burden of the consideration on which it held the common property of the nation, and saddled it on the people at large in the taxation of all consumers. Both actions were hailed, and doubtless intended by lovers of freedom, as steps in advance, but to those who think with me they were the most disastrous of mistakes. We think that if these feudal dues of monopoly were now in force, changed only in form for adaptation to the changed times, and if monopoly and privilege paid to the community which guarantees them existence, the due pecuniary reward or compensation justly and properly chargeable to them, all other taxation could be abolished, and that all which makes law instituted monopoly and privilege, the enemy of labor and capital, would be thereby destroyed. Of the products of labor and capital there would be two parts, one going to the individual producers according to the part each had taken in the work of production, the other to the community as a whole, to be distributed in public benefits to all its members.

It is no part of my purpose to attempt in this paper, at this time, to sustain this practical proposition for the improvement in present social conditions.

I have tried only to point out that the antagonism is not between labor and capital, that it is between labor and monopoly, that the right of labor is liberty to enjoy the fruits of its exertion, that the problem is not to define the duties of capital, but of monopoly and privilege. How well I have succeeded it is for you to judge, but this I know, that nowhere is a fitter place to discuss the social problem and to find its solution than in the societies of the Holy Church; nowhere are men more clearly called to the work than are the clergy and laity of his Church, who summed up his teachings in social philosophy in the sublime utterance, "Whatsoever ye would that men should do unto you, do ye even so to them."

A justice of the supreme court of the United States, in a remarkably inapt phrase, as it seems to me, addressing students of a law school in one of the great universities, spoke recently of the age-long struggle between "private rights and public greed."

In a more truthful, and I hope a more truth-loving spirit, I suggest to you that "the rights of labor, the duties of monopoly" are involved in the age-long struggle between private greed and public rights.

That in that great struggle the Catholic Church, which gave liberty to the slave, which emancipated woman, which has ever been the greatest of all bulwarks and defenders of human liberty, will give her countenance and aid to the oppressed and struggling masses, is certain. It is proven by her history. It is a part of her mission. To doubt it were impiety and heresy.

A paper on the same theme, by another eminent member of the Chicago bar, John Gibbon, LL.D., was substantially as follows:

THE LABOR PROBLEM.

The unrest and discontent felt and heard in every line of social and industrial life are but the protests of a struggling humanity against hardships and oppressions which are the necessary outgrowth of the strained and abnormal conditions existing between labor and capital,—conditions which if not speedily remedied, may work the debasement of the one, and the destruction of the other. The folly of labor is no more reprehensible for these conditions than the greed of capital. For years the tendency of the times has been toward the enslavement of the individual through the domination of the masses on the one hand, and the monopoly of capital through trusts and combines on the other, and whoever imagines that there is in legislation or statecraft, a short cut by which the conditions wrought by both these causes may be reached, adjusted, harmonized, and remedied other than by mutual concessions based upon mutual interests is shortsighted, if not visionary. That legislation is beneficial, and sometimes necessary to compel the performance of duties which ought to be discharged voluntarily, I admit, but in respect to matters of a social and industrial nature, which are so largely dependent upon natural conditions, legislation may aid, but can not create them.

That hardships and oppressions have existed for all time does not prove that they are a heritage of the human family. "And there shall be no poor nor beggar among you," is a divine command, while "the poor ye shall have always with you," is but the voice of prophecy. The former is the law proclaimed, the latter the result of its nonobservance. Every man born into the world owes certain duties to society, and paramount to all others is the duty to support himself, and those naturally dependent upon him, and of equal importance in the scale of primary duties are obedience to law and respect for the rights of others. The performance of these primary obligations no man should be permitted to evade or ignore.

In the proposals we advance, if we hope thereby to accomplish beneficial results, we must recognize the changes which are constantly occurring in natural conditions, for these changes necessarily affect the industrial life of the people. The conditions which existed fifty, or even twenty-five, years ago do not exist to-day. Fifty years ago the surplus labor of the country found employment in reclaiming and cultivating the waste lands of the fruitful West; but now nearly all the available lands have been appropriated, so that surplus labor no longer finds remunerative employment there, and the stream of immigration has ceased to flow toward the setting sun.

Thirty years ago surplus labor found employment in the army, in the building of railways, in the improvement of rivers and harbors, and in many other enterprises which existed as a result of the war then being waged for national supremacy. These changes which are wrought by what may be termed natural causes only, serve to emphasize the

ARCHBISHOP KAIN,
ST. LOUIS.
ARCHBISHOP WALSH,
TORONTO.
ARCHBISHOP ELDER,
CINCINNATI.

CARDINAL TASCHEREAU,
QUEBEC.

ARCHBISHOP WILLIAMS,
BOSTON.
ARCHBISHOP GROSS,
OREGON.
ARCHBISHOP KENRICK,
ST. LOUIS.

fact that in the field of labor, as in the whole domain of industry, supply and demand must ever be controlling factors, and the economist who ignores this fundamental truth in seeking a wise solution of the all-important problem now agitating the public is a dreamer or a demagogue.

Whatever speculations or theories we may advance or proclaim it should be conceded that unless labor is reduced to a condition of servitude, the amount of wages to be paid and the amount of work to be done at a certain price must always remain the objects of free and open bargain. Under such circumstances, the connection between employer and employed has the advantage of a voluntary association, in which each party is conscious of benefit, and each feels that his own welfare depends, to a great extent, on the welfare of the other. But the instant wages ceases to be a bargain, the instant the laborer is paid—not according to his value, but to an established scale; both employer and employed are no longer free agents, and all the incentives to mutual advantages are taken away, and the kindness which naturally arises from a voluntary association, as well as the mutual benefits, is wanting.

It must also be conceded that trades unions and associations of that nature, when properly conducted, are designed to do much good. They will prove beneficial in educating the workmen, in inviting discussion respecting proposals advanced looking to the elevation of labor—beneficial in assisting members to obtain employment, beneficial in bringing before the public their wants and molding public opinion in favor of granting them—beneficial from a political point of view, because by united action they may obtain legislation which as individuals they could not secure. But when they go beyond these objects, as they sometimes do, the state, rather than the trades unions, is to blame in not making adequate provision for the adjustment of differences which inevitably grow out of the relation of capital to labor. In every other department of life the differences which emanate from contractual relations are regulated by common or statute law, and why should the conflicts arising between labor and capital be left to the will or caprice of the haughty capitalist on the one hand, or the aggrieved laborer on the other?

The right to enjoy life and to strive in the pursuit of happiness may be classed among the absolute rights of man. The right to sustain life in case of necessity—the right of a starving man to a portion of his neighbor's food—is paramount to all human enactments. But the right to live, in the ordinary acceptation of the term, does not mean merely the right to exist. The man who tills the soil, the man who forges the iron, the man who pushes the plane, ought to be afforded the opportunity of providing for himself food, raiment, and shelter. Moreover, as the family is ordained of God, and the basis of all human society, the head of the family is not only entitled to all these things for himself but for his wife, children, and all those of his household. Hence when a powerful manufacturer draws around him a community of men, women and children, his duty toward them is not fully discharged by the mere payment of wages. The conditions which he has created impose upon him corresponding duties, and it is no answer to the neglect or refusal to perform them to say that they are not imposed by the law of the land, or that they do not grow out of any compact or agreement with the community thus organized.

This moral duty has been given practical effect, with excellent results, at Essen and Altendorf, Germany. For example, the number of men employed by the Krupps is 25,200, who, with their families, amount to 87,900 people. The corporation builds and rents all dwellings for its workmen, provides co-operative stores, and boarding accommodations for unmarried men, and attends to the prevention of sickness by careful sanitary regulations. The death rate is smaller than any other community in Europe. The lives of the employes are required to be insured, and in addition Mr. Krupp provides pension and relief funds for the injured and bereaved. He also provides schools for the children of his employes, and churches for the religious training of all connected with his establishment.

The Krupps have been able, through their social work, to center so fully the interests of their employes in the neighborhood in which they live, and so to unite them with the interests of the firm, that their men have exhibited less desire to change employment and have been less affected by labor disturbances than in any other parts of the country. Co-operation and profit-sharing have been conducted with satisfactory results in many lines of industry both here and in Europe, and from the harmony existing in these communities between employer and the employed, it is safe to conclude that the vexed labor problem may be solved through mutual concessions based on mutual advantages.

The idea of master and servant grows out of the domestic relations, and while it may be less culpable for a man to neglect providing for the support and comfort of his servants than it would his wife and children, still it is a crime against the natural and divine law for him to do so. Whoever neglects this moral duty in the one case is amenable to the law of the land, and why not extend that law to include those who disregard it in the other? My contention is that what has been accomplished by voluntary action, and as a moral obligation on the part of humane employers, might be enforced as a legal duty in respect to those who regard their workmen as merchantable commodities.

In the abstract it is perceived that everyone has a natural right to use and enjoy his property in such manner as he pleases, and if an employer of labor it is his privilege to employ whom he will, at the best prices he may; but abstract principles and natural rights are subordinate to the laws of human necessities and the well-being of the people. The absolute right of man to the enjoyment of his own property exists only in a state of nature where no relative rights intervene and so long as he is able to defend his possession. But as soon as society is organized and the individual becomes dependent upon the community for all the rights and privileges which he enjoys, corresponding duties arise, which grow out of the compact and are binding upon him whether he wills it or not, and whether defined by law or stipulated by contract.

Justice to labor does not imperil or impair capital. The stability and progress of a country must depend upon the character of the industrial classes, and whether the standing of the working population is to be debased or elevated must depend upon the relation they sustain to the common conditions of their country. Ownership of property is the true status of liberty, and as the idea of home is the initial point around which clusters every ennobling virtue, it should be the duty of corporations and individuals who establish industrial centers and manufacturing communities to provide homes for men and families engaged in their employment. All honor is due to the noble, charitable, and humane men and women who devote their time and contribute their means for the care, nourishment, and comfort of children whose mothers are forced to toil for bread, but there should be no occasion for the infants' corral or the robust man's almshouse in well-governed communities. Their existence belies social progress and is repugnant to the plan of a wisely governed state.

The highway of nations is strewn with the ruins of the democracies of the past. Their decline and fall can be truthfully ascribed to the defect in their policy, which, while recognizing and protecting political equality, failed to provide for an equality of conditions such as would have prevented the conflicts between the rich and the poor, conflicts which grow into the revolution that results in despotism. The struggle between the rich and the poor, between those who own property and those without property, is now more general, if not more alarming, than ever before in the history of the world. This struggle must increase in scope and intensity until in our political economy man is acknowledged to be superior to wealth, and, as a consequence, that the rights of the many are paramount to the privileges of the few. Then will follow the complete emancipation of labor from the practical ownership which now holds it in bondage, and unto it will be given an equitable portion of the wealth it produces in alliance with capital.

So far as my observation goes, I am led to believe that the conflicts between employer and employed find their origin in the false relations existing between the people and the land, and between labor and capital; and until we unite labor and capital in a closer union based upon a more equitable division of profits, and effect a more general distribution of the land among the subordinate holders of power, these evils will be intensified even unto the utter destruction of our democracy.

Next to the right of life and liberty there is nothing so sacred to an American as the right of property; and in our efforts to rectify the wrongs of labor and to bring about a more equitable division of the land among the people, they must be accomplished not by subversion of justice, not by invasion of right, not by destruction of tenures, not by forfeiture of titles, not by community of property, not by single tax upon land, not by shackling individual exertion, not by blasting personal ambition, not by turning the hands of progress back upon the dial of time, not by overthrowing established institutions which have been replenished, fostered, and fortified by the worth and wisdom of the best thinkers and purest men of all the ages that have gone before, but by marching onward and upward along the lines of duty and law, using the materials at our command to improve the condition of men as we find them.

It may be that there shall come no time, indeed, when there will not be, in lamentable contrast, poverty and wealth, suffering and affluence, misery and luxury. It may be that there shall come no day which will not see one class of men with only the labor of their hands to sell and another whose business it is to buy this primal commodity; and that the one shall endeavor to market his only ware at the highest obtainable price, and the instinct of greed compel the other to buy as cheaply as he can. But I believe that there shall be, in time to come, a vast improvement in the aggregate comfort and independence of the laboring class, between the power of money in that coming day and its influence in the present. Another epoch, as I believe, will turn away in horror from the pestilential tenement houses and the hordes of hungry and homeless ones of the 19th century.

The troubles and dangers that confront us as a nation must be met and conquered within our own borders. There is no other possible escape. Emigration has been the safety and salvation of Eastern lands. There can be no emigration from America. This is the Mecca of the human race, the final resting-place of restless humanity.

Earth's imperial people have ever moved westward as if impelled by a resistless power divine, and parallel with their migrations civilization and sovereignty moved. The world's sceptre has made the circuit of the earth. First raised and wielded in Egypt, it passed to Greece, from Greece to Rome, from Rome to France, from France to England, and from England it is passing unto America, here to remain, for the Orient is just beyond us—the land where it first arose. By the logic of causes, that knows no change, the solution of the problem—mighty and grave—that confronts us as a people must be reached through agencies of our own, and that solution not only involves the life of the nation, but comprehends the future of the world.

An eloquent and instructive review was that of the Paulist Father, Rev. Walter Elliott, on the "Missionary Work of the Church in the United States." It ran as follows:

FATHER ELLIOTT ON CATHOLIC MISSIONARY WORK.

He stands erect and has a far outlook whose feet rest upon the mountain of the Lord. The ages move in review, the nations march past; his outlook is universal.

The outlook in the United States is many millions of independent men and women whose characteristics are liberty and intelligence. Their eternal destiny and the means of arriving at it are eagerly discussed, but amid a bewildering conflict of opinions. This most modern of nations yet holds to a vague idea of Christ as the world's redeemer, of the Bible as God's book; for the rest, the only common creed is progress, human dignity, and the destiny of the great Republic. Any claimant for a hearing in religious matters must before all else be able to square his fundamental principles with these beliefs.

Catholics are mingled among this people in the proportion of about one to six, and are the only perfectly organized body of Christians. These are also distinguished by liberty and intelligence, though fully half are new-comers or their children. They are endowed with an absolutely certain knowledge of man's eternal destiny as well as of all the means of arriving at it, and are masters of the most renowned of intellectual forces—the faith of the Catholic, Apostolic, Roman Church. The problem is how to place this virtue of Catholic faith in a missionary attitude and secure it a hearing; how to turn all the organic and personal force of Catholic faith into apostolic zeal for the eternal salvation of the entire nation.

As a matter of fact, we are only beginning to act as if we felt that our fellow-citizens were our brethren in sore need of the truth of God. We have as yet failed, as a body, to take the entire American nation into account in a religious point of view, have not felt it a duty to proclaim to them that the certainty of Christ's truth is with us, that the pardon of sins is in the contrition, confession, and satisfaction of the sacrament of penance, that the union of their souls with God is in the communion of his Son's body and blood in the Eucharist—and the other necessary means of enlightenment and sanctification.

The problem is, how to induce Catholics to attempt the conversion of non-Catholics, and to realize that until they offer them the true religion there is a cloud upon their own title to it.

God would have us missionaries to the American people. Does any Catholic dare to contradict that? If so, let us hear from him.

Suppose that my neighbor's house and mine were separated by a dense wood, and that some morning I should wake to find a noble avenue cut through between us; what would such a miracle mean? That God willed me to make my neighbor my friend, to visit him familiarly, and to love him. God has done more than this with Catholics and non-Catholics in America, and by community of all that is good in civil and industrial life, by close social ties and personal friendships, has opened our hearts mutually to each other. Let us be friends in the truest sense of the term, the religious.

The dense and tangled forest of prejudice has already been pierced. That vice of honest minds is now chiefly to be found among the more ignorant. Few converts but will tell you that their first step was surprise that Catholics had been falsely accused. There are men and women all round us who have but to learn *just what we are* as a religious body, to be led on to conversion; they already know that we have been basely calumniated. In the better class of minds we shall have to contend mainly with such difficulties as lie in the way of all supernatural religion—timidity, dread of the mysterious or a false view of reason's prerogatives, unwillingness to submit to the unchangeable truth. And in a multitude of other cases men and women fail to become Catholics only for the same reason that many of our own people refuse to be good Catholics—worldliness, sensuality, fastidious objection to our vulgar crowds, family pride, human respect. St. Paul's example shows how to deal with these: "And as he reasoned of temperance, and righteousness, and judgment to come, Felix trembled." If even that wretched bribe-taker trembled, our honest fellow-citizens will do more. Let us but manage to bring to bear a patient and intelligent exposition of what our religion actually does for us in our inner and outer life, and then a realization of the need of salvation, the shortness of life, and the rigors of the judgment will do the rest.

There can be but one excuse for a Catholic, especially one of intelligence, and above all a priest, not addressing our erring brethren: that they can not be induced to listen to him. And who has ever fairly sought a hearing and been denied it? How many instances are there where men of no peculiar gifts have filled their churches, and even public halls, with audiences full of Protestants, giving respectful attention to Catholic truth. The trouble is not want of audiences, but want of men and methods persistently to follow up the work.

The collapse of dogmatic Protestantism is our opportunity. Denominations, and "creeds," and "schools," and "confessions" are going to pieces before our eyes. Great men built them, and little men can demolish them. This new nation can not but regard with disdain institutions hardly double its own short life, and yet utterly decrepit; can not but regard with awe an institution in whose life the great Republic could have gone through its career nearly a score of times. I tell you that the vigor of national youth must be amazed at the freshness of perennial religion, and must soon salute it as divine. The dogmas of older Protestantism are fading out of our people's minds, or are being thrust out. It is not against the religion of men's ancestors, but against each one's religion of yesterday, as unsteady in grasp as it is recent in acquisition, that we have to contend—we who speak for Him who is of yesterday, and to-day, and the same forever.

Consider, then, how it is with our noble-hearted friends: in their case it is religion wandering here and there in search of a Church. How many earnest souls are about us, weary of doubtful teachings, glad to harken to, ay and to believe, anyone who promises them relief.

See, too, and admire, how their religious instincts strive after organic life. As Calvinism dies, Christian Endeavor is born and counts a million members in a day—good works making little of faith, as at first faith made little of good works. See that while Methodism leaves the slums and is petrifying in lordly temples and in universities, the Salvation Army scours the gutters it has turned from with loathing.

I tell you that the people around us are religious, that they long for God and are ready for those divine rules of the higher life called Catholicity.

No form of belief faces civilized irreligion with half the courage of Catholicity. A vigorous man exults in the trial of his strength. It is incredible that an intelligent Catholic shall not command the attention of thoughtful minds on questions of such absorbing interest as—What becomes of our dead?—Can we communicate with them? —Can we get along without the Bible?—What think you of Christ, whose son is He? We have the truth on all such vital questions; Catholic truth is simple, accredits itself, and is in the highest degree commendatory of the Church as compared with the Protestant denominations.

Only make a parallel of Catholic principles and American fundamental ideas on human dignity, and you will perceive that we are up to the times and kindred to the nation. There can be little doubt that this Republic shall be made Catholic if we love its people as God would have us.

We are right, and we can prove it. How very much that means. It is God's will with men that those who are right shall know how to prove it, and those who are wrong shall be brought to listen to them. If all that we had to give were a right scheme of social amelioration, we should win the people, because we should be right; or if it were a true discovery of how to fully develop electrical forces, we should win the world of science and industry. But oh! it is the true religion of God about which we are right

—every man's sorest need, every man's sweetest joy. That is in our case the tremendous meaning of the claim, We are right, and we can prove it. The cruel fact is, that dreamers of social reform work harder and succeed better than we who are the children of light, and they whose only end is money are the best models in our day of devoted and well-directed endeavor.

Why, when it was to fly in the face of high Rome, to be burned to death, to be devoured by wild beasts, countless thousands yearly rushed into the Church. And now it is to float into the heaven of peace and joy, it is to taste the sweetness of the Lord Jesus Christ without any persecution, it is to embrace a religion whose dogma of human dignity and equality—listen to Leo XIII. as he expounds it!—adds to American greatness the placit of higher Rome.

I do not want to believe those prophets of ill-omen who tell us that we are shortly to find ourselves in the midst of a nation which has lost the knowledge of Jesus Christ as its redeemer, which knows no heaven or hell but the sorrows and joys of this fleeting life; but there is much to confirm that gloomy view. And what voice shall call them back from so dark a doom but the trumpet note of Catholic truth? Who should be foremost in print and on platform and in the intercourse of private life, pleading for Christ and offering his promises of eternal joy, if not Catholic bishops, priests, and laity?

The first element of hope in any enterprise is that the right sort of men and women are undertaking it. The sanctified soul makes the best missionary. Good men and women are the power of God unto salvation. The Bible is the Word of God, and it enlightens me; but a zealous Christian is another Christ to me. The union of men with truth is not union with books, or even ideas, but with God, and with each other; and that immediately.

The diffusion of Catholics among non-Catholics makes a personal and independent tone of Catholicity necessary in any case, but it also distributes missionaries everywhere, independent religious characters who can maintain the truth with the least possible external help. It is God's way. One by one men are born, become conscious of responsibility, die, are judged. One by one, and by personal influence, non-Catholics are made aware that *they are wrong;* and then one, and again another, of their Catholic friends personally influences them to understand that Catholicity is right.

Combined action can do much, but the supreme combination is that of virtue, and sympathetic interest in a single person. Family, social, business relations are made by Providence for this end; that they may become channels of heavenly influence.

Councils have done much for religion, but men and women have done more, for they made the councils. There were great councils during the two hundred years before Trent, and with them, and between them, matters grew worse. Why did Trent succeed?—held amid wars, interrupted, almost disjointed. Because the right sort of men at last had come: popes, bishops, theologians. It was not new enactments that saved us but new men—Ignatius and Philip Neri, Teresa and Francis de Sales, and Vincent de Paul, and their like.

The real force of life is personal, is soul upon soul, and must be our real missionary force.

Catholics are, therefore, to be made missionary by personal qualities which shall attract their non-Catholic acquaintances—the American virtue of self-control, independence of character, love of liberty and of intelligence, these must shine out with a Catholic lustre. To them must be added other natural virtues dear to our countrymen, such as truthfulness, candor, temperance, industry, fair dealing; these must find heroes and exemplars plentifully among us. All this is necessary to introduce the supernatural life, divine faith, and hope, and love; Catholic unity; confession and communion. "First the natural man and then the spiritual man," says the apostle. Give us fervent Catholics who are typical Americans, and brotherly love will do the rest. If non-Catholics are felt to be brethren by nationality, soon St. John's test will claim its application: "We know that we have passed from death to life because we love the brethren."

Interest in the advancement of God's kingdom must become a note of personal Catholicity. We must open our hearts to non-Catholics as to brothers and sisters; each of them who reaches the circle of our influence must feel our kindly interest in his religious state, if it be no more than sympathy with his sincere belief in what is common to all.

The men and women who are right will persuade those who are wrong, if they want to. Truth is mighty; but that means truth thrilling upon the lips of men and women, gleaming in their eyes, beautiful in their lives. We need not pray for orators; he that speaks from the heart is eloquent enough. If a man loves American souls because Christ died for them, he will win his way to save them.

The personal use we make of the truth of God is a good test of our valuation of it. It is this way in the gift of the truth: if it is not worth sharing it is not worth keeping. A people not eager to share Catholicity with kindly neighbors and fellow-citizens are not likely to live up to it themselves; certainly they are not worthy to enjoy it, much less to transmit it to their children.

The biographer of St. Philip Neri, speaking of the singular power and warmth of the saint's heart-beat, says that "when he knew anyone to be tempted, especially with sensual temptations, he would draw him tenderly to his breast, and so dispel the temptation at once, and fill his soul with a sweet serenity and heavenly peace." Take your doubting non-Catholic friend to your heart, at least figuratively, and your words by their very tones of sympathy will dispel his errors.

The following lines from Cardinal Newman, entitled "The Religion of Cain," and headed by the text "Am I my brother's keeper?" are instructive:

> The time has been, it seemed a precept plain
> Of the true Faith, Christ's tokens to display;
> And in life's commerce still the thought retain,
> That men have souls and wait a judgment day;
> Kings used their gifts as ministers of heaven,
> Nor stripped their zeal for God of means which God had given.
>
> 'Tis altered now; for Adam's eldest born
> Has trained our practice in a selfish rule—
> Each stands alone, Christ's bonds asunder torn;
> Each has his private thought, selects his school,
> Conceals his creed and lives in closest tie
> Of fellowship with those who count it blasphemy.
>
> Brothers! spare reasoning; men have settled long
> That ye are out of date and they are wise;
> Use their own weapons; let your words be strong,
> Your cry be loud, till each sacred boaster flies.
> Thus the Apostles tamed the pagan breast,
> They argued not but preached; and conscience did the rest.

Religion can not exist in the soul without a principle of fecundity by which it demands to be communicated. Selfishness, besides being a vice, is a malady. It was the primary evil of Protestantism, and it has proved its ruin. The Bible is the common heritage of God's children; the Reformers made it each man's private property; hence disunion and then doubt. And any Catholic who fancies that he can use his Faith as if it were his own exclusive property is in error, and is in danger of being decatholicized.

The missionary spirit is needed for our own inner life, in order that racial, local, family influences may be restricted to their subordinate spheres. These tend to supplant the universal. Nothing tends to make a man universal, catholic, better than the noble virtue of zeal for souls. "Blessed is the man who hath found a new friend" is perfectly true in its converse: blessed is the man who is true friend to another.

It is easy to see, therefore, that a spirit of defense is not the missionary spirit, but one of aggressive charity. The dread of defection, and the tendency to mournful exercises of reparation, indicate a tone of mind quite unmissionary. Catholic Faith is too often and too closely identified with religious traditions and practices brought from the Old World, producing a narrow and suspicious disposition. The sensation of exile is injurious to the missionary vocation. "To the Greek and to the barbarian, to the wise and to the unwise, I am a debtor."

To my mind our very dissensions, whether on matters of principle or of policy, are reason for encouragement, for they have shown an independence of conviction which yields to no human tribunal, and in bowing to a divine tribunal does so frankly and without cringing. Turn this independence of thought into missionary channels, and the results will be equal to our deep personal sincerity multiplied by the incalculable power of our divine organization.

How to go to work is an easy problem, since we have a perfect organization which can utilize the resources of modern civilization. Let us but have the determined purpose—the men of action bent upon success—and the ways and means are the divine methods of the Church and the modern opportunities of the press, the platform, and the incessant intercommunication of all classes in America.

American bishops, priests, and laity working together in an apostolic spirit will missionize the entire land in half a decade of years. The immediate effect will be to throw every form of error upon the defensive, to set every religiously disposed person to sorting out and dividing calumny from fact, to start a small and perceptible stream of conversions in every locality. It seems like a dream, but it is really a vision of the future, and the not distant future either. Having done nothing, we have many thousands of converts. What may we not hope from a universal apostolate?

If what I have been saying is true, the practical suggestion which follows is that every diocese should have at least one or two priests who shall be exclusively missionary—I mean, of course, secular priests, and missionaries to non-Catholics.

As the bishop has one of his more experienced clergy to do bishop's work as Vicar-General, one of the younger priests to do bishop's work as secretary, an expert to do bishop's legal work as chancellor, so should there be one or two priests to do bishop's work as missionary to his "other sheep not of this fold," wholly devoted to arousing the consciences of non-Catholics. If there is an administrative need of help, and an epistolary and a legal need of help, so is there a missionary one.

And this is the answer to the difficulty. "The bishop hasn't got priests enough to take care of the parishes." If this were absolutely true he would dismiss his secretary to a parish, recall the professors in the seminary to parishes; if he can not take care of the necessary routine and educational work of the diocese without sharing it with the priests, neither can he the apostolic work without a missionary. Or is it not to be deemed a necessary work? Did the Holy Ghost say only that bishops were to *rule* the Church of God committed to them? Who was it that said, "Go forth into all the world and preach the Gospel to every creature?" Have this and kindred texts no meaning for the Church in America?

The diocesan missionary should be the bishop's right arm, as the Roman Propaganda is the Pope's.

What can a priest do in his parish? He can give courses of doctrinal sermons, inviting the presence of all thinking men and women through the press—or he can get his neighbors to do this in his church for him. He can act and look and speak as belonging to this people and nation, deeply in the common welfare. He is the appointed champion of religion and morality in his parish, and he should act accordingly. He should be the public foe of all vice. In him gambling, and saloon-keeping and saloon-going, bribe-taking, and oath-breaking, should find their bitterest antagonist. He should be the known advocate of every good cause of whatever kind—well known as the friend of all good men. "I became all things to all men that I might gain some"—a saying often quoted, little understood, and less practiced.

All this is parochial duty anyway; but it is pertinent to our subject that such conduct builds the Catholic priest a pulpit in every household in his town, and enables him to introduce the Catholic religion to men's notice under the most favorable circumstances.

The parish priest should watch the local papers, and defend and advocate the truths of religion, natural and revealed. He should carefully provide that Catholic journals come to each family, and see to the distribution of the printed truth generally.

And this opens to view one of the mightiest of apostolates—the Apostolate of the Press.

In most places the secular press carefully excludes everything hostile to Catholicity, and opens its columns to communications from respectable Catholics, especially the clergy. Oh! why is not this golden and universal opportunity better utilized? There are multitudes of converts who were first drawn to us by a paragraph in the daily paper.

A small band of laymen in the city of St. Paul put their heads together and then their limited means, and the Catholic Truth Society of America is the result, beginning a glorious propaganda of the printed truth. One man in New Orleans, Judge Frank McGloin, has devoted the recent years of his life to the same work, and with marvelous success. Faithful souls are to be found in every parish who ask, "What can we do to save our neighbors and friends?" The answer is the Apostolate of the Press. The Catholic weekly and monthly press has a limitless missionary field, and is daily seeing its way better to cultivate it.

What gives much promise is that the Apostolate of Prayer is spreading everywhere. Many if not all the contemplative communities are engaged in it, and most heartily so. Men and women everywhere are being stirred by a secret thought—Let us pray for conversions. Those actively engaged say—Will they accept a book, leaflet, a Catholic magazine? If so, I leave to God the rest. Give me a non-Catholic audience, says the apostolical priest, and I leave to God the rest; it is God's will that I should seek a hearing from them. Prayer will do the rest. As a result of this apostolate of prayer, men and women will everywhere arise among us gifted from on high with a life-mission to impart the truth to their fellow-countrymen.

You see, then, how to go about it. Not alone by spasmodic efforts of zeal (though even these are useful), not only by starting societies (though there is a wide field for all such, new and old), but each Catholic must have a missionary element in his personal belief and practice of religion. And the Church is herself essentially a missionary society, not excepting her ordinary form of diocese and parish. Utilize this divine missionary society to its full capacity, but above all encourage personal zeal.

Let every parish have its stated courses of lectures and sermons for non-Catholics, and public prayers for their conversion, just as regular as the yearly Forty Hours' Devotions and the Lenten and Advent courses. Let there be a class of converts in all the larger parishes.

Let every Catholic periodical have its convert's department.

Let every diocese have at least one diocesan missionary.

Let every family have its little library of doctrinal and controversial books and pamphlets, its Catholic paper and magazine; every man and woman their little list of non-Catholic friends for whom they are ever praying and ever asking prayers, to whom they are ever talking and ever lending books.

Let the entire American Church face onward and move on, working and praying, toward the greatest victory of the Holy Spirit this thousand years—the conversion of the great Republic.

Of course objections are heard. For example: Keep to your place. I dread lest you will precipitate a public controversy in my parish. You are taking on yourself the work of the bishops. Why don't the bishops do it? Why don't the priests take up the work? Why don't the laity do their part? It's dangerous to make experiments. Where's your eloquence? Where's your learning? Have you ever made a course of philosophy? Don't be a crank, don't attempt the impossible. Don't be deluded by your study of early days—the Church is not what it once was. (That is to confess that it is now racial and not universal, no longer youthful, but old and stiff-jointed. Our Holy Mother, the Church, has passed the age of child-bearing.) Be safe. There s a line in the way. Where's the money to come from? Are you the dynamite that's going to blow up the Presbyterian religion, the Episcopal, the Baptist, the Methodist—or the big religion which says mind your own business? John Hughes failed, John England and Martin Spalding failed—are you impertinent enough to think *you* can succeed?

Or other objections: They don't want you—they have no use for Catholicity. Establish my little sodality—that's the best thing to do. They are a rotten race and totally depraved; let's huddle ourselves and our little ones away from them, or they will contaminate us. They are as bad as outright apostates, nearly all in bad faith. A race that once has renounced the truth has never been known to return to it, etc.

Yes. Appeals to cowardice. Appeals to race hatred, to sloth, to despair. Such croakings once had weight, but that day is passed.

We everywhere behold signs of the opposite spirit. The diocese of Covington is given a farm, and the bishop sets it apart to support missionaries to non-Catholics.

Another bishop has engaged a missionary to assemble and address non-Catholic audiences in public halls in the smaller towns of his diocese; and several other bishops would be glad to make the same arrangement.

A zealous parish priest is inspired to pray for conversions, and from looking about him for company he prints a little prayer, and in less than a year more than a hundred thousand copies of it are asked for and distributed.

For the colored non-Catholics there is a young society, the Josephites, small in number but full of courage and hope, and equipped with a college and seminary for the training of missionaries. Associated with them is a body of apostolic women, the Mission Helpers. "The Spirit of the Lord hath filled the whole earth," and "his gifts and calling are without repentance."

Multitudes among the surging crowds about us are now subject to a mysterious yearning toward the ancient religion of God, the ever-youthful Bride of the Lamb. One word from your heart, one glimpse of your shining altar, and the riddle of life is solved. All about us are minds darkened by passion, enslaved by lust, blinded by pride of wealth, in despair from poverty, sickness, disgrace; you have the cure upon your tongue if you have the love in your heart. They need the grace of God a thousand times more than you do. Will you not strive to give it to them?

They suffer from the deep wounds of adversity, and have no such balm of consolation as your good confession and happy communion. The toys of prosperity mislead them, for they have no such appreciation of the transitoriness of this life as the

Catholic religion imparts. They are just beginning life, and you offer them not the chart and comfort of heavenly truth—you who read the heavens and who know the paths of the great deep. They are dying on the burning desert, and you will not cry out to them, Ho ye that thirst! come to the waters.

How many of them look into human life and behold only vice and its writhing victims, and beyond this life only the blank of agnosticism; and you can people the air about them with many thousands of the angels, and the spirits of the just made perfect.

Young men are there, buffeting the flames of sensuality, and the sacrament of penance with its unearthing of the secret demon, and its finding of the true friend—which of you will not tell them of it? It saved you in youth, will not you offer it to them? How can we enjoy the grace of God, and be conscious that we have done positively nothing for those who are perishing for lack of it?

Come, then, Bishops of the Church of God! open wide your eyes, and from your mountain-tops see the States of America white for the harvest. "And Jesus when he came out saw much people, and was moved with compassion toward them, because they were as sheep not having a shepherd, and he began to teach them many things." (*Matt. vi. 34.*)

Come, ye priests of God, and join your voice with him who said: "And other sheep I have which are not of this fold; *them also must I bring*, and there shall be one fold and one shepherd."

Come, ye men and women of the faithful laity, and join the glorious work of converting America; for the spirit of God is waiting to choose you all to be his messengers.

"Sing unto the Lord a new song: sing unto the Lord all the earth. Sing unto the Lord, bless his name, declare well his salvation from day to day, declare his glory among the nations, among all people his wonderful things." (*Ps. 96.*)

We may find no more fitting place for an admirable paper by George Parsons Lathrop, the distinguished New England convert, on the "Consequences and Results of the Discovery of the New World." It ran as follows:

GEORGE PARSONS LATHROP'S ADDRESS.

To trace the consequences to religion, brought about by the discovery of America, would indeed be a long and laborious task. Those consequences, as I understand the term, were *immediate* influences on the human mind, and on human action. Under this head must be ranged the prodigious stir caused in Europe by the finding of another continent; the quickening of thought, the wider views it produced, and the fresh openings it made for worldly ambition or energy, as well as for piety, charity, and zeal.

The greed or enterprise of monarchs and merchants, of explorers, soldiers, adventurers, formed a part of the consequences that worked their effect at least on the outward history of religion. But what is more important is that the voyage of Columbus, prompted by an over-ruling desire to serve the cause of Christ—and aided in the same spirit by the benignant will of Isabella the Catholic—opened the channel for a new, a deep, and steady outpour of that apostolic zeal always inherent in the Church.

Nature abhors a vacuum; and so does religion, which always rushes in to fill the void of heathen ignorance or agnostic misbelief. The Church in the Old World, therefore, was thrilled and aroused by a desire to occupy and illuminate the whole of America with Christian life and knowledge. This was a consequence of farthest reach; and afterward it branched out in many other directions. The work and the triumph of Columbus gave a powerful stimulus to further voyages, and to commerce with distant places, in all quarters of the globe. We may say that the great Admiral's flag, as it fluttered over the Atlantic solitudes, became a signal which, in the next two centuries, was answered by hundreds of pennants hovering in remote seas, and marking the billowy paths pursued by countless missionaries.

It is impossible, in a short paper like this, to discuss the first part of the subject with anything like fullness; and the question of results is that which will need most attention.

Consequences are the rush of the torrent of deeds, as it cleaves its way. Results may be likened to the fixed course of the stream, after it has found its bed; together with the new beauties it has unfolded, the ruin it may have caused at certain points, or the benefit which it confers, and the sparkling gold it sometimes brings to light. Consequence is motion, following from a first motion, a current of actions or events. Result is the fact which is established by the flowing of that current. Briefly, results are the summing up of consequences. Hence, it is chiefly with results that we have now to deal.

But, first, let no one rest content or indifferent with imagining that this subject is "un-practical." I know it is often said of congresses, schools, or lectures, that, if they do not incessantly treat the hard, gritty, grubby facts which confront us all individually, in our business or professional careers and daily problems, they are not "practical." I fully believe in the value and necessity of the immediate, every-day, direct view of things, and of instruction adapted to it. But that is simply the limited "practical." There is an unlimited practical, which is far more comprehensive and just as necessary. And nothing can be more unlimited and comprehensive in its practicality than the history and science of results.

In the vast field at which we are glancing, the first effect to be observed is the reflex action of the discovery of America upon Europe; and then we have to note the gradual shaping of results in America itself.

Spain's foothold in the Western hemisphere added immensely to her power among the nations—a fact which had much to do with later complications, political and religious. The jealousy which other European countries felt toward the peninsular empire, on account of this increased importance and control, arrayed some of them against it and also intensified the fervor with which they espoused the heresies of the "Reformation," since these were unrelentingly combated by Philip II. of Spain. Motley, who has celebrated the Rise of the Dutch Republic and the story of the United Netherlands as a grand campaign of Protestantism in conflict with Catholicity, says: "The object of the war between the Netherlands and Spain was not, therefore, primarily, a rebellion against established authority, for the maintenance of civil rights. To preserve these rights was secondary. *The first cause was religion.* The provinces had been fighting for years against the Inquisition. Had they not taken arms, the Inquisition would have been established in the Netherlands, and very probably in England, and England might have become in its turn a province of the Spanish Empire."

This, to Motley, is a thought quite unbearable; and it is upon his repugnance to it that he bases his whole treatment of the Netherlands matter. It seems to me that in so doing he reads and writes history backward, from the present into the past, instead of forward and straight forward from the past to the present. He injects into the coloring of his own idea or prejudice as to what might have happened, and turns his narrative into a partisan justification. Thus he becomes one-sided and takes the tone of an advocate, instead of tracing events and results impartially. But the passage just quoted from him shows well enough how—a hundred years after the American discovery—Europeans mixed a good deal of religion with their warfare and put a good deal of war into their religion. That mingling of the two will explain why some of the consequences of the discovery were not immediately or wholly favorable to religion pure and simple. Motley also tells us of the counsel given by one Roger Williams, a Welshman—not the Welsh Roger Williams of Rhode Island, so conspicuous in the 17th century, but an earlier though equally pugnacious Roger, who served England and the States General as a soldier of fortune in 1584 and thereabouts. He advised a combined attack by sea on the colonies of Spain. Such an attack the English and Dutch afterward made successfully. Here we have the first momentous example of the manner in which the New World affected the civil and religious situation of the Old, and was in turn involved and affected by it.

At the same time single-minded Faith—apart from worldly considerations—had turned many hearts in Europe toward America and kindled the eyes of holy men with the light of a vision. For the first time the sun seemed to rise in the West. The land of the Occident was now the Morning Land to Christian hopes. The period of crusades to the Orient to rescue the sepulcher of Christ had gone by; but the new, more peaceful crusade of the 16th century had for its object the rescue of souls in America from the sepulchral darkness of heathenism. A great breeze of apostolic zeal streamed in that direction. Nevertheless the earliest consequences and even some of the later results appeared, or at least might be fancied, discouraging to the cause of religion or inadequate to its high standard.

The first gold taken by Columbus to Europe was made into a chalice, which is now preserved in the Cathedral of Seville; and it could well have been hoped that all the other first-fruits of the New World would be equally dedicated to the service of God. But the first settlements planted on Hispaniola became—notwithstanding the aspirations of their founder, and the religious devotion connected with them—a scene of strife, moral disorder, injustice, and cruelty. Columbus, himself in one way the chief sufferer from these evils, also inflicted a great evil upon the original inhabitants, by sending home cargoes of them to be sold as slaves. And yet from this enslavement of the natives, destructive though it afterward was to them, arose Isabella's noble indignation at the traffic, and the first protest against human slavery in America, uttered by Father Anthony de Montesinos, in 1511.

The San Domingan cities of Columbus crumbled; his colonies faded away, and have been overgrown by something little better than the wild weed of civilization. Still, the country he first occupied has never again become un-Christianized. And, on the other hand, as an example of the complete triumph of gentle religion, we have the mission of Las Casas, afterward Bishop of Chiapa, in Mexico, who throughout his life successfully defended the Indians through slavery and oppression. Near Guatemala there was a province, Tuzulutlan, which the Spanish had invaded three times, suffering each time a bloody repulse. They called it "The Land of War," and did not dare approach it again. Las Casas offered to subdue it, but on condition that only spiritual weapons should be used, and that no Spanish colonist or soldier should be allowed to enter the territory for five years. This being agreed to, he penetrated with other Dominican fathers among the hostile dwellers there. In a few years they tranquilized and made Christians of the natives; and, in consequence of this, what had been so long "The Land of War" received from Charles V. the name which it bears to-day—that is Vera Paz, or "Land of Peace." Soon afterward Las Casas received the brief of Pope Paul III., which pronounced excommunication against all who should enslave or rob the Indians.

In the next century we find the great Franciscan, St. Francis de Solano, the apostle of Peru, overcoming alone and unarmed a furious multitude of savage warriors who were about to attack his native neophytes; and, eventually, spreading the gospel among those dusky swarms. When he died, a hundred tribes, throughout a tract of two thousand miles, burned lamps day and night in his honor, and besought him as their advocate in heaven. Although Urban VIII. forbade public devotion to Francis Solano until the claims of the saint should be further examined, the Indians—although faithful and docile in everything else—refused, for the space of twenty years, to cease from their open veneration. Then, realizing at last that they were doing their beloved apostle no honor by opposing the command of the Vicar of Christ, they brought in and surrendered all their lamps, and waited nineteen years longer for the decree of Beatification.

Thus, as Las Casas had taught the Indians of Tuzulutlan the lesson of peace and had impressed its name upon their very country, so the natives of Peru learned, through St. Francis Solano, the lesson of true obedience.

Marvelous were the achievements of these and other missionaries, and wonderful was the fabric of spiritual culture which they reared among the peoples of Southern and Central America and Mexico. Many suffered martyrdom, and all would gladly and gratefully have accepted it, had it come to them. The thought of violent death in such a cause had no power to alarm or deter them; but the violence and cruelty of some among their nominal followers, Spanish adventurers and soldiers of the baser sort, toward the natives, must have been hard to meet and endure. This was a consequence detrimental, indeed, to religion; and reference to it has often been made by men of later generations, to show that because the name of religion was sullied by these unworthy hangers-on, therefore religion itself must be false or unworthy. But do we not find records of similar cruelties in New England, toward both the red and the white man, and in the injustice perpetrated upon North American Indians in this great country of ours, not by arbitrary and lawless invaders or soldier governors, but by the lawful authorities of a constitutional government, which makes a special claim of loving justice and of maintaining the freedom and equality of all men? The truth is that every age and every race has exhibited the same conjunction of the sordid and sublime. Evil seems to delight in settling down as the next-door neighbor of good.

But, by the very contrast which the misdeeds of some of the Spanish invaders offer, the pure, unselfish course and the holy labor of monks and missioners glow with a luster all the more clear and brilliant. They counteracted even this drawback, and overcame every other obstacle by a power more than human. Instead of allowing the native races to be swept away by fire and sword, they saved them body and soul, and drew them gently into the fold of the One Shepherd. And there those races remain to-day. Some small portion of them are still unconverted; but a modern French naturalist, Alcide d'Orbigny, who personally visited thirty-nine nations of pure American race in South America, and gathered accurate statistics concerning them, found that among all these nations or tribes there were only 94,000 pagans, while in the same district the native Christians numbered 1,600,000.

In his comprehensive and valuable report on Christian missions, T. W. M. Marshall says: "When nature divided the great American continent into two parts, she seems to have prepared by anticipation a separate theater for the events of which each was to be the scene, and for the actors who were destined to perform in either a part so widely dissimilar. The one was to be the exclusive domain of the Church, the other the battlefield of all the sects."

We who do not measure progress by material things only, or by mere smartness and superficial popular education, can rejoice heartily in the noble Christianizing of Southern America—which Mr. Marshall calls the Church's domain—and the thorough education, ingrained with religion, which the Church established there. In the later days of some of those Spanish-American countries, churches, convents, and colleges have been robbed or crippled by selfish, ambitious, and sometimes wholly irreligious men, who have masqueraded as republican leaders. But the damage appears to be on the surface only. The people are still Catholic. It is easier to rob churches than to steal souls.

These disasters came late in Southern America. Turning to North America, "the battlefield of all the sects," we see that things there have gone just the other way; disaster, which for a time seemed overwhelming, came first, and now a prosperity of the Church has resulted, which even 100 years ago would have been regarded as impossible of realization.

In the region which is now the United States, as Gilmary Shea well remarks, the Church did not wait for the formation of colonies. "Her priests," he said, "were among the explorers of the coast, were the pioneers of the vast interior; with Catholic settlers came the minister of God, and Mass was said, to hallow the land and draw down the blessing of heaven, before the first step was taken to rear a human habitation. The altar was older than the hearth."

To this terse and striking statement we may fitly add the remainder that these firstcomers sought to give the new country a kind of consecration, in the very names that they bestowed. Santo Domingo means "Holy Sunday." Another great island in the Spanish Main was called Trinidad, or "Trinity." Ponce de Leon in 1513 sighted the coast on Easter Sunday, which is known in Spanish as Pascua de Flores; and hence the present name of Florida commemorates the sacred season of Easter. Wherever Catholics went, throughout North America, this delicate yet pervasive aroma of beautiful religious names and associations went with them and diffused itself like the perfume of incense, which lingers in the air and the memory. The spot where Mass was first said at St. Augustine was marked for a long time, on Spanish maps, as *Nombre de Dios:* that is, "Name of God." San Francisco, in California, keeps before us, by its name at least, the recollection of St. Francis of Assisi. In the middle West there is a peak still known as the "Mountain of the Holy Cross," from the cruciform mark of snow in the deep ravines of its rocky height. Many of the old religious names of places have been changed and effaced. But Santa Fé—signifying "Holy Faith"—yet survives in New Mexico. Maryland was named for that pious Queen of England, Henrietta Maria, whose second name of Maria—or Mary—was chosen for the Catholic colony because it was the name of the Blessed Virgin.

These may seem remote considerations. But there is a great significance in names and the way in which they are applied. Certainly it is interesting to observe that our country—which many persons are pleased to call, without authorization, a "Protestant country"—is so clearly marked in every direction with holy Catholic names, as well as with heroic Catholic traditions. The fact that these names have remained is emblematic of that other and deeper fact that the Faith itself has remained and increased, although at one time it seemed probable that nothing would be left of Catholicity here, *except* its names.

Within a period of 250 years from the first Catholic foundations in North America, nearly everything established by them had, to all appearance, been blasted. The settlements in Florida were devastated and burned by the Anglicans of South Carolina, and the territory itself was finally given up by Spain to England. Later on, Maryland—which, as a purely Catholic colony, offered peaceful life, liberty, and freedom of worship to people of every sect—had been treacherously undermined by Protestant immigrants, who overpowered the Catholics and condemned them to proscription. The great Catholic missionary organization in Canada had been destroyed. The Puritans had set up, and were maintaining immovably, their absolute intolerance and oppression in New England. Everywhere east of the Mississippi, Catholics were weighed down by an arbitrary power, which deprived them of civil rights and could at any moment seize their property and drive them into exile. Even in the West and Southwest, where Catholics were still free under Catholic governments, the suppression of the Jesuits had stripped many districts of their priests and had left the faithful exposed to the dangers of isolation and religious decay.

This was the state of things in 1763, a dozen years before the American Revolution. Then came the Revolutionary War; and suppressed Catholic Maryland was promptly liberated and Catholic citizens were restored to their rights, because the other colonists knew and admitted that — when the pinch came — these citizens were absolutely loyal to the country, notwithstanding the wrongs it had inflicted upon them, and were essential to the success of its cause.

From the time when Catholic emancipation was declared on our shores, and ratified by the Constitution of the United States, which guarantee to every one the religious freedom that Lord Baltimore inaugurated on this continent; — from that time, the Catholic and Apostolic Church has flourished amazingly within our North American borders. It was a good thing that all the sects found outlet here, and were enabled to carry on their battle to the fullest extent. It was a good thing that the Puritans should enter freely and have their way, and fancy that they possessed the whole land. Spain, France, and England — these three powers vied with each other in colonizing and trying to possess the New World, and especially this northern part of it. France and Spain were Catholic, and they rendered us the service of tingeing the country deeply with their faith. England became anti-Catholic and did her best to expunge the Faith from this realm which came under her rule. Yet, as history has resulted, the Church at last found her surest foothold in this country under the anti-Catholic dominion of England, which had tried so hard to suppress her; and the Church has since attained here, in a single century of freedom, a growth never paralleled in modern history.

This, then, is one of the most important results to religion of the discovery of America.

It was largely brought about, humanly speaking, as the Vicomte de Meaux tells us, in his recent book on "The Catholic Church and Liberty in the United States," by "the advent of the Celts of Ireland, and the Teutons of Germany to the first rank of Catholic peoples," in the United States; which he declares, "is the most astonishing phenomenon that the New World, at the end of this century, can offer to the contemplation of the Old World." In former times Frenchmen and Spaniards, both Catholic, strove against each other in North America; sometimes to the detriment of religious progress. Even the English James, Duke of York, also a Catholic, tried to oppose the French in Canada — for political and state reasons — by setting up in the province of New York an Iroquois village under charge of Jesuit priests, as a hostile offset to the French Indian villages supervised by Jesuits in Canada. To-day, certain rivalries between German and Celtic Catholics in the United States are not altogether unknown. Yet here we have this French Catholic of our time, the Vicomte de Meaux, honestly sinking all prejudices of the past or the present, and surrrendering himself completely to admiration of the way in which — by unforeseen means — the Irish and the Germans, oppressed at home, have become the central and immediate forces of Catholic advancement in America. Ought we not all to learn some pertinent and peaceful lesson from the struggles of the past, and this calm, impartial tribute of a modern Frenchman?

True liberty is what the Church most inculcates, and what it most needs. It has found it at last in this country, where at first its prospect of doing so seemed most unlikely. It is by such paradoxes that the divine power works, regardless of the self-interest, or even the most unselfish foresight and planning, of men. The complete separation of Church from state, which exists here, has been an immense advantage to religion, and will continue to be so by assuring it of entire independence in the pursuit of its spiritual aims.

But see: The development of this independence was opposed by nearly all the human forces which were in action during the period when it was maturing. The Puritans themselves, though rebels against Church authority, formed the closest kind of union between their own particular religious organization and their own form of civil government. When it became necessary to admit Catholics as political equals and fellow-citizens, the Puritans, who were in terror of the "Romish" influence that might be exerted upon the state, were obliged to abandon their own system of controlling the state by religious authorities, and to join in forbidding all connection of Church with state; so that they might be sure of shutting out the "Romanists" from such control. And this separation of Church and state proved to be precisely the most beneficial thing that could have happened for the progress of Catholic Christianity.

If Catholics had been able to establish, when they first set out to do so, a series of flourishing colonies along the seaboard of North America, and to maintain them unopposed, they would have built a rampart which the Pilgrims and later legions of Protestants would hardly have ventured to pass. As it was, the attempts of Sir Humphrey Gilbert and Weymouth to plant Catholic colonies in New England failed; and wherever Catholic settlements *were* made along their coasts, from Florida to the St. Lawrence, they were overturned, cut down, or rendered powerless. So it came to pass that other elements pressed in, which, under different circumstances, would scarcely have ventured to do so. They throve, and came to believe that this portion of the continent was theirs. Their successors streamed in and believed the same. Circumstances led them—while they were opening the gates to every element of warring religious belief—to establish complete civil liberty and freedom of conscience; thereby opening the gates, also, to the one religion which does not mean endless division and war, but means peace. And everywhere they have gone, through all the great expanse of territory, they have come upon the old monuments and tokens of this religion which had preceded them—in Florida, in Maryland, in New York, up and down the Mississippi, in Canada, in New England itself, and in far-off California, where the restless tide of pioneer invasion ceased on the shores of the Pacific, at the feet of the old Catholic missions along that coast.

The whole country is surrounded by the early outposts of the ancient Faith. Their garrisons may have seemed dead, but they were only sleeping. The saints and missionaries of the past have apparently come to life once more, in all those little strongholds which enring the land and seemed to be ruins, but suddenly prove to be in full vigor of existence again. And in the train of these reviving memories and associations, an immense army of Irish, German, Italian, French, Polish Catholics have come upon the field.

Let them learn from the past, and avoid all strife, jealousy, or rivalry among races or families, which may retard religious and national progress.

When we perceive and comprehend how the apparent failure of early Catholic institutions in North America was the essential factor in bringing multitudes of non-Catholics hither—where they have developed within a cordon of Catholic historic associations, and have become mingled with a great body of living Catholics—and when we realize how it has taken 400 years for this country to realize that the hero, Columbus, whom the entire nation unitedly celebrates in 1893, was the coloseal Catholic pioneer, then we shall begin to have some conception of the immense scale on which God works, and the patience with which he works.

When we realize, also, that the present condition of the true Faith in this country—with its millions of communicants, its thousands of church buildings and charitable institutions—has grown up against the opposition of those who attempted to mould the national life in a totally different direction, we can appreciate what St. Francis de Sales meant, when he said: "God makes people co-operate with him, when they are least aware of it."

THIRD DAY.

In its morning session of Wednesday the Congress was favored by the presence of the Most Rev. Archbishop of New York, who, on being introduced by the Chairman, was greeted with hearty applause, which he acknowledged in these gracious terms:

ARCHBISHOP CORRIGAN'S ADDRESS.

Mr. Chairman, Ladies and Gentlemen: I rise to thank you most sincerely for the very kind manner in which you have seconded the suggestion just proposed, and I am indebted to the delegation of New York for the words of welcome given through their president. I especially prize the welcome given by the audience in general, to nearly all of whom I am a stranger, and therefore their action is one of pure veneration for the episcopal office. It is, I need not say, a heartfelt pleasure to attend a celebration which is so appropriate an incident of this great Columbian Exposition.

Let us look back awhile. What were the motives of Columbus in undertaking his voyage of discovery? If we read his own letters, which are the authentic exposition of his reasons, we shall see that he was dominated by three great principles: First, the love of scientific knowledge; next, the love of his adopted country, and lastly, but most of all, the love of Holy Faith. He was impelled to his journey of discovery by a love of scientific knowledge, because he had long held that the world was round, and he felt that by continually journeying westward across the ocean he would come to some undiscovered continent, and that scientific fact would be established for all time. Then to this love of science was added the debt of gratitude to Ferdinand and Isabella, particularly to that large-minded queen who was willing to pledge her jewels that the enterprise might be carried to a successful termination. Therefore in return for the assistance and encouragement of this noble-hearted queen he wished to add new jewels to the crown of Spain in the shape of lands not yet known to the civilized world. And far beyond this sentiment was the underlying love of the Faith, the love of converting souls and of bringing them into the light which shines from heaven.

Now, what are your motives in coming to this Columbian Catholic Congress? Are they not the same as those which guided Columbus? You show a love of knowledge by meeting to discuss the great problems which now agitate the world; and just as Columbus had a safe guide in that mariner's compass which kept him in his western course, so have you, in the teachings of the Holy Father, an unfailing guide which will bring you also to the land of promise. Then as to the love of country; are we not, we who are Catholics, all animated by the same feeling? Do we not love our country as the best land on earth? Does not all the devotion of our hearts go out toward it? And if Columbus desired to show his affection and gratitude to Isabella and the land of his adoption, I am sure that each one of us feels his heart swell with similar emotion. We have great pride in loving our country, for we feel that just as the Lord in the miraculous multiplication of the wine at the wedding feast saved the best for the last, so in the order of Providence, the land last to be discovered was our own fair land and the best. Then, again, you have come together as Catholics through love for the Church, love for the truth, love for souls. All of us here, from every part of the United States, with our brethren from abroad, are animated with the one faith and the one feeling that guided Columbus—the one love for our Divine Master; this is the mainspring of all our deliberations, and we are assured in advance that that guiding star will lead us safely to the haven of rest. And now, Mr. Chairman and ladies and gentlemen, I have no right to interfere with the order of the day's proceedings and divert your attention from important papers, prepared with great care by those who are to address you. Therefore, simply, let me say in conclusion, that I trust the success of your deliberations will be commensurate to the noble aim you have proposed yourself, worthy of the great occasion that has called you to this Columbian Congress, and worthy of the queenly city that gives us such a hospitable welcome.

A still more fervent special ovation greeted the same distinguished Archbishop in the Thursday evening session, which was attended by many other illustrious prelates, following being the eloquent expression of

ARCHBISHOP CORRIGAN'S THANKS.

Most Reverend and Right Reverend Prelates, Ladies and Gentlemen: As an honest confession is said to be good for the soul, permit me, while gratefully acknowledging your most cordial welcome, to say how utterly abashed and overwhelmed I am at this immense outpouring and unexpected demonstration. When your Chairman kindly invited me to attend a reception to be offered by members of my own Diocese, I had no idea that this hall would be filled to overflowing; and I expected merely to say a few pleasant words and to pass the time in friendly conversation. Instead of this, an address is looked for from one who is almost totally unprepared to answer such expectations. However, if a speech must be made, let me try to analyze the cause of this most generous welcome.

In the first place, the poet says: "One touch of nature makes the whole world akin." If this be true, and we all feel the sympathetic thrill of our common humanity, much more does unity of faith bind together the children of God with the links of common origin, of commmon aspirations and common destiny. It is hard for us to realize the fact now, but nevertheless it is quite true, that until the blessed day when the Sermon on the Mount was preached, men were strongly divided against each other, and the idea of a common brotherhood was unrecognized. The weaker class was driven to the wall, becoming the prey of its more powerful neighbors. In Imperial Rome itself, in the days of its highest material splendor, by far the largest part of its population were slaves, over whom their masters wielded the right of life and death, with a recklessness that can only be fitly characterized as brutal. In the eyes of the law, slaves were not regarded as men, but as chattels. Now the law gives a man the right to use his goods and chattels, as he pleases.

As a sunbeam of light piercing a dark dungeon, as a strain of exquisite and heavenly music wafted to captives languishing in exile, was the letter of St. Paul, the

Apostle, to Philemon on behalf of a fugitive slave, a slave to be received by his Christian master, not now as a chattel, not even as a runaway to be punished for his transgression, but, as the Apostle says, "as a most dear brother." This incident alone shows how the Church began to knit together the ties of our common humanity, from the beginning. Again, take the well-known story of Fabiola, with which you are all familiar, a work of fiction, it is true, but one which faithfully portrays the state of Roman society in the 3d and 4th centuries. Probably you all remember the striking passage in which the writer describes the perplexity of Fabiola, on discovering by chance a passage of the Gospel in which the love of God for all His creatures is intimated, for "He makes His sun to shine on the good and the bad, and the rain to fall on the just and the unjust." Cardinal Wiseman, speaking of the embarrassment of Fabiola on reading such a declaration, compares it to the perplexity of an untutored mind in finding some shining stone by the wayside, unable to decide whether it be a precious gem or a worthless pebble. Even so, the beautiful doctrines of Christianity, now universally recognized, struck the Pagan mind, as late as the 4th century, as an enigma; for the Pagans doubted whether they were the revelation of a new and sublime philosophy, encircling all humanity in the folds of divine love, or whether they were mere idle speculations, pleasant, indeed, but never to be realized. It is evident that once the truth of our common origin, our common destiny, our redemption by the outpouring of the same Precious Blood, permeated man's intelligence, the value of the human soul would begin to be appreciated at the same time, and consequently man soon perceived the consoling truth that the children of men, being creatures of the same Heavenly Father, constitute but one great family. From the same truth evidently flowed the burning zeal of the Catholic Church, from the beginning, for the salvation of souls.

Without glancing even for a moment at the missionary spirit of the Catholic Church throughout the onward course of its existence, let us confine our attention to one or two instances that bear on the present celebration. It was this grand and inspiring motive of the value of the human soul that, more than anything else, impelled Columbus to tempt unknown seas in order to spread the Gospel of Christ. Discouraged and despondent by many rebuffs, Columbus turned his steps to the Convent of La Rabida. Father Juan Peroz, the hospitable guardian, was interested, it is true, in scientific discoveries, but his sacerdotal heart was still more touched at the possibility of leading innumerable souls to heavenly light, and he determined that Columbus should obtain the aid necessary to promote his enterprise. King Ferdinand, cool and calculating statesman that he was, could not be insensible to the manifold advantages that might accrue to Spain from the discovery of the new territories, yet he hesitated, wavered, and delayed to act. Isabella listened to the selfsame story, and her instinct of piety was aroused, and she resolved that as souls might thereby be gained to God, she would give strong and efficacious help. Again, it is a striking fact, and one perhaps not generally known, that the flag of the Santa Maria in which the great admiral sailed was no other than the white and green banner of the holy office. What! was America discovered under the flag of the Inquisition? Even so. And here, again, we find a luminous proof, not only that the Church did not retard the progress of science by forbidding, as has often been asserted, the belief that the earth was round, but, furthermore, that the most severe ecclesiastical tribunal on earth actually gave aid and encouragement to the discovery of this continent. Now, what was the reason of this encouragement? for reason there must have been. Can you assign a stronger motive or a better reason than the love of advancing the Christian religion and of securing the salvation of souls—the spirit of faith?

BISHOP GABRIELS,
OGDENSBURG.

BISHOP MAIS,
COVINGTON.

BISHOP JENSEN,
BELLVILLE.

BISHOP SPALDING,
PEORIA.

BISHOP COSGROVE,
DAVENPORT.

BISHOP BRADLEY,
MANCHESTER.

BISHOP McCLOSKY,
LOUISVILLE.

BISHOP RYAN,
ALTON.

Passing by four centuries and coming to our own days, what was the character of the Columbian Celebration in the city of New York on the 12th of last October, and a little later in the city of Chicago? I mention these two cities because I had the privilege of participating in both celebrations. Without wishing to give offense, I think we can modestly claim that these were both distinctively Catholic celebrations. As a friend from Boston said to me at the time, the public-school children properly appeared first, and gave us a standard by which we might form our judgments, and then the Catholic children of our free schools followed, and, according to the testimony of the secular press itself, by their neatness, their proficiency in drill, their manly appearance, they undoubtedly carried off the palm. A similar scene was displayed in the long line of our 30,000 young men attached to various religious or literary societies. I had the honor, that evening, of being seated near the Vice-President of the United States, as well as our own chief executive, His Excellency, Governor Flower. Both were most favorably impressed by the numerical strength and bearing of our societies, and they added that young men so carefully nurtured by the conservative spirit of the Church could not fail to be patriotic and sterling citizens.

Permit me to point out still another manifestation of the same spirit of faith in the Catholic Educational Exhibit in the World's Fair. I hope all here present have seen this exhibition, and more than this, that our fellow-citizens at large will carefully examine the magnificent display made by our schools and academies. This exhibit speaks volumes for the self-devotion and enthusiastic service of our Catholic teachers, of our patient sisters and brothers, in the great cause of education. Without state aid, and contending with many obstacles, "they sow in tears," according to the Holy Scripture, "but they reap in joy." What is this, then, but a silent and yet most eloquent testimony of their faith? They recognize in the young child, humble and uncouth, if you will, a soul for whom the loving Saviour died, and of whom He said: "Forbid them not, but permit them, for theirs is the Kingdom of Heaven." Says St. John Chrysostom: "Noble, indeed, is the profession of the painter and the sculptor, who make the canvas breathe and the marble glow with instinct of life, yet nobler far is the work of him who forms the soul and the character of youth, and who moulds and fashions them to the lineaments of Christian virtue."

Such is the work accomplished quietly, patiently, perseveringly, in our Christian schools. Those who enjoy their benefits not only are devoted children of the Church but they will make the best citizens of the State. Among those educated in our schools you will find no anarchists or socialists, but thousands and thousands of brave men and true, who love their country, not only for its own sake but for conscience' sake; who willingly obey its laws, and who would shed their blood in its defense; men such as those of whom the poet sang in the person of Sir Galahad:

> His strength was as the strength of ten,
> Because his heart was pure.

These few remarks sufficiently prove the strong links which bind us together, and shed a new light on the meaning of the old Pagan, who, observing the conduct of our forefathers in the faith 1400 years ago, exclaimed, with as much sagacity as truth: "See how these Christians love one another!"

Among the excellent papers of Wednesday's session a chief place must be given to that of F. M. Euselas on "Woman's Work in Religious Communities," or

THE CATHOLIC SISTERHOODS.

To compass within the prescribed limits an account of "Woman's Work in Religious Communities" is not less difficult than "to do" the Columbian Exposition in the few months allotted to its existence, remembering, as we are told, that allowing three minutes for each exhibit, one hundred years would hardly suffice for the task. In either case only a cursory view can be taken, leaving the rest to be inferred.

Monachism, or the state of religious seclusion more or less complete, antedates Christianity, being found among the Jews in the time of Elias. It is also a prominent feature of Brahminism; even to-day the lamaseries of Thibet exceed in number the monasteries of Italy or Spain. China, too, has its cloisters of Buddhist nuns, Kuanyim, the goddess of mercy, being their patron saint.

Its primitive form among Christians dates from the persecution under the Roman emperors, when converts took refuge in caves and deserts. Later on, preference for seclusion continued what necessity commenced, developing the community life, at first purely contemplative, then combined with the active; within the last century, the latter far outnumbered the spirit of the age, one of active zeal for human welfare, largely shaping vocations for such service; or, with fuller meaning, God thus guided means and instruments toward creation's destined end.

Nature is indeed a great diversifier; she "never rhymes her children, or makes two alike," thus meeting the ever-varying, never-ending needs of humanity. Vocations for so many different orders and for the myriad duties of each show how Infinite Wisdom ever adapts the demand to the supply, constantly giving us new orders or modifications of the old, using the feeblest instruments for the greatest designs, the poor and insignificant of earth being founders of the most efficient orders. "The weak things of this world hath God chosen to confound the mighty."

Our grand discoveries and inventions equally prove this fact, and we hold our breath in astonishment at the outcome. We say this or that man, almost by chance, perhaps, originated such an idea or wrought out a new principle in science. Galileo, grinding his lenses in a fortunate way, gave his magnifiers, then the telescope, our first refractor being from the brain and hands of the great Italian.

The experiments of Galvani upon the nervous condition of cold-blooded animals revealed their electricity, which Volta's genius utilized as an agent of wondrous importance. Later on still further developments were made by Franklin, Ampere, Davy, Faraday, Bunsen, and others, down to our own Morse and Edison, who have caught and chained the lightning's bolt, making it the electric motor in our mechanic and other arts.

How wonderful, we say, these discoveries of man's skill and genius! And so it is, of material things we take only a material view, always on the same dead level. Thus is our material nature stamped and reflected in opinions uttered or unexpressed. But, look higher; give the spiritual forces a chance, awaken their latent powers, what a change! Before, we saw through a glass darkly, now face to face, revealing the Divine Master behind Galileo, Newton, Herschel, and their confreres, giving inspiration and guidance. He was compass, rudder, and barometer for Columbus and other early navigators, sending their rude barks over unknown seas to this "land of the free and the home of the brave."

Alas, that we should lose sight of this fact in our mad rush for—we hardly know what. Weak man can originate and idea, when he can not even create a single grain of sand!

Through these mistaken views of life and its bearings, through our false standards of right and wrong, the greater part of time is spent in making and unmaking ourselves, in unlearning the world's wisdom, "which is foolishness before God."

Standing to-day proudest among earth's nations, since we welcome them all as friends and brothers to our shores, as they come laden with marvels of genius and industry never before dreamed by poet, painter, or prophet, we shall trace through all the great Master carrying out His designs. In God's creation each sentient being stands in an allotted niche, a spectacle to angels and men. Rightly measuring the scope of her being with the means at hand, she will work out that true mission.

Animated by these ideas, we see that by no other means could the great work of the sisterhood be accomplished. How simple the origin, how grand the consummation! Prayer for the salvation of their own and others' souls initiated the plan, giving relief to the poor, sick, and outcasts opened a broader field for devoted charity, bodily wants supplied, ignorance must be enlightened and religious truths inculcated. Thus, education through the progressive spirit of the age, rounded up the religious life in its beauty and completeness.

Viewed in this light sisters are before the world as representative women in its best sense, not as relics of a buried past, as fossils for spiritual geologists to examine, classify, and put behind glass doors to be labeled "Footprints of Creation," the first perhaps after the Azoic age. No, none of this; let them be the incarnate idea of the golden rule, the eleventh commandment clothed in flesh and blood, to whom its great author gives this consoling assurance: "Inasmuch as ye have done it unto the least of these, my brethren, ye have done it unto me."

The history of different religious orders and of the houses branching therefrom reads more like some legend of remote ages or a tale coined from the brain of a Jules Verne than a reality, so utterly opposed do methods and results appear. The laws of finance or the most ordinary business forms seem utterly ignored by sisters in general, the plans of architects and contractors set at naught to follow their own sweet will. Wading up to their eyes in seas of difficulty, personal, social, and financial, even in spite of these, by ways and means past finding out, save to the great-hearted and never-to-be-rebuffed nuns, they manage to come out of the fray with flying colors. Sacrifices that few would face count for nothing with them; to see a need is to meet it, urged on by that supreme motive, the salvation of souls at any cost.

Unlimited confidence is the backbone of their success; call it presumption, a tempting of God if you will, yet none the less effective is the result. Look at Mother Irene in charge of the largest foundling home in New York. In her simple faith she says:

"Father, please make a memento for my intention, I just want this piece of land adjoining our grounds."

"That property, mother! Why, do you know its worth? A quarter of a million at least."

"Yes, father, but I must have it as a playground for our poor little orphans."

"Well, mother, how much money have you now?"

"Not a cent yet, but never mind, prayer will win the day."

And it did.

Every religious house is more or less the fruit of earnest, confiding prayer. To understand this the better, we must deepen and intensify the true conception of a sister's life and work by a fair and critical examination, making due allowance for the defects and defections that more or less mark every organization, perfection never being found this side of heaven.

What then are the qualities insuring a sister's vocation? While the purest and holiest motives should be the animus of her work, a large fund of common sense, a practical matter-of-fact shrewdness must supplement the higher instincts; for remember your real Sister of Charity is not an angel plumed for her heavenly flight; she isn't expected to spend the day in perpetual adoration, while her orphans and pupils, the poor and the sick are—she doesn't know where. As the handmaid of our Lord, He wont do His work and hers too. She must be a minute-woman, ever on the alert, ready for the Master's call. She realizes that the highest aim and purpose, love being the exponent, are sent through her, the lowest organ. Herein lies her true sanctity, none other will pass current. Intense activity without the enthusiasm of impulse, constant devotion to present duty, with a sort of fiery patriotism, so loyal and unswerving as to care for naught save winning souls from their great enemy, mark the high and perfect aim of her whole life.

Do not mistake means for the end, the shadow for the substance; the whole is always greater than a part. It is not because of her high or low estate; it is not place, surroundings, or circumstances, prosperous or adverse, not her brilliant qualities, her this or that, which perfect a sister's life. It is herself—the great soul incarnate through and through—that does the work; it is the assurance of certain conviction and the eternal peace of an unshaken faith; it is her inner life, with its principles stable as a rock, pure as the diamond, that make her proof against any hindrance. No difficulty can be an obstacle to such a soul when that noble aim and high endeavor surcharge her whole being. Let duty call her to the battlefield or to the halls of science, to the leper's hut or the palace of princes, it is all one to her. A true religion still carries the selfsame purpose everywhere. God behind her, as His instrument, she is what she is, does what she does, and her end is gained. Hers is "the repose of a heart set deep in God." Let the world fully realize this, and, ceasing to criticise and cavil, it will admire and imitate.

We live in an age of thought, deep, critical, far-reaching, and sisters are no small factors here. Everything is on the alert. What has been, is, and shall yet be, are questions forcing themselves upon us, not as mere isolated events, like separate blades of grass in a field, but as links in God's great chain, girdling humanity and reaching from eternity to eternity.

It is an every-day wonder, both to those within and without the Church, that persons of sense and judgment should leave the world and all it holds dear for a convent life, impelled, as cynics say, by an ascetic whim, a sentimental notion, proof of a soft, weak spot somewhere. Passing strange indeed would it be if this were all; and, believe me, none would decry such a step more than the religious themselves. Let anyone thus impressed step into a Sister's shoes and look through her eyeglasses. A few whiffs of convent air would show her the mistake. A mere passing whim stand the test of a religious vocation! Why, the very assertion defeats itself, since the indispensables are wanting—intellectual power, moral force, and an intense sacred purpose that never counts the cost. Flesh and blood with sentimental notions are spurned beneath their feet as utterly unworthy of notice.

Call the Sisters cranks and idiots, if you will, their work a sham, but remember soft-brained people are liable to dub as a sham whatever they can not grasp. Tell me, could the mind of a crank plan and perfect such enterprises as we daily see carried on, year in and year out, century after century, to the remotest corners of God's universe? Their ideas mere pretension! Show me one solid, noble act ever built on a pretension, and it will be the first of its kind. Far easier to base the great pyramid of Ghizeh on a basket of eggs or a bag of feathers.

Sham ideas never started the first steam engine, never stamped our alphabet in type metal, never laid between Washington and Baltimore the first electric wire that now in long-drawn threads and cables is our master of masters and servant of servants. Still less could pretension lay the foundation of schools and orphanages, asylums and hospitals. Look a little farther, dig a little deeper, before laying such a charge at the door of the sisterhood. Little wonder that Job's comforters, predicting a failure, soon with astonishment say: "How is this? how do they manage it all?" Though puzzled ignorance may still jeer and laugh, thank God the number of censors is rapidly diminishing; experience and sound judgment are fast grinding the yeas and nays of old-time prejudice, giving a favorable verdict and above appeal. That which is seen with the eyes, heard with the ears, and which our hands have handled, is sufficient refutation. In letters of light, stamped by the Almighty, may be read their sacred purpose, noble work, and its marvelous results. The admission of non-Catholics, though tardy and almost perforce, only the more surely confirms this. "Don't know how it is," says one; "make up my mind a hundred times that I'll say 'no' to the Sisters' appeals, but they always get the better of me, and I'm a V or an X poorer each time"—richer, would it not be better to say?—"and now would you believe it, I actually stop them on the street."

Motives, measures, actions; real character stamps one for better or for worse; there is your true gauge, my friend, for the worth of a religious; it must out; if valuable it will be valued, if estimable, esteemed. It is the whole court of heaven speaking through the heart of mankind and saying, "Well done, good and faithful servant."

Nor is this so strange after all, for, taking an all-round view of woman, she seems possessed with an insatiable desire to have a finger in every benevolent pie, whether it's rubbing goose-oil on Mrs. Neighbor's croupy baby or working out some great plan for the world's reformation. This master passion of her nature defies all restraint; bluff it on one side, sniff it on the other, hydra-headed, it still crops out, and we who know its blessed effects thank God for it.

The work of religious communities through all its ramifications represents the practical wisdom, intensified by critical observation, varied experience, and well-tried sanctity of generations upon generations, whose traditions become in turn stepping-stones for their successors. What have they done? Far easier to tell what they have not done. Their ubiquity is proverbial. Put your finger upon any spot of the habitable globe, and there will they be found. "It is a corner of God's earth," they say, "His footprints are already there; since He leads the way shall we not follow?"

The great success attending Sisters' work, with means so limited, is unquestionably due to the admirable system that marks the plan of each founder, as meeting the special ends in view. With wisely directed foresight the various rules and constitutions enter into minutest as well as most essential details. Each department has its special staff of officers and aids, directly responsible to the superior for efficiency. An interchange of officers from time to time is of mutual advantage; latent talent thus brought out adds to the general good of the community. Convent life is a wonderful developer. No delicately sensitized plate of the photographer ever evolved more marvelous effects. Out of an embryo Sister, seemingly inefficient every way, a shrewd novice mistress and wise superior will develop a true woman fitted for many and varied duties. Sudden emergencies throw the novice upon her own resources, and necessity becomes the mother of invention. One of these, timid to excess, left in charge of her class, thus relates her experience:

"They were only little tots, to be sure, but none the less did I quake when meeting that row of eager faces. One glance told me they were ready for frolic if I gave them half a chance; that wouldn't do. I must 'head them,' as the boys say, and I did, gaining a victory over them, but, still better, over my weak, foolish nature, making me a woman from that day to this."

Through such perfected system the work seems to do itself. Each new-born day, of course, is consecrated by the baptism of prayer, which, with other spiritual exercises, is renewed at intervals, closing with the same benediction; otherwise the routine is similar to that in any well regulated family. Each member, animated by the spirit of her order, feels in a measure responsible for its success, doing all she can to insure it. No honors whatever are attached to any appointments; if there are no mean offices in the courts of kings much less should there be in that of the King of Kings. Merit and ability must mark the positions held; these being interchangeable help to secure that perfect equality.

This practical view of a Sister's life will no doubt sadly disappoint many who regard it as a sort of saintly romance—an ethereal existence encircled by a mysterious halo. Let such remember that only out of these plain, every-day materials are wrought the saints whom we daily meet by hundreds and thousands, ever intent on some errand of mercy, since through all the spiritual life and motive give their touch and spur to every duty. They are the visible conductors of God's magnetism and electricity. Charged with this they must do his bidding.

Here, at our great Exposition, are seen Sisters with pencil and note-book in hand harvesting the ripened fruit and grain for their pupils. Tangible proofs of what they do for education are here before your eyes. Go to the southeast end of the gallery in the Liberal Arts Building, next to the French exhibit, and see for yourselves. While the practical side of life receives due attention, not less does the æsthetic. Their skill with the brush, pencil, and needle is proverbial. The Dominican Sisters of New Orleans, Sisters of the Precious Blood, of Charity, of Notre Dame, etc., give an exhibit that only true artists can furnish, yet these are but types of what may be seen in almost every convent throughout the world. Art is indeed innate, intuitive with the sisterhood; the love of the beautiful as a reflection of its divine author must ever be linked with love of Him to whom their lives are consecrated.

Here in the United States are 3,585 parochial schools, besides 245 orphanages and 463 other charitable institutions, in addition to 656 academies, using a total of 5,975 buildings, which, at a valuation of $3,900 each, represent an investment of $17,975,000. In addition to this the annual running expenses of these establishments, except the academies, which are supposed to be self-supporting, will not be less than $10,732,500. Besides thus providing for the common and higher education of the children, a large number of whom in charitable institutions are taken from the slums, many a reformatory, jail, and penitentiary with its staff of officers would be an additional tax upon the public purse. Let not this be overlooked in our estimate of results.

Nevertheless, great as is this material work, linked with it and far more effective is the higher and spiritual life infused into those under the Sisters' charge, from the frail infant, fresh from the hands of its Maker, on to the highest prelate whose first lessons in the principles of theology received from them, became the impetus and underlying current of his whole life.

The great question of religion or no religion, God or no God, in our school system, agitating, dividing, and colliding our educational leaders, here finds its solution in the Sisters' work. The grand motive urging, driving them on is that the life of Christ, in its fullness and beauty, in its strength and sanctity, and in its sublime perfection, as far as possible, may be first implanted and then wrought out of those who otherwise might know little of Christianity beyond a few formulas and a code of morals, shaped too often by human ideals and interests. Tell me in all sincerity, will your child be the worse for such training? Yet more. Side by side with each lesson, and running through it, the Sisters aim to put Jesus Christ, making him the inspiration, life, and motive of whatever is thought, said, and done. Trying to live his divine life themselves, and finding how blessed it is, they desire nothing less, yea, can give nothing more to these lambs of his flock. Indeed, there can be no more interesting study for the theorist and the reformer, the optimist and the pessimist, the conservative and the liberal than the origin, growth, and marvelous results of their work. In noting the lines taken by different orders, this fact may well be emphasized as a clew to their success, that in singleness of aim and purity of intention, all unite in the one endeavor of making the world better, wiser, and happier through their efforts; thus do they help on the federation of the human race, that glorious ideal of to-day to be merged into a more glorious reality of to-morrow.

The session of Wednesday evening was held in a densely packed hall, the enthusiasm of the gathering being especially awakened by this brilliant address of Most Rev. Archbishop Ireland on the subject of

THE CATHOLIC CHURCH AND CHARITY.

I am sure that from this Congress dates a new era, an era in which, more than in the last, we shall go forth showing to the world that we are Catholics and Americans bearing, as the Apostolic Delegate said yesterday in magnificent words, in one hand the Gospel of Truth and in the other the Constitution of the United States. We need mottoes for our great work, and the motto was given to us yesterday in these words by the representative of the immortal Leo XIII. In one hand the Gospel of Truth—your faith to which you are to be absolutely loyal in all your thoughts, words, and actions; in the other the Constitution of the United States—showing yourselves to be, because you are Catholics, the best, warmest, and most loyal of Americans. There are Catholics —few of them, thank God!—who dare at times to criticise our manifestations of patriotism, calling these manifestations, as one lately has dared, travesties upon real patriotism. I believe those men speak from their own souls. There is no patriotism in their souls, and they can not see that there is patriotism in the souls of others. Why should we not be loud in our manifestations of patriotism? We love what is great and good; therefore we love the Republic.

We love what is given us by its institutions, liberty, and prosperity, and because we are Catholics we ought, if it were possible, to be more patriotic than others, because patriotism, for Catholics, is a virtue naturally, and a virtue supernaturally; because we are Catholics, we love with all the strength of our Catholic hearts the banner of the United States which sheds throughout the whole world the sweet perfume of liberty. We love the Constitution of the United States which grants to the Catholic Church, liberty such as she has nowhere else. We love America because there is here a country great and glorious, offering to the zeal and Faith of the Church a promising and fertile field, such as no ocean laves, such as no continent opens.

And let me counsel you to be always enthusiastically patriotic, and let it be known throughout the whole country that Catholics are, as I said, if possible more patriotic than other fellow-citizens, so that we show to the whole country what are the lessons of our Faith. We show to the whole country that in the hands of none others, in the hearts of none others, are the liberties and institutions of the Republic of the United States safer. This then the motto: The Gospel in one hand, and the Constitution of the United States in the other.

But a word on the Catholic Congress itself. It is held to bring out before the people the meaning of the encyclical of Leo XIII. on the social question. The Gospel of Christ is summed up by the Lord himself in these words: "Love God with all thy heart and soul, and thy neighbor as thyself." Christianity puts before us the two objects of our love. A religion which would confine our affections to God Himself would not be divine; it would not be a religion of the Gospel; God would not be satisfied with it.

Precisely because we love Him we must love all that He loves, and love, therefore, our fellow-man. Nor would it be sufficient to love the spiritual good of the neighbor; we must also love the temporal good; we must love him in soul and body; we must love him for the life to come and the life there is. The Gospel was throughout a great book of holy social work for men. The miracles of our blessed Lord were primarily exercised for the good of the body, for the temporal felicity of man, aiming, of course, through those miracles, to the spiritual good of man. God gave the earth for the children of men that they may live. He gave it to all, and while, because of the nature and necessary conditions of mankind, private property is required, yet God never so sanctified private ownership that, because of private ownership, any children of the Great Father of all should suffer from starvation.

It was God's intention that there should be a sufficiency for all, and it is the duty of each and every one to see that God's intentions are realized. God's will is that those who have an abundance of good things for themselves think of those who are in want, think of them as brothers and sisters of the same family; and when they refuse this universal charity, they lie in their prayers when they look up to the skies and say, "Our Father, Who art in Heaven."

This is the true Gospel of Christ. This is the true teaching of the Catholic Church. To-day the world, alas, is drifting away from its Christian moorings. It is our duty to mark before all eyes the path of peace and blessedness, to spread before the nations the divine treasures in the bosom of the Church. Are you going to convert the world by argument? By no means. Argument convinces the mind; it does not move the soul. The age, moreover, is tired of argument. The age has told us the evidence it demands, and I admire the good sense of the age.

This age says to us, you profess to be the Church of the Gospel. Give us the Gospel in daily life; we judge the tree by its fruits. And in so saying it accepts our own challenge. The age is an age of humanity. It has caught up some of the lofty aspirations of the Christian soul in its great love for humanity, in the very profession of this love. The age demands charity, love for all of every language, every race, and every color — love of man as he came forth from the hands of his Creator. Our country is well filled with good works, charities of all kinds. Asylums are built for the poor and the blind, and the mute and the imbecile. The American state is essentially, in its instincts and aspirations, Catholic. Let us then take hold of these instincts and aspirations and show that they have all been perpetrated by our Church in the past.

The encyclical on the condition of labor is timely. This is what is needed—Catholic social work—social work to be done by all bishops, priests, nuns, and women and here precisely are our present efforts. Catholics have been half-inclined in the past to perform their social duties through representatives. It will not do to leave all this work to the priests and the sisters and the religieuse. Catholic laymen have been too quiet in the past. The Catholic laity have an individual duty in all these social questions, in all the works of humanity and of charity. In these matters we should not be afraid, as some have seemed to be, to co-operate with all who are doing good, whether they are just our kind of people or not, whether they be Catholics or not.

We say this is a glorious Church of ours—as, indeed, she is—and yet what a fearfully large proportion of those so-called saloons are held by Catholics and a fearfully large proportion who lose in them their souls are children of the Church. Here is work for all, here is work into which we ought to put all our religion, all our social and political energies, until our country is freed from these dreadful evils. We think we are good Catholics so long as our own private lives are not contrary to the law of God, but we have grave responsibilities besides this in our social relations and in our political life, and Catholics who vote for bad laws, who vote not for the suppression of great social evils, contradict the God of purity and holiness, contradict the Gospel of Christ and murder souls.

There is much we can do in many directions. Let not the laymen wait for the laymen, let not laymen wait for priest, let not priest wait for bishop, and let not bishop wait for the Pope. But let all go on in well-doing along the great road of social charity, and then we are living out Christ's Gospel and are leading the age, for which it hungers and thirsts, to that shrine which, when the nation comes to it, shall bear over its portals the name of the Catholic Church.

In the same session Rev. Father Patrick Cronin of Buffalo, N. Y., spoke vigorously as follows, on "The Church and the Republic":

This land, discovered by Catholic genius, explored by Catholic missionary zeal, baptized in the blood of the Catholic revolutionary heroes, and preserved in unified glory by the prowess of Catholic arms on many a gory field—is it any marvel that the Church should have phenomenally grown and flourished here?

The same showering mercies of the skies which fructified the labors of the missionaries were not and are not absent during our episcopal rule. When Bishop Carroll took possession of his see in Baltimore the Catholic population of the Republic was not more than 50,000. What is it to-day? Surely not less than 10,000,000! The Flagets, the Cheveruses, the Kenricks, the Timons, the Spaldings, are names not born to die; and their successors to-day are well worthy of their great prototypes.

The American hierarchy stands peerless before the world. Yet among them there have been and there are giants. Three especially were sent by God, whose names were John, whose deeds will ever be golden-urned in the heart of the American Church—John England, John Hughes, John Ireland. The first, a marvel of eloquence, learning, and courage, could scarce find place to lay his weary head when first he bore the cross to the haughty South. On the day of his all-too-early death the whole city of Charleston was in tears. The second, a man of metropolitan largeness, whose heart never quailed before a foe, stood at the chief gateway of our immigration, gathered his people around him with paternal solicitude, and, like another Jonathan, slew, with pen and tongue, the Know-nothing philistine who dared to trespass upon their rights!

The third. What shall I say of him? Happily he still lives. You all know him as well as I. As yet in the midsummer of his days, he has already written his name in characters of golden light upon the heart and brain of the American Church. To the eloquence, activity, and learning of John England, John Ireland adds the combative courage and progressive leadership of John Hughes. Loyal to the core to Rome and to its every teaching, he is intensely American, and cherishes as the apple of his eye the free institutions of this Republic. He has a hold upon the popular heart which, with the possible sole exception of the Cardinal Archbishop of Baltimore, no other American prelate ever held. Such men are the Church's jewels, which she cherishes with more than a Cornelia's pride.

I now come to the latest manifestation in the Church's development in the United States. Need I say that it is symbolized by the magic name Satolli! A name hailed and revered by the whole American people. Why? Because it means law, justice, liberty, and peace! Because it means progress and not reaction. Because it means home rule and not rule of 4,000 miles away, with all its chronic difficulties and proverbial tardiness. Because it means that henceforth the church is to be governed in the United States by her established canons, and not by the caprice of any individual, however learned or holy. Because it means that the Church, now grown to maturity, has burst her missionary swathing bands; that she stands forth not only emancipated forevermore, but that "divinely tall and most divinely fair," she shall no longer be covered with the moth-eaten rags of a dead and buried past, but shall henceforth be clothed in the queenly splendor of her rightful inheritance.

But Satollicism means even more than this. It is no longer a question whether America is hostile to the institutions of the Catholic Church. The burning question is, whether the Catholic Church is hostile to the free institutions of America. The coming of Satolli is a final and irrevocable answer to the latter, while the universal outburst of acclaim that signalized his advent shows the hearty friendship with which America hails the co-operation of the Church.

I shall only add that Satolli's mission here is beyond recall. He is here with the permanency of Rome's everlasting rock. All blessing and glory to that mission and to the person of America's first resident apostolic delegate, and fadeless laurels for the peerless Pontiff that sent him.

A valuable and suggestive paper was read during this session, by its author, Rev. James M. Cleary of Minneapolis, on the subject of

THE DRINK EVIL.

No congress of earnest men in our time and country can justly consult the best interests of their fellowmen, and ignore a thoughtful consideration of the drink evil. Many honest and conservative men hesitate to enter upon a discussion of the evils of intemperance, and to openly ally themselves with temperance workers lest they be accused of fanaticism or misunderstood by those whose good opinion they highly esteem. Every great and noble work in the history of human progress has suffered from the intemperate zeal of its friends and from the hypocrisy of its avowed advocates. But the temperance cause has suffered more, I imagine, from the apathy of timid friends than it has from either hypocrisy or fanaticism. It is a cause that in a special manner needs the support of honest, conservative, and thoughtful men.

Intemperance is a crying sin of our land, and with marvelous ingenuity has kept pace on its onward march with our unrivaled prosperity and progress. Something over nine times as much intoxicating drink is consumed in the United States to-day as there was forty years ago, and we have only about three times as many people as we had then within our borders. No evil existing among us menaces so boldly the peace, prosperity, happiness, and moral and religious welfare of our people as the evil of excessive drinking. No other social evil disturbs the family relation and renders the domestic life of men, women, and children so inhuman and hopeless as the evil of excessive and habitual indulgence in strong drink. Intemperance unfits husband and wife for the duties of parentage, the most sacred and solemn in the entire catalogue of human obligations. It destroys the sense of decency and honor, silences conscience, and deadens the best instincts of the human heart. There is no bright side to the picture of strong drink in the home. This hideous and brutalizing vice can not be condemned too severely, and those who have experienced much suffering from its influence may be pardoned if they are unsparing against every effort that tends to widen the way for the spread of habitual drinking among us.

The Church, through the united voice of our bishops assembled in the Third Plenary Council of Baltimore, warns its members against the dangers of the drink habit and the temptations of the saloon. The same Council warns our Catholic people against the business of saloon-keeping, as "An Unbecoming Way of Making a Living." A man can not be a good Catholic, a loyal follower of the teachings of the Church, and be a good friend of the saloon. We should at least have the courage to follow where our chief pastors lead, and our Catholic loyalty is not above suspicion if we are not as ready to condemn the drink evil as our bishops, who have been placed over us to rule the Church of God.

It is the crowning glory of the Catholic Church that, true to the spirit of her Divine Founder, she has never become the Church of any special class, as also she has not permitted herself to be narrowed down as the Church of any particular nation or generation of men. She is the Church of all times, all nations, and all classes and conditions of men. She is the living voice of God to cheer, instruct, and comfort all the people. But in this country, owing to the mighty wave of immigration from less favored lands during the past half-century, bearing a noble army of toilers to our hospitable shores, the great body of the wage-earners, the masses of the people, crowd around our altars, and with loyal honest hearts appeal to our Church to devote her best efforts to their moral and spiritual welfare. The great army of labor, the sinew of the nation, acknowledges a loyal allegiance to the Catholic Church. The debasing, brutalizing influence of excessive drinking, and the saloon environments fall upon the laboring classes of our people with more disastrous effect than upon those better favored by fortune. The dreadful vice of intemperance has made frightful havoc among our hard-working Catholic people.

What else but this spendthrift vice could afflict a large portion of our people with poverty so hopeless as to be like an incurable disease, a people to whom countless millions are yearly paid? What else huddles so many of them into the swarming tenement houses? I make no odious comparison between the intemperance of the wealthy and the intemperance of the poor. The heathenish vice of drunkenness is an abomination wherever its foul presence is known. I only state a fact which can not be set aside; a fact which the philanthropist and the statesman can not ignore, namely, that the greatest curse blighting the lives and desecrating the homes of the poor in this country to-day is the curse of drink. That homes of comfort are, alas, too often blighted by the presence of the demon of intemperance and drunkenness among the wealthier classes of the people is equally odious and even more disgraceful than among the poor. But the poor are greater sufferers, and hence enlist our deeper sympathy when intemperance blights their lifes, for in addition to the heartache and sorrow which the vice entails equally upon rich and poor, it adds the horrors of penury, beggary, and hopeless degradation to the lives of the children of toil.

Great and long-standing evils are not remedied in an hour. When we have to deal with human passion and human weakness, when we must conquer bad habits and diseased appetites, our progress will not be rapid, and discouragement and failure will often be our reward. Evil there will always be in the world, and human energy must not slumber because wickedness and sin remain.

The people look with longing and hope to the Catholic Church to lead them away from the bondage of drink. The Church that civilized the savage and that preserved the civilization which it erected on the ruins of barbarism, is able to rescue the masses of the people in this country to-day from the cruel thralldom of drink. The drink-curse is intrenched in custom, hence we must follow it into society. At all social assemblages of Catholics let them deny themselves the indulgence in intoxicating liquors and thus publicly proclaim their recognition of the principles of self-denial. At the reunion of friends and family connections, whether occasions of joy or of sorrow, let Catholics show their horror of drunkenness by denying themselves the use of strong drink. There is no gratification worthy of a Christian that can not be enjoyed without the use of intoxicating liquors. As an act of reparation for what our religion has suffered from intemperance, let our Catholic people proscribe intoxicants at all their public gatherings. Let there be such an earnest and potent public sentiment among our Catholic people that no liquor-saloon can crowd itself right up to the doors of our churches and thus, by its foul presence, tempt weak and unwary men to wickedness under the very shadow of the cross. If our prelates, priests, and people join hands together to work in harmony and strength for the realization of the admonitions of our plenary councils, the awful curse of intemperance can be almost entirely eradicated from among us. We must encourage, then, our total abstinence societies by every means at our command. We priests, mindful of Pope Leo's words, must "shine as models of abstinence," and by exhortation and preaching avert the many calamities with which the vice threatens Church and State.

Let there be a general and generous distribution of temperance literature, tracts, lectures, statistics, and good reading among our people. And this work and agitation in favor of sobriety and temperance must be constant and active. The allurements of drinks are ever thrusting themselves in the pathway of men. Near to the house of prayer the workingman finds the drinking-saloon, cheerful, enticing, and hospitable, as he goes to worship God on Sunday morning. Close to the gates of the factory or mill the agents of alcohol ply their trade and tempt the weary toiler to spend for a moment's gratification his hard-earned money that is much needed in his humble home. Surrounded thus by attractive temptations, men need constant warnings, repeated admonitions and such wholesome influences as will strengthen and safeguard them against the overpowering spell of drink.

FOURTH DAY.

Thursday, the fourth day of the Congress, might well be called Woman's Day, the claims and glories of the gentler sex being eloquently presented by some famous Catholic ladies. The first of these was introduced by Right Reverend Bishop Burke of St. Joseph, Mo., in the following terms:

I came here to-day for the purpose of listening to a lady who deserves well of the Catholics throughout the United States, one whose name is a household word in every Catholic family throughout the land, who has written and lectured on the beauty, and culture, and refinement of the Christian art set forth by the Church in her galleries throughout Europe, the product of Christian artists, in a manner that is hers especially. She has had no equal among us in this respect. I came here to-day to listen to her, and to show my sympathy with the great work of this Catholic Congress, and not to address you. I will only say that it is an exceeding pleasure for me, and for every ecclesiastic who has witnessed this grand assembly, and listened to the eloquent discourses; we have been in admiration with all the people of this great city at this outpouring, at this manifestation of Catholic doctrine and Catholic activity, and culture and refinement.

It has been said by some of the public speakers who have given expression to their views during the past few days, that the United States is a country of great possibilities, a country where everything can be accomplished that is attempted by man; and it has been said, too, that all that the Catholic Church requires, is to be set forth before the eyes of our countrymen to be appreciated, loved, and respected throughout the land. I believe never before in the history of the American Church has this been done so eloquently, so magnificently as it has been by this grand Congress, or Congresses. In every part of this building there are persons setting forth the glory, and the power, and magnificence of the Church of one living God; and the newspapers of this great city are full of our doings. They are flashed to the ends of the country, and our name to-day is held in benediction because we have appeared to the people, I believe, as we have never appeared before.

The great questions that have agitated the human mind throughout the world have been treated here in the most masterly manner, and thoughts and problems and solutions have been set forth, based on the solid foundation of Christian truth and conducted in the spirit of Christian charity, in a manner that is marvelous and that is appreciated by the whole community in which we live. I say to you, however, not to be content with what you see and hear from this platform, but when you go forth to the World's Exposition fail not to see the works of Catholic charity, of Catholic intellect, of Catholic culture, set forth for the admiration of the world as they have never been set forth before. See the works of the holy nuns who are hidden from our gaze in their cloisters, unknown to the world except through the little ones of Christ as they grow up before us, as Jesus Christ of Nazareth did, advancing in age and wisdom before God and man.

See the works of education, the product of Christian education, refinement, and culture, and you shall be astonished, and it shall not be necessary for ecclesiastics to set forth before you the necessity of Christian education, for there is an object-lesson that lights up the charity of Christ, to impress you with the work that is being done in this great country. There is this remarkable about the exhibit: It is an evidence of Catholic education that can not be witnessed in any other department of the great Exposition; it is one in which to the knowledge of natural things there is given a refinement, a culture, and development of the moral nature in man.

I am sure that the hearts of the ladies will rejoice to-day when the venerable form of Miss Eliza Allen Starr shall be presented to you, and you shall hear from her lips words of beauty and eloquence, describing the magnificence and the beauty of Christian art.

Beauty, expressed under visible forms, may be called the soul of that art which, under its almost infinite variety of mediums, marks the progress of the human race, is one of the tests of the human race, is one of the tests applied to nations and to epochs. What share has woman had in this beginning—that is, from Eve to the women of our own generation? For we must go quite one side of the book of Genesis, and quite one side of all the traditions of art, not to recognize that Eve, "the mother of all the living," contained in herself, as did Adam, the germs of those wonder-working periods in the liberal arts and sciences which have won our admiration.

"A perfect woman, nobly planned," was Eve, and we, her daughters, look back over the world's five thousand and almost nine hundred years, to claim for her those endowments which grace the highest civilization of to-day. No mention is made of her actual occupation in Genesis, but the old rhyme of Adam delving and Eve spinning, which the artists laid hold of even on the walls of Campo Santo, Pisa, gives us the impression that the first exercise in decorative art for the human race might have come, very naturally, from the hand of Eve, while the woman who remembered the loveliness of Eden must have had images of beauty in her mind which found expression under her skillful fingers. Tubal Cain may have taken from his mother, Zillah, what gave grace of form, as well as sweetness of sound to the musical instruments of the antediluvian artificer in metals; and we are quite sure that Joseph's coat of many colors owed its beauty to feminine hands.

No sooner, however, do we come to the Mosaic ritual than the skill, which monuments existing to-day prove to have belonged to the women of Assyria and Egypt, is found to have been practiced to a high degree by the Hebrew women under the shadow of Mount Sinai. The Greek scholar is never allowed to forget the web woven by the faithful Penelope, which not only gave evidence of her industry but of the imagination which endeavored to express, in the overshot figures of her tapestry, her admiration for her husband, Ulysses; while no barbarous tribe has yet come to light without giving numberless examples of the instinctive expression of beauty under visible forms at the hands of its women.

This universality of endowment, and this universality of its exercise, giving the foundation for woman's work in art hitherto, will continue to be the foundation on which her achievements in art will be based, furnishing an argument for our educators which will be fruitful of results favorable to those virtues that show most fair in woman.

Greece, pre-eminently the home of beauty, which gave heroes and poets to sing their praises, gave sculptors, also, to perpetuate their deeds in immortal marble; and to a daughter of Greece, Kora, who helped her father, Dibutades, in his modeling, we owe the reliefs which enabled the Attic sculptors to tell the stories of the gods on the pediments of their temples; for rilievo must always be regarded as the sculptor's medium of narration.

Of those who worked in color, we hear of Helena, belonging to the age of Alexander the Great, who painted for one of the Ptolemies the scene in which Alexander vanquishes Darius, a painting which is supposed to have been the original of a famous mosaic found at Pompeii; while an artist, Calypso, executed a picture which has been transferred from Pompeii to Naples under the title of "A Mother Superintending Her Daughter's Toilet." A Greek girl, Lala, a contemporary of Cleopatra, was so celebrated for her busts in ivory that the Romans erected a statue to her memory; and a Roman paintress, Lava, using her brush some seventy-nine years before the coming of our Lord, is the first person spoken of as painting miniature likenesses on ivory, which she executed with marvelous rapidity. According to Pliny, she ranked among the most famous artists of her time.

We shall refer to this miniaturist again, but to preserve a chronological thread on which to string our facts, we will mention here that benefactress to all succeeding time, Galia Placidia, daughter of Theodosius the Great, who, in 440, or during the pontificate of that Leo, the first of all pontiffs to be called great, caused to be executed, under his approbation, that arch of triumph which glorifies even the new Basilica of St. Paul outside the walls; this mosaic being, as Cardinal Wiseman declares in his "Recollections of the Last Four Popes," "the title-deed of the modern Church," to the veneration of Christendom. Not only this venerable monument, but very interesting mosaics were executed under her order at Ravenna, before which the traveler pauses under the spell of their Christian significance as well as beauty.

To return to our miniaturist, Laya, who may be said to lead one of the most beautiful processions in the story of art, for she was followed by legions of monastic workers in the European cloisters, who, in the silence of monastic scriptoriums, adorned those choir books which are the ever increasing wonder of the lovers of art. Many of these monks are high on the roll of fame; but, working even more hiddenly than the monks of St. Columbkill's time, were legions of women, working so hiddenly, in truth, that it is only by the slip of a pen like Montalembert's that we are likely to hear of these nuns whose names were caught by the quick ear of Saint Bede the venerable; but the names of Saint Lioba, the cousin of Saint Boniface, of Saint Walburga, sister of Saint Wilibald, the nuns of Eiken and their two abbesses, Harlinda and Renilda, have come down to us by the fame of their pious labors over psalter and gospel; and all this in the 7th century, supplying links to the traditions of art which would prepare it for more favored periods.

Agnes, Abbess of Quidlenberg, was celebrated as a miniature painter in the 12th century, and some of her works are still so well preserved as to excite admiration. We know that at this present time painting in miniature, on vellum or paper, is practiced to a marvelous degree of perfection in our convents; and I can not refrain from speaking of a volume of transcribed poetry from the convent of the Benedictine nuns in our own city, with charming marginal decorations in gold and color by a Benedictine nun; while in the Convent of the Holy Cross, St. Mary's, Ind., are designs on panel, silk, vellum, paper, which will compare with the celebrated works of the 13th and 14th centuries.

In the 14th century, Sister Plautilla, a Dominican nun, won fame which compelled Vasari to name her pictures with praise; especially a Madonna bearing her Divine Child on her knees as he is adored by the magi, of which I have a photograph.

Alongside the Van Eycks, Hubert and John, is found their sister, Margaret Van Eyck, who worked in miniature under the patronage of the court of Burgundy, her fame extending to the far South. Often she worked with her brothers on their pictures, much in the way that the Robbia family worked together on the same compositions, showing that her style or handling was not inferior to that of her renowned brothers.

From these delicate and, as they are often called, feminine labors, we pass to the plastic art, in which Properzia di Rossi, of Bologna, so distinguished herself that Clement VII., having gone to Bologna to crown the emperor, Charles V., inquired for her, greatly desiring to see her; but, to his deep regret, was told that she had died but a few days before his arrival, not having completed her thirtieth year. Her works are still to be seen in the cathedral at Bologna.

It was to Sabina, daughter of that Erwin von Steinback, whose monument is the Strasburg Cathedral, that the ornamentation of this wonder of ages was in a great part committed. Not only did she complete the spire after her father's death, but designed and executed the sculptured groups of the portals, especially that of the southern isle. The name of De Pazzi, associated as it is with some of the choicest pages of saintly lore, is associated also with art. Caterina de Pazzi was born in 1566, of the old Florentine family, and retired, while still young, to a Carmelite convent, under the name of Maria Maddelina. There, under the protection and, we must believe, the encouragement of her superiors, she threw the energy of her ardent and noble soul into the works of her pencil and brush, which are still to be found in the cloisters of the Carmelites at Parma and in Santa Maria, in Rome. She was canonized by Clement IX.

As was to be expected, the cold wave which passed over Europe under the name of the reformation, chilling so many poetic and artistic souls, affected, in a special manner, the sensitive imaginations of women. Hitherto their ideals had been formed by that Faith which had so generously nourished arts and letters as well as souls. With a recoil which kept the traces of inherent delicacy, the women of those ages turned to nature, studying flowers, fruits, and landscapes; practicing, also, artistic industries, such as engraving, etching, lithography, indeed, every art medium which united them to the world of letters. One of these lovers of nature was Maria Sybilla Merian, who devoted herself not only to the study and classification of plants and insects, but to their representation with her brush. Not contented with these artistic labors in her native Holland, she visited, in 1869, Dutch Guiana, especially Surinam, remaining two years in America. On her return to Holland the admiration excited by her work was so great that she was induced to publish her researches in books which enjoyed a sale of successive editions.

The 18th century was beautified by a genius which has never lost its charm—Maria Anne Angelica Kaufman. Her mind turned instinctively to painting, which she enjoyed as other children enjoy play, and at a very early age she painted the Bishop of Como. In 1754 her father settled at Milan, when Angelica came directly under the influence of the works left by that master of Greece, Leonardo da Vinci, and of the more tender Luini. The decoration of a church in a secluded region was entrusted to her father and herself, her own share winning the enthusiastic admiration of the Bishop of Constance. At Florence, and again at Rome, she enjoyed the society and instruction of the venerable Winckelmann. Goethe, with his æsthetically critical eye, was compelled to praise Angelica Kaufman. Art was to her the breath of life, and labor was her greatest delight. She died at Rome in November, 1807. All the members of the Academy of St. Luke assisted at her obsequies, and as with Raphael, her last picture was borne after her bier.

The 19th century brought to us of America, a warm breath from the realms of imagination. One hardly knows how it found its way to the sparsely adorned Puritan homes, and to the secluded ways of the daughters and granddaughters of revolutionary heroes. But the fact is all the same, and the growth of artistic ideas, moreover, seemed an indigenous one. Among the very first of our American women to give herself to art, was Sarah Freeman Clarke, the only daughter of a physician in Newton, Mass. Very scanty instruction in drawing, of any sort, was given in those days; but she got a glimpse, in some way, of drawing from nature, and it was her delight to wander over the picturesque country around her and bring home sketches of hills, and valleys, and homesteads.

One day as she was thus engaged, she heard some one come up behind her, look over her shoulder, then turn away, saying: "Oh, I thought it was Mis' James!" Who could this Mis' James be who had the same tastes as herself? She determined to find out, but even the doctor, her father, failed to have any knowledge of Mis' James, when the washwoman was questioned as a last resort. "Mis' James! Don't you know who Mis' James is? The crazy woman what takes her knitting and sets on her husband's grave!" "And thus," Miss Clarke says, "my first artistic studies were coupled with insanity."

Some years after a friend mentioned her case to Washington Allston, who invited her to bring her sketches to him, and he went so far as to paint a picture with her—his way of giving lessons. Thus Miss Clarke was Allston's first and only pupil. She visited Europe afterward with her mother and brother William, who is associated with the early days of Chicago. On their return, she accompanied him to our Lake City, and during her expeditions with him "the beauty," as she says, "of the prairie was made known to her."

She was the first person to open a studio in Chicago, and her magnificent pictures of oak openings and prairie adorned the homes of such lovers of art as William B. Ogden and Mr. Newberry. All of these, however, were lost in the great fire of 1871. One of her most remarkable pictures is a fragment of the temple of Esnah, Egypt, painted for Mrs. Alexander Mitchell, of Milwaukee, for whom she made her remarkable collection of Dante sketches, being pen and ink drawings of the spots mentioned by Dante in his "Divina Commedia," and which made one of the treasures of the Centennial Exposition, in Philadelphia, in 1876. A duplicate of this collection was made for Lady Ashburton.

Following closely after Miss Clarke was Caroline Negus, born among the hills of Petersham, Worcester County, Mass. Caroline's ambition was to be a miniature painter; to learn her art of those who knew Malbone, and to do this, she not only taught the small school in our neighborhood, to which I was sent as a child, but practiced every industry her facile fingers could lay hold upon. It was under her that my own young fingers found guidance, and I well remember her charge to my mother: "Never allow her to copy anything but nature." Her career was eminently successful, her pictures on ivory, of such men as Emerson, placing her in the highest rank of American portrait artists.

The first sculptress to win recognition from Europe as well as America was the daughter of a physician near Boston, who gave her what he intended to be a training for health, but which developed in her the taste for plastic art. Every opportunity for a thorough course of sculpture which Boston possessed at that time was given to her, but as St. Louis gave more special advantages for anatomical studies she went to that city, and, in 1852, found in the sculptor Gibson, residing in Rome, what made her mistress of the technicalities of her art.

Although her works are to be seen in Europe and America, for she has enjoyed a singularly wide distinction, perhaps her most charmingly characteristic creation is that of Puck, which is as Shakspearean as Shakespeare himself in its poesy and drollery, is an exquisite piece of modeling and finished with untold pains. But it is to her latest work, Isabella of Castile giving her jewels to Columbus to defray the expenses of his first voyage, resulting in the discovery of America, that Harriet G. Hosmer has intrusted her fame. This was modeled in Rome from studies, as to likeness and costume, made most carefully from authorized monuments during the winters of 1890, 1891, and 1892.

The commission for this statue was given to Miss Hosmer by the Queen Isabella Association to be cast in bronze and of heroic size for "The World's Columbian Exposition," as a tribute from American women to the co-discoverer of America. The full-sized model of this statue, on a pedestal, designed by the best architect in Rome, in a beautiful material fitted for indoor exhibition, stands in the Isabella pavilion, just outside the walls of "the World's Columbian Exposition" grounds; but the statue which is now coming through the foundry of Signor Nelli, Rome, to appear in all the glory of bronze, with that perfection of workmanship which belongs to the eternal city, will stand in some one of the beautiful parks of our City of the Lake as a proof, not only of the noble intention of the Queen Isabella Association to honor Isabella, the co-discoverer of America, thus winning for itself the administration and best wishes of the Holy Father, Leo XIII., but of the determination of the Catholics of America, above all, of the Catholics of Chicago, to do poetic as well as historical justice to this noblest of uncanonized women and peerless Christian queen.

The fame of a Rosa Bonheur as a painter, not merely of animals, but of animals under the influence of maternal affection or under the inspiration of the national shows, the fame, too, of an Elizabeth Thompson, who has brought to our eyes not only the horrors of war, but, with a most womanly instinct, its grandest pathos, show how wide the pendulum of a woman's genius may swing and how readily the technique of modern schools is appropriated by women.

Who was it that lighted up, with a beauty all celestial, the gloomy depths of a catacomb chamber in the cemetery of Santa Priscilla before the close of the 1st century of the Christian era—before St. Peter and St. Paul had won their crowns or their palms? Lighted it up, not merely by her own maternal loveliness, but by the divine charms of the infant nourished at her virgin breast, and before whom stands the prophet Isaiah, pointing to the star above her head as typifying the star which had arisen out of Jacob, according to the prediction?

Who is it that is found again and again in the subterranean crypts not only of Santa Priscilla, but of Santa Domitilla and Santa Agnes, and of every catacomb lying under the smiling Campagna and vineyards of Rome, until we see her in the year 432, in all the beauty of imperishable mosaic, on the arch of triumph in Santa Maria Maggiore; thence onward, on the apses of Rome's loveliest basilicas, all through the hidden period of antiphonals and psalters, until art effloresced under Cimabue and Giotto and the holy breath of St. Francis and St. Dominic; onward still through the ages of Vienese and Florentine art, until Raphael, under what has always seemed a direct inspiration, gave to the world that hitherto unrivaled conception of Mary, the Mother of God, in what we know and reverence as the Madonna Sistina? There was not one great artist in all those ages, whether monk, or nun, or courtier, who did not invoke the patronage of Mary, nor is there a school or academy that can furnish ideals like those which Mary gives to the hearts of her faithful sons. Can she do less for her faithful daughters?

Therefore I say to the women of my own nation—put not your trust in academies or in schools of technique; but whether in the cloister or in the world, make Mary your art mistress, your guide, your inspiration, and she will bring to your imaginations what you will seek for in vain elsewhere. She will speak, also through your pictures and your sculptures to your generation, until they demand, like those ages of which we read, the works of your brush and of your chisel to kindle their devotion and urge them onward in the heavenly way. Do not tell me that the atmosphere of your native land is chilling to devotion. Make your own atmosphere; make it by frequenting the sacraments, by lives of loving devotion to the saints, by a frequent observance of, and attendance upon, all festivals; and not only will your own atmosphere be one springing forth lilies and roses, but it will be caught by your countrywomen, so that you will be asked for in their homes, will be placed before their children, and—glory of glories to a true Christian painter or sculptor—you will live and speak to them from the altar-piece and altar-niche.

Rouse then, oh my countrywomen, to the fullness of your vocation as artists! Use all the opportunities afforded you, not to win the poor fame awarded by gallery or salon, but aspire to that ideal which we have seen consistent with a life of a consecrated nun and even that of the saint—the Christian work of a Christian woman in Christian art.

In an essay entitled "Women and Mammon," Mrs. Rose Hawthorne Lathrop, daughter of America's famous novelist, Nathaniel Hawthorne, pictured in words of beauty the ideal woman, and then drew impressive contrasts and teachings. Among many bright passages were these:

WOMAN AND MAMMON.

The word man conveys to us the meaning at once only of courage, energy, constructive force. But when the word woman is presented to the mind, two diametrically opposed types are surely evoked — the woman who is pure and elevating and the woman who is at most pure in a limited sense, and who lives in an atmosphere of such attractiveness as is not elevating. This is the sort of woman who would rather disenchant her husband with life than give up the approving glances of a half-dozen admirers.

We will not describe her any more minutely, for it would be a picture of a frequent companion. A companion not all wicked, shining brightly in her beauty, seemingly sweeter than the women of true hearts, petted, clever, and gracious. But she worships mammon in that half-conscious way in which so many of us are guilty of evil. It is only righteousness which is always awake to its responsibilities, eager for its success in meeting them, and quick to detect the ease and unkindness of low principles.

Mrs. Lathrop described at length the influence upon the world of these two classes of women and concluded as follows:

Can it be that woman is, in the majority, forever to serve mammon? Is she, who is the mother of all perfect impulses, to be represented anywhere forever as the adorer of vanity? Is she always anywhere to appear laden with jewels, like a jeweler's show-case, and with jewels that are very likely gathered upon her bosom at the expense of health, or even the honesty of her husband? Must woman, who stands for the highest note of human perfection, who should, above all created beings, worship God, erect, upward-looking, must she stoop to mammon in coquettish courtesy, anywhere in this world of God? Oh, woman, the hour has struck when you are to arise and defend your rights, your abilities for competition with men, intellect, and professional endurance. The hour when your are to prove that purity and generosity are for the nation as well as for the home. If it is well for you to imitate the profoundest students, the keenest business minds, the sublimest patriots, is it not well for you to imitate the noblest and tenderest of your sex?

A most instructive and eloquent paper by Miss Eleanor C. Donnelly of Philadelphia, Pa., was next read to the Congress on the subject of

WOMAN IN LITERATURE.

It was the genius of a woman, the generosity of a woman, that first made possible the discovery of America. But years before Isabella offered to sacrifice her jewels that Columbus might sail out of Palos, an Essex-born woman over in England, near St. Albans, had launched her little bark upon a sea almost as wide and trackless, almost as dim and perilous, as that through which the Santa Maria was later to plough its way. Dame Juliana Barnes, or Berners, a Catholic nun of Herefordshire, was the first person to write English verse. The father of Anglo-Saxon poesy was Caedmon, the monk of Whitby. The mother of English female authorship was Juliana, prioress of Sopewell Nunnery.

Food is here for much triumphant exultation in the glories of creed and sex. Our bosoms make haste to swell with honest pride, with womanly self-gratulation. But, my sisters, festina lente! The iconoclasts, alas, are busy and almost cruel. Modern and most destructive biographers rudely dispel the flattering illusions that have long veiled the memory of our literary primogenitrix.

Remorselessly they tell us that the venerable Dame Berners wrote verses on the most unfeminine, the most un-nunlike themes; that the "Book of St. Albans," published at Westminster in 1486 from some old, discarded type of Caxton, contained her three rhyming treatises on — on — (stop your ears, oh, outraged shades of the mystic and æsthetic nine) — on "Hunting," "Hawking," and "Coat Armor."

In the shock of this early English revelation, in the shame-faced effort to marry the mythical prioress to her verse, we remind ourselves that Dame Juliana was a lady of high degree, when the wine of youth ran red and hot in her veins, a 15th century Diana, in plumed hat and flying robes, following the chase with the gay knights and ladies of the court, and we say to ourselves: before this valiant woman hid her noble presence and masterful mind behind the convent grille she posed on her palfry among the gallants of the greenwood, her soul straining at its social restraints, and sounding the warning chime of its deliverance, even as the hooded falcon on her wrist strained at its silken jesses and jingled its silver bells.

If Bales describes the noble Juliana as "an ingenious virago," he frankly admits that her personal and mental endowments were of the highest character; and he goes on to explain, that, "among the many solaces of human life, she held the sports of the field in great estimation, and was desirous of conveying these arts, by her writing, to the youth, as the first elements of nobility." In the three centuries following the prioress of Sopewell Nunnery, few of her own countrywomen ventured after her into the new world of letters.

Germany had produced her sacred poet and dramatist, the Benedictine, Dame Hrosvitha, Italy her Catherine of Sienna, her Caterina Adorni, her Victoria Colonna. Spain had given birth to the mystical Teresa Ahumada (better known as Saint Teresa of Jesus); and the eldest daughter of the Church rejoiced in the brilliant glory reflected on her by the works of Marie de France, Marie de Gourney, Madame Guyon, Madame de Sevigne, and Madame Deshonilliere.

But, up to the middle of the 18th century the number of English women writers of any note could be reckoned on the fingers of one hand. To the originality and keen perceptions of one noble poetess, however (to Annie, Countess of Winchelsae, who wrote in the 17th century), Mr. Wadsworth pays this tribute: "It is remarkable that, excepting the "Nocturnal Reverie" by Lady Anne, and a passage or two in Pope's "Windsor Forest," the poetry of the period intervening between the publication of "Paradise Lost" and the "Seasons," does not contain a single new image of external nature.

"Literature," says Dr. Brownson, "can not come before its time. We can not obtain the oracle before the pythoness feels the God." And he further directs attention to the fact that "there is no literature, ancient or modern, which is not indebted for its existence to some social fermentation, or some social change or revolution.

The intellectual life of the 18th century seems to have been fermented by the strongest leaven of "social change," even as its civil atmosphere was surcharged with the electric currents of widespread revolution. Amid the upheaval of nations and the dismemberment of kingdoms certain volcanic tremors foretold the coming emancipation of woman's intellect.

Prior to the Augustian age of English literature there were few inducements, few opportunities for secular women to enter the arena of letters. Men barely tolerated their literary sisters, or cauterized them, if successful, with sneers and satires.

The very soubriquet "Blue Stocking," originated in 1786, as a term of derision for literary ladies; and the measure of approval accorded, at that era, to the works of Hannah More was mainly due, we are told, to the egotistic patronage of Garrick and Dr. Johnson. Sara Coleridge, daughter of the poet, does not hesitate to say in one of her letters: "The great mogul of literature (Johnson) was gracious to a pretender, whose highest ambition was to follow him at a humble distance. He would have sneered to death a writer of far subtler intellect and more excursive imagination who dared to deviate from the track to which he pronounced it good sense to be confined. He even sneered a little at his dear pet, Fanny Burney. She had set up shop for herself, to use a vulgarism; she had ventured to be original."

In truth, although Johnson protested to Mrs. Trale that "there were passages in Evelina which might do honor to Richardson," no one can read the "Diary and Letters of Fanny Burney" (Madame d'Arblay), gossipy and self-conceived as they are, without discerning the difficulties that handicapped the career of a lady of letters, even in the time of the third George. That boorish king rehearsing to one of his court ladies a certain interview with Dr. Burney reveals the latter's extraordinary terror at the discovery of his daughter's authorship. "Her father," said the king, "told me the whole history of her Evelina, and I shall never forget his face when he spoke of his feelings at first taking up the book; he looked quite frightened, just as if he were doing it at that moment. I can never forget his face while I live."

But, thank heaven, the day of class prejudice and narrow jealousies anent woman's work in literature has forever passed away. Through the widening of woman's sphere, through the opening of innumerable avenues to her higher education and intellectual advancement, the queen hath come at last to her own. The barefooted beggar maid before King Cophetua hath been lifted at last to her rightful throne at his side in the kingdom of letters.

While we agree with Brownson that woman was made for man and "in herself is only an inchoate man"—from a literary standpoint we must be willing to admit with Tennyson that

Woman is not undevelopt man,
But diverse.
Not like to like, but like a difference.

REV. PATRICK CRONIN, BUFFALO.
BROTHER AMBROSE, CHICAGO.
REV. WALTER ELLIOTT, C. S. P., NEW YORK.
REV. J. M. CLEARY, MINNEAPOLIS.
CHANCELLOR MULDOON, CHICAGO.
REV. F. J. MAGUIRE, ALBANY.
REV. F. G. LENTZ, BEMENT, ILL.
BROTHER MAURELIAN, CHICAGO.
REV. JOS. L. ANDREIS, BALTIMORE.

And be willing to accept from the same standpoint the dead Laureate's prophecy that

> In the long years liker must they grow;
> The man be more of woman, she of man;
> He gain in sweetness and in moral height,
> She, mental breadth, nor fail in childward care.

"Till at length her work shall set itself to man's like perfect music into noble words." If she be the queen of beauty in the tournament of the world's thought, she must also be the queen of truth and purity. Like the woman of the gospel, she must hide her leaven in her three measures of meal; she must hide the truth of Christ, the purity of Christ, in poesy, fiction, and journalism, until the whole is leavened.

As Cardinal Newman said of Philip Neri's work in Rome, she must make use, in a corrupt and faithless generation, of the great counter fascinations of purity and truth; she must direct the current which she can not stop; sweeten and sanctify what God has made good, but man has corrupted and profaned.

Not mere elegance of diction, brilliancy of style, or perfection of technique, shall serve her ends. Her mission is a higher and holier one than the polishing of clever verses, or the perfecting of "a filigree tale in a paper cover."

Artificial flowers, fashioned by a Parisian hand, may be exquisite in form and color, but they lack nature's fragrance and honey-dew. All the pressure in the world can not distil from them one drop of the attar of roses, such as is yielded by the smallest bud in the rose gardens of Ghazebor.

An elaborate setting is employed to enhance an inferior gem; and the meretricious glitter of stage jewels often does duty for the pure radiance of diamonds of the first water.

"We are not," says Ruskin, "to set the meaner thing, in its narrow accomplishment, above the nobler thing, in its mighty progress; not to esteem smooth minuteness above shattered majesty."

Thought must be great enough, wise enough, strong enough to seize and shape its vehicle, making style ever secondary to sentiment.

"Landscape Gardening" is Emerson's synonym for an over-devotion to technique, and close and stifling is the confined atmosphere of Boyle O'Reilly's carver of cherry-stones in the "Art Master."

> For such rude hands as dealt with wrongs and passions,
> And throbbing hearts, he had a pitying smile,
> Serene his ways through surging years and fashions.
> While heaven gave him his cherry-stones and file!

If, perforce, the queen must step down from her royal dais to champion the "rude hands" of social reformers, or to deal in her own realm with "wrongs and passions and throbbing hearts," she must not soil her white sandals or bedraggle the trailing splendor of her fair robes in the mire of the slums. It is proverbial that the worst corruption is of the best. Woman's influence in letters can never be an uncertain or negative one. If she does not elevate and strengthen she degrades and enervates.

The day was, when the startling realism of the Brontë sisters (to put it mildly) met with the sternest censure and fiercest ostracism of right-thinking people. Dr. Brownson goes the length of declaring that "there are passages in 'Jane Eyre' which show that women can enter into, and describe with minute accuracy, the grossest passions of man's nature, which men could not describe to their own sex without a blush." And yet, in their biography of its author, Mrs. Gaskill would have us believe that when Charlotte Brontë violated convention (again, to put it mildly), she did so unwittingly; and that the daring utterances of the Yorkshire curate's daughters were simply the innocent expression of morbid temperaments acted on by exceptional environments. Apologists have also been found for the agnostic sophisms and psychological subtleties of Mrs. Humphrey Ward, on the grounds that they are not set forth in "Robert Elsmere" and "David Grieve" with malice prepense and aforethought, for the destruction of believing souls, but that they are merely the grave, troubled exposition of the writer's private uncertainties in ethics, her own personal perplexities in dogma and doctrine. But, whether it be a question of murder or manslaughter, whether it be an indeliberate slaying of souls or a cold-blooded intent to kill, woe betide the woman who unsettles or confuses convictions of right and wrong in her readers' minds, or who leads them astray in issues of the affections or of the marriage relations! Like the fisherman of the Arabian legend, she has let forth unto destruction an evil and powerful genii whom she will never again be able to imprison in the gloomy casket of her own fancy.

It is in the field of fiction that the woman writer of the 19th century has attained her highest success, has won her most enduring fame. Yet, sorrowful to say, the crab-like tendency of some of our modern women novelists seems to be to work backward to the contemplation and delineation of pagan models. They forget that the passionate song of Sappho must give way to the chaste "Magnificat" of Mary. Their gross indelicacy is due either to greed for gain or itch for notoriety. It is even said that a young authoress once begged an editor to denounce her work as indecent, in the hope that the scathing review might do for her novel what barring the mails did for "Kreutzer Sonata"—sellhalf a million copies of it! Too often, however, the women who befoul their pens in the cesspools of lewd sensualism and erotic romance (like certain delineators of the nude in art), pander unblushingly to the pruriency of the fleshly. They, indeed, create "words that burn"—yea, that burn with the lurid and unquenchable fires of hell, not with the pure and cleansing flame of Isaiah's celestial coal. Their muse, instead of swinging before the Most High a golden censer, sending forth delicious incense from consecrated resins, flourishes before the golden calf a brasier of dusky, smoldering charcoal, whence issue the deadly fumes of asphyxiation to all that is pure and noble in humanity.

Such women are the "Dorothy Draggletails" of literature. They may have learned, in common parlance, "to call a spade a spade," but in so doing they have furnished themselves with a spade to dig the grave of their own womanly delicacy and self-respect.

> Ye nymphs, that reign o'er sewers and sinks,
> The river Rhine it is well known
> Doth wash your city of Cologne;
> But, tell me, nymphs, what power divine
> Shall henceforth wash the river Rhine.

Commenting upon the assertion of Julian Hawthorne and others, that "literature in America is emasculated by convention," a reviewer not long since boldly declared in a leading Eastern magazine that "it is the fear of the young that emasculates it!"

Surely, this out-Herods Herod.

Accursed is the age, accursed the commonwealth, that ceases to respect, to reverence, the innocence of the young. Even the pagans wrote: "Maxima debetur puero reverentia;" and the ancient Egyptians at the obsequies of their dead, proclaimed the departed spirit damned or saved, according as it had wronged or reverenced little children during life. Conscientiously careful, tenderly strong, must be the pen that traces the first impressions upon the soft, pure wax of the virgin mind. Those gravings will outlive the inscriptions cut upon bronze and granite. "Take your vase of Venice glass out of the furnace," says Ruskin: "and strew chaff over in its transparent heat, and recover that to its clearness and rubied glory, when the north wind has blown upon it; but do not think to strew chaff over the child fresh from God's presence, and to bring back the heavenly colors to him, at least in this world."

What Christian father would dare read aloud to his young sons the immoral tragedies or the disgraceful figures of George Sand? What Christian mother would dare lay open before the innocent eyes of her young daughters the shameless pages of "The Quick and the Dead," or "The Doomswoman," or deliberately put into their hands the lucubrations of Miss Braddon, or of that hydraheaded and sensuous gorgon of romance, yclept the Duchess?

Literature, it is true, as Cardinal Newman reminds us, can never be anything else than the manifestations of human nature in a human language; that, as science is the reflection of physical nature, literature is the reflection of nature moral and social. We can not eliminate the evidences of human passion from the records of human life, and our age of fiction is pre-eminently introspective and analytical. But surely, my sisters, in order to be true to nature, we are not called upon to dip our pens into the stinking slush of foul and debasing passions. In order to be faithful to reality we are not obliged to lay bare to the vulgar the most sacred esoteric mysteries; to make our toilets in public; to expose ourselves, as a master mind has phrased it, unveiled in the market-place, unveiled and unrobed to the gaze of a profane world.

Surgeons do not dissect their subjects on street corners. There is a native delicacy in true science as well as true art. Of Rembrandt's famous picture, "The Lesson in Anatomy," it has been remarked that the artist rivets the gazer's attention on the glowing, lifelike figures of the professor and his students rather than on the vivid, repulsive corpse that lies before them on the dissecting table.

If we must faithfully portray nature in our works, my sisters and colaborers, let us not forget the God of nature in his works. Let us give to the world something better than the vintage of an intoxicating and effervescing romance pressed from the dried grapes of exhausted passion and erotic pruriency. Let us offer it, not "devil's wine," but "God's wine"—a distillation from the fresh herbs and sweet-smelling simples of a chaste pasturage, giving to fainting souls and faltering heart the royal cordial of the golden and La Grande Chartreuse. The dove that goes forth from the saving ark of a purified literature must not pause to dissect the putrid carcasses tossed upon the rocks by the receding deluge of human passions.

"Let the carrion rot." Leave it to glut the rapacious raven, which shall return no more to gladden the yearning eyes of the watchers; which surfeited with rottenness shall never bring back to any longing soul the olive branch of God's eternal peace.

Once, in a literary circle of unusual brilliancy and culture, an American writer of some note read a paper to prove that there had never really existed a female poet! Beginning with poor, "sweet, smiling, violet-crowned Sappho," whose broken snatch of Grecian melody, sounding through twenty centuries, he scoffed at to the echo, he ran the gamut of the fair singers of the ages, dealing death to their pretensions and destruction to their fame. His coup-de-grace was a showing of the post-mortem decline of Mrs. Browning's literary repute. He enlarged upon the fact that during her lifetime, when any pilgrim visited the home of the Brownings in Italy, it was less with the view of meeting Robert Browning than his gifted wife, Elizabeth Barrett. But that, strange to say, since the latter's death, the star of her glory has been steadily declining, whilst the orb of her husband's fame had been as steadily mounting to its zenith.

A listener suggested that this might be because an age devoted to technique had launched its fiat against effusions which Miss Barrett wrote rapidly and from impulse, glorying, as Mr. Bethune remarks, "in her expedients to save time, though they took the shape of false rhymes or distorted syllables." But, when it was presently shown that a like decadence had waited upon the fame of Mrs. Hemans, Mrs. Osgood, Miss Landon, the Carey sisters, and others, whose technical expression was more painstaking and polished, we were forced to conclude, with Emerson, that some of the immortals were merely contemporaries; that, as a lady writer in the *Century* has lately shown in commenting on the oblivion fast closing around the name and works of the American, Margaret Fuller, it is to a strong personality that , in popular songstresses have owed their power over men, and that, with the vanishing of their personality, their power has ceased to exist. This is especially true of women of the transcendental school.

But to the 19th century alone belongs the authorship of American Catholic women. It has scarcely more than reached, indeed, its golden jubilee of existence. Yet while England points with pride to Adelaide Proctor, Lady Fullerton, Lady Herbert, Mary Howitt, Alice Meynell, Emily Bowles, and Mother Theodosia Drane, Ireland to Rosa Mulholland, Julia Kavanagh, Kathleen O'Meara, Cecelia Caddell, Ellen Downing, Katherine Tynan, and Mrs. Cashel-Hoey, France to Eugenie de Guerin and Mrs. Craven, Germany to Countess Hahn-Hahn, Spain to Cecelia Bohl de Faber, and Italy to Maria Brunnamonti, America enshrines in her Catholic heart of hearts the names of Anna Hanson Dorsey, Elizabeth Allen Starr, Margaret Sullivan, Christian Reid, Louise Guiney, Katherine Conway, Sara Trainor Smith, Agnes Repplier, Mary Elizabeth Blake, Harriet Skidmore, Ella Dorsey, the gifted Sadliers (mother and daughters), Ellen Ford, Mary Josephine Onahan, Helen and Grace Smith, the cloistered singers, Mercedes and Mother Austin Carroll, and a host of others who blend their sweet voices in the grand cantata of Columbian Catholic literature.

No meed of earthly glory shall fill the aspirations of the true Catholic woman writer. No crown of laurel or of pine shall satisfy the brow created for the amaranth of eternity. Her face is set toward the white city of the heavenly Jerusalem; her pen is illumined with the splendor that streameth from its gates of pearl; her highest ambition is to write her name in the book of life, beside the names of those whom her genius has ennobled, whom her gifts have drawn closer to God, whom her works have established in the perfection of his law. She may not be crowned after death as one of fame's immortals; her memory and her writings may not long survive her own day and generation, but, having done what she could, in her time, with the talent that was intrusted to her (and with it instructed "many unto justice"), she shall be crowned by the Lord God in his everlasting kingdom as one of those blessed toilers

Whose works shall last,
Whose names shall shine as the stars on high,
When deep in the dust of a ruined past
The labors of selfish souls shall lie!

The history and workings of St. Vincent de Paul's Society, whose delegates had been holding their Convention in one of the lesser halls, were thus presented to the Congress by Joseph A. Kernan, Jr., of Philadelphia.

THE WORK OF ST. VINCENT DE PAUL.

Before an audience of Catholics it would seem hardly necessary to say anything in explanation of the origin and aims of the Society of St. Vincent de Paul, now in existence in France for sixty years and in our own country for almost half a century, and yet there is evidently a very imperfect knowledge of it, except in a general way. It is not unusual to hear even clergymen speak of the society as it now exists as being founded by its illustrious patron, St. Vincent himself, which is a natural error; but much graver ones are the result of ignorance on the subject. To those who have read the highly interesting life of Frederick Ozanam, by the late Kathleen O'Meara, some portion of this paper will be a repetition of what they have already learned, but as there are still good, active Vincentians who zealously follow in the footsteps of their founder and yet are ignorant of this charming book, it may safely be presumed that there are others in the same category.

What St. Vincent de Paul accomplished in the cause of charity is incorporated in the "Lives of the Saints" and in the "History of the Church in France," and existing monuments in the shape of institutions which owe their origin to his great zeal, for the poor are daily reminders of his wonderful success. More effective still, perhaps, in recalling and perpetuating his memory, are his "Daughters of Charity," as they were originally called, but whom we now recognize as "Sisters of Charity," known throughout the world, and especially in France, where their services in the hospitals and upon the field of battle have been honored by a government which ignores the crucifix they bear—the image of one whose religion that government seeks to abolish. In our own sad days of strife they rendered like service, and in these "piping times of peace," which may God prolong indefinitely, they quietly succor the orphan and the afflicted and allay the sufferings of the sick with their kindly care and ministrations; but the society of St. Vincent de Paul is everywhere a living witness to the great spirit of charity for which the saint's name has been so long a synonym.

In 1833, the year of its foundation, France had, within a few decades, passed through two revolutions, had gloried in its first empire, and was not entirely free from the influence of the prestige of the great conqueror who founded it. She had seen three restorations of the old monarchy, and was drifting toward another revolution, and that republic which was, in its turn, to be wiped out by a coup d'etat, and followed, or swallowed up, by the second empire. As has been said, the shadow of the first Napoleon, who had sought to subjugate the Church, yet brooded over her. There was still the pride of race in the hearts of her old nobility, there was revolutionary blood in the veins of her citizens, and these were irreconcilable. The teachings of Voltaire were widespread, the indifference of the self-styled Catholics was demoralizing, the general discontent of the masses apparent. The Church was fettered; her clergy had not the influence to be expected in a nation called the "eldest daughter of the Church," but happily France, with all her faults and her decadence, was never wanting in champions of the Faith. In every age she had faithful, exemplary, and valiant sons and daughters among the clergy, the religious, and the laity, to fight her battles against infidelity and indifference; to take a stand for law and order and Christian civilization against anarchy and its causes, and, if need be, to lay down their lives.

The government of the period was, practically, in the hands of men who were not Christians; Guizot, Cousin, Hugo, Lamartine were the prominent men of the day, the last of these being classed among the dilettante order of Catholics. At the same time, that restless and restive spirit, the Abbe de Lammenais, then in the zenith of his popularity, together with his milder, but not less distinguished associates, Lacordaire, Chateaubriand, and Montalembert, were battling for the Church and its rights and privileges.

De Lammenais seemed the most brilliant star of the galaxy, but his "nonserviam" was a serious misfortune to the cause of Catholicity and still more disastrous to himself, for the great master mind, which could not learn humility and brook submission to the universal pastor, soon lost his influence and suffered the inevitable eclipse which attends all refractory children of the Church. But Lacordaire was faithful, and Montalembert and the others stood firm, and they gathered about them lesser lights but devoted followers. The spirit of faith and practical Catholicity in daily life among the laity was to be revived by the fervid eloquence of the great Dominican, and the ardor of the rank and file to be awakened and strengthened by the writings of his associates and their arguments in the senate and assembly.

The old college of the Sorbonne (now demolished, in part, to make way for a new structure), with its souvenirs of its founder, and, also, of its famous patron, Cardinal Richelieu, was the great center of learning; but none of its scientific or even philosophical teachings were allied to religion; on the contrary, its lecture halls resounded with the logic of materialism. Students of the Lyceum, the College Stanislas, and other smaller schools of learning, where they either imbibed their faith or were taught to preserve it, were here exposed to the danger of losing it, unless they were fervent, steadfast souls. Among these were a few youths, of one of whom especially we have to speak.

Frederick Ozanam was born in 1813, at Milan, where his father settled during the first empire. The family traced its origin not only back to the period when, hundreds of years before, it became Christianized in France, but also to that Hebrew race, which formed the chosen people of the Old Testament, and whose genealogies are to be found in the Bible. Ozanam's father had served with distinction under the consulate, but when the first consul made himself emperor, the faithful officer, who seemed to be neither royalist nor imperialist, became disgusted with the new régime and refused a position under the imperial government, preferring to take up his residence in Milan, where he became an accomplished and successful physician. He was an exemplary Catholic, and it was natural that with such a sire and such a mother as was Madame Ozanam, Frederick should have passed his boyhood in the practice of the faith. His later environment in Paris exposed him, as it did a great many others, to temptations to waver, but his early training made him strong, and so we find him, at twenty, a youth of steadfast character, serious but enthusiastic. He went to Paris to pursue his law studies with assiduity and thoroughness, and later on—his ability being duly recognized—he received the appointment of professor of commercial law in Lyons, and subsequently, was made professor of foreign literature at the Sorbonne. It was in this position that his genius shone out most brilliantly, and his Faith as well. He also entered the field of journalism and did good service for the cause of religion. His natural leanings were toward democracy, with more or less utopian ideas of the grand republic that was to be the great remedy for all political difficulties, the panacea for all social grievances, the great millennium for the poor and the oppressed. Like all earnest minds, he dreamed of the days that were never to come, of the ways that were never to be adopted, and he descanted upon those possibilities of the future which were never even to take the shape of probabilities. He was, however, in no sense a dreamer, but a practical Christian and a valiant champion of the right.

When fame and position were achieved and from the rostrum of that same old college of the Sorbonne he, in his turn, lectured the students who loved him so well, nothing deterred him from defending the truth and exposing error, and he seemed to have had the peculiar gift of ably answering the sophistry of his opponents and bringing their fallacious arguments to naught. His contributions to literature indicate the high order of talent, patient research, and convincing logic which characterized his lectures and his writings. It was at the early period of his life from which the society dates that Ozanam felt the lack of Christian teaching and the support of Christian example and companionship, as well as the longing for something higher and purer to actuate every-day life than the average student was satisfied with. Hence, in response to these aspirations and in direct answer to the taunts of his sneering associates, who asked for some tangible proof of his disposition to accomplish something practical, he and a few kindred spirits, encouraged by a friend of maturer years, M. Bailly, started the first "Conference of Charity," which was the nucleus of the present wide-spread society. They first put themselves under the protection of the Mother of God, making the sanctification of their own souls their main object. Their next aim was the alleviation of the sufferings of the poor, their moral and physical ailments—the former to be reached by assiduously caring for the latter.

A brief life, but a noble one, was that of Frederick Ozanam. We have only an imperfect portrait of him; a pen and ink sketch, which shows little more than a profile of a serious face upon which much study and the conscientious discharge of laborious duty, together with the suffering entailed by disease, have left their unmistakable traces; but he was cheerful and patient withal, a good son, brother, husband, and father, faithful to his friends and charitable to his enemies—if he had any. Although cut off in the prime of manhood, he lived to see the great success of the society which he had helped to establish, for he always disclaimed the honor of being the sole founder. For some time before his death, failing health forced him to intermit his duties, and he traveled in Italy and Spain, where his footsteps were marked by the establishment of conferences. The last of his excursions was to the little seaport of Antignano, which he left in the fall of 1853, hoping to breathe his last in Paris, the scene of his labors, but the Lord willed otherwise, and shortly after his arrival in Marseilles the closing scene set in and he died there on the 8th of September.

He has long ago, we trust, received his reward, and his confrères continue to cherish his memory with a respect and affection which will long survive the appreciation of his literary labors. He has had many worthy successors, also men of talent and distinction, in the government of the society—particularly in the council-general in Paris—and before giving a brief sketch of its progress and position in America, it may not be out of place to make, parenthetically, a few reflections on the influence of such men in the community. While we know that God has usually chosen the humblest instruments to propagate his Church, and, at times, some special devotion, still we all recognize the marked effect in our own day of good example, notably among that higher class of the laity to whom we are naturally inclined to look for models. We may recur to an incident in the life of Ozanam himself, as an illustration of this.

A prey, momentarily, to that weakness which is most fitly called human respect—a powerful motive, especially with Frenchmen—he entered a church in passing (for he was a devout man always), and there he saw, kneeling absorbed in prayer before the altar of Our Lady, that great scholar, the elder Ampère, in whose family he had happily found a home at a critical time. The young man confessed, afterward, that he was indescribably impressed and strengthened by the spectacle.

There are brave men, we know, in the humblest walks of life, but their deeds are not so manifest nor so likely to inspire emulation as the example of those in higher positions. The private in the ranks is as gallant and daring as his commanding officer, but when the latter is at the head of the charging columns all eyes are fixed on him and all hearts filled with the resolution to follow his valiant leadership.

While the practical work of the conferences was the fundamental one of relieving the poor by personal visits and direct assistance, no work of charity was ever to be foreign to the society; and so we find it, notably in France, taking up and developing the patronages, which have been so successful, and which were really the foundation of institutions of a kindred nature now so widespread, and which have taken the shape, with our Protestant friends, of Young Men's Christian Associations. All the needs of the poor, both spiritual and temporal, have become the special care of the society, which also occupies itself with remedying the causes of poverty. Hence its exhortations to temperance and economy in both old and young; the establishment of "penny banks" in England, following the example of our French confrères, who have also many other expedients, such as co-operative kitchens, and the various plans which have been found practical for the prevention as well as the alleviation of the misery entailed by ignorance and improvidence. Thus it will be seen that there is no limit to the projects and labors of a Vincentian in the field of charity. He has penetrated into the northern wilds of the British possessions on our own continent, and although we can not trace his footsteps as far as Cape Horn, he is to be found in various points in the intervening land, from Maine to California, in Mexico, Central and South America. Conferences exist in all the great nations of Europe with the exception of Russia; in Asia, embracing Arabia and the Holy Land, and we know of at least one native Arabian conference. On the "dark continent" in Egypt, upon the banks of old father Nile and not far from the great pyramids, whence "forty centuries look down on them," brethren are to be met with; and in this connection we may mention that our fellow-citizens of African descent have been gathered into the fold in Washington and Boston, St. Louis and Indianapolis. If not "Greenland's icy mountains to India's coral strand," we count at least members in Norway and Denmark; they gather together also upon the classic soil of Greece, as well as under the dominion of the turbaned Turk and amid the gorgeous paganism of the Indies. China has been long since invaded, and in distant Australasia Macaulay's dreaded New Zealander (who is supposed to be cultivating an artistic eye for prospective English ruins) has in his midst the disciples of St. Vincent de Paul.

From the latest statistics in our possession the present condition of the society may be summed up in the following figures:

In the United States about 500 conferences, with an active membership of about 9,000, while the total membership of the society is about 90,000, and the number of conferences 5,000.

The work of the patronages has reached, in France, a development which dwarfs our efforts here, and these efforts seem insignificant in comparison with what our Protestant brethren accomplish in the same field, having borrowed from our society the idea, and elaborated it, thanks to their ample means. Unfortunately for us, our resources are extremely limited, and where our Catholic brethren are wealthy there does not seem to be so much liberality in helping to found and sustain these institutions. In Paris they have established auxiliary societies of lady patronesses of all walks of life, whose efforts are bent to secure the funds necessary for the support and maintenance of these noble institutions. In London the same work has been already taken in hand quite energetically.

In Boston, especially, the children of the poor are looked after in the most thorough manner. As in New York, they have agents at the courts to rescue Catholic children from commitment to Protestant homes; Catholic ones are provided; occupations are found for those who are old enough to work, and it is highly interesting to read of the ingenuity exercised in amusing the children on the "outings" given them in pleasant weather. The abandoned or neglected infants, through the paternal care of the conferences, get the next best thing to proper maternal nursing, arrangements having been made to place them in good hands, which has resulted in materially reducing the mortality among these little ones. Thus the society in Boston is doing the work of a foundling asylum.

The organization of its early days obtained the approval of the late Pope Pius IX. of blessed memory, who enriched it with many spiritual favors, and our present Pontiff, Leo XIII., has endowed it with like testimonials of his paternal affection. The last council of Baltimore spoke in flattering terms of the society, and placed it in the front rank of lay organizations. Those of the hierarchy and the clergy who know best its objects and its aims and what it accomplishes, are anxious for its establishment, propagation, and success, and always give it their heartiest support. Even our municipal authorities recognize it in a most practical way by giving it, in some places, a share in the distribution of the public funds devoted to charity, because they realize that the application of the money will be direct and undiminished by salaries of distributors; and it has conquered the respect and, in many instances, the co-operation of our separated brethren, who admit its quiet efficacy in succoring the poor. It is essentially a lay society, seeking always to work in harmony with the clergy, to whom it is a valuable aid, and it is par excellence the most important lay society in the Church. It remains therefore for Catholic laymen to recruit its ranks. Its rules are simple; no great sacrifices are exacted; no very onerous duties are imposed.

We should have many more upon our rolls of active membership; men of all classes and conditions. In Europe, and especially in France, conferences are thus composed; while in America we see few names of the wealthy and distinguished upon the conference lists. With accessions from this class, dare we not hope that in addition to its multifarious works of charity, it may have its humble share in solving the serious problem which agitates all nations and peoples, the great living question of the relations between the rich and the poor; the conflict between capital and labor, and the other social questions involved. Only faith and hope and charity can surmount the obstacles which these antagonisms present, and lead to a better understanding of relative rights and mutual duties. "And the greatest of these is charity;" "for the poor we have always with us."

"Indian Rights" was next stated by Rt. Rev. Bishop McGolrick, of Duluth, Minn., his address embodying a mass of statistics not deemed appropriate here.

THE INDIAN IN THIS REPUBLIC.

Our young Republic, but now in the beginning of its development, has, for the most part, pursued a policy of conciliation in its treatment of the Indian tribes. To those who were supposed to represent the Government, to its agents and officers, must be generally attributed the evils which have fallen on those wards of the nation, which have well-nigh blotted out a nomadic race, about whose extinction there appears to be slight doubt, as they recede before the white man's advancing tread.

The commission of nine appointed by General Grant in 1869, after enumerating the many notorious grievances of the Indians, summed up by declaring that "the history of the Government connections with the Indians is a shameful record of broken treaties and unfulfilled promises." "Theft, lying, robbery, broken promises"—such is the summing up of Helen Hunt Jackson, when, in pleading for the rights of the Indians, she recounts the story of their woes.

Professor Painter, agent of the Indian Rights Association, in his report of 1888, states as his conclusion, after a careful investigation, that "the whole management of Indians has been abnormal, with little or absolutely no opportunity for the natural laws regulating social life to operate."

"The aboriginal population of the West Indies, of Mexico, of Central and South America," writes Rt. Rev. Bishop Marty, so well known for his active interest in the

Indians, "was preserved, Christianized, and in great part civilized. Forty-six millions of Catholic people now inhabit those countries, with a proportion of white people to the mixed and purely aboriginal elements nearly everywhere the same—20 per cent. white; 43 per cent. mixed; 37 per cent. aboriginal. North of Mexico, the fate of the aborigines has been extermination."

In the report of the commission, charged with the distribution of the fund for Catholic mission work among the negroes and Indians, and of which His Eminence, Cardinal Gibbons, is the chairman, the Indian population is marked as being about 285,730. The report of the Government Commissioner of Indian affairs for 1892 gives the Indian population, exclusive of Alaska, as 248,340; with about 3,000 employés. The location of the Indian population, together with the statistics of Catholic Indians, churches, sisterhoods, and religions for the year 1892, makes very interesting reading.

In 1891 the total Indian population was given as 249,273, and of these 80,891 were Catholics. In the statistics of 1876 there were enumerated 260 different tribes in the United States, amounting to about 300,000 Indians. These were widely scattered, roaming around in the chase during the year and only settled in their camping grounds during the winter and early spring. For many of these tribes the Government holds in trust certain funds belonging to them and for which they receive the annual interest.

Five tribes, civilized, the Cherokees, Chickasaws, Choctaws, Seminoles, and Creeks, have a trust fund of $8,008,525.99, with an annual interest of $413,790.11, while thirty other tribes have about $16,000,000 for their benefit. This fund, if well managed and properly disbursed would be a great assistance to the Indians, but the commissioners, clerks, inspectors, supervisors, agents, boss farmers, physicians, teachers, and all the rest of the multitude to whom the Indian is so valuable, take to themselves a very large percentage of the fund belonging to these poor people.

The constant advance of the white man, and the ever-increasing demand for land, gradually drove back the Indian to remote western wilds. Before the shrewd and often unscrupulous pioneer the Indian had to retreat or become completely helpless.

The general government was gradually forced to exercise unlimited control over the aborigines and their property. They became wards of the nation, to be governed and directed in all their affairs until they could be formed into civilized men. Prisoners in their own homes, they are strictly kept within lines called reservations. There they are forced to remain, and can not leave but by special permission and with a pass, on which is marked the number of days they are allowed to be absent. The agent has full power over these people, and, if he be tyrannical, can govern more absolutely than the Czar of Russia.

The number of these reservations and agencies increased up to 1870, when General Grant inaugurated the Indian peace policy. Of the seventy agencies under this new system eight were assigned to the Catholic Church. In other agencies, where the large number of Indians were Catholics, their demands for a Catholic priest were ignored, and they were handed over, body and soul, to those who were in many cases hostile to Catholicity.

At this period, twenty-three years ago, more than forty mission houses, with over 300 stations, at which 100,000 Indians received instruction and the sacraments, were built up, but under this new system complaints grew ever louder, showing that the Government agents were using all their powers to counteract the labors of Catholic missionaries, to prevent their mission work and destroy their control of the Indians. In many places the Catholic missionaries were driven out of the reservations, and, as Archbishop Bailey declared, "this action was taken under a government policy of itself wise and humane."

Under this policy, non-Catholic missions and schools were erected and established among the Indians already Catholic, and amongst pagans who for years had been petitioning for schools and churches under the influence of Catholic missionaries.

The sad story, which can only be hinted at, of the gross immorality of white men and Indians in many of the reservations; the dissolute white man and the savage in league to destroy every remnant of purity in the poor Indian girl; the parents themselves, the natural guardians of the children for whom they have such warm love, engaged in forcing their daughters to lives of shame—alas! how often has all this been rehearsed as the common tale of the reservations!

But what a change when the good Sisters came amongst the children of these wretched people! In the midst of privations and trials, these brave women fighting the good fight against superstition and darkest temptation preserved the children entrusted to them pure and holy; gave the Indian mother a new life of freedom, before unknown, and investing them with Christian purity made the Indian family a fit subject of rejoicing both to angels and to men.

"Give us," said the chief of the Gull Lake band of Chippewas, Minnesota, speaking in July, 1892, to the bishop of Duluth, "give us a black-gown to teach ourselves and our children."

"I have been twenty years on the reservation here," said an old chief, "and the promises made to us I never saw fulfilled; give us a priest and a school for our children and we will be satisfied."

Many of these were pagans, but they had centered their hopes for their children in the sisters' school.

The act of Congress, February 8, 1887, giving the Indians an individual title to certain lands, and thus bringing them under the ordinary laws of regular citizens of the country is the last, and it would seem final attempt to settle the Indian question.

The amount of land given to each Indian varies with the locality; the Modocs received forty acres each; the Senecas, 160 acres; and the Quapaws, 200 acres each.

From February, 1887, to November 30, 1892, there were made 15,482 allotments on reservations under the general allotment act; 4,550 allotments by special act of Congress; 1,242 allotments on public domain outside reservation.

As the Indian's mode of life and traditions are altogether opposed to this settled life, it will be wise on the part of the Government to see that these people, rendered so helpless by long years of reliance on the Government care, may be protected in their rights and prepared gradually for the change to regular citizenship. Children of nature, careless of future needs, if present wants be satisfied, never, in any period of their history, do they need more the advice and encouragement of the faithful missionary.

Amongst them the demon of intemperance has had its thousands of victims. This, their greatest curse, of itself, would complete their destruction, but the Government, by wise restrictive laws, aided in diminishing the evil. Still there were ever hordes of white men watching to supply, through greed of gain, the "fire-water" which changed the Indian into a devil.

The Catholic Church in the United States had from the commencement to deal with a population ever increasing at a rate unparalleled in any other country in the world. Her missionaries were few, unable for many years to meet the wants of the growing towns and with little possibility of attending the new settlers scattered over a country of immense distances. Many, too, had come to make this land their home, whose traditions taught a hatred of Catholicity. History, which should have been a record of the truth, became the medium of shameless lying and the disseminator of calumny. Catholics and Catholicity were judged and condemned on such testimony; so we need now the active co-operation of the religious orders. Let them prepare men and women missionaries well schooled in the various Indian languages and dialects; let them prepare such useful books as may suit the present generation, and the future is in the hands of the Church.

The day of the nomadic Indian is gone; soon to be settled on the lands, many of the difficulties of the old missionary work will have passed away, but this is the critical period, and the Church naturally turns to her reserve corps for self-sacrificing men, now as in the past.

How sad it is to read the letter of Archbishop Salpointe, who tells us of 20,000 Navajoes "that the Gospel has never been preached to them; that they are intelligent and many of them would be won over easily to Catholicity." Priests are wanting. Sadder still is it to learn from the same source that the agents of government commissioners, hostile to the Church, "do all in their power to ruin our schools and to pervert our poor Catholic Indians, by means fair and foul; their efforts being especially directed against the faith and Catholic allegiance of the Pueblos."

Nearly every bishop who has to deal with the Indians has a like story of poverty, of difficulty in finding missionaries and of bigoted obstruction. Yet is it not consoling, in the face of all these troubles, to find that over 2,000 Indians have been received into the Church in the last year, 1892?

Bright are the prospects of the future. "We have good hopes," writes Bishop Lemmens, of Vancouver, "that all the Indians on the west coast will ultimately be Catholics; the majority are so now. The missions on the Yukon River and in the southwest of Alaska are very successful."

The red man turns to the Catholic Church as to a true friend. May we in our day find missionaries as of old, ready to acquit themselves as men of God to win to the civilizing influences of religion the souls of these poor wanderers from light and life. The question for earnest discussion, and which must meet with prompt response is this: "Can we devise a plan by which the present demands of our Indian population may be answered?" In this new phase of the Indian question are we equal to our golden opportunity?

The Catholic Young Men's National Union held its convention in the hall of Washington, in the Art Institute.

This convention was a notable gathering of the representatives of the rising generation of Catholics in the United States. The proceedings were enlivened by the opening address by James F. O'Connor, president of the Chicago branch of the Union; an address by Rev. Francis McGuire, of Albany, N. Y., President of the Union, and a paper by Warren E. Mosher, of Youngstown, Ohio, all of which will be found later on in this book under the fifth day's proceedings.

Archbishop Ryan, of Philadelphia, made a short address, among other things he advised them to cultivate a spirit of manly independence, self-respect, and regard for the rights of others. He said that the old prejudice against the Catholic religion was fast dying out, and the time had now come when men were regarded from the point of view of character more than on the account of their religious convictions. He solemnly impressed upon them their great responsibility as young men, and said they were accountable to Almighty God for the influence they exerted on society. He advised them to read the writings of Edmund Burke, and try to catch therefrom something of the ideals which that great statesman held up for the guidance of men in public life. The young men, he said, should adopt that grand old maxim of that grand old statesman, Henry Clay, the saying: "I would rather be right than be President." He mentioned William E. Gladstone, a name that brought forth a storm of cheers, as a man that always had the courage to do his duty in the face of opposition, misunderstanding, and calumny, and who always felt his responsibility to God and to the public. He said that no better type of a public man could be mentioned than that of Grover Cleveland. Mr. Cleveland represented the people of the United States perhaps better than any man who had occupied the presidential chair since the days of Washington.

After an address by Right Rev. Bishop Burke, of St. Joseph, Mo., the regular work of the Convention was taken up by the reading and discussion of numerous valuable papers. On this fourth day, the C. Y. M. Union heard other papers and eloquent addresses from Right Rev. Bishop Gabriel, of Ogdensburgh, and Rev. Dr. Dolan, of Albany, N. Y., and also from Father J. B. Daley, of New York City Cathedral. Besides its election of officers and other customary business, the Union then passed the following resolutions.

C. Y. M. N. U. RESOLUTIONS.

Resolved, That the Catholic Young Men's National Union, in convention assembled, tender to our most Holy Father, Pope Leo XIII., assurance of our love and devotion.

Resolved, That we renew our belief in him as the infallible representative of Christ, and express our filial devotion to him, and, also, to his representative, Mgr. Satolli, whom he has appointed the Apostolic Delegate to America.

Resolved, That each society make especial effort to lend itself to literary work, and, also, to the establishment of classes in the ordinary, and, if convenient, in the particular branches of learning for the boys of our colleges and parochial schools; and, also, for our working boys, believing that the great cause of the young men can be best served by taking care of the boys and molding their character.

Resolved, That it is with gratification and a keen sense of its far-reaching usefulness we have watched the work and progress of the Catholic Summer School of America, and that we do heartily indorse the aim and objects for which it was established, and would recommend the establishment of some plan or movement by which the young men's societies can make use of the benefits of the Catholic Summer School.

Resolved, That we heartily commend the work of the Bishop's Memorial Hall, conducted by Professor Edwards, of Notre Dame University, and of the American Catholic Historical Society, of Philadelphia, whose special object is the collection of all material pertaining to the history of the Church in this country, and the publication of articles making known important events in our history.

Resolved, That we congratulate the young ladies of many sections of the country upon the successful establishment of reading circles, and that we encourage female societies to aid us in our laudable object of spiritual, intellectual, and social advancement.

FIFTH DAY.

The fifth day of the Columbian Congress was chiefly devoted to the great question of education, and was signalized by the delivery of a momentous paper on "Catholic Higher Education" by the Rt. Rev. Rector of the Catholic University at Washington. Following is

BISHOP KEANE'S ADDRESS.

For the right understanding of the subject which I have been requested to treat, it is necessary, in the first place, to form a clear idea of what is meant by higher education as compared with elementary and secondary education.

Elementary education is the education of the child up to the age of twelve or fourteen. It consists of a knowledge of "the three R's," which are the first instruments of all learning, and it ought to impart through these instrumentalities an elementary acquaintance with the three great books which lie ever open before human eyes—the book of nature, the book of man, and the Book of God. Elementary education is ordinarily imparted, all the world over, in schools.

Secondary education is the education of youth, from the age of twelve or fourteen up to seventeen or nineteen. It consists in acquiring the use of other instrumentalities of learning, namely, languages ancient and modern, and of arriving through these at a more thorough acquaintance with nature or science, with the thoughts and achievements of men in literature and history, and with divine things in themselves and in their influence on the life of mankind. In different countries different names are given to the institutions in which secondary education is imparted. In Germany they are called gymnasia; in France, lycées; in England and America, high schools or colleges.

Higher education is the education of man, of one who has passed through the elementary and the secondary, and who presses on in the paths of learning, usually from the age of seventeen or eighteen up to twenty-four or twenty-five. And here let me remark, once for all, that in speaking of the education of man, I have no intention of excluding women. On the contrary, I firmly believe in giving her every educational advantage which she desires and which she finds profitable to her. Waiving for the present as not now concerning us, the practical question this involves, I wish it understood that I use the word man in the generic sense, concerning both sexes as far as the subject concerns them both.

The youth leaving college at eighteen must know that he is not a learned man. If he thinks he is, then he had better close his books, for further study will be apt to do him but little good. But if he has in him the stuff to make a learned man, then he knows that he has only seen what learning is and the way to it.

He knows that he can not hope to obtain it in the busy struggle of life; he craves more time for deeper and wider and more philosophical study, study that he will carry on with the seriousness of a man, of a disciplined mind. His aim may be a learned profession, law or medicine, giving position and emolument. It may be to master the great social, political, and economic problems, and thus become not only an intelligent citizen, but a leader of public thought, a moving and guiding power in the life of the community. Or his fitness or taste may run in the direction of the natural sciences, and then his aim will be to acquire that profound acquaintance with some one of them or some group of them, which may not only give him skill but scholarly eminence in some of the various lines of engineering or applied science; or fit him to be one of those scientific investigators who benefit mankind, and perhaps earn fame, by extending the boundaries of human knowledge. Or he may have chosen literature for the field of his life-work, and he longs for time and opportunity to acquire that acquaintance with the best thoughts of the best writers; that thorough mastery of the special line of subjects on which he would wish to write; that wide knowledge of the facts of nature and history from which he is to draw themes and illustrations; that correctness and dignity and beauty of style—in a word, to acquire such share as he is capable of in that combination of qualities which make the great writer. Or God may have put into his soul the noble ambition to perfect himself in one or another line of sacred studies, or more thoroughly grasp their entirety, in order to do nobler work for religion and for the highest welfare of mankind than the training of the ordinary theological seminary would suffice to fit him for.

In whichever of all these various directions the cravings of his soul may turn, the object of his desires is what we call the higher education, and the places in which it is to be found is all the world over called the university.

Owing to the present tendency to specialization, many institutions may be found which are special schools or institutes aiming at the exclusive development of one or another of these lines of higher study. But these special schools are really departments of the university that have gone off to themselves, and the notion of a complete university, it is now generally recognized, includes them all.

In the next place, we must consider the relative importance of these various degrees of education.

Multitudes receive only the elementary. Probably it will always be so with the bulk of the sons of toil. To supply it to them all and of as excellent a quality as possible is one of the most imperative duties of civilization.

Secondary education is reached by that more fortunate portion of the community who are ordinarily styled the "middle classes." Such classes will naturally be formed wherever industrial freedom exists, wherever energy and ability have a chance to rise. It is manifestly necessary that they should advance in culture, as they rise in the social respectability which their improved condition entails. Thus high schools and colleges become a necessity of every civilized community, and the increase in the number of their students may be considered a good criterion of the community's advance in civilization and the increase of popular prosperity.

But God has put into the hearts of his creatures an instinctive craving, not only for the good and the better, but also and especially for the best. Knowledge acquired makes the mind hunger for the greater abundance of knowledge which it sees beyond it, and by following the craving the soul develops its noblest faculty and grows in the dignity and beauty of its being. God wills it so. And knowledge is a mighty power, not only for one's own improvement, but also for the utility of our fellow-men. This is another reason for the providential instinct which impels the mind toward its fullest improvement.

Hence, with the development of civilization has ever advanced the development of the educational system. The truest pride of a civilized nation is in the universal spread of its schools, in the multiplication of its colleges; but its chief glory is in the number and excellence of its universities.

Since the Son of God sent forth his Church to be the light of the world, she has ever been the foremost promoter of education in all its degrees. She knows well that her divine mission can never be furthered by darkness, by ignorance or stupidity, for "God is the light, and there is no darkness in Him." She has ever blessed and guided minds emerging into the first beginnings of knowledge; she has fostered the sacred thirst for knowledge as it grew, and has everywhere encouraged and directed the establishment of the colleges which fanned the sacred flame and led onward into the light; she has, with special affection and care, encouraged and spurred on those minds of noblest calibre, that longed for the deepest draughts of the waters of truth, and in nothing does she more fondly glory than in being the mother of nearly all the great universities of the world. She knows that it is God who has implanted in man that craving for the fullest truth, and, in her perfect loyalty to both God and to humanity, she fosters the craving and does all in her power to satisfy it. She knows it is "the Father of Lights, from whom every good and perfect gift cometh," who has given to superior knowledge its present influence among mankind, and for the world's good she desires to see that influence brought to the utmost perfection, and used by good men through noblest motives for the best ends. This is the reason of the part she has taken in education, and especially in its highest, noblest, and most influential department.

In our age, more than in any that has preceded it, and in our country, more than in any other country in the world, reasons of special importance urge both on the Church and on civilization the necessity of encouraging and diffusing the advantages of the higher education, and of making it as complete and as sound as possible.

Human society is passing through the agonies of a very deep and wide reconstruction. Social conditions are being leveled upward. Privileged classes are passing away, and lingering vestiges of caste, of feudal arrogance, of autocratic Cæsarism, evoke only protest and indignation. Natural inequalities have to be accepted, but artificial inequalities are dams and dikes which will not long withstand the flood-tide. In this condition of things, the existence of which no man can question, there are grave dangers to be guarded against; but there are also weighty principles of right which have to be respected and, above all, there is a world-transformation which it is the duty of prudence to foresee and to provide for.

Now, how are these tendencies to be wisely directed? How is the future to be wisely molded? In one word, the process of leveling up must be encouraged and helped. Loyalty to humanity demands it; loyalty to the Creator of humanity, to the-blessed Father of us all, demands it; it can be discountenanced and resisted only through loyalty to traditions of men which too often make void the will of God.

And how is that leveling up to be safely accomplished? Through education; by making elementary education more and more universal and steadily elevating its level; by lifting larger and larger numbers from elementary into secondary education, till the multitudes in the schools be rivaled by the multitudes in the colleges; and in a special manner, by bringing the advantages of the very highest education within the reach of every child of the masses to whom God has given the highest qualities of brain. The day is past when it could be pretended that the finest quality of brain could be found only in the privileged classes. Intellectual power is a gift which God dispenses as He will, and wherever God has given it He has given with it a right to its full development. And the day is past—nay, the day never has been—when privilege and conventionality of any kind could look down on intellectual pre-eminence. Therein lies the highest respectability, the loftiest influence, a dignity before which artificialties of position must bow, a power which even the might of wealth can not lastingly withstand. Place these advantages bounteously within the reach of everyone whom God's providence has made fit for them; bring them especially within reach of the gifted poor; let it be distinctly understood that poverty shall debar no man from the intellectual pre-eminence for which God has fitted him; let the offspring of the sons of toil mount to that degree of learning, and consequent respectability and influence, to which their Creator by their endowments calls them—thus, better than by any or all other means, shall the social problem of the future be solved. Thus shall complaints of injustice and chafing against inequalities be stilled. Thus shall human society be leveled up, as far as God and nature mean that this should be done. Thus shall the wrongs of humanity be righted and its rights secured—not by violence, which only entails reaction and worse disaster, but by the gentle, irresistible force of the true and the just, acting together in God's ways for the real and lasting elevation of His creatures.

In the reconstruction of the world, Divine Providence has given a mission of special influence in America. She is giving the keynote of the world's future; and God has meant her to do so. In America, therefore, above all, must that universal abundance and excellence of elementary education, and that universal freedom and facility of the highest education, prevail.

But here we are faced by a thought of tremendous importance. Intellectual power, like any other power, may be used for purposes of evil as well as purposes of good, may be a curse or a blessing to its possessor and to those who come within its influence. It may do the work of the Father of Light, leading to light and peace and welfare, temporal and eternal; or it may do the work of Lucifer, who ever, as in Eden, offers what he claims to be a higher knowledge, ending in darkness and disaster.

Hence the natural relationship of the Church of God to education. Hence especially her relation to the higher education, since it is this which forms the men of intellectual power and influence, who shape the thought and action of their generation and lead the millions through true principles or false ones in the ways of wisdom or of folly and evil. Having in her custody both the philosophy of human experience in all ages, and the far higher philosophy of divine revelation, being the divinely established power for the world's moral and spiritual improvement, hers is naturally the influence which perfects education, which breathes a living soul into it, which insures its tending toward heaven's appointed ends, and its being used for the temporal and eternal welfare of mankind. That is why Providence made her the civilizer of the barbarians and the educator of the modern world; that is why her influence never can be spared from education and why its absence is always a grave danger to human society.

Therefore does she stand amid the surging mass of mankind blessing its upward aspirations, smiling maternal approval on the "excelsior" which ever sounds forth from its heart. Again and again of late we have heard that word of benediction on the aspirations of humanity from the lips of Leo XIII., and the world has rejoiced at the sound.

Therefore does she exult at the mighty energies which God has put into our young America, and with uplifted hands pray that these energies may ever be used for the world's good. Therefore does she bend all her powers to bestow on this favored land the fullest blessings of Christian education. Therefore does she long to see the multiplication of schools in which the knowledge of God and of Christ shall be the soul of the education there imparted. Therefore does she strive in like manner to multiply Christian colleges and to spur her people to the noble ambition of making their advance in educational advantages keep pace with their advance in earthly means and in social position. Therefore has she, for over thirty years, as the proceedings of her councils show, longed to crown the system of Christian education with a university that would be worthy of her, worthy of our age, worthy of America. From the Fathers of the Second Plenary Council in 1866 that wish burst forth as a longing and a prayer, for the realization of which the condition of the Catholic flock was not yet ready. From the Fathers of the Third Plenary Council in 1884 it thundered forth as a resolution no longer to be delayed, and at last, blessed and spurred on by the approval and exhortations of Leo XIII., the hierarchy of the United States laid the foundations of the Catholic University of America.

A woman was the instrument of Providence to supply the means for the beginning of the great work. May her name stand forever in honor among the women of America. Other women, and some men, too, emulate the noble example. From among the clergy and the people of the country hundreds—whose names shall ever form a roll of honor in our country and history—responded to the appeal of the hierarchy, and to the soul-stirring exhortation of the Vicar of Christ, that all should rally with united devotedness to the accomplishment of this great work. National associations and unions have recognized in it an object worthy of their united endeavor, the worthiest means of rendering monumental honor to great names which they wished to immortalize.

Here let me especially pay a tribute of grateful acknowledgement to the Catholic Total Abstinence Union of America for having, by the endowment—though not yet complete—of a professorial chair in the university, erected the worthiest of centennial monuments to the apostle of temperance. I regret that the endowment was received after our official announcements for the next scholastic year had already been printed, and that the Union does not, therefore, appear in the list of the founders of chairs. But I am happy to make this public announcement of their noble deed, which shall forever stand inscribed in the university's official documents, as well as in the imperishable tablets on her walls.

And so the beginning of the great work has been made. It is as yet only a beginning, but yet such a beginning as to have already outstripped any previously existing work of Catholic education in the land and to give noble presage and encouragement for a great future. One faculty is already established and endowed in perpetuity, secure, as far as human things can be secure, against all possibilities of financial embarrassment—and that one the noblest of all the faculties, the faculty of divinity, which places God and Christ in the center of the whole work as its inspiration and guide forever, and which, for four years past, has already been bestowing on the clergy of America the first-fruits of the intellectual blessings so ardently sighed for by our predecessors in the Lord's vineyard.

Now, responsive to the repeated exhortations of our glorious founder, Leo XIII., all efforts are being made to establish and endow another great faculty, the faculty of philosophy, science, and letters, which will throw open to the laity the beginning of those educational advantages which are meant, in God's good time, to rival the best which advancing civilization and the Church of God have offered to eager intellects in the grand seats of learning in the Old World. How soon that opening will be made—how ample will be the learned training and opportunities which from the beginning it will be able to offer; how rapidly its development shall go on; how soon there shall bud forth from it the faculties of law and medicine; how soon the university shall stand before the eyes of America and of the world, in the full proportions which Leo XIII. craves to have it attain—all this depends on the good will of the Catholics of America, on their appreciation of the supreme importance of the work, and of that national character impressed on it by the Holy Father, which he meant should bring it home to the sympathies and to the honest pride of every Catholic in the land.

It takes time for every great idea to reach its full appreciation and welcome, and we are willing to be patient. Nay, more; every great idea must expect to be disputed and contradicted, and we are quite willing to take our share in the crucible. There are naturally those who, when the project was first proposed, believed it inopportune; who, when its plan was determined by competent authority, believe it mistaken; who, when the attempt was made, considered it doomed to failure, and who, naturally, would be somewhat glad to wag their heads and say, "I told you so." Some people are proof even against Papal pronouncements, and invulnerable against the logic of accomplished facts. Their imagination, having made up its mind to the worst, can see chimeras dire peeping over the walls of the new institution, threatening the destruction of all orthodoxy in the land. The Pope and his delegate say the contrary. "But that makes no difference, you know; you see we know better." Nay, they even discover that it is an ogre plotting the overthrow of the Catholic school system in our country. True, it is an integral part of the system of Catholic education, and it is rather an unheard-of thing for the superstructure of a house to plot against its own foundations; true, the utterances of its rector have always, as is well known, been strongly in advocacy of Catholic education in all its departments. "But, nevertheless," say these wiseacres, "we know it is so and the university is laboring to destroy our schools."

Well, we are willing to have patience with all this silly misrepresentation, sorry for those who disseminate or believe it, and regarding the hindrance which it may throw in the way of the work as only a ripple at its prow. The work of the hierarchy of the United States and of Leo XIII. can afford to be magnanimous with such obstacles, and to press on.

Only a few weeks ago the glorious Pontiff, in long private audience, most lovingly granted to one of the professors of the university, discoursed with him at great length on the progress thus far made by the university, and on the difficulties and hindrances which it had to encounter. Then the Holy Father reminded the professor how he, when Nuncio, in Belgium, had seen the early struggles and difficulties of the University of Louvain; how he had sympathized with the university and aided it in its struggles, and how he had lived to see it the glory of Catholic Belgium, with 2,000 eager students crowding its academic halls. "Such," said the Holy Father, "has been, and shall be my course in regard to the Catholic University of America. It is my work; I am its founder; I shall be its protector; and it, too, must yet see the day when its students shall be numbered by the thousand." Such words from the heart and lips of the Vicar of Christ are for us answer enough to all objections, and assurance enough against all prognostications of evil. They and the apostolic benediction that went with them will sink into the hearts of the Catholics of America, and bring forth the fruit so earnestly desired by the Vicar of Christ. Like the crusaders of old, they will exclaim together "God wills it," and strive with an eagerness and a generosity worthy of the Church's mission in America to make this the noblest national seat of Christian learning that the world has yet beheld; a great power of higher education, exerting a beneficent, elevating influence on the whole system of Catholic education throughout the United States; a great beacon-light of sweetly blended natural and supernatural truth, shining forth from our country's capital city, a guide in the pathway of our country's future.

The gifted Brother Ambrose of De La Salle Institute, Chicago, next read a paper entitled, "Lessons of the Catholic Educational Exhibit," referring to the magnificent display of the work of Catholic schools, etc., which had formed a most attractive feature of the great Columbian Exposition:

A VOICE FROM DE LA SALLE.

The district school teacher and the hedge schoolmaster have passed away. In their place we have the educator. He is no longer the coming man; he is here. To-day his work is admitted to be the aristocracy of the labors. The world had to be taught that truth. Those old-time monks and shaven priests and long dead martyrs knew it well. The Gersons and the Roger Bacons and the Bedes and the Cassians put their energies into it. They knew the school-house was a giant factor in civilization. They left the glories of the battlefield to their masters, but kept for themselves the struggles of the mind. And they won; won everlasting victories. They soon taught the world that to-day there are schools for everything. Apprenticeships as served forty years ago are virtually dead. Murillos of to-day send their Sebastians to art schools. The chisel, the brush, the rudest handicraft, as well as that which requires the greatest deftness —each has its school. There are schools of architecture and schools of design, schools of pottery-making as well as schools of medicine, law schools and schools of agriculture, schools of art and schools of science.

Let not our modern educators deceive themselves in the belief that these good things have come with them and because of them. The truth is, they have happened along about the time the world caught the idea that Christianity has been thrusting before its mental eye for centuries. "We will dignify labor," cry the advocates of manual training. "Laborare est orare," centuries back, said the old Benedictine monk, whether he illumined the page or taught the feudal farmer to care for his crops. And farther back than he the Fathers in their homilies on the text "Pray always," made the explanation that gave the Benedictine the idea he so tersely expressed. And still farther back than they, the warm wind that blew over the sea of Tiberias kissed the lips of Him that uttered the sweet command "Pray always." And so, all that is good, and all that is true, and all that is beautiful in modern civilization may be traced back to the gentle Jesus of Nazareth. He was the inspirer of the old masters; He and His mother and His saints and angels gave themes to the sculptor's chisel and the artist's brush. If the world to-day has the literature of the ancients, it is because there were Christian monks who treasured it. If Europe to-day has a single university, the name of some Christian bishop, prince, or priest is written on its foundation stones. It was the Christian monk, Alcuin, who would have made France a Christian Athens. If the decree of the eternal brotherhood of man has at last been accepted, the slave whose shackles have been stricken off must bend his knee in thanksgiving to the God-man, Christ. If to-day woman is admitted into this eternal brotherhood, if yesterday chivalry raised her on a pedestal and worshiped her with reverence untold, it is and it was because the Virgin Mother of Jesus was the peerless woman of prophecy, the Immaculate Virgin, Mary.

Our silver dollars bear the legend "In God we trust." We are a Christian people. The Constitution of our country is, in its very essence, Christian. Our standing army has its Christian chaplains. Our President each year sets aside one day on which to return thanks to the God of the Christians for the favors received at his hands. The very birthday of the founder of Christianity is a legal holiday. But in our State schools the tenets of Christianity may not be taught. The army may have its chaplains, the nation its days of thanksgiving, the people their churches, but the young in their class hours must be without the God whose name is graven on the dollars with which their teachers are paid. Oh! well might the prophet of old take down his harp from the weeping willow, and tuning its strings to the minor keys sing as once he sang by the rivers of Babylon: "The little ones have asked for bread, but there are none to break it unto them." Oh! well indeed could he so sing to-day, if Christ had never come. But Christ has come; and the centuries that have passed bear evidence to the quickening activity of His philosophy. That philosophy accepted is Christian faith. And Christian Faith has stimulated private enterprise to sprinkle the land with schools in which the tenets are taught.

Now, if the religion of Christ was the force that changed the savage to the gentleman, that taught him the arts of peace, that struck the shackles off the slave, that welded woman unto the brotherhood of man, that laid the foundation stone of the ivy-mantled universities to serve as beacon lights in the darkness of ignorance, that induced men and women to forego every legitimate pleasure in life that they might "break the bread to the little ones," that to-day urges the Catholics who can to add their mite to the support of schools wherein the influence of Christian truth may be made active, tell us what are these Christian schools doing for truth and for light?

At creation's dawn God said, "Let there be light," and light was. At Christianity's dawn the Church said: "Let there be light." Go out to the Catholic educational exhibit at the World's Columbian Exposition and there behold! "Light is." Far be it from me to worry you with the recital of the history of that display. You have heard it, you have read it over and over again. Those whose efforts shaped it need no commendation from my poor lips. Their monument is their deed. Catholic education in its minutest detail is there. If you wish the full force of its grandeur and magnificence to strike you, examine the educational exhibits by which it is surrounded. When you have done you will pass away with a luscious sense of honest pride you never felt before. Then go to your homes in the East and the West, the North and the South. That school-house in the shadow of your parish church, be it bright with its newness or dingy with age, will henceforth wear a lustre to your eye. You never dared to dream that through its humble portals such evidences of success could be sent forth. Then tell the people who, with you, Sunday after Sunday, heard the hard-working pastor ding-donging for the dimes and the dollars that built the schools and put the teachers in them—tell them what has been done, because they made the necessary sacrifices. Bring them the good news and give them the taste of the sweet peace of joy. They will bless you for it, and they will know "How beautiful upon the mountain are the feet of him that bringeth good tidings and shall preach peace."

Ignorance is not the evil of this day. Quantitative doses of religious instruction given half-hourly each day are not the "cure all" for the world's ills. The woods are filled with people who know better than they do. Their heads are right. The wrong is with their hearts. To set hearts right is the real object of the Catholic school. Religious education, not religious instruction, is their real support. To accomplish this is the why and the wherefore of religious teaching orders of the Catholic Church. Fifty-two bodies of religious teaching orders have done the actual work that produced the results displayed in the Catholic educational exhibit. How many Catholic schools would there be in this wide land of ours were it not for these religious educators? They have made the vast majority of these schools a possibility. Go out to the Catholic

BISHOP FOLEY, DETROIT.
BISHOP BURKE, ST. JOSEPH.
BISHOP HEALY, PORTLAND.
BISHOP RADAMACHER, FT. WAYNE.
BISHOP McGOLRICK, DULUTH.
BISHOP SCANNELL, OMAHA.
BISHOP KEANE, WASHINGTON.
BISHOP MESSMER, GREEN BAY.

educational exhibit and see if the cassock and the cowl and the nun's dark veil throw the shadows of gloom upon the minds of the little ones and keep from them the light of to-day.

I hold as a psychological axiom that soul is best fitted to raise others to higher things which is freest from purely natural affections. Witness Diogenes when he would elevate his followers. Witness Plato, who at twenty followed Socrates, renounced marriage, and, like his master, lived content with the barest necessaries, in order to give himself entirely to the things of the mind. The religious teachers of to-day are untrammeled. Look on this young man or that young woman, clothed in the religious habit, standing before the students in a Catholic school-room. Do you for a moment appreciate all the sacrifices they have made to be there? They stood before God's altar, and, taking their heart strings in their hands, they wrenched them from the bleeding, quivering heart that they dashed to the floor. Then, kneeling down, they swore away their liberty, by oath renounced the right of ownership, and thus made themselves more penniless than the pauper. Do you think they did not feel it? Ay! they did and they do. But onward they move, forgetful of all things save Christ and his little ones. Thus do they "rise on stepping-stones of their dead selves to higher things." There is nothing to come between them and the cause they have wedded. Ambition? Wealth? The pleasures of life? Whoever knew of them between the nun's fair veil or the sombre cassock of the religious? The treadmill of the class-room affords no opportunity for the play of such passions. The love of home, of father, of mother, of brother and sister—oh! it burns in their hearts with a steady flame, and the days make it stronger and the years make it brighter. But the voice of Christ is sounding in their hearts and they may not leave His side. Age comes with its wrinkles, disease with its pains, and still they are feeding the lambs of Christ's flock. This is devotion. Look for it where you will, it is to be found only in the Church of Christ. Tell me, is there beneath God's blessed sky a grander thing than such devotion and such sacrifices? The world is filled with men and women who are courting its joys and sipping its cups of pleasure. Anybody can do that! But it is only the chosen few who can rise to the grandeur of the deed done by those who have labored in the class-rooms from whence have come the glories of the Catholic educational exhibit.

Priceless gifts of heaven, you Catholic educators, I salute you! Bright jewels in the crown of Holy Church, I hail you! Your sombre robes, your simple homes, your sweet, retiring ways can never dim the lustre of your deeds. Jewels of Mother Church on earth, yours shall it be to shine as stars in heaven for all eternity.

H. L. Spannhorst of St. Louis, in a paper upon "Catholic Societies," gave valuable suggestions to the Congress, as follows, upon the subject of

CATHOLIC ORGANIZATION.

I shall speak of such societies which were meant by the pastoral letter of the archbishops and bishops assembled at Baltimore in 1884, when they said: "It is not enough for Catholics to shun bad or dangerous societies; they ought to take part in good and useful ones." Again has the voice of the Vicar of Christ been heard, giving approval and encouragement to many kinds of Catholic associations, not only as a safeguard against the elements of secret societies but also as a powerful means of accomplishing much of the good that our times stand in need of. Not only should the pastors of the Church be diligent in building up "the spiritual house," the tabernacle of God with men, "but every hand among the people of God should share in the labor."

We find sufficient ground for the encouragement of organizations and the sustenance of Catholic societies. We find, furthermore, that which is mentioned as desired has become a necessity in our time, and, I may say, more so than at the time since the mentioned pastoral was issued. It is not simply the name which constitutes a society Catholic, but it is the effect the organization creates and sustains upon its members in the practice of their religion in every day's life.

The Catholic Church is the church in which all are alike; station or position with it in a spiritual sense cuts no figure; the Confessional and Holy Sacraments are for all, and approachable by all through the same source and channel. The Church has time and again told us to organize Catholic societies—or rather Catholics into societies. Look at the roll of your societies of Catholic men. Who are they? Generally men of small means and humble stations; many of them look upon the societies of which they have become members as their protectors and supporters in time of reverses, sickness, and need. Why then not join in and become members of a society with an object so noble, a work of two-fold charity?

To help support your brother when in need, and also to give proof of your love and affection toward him, who is your equal before God, is a duty for every person. Catholic societies are the need of our time. Under the circumstances surrounding us, it is to be feared that not a few of our own people, who are not too practical in their duties, may for various considerations be entrapped, and finally, through indifference and constant association, led astray and either through ignorance or indifference lose their faith and become enemies of their mother Church; we must, through our own activity, stop this and regain what has already been lost.

I am well aware of the fact that many of our Catholic men look upon societies with indifference as being a matter to be left entirely to those who may need at some time, through adversities, sickness, or other ailings, assistance and help, they believing themselves so well fixed, not expecting want of any kind or help, thus forgetting their duty toward their fellowman, commanded by our Saviour when He said: "Do unto others as you would have them do unto you."

When I speak of the societies which, in my judgment, are best adapted to accomplish the most good in our time, I mean and recommend so-called benevolent societies, which years ago were so very popular. If to-day they are not so popular as fifteen and twenty years ago, there must be a reason for this, which I find in the fact that men of Catholic societies are gradually falling into classes, i. e., those who have been successful in acquiring a better condition of life during their days, have by toil or some successful stroke, operation, or speculation—the latter the most ruinous of all operations of our day, and, I am sorry to say, pretty widespread—housed their share of worldly rewards, this class actually believing themselves better than the poorer and laborer. The latter, who in many cases is a better Christian, has remained practical, and brings up his family in the faith and in the practice of religion.

There was a time when benevolent societies, i. e., societies which, generally mostly by monthly contributions by its members, paid to a member or his family a certain sum weekly during his inability to follow his daily vocation, or in case of death provided for the widow or orphan left behind. To the credit of the German Catholics, it must be said that this class of societies is to-day in its prime. There are about 550 societies, numbering between 55,000 and 60,000 Catholic men throughout the United States. This organization, known as the "German Roman Catholic Central Verein," will hold its thirty-eighth annual convention in St. Louis, commencing September 17th. None of these societies is yet fifty years old.

These societies have contributed to sufferers by calamities, fires, etc., including $3,142.98 for the Peter's pence, $28,682.35. During the last twelve years they have paid to 57,624 sick calls $1,348,290.19; to widows and orphans of deceased members $1,328,538.73.

The Bohemians and Poles work in entire harmony and successfully. The Irish Catholic Benevolent Union, too, is an organization working in the same direction. Within the last twenty years numerous organizations have been formed which make a specialty of what is termed life insurance upon principles different from that followed by the substantial and tried life insurance proper.

As a result of the withdrawal from some Southern States of the regular life-insurance companies, people were left without life insurance or chances to get any. Plans were adopted which have since become popular—one by assessment, the other by the contributing plan. By the first, assessments are made on every living member, generally according to their ages, to pay for the death losses occurring, limiting the amount of benefit from $1,000 to $2,000. The other plan is, each living member contributes for each death occurring a stipulated sum, thus creating a fund out of which deaths occurring are paid.

Upon those who are interested in the management of such institutions, and those who organize them, there rests a great responsibility. Two items must not be forgotten, that, like in regular life insurance, the largest number of laboring and middle classes would not seek and acquire life insurance, unless urged thereto; and that, secondly, but a small per centum acquire the age allotted them by the experience tables of life insurance, and where there is no reserve fund there is no surety.

In conclusion I will say that I deem benevolent societies, to which I have referred, of great benefit for any parish; not only because of the immediate contribution, but also because a united body of men, organized into a society by the advice and with the consent of the pastor in a congregation, can always be made a telling instrument for good.

Dr. Maurice Francis Egan, of Notre Dame University, Indiana, presented a very instructive paper on "The Needs of Catholic Colleges," which is given in substance as follows:

The object of the writer of this paper is not to find fault with existing institutions, or the management of them, but to accentuate the fact—sufficiently well known, but not enough considered—that a crisis has come in higher Catholic American education, and that if it remain stationary now it must eventually go backward. The primary object of this paper, then, is to point out means by which a forward movement may be carried out.

Catholic colleges have suffered both from ignorant fault-finders and equally ignorant or narrow-minded supporters. More than all, from that almost slavish adherence to tradition which goes by the name of conservatism. However satisfactory this state of affairs may be to those who do not actually suffer from it, we can not believe that it is satisfactory to those who are not content to remain within the Chinese walls which such conservatism would build around them. However we may strive to excuse ourselves for our isolation with the saying that the outside world is bad, we can not prevent our children from taking their part as men in it, nor can we afford to neglect due preparation for their struggle in this world. I can best justify this paper by quotation from Cardinal Newman's "Idea of a University," which I shall take as my text. On page 15 of his preface he says:

"Our ecclesiastical rulers view it as prejudicial to the interests of religion that there should be any cultivation of mind bestowed upon Protestants which is not given to their own youths also. Protestant youths, who can spare the time, continue their studies to the age of twenty-one or twenty-two. * * * I conceive that our prelates are impressed with the fact and its consequences that a youth who ends his education at seventeen is no match for one who ends it at twenty-two.

"All classes, indeed, of the community are impressed with a fact so obvious as this. The consequence is that Catholics who aspire to be on a level with Protestants in discipline and refinement of intellect have recourse to Protestant universities to obtain what they can not find at home. Assuming (as rescripts from propaganda allow me to do) that Protestant education is inexpedient for our youth, we see here an additional reason why those advantages, whatever they are, which Protestant communities dispense through the medium of Protestantism should be accessible to Catholics in a Catholic form."

The need of a Catholic university and of the most adequate colleges is as great in this country as it ever was in England. We have much to learn from the example of the English in higher educational matters; but the lessons we gain from them are in the nature of warnings. We Catholics in the United States are not so isolated from our non-Catholic neighbors as the Catholic English are. We know that some of their greatest minds have regretted this isolation, and we know, too, that the same spirit of conservatism which would make them content with an inferiority of instruction and education in this world, under a false impression that they may be helped by it to be among the aristocrats in the next, would, if permitted, produce similar effects on the Catholic body here. If it be the duty of a Catholic to consider himself as a being apart, with no duty to any of his neighbors except to those of his own faith, then men like

Cardinal Newman and the late Lord Petre have tried to place a visionary and useless object before their fellow-countrymen. The nature of our American social system and government has prevented the tendencies to exclusiveness and appalling narrowness, which, in addition to bigoted restrictions, deprive the whole system of Catholic higher education in England of any stimulus or hope for us.

In truth, we can not look abroad for models. In that other English-speaking country, Ireland, which might afford us some help, we have had the mortification of seeing a great university to which our fathers liberally contributed become a failure. And the present condition of Catholic education in Ireland is in its highest branches dependent on the future action of the bishops and the political parties. But fortunately we have not upon us the weight of English conservatism, nor are we dependent —and we can thank God for it—on any political movement. We have it in our own power to decide whether the number of Catholic young men—serious and earnest young men— shall increase every year at such secular institutions as Harvard, Yale, Cornell, Ann Arbor, and Johns Hopkins, or enable them to gain under true religious influences such an equipment as the world of to-day demands.

We believe that no height of culture, no amount of skill, no success in the world will compensate for the absence of a knowledge of the purest morality and philosophy and the intention to inculcate their precepts by our example. The church is truth, and we fail to fulfil the greatest of all commands, which is to love our neighbor as ourselves, if we selfishly refuse to let the light within us shine before men. The highest patriotism is the highest Catholicity; it is the tenderest charity; it is the first Christian duty. Our experience teaches us that ideals, no matter how fine, if clothed in forms that are unsympathetic or impracticable, fail of their influence. We make high claims for Catholic education. We are not, with all our humility, above praising what we have done. The Catholic press has been uniformly kind to our colleges. The annual commencement is never unaccompanied by amiable comments which give great consolation to the optimist and corroborate Pope's dictum, "that whatever is, is right." Nevertheless, in spite of the efforts of noble men who in religious communities have laid the corner-stone of Catholic education in their life blood, our colleges have achieved only a limited influence in American social life. They need much more than they have to make them widely effective. The time has come when they must broaden their scope, when they must reach the people at large or be content to remain small and isolated eddies apart from the main stream. We who are the heirs of the ages ought to be men of our time. Ascetical or mystical models need to be fitted to a modern environment to be of any use at all. We can not reasonably close our eyes to facts, and this fact is evident, that, no matter how ascetic or mystical the theories of the Catholic teacher among us may be, he is seldom averse to acknowledge the value of material success. We need, first of all in our Catholic colleges, a firm insistence on some system which will make men rather than exotics. We need a system of discipline which will lay more stress on the honor of the youth and less on the subtle distinctions between venial and mortal sin.

Another need of our Catholic colleges is that they should have more students. The transient element—that element which comes into them without special aim, and which obtains only a partial benefit from them—has always been too large. It is an axiom that no school can be entirely efficient while it is dependent on the fees of its students. The necessity of considering the financial question very carefully has forced some of our colleges to accept as inmate or boarder (I wish to make a distinction between the student and the mere boarder), any lad not absolutely a criminal, and the same necessity obliged some of them to take pupils without proper conditions or adequate examination. Whether this be true of other American schools is another question; I am solely concerned with the Catholic schools. The necessary attention given to the ways and means by which the expenses of the Catholic colleges should be paid has occupied attention and absorbed energies which are required in other directions. It is the duty of all laymen interested in the present and future of the highest form of education to assist in any plan by which these energies may be directed into their proper channel. They must be helped to the greater glory of God and a better development of society. At present the Catholic college does not obtain its proper quota of real students because it must, in order to exist, accept boarders—mere sojourners sent to be kept until called for. When the boarding-house anomaly and the reformatory atmosphere are eliminated in the public mind from the reputation of some of our colleges higher education will have begun to progress. It is well that the college should keep its students beneath its own roof, but let them all be students.

The Catholic College needs more men who want to be students. At present there is a gap between it and the higher parochial or public school which ought to be filled. Harvard, Yale and Cornell and Ann Arbor have brought themselves by means of scholarships directly in contact with the most studious and worthy classes of our young men. The pupil of the parochial school, no matter how industrious and clever he may be, no matter how ambitious, must in order to obtain further instruction be financially well off or have a friend who will pay his tuition at a Catholic college. Failing in these things, he can obtain through some of the public high schools a scholarship in one of the secular colleges. This accounts in some manner for the rapidly increasing number of Catholic students at secular colleges. It is evident that the pupil of the parochial school has no advancement in a logical direction to look forward to unless he has money. The Catholic college must have fees in order to live; it lives solely by its fees; it is without endowment, except the gratuitous services of self-sacrificing Christians. Its fees, including board, are, owing to this flesh-and-blood endowment, comparatively low, and yet the endowments in money and the scholarships which reduce the expenses of the student at secular colleges place our colleges in immediate competition with them. And the prestige in the public eye of certain secular colleges seems an additional advantage to the graduate.

Our colleges need at present not only more students but more ambitious and persevering students. These come, as a rule, from that class whose grip on the world is dependent on its own exertions, and yet this is the class which the colleges find it most difficult to reach. It costs from $400 to $500 a year to keep a student decently at the best of our colleges—this lowest estimate includes traveling expenses and clothes. But there is no way of lessening it unless, as at Notre Dame, there are some opportunities of a student's paying part of his tuition in manual or other labor. At Harvard, for instance, a scholarship very frequently reduces the yearly expenses of the student to the one-fifth part of $500. It is no wonder, then, that the sons of the people are always well represented in the graduating classes at Harvard, and that at Cornell the poorer Catholic who has secured a scholarship is enabled to gratify his ambition to stand as the equal of any man in his fight for a place in society.

The reason, then, why our colleges do not attract the hardest working class of students is because the Catholic pupil in the parochial school is cut off from gaining, by his own exertions, the benefits of the higher Christian education. This condition of affairs has, no doubt, led some of our bishops to encourage the establishment of Catholic clubs and libraries as part of the secular university system. The recent founding of guilds, under Catholic auspices, at Harvard, Cornell, and Ann Arbor, show that these far-seeing prelates have chosen to make the best of what we can only regard, at its best, as an expedient. The attendance of Catholics at the secular universities can be accurately characterized by no other term.

The Catholic colleges need endowment. But, more than all, they need scholarships. And with the scholarships will come just such students as they ought to have. And with such students will cease the maintenance of a system of discipline which can only be justified on the presumption that each older student is possessed of a devil which can not be exorcised, but which must be caged. Lay professors of character and of acquirement are needed, too. No college which is entirely manned by ecclesiastics can thoroughly do its work or obtain its proper effect on society in America. This is admitted by thoughtful and observant men who talk and write on the subject of higher Catholic education. Happily there is now no Catholic college in the country in which, when a vacancy occurs, the place can be supplied by any layman, with or without character, who is willing to work for a mere pittance. And there is now no Catholic college in this country where the sacrament of holy orders is supposed to give a man all the requisites of an ideal character.

It lies with us laymen to supply the present need of the Catholic colleges. We can no longer wait for the bishops or the religious communities to take the initiative. We are primarily responsible for the souls of our children. We only are responsible before our fellow-citizens for the position we, as a body, take in the intellectual and social life of our country, and we feel most heavily the results of any system of education which would leave us in the rear of the onward march of American progress. Besides, a sentiment of gratitude to those self-sacrificing men who, by their own devotion, have given us the foundations of the higher education ought to lead us to crown their work through our own exertions. We who come in daily contact with the world know better than even the most learned and pious priests the requirements for legitimate success in life.

The needs of Catholic colleges are chiefly money and the right kind of students. Endowments for professorships we can not hope for at once. But we can have scholarships at once. If every man with an income of $1,500 a year would contribute $10 and every man with $3,000 a year $20, we should have a fund which would give each ambitious and deserving Catholic boy in this country, whether in a parochial or public school, an opportunity of securing that education which, in the present condition of things, he can not get.

We must put our brains, our hearts, and our sympathy into this work. We can not look to the rich; we ought not to look wholly to them. Let us put our shoulders to the keel of this ship of education which is lying on the dock waiting for the tide which may never come. One good push, gentlemen, one strong effort, and we can send it steadily into midstream, onward to the rising sun.

A deeply interesting paper by Katherine E. Conway, of Boston, on "The Catholic Summer School and the Reading Circles," was one of the features of the Congress. The paper was as follows:

"Your mission is to make America Catholic." This was Archbishop Ireland's greeting to the assembled delegates at the Catholic Centenary Congress in Baltimore four years ago. And this was the charge with which he sent them back to their homes. Patriotic and religious enthusiasm were at flood-tide, and all hearts were willing to respond, like the first Crusaders at the call of Peter the Hermit, "God wills it."

The archbishop's charge was mainly to the laity, and the apostolate to which he pledged them was on the lines of secular opportunity. But, with dispersion, the electric current of brotherly sympathy was broken. Individuals stood apart, each no longer feeling the strength of 1,000 behind his own good intent. Men questioned, not in doubt, not in discouragement, but in reverent expectation of an answer: "How shall this be done?"

The answer came, and we know one term of it by the resultant action. "First fit yourselves for the mission. Foster the community spirit among Catholics. Raise the Catholic intellectual average. Prove your strength in the mass."

Association became the watchword of the time. New organizations sprang up on every side, and new life was transfused through existing bodies. The first immediate result of the Congress on this line was the Catholic Truth Society, whose aims and achievements have already been so well presented here. But that was a consequence of the second term of the answer, and aimed directly at missionary work among non-Catholics.

This paper is concerned rather with those other associations whose origin was in their members' conviction of the primal need of missionary work among Catholics themselves, but through agencies heretofore untried among us.

Our opponents are often our best teachers; yet, not every plan resorted to by non-Catholics or distinctly anti-Catholic bodies in missionary and reformatory work, not to speak of less well-intentioned effort, is adaptable to the Catholic purpose. Would that this were never forgotten! We don't want, for example, a Catholic political party, because some fanatics have organized a Protestant party in the shape of the mis-called American Protective Association. We don't want a "Secular Solidarity"—whatever that may be—of Catholic women for public-reform work, because such an association prospers among Protestant women. We don't want Catholic camp-meetings, nor Catholic women-suffrage leagues, nor Catholic dress-reform circles. We don't want to be so ignorant of the history and spirit of our own religion as not to know what true Americanism has drawn from it; much less to humor by our servile attitude the erroneous notion popular in certain circles that Catholicity can not make its way except in borrowed attire.

The noblest and loveliest can be made to look grotesque by misfit garments.

But there are examples set by the various Protestant bodies of so splendid utility and suggestiveness that we shall not be blameless if they are lost upon us. What thoughtful Catholic has not blushed to see how far ahead of us they are in practical and attractive methods for holding their young people—and alas! sometimes drawing our own away—by societies combining business and social advantages with religious affiliation? See the network of Young Men's and Young Women's Christian Associations which overspread the land; the Christian Endeavor Societies, the Chautauquan reading circles, and the Chautauquan summer school, and radiating from it to every section of the country its local assemblies.

What is the secret of the growth and permanence of all these things? One double word in its most comprehensive sense—lay co-operation. Protestant men and women of every class, being actively benefited by these societies, are actively interested in them. Protestant men of means have put them on a sound business basis.

Oh, it is true that they out number us and have an overwhelmingly larger share of this world's goods. But this does not explain everything. Is there even a slight foundation for the reproach sometimes made us, that we are lacking in capacity for organization, that we have enthusiasm in excess and perseverance in defect?

Let us honor the men—young men they were, too—who, long before the days of Catholic congresses, anticipated these questions. Indifferent or short-sighted Catholics who ask scornfully to-day, " What's the use of your Catholic Congress?" asked twenty years ago, " What's the use of your Catholic Young Men's National Union?" The union might have answered then, " We mean to train leaders for you." It might say to-day, "We have kept our promise;" for few among the priests and laymen whom we instinctively write on the roll-call of our national men but have developed themselves in the Catholic Young Men's National Union. And what good work of national magnitude but has had, if not its inception, at least a generous fostering in the same association?

At least, the reading-circle movement and the Catholic summer school have their roots in it. A layman, Warren E. Mosher, a zealous member of the union, deeply impressed by the adaptability of the Chautauquan methods to Catholic needs and uses, familiarized himself with them, started a reading circle in his native city, Youngstown, Ohio, and seized all Catholic occasions, local and national, for the advocacy of a reading union and a Catholic summer school.

Lay co-operation in church work among Catholics—a word not of new coinage, but merely of new emphasis—is sometimes spoken of by people who forget, for the moment, the direct and special service to religion of Orestes A. Brownson and John Gilmary Shea, and in another line, of Ellen Ewing Sherman and Sarah Peters, as if it were a novel idea—an experiment which may possibly result in disaster to church and people. And yet inter-relation and inter-dependence among all degrees and orders seem inevitable, so long as we can't even get our bishops and priests from another race of beings grown in another planet.

The need is of more lay co-operation. George Parsons Lathrop has well described the power of the Catholic laity as a moral Niagara allowed to run to waste. Archbishop Ireland has spoken not simply for lay co-operation, but for lay initiative in certain good works. Mr. Mosher took the initiative in his summer-school project, and found priests ready to co-operate with him. We may name among them those who later have successively held the presidency of the school—the Rev. Morgan M. Sheedy, of Pittsburg; the Rev. Dr. James F. Loughlin, of Philadelphia; the Rev. Dr. Thomas J. Conaty, of Worcester, the present executive, and the Rev. Thomas McMillan, of the Paulists, the present chairman of the board of studies. All these priests are identified also with the work of the Catholic Young Men's National Union.

To mention the Paulist fathers is to recall an American Catholic literary movement of missionary intent, long preceding and preparing the way for our reading-circle movement and Catholic summer school—that begun by Father Isaac T. Hecker when he founded the American Catholic Publication Society, the *Catholic World*, and he *Young Catholic*, and carried on so faithfully and fruitfully ever since by his disciples, the Paulists. To them he said, as Archbishop Ireland later said, to all American Catholics, "Your mission is to make America Catholic."

And whether working directly on the non-Catholic body, like Father Walter Elliott, in his missions, or indirectly, like the home missionaries, by unifying the Catholic people and raising their spiritual and intellectual standard, this end is ever before the Paulists.

If the first local reading circles were Mr. Mosher's, the first National Reading Union was that of the Paulist fathers, starting in 1889, with headquarters in New York, and Rev. Thomas McMillan, director. Under its protection reading circles were founded East and West, till in 1890, Mr. Mosher established his Catholic Educational Union, centralized at Youngstown, Ohio, to share, not to divide, a field too large for any one organization to work effectively alone.

The reading circles of the Columbian Reading Union had for chronicle and medium of inter-communication a department of the *Catholic World;* the circles of the Catholic Educational Union and the *Catholic Reading Circle Review*, founded and edited by Mr. Mosher. But the printed word is, after all, a cold and tedious process for the fostering of that community spirit needed in the establishment of a work of general advantage.

When the Paulist fathers, in January, 1892, effected a national gathering of Catholics, mostly literary workers, journalists, and philanthropists, for the promotion of the apostolate of the press they founded no new organization. The convention did not aim even at repeating itself. It met on the Epiphany and in the spirit of the feast, the dominant thought being how to manifest, through the press, the church of Christ to the non-Catholic American people.

Again and yet again the answer, "Unite and raise the Catholic spiritual and intellectual average first of all."

The reading unions as embodying this idea were both represented by their heads. So were a number of Catholic literary societies and alumnæ associations of like aim. The most successful man in the Catholic popular library work, Rev. Joseph H. McMahon, of New York, set forth the intellectual needs and risks of the young American Catholic. New England's great contingent of Catholic men and women of letters—she sent the most because she has the most to send—spoke less, on the whole, for direct missionary work among non-Catholics than for strengthening and unifying our own forces and reclaiming our own estrays.

The apostolate of the press has done infinite good in many directions. For one thing it was the hot-house in which the sapling of the Catholic summer-school idea was hastened to flower and fruit. Almost immediately thereafter Mr. Mosher appealed for an expression of opinion to the membership of this educational union and Catholics generally, through the *Catholic Reading Circle Review*. It was heartily favored and received, moreover, the cordial approval of many bishops and priests.

In the May following a permanent organization was effected; Rev. Morgan M. Sheedy, of Pittsburg, presided, a programme of lecture courses and single lectures arranged by Rev. Joseph H. McMahon, first chairman of the board of studies, and the first session successfully held in New London, Conn., from July 31st till August 20th following. The secular press and the non-Catholic public generally followed the experiment with interest.

The summer school let loose a good deal of money in New London and on the various railroads leading thither. When it became known that the school was seeking a permanent site, public-spirited people in various sections began to offer inducements to its trustees. The best offer came from the town of Plattsburgh, N. Y., on the Delaware and Hudson River Railroad—a site of 450 acres at Bluff Point, overlooking Lake Champlain, with the opportunity of incorporation under the board of regents of the University of the State of New York.

This was accepted, a reorganization was effected and the enterprise was incorporated under the title of "The Catholic Summer School of America."

Smith Weed, of Plattsburg, donated the use of the opera-house for the lectures, the town the use of the Plattsburg high school for a house of studies, and the Grey Nuns their academy hall for social purposes, pending the erection of the summer-school's own buildings, and the second session was held from July 15th till August 7th, inclusive, with larger attendance of students, a better programme of lectures, and a great increase of general interest over the first year. And this despite the tremendous counter-attraction of your great World's Fair at Chicago.

The attendance represented sixteen States, though New York and New England still furnished the bulk of students. As at New London, a few non-Catholics attended the lectures, and a Jewish Rabbi, Dr. Veld, from Montreal, followed the whole course.

The ubiquitous and irrepressible Fadladeen criticised the trial session of the summer school on the ground that the great majority of the students were young women. But even Fadladeen could not be blind to a change (may we say an improvement?) in this respect at the second session. It should be said, parenthetically, in extenuation of our too numerous presence, that we women are naturally drawn to any enterprise started under religious patronage, though we are perhaps over-demonstrative in recording our adhesion.

A young preacher, in one of our surburban churches a few years ago, was remonstrating with the men of his congregation for their delay in attending to some spiritual duty. "The means of salvation," he said, "are not exclusively for women. You, also, want to go to heaven. Indeed," he went on, warming to his theme, "heaven would not be heaven if it were peopled exclusively by——"

He stopped abruptly, and passed to another aspect of his subject, but every woman in the church completed the sentence according to the preacher's mind, and heartily agreed with him.

Similarly, the women would not, if they could, monopolize the advantages of the summer school. This year there was a perceptible increase in the attendance of young men; and, even a better sign, there were a number of family parties—father or mother, in a few cases both, remaining for a week with their young sons and daughters.

When, in the last season, that part of the summer-school property not needed for the summer-school buildings was put up for sale in lots, twenty were disposed of within a few days. This means the speedy erection of cottages, and a Catholic family summer settlement behind the Catholic summer school—one of the best possible guarantees of its permanent success.

But only one of them. If the summer school were to depend for students on the family settlement at Plattsburgh, the scope of its influence would be restricted to a comparatively small number of rich or well-to-do people; and we should have as a result, not an increase of the Catholic community spirit, but of the un-Christian spirit of caste. The Catholic summer school of America is for all the people, to bring all together on a plane of high, but equal, intellectual advantage. It is democratic in the best sense. Christian democracy means leveling up. The Catholic summer school is an outgrowth of the reading circles which have been organized and which work in this Christian democratic spirit.

The family summer settlement will do much for the social and recreative side; but, for students, the reading circles and other societies of like aim, of which a word later—must be the feeders of the summer school. They must be also the channels through which its achievement and influence shall be redistributed, extended, and continued throughout the year.

As a long-time reading-circle worker it is my conviction that extensions of the summer-school work in the shape of winter courses mapped out and disseminated through the printed page will hardly succeed among us. This method of instruction is too indirect and impersonal to suit the character of our people. We are more easily drawn by the spoken word.

There is, besides, too great diversity of condition, education, and environment among our Catholic young people to make it possible, or desirable, that the circles organized under the Columbian Reading Union of the Catholic Educational Union should all follow even the reading lists given in the organs of each. These lists **must** be suggestive, rather than prescriptive.

National reading unions can not be more than the loosest of confederations, within which every circle shall enjoy, as Father McMillan puts it, the largest possible degree of home rule. Some circles devote themselves to distinctly Catholic literature, feeling that, however otherwise advanced, in this especial point the literary education of their members has been defective. Others study English literature in general, with a Catholic light upon it. Still others have adventured into French and Italian literature. Some are pursuing a course of church history and some are re-reading the history of America in the light of that star which led Columbus thither. Many give much time to the biographies of eminent modern Catholics of Europe and America. Not a few concentrate their study on points of controversy.

What shall the delegations from the strangely varied circles find, each for its special need, at the summer school, and what shall they bring back to the circle and to the community from which the circle is recruited? Why not a winter lecture course? In this way summer-school extension has been opened. Thus far we see no better way.

The total of lectures on the regular programme of the summer school was forty-two, besides addresses before the teachers' conferences. These cover so great a variety of topics that every reading-circle's representatives must find one or several lectures in line with its own special work, and which they would like to have repeated in their own town or city.

An immediate reaction of the summer school on the reading-circle work was the organizing of courses of lectures under reading-circle management in several parts of the country. The lecturers in all these courses were chosen wholly or in part from those appearing at the New London session of the school. In one city, four circles combined for a course of four lectures. The John Boyle O'Reilly circle, of Boston, has instituted an annual course of three lectures. These courses are on a business basis. They serve a double purpose. Through them the circle acts directly on the community, raising the intellectual standard and fostering the Catholic community spirit. Through them, again, the circle does its part toward creating a public demand for the lecturers and literary workers of our own faith.

Before the days of Catholic national associations and Catholic congresses and Catholic summer schools, how little we 10,000,000 Catholics knew of our own eminent men. The Catholic summer-school movement, especially, has helped to show the world how rich we are in such men. The secular priesthood, the religious orders, whether the Jesuits, pioneers in American religious and civil life, or the Paulists, the latest of our native born, have but begun to reveal their resources. What splendidly gifted men are building their very lives into the manhood and priesthood of the American Catholic body in our classical colleges and ecclesiastical training schools!

How the cause has moved on, as the lamented John Boyle O'Reilly used to phrase it, on the citizen lines; and what a host of men whose names have stood in the popular mind for eminence in statesmanship, or law, or medicine, or literature, or oratory, or journalism, have been shown forth, through the stress of this Catholic intellectual movement, as earnest Catholics also. Truly, it is not the least of the glories of the Catholic summer school to have shown to our timid and self-distrustful, by shining examples, that the Catholic faith has not been an obstacle even to the worldly success of its professors.

The man who said, after the first Catholic Congress, "For the first time in my life I was proud of being a Catholic," did not express precisely the heroic spirit of Catholicity; but he voiced, I fear, a sad experience, by no means individual.

Let us not forget, in our citadels, the young and the weak on the undefended marches. It is easy for a Catholic to be brave and proud in New York, or Chicago, or Philadelphia, or Boston, to name but a few of our strongholds, but it takes something close akin to the spirit of a martyr to wear our profession cross unflinchingly under the supercilious eyes of the social despots of the provincial town where we are the unpopular majority.

It should be the aim of every reading circle to send to the summer school as large a delegation as possible, and to choose from among the lectures at least one to be repeated under its patronage the following winter. Remember, there are now 150 reading circles organized under the Catholic Educational Union with an aggregate membership of nearly 5,000, and 100 circles under the Columbian Reading Union with 5,000 aggregate membership. Remember also that an immediate consequence of every summer-school session is more reading circles. Moreover, a fixed feature of the summer school is the reading-circle convention. The interchange of experiences as to local work and local needs may be not only mutually suggestive among reading-circle workers, but suggestive also to the board of studies in the choosing of topics and lecturers for the summer school itself.

Already our leaders have learned that there is nothing too good in the intellectual order for the keen, earnest, and persevering young men and women who have been moved to seek the higher education on Catholic lines. It would be a grave mistake to talk down to those. They can appreciate and assimilate the best. They want instruction, not diversion, and are quick to resent the ill-considered, superficial, or spectacular. There is only one basis of selection for the instruction of such students as are drawn to the summer school—well attested personal fitness; and without this, sectional, partisan, and institutional claims should count for nothing.

It may be mentioned here that the reading-circle membership includes a very large proportion of public-school teachers. The religious orders of teachers are beginning to send representatives to the summer school. The friendly meeting, with interchange of experience and opinion between these two bodies of teachers, can not fail to be of advantage to the cause of education in general.

But who shall speak again for the teachers and the schools as did that gentlest of scholars and most earnest of teachers, Brother Azarias, whose untimely death, the result of his work in the summer-school's interest, we, in common with all Catholics, deplore. He has left to the reading circles the foundation of a library of Catholic literary criticism with especial advertence to the young American Catholic's needs; and he has not wholly passed from the councils of the summer school, for the light of his example shines unquenchably.

The reading circles can further help the summer school by holding, at the close of every season's work, public meetings in its interest. This was done last June in New York and Boston, and in result and students these two cities, like a pair of Abou ben Adhems, led all the rest. One Boston circle proudly, and, we think, justly, claims thus to have sent fifty-seven visitors and students to Plattsburgh. The same circle sets another example in the summer-school interest which will doubtless be widely followed —it proposes to buy a lot and build a reading-circle cottage for the use of its own members attending the school.

Mixed membership in the reading circles is an open question. The Catholic Educational Union seems to favor it. In the East and South, however, most of the reading circles are composed exclusively of young women. Our Boston circles so composed, however, are fortunate enough to revolve around the Catholic Union of Boston, and have the Union's membership to draw upon for presiding officers for our lecture courses and other indispensable aid. As between the attracting and distracting consequences of the admission of young men to the study meetings, distraction would tip the scale. Moreover, the reading-circle methods are not, to our thinking, quite adapted for young men. A corresponding plan for their intellectual advantage, however, is evolving itself in the East, and perhaps elsewhere, as the same condition must exist at least in the older sections.

The reading circles aim not to raise a crop of women publicists, disputants, and debaters, but simply to increase the good influence which we can exercise on the normal womanly lines by making us more numerously able to write, at need, a plain statement of fact or opinion; increasing our resources for dull and lonely days, making us more tolerant and reasonable and therefore more companionable in our home and social life.

The reading circle will act on the general community through its public lecture courses and occasional social gatherings; but its plan of study must be for the direct benefit of its immediate membership. May I venture to suggest that the relation between our summer school and the reading circles, and their reciprocal action, sets forth a relation and a reciprocity of service possible and most desirable between the summer school and the college and convent alumni associations and Catholic literary societies generally. And this will be equally true, in the day, doubtless near at hand, when the Catholic summer school, at Plattsburgh, will cease to have the right to add "of America" to its name.

It is much for the Catholic summer school to enter into the work of the Catholic Columbian Congress. It will be more for the school and for every Catholic interest when the Catholic Congress three years hence comes in its increased strength and splendor to the first permanent home of the Catholic summer school, at Lake Champlain, to be its desired and honored guest.

Meantime, see the fields and the harvests for Catholic Endeavor. Let us unite for the reaping on a plane high above partisanship or sectionalism. Our mission is to make America Catholic. Yes; and we shall do it mainly by making ourselves better Catholics—more intellectual, more refined, more prosperous, united, and public-spirited Catholics. Thus shall we become a leaven, interpenetrating and uplifting the whole body of our citizenship. The desire to advance God's cause gives a pure motive to every man and woman for self-advancement. It gives the greatest impetus to discovery, exploration, the pursuit of science, and the development of art and literature.

We need faith in ourselves, faith in our cause. The word of faith creates. The magnet of faith moves the mountains. Had Christians kept intact the faith, the community spirit, and the disinterestedness of the apostolic age, the new world had been discovered a thousand years sooner; the crusades, with other purpose than the rescue of Christ's tomb from misbelievers, had had the aid of the printing press and the telegraph and the cable, the railroad, the steamboat, and the electric light; and the crosses raised in pure hands, nerved from martyr hearts, had drawn the whole world in the unity of the truth to God.

Rev. John T. Murphy, president of Holy Ghost College, Pittsburg, Pa., made a strong and eloquent plea for the establishment of free Catholic high schools. He said:

Anyone who considers carefully our present educational system in the light of our educational needs must readily be convinced that there is a great lacuna yet to be filled up. A complete educational system embraces primary, secondary, and university education. It is not necessary, or even advisable, that all should be initiated into each part of this complete system, but it is absolutely necessary that such Catholic children as have the proper aptitude should have in the system we offer and partly impose upon them the means for obtaining the very highest education.

The third plenary council of Baltimore planned and enjoined a system of primary education which, if fully carried out under favorable circumstances, seems to be all-sufficient for the educational sphere for which it was intended. Since the close of the council, and in accordance with its strongly expressed wishes, important steps have been taken to put university education within the reach of both Catholic clergy and laity. But so far no corporate, organized measures have been taken by the church in the United States to cover the very important ground that lies between the primary school and the university. The foundation and basement of our educational edifice have been built, a goodly portion of the roof has been put on, but nothing has been done to the walls; only a stray pillar here and there, erected for the most part by private enterprise, connects the basement of primary with the roof and pinnacles of university education and saves the latter from being a palace top suspended in the air. The stray pillars I refer to will easily be recognized as those private Catholic colleges and academies spread throughout the land. While everyone will admit the good which these institutions accomplish, serving as they do to save us the semblance of an educational system, yet it must be avowed that they do not, can not supply the missing link of the chain, the continuous walls of the edifice.

In other words, our present educational system is so radically defective that it can not well claim the name of a system. It takes up the Catholic child from its mother's arms, supplies it with education, mental and moral, till about the age of thirteen, and then ceases as a system to take further cognizance of its education. It points out to the young boy, it is true, the towers of the university looming in the distance, but it supplies him not with the means of reaching them. If the boy has money and time at his disposal he can go for his secondary education to one of the private Catholic colleges; and the girl can, under similar conditions, go to one of the convent schools or academies. But the vast body of Catholic youth are debarred from entering these private unendowed institutions, and are simply cast adrift when their primary schooling is over. Withal, they are expected to meet in the battle of life their neighbors' children of a like station who have been trained at the public expense in richly-endowed and well-equipped high schools and State universities. Of course, such a contest is utterly unequal. It is a contest of raw recruits against disciplined troops. Native valor, natural genius, indomitable endurance may secure partial victories for the former, but eventually the random shot from the rusty gun must yield to the unerring aim of the repeating rifle, the straggling onslaught to the serried ranks of the square, the club, the claymore, or assegai to the keen edge in the hands of the well-trained swordsman. So, too, the contest in life's struggle between the comparatively raw parochial school boy or girl and the well-trained high-school graduates can have only one issue, the supremacy in secular matters of the latter. Exceptional talent and character will occasionally carry some of the former to the front, in spite of the disadvantage under which they labor, but the rank and file will have to bite the dust.

Surely the church in the United States, after having undertaken an educational system of her own, can not afford to allow this stigma of inferiority to remain branded upon it. It would be an evil day for the church in this country were her children to realize that on account of their religion they were precluded from their just rights to the secular advantages of life. Nothing could be farther from the mind of the church, of her supreme head, and of the fathers of the Third Plenary Council than the acknowledgment of the necessity of any such inferiority. Still, it exists, as I have shown, and will continue to exist until adequate, systematic provisions are made for providing secondary, or high-school education for Catholics. It is, therefore, a matter of the greatest importance to consider what means ought and can be taken to remedy this glaring and grievous defect in our educational system. Before proceeding to suggest what I consider adequate and feasible means, I may be permitted to refer to some remedies that are already being employed.

The manifest need that exists for giving Catholic children something more than a mere parochial-school education has given rise to two practices. The one is to tack on to or blend with the parochial school a portion of a high-school course. Thus we find many parochial schools embracing studies that range from the first elements to quite a number of the "ologies." This practice seems to me objectionable for this reason, that this blending of two different courses of study is injurious to both. The proper work of the parochial school is liable to be neglected, or glossed over, on the part of both teachers and pupils in the eagerness to reach the higher and more brilliant studies. Those exhibits of fancy or advanced work of parochial schools, of which we so frequently hear, are usually made at the cost of solidity and thoroughness in the subjects which properly belong to them. Of course it would be very commendable to have a real high school attached to every large parochial school, but it is scarcely conceivable that any one congregation could afford to carry out a complete system of both primary and secondary education. And, as it is not possible to have both, it is better to have the one thorough than to have the two spoiled.

Another practice which largely prevails is to have in the parochial schools what is known as a high-school class, where a select number of children are prepared for the public high schools. I think that this practice is not admissible for the reason that the danger to faith and morals which are inherent to the public-school system are multiplied for those children whose elementary training has been acquired in the parochial schools. The change of discipline and method and the sudden elimination of religious teaching can not but exercise on children of that age a reactionary influence. To my mind, it were better to frankly accept the public-school system as a whole, and counteract its ignoring of religion by extra religious training at home and in church, than to subject children to contrary systems of education at a time of life when they are so susceptible of impressions and so incapable of independent reasoning. It seems to me that there is far less danger in sending Catholic young men to non-Catholic institutions and professional schools than in transplanting parochial-school children to the public high schools.

Since, then, neither of these remedies is calculated to cure the great defect which exists in our educational system, it behooves us to consider what right and feasible remedy should be employed. To every one will occur at once the rational remedy of supplementing our parochial or primary school systems by an organized system of secondary or high schools. This is what the State has done all around us; and, as long as we find ourselves obliged to recommend Catholic children not to frequent the State schools, we are bound to supply them with schools equally good.

But how establish and conduct these Catholic high schools? The first question admits, I think, of three solutions. One would be the establishment and endowment of high schools in different localities by private munificence. This is the solution arrived at in Philadelphia, where the late Mr. Cahill founded and endowed forever the high school which bears his name. It is possible that his noble example may be followed elsewhere. It is certain that the greatest benefactors of their day and of their kind would be those who would erect and endow such institutions for the higher education of Catholic youth. For knowledge is power. The earth belongs to man, that is to the disciplined intellect of man, and the future position of our Catholic people in this country will depend chiefly on the extent and quality of their education. Add to the morality and fruitfulness of our people the cultured intellect and the disciplined character, and you have a power that is irresistible and securely triumphant in spreading the kingdom of God. What nobler use could a man make of the superabundance of his means than to devote it to achieving such far-reaching results?

As this solution, depending on private munificence, can reach only a very limited number of centers, some other must be found capable of general application. Such a solution would be to have all the Catholic elements of a given center unite in founding and supporting a Catholic high school. Building and equipments might be m re or less imposing, according to the means at the disposal of the body corporate, but the teaching should equal, at least, that given in the public high school of the place.

It appears to me quite feasible to establish and support a free Catholic high school in every important center. It is true that our people are already heavily taxed, first to educate everybody else's children, and then taxed again to educate their own. But the generosity which has done such wonders in the way of building up churches and schools will be found equal to the task of completing the good work begun in the parochial schools, once it becomes convinced of the necessity of such sacrifices. It is difficult to calculate exactly the expense which the establishment of a high school would entail on the several parishes of a district. It would largely depend on the number and sizes of the parishes. It may, however, be safely said that $50 a year for each pupil sent to the high school would cover all expenses. Some understanding could be entered into between the several parishes whereby would be regulated the maximum and the minimum number of pupils which each would be expected to maintain in the high school.

We, the Catholics of the United States, are committed, for the present at least, not of choice but of necessity, to an educational system of our own. Duty, honor, and self-interest imperatively call on us to make our system as perfect as possible. Every instruction on this subject sent by the Holy See—from the celebrated one given by the propaganda to the American bishops before the council of Baltimore down to the latest utterance of Leo XIII., who quotes approvingly the idea of his delegate, "omni tamen ratione et ope connitendum esse ut scholae Catholicae quam plures suit numero omnique re ornatae et perfectae"—every instruction from the Holy See insists as a condition of the existence of our schools that they be made at least as efficient as those of the State. Justice to the secular interests of our people demands this. The honor of our olden church demands it. And there is no reason why our united efforts and sacrifices should not be equal to the demand. Our primary and parochial schools are already on a good footing, and once all the dioceses will have exerted themselves to carry out the letter and spirit of the Third Plenary Council regarding them we shall have our primary schools efficient and well equipped—"omni re perfectae et ornatae."

But we must not rest satisfied with this. We must not constrain our people to delve all their lives in the lowlands whilst their neighbors are carried up by higher education to the rich and beautiful plateaus. Not only the material interests of our people, but the interests of education itself require that we supplement our primary schools by well-equipped high schools. The entrance examinations to high school, the value of free scholarships therein, the competition to obtain them, would be a most powerful stimulus to the lower schools. Again the high school would serve as a feeder for seminary and university.

And what more suitable occasion could there be for considering and promoting such a project? Here in this Catholic Congress we have gathered together bishops, priests, and laity. It were well if the laity took a more active part in the carrying out of our educational system. It seems to me that too much burden has been thrown in the past on the shoulders of the clergy and of the religious communities. There is no portion of the church that can do so much for secular education as a loyal and progressive laity. The composition of this Congress is a proof that the church in America possesses such a laity, loyal to the unchangeable teachings of divine faith, progressive with the best progress of modern times and civilization. It is with them will lie the carrying into practical effect what I have been pleading for. And I trust, in conclusion, that the importance of the subject, the pressing needs of our people, the opportuneness of the time and the suitableness of the occasion will add in the minds of all the members of this Congress—bishops, priests, and laymen—a thousandfold force to this, my poor plea for free Catholic high schools.

"Young Men's Societies" was the subject of a paper presented by Warren E. Mosher, of Youngstown, Ohio. The reading of this paper was listened to with marked attention, and it is given here in full for the benefit and enlightenment of the rising generation of the Catholics of the United States:

In its battle against evil the church to-day is working without what should be its most powerful force—a vigorous, enthusiastic, zealous, and united young manhood. How to win this support is one of the most important problems now confronting the Catholics of America.

The improvement of the young men has ever been a vital question in all ages and among all classes. The spiritual, intellectual, and moral advancement of young men means the advancement of social conditions generally. It means a decrease in the statistics of crime and in the occupants of prisons, and an increase of those institutions beneficial to the arts and manufactures—it means the advancement of higher civilization. It means happy homes, with mothers peacefully secure in the possession of sons guarded by the armor of strong, manly character and Christian virtues, and with wives blessed in the possession of husbands conscious of the sanctity of marriage and with the nobility to faithfully discharge the duties of their state.

There are three great and powerful agencies at work in molding the character and shaping the destiny of young men—the church, the home, and society. The former is constantly striving to rescue them from the vices acquired in most cases, and fostered by the licenses granted by society.

Society indulges the human passions of young men, and gives them the license and opportunity to gratify them. And finally, when, from the excess of indulgence, society suffers from outrages committed against her by the victims she has created and the vices she has encouraged, she pays back the revenue she has derived from the licensing of necessary evils in the maintenance of institutions of correction and reform. The home, according to its teachings, increases the evils of society or the blessings of the church. That these three great agencies do not always work in harmony and union is a deplorable fact.

Among the many institutions established and encouraged by the church as a safeguard for young men are young men's societies having for their object their religious, intellectual, social, physical, and material improvement.

The Third Plenary Council of Baltimore has ruled on this question in a manner that leaves it unnecessary to discuss the advisability of organizing young men's societies, as follows: "Since the young men are exposed to greater danger, we wish that special care be taken of them. Hence we decree that in every parish or mission where a sufficient number of them can be found, special societies be established for them by the rector, and that they be cherished with all possible care. For without associations of this nature the work begun in the parochial schools of saving the Catholic youth will, for the most part, have been in vain, and our young men, who have been so carefully guarded from their infancy, will be seduced by the allurements of the world, and will be swallowed up in the vortex of the forbidden societies. But when banded together in respectable societies, they will, while pursuing some temporal object, be readily induced by a prudent pastor to join thereto the cultivation of piety."—Title viii., par. 257.

That the parish society, under the direction of a zealous priest and with the co-operation of earnest, self-sacrificing young men, has a great influence for good is unquestioned. The methods of conducting parish societies may vary with the various conditions of young men in the different parts of the country, but the object is one and specific.

That the parish society is not accomplishing all that could be desired or all that it might is also unquestioned. The cry for improvement is to-day ringing out from pulpit, press, and convention hall. It is engaging the attention of every thoughtful man anxious for the preservation of youth; and noble men have spent the best part of their life and brain in devising means for saving our young men. It is only necessary to read the reports of our annual conventions to learn how much attention is given to this subject, and how clearly and eloquently innumerable methods have been set forth by all champions of young men. There is no lack of good features, no lack of excellent suggestions for improvement, but a great lack of young men who will act upon the suggestions proposed, even while admitting they are good.

As the work for the improvement of young men by means of societies goes on, it is assailed by the snarling and carping criticism of some, and neglected by the almost criminal indifference of others, while comparatively a handful of young men, in the face of the most discouraging difficulties, without system and without means, are struggling valiantly in the cause; and these young men are not the ones most in need of society influences.

I believe the existing condition of affairs can be improved, and in submitting the following suggestions to the Columbian Catholic Congress I also offer my humble services to practically execute them in order to demonstrate their success or failure.

In order to create among existing societies an intelligent system of co-operation, to quicken the feelings of sympathy and fellowship, and to promote a friendly and practical union, I would suggest that State organizations be formed, subdivided by dioceses, and that in each State paid secretaries be appointed by the bishops of the State, or elected by the several societies, who would give their whole time to the work of young men's societies. These men should be thoroughly familiar with the wants of our young men's institutes. They should be from among the very ablest of our ranks. They should visit cities and towns where societies are already established and infuse new life into them, and awaken the ambition to achieve their highest aims. Where no societies exist, they should organize them, always, of course, with the approval and, if possible, the co-operation of the clergy. They should assist in establishing lecture courses, and take an active part in every plan for improvement. Ex-officio, they could be members of all societies. These men would exert a vivifying influence, they would be the link connecting all the societies of the State into one strong cohesive chain; their visits would always stimulate activity, bringing, as they would, fresh ideas, or shedding brighter luster over already successful methods.

There should also be paid national secretaries and a national bureau.

It would be difficult to find young men to do this work, even though the means were at hand; for a young man with the qualifications necessary for such work can command better compensation in many pursuits offering distinction and honor, notwithstanding that there could be no nobler occupation.

The men eminently fitted for this work are active young priests. Their education and training, and above all, their profession, qualify them above other men. They would command respect and attention where a layman would be ignored or snubbed. Can our bishops spare them for this work? Will they spare them? It is one of the most fruitful fields for missionary labor within the domain of the church, and I believe the results would amply repay the efforts expended.

1. The expenses of these secretaries could be borne by the societies of the State.

One of the greatest necessities of the present day is the establishment of a system of young men's institutions, combining, to some extent, the polytechnic, the lyceum, and the social association. Every city that can afford such an institution should have one, the metropolitan cities many.

In a few places Catholic young men have erected their own homes; there are many cities amply able to do likewise. To succeed, parish barriers must be thrown down. Few parishes can afford to maintain alone such an institution, but by a concentration of forces an association building might be erected for the Catholics of the whole community.

The Catholic young men of to-day must keep pace with the progress of the country. The days of the back room and top story are past, and the commodious, centrally located building, equipped and adjusted to the special needs of young men, will supplant them, as they should.

2. The only saving power of our young men is the faithful practice of their religion. With all the societies for the cultivation of piety among the laity now existing within the church it is a noted fact that their membership is composed almost entirely of women. There is not to-day an auxiliary league of the church that appeals as successfully to the religious sentiment in young men as it does to this sentiment in young women. It may not be possible to accomplish this equality, but I believe the inequality can be lessened. I do not believe the days of chivalry died with the ages of the Crusades. An appeal to the manhood of young men would arouse them in this age as it did in previous times, and for this purpose I suggest the institution of a league of young men to be known as the Loyal Catholic Legion, or by some such significant title, the members of which shall subscribe to the faithful observance of the principles of honor, purity, knightly conduct, and practical Catholicity. There might be degrees in this league and special indulgences, as in the League of the Sacred Heart and other orders, and leaders and promoters appointed.

This order would not conflict with existing orders. It would be open to all young men, whether members of societies or of no society. There need be no fees, or simply a nominal fee for offerings. Several young men in a society might institute a branch of the league voluntarily for the observance of these principles; and young men not of the society could be members of the same local branch. An independent headquarters with general directors might be established, or the league might be under the direction of the directors of the League of the Sacred Heart, or some other established order.

This idea of putting young men on their honor by the institution of such a league occurred to me several months ago with a suddenness that thrilled me. It has impressed me with a most singular power, and my confidence in its efficacy is very great. I have consulted my pastor and several distinguished priests and laymen, who expressed their earnest approval of the idea. There is a charm, a fascination in it that engenders an intense, fervent feeling for manly perfection and religious piety. It appeals to the manhood of young men.

Let us resurrect this spirit of chivalry among young men. The spirit of manliness is not dead but sleeping, and the spark of chivalry in the breasts of young American Catholics might be fanned into a flame that would develop knights as true as ever gave up their lives in the cause of righteousness or for the possession of the Holy Sepulchre.

For the improvement of young men and young men's societies, I therefore urge the adoption of these three movements: (1) Traveling leaders or organizers, who shall, if possible, be young, active priests. (2) The establishment of special buildings adapted for the requirements of young men, with salaried secretaries. (3) A league of Catholic young men on the lines suggested above. The adoption of the first suggestion would ultimately bring the other two into practical operation, for men traveling in this cause could establish such a society as the needs of a place demanded and as it could support, whether it be the parish society or the general institute.

Let us throw open our young men's institutions to every Catholic young man, whether he be an active paying member or not. At least give them all some privileges, such as free reading-rooms and comfortable sitting-rooms. Under our present system there is an exclusiveness that repels rather than attracts our young men. We must come in contact with them and endeavor to bring them within a pure atmosphere and among pure associations. The less restraint we put in their way the better. The church closes its doors to none, whether they give much or nothing to its support. Then why not have a home for young men supported by all the Catholics of our communities, as free as our churches, and whose doors shall be open to a limited share of our privileges without all the qualifications of perfect young manhood? This is a kind of institution needed in our day.

There is a barrier growing up between Catholic young men and women, which is getting stronger year by year—the barrier of education and refinement. The only remedy that I can suggest for this impediment between our young people is to cultivate with equal zeal and in equal numbers the advantages offered for the acquirement of these accomplishments.

There is an object lesson for the young men here to-day in the City of Chicago that should appeal to their better parts more strongly than all the sermons and essays they ever heard. Here is the greatest exhibition of human skill and material wealth the world has ever seen, and its accomplishment was made possible by Catholic genius.

HON. C. C. BONNEY,
CHICAGO.
JOHN GIBBONS, LL. D.,
CHICAGO.
THOMAS F. RING,
BOSTON.

DR. AUGUST KAISER,
DETROIT.

MAURICE F. EGAN, LL. D.
NOTRE DAME, IND.

COL. R. M. DOUGLAS, LL. D.
GREENBORO.
HENRY C. SEMPLE,
MONTGOMERY.
E. O. BROWN,
CHICAGO.

In conclusion, let me appeal to this distinguished body to give generously of their time and means for the preservation of our Catholic youth. Think of the energy that is lost in the cause of religion by the apathy and indifference of young men! Watch a political campaign and notice the enthusiasm displayed. If half the amount were expended in the following of Christ that is wasted on political demagogues frequently, what a reform there would be in civil government. Watch a baseball game and reflect on the result that would follow such energy exercised for religion. Listen to the mighty shouts that ascend to heaven over the victory of some brutal champion of the prize ring and see the indifference shown to the hero of Molokai. We want this force, this unbounded energy of young manhood harnessed to the chariot of practical Christianity, and until we secure it the race for the salvation of souls will be run against tremendous odds.

Let us love the young men, encourage them, aid them, not for what they are but for the temptations which are theirs and for the glorious manhood that might be theirs.

"Working Men's Organizations and Societies for Young Men," was the subject of a paper read by Rev. F. J. McGuire, of Albany, N. Y., President of the Catholic Young Men's National Union of the United States. This is what he said:

The genius of our national being is peculiarly suggestive of union and combination. Composed of many states and communities, these made up of various people to whom is given a common adhesive principle, and on all of whom it is impressed that unity of purpose and of government is the chief security of their national existence, the rational aim of all who have part in the framing of our laws, or of those who are clothed with the dignity of administering them, should be to foster and strengthen a spirit of union among the people.

The public "society" of St. Thomas, wherein "Men may communicate with one another in the setting up of a commonwealth," exists here in its fullness, but it is enriched and made doubly lasting, in that it possesses all the features and benefits of the more "private society, wherein a few may be conjoined for the following and attaining of a common purpose." For, the first and ordinary object of our common citizenship is to perpetuate union of the many for the good of all; for we are all equal on the plane of our national constitution, and equal in the rights of liberty which it secures to us. Hence there is a congenial abode in our country for that "propensity" called natural "of man to live in society," which has its foundation in the natural law which is sanctioned in the sacred scriptures, and in whose favor our Sovereign Pontiff, Pope Leo XIII., has addressed the universal church so earnestly.

From the first years of her existence the United States has been a prolific mother of societies of men. Her great political parties, which have aimed at a balancing of power, whose struggles, successes, or failures have been marked by the ruling for a time of one, to be in turn succeeded by the other, has been simply the organizing of many societies into one, the welding together of many for a common purpose. In earlier years she fashioned associations for military exercise ostensibly, which, being without governmental control, for a long time were so many private or even social societies of free men. Yet, in her day of need, these evolved into the grandest armies the world had seen, and achieved victories among the most valued of all history.

In equally gigantic form have we witnessed the growth in our land of the extensive railroad and telegraphic combinations, which were originally fondled by our government, as promising many facilities and advantages to the commonwealth, but which latterly penetrating every corner of the public domain, and, absorbing less powerful enterprise, have again and again excited the anxiety or provoked the condemnation of many of the most sincere friends of our national interest.

Here, too, individuals have united for the promotion or accomplishment of almost every lesser object. The practice of religious tenets, the diffusion of knowledge, the protection of art and science, the perfection of varied skill of the mechanic or laborer, the alleviation of the miseries to which man is heir, and security from the results which come with accident and death, have in turn formed pretext for association; and in this feature our country is said to be a leading representative among the nations.

Such is the prospect which greets the view of the observer of to-day. The Catholic American, enriched with the birthright of true citizenship, is especially interested in this prospect; and so, as well because of facilities which it presents to him, as because of his peculiar fitness to reap rich advantage and the magnificent consequences to his church and to mankind which may result. Our holy religion teaches us that the perfection of Christian effort does not dwell alone in aiming at the loving and serving of God, but must reach out into a love for the welfare of neighbor, and the Catholic watchword must be the twofold sentiment, "God and our neighbor." His duty is not alone to build up churches which are to be the outward sign of an inward sacred and spiritual trust, but he is to build up by his word, his example, and his fidelity to profession, that holier edifice, the Catholic Faith, which, not built by hands, is as imperishable as her Divine Founder.

What are his facilities? Our brethren, guided by pious promptings, were the first of the civilized world to tread this continent and they offered it to God to be His in perpetuum. As the years revolved others came upon the scene, and for a long time the principles of our holy faith held but a tolerated existence here. It required the blood of some martyrs, the painful labors of some of the most illustrious saints and scholars of the last century to retrieve the liberty which Catholics first secured by the right of discovery here.

Meantime, in this fair field an enemy hath sown cockle. Here we find every species of belief or practice which has been known in the history of the human race. The consequence is a state of society not only detrimental to the immediate interests of Christ, but even menacing to that destiny of perpetuated greatness to which the American nation seems to have been called by the Creator.

As friends of humanity we can not afford to belittle the goodness of life of many outside the Catholic Church, of which goodness we have been frequent witnesses; but still we must not refrain from proclaiming that the Catholic Church, which gave to the nations of the earth all that has sustained and made them worthy of the respect of succeeding ages, is still, as representing her Divine Founder, "The only name under heaven given to men whereby they can be saved." It is for us duty and obligation to declare this by work as well as by word. In conjunction with the pulpit, then, may we not find in Catholic societies a most perfectly adapted channel for the conducting of this spirit to the people? Nay, do we not perceive with our Sovereign Pontiff, that in such associating together of our people "there is cheering hope for the future of the church" in America? Associating them not simply for the purpose of presenting a united front against those who may oppose us, but for the purpose of cultivating such a spirit of Christianity as will make each individual Catholic a power for good "terrible as an army set in array."

I have referred to the peculiar fitness of our Catholics for society rule and life. The Catholic who knows his church or is accustomed to scrutinize her sacred character has learned to love her for her unity and the unity which she inculcates. Likened to the mysterious unity existing between her Divine Founder and herself—one in doctrine, in doctors, and in pupils; one on earth and in heaven—in the midst of this world's kingdom, which is ever and in all things divided,and hence ever falling,this solitary claimant of perpetual oneness must gladden and delight the heart that loves unchanging truth. He knows, too, that so close is the unity which must exist, that in this family of God there can be no distinction of any kind. The poor are enriched with blessedness; the wayward or hurtful are to be forgiven; the richest possessions of one are most precious inasmuch as they can alleviate the needs of another, and the only badge of discipleship in Christ that is prescribed is the love which one bears toward another.

Graced with such a spirit of unity and manifesting it in each society duty, what a magnificent form of organization is within the capabilities of the good Catholic man! How far superior in its aims and in the actual results of its existence as compared to societies which have for their object a pretense of righteousness, or which often have expended their best ambition when they have destroyed by proselytism the only dignity or worth which their victims possessed. A truly Catholic society can be a bulwark of all that is calculated to subserve the public good. Morality will be a distinguishing characteristic of its members; temperance and all the virtues will flourish under its sway, and the community in which it exists must acknowledge the charity from which it came forth and the Faith which sustains it.

But our Holy Father voices the actual state of our country when he says in his encyclical, "There is a good deal of evidence which goes to prove that many existing societies are in the hands of invisible leaders, and are managed on principles far from compatible with Christianity and the public well-being." In the presence of this well-known fact, what is the plain duty of Christians if it be not to seek desired good through societies of their own founding and management? Or, as our Holy Father again expresses it, "Unite their forces and courageously shake off the yoke of unjust and intolerable oppression."

Aside from the essential features of "unity of purpose and harmony of action," it would be difficult to prescribe detailed formulas or to set precise rules for the regulating of Catholic societies, since the vastness of our country in region, in disposition, and needs of our brethren is so varied. The experience and practice of those who have been prominent in such works (and they are not a few in our midst) should be consulted. Let us bear in mind the fact that the Christian family should be the foundation of the life of the Catholic society. Here, as all agree, there should be capable supervision, reasonable discipline in its fullness, unquestioning respect, and obedience and interest for the common good. I believe to the absence of this family training chiefly may we trace all the obstacles which lie in the way of Catholic society work, whether in the founding or conducting of such. It will seldom be difficult to continue and develop in the society the work which has been nurtured in the bosom of the Christian home. The boy who enters his sodality with the graces of the first sacraments on him will quickly learn to love the petty strifes and contentions by which he may pardonably hope to evince his superior gifts or command the respect of his associates. Early will he develop the characteristics and powers which will make him useful in the parish association, or in turn command respect for the organization which affords scope and opportunity for the exercise of the gifts of his maturer years.

After due consideration of the matter of grading, especially as to age, which should be observed in the membership of an association, it remains to be said that societies whose every prompting tends to the seeking of God and His justice, to the end that the members may be increased in all lesser things, are the best. In other words, societies under the supervision of the pastors. In these, mental and physical attainments might be ambitioned, and the members, while protected from the dangers of evil associations, might find reasonable recreation; but in these must be exercised such influences only as can tend toward the development of true Catholic manhood. It is an obvious fact that many of our American Catholic men, and, indeed, in some sections of the country, our women as well, are entering societies that are ruinous to their best spiritual interests. Especially is this true of our young men. It has been computed that not three-tenths of the Catholic young men of the United States are connected with any Catholic society. For the sake of their qualities of body and mind they are being sought after by those who have no desire for their souls' welfare; or they are allured by tempting immunity given in return for their sacrifice of faith. In these ways the interest and active co-operation of thousands of her young men are being lost to the church annually.

What means have we to reach and use and save this portion of the flock of Christ—this multitude so full of the vanity and the pride peculiar to their years, yet ever so dear to the heart of Jesus—other than by gathering them into societies especially established for them? It costs effort, but is there any work more worthy the zeal of an apostolic man than is this? In some European countries it is said the children are kept in religious training until their first communion, or twelfth year, and after that time they are committed to the keeping of the secular studies. Some have traced to this very cause the Catholic indifference or defection so painfully remarkable in Europe during the past quarter of a century. We know from our sad experience that in our own country it frequently happens that the study of religion ceases on the day of first communion, to be resumed no more—not, indeed, because sufficient has been learned, but because of fatigue from restraint, or because of joy at having been admitted to the sacred privileges of their elders, young people are loath to continue a formal study of religion. Well regulated societies in which the priest and young man may continue to meet, and in which the sacred relation of pastor and child may be perpetuated, is a tried and effectual means of avoiding evil of so great magnitude.

An oft-proposed query is, what is the best form or rule for a Catholic society? Some advocates of men's societies find scope for their zeal in the admirable institute known as the Young Men's Sodality, and certainly a more perfect rule, or one that is permissive of more that can benefit or enrich manly character, is not known. The purely literary association with the athletic feature annexed has proved its value by extraordinary examples of success in many portions of the United States. The strictly beneficiary society, with what is called social accompaniments, as under the management of the Catholic Benevolent Legion or Catholic Mutual Benevolent Association, is a scheme that has been warmly received by our people, and the admirable supervision during the past decade of these associations has elicited the respect and confidence of the public generally. There is no doubt that these societies are gradually destroying the hurtful influence which Masonry, Oddfellowism, and other objectionable organizations have heretofore wielded over careless Catholics. The financial benefits which they confer have done much to lessen poverty and to establish families in thrifty ways, and their continued success is worthy the deepest attention of all interested in the welfare of the Catholic community.

Surely there is no dearth of admirable forms for association. Yet it would be difficult to account for the fact that there are so many well-established congregations in the United States in which there are no societies for men. It would be equally difficult to account for the indifference to Catholic associations, especially on the part of our young men, in places where good societies are established and where need and facilities for work such as theirs are so pronounced. Certainly this class of our people, the future hope of the church, ought to be a source of concern and object of our care. Theirs is a time of life which craves for association or such companionship as will increase the pleasurable occupations of life. Does it not seem that we should, if necessary, make sacrifices for them as we do for other church works? Should not the church afford them meeting places, or any facility which might induce them to come and attract them to remain in Catholic societies? This would imply expenditure. We rightly contribute to convert and civilize the pagan. Is there anything less laudable in similar effort to save our youth from degradation? Give them a positive rule for their association and exact their observance, but allow them such liberty as is consistent with propriety. Especially do not treat them as infants whose every fault demands humiliating punishment, but labor to develop (again I repeat it) a character of dignified manhood. The natural spirit of young American manhood is pride and independence. Legions of satans, like roaring lions, are daily devouring the youth of our church for this very fact; but, friends of Catholic young men, if we can sanctify this spirit by religionizing it, we will thereby secure to our church generations of devoted men, and to our country a spirit of intelligence and patriotism that can ennoble her institutions or save her in her day of trial.

It has occurred more than once within our knowledge that men who have assumed and graced most exalted positions in public life have had little other advantages than these which they had secured in the Catholic society room, where, under the inspiration of devoted priests, they have imbibed rich principles of manhood, and attained a perfection in gracious talent which have made them objects of pride to their friends and of pleasurable envy to their less-gifted fellows.

Brother Azarias, of Manhattan College, died since preparing his most eloquent address upon " Our Catholic School System." His name upon the programme was appropriately bordered with black. The paper was read by his learned brother, Rev. John F. Mullaney, of Syracuse, N. Y. As an enthusiast on the subject of Catholic education, Brother Azarias had no equal, and when the paper was read, touching reference was made to the brother's interest in the subject upon which he wrote substantially as follows:

Our Catholic school system embraces all grades of institutions from the kindergarten to the university. Each religious teaching order has its own methods. But in the midst of variety a unity of purpose runs through all our educational institutions. This purpose is to impart a thorough Catholic training to our Catholic children.

That portion of our system most cherished is the parochial school. It has been erected and it is maintained at many sacrifices. It is indispensable for the preservation of the Catholic faith in the hearts of Catholic children. There may be difference of opinion as to the ways and means by which Catholic education is to be imparted and Catholic schools are to be supported, but there can be none regarding the self-evident truth that the church in America is to be perpetuated in a robust, God-fearing and God-serving Catholicity, it is only by the establishment of a Catholic school in every Catholic parish. The Catholic school is the nursery of the Catholic congregation, the inclosed garden in which are fostered vocations to the priesthood and to religious life; in a word, the hope and the mainstay of the church in the future.

When we consider the history of Catholic education during the fifty years that have just elapsed, and note the many serious obstacles our Catholic schools have had to contend with, and at the same time go over the roll-call of prominent Catholics who have had their early training in these schools—archbishops and bishops and priests, and religious men and women whose vocations have been fostered in them; eminent laymen now filling positions of trust and honor, whose consciences were there formed, and who had there learned to be proud of their faith and to praise its teachings to the best of their ability—we are compelled to regard these schools, even in their least efficient forms, with great respect. In no sense are they failures; in no sense are they to be abandoned or neglected; rather, in the very words of Leo XIII. concerning these schools, "every effort should be made to multiply Catholic schools, and to bring them to perfect equipment."

Next in importance to the parish school is the convent school. It is a choice garden attached to the Lord's household, in which the sweetest flowers of virtue are tendered and fostered by women of piety, zeal, and culture. Its influence extends far and wide throughout the land. Among the leading social forces in America to-day, the women whose power for good is most far-reaching are pupils of the convent school. The tendency in these latter days is to make woman as independent as she possibly can become.

There are still untried possibilities in our Catholic school system. Why, for instance, may we not have large commercial schools in our principal cities? Not mere business academies, in which a knowledge of penmanship and accounts is imparted, but schools established on a broad basis, in which chemistry and the sciences as applied to the industries and manufactures would be taught, in which political economy, and common law, and history, and literature would be studied from the Catholic point of view. Such schools would benefit a large class of our Catholic young men.

Again, there are Catholic boys who have been obliged to quit school at an early age for the workshop or the factory, and who with riper years and larger experience feel the necessity of making up for early deficiencies. What accommodation have we for this class? Practically none. Could not Catholic night schools flourish in our larger cities? They would be a great boon to our working boys and working girls. It is painful to witness in large cities the active aggressiveness of those who misunderstand and misrepresent our faith. They attract to their soup-houses and night schools hordes of our Catholic Italian and Bohemian children and inoculate them with un-Catholic and anti-Catholic ideas, while little or nothing is done to counteract their machinations. This is work for our Catholic laity.

The more cultured class of Catholic young men and women are now supplementing their school studies by reading circles and literary clubs. These are so many annexes to our educational system, and as such are not to be overlooked.

Another institution that has grown out of our reading circles, and that bids fair to become an intimate portion of our Catholic system of education, is the Catholic summer school. In this manner is an antidote administered against the intellectual and moral poison that is imbibed from the secular journals, magazines, and reviews.

For the completion of our Catholic school system we look forward to the time when our Catholic university shall be able to supply our colleges and academies with specialists in the various branches taught, and when we will have Catholic normal schools to supply Catholic teachers to our parochial schools. The State normal schools do not suffice. They prepare teachers, but not Catholic teachers. In their books on educational methods they ignore or condemn our great Catholic educators. Moreover, the Catholic teacher whose faith during the whole course of his training has been ignored in its historical, literary, and religious aspects, whose mind has become imbued directly or indirectly with Protestant estimates of men and events, whose training has been purely negative so far as his religion with all its glories in art, in history, and literature is concerned—such a teacher is no longer fitted to take charge of a Catholic school. He is lacking in religious knowledge, in devotion, and in a robust Catholic spirit. He is timid where his faith is concerned. He is afraid to assert his Catholicity lest he give offense. He lacks that delicate sense of appreciation of the spiritual and supernatural —that ideal standard of worth which prizes the salvation of a soul above all other things.

There are exceptions to this estimate. But those exceptions will be the first to confirm it, and to prove that if we are to have Catholic teachers worthy of the name to aid and strengthen the work of our religious teaching orders, they should be trained in Catholic normal schools.

The committee appointed by the Fourth Congress of Colored Catholics to prepare an address to the clergy and laity issued the document contemplated by its appointment. The address covers the points discussed in the sessions of the Congress, and represents its work and conclusions. It is as follows:

COLORED CATHOLICS ADDRESS.

At this point a motion was made by a Texas delegate to invite the members of the Colored Catholic Congress and the other associations meeting in the building to the floor of the Congress.

Archbishop Ireland came forward again. "I beg leave to express the utmost delight of my heart," he said, "that a proposition was made to invite here the members of the Catholic Colored Congress. Let us, the members of the Catholic Columbian Congress, show our thorough Catholicity, and in God's name invite them all. I have but one regret—that they are not one hundred fold more numerous."

Colored Catholics opened their Congress in hall 6. Delegates were in attendance from New York, Pennsylvania, Maryland, South Carolina, Ohio, Louisiana, Minnesota, Missouri, and the District of Columbia, and in addition to these there was a large general attendance of colored communicants of the church.

James A. Spencer, of South Carolina, was the presiding officer, and Dr. W. S. Lofton, of Washington, D. C., and D. A. Rudd, of Ohio, were the secretaries. The meeting was opened with prayer by Rev. Father Tolton. Then followed an address of welcome by L. C. Valle, to which an appropriate response was made by W. Edgar Easton, of Texas. Brief addresses were also made by F. L. McGhee, of St. Paul, and Mr. Reed, of Pennsylvania. Committees were then appointed as follows:

Credentials—C. H. Butler, Washington, D. C.; S. P. Havis, Arkansas; L. C. Valle, Illinois; R. N. Wood, New York.

Permanent organization—R. N. Wood, New York; W. J. Smith, Washington, D. C.; S. K. Govern, Pennsylvania; W. E. Easton, Texas; D. A. Rudd, Ohio.

Rules and order of business—S. K. Govern, Pennsylvania; F. L. McGhee, Minnesota; D. A. Rudd, Ohio.

The Congress adjourned to this morning at 9 o'clock.

J. J. Smith, of Davenport, Iowa; J. F. Brown, of Galveston, Texas; T. C. Driscoll, of Hartford, Conn.; David Garrity, of Milwaukee, and Felix McGill, of Mobile, Ala., were appointed a committee to carry out the wishes of the Congress in this respect. Then the meeting settled down to listen to prepared papers on the social problems of the day.

The Congress of Colored Catholics sat with closed doors most of the day, considering questions relating exclusively to the interests of the colored man. The invitation to join the great Columbian Catholic Congress was accepted, and the colored men immediately took a recess and visited that body. In the afternoon a committee was appointed to prepare an address. It consists of W. Edgar Easton, Texas; F. L. McGhee, Minnesota; C. H. Butler, District of Columbia; L. C. Valle, Illinois; Daniel A. Rudd, Ohio; W. J. Smith, District of Columbia; S. K. Govern, Pennsylvania; W. S. Lofton, District of Columbia; S. P. Havis, Arkansas. Miss Jessie Schley proposed as a question of discussion, "Why Should Not the Negro Go Back to Africa?" The remainder of the afternoon was occupied in discussing the subject.

Charles H. Butler, of Washington, D. C., read the following paper on "The Condition and Future of the Negro Race in the United States."

THE FUTURE OF THE NEGRO RACE.

The subject of the paper that I have been invited to prepare for your consideration, "The Condition and Future of the Negro Race in the United States," can in no sense be considered a new one. It has been constantly before the people of this country since the establishment of the government itself. It has been discussed in the church, on the rostrum and in politics. The negro has been a conspicuous figure in our body politic, and like the ghost in Macbeth, "It will not down." I come from the common people, with no special ability to produce a paper with well-set phrases, or to say anything new upon an old and well-worn subject. But I shall a plain unvarnished tale deliver and leave the rest to you and God.

Passing over the terrible story of the negro's sufferings in slavery days, I would date his existence from the time of his emancipation. From that day, by reason of a great war necessity, the President of the United States signed with his hand, and caused the seal of the United States to be placed upon it, that immortal instrument which struck the shackles from millions of human beings. I would mark his existence as a man from that January morning, when he whom God had created in His own image and likeness was declared free. Free without a dollar, without education. His best and most sincere friends believed that he could not exist, but that he would be swept from the face of the earth. The Most Reverend Archbishop of Philadelphia, in his address of welcome to the Third Colored Catholic Congress held in Philadelphia, January 1892, said: "Many trembled at the proclamation of emancipation. Even the friends of the colored race believed that the time had not come." I frankly admit that at that time there was much to justify the belief. The greater part of the emancipated slaves remained in the midst of their former oppressions, and sought to work out their own salvation through fear and trembling.

The history of their sufferings has been recorded by Him who knows the secrets of all hearts. Their sufferings were not unlike the sufferings of the Israelites of old, who were held in bondage for 400 years. History oft repeats itself. A chain of unfortunate circumstances followed the emancipation in rapid succession and placed the negro at a disadvantage. The period of reconstruction followed. The interests of the negro fell into the hands of men, many of whom were selfish and unscrupulous, who cared very little for his welfare and valued nothing but his vote.

It can not be said that during this period he made much progress, mentally or morally. True, now and then a single man under favorable circumstances rose up by force of intellect and did attain a respectable and commanding position. But his eminence served only to mark with greater emphasis the inferior condition of the race to which he belonged.

There is one thing that can be said to the credit of the reconstructed party. They established schools for the poor and illiterate, both white and black, and when they fell the school system remained. But the exit of this party left no kindly feeling toward the negro. He was the visible representative of antagonism. The white man held the negro responsible for the unhappy conflict that brought ruin financially to his nation's soil. He was held responsible for the acts of men who did not represent him, although they used him, and for those acts the negro paid dearly, being made the victim of political murders and outrages, the subject of a bitter ostracism that denied him any chance to improve his condition, and finally forced him to become an outcast from his native soil.

I have not the time to touch upon the exodus of the negro race from the Southern States, but it is one of the most thrilling incidents in his struggle for life, liberty, and the pursuit of happiness. I do not think I would be doing justice to my subject if I did not here make mention of it. That movement has often been referred to as a political movement and passed upon lightly by our white fellow-citizens; but it was a natural operation of divine law that moved those communities of negroes to turn their faces towards the setting sun. They were willing to endure any hardship short of death to reach a land where, under their own vine and fig trees, they could enjoy the life our Creator intended for them.

The failure of that institution organized and chartered by the government, known as the Freedman's Savings Bank, did much to sow the seeds of distrust among the freedmen of the South. Sixty-two thousand one hundred and thirty-one depositors had faithfully carried their wages to the government bank. The books of that institution showed that $3,000,000 had been placed to their credit, for freedom had inspired them, and they were using its opportunity to secure a competency in the hope of becoming, some day, property owners, and of holding up their heads as men in the land where they had once been slaves. Because of the failure of that bank they did not lose heart. They tried again, and to-day own $263,000,000 worth of property. In the Southern States it is said the negroes' wealth is as follows:

Alabama	$ 4,200,125
Florida	7,900,400
Arkansas	8,010,315
Georgia	10,415,330
Kentucky	5,900,400
Mississippi	13,490,213
North Carolina	11,010,652
Texas	18,010,545

Virginia 4,900,000
Louisiana 18,100,528
Missouri 6,600,343
South Carolina 12,500,000
Tennessee 10,400,211

Since history tells us that it took the proud and mighty Saxons a thousand years to emerge from the thralldom of the Roman conquest and to reach a condition akin to modern civilization, I ask all fair-minded persons if this is not a remarkable showing? Let those who oppose the negro and who claim that he has made no progress point to any period of the world's history where any race, even the most favored and under the most favorable conditions, has made as much genuine progress in thirty years as has the despised one.

In the struggle of the negro in the United States I am reminded of the struggle of the Holy Church in America, when prejudice ran riot and it was considered no crime to place the torch to the church or the orphan asylum. But, thank God, those days have passed, and we live in an age when every man's religious convictions are respected and no one is persecuted for opinion's sake. The negro has made mistakes, but they should not be held against him with more force than against any other race. And what race has not made mistakes? Those made by the early leaders of the negro are now being remedied and corrected by the young, more advanced generation of to-day, who are educating the race that they may develop true manhood and character.

It is to be regretted that the Catholic Church did not take earlier steps in the missionary work among the emancipated slaves of the South. Then their calling and election would be sure. The reputation of the church for civilizing and educating nations is established in history. It seems, however, to have been left for the Plenary Council of Baltimore to issue the mandate which called the attention of the Catholics of this country to a sense of duty in this matter. That little mustard seed, planted by Rev. Father Slattery and his co-laborers in Baltimore, is bearing fruit that will have its ultimate result in Catholic schools, with industrial facilities, that will be a most powerful factor in solving the negro problem in the United States. The Protestant Church is greatly in advance of us, for their colleges and industrial schools, supported by white philanthropists of the North, are dotted all over the Southland.

What shall I say of the future of the negro race in the United States? His future depends upon his treatment in a great measure by the white man; whether the proud Anglo-Saxon intends to dispossess himself of mere race prejudice and accord his black brother simple justice. If continual warfare is to be carried on against him because of the accident of color, then all his efforts are in vain. But I am strong to believe that the dust of American prejudice will be cleared from the eyes of our white fellow-citizens, they will learn to discriminate, not by the color of a man's skin, but by the test that all men should adhere to—character and ability.

There is one subject upon which the negro has been greatly misunderstood by his friends, and purposely so by his enemies—they have made the clear and definite term "civil equality" synonymous with that other definite term of entirely different significance, "social equality." If civil equality and social equality had the same application there would be room for complaint, and justly so, but upon a calm and dispassionate thought it must be apparent to all intelligent men that such a thing would be as distasteful to the negro as to the white man. Civil equality makes no such proposal, bears no such result. Public society and civil society comprise one distinct group of mutual relations and private society entirely another, and it is evil to confuse the two. Professor A. F. Hilyer, of Washington, D. C., in treating his subject, said:

"We can take care of ourselves in a social way, but when prejudice sets up an invidious distinction and discrimination in public licensed dining-halls, hotels, and places of amusement, and make them want to exclude us from the avenues of remunerative employments of the commercial world, and make them deny to the most cultured and aspiring among us admission to their best professional, scientific, and literary associations, we think it is a hardship which we, as loyal American citizens, ought not to be compelled to endure."

My voice has been lifted upon many occasions upon this subject of caste prejudice. I have pleaded with all the earnestness of my soul that all the avenues of human activity be opened to the negro race, and that they be given a fair and impartial trial. Will this be done? For upon this rests their case. I can not dismiss this consideration without saying a word to those who would carry their prejudices into the sacred confines of God's holy church, and relegate the negro to an obscure corner of the church, and endeavor to make him feel that he is not as good as the rest of God's creatures for the reason of the accident of his color. How long, oh Lord, are we to endure this hardship in the house of our friends?

We celebrate the 400th year of the discovery of America. Lo, all the nations of the earth are here to do us homage with their presence. I here appeal to you, first as American citizens, second as loyal sons of our Holy Mother, the Church, to assist us to strike down that hybrid monster, color prejudice, which is unworthy of this glorious Republic. We ask it not alone for charity's sake, but as a right that has been dearly paid for. Our labor in concert with the other laborers of the land, has made this World's Columbian Exposition possible. Our valor has been tested in all the three great wars of the Republic. The first man that lost his life in defense of this country in the Revolutionary War, was Crispus Attucks, a negro. Let us quote the language of that immortal bard, the lover of all humanity, John Boyle O'Reilly:

> And honor to Crispus Attucks, who was leader and voice that day,
> The first to defy, and the first to die with Maverick, Carr, and Gray,
> Call it a riot or revolution, his hand first clinched at the crown;
> His feet were the first in perilous place to pull the King's flag down;
> His breast was the first one rent apart that liberty's stream might flow;
> For our freedom now and forever, his head was the first laid low.

William F. Markoe, corresponding secretary of the Catholic Truth Society of America, read the following paper on the possibilities of the society in the United States:

The Catholic Truth Society of America, as declared in its prospectus, is one of the results of the first American Catholic Congress of Baltimore. It is highly proper, therefore, that it should give an account of its origin and progress to the second great American Catholic Congress of Chicago. As many of my hearers may remember, the delegates to that first remarkable gathering had listened to the burning eloquence of some of the most gifted Catholic minds of the country. They are reminded in the most forcible manner that the mission of the church in this country was "To make America Catholic;" that the second century of American Catholic history would be what they made it, and that this was a missionary land in which every Catholic man, woman, and child owed a duty to his neighbor for the performance of which posterity would demand a strict account. Like the apostles issuing from the upper chamber on the day of Pentecost, those delegates returned to their homes filled with religious zeal and patriotic enthusiasm. "Lay action" became the motto of the hour. The question was how could the laity co-operate with the church in her glorious work.

As a result of the interest thus awakened in the matter by the Congress of Baltimore, the Catholic Truth Society was organized on the evening of March 1, 1890, in the archepiscopal residence of St. Paul, Minn., with nine original members, and its avowed object was to "enable Catholic laymen to perform their share of the work in the dissemination of Catholic truth, and the encouragement of wholesome Catholic reading." Though the original founders of the American society possessed at that time little, if any, knowledge of the work of a similar society in England, it was discovered later that their objects were identical, and their methods differed only in the greater prominence given to newspaper work in the new organization. The principal means adopted by the American society for attaining its object were as follows:

1. The publication of short timely articles in the secular press (to be paid for if necessary) on Catholic doctrines.
2. The prompt and systematic correction of misrepresentations, slanders, and libels against Catholicity.
3. The promulgation of reliable and edifying Catholic news of the day, as church dedications, opening of asylums and hospitals, the workings of Catholic charitable institutions, abstracts of sermons, and anything calculated to spread the knowledge of the vast amount of good being accomplished by the Catholic church.
4. The publication of pamphlets, tracts, and leaflets; the circulation of pamphlets, tracts, leaflets, and Catholic newspapers.
5. Occasional public lectures on subjects of Catholic interest.
6. Supplying jails and reformatories with good and wholesome reading matter.

Thus it is seen that our society offers a variety of methods sufficient to suit the talents and tastes of all, yet its very life and essence consist in disseminating Catholic truth through the medium of the press. It does this in two ways: First, it endeavors to reach the vast American reading public through those great channels of popular information, the secular dailies. It would seem as though Providence had permitted these great journals to attain their enormous circulation in order to afford Catholics an easy and efficient means of conveying the priceless treasure of Christian faith which they possess to the countless millions in search of Divine truth. On the day of Pentecost he worked a miracle to enable the apostles to speak in all languages at once and thus reach thousands of hearers in a moment. In our days he puts at our disposal the modern newspaper, by which a sermon can be conveyed in an hour to millions of readers.

Have you ever thought of that, my friends? Can we shut our eyes to this modern miracle of Pentecost? This use of the secular press, which we are willing to pay for, if necessary, is a method of "carrying the war into Africa?" Of course, no intelligent Catholic will dispute for a moment the power of the Catholic press, the importance of the field it occupies, or the value of the results it has obtained. But what do non-Catholics know about the Catholic press? How many of them ever read a Catholic journal? With many, alas! the very word "Catholic" is sufficient to excite suspicion and thwart the good that is intended; hence, we are forced to admit that "when the mountain will not come to the prophet, the prophet must go to the mountain."

Another reason makes it necessary for us to have recourse to the secular rather than the Catholic press in this work. "Mis-statements, slanders, and libels against Catholic truth" do not usually appear in Catholic papers; hence, that is hardly the place to correct them. Moreover, the value of a correction depends largely upon the promptness with which the truth is sent traveling on the heels of error. This promptness can never be secured in the columns of the Catholic weeklies. The damage is done in the secular dailies, and they are the ones that must repair it. Nor is this an unreasonable demand to make on the secular press. Newspapers do not, as a rule, willfully or knowingly, slander their readers. They aim to give the news impartially and correctly, and are always glad to receive it from reliable sources.

To guard, however, against the danger of incompetent persons attempting too much, ample provision is made in the constitution of the Catholic Truth Society directing how such newspaper work shall be done; yet, as all can not write, we follow in this the motto of the Catholic Truth Society of England : "For ten who can write 10,000 can subscribe and 100,000 can scatter the seed."

Hence, the second way in which we work through the press is by furnishing all our members with an inexhaustible supply of new, cheap, and original literature, especially designed for our work, and presumably the most useful, suitable, and appropriate for the purpose that can possibly be produced. Our plan of publication, briefly stated, is as follows:

Pamphlets, tracts, and leaflets are solicited without remuneration from the ablest ecclesiastics and laymen whom the society can interest in its work, and furnished to all its members and affiliated branches at a nominal price, based on the cost of an electrotype edition of not less than 10,000 copies. We trust to the annual initiation fee of our members and the energy of our local branches throughout the country to meet the necessary pecuniary outlay and to dispose of our publications. The slight profit that may then remain is used in distributing our literature gratis among non-Catholics, where it will do the most good. Thus it is evident that with 100,000 members we could flood the land with Catholic literature almost gratis.

The Catholic Truth Society of America has not failed to win during its short career the hearty approval of the American hierarchy and of our Holy Father, the Pope himself. We have received earnest letters of approval from his eminence, Cardinal Gibbons, from four archbishops, and thirteen bishops. On March 10th we received the special blessing of our Holy Father by cable, and on March 10, 1893, we received a papal indult, dated February 19th, granting special plenary and partial indulgences for five years to the members, of the Catholic Truth Society of America, and all who write, publish, or promote the spread of the society's literature. What more can we ask?

As the Catholic Truth Society and its work becomes better known, it would seem a difficult matter for any earnest Catholic, who loves his church and his country, to find an excuse for not joining it. As its affairs are conducted by a board of directors, who hold monthly meetings for the transaction of all its business without pecuniary compensation, membership involves no irksome duties; there are no compulsory meetings; no fines or penalties, and the annual subscription is only nominal; it interferes with no other society in existence, for its ultimate object being to "Bring other sheep into the fold," its ultimate effect must naturally be to strengthen and increase the membership of all other Catholic societies.

The individual member has full liberty to work according to his ability and opportunities in the manner his judgment and inclination may suggest. He may write for the press, disseminating Catholic truth, correcting misstatements and furnishing edifying Catholic news, always, however, taking care not to compromise the society; or if he can not write, at least he can distribute an occasional tract, attend the lectures, and bring a non-Catholic friend, carry the literature furnished by the secretary to the imprisoned, secure new members, and aid the good cause in countless other ways as occasion offers.

So much for the work of the Catholic Truth Society of America. Of its possibilities in the United States, time will permit of a few words only. Never, perhaps, in the history of the church was field of labor more glorious, open to the efforts of her children than in our own age and land. This country owes its very discovery to the heroic faith of a devout son of the church who undertook the search for a new world that he might sow therein the seeds of divine faith—the immortal Christopher Columbus. Nor is this soil unfriendly to the Christian religion. The United States government has never, like so many European governments, made war on the Pope, or cast off the authority of the church. This nation since its birth has never performed one act of hostility to the Catholic religion, martyred or persecuted a single Catholic, and its first act on winning independence was to repair the injustice of the mother country and to place Catholicity on an equal footing with Protestantism.

Indeed, there seems to be a natural affinity between the Catholic Church and the American Republic. In the language of Chief Justice Shea, of the Marine Court of New York, "Our own government and the laws which administer it, like those of Alfred the Great, are in every part—legislative, judicial, and executive—Christian in nature, form, and purpose."

In the still plainer words of the illustrious Dr. Brownson, than whom America has produced no deeper thinker, " the American State recognizes only the Catholic religion. It eschews all sectarianism, and none of the sects have been able to get their peculiarities incorporated into its constitution or its laws. The State conforms to what each holds that is Catholic—that is always and everywhere religion; and whatever is not Catholic it leaves as outside of its province, to live or die according to its own inherent vitality or want of vitality."

Thus, where Columbus and our Catholic ancestors have sown the seed it is ours to reap the harvest. Amid the universal crumbling of creeds and wreck of religions, the ship of Peter alone sails majestically onward and upward, and it is for us who are on board of her to cast the nets in which the souls of men must be saved from religious shipwreck.

The opportunity is before us. The Catholic Truth Society supplies the means. Let us not be recreant to a duty so noble. A nation whose mottoes are "In God we trust," and "E pluribus unum," must soon recognize the necessity of unity in religion, and that religion alone can safeguard it. When that day comes, Catholicity will dawn like a new revelation on the American mind. Then may be realized those prophetic words of John Bright: "I see another and a brighter vision before my gaze. It may be only a vision, but I cherish it. I see one vast confederation stretching from the frozen North to the glowing South, and from the wild billows of the Atlantic to the calmer waters of the Pacific main; and I see one people, one language, one law, and one faith; and all over that wide continent, the home of freedom, and a refuge for the oppressed of every race and clime."

Richard R. Elliott, of Detroit, contributed a paper on "Public and Private Charities," in which he considered the question from the Catholic as well as from a practical standpoint. The substance of his paper follows:

It is not difficult to explain the evil tendencies and results of public outdoor relief in a Catholic parish in connection with the work of a pastor, who is aided in caring for the poor by such auxiliary charitable societies as may be established in his parish. The pastor of a city parish, having a census of the members of his congregation, will most probably know the status of the religious and temporal condition of each family or member. He knows the location of the homes of the wealthy, of the well-to-do, of the self-supporting, as also the abodes of those who may be classed as poor families. He has either a St. Vincent de Paul conference or a parochial relief society to aid him in such charitable work as may be found necessary. His attention is called to a family in distress, whose condition is investigated and found to be worthy, and its care is relegated to the Vincentian conference or some other organization. If there be children old enough to go to school and they are not attending the parish school this will be changed, and such other remedies applied as may be necessary to ward off poverty and its consequences if possible.

The condition of such families when first discovered differ greatly. Often, indeed, is the widowed or deserted mother in charge found to be a heroine deserving the warmest sympathy for her efforts to keep her little ones together, to shelter them from the cold, to feed and to clothe them, and to shield them from contaminating influence by companionship or from vicious surroundings. She has to do this by her individual efforts. Whatever may have brought this family to a state of poverty is immaterial. There it is found existing in this parish. Assistance by Vincentian methods continue; as the children grow in years they are educated and instructed in their religion, in time they receive the sacraments, and one or more may then be found employment, by which the burden of the heroic mother is lightened more and more as her children mature. Such is the experience of many devoted pastors who have worked for the improvement of the condition of the poor within their parochial limits. It is not an uncommon result, but if it were so it would nevertheless console that pastor for other bitter disappointments.

Very much depends upon the character of the mother. Her neighbors in similar condition, of the same faith, may be lazy, indifferent, and intemperate. They will ridicule the heroic efforts of this honest Christian mother, ridicule the practice of her religious duties and her obedience to pastoral advice. They will say to her, "You are so foolish to work so hard day after day; do as we do; go to the office of the director of the poor and demand assistance, as thousands of others do; he can't refuse you, for you have children, and he will supply you with coal and give you an order for provisions once a week."

It would be a sore temptation to this inexperienced soul. Half a ton of coal a month and $5 or $6 worth of provisions would be equal to the proceeds of two or more days' work each week, which she was not always certain to obtain. This would add so much to the comfort of herself and her children, and she would not be obliged to ask so much aid from the priest.

Should she yield to the temptation, what would be the result? She goes to the office of the secretary of the poor and enters an anteroom whose atmosphere is sickening, and finds herself one among hundreds of filthy-looking and degraded-appearing people, who are waiting their turn to approach the official window from which outdoor municipal relief is given. She becomes disheartened, sick; but her courage nerves her, and she consoles herself with the reflection that she is there for her children, not for herself. Her turn comes; she goes to the official window and makes her demand; her appearance is favorable, she receives an order for provisions and a promise for coal if, upon investigation, her statements are found to be correct. These prove favorable, she receives a load of coal, and once each week she goes through the same ordeal during the winter season and receives an order for provisions and, when necessary, coal.

This is the practical method of outdoor municipal relief. What are its consequences? The recipient of this charity has, in fact, become what is legally termed a pauper. She has fallen an immeasurable distance below the Christian mother she was in her respectable poverty, because, in obtaining this relief in the manner she did, she lost her self-respect. She and her children are to be nourished with pauper food, and warmed with pauper coal. Can she conceal this fact from her children; can she conceal it from others? Unfortunately, she can not; and it remains for the future a stigma upon herself and her children.

But there are other consequences. The fact that she receives public outdoor relief may not come to the knowledge of her pastor; when, therefore, he finds the object of his solicitude less docile, he is at a loss to account for the cause. But it will soon be developed that this deserving mother has become in a measure independent of his control. She may still be saved from the consequences, but it is doubtful; her self-respect gone, she can only weep at the degradation she has brought upon herself and her children. Were there no system of outdoor aid, had a mother who could get along during the summer season fairly well by her own labor, but who required assistance during the winter season, no recourse to outdoor aid, she would be guided by the advice of her pastor or of other private charitable agencies, who would render her temporary assistance from time to time, and tide her over an inclement season or a period of stagnation when work would be scarce; she would be saved from the disgrace of pauperism, her children would be properly educated and instructed in their religious duties, and in time this family would become self-supporting.

There is a brighter side to the administration of public outdoor aid. It may be temporarily given, and the home and status of the applicant is then pretty fairly investigated, for an excellent system of investigation has been the rule for some years. If the official visitor's report be favorable the aid may be continued until poverty no longer exists in the family aided, or the director may contribute indefinitely in such a manner as to supplement the means of support the family may have been deprived of, and in most cases this is a worthy bestowal of public aid; but even in such cases it operates unfavorably to the recipient, for, unfortunately, the records of the relieving officer disclose the fact that the names of nearly all recipients of such aid recur year after year until death, some fortunate event, or removal from the city brings the account to a close.

But it may be safely asserted that in all American cities the poor or dependent classes, as they may become so, can and should be properly cared for by charitable methods independent of official outdoor relief. As this system interferes with the efforts of private charities to restore these dependent classes to self-support, as it interferes to thwart organized effort for their religious and temporal improvement, as it encourages begging, imposition, and laziness, and breeds pauperism, it may be claimed that public and private charities would become more effective by the general abolition of the system of outdoor relief as heretofore administered in cities.

"The only really perfect way of caring for the poor," said Bishop Chatard, "is where, to prudence in dispensing through organized effort, is added the presiding influence of religion, for the needs of the soul are more important than those of the body. What is noble of man is his soul; the body is to perish. As the man who destroys another's faith in Christianity is the most of all wanting in charity, so he who helps a man to be a Christian shows himself to be truly charitable."

Among the lay associations, numerous in every time, in this day stands prominent the Society of Saint Vincent de Paul, which has made the name of its founder, Ozanam, famous throughout the world. The system they follow is one in which out-door relief is especially looked to, and every kind of distress is their object to meet. "And the reason why their work is so thorough, and so permanent, and so persevering," Dr. Chatard concludes, "is because it is material aid bestowed by charity enlightened by religion."

But the social problem, how to improve the condition of the poor and prevent pauperism, which for so many years has been fruitlessly discussed in this country, has been solved in Europe, and by methods based on the principles as explained by Bishop Chatard. Where? Was it solved in London, distinguished of all other cities for the extent and debased condition of its poorer classes? No. It was solved in Vienna, whose population is about one-fourth that of the capital of the British Empire, whose Empress, figuratively speaking, rules a free people; while the Emperor of Austria-Hungary rules as a paternal autocrat.

But once each year the Austrian monarch teaches the sublime lesson of charity by publicly washing the feet of twelve of the poorest subjects of his great empire. Fancy Queen Victoria washing the feet of twelve poor wretches from a London workhouse, or President Cleveland those of twelve of the poorest negroes in the American capital! But when a Catholic monarch, before the highest dignitaries of church and state, and with all the *eclát* a brilliant court can add to the surroundings, offers this example of Christian charity to his subjects, the time-honored scene is not without its effect. And behind this ceremony there exists probably the only successful practical method known in Christendom, of improving the condition of the poor from the foundling waif to the last age of man under religious direction.

It is much to be regretted that the chivalrous impulse which adds to the membership of the conferences of the society of Saint Vincent de Paul from the highest classes in Europe does not exist to the same extent in this country. Time may develop a change, and it would be well if the ordinaries publicly encouraged the formation of conferences in city parishes. To make such a conference effective there should be one master spirit to lead, either the president or secretary; for much depends upon a prudent, zealous, and active leader. Thorough investigation should be the rule, and information sought from all relieving agencies; for without diligent scrutiny it is impossible to avoid imposition. All reports should be in writing, to enable the secretary to comply with the manual, by having the record of existing cases of relief written up each week. It is all important that conference meetings be held on week day instead of on Sunday mornings, when members would perhaps prefer to be eating breakfast. At an evening meeting time will permit a free discussion of the merits of each beneficiary, and consultation of the vital subject of obtaining employment for such as are in need of work, and the spiritual exercises and reading. It is impossible to accomplish the requirements of the manual in a morning session of an hour. It is probable that no conference work in a city can be satisfactorily done at Sunday morning meetings.

Auxiliary assistance may be provided by a pastor of a city parish for Vincentian work by a ladies' society, to visit the poor in their homes; for such visitors are more observing than men, and can discover defects and wants which a man can not, but the most important auxiliary aid a conference can have is a temperance society, for perhaps 50 per cent of the cause of poverty arises from intemperance, and such a great factor of misery should be counteracted in every parish. A very simple arrangement may provide a labor intelligence office in each parish by providing a register in some office or store, nearest the church, where those in need of work could leave their names, occupations, and address, and those needing servants or others for work could avail themselves of this method.

Knowing what I do of the imposition practiced by applicants for aid, and the necessity existing for educating members to detect such fraud, if I were the president of a conference, I would have read once a month, at least, a chapter from Dr. S. Humphrey Gurteen's "Handbook of Charity," which contains much valuable information and many useful suggestions in connection with the treatment of the poor in American cities.

"Pauperism. The Cause and the Remedy," was the subject of a paper read by Thomas Dwight, M. D., of Boston, which follows:

Those who would honor God by serving His poor must, if they would do their whole duty, bring all that they have to that service. It is to be undertaken deliberately, seriously. Not only the force of the body, but the powers of the soul must be brought to bear. As rational beings, undertaking a serious work, it is for us first deliberately to apply our reason to the matter, to study it as we should study any commercial enterprise in which we were about to embark, any scientific question which we hoped to solve. Instinctive charity is good. We have a kindly feeling for Goldsmith's village preacher in his dealings with the poor:

> Careless their merits or their faults to scan,
> His pity gave ere charity began.

But charity guided by reason is something higher.

Pauperism and poverty are not the same. Every poor man is not a pauper. The pauper is one who habitually lives in a state of destitution, without recognized means of support, without purpose or hope of bettering his condition. Of course there are paupers of all grades. Of course this species is not always easily recognized. There are transitional forms. The poor man, falling under discouragement, is not far removed from the pauper who, as yet, is not quite hopeless. At the other extreme the pilfering pauper merges by degrees into the habitual criminal. I should hesitate to class as paupers those who, near the close of an industrious life, fall into destitution. But in spite of uncommon instances, the pauper is, on the whole, a fairly distinct type.

Let us try to see him as he is, without Pharisaical condemnation on the one hand or sentimental gush on the other. Like other people, he may be married or single. The married pauper is the one we are most concerned with in large cities, for the unmarried speedily become something else. If caught and saved early he may rise to something better, otherwise he becomes a tramp in summer, an inmate of a penal or charitable institution in winter, or too often an habitual criminal. Though the more picturesque type of the two, let us leave him to attend chiefly to the one, who, if not more to be pitied, seems at least more deserving of pity. He has a wife and many children. They live crowded together in a dirty tenement. One shudders to think of the well-nigh inevitable want of all the most elementary decencies of civilized life. The room is foul, the air is foul from want of ventilation and drainage, the bodies are foul from want of water, and often from disease. Think not that I lay this dirt to their charge. How could it be otherwise? If the family have fallen to this from something higher, we may be sure that it was by degrees that one sign of self-respect fled after another. The man is lazy. Perhaps he was not so always. He may have worked well and willingly once, but hard times, improvidence, sickness, dissipation (perhaps even a casual, almost an innocent, deviation may have cost him a place), misfortune, in short, of many kinds may have brought him low, until, by degrees, hope has changed to despair. He drinks, of course. There is at least a temporary comfort in it. Many in other stations drink more with far less excess. But bad liquor in vile surroundings does not make glad the heart of man. The lowest passions, the violence, the brutality in the depths of the rough nature are brought to the surface. His wife drinks, too. Why should she not? she says to herself. If he is to come home drunk and brutal, why should he find her sober? It will be easier to bear if she is drunk, too. It is needless to complete the picture, for we can read the sequel any day in the police reports.

And the children! No prophet is needed to foretell their future. Happily the mortality below five years is very large. But this speedy release is not for all. Who teaches their prayers to the little ones? What do they know of God but as a name to swear with? Even if of a Sunday they occasionally pass an hour in the crowded basement of a church, they may grow up without understanding how to make even an act of contrition. How will they resist the temptations around them at their very doors? The father may have been originally a fairly well-living man, but as he went deeper into the mire of pauperism he had to take such neighbors as he found. The drunken, the riotous, the lewd swarm on the same staircase, perhaps on the same floor. What future is before his little girls there! It is enough to make him drink the deeper if, in a lucid moment, he thinks of it.

How does he live? Of course he must have food, and he must, at times, at least, have money to pay for his liquor. How he does it is a mystery; a question which I incline to think very few but those living on the spot can answer fully. He does odd jobs when he gets them and feels like it. He is helped very often by municipal or private charity, but to eke his living out he must have occult ways of which we know little. A common one is the illegal sale of liquor; another is receiving night lodgers in his crowded tenement. When charitable visitors come he sometimes fawns and sometimes snarls; this is according to the nature of the man, his degree of degradation and his idea of his own interest; but he, practically, always lies. Let us not blame him too much for this. Why should he feel called upon to tell all his secrets? They can not be bought by an order for groceries, still less by a system of taking notes and giving good advice. He may well be excused for declining to expose to public scrutiny a life ill-fitted for close inspection.

Such is the condition of the typical married pauper in a great city. I believe it is a fair average specimen. There are both better and worse. It is certainly a ghastly picture. Too many of the rich turn away from it as too repulsive. What feelings of brotherhood have they with this dirty, drunken, shiftless, lying pauper? Each epithet is but too well deserved, but what has made him all this? Is it wholly his own fault? Is it wholly our own virtue that has made us something else? Have we any reason to believe that in his place we should have been less dirty, drunken, shiftless, and debauched than he? It is humiliating to think how Pharisaical one is. How we feel that the poor man should be resigned, cheerful, industrious, temperate, neat in dress, polite in speech, and, above all, candid to our questions. This is a part of the system of weighing with an unjust balance, which the Lord hateth. "Clear your mind from cant," was the advice of Dr. Johnson. It is an excellent preliminary to the study of these questions.

Many paupers have been such from their childhood up. They have been bred literally in the slum and gutter. Their bodies bear in their most intimate tissues the inheritance of vice. Unnatural and debased cravings are inherited also. Such a one can not remember the time when his body was sound and his mind pure. He is a pauper both in soul and body. To those ignorant of these matters it were as easy to conceive the physical conditions of life on a planet circling round a red sun with a blue companion, as to grasp the feelings toward society of such a young pauper, who does not know God, and knows man, that is, the man of his world, only too well. Kindness is unknown, justice incomprehensible. Who ever made a bargain with him who did not exact the most work for the least pay? If ever a man gave him alms, it was as to a dog or with a sneer. Gratitude could go no further than to thank fortune for putting a fool in his path.

What good has he ever received from his fellows? Wrongs and insults he can recall by the score; but what good? How many civil, not to say kindly, words have ever been spoken to him? He knows that there is no love given with the food which society feels forced to supply to him. What has he to be grateful for?

Grown familiar with disfavor,
Grown familiar with the savor
Of the bread by which men die—

he has an instinctive distrust of society which needs but little to become hatred. Or granting that occasionally he has fallen in with charitable persons, the distorting medium through which impressions reach him makes it all incomprehensible to him. We can guess at his temptations, but not at his idea of duty or at his accountability.

There is a very suggestive passage in Dickens' novel "Great Expectations," where the convict gives some account of his early years. He remembers himself first in the country stealing turnips for a living.

"I know'd my name to be Magwitch, chrisen'd Abel. How did I know it? Much as I know'd the birds' names in the hedges to be chaffinch, sparrer, thrush. I might have thought it was all lies together, only as the birds' names come out true, I supposed mine did.

"So far as I could find, there warn't a soul that see young Abel Magwitch, with as little on him as in him, but wot caught fright at him and either drove him off or took him up. I was took up, took up, took up to that extent that I reg'larly grow'd up took up.

"This is the way it was that when I was a ragged little creetur, as much to be pitied as ever I see—not that I looked in the glass, for there warn't many insides of furnished houses known to me—I got the name of being hardened. 'This is a terrible hardened one,' they says to prison visitors, picking me out. 'May be said to live in jails, this boy.' Then they looked at me, and I looked at them, and they measured my head, some on 'em—they had better measured my stomach—and others on 'em give me tracts what I couldn't read and made me speeches what I couldn't understand. They always went on agen me about the devil, but what the devil was I to do? I must put something into my stomach, musn't I?

"Tramping, begging, thieving, working sometimes, when I could—though that warn't as often as you may think, till you put the question whether you would ha' been over ready to give me work yourselves—a bit of a poacher, a bit of a laborer, a bit of a waggoner, a bit of a haymaker, a bit of a hawker, a bit of most things that don't pay and lead to trouble, I got to be a man."

Thus the pauper, as a rule, is one morally as well as physically. He is only moderately dangerous to the State just so long as he does not think. But thought is now in the air; it is everywhere, for good and for evil. Wise men now appreciate that the old saying, one half of the world does not know how the other half lives, cannot hold true much longer. The under half is determined, and rightly, that the other half shall know it. How long will the pauper stand his misery when the horrible inequality of this world is brought home to him, without the explanation which religion alone offers? His hand is ready for the dynamite which the infamous anarchist will put into it. Against such society protects herself with the Gatling gun and the gallows. All honor to the commonwealth that does not shrink from their use when the crisis comes! But let no one flatter himself that such measures are any cure for the evil. They are dread necessities for the putting down of violence; that is all. They do not remove the deep sense of wrong which is at the root.

What reason is there that the pauper should bear his sufferings patiently? The more he thinks of them the worse they seem. This is not due only to the effect of self-love in distorting his vision. It is because in very truth these evils will not bear thinking of. Thought reveals only the more clearly the monstrous injustice of his position, seen from the natural standpoint alone.

Such being the evil, what is the remedy?

It is to make the pauper a Christian. With a Catholic audience, it is superfluous to prove this point. We have the great advantage over others that we bring to the study of great questions certain fundamental truths as starting points which to them are still objects of speculation. We are not to be deceived by the shallow fallacies that crime is a form of physical disease; that learning without religion deters from vice; that to accumulate money only is to become respectable.

We have learned also to look at questions from a supernatural standpoint. Were I an atheist I should emphatically deny that there is any reason for loving one's neighbor. As Catholics, we know that there are great ones. There is first our Lord's command; then we know that every one of the human race was created for an eternity of glory which it has not entered into the heart of man to conceive, and finally that the soul of the lowest is of such value that the Son of God died to save it. But these are all supernatural reasons which we hold as Christians. Mere humanitarianism without faith has no logical basis.

Hence we reach at once our conclusion that the pauper is to be made a Christian to be raised from his degradation of soul and body. Hence comes also the corollary, that it is for us Catholics to do it. We may thankfully accept all help that the State and our friends outside the church will give us, but we must entrust this work to none.

It is easy to say that the pauper must be made a Christian. So easy to say and so hard to do that it sounds like cant. But let it sound as it may, this is the problem before us. Let us then discuss the means.

The pauper is essentially a degraded type. If the degradation could be stopped the type would die out. It is far easier to save a man, still more to save a child from becoming a pauper than to reform the deformed individual. We must, therefore, consider both prevention and cure. Practically, as will soon appear, the two processes are hardly distinct. The difference is only in the greater difficulty, humanly speaking, in

JAMES F. O'CONNOR, Sec'y,   THOMAS LAWLER, Sec'y,   JOHN M. DUFFY, Sec'y,
CHICAGO.   PRAIRIE DU CHIEN.   CHICAGO.
THOMAS DWIGHT, M. D.,   HON. MORGAN J. O'BRIEN,   RICHARD H. CLARKE, LL.D.
BOSTON.   Chairman,   NEW YORK.
                        NEW YORK.

the hopelessness of saving the confirmed pauper. The latter has no correct notions about anything. Society seems in league against him. Law is but an engine of oppression. Nothing but the doctrines of Christianity can give him light on the inequality of things here below. That his burdens should become bearable they must be seen in the light of the supernatural. He must learn the brotherhood of man.

But how is he to learn it if there is none to teach? Moreover, it is a branch of knowledge that must be taught by object lessons. What he needs is a friend. One who will do more than say a kind word as he leaves an order for relief, one who will take a true interest in his concerns, who will spend hours, if need be, in his company, who by weeks and months of patience will find time to speak to him of his soul, and above all shall show him that he does it for the love of God. This is the work done by the Society of St. Vincent de Paul among poor and paupers alike. If in practice it too often falls short of this ideal, instances of surpassing it are not wanting.

The sick poor should be cared for at their homes, when practicable, as is done by the Little Sisters of the Assumption. It is needless to enumerate, in great detail, the auxiliary works that are called for. They suggest themselves readily enough to all who have thought on the subject. There must be night asylums for the homeless. Wayfarers' lodges, giving a bed and breakfast in exchange for moderate work. There should be institutions for savings, there should be plans for rational amusement.

All these should be distinctly Catholic. That is to say, under Catholic management, but open to all. While religion should be forced upon none, its consolations should be offered to all who will have them. The ground principle that the love of man comes from the love of God should appear. All this would cut off one source of pauperism by preventing those on its verge from falling in. It would go far to remove discontent by doing away with the rankling feeling of wrong. The effect will go beyond the poor thus helped to confirmed paupers themselves. Even if they rejected these advances, they will know that they have been made. Their wives and children may have profited by them.

The children, indeed, must not be forgotten, not only on account of their intrinsic value, but because by saving them we choke up another, probably the greatest, source of pauperism. There must be sewing schools for the girls, and clubs for the boys, all tending to the same end, to keep them out of mischief, to give them instruction, and, above all, to make them good Catholics. These are for the children of the poor, and of paupers also, but in the case of very many of the latter, more will be needed. They can not be left in their tainted homes. They must be placed in institutions for a time at least. In this matter above all we must see to it that the institution, be it refuge or reform school, must be Catholic. True, as American citizens, we can demand that in public institutions nothing hostile to our religion shall be taught. The sense of justice of our fellow-countrymen gives more and more freely the right of religious instruction by ministers of our own religion in such institutions. Still, when the whole bringing up of the neglected child is at stake, it is clear that nothing should be left undone to have it carried on under Catholic influences.

Such is the outline of our task. Now comes the most practical question of all—how is it to be done? Have we the means ready at our hands or must we seek new ones? The answer is not quite clear, but this much is certain, that our present means are ample for great good. When they have been exhausted, or when it is certain that others are needed, new ones will doubtless be found.

First, then, it is essential that Catholics should be brought thoroughly to understand the vastness of the issue, and that the cure is in their hands. Let this great truth be brought home to them in season and out of season, till it is accepted as a matter of course. This being once accomplished they will spare nothing to strengthen the societies and charitable associations by which the actual work is to be done. We shall then no longer hear presidents of conferences of the Society of St. Vincent de Paul complain, that, as the members grow old and fall off, young men, and especially young men of education, do not come forward to take their places. This is a crying need, for this society is the one that alone should do a large share of the work. Let all remember that no man can bring to this society anything to equal the advantages he himself receives from it.

Societies of women are needed, also. It would be well that these should be associated, as much as possible, with religious orders. Under the guidance of the Little Sisters of the Assumption, young women might go further than were otherwise prudent. The work will not stop here. Everything will be done to support asylums, training schools, and all necessary institutions. But, above all, if real good is to come out of this, we must frankly realize that works of bodily mercy alone are inadequate.

The evil is of soul as well as of body; we attack it from supernatural motives. Our means, in part at least, must be supernatural also.

As has been said before, the pauper is such both in soul and body. While we must not mock him with "tracts which he cannot read and speeches which he cannot understand" when what he wants is food and clothing, neither must we think that when he is filled and warmed the evil spirit of pauperism has been exorcised. Our warfare is not with want and dirt and ignorance only, but "with principalities and powers." The old tendencies to evil, to say nothing of shiftless ways, are not so easily overcome. Till they shall be, till the man shall begin to understand Christian charity, to see things, though confusedly, in the light of God's will, all improvement will be skin-deep. Physical help must indeed come first, but our supernatural motives for giving that help should be made apparent.

At first the pauper will care little whether our motives are from above or from below, so long as the help is his, but their effect may come in time. By degrees his Catholic instincts will revive. The little picture of "Our Lady of Good Counsel," which we have placed on his wall, may say more to him than we know of. Above all in the case of those who are still practical Catholics some fellowship in worship between the helpers and helped is to be greatly wished for. The wonderful spectacle which we have lately seen of an Eucharistic Congress at Jerusalem is but another proof that the great devotion of the coming century is to be the adoration of the most Blessed Sacrament. Let everything be done to encourage its practice among the poor. Nowhere do we feel the love of our neighbor so strongly as at the foot of the altar.

These are the lines which we must follow. As we go on, the needs will become clearer. It may be that in time one or more semi-religious associations may arise for this work; but that time is not yet. The first and most important step is to rouse Catholics to the conviction that the need is pressing. The good of society, as well as Christian charity, demands that the remedy be found and found speedily. Next, we must feel that the work is ours, and, lastly, that it is a supernatural work far more than a physical one. We need to have preached a crusade against pauperism.

It is not the part of wisdom to underrate one's task, nor that of honesty to raise enthusiasm by concealing difficulties. This is not the work of a year nor of a generation. There are those, unfortunately, who refuse to be saved. While they live, they will be what they are. Neither can their children always free themselves so fully from inherited trammels as to be quite like others. The prospect for the grandchildren is brighter. But the struggle is to end only with the world. The poor will always be with us, and while human nature is what it is, there will be paupers among them. What the proportion of them is to be depends in part upon us. Each generation is the trustee of the succeeding one. The child, moreover, is the father of the man. In bringing up a generation of good Catholics and good citizens out of what else would have been paupers we exercise an influence which may be felt through centuries.

The subject of the address delivered by H. C. Semple, of Montgomery, Ala., was "Pope Leo XIII. on The Condition of Labor." He said:

The platform of Catholics on the condition of labor was announced by Leo XIII. in the encyclical "Rerum Novarum." This paper seeks to gather a syllabus of leading social principles from that immortal document which called for letters of thanks from the Emperor of Germany and the President of the French Republic, and which shows the head of the church as the reverend counsellor of states, the father of Christians, and the friend of the people.

What task more arduous than to define the rights and the duties of the rich and of the poor, of capital and of labor? What more perilous than to discuss the foundations of society when every word is scanned by crafty agitators, enemies of peace and order? Yet what more humane than to extinguish the embers of the mighty conflict which threatens the very foundations of society, than to alleviate the hardships suffered by the defenseless victims of un-Christian laws, greedy competition, rapacious usury and despotic monopolies and trusts?

All agree, and no one can deny, that some remedy must be found, and quickly found, for the misery and wretchedness which press so heavily at this moment on the large majority of the very poor. But where is it to be found?

Socialism steps forward and answers: I have found it: I am the redeemer of society. I will invest all property in the State, I will give it the sole administration, and it shall distribute to each according to his needs. Thus I will abolish poverty and bring back the golden age of universal equality.

No, replies the Holy Father. Your project is at once futile, unjust and pernicious. It is futile, for if all goods must forever remain common, where is the workingman's hope of bettering his condition by industry and economy? Where is his liberty, his inalienable right to invest his wages permanently and profitably, to dispose freely of the fruit of his sweat?

But, above all, it is emphatically unjust. Centralization of property in the State violates natural rights. The State cannot take away the right to acquire property, for this right is from God, who made man in His own image and likeness, and said, "Let him have dominion over the fishes of the sea, and the fowls of the air, and the beasts, and the whole earth, and every creeping thing." We see this natural right by the light of pure reason, and see it in our ever-recurring necessities, and in nature's first law of self-preservation. We see it in our intelligence, which surveys the vast outward world of countless objects necessary and useful for the support of life, and which joins the future to the present. We see it in our free will, which directs and guides us under Providence, and which enables us to select from the multitude of earthly goods those things best suited to each of us. And no matter how primitive a condition of man be conceived, even though no state existed, yet if a man occupy for his exclusive use any of the goods of earth or any spot on its surface which no other has occupied, it becomes his, and if besides occupying it, he expends on it the labor of his hand or his mind, he stamps it with his own personality, and to dispossess him would be to rob him of his labor.

This natural right to acquire and hold property is manifested more clearly still in the rights and duties of the father of the family. What right more clear, what duty more sacred for the father than to provide for his offspring against the wretchedness of want in this mortal life? Yet by what other means can this sacred duty be fulfilled than by the acquisition and ownership of permanent property, to be transmitted by inheritance?

True, the State may regulate the exercise of these natural rights. And in the exercise of this power to regulate the transmission of property by inheritance, or testamentary gift, may it not correct to some extent the great evil of our times, the accumulation of millions on millions by single individuals or families, by the imposition of such inheritance taxes as will not only provide some relief to the suffering poor from the heavy burdens of taxation, but secure a fund for the merely frugal support of industrious workingmen in times of hardship. The State may even enter the domestic circle to protect the members of the family, but the State cannot usurp or absorb the parental authority, or destroy its very life, by assuming the control of all property.

But has not God given the earth to all men? He has given to each man the right to live, and sustenance necessarily comes from the land. But we may procure its fruits by our labor, without all becoming proprietors. God has given to each man the right to acquire property in land, but he has left the limits of property to be determined by the industry of individuals and the laws of states. He has not vested the property of the earth in the human race promiscuously, nor in the organized state.

It is asked: "Did not God make all men equal?" Yes; and no. He made all equal in the possession of human bodies and immortal souls, equal in origin from God, in destiny for heaven, in the right to live and to save their souls, but he made them unequal in strength of body, in the faculties of the mind, and in energy of purpose. And these inequalities of nature have always produced inequalities of fortune, absolutely inseparable from our very nature.

Socialism would introduce discord and confusion, dry up the very sources of production, and destroy the chief spur of genius, and its boasted equality would be an equality in wretchedness and misery and of universal enslavement to the State. Nothing could be more unjust or more disastrous than thus to deny man's natural rights, so manifest to our reason and so strongly confirmed by the morally universal consent of mankind, by the practice of all ages, by the sanction of positive human laws, by the divine law itself, which forbids us even to cast a covetous look on our neighbour's house, or his field, or anything that is his. Therefore socialism is manifestly futile, unjust, and pernicious, and cannot be the remedy which we seek.

How, then, shall we soften the asperities arising from the friction of labor and capital? For they are not naturally hostile, but friends.

The Vicar of the Prince of Peace declares that this blessed result demands the harmonious co-operation of all the agencies involved, of the laborer and the capitalist, the rich and the poor, the State and private societies. But, he adds, that all their efforts will be vain without the aid of religion, with the principles which she brings forth from the gospel. For, in the first place, religion, as the herald of God, teaches men their duties of justice. It says to the workingman: "Perform faithfully and scrupulously the labor which you have freely and fairly promised. Respect the person and property of your employer. Never resort to violence, even in representing your just rights. Above all, shun the company of men of evil principles, of men who delude you with vain hopes and lead you to disaster, denying the necessity of that painful labor which was imposed by our Maker and not done away with by our blessed Redeemer, but only sweetened by His example, and grace, and promises."

To the capitalist religion cries out in warning, "Beware of regarding and treating the laborer as a slave, or mere muscle, as a tool for making money. He is of the same blood; the same divine origin—the same destiny for heaven. Your fellow-image and likeness of God, your fellow-Christian and your brother.

It is your duty to see that he has rest and leisure to attend to the affairs of his soul. It is your duty to ward off from him the allurements to vice and temptations to neglect home life. Beware of overtaxing age, or sex, or tender youth, and above all remember that to defraud him of his honest hire, or unfairly to cut down his wages is a sin which cries to heaven for vengeance."

Such are the duties of justice, but where justice ends charity begins, which, though not enforced by the State, is most binding in the eternal law. For there is a future life, of which the present is only the beginning, where wealth and luxury here below do not insure beatitude, but rather endanger it.

The Son of God was Himself a poor man and a carpenter, and he made it plain to all ages by His example that dignity is in worth and not in wealth, and He taught us that the only path to heaven is that stained by His bloody footprints.

Religion says to the rich, "Your wealth is yours to possess, but not to use as you please; it is a talent of which you are only the steward, and a rigid account awaits you not only for its just but its charitable use." It is a mistake to suppose that religion is so engrossed by the care of man's spiritual welfare as to neglect his material wants. While consoling us, under the wretchedness of poverty, and pointing to the compensation of the blessed future, she earnestly desires and actively strives to help all to rise above the pressure of want and acquire property as an instrument of virtue. And what can be more conducive to this than the practice of Christian morality, which at once merits and enjoys the blessings of Providence, restrains inordinate lust of gain and lust of pleasure, and represses those vices which destroy honest industry and eat up so many goodly inheritances. She not only does this by her teachings but by active intervention for the help of the poor. So active was this charity among the early Christians that the Acts of the Apostles record that "neither was there any poor among them."

St. Paul, though burdened with the care of all the churches, made long journeys to distribute alms of the charitable to the needy. The order of deacons was instituted to administer the patrimony of the church, which has been ever guarded by her as the sacred heritage of the poor. The heroism of Christian charity has founded religious orders for the relief of nearly every description of poverty and human misery, and some of the heathen, and even some in our time, have reproached the church for her charity, but there can be found no adequate substitute in any State organization for that divine charity which springs from the heart of Jesus.

Such are the doctrines and practices which the Holy Church, through her bishops and priests, has diffused far and wide throughout the world. Through agencies instituted and assisted by God, she applies them to the mind, the conscience, and the heart of the individual, and makes them a part of his daily life; and he learns to act from a motive of duty to resist his evil appetites and passions, and history records that the teachings of the church and the example of the life of Christ subdued in a great measure the pride of wealth and impregnated all races and nations which came under their influences, exalted the human character, and elevated a debased and degenerated society.

How, then, can society be cured in our day? By a return to a pure Christianity and submission to its health-giving precepts and practices. What are the counsels of the Holy Father to the State for the improvement of the condition of labor? The State is reminded that while it exists for the common good, it has a special duty to workingmen and to the poor. For they are the most numerous class, and are so engrossed by their daily necessities as to have little leisure or capacity for the thoughtful and prudent consideration of their own special interests; while the capitalists and employers, fewer in number, strong in wealth, and with an abundance of leisure, may spend their days and nights in scheming to add more and more to their gain; and striving to diminish yet more the share of the workman in the product of his labor. The power of the State should be exerted in behalf of the weak to lighten their burdens by wise and wholesome administration and by striving to secure to them a reasonable subsistence as the price of their toil and some provision for their necessities in times of hardship. This it may well do without suspicion of undue partiality, for it comes to the help of the weak.

It is a mistake to suppose that the State should not intervene except in the case of the tumultuous refusal of the workman to do his promised work, or of the employer to pay the promised wages; for labor is not only personal, as belonging to him who exerts his powers, but it is also necessary for his support. It is true that wages should generally be determined by contract, but it is a dictate of nature more ancient and imperious than any bargain of men that the remuneration of the workman must be sufficient for his reasonable and frugal support, for he has the right to live and all property is held subject to this right. True, he may not enforce it by violence; he must exhaust every other means of redress and must appeal to boards and societies; he must cry out for the intervention of some great and good man, like the late Cardinal Manning, for his mighty assistance, and finally appeal to the State for approval and protection. And if through necessity, and because the employer will go no farther, he has accepted hard and unreasonable conditions, he is, in fact, a victim of injustice, which it will be wise for the State to correct.

The State may regulate the natural right to acquire property, but it has no authority to abolish it by the drain and exhaustion of excessive taxation. At present one of the greatest evils we endure is that society is too nearly divided into classes of the very rich and the very poor. One of these exercises the great power of wealth. It grasps all labor and all trade, it manipulates for its own profit all the sources of supply, and is always powerfully represented in the councils of the State. On the other side stand the sore and suffering multitude, always ready in their distress to listen to the extravagant promises of irresponsible advisers, and prone to violence.

The working man should be encouraged to look forward to obtaining, and the law should facilitate the ready acquisition of, parcels of land. Thus a class will be established which will be the best defenders of the order and the bulwark of the State. The providence of the State should foresee and endeavor to remove all grievances which paralyze labor by strikes, often the result of injustice and the fruitful cause of strife and violence. It should not be indifferent, but sternly interfere when greedy contractors impose burdens which exceed human strength, stupefy the mind, and are incompatible with human dignity, which blight the buds of childish promise, expose the modesty of woman, and detain the mother from her sphere of domestic duty and the care and training of her children.

It is also incumbent on the State to protect the workingman's enjoyment of the Sunday rest; not to be devoted to vicious excess, but that he may forget, at least for one day in the week, mere worldly cares, and turn his face and his thoughts upward to his Maker. For nothing is more conducive to the strength of the State than the morality of her citizens, and true morality is always founded on religion. The workman himself can not agree to the servitude of his soul, and no one has a right to stand in the way of his enjoyment of that higher life which prepares him for the joys of Heaven.

The various religious orders founded and directed by the heroic spirit of supernatural charity, have, in all ages, wrought wonders for the relief of suffering humanity. Each devoted to its own special object, moved by the spirit of self-sacrifice and self-denial, they have astounded the world by their achievements, and brought thousands to the faith from the contemplation of the fruits of their labors. Yet the veneration of the faithful for these orders has too often aroused the jealousy of States and caused them to suppress rather than encourage them. And sometimes they have ruthlessly grasped the property which the piety and charity of good men had bestowed for the furtherance of their sacred ends, and thus robbed at once the founders of their benefactions and the poor of that which was so wisely administered for their relief.

The last element treated by the Holy Father is the association of individuals in private societies for mutual protection, which he commends. He reminds us of the benefits of association, which appeal to each individual from his consciousness of his weakness in standing alone, as compared with the strength of organization. He refers to the history of the ancient Catholic guilds, so full of instruction as to the advantages of association; he contrasts their benefits with the dangers of those fierce and turbulent societies, often bound by secret oaths, which seek to persuade the workingmen that there is no hope for them, but in the terror of capitalists at revolution; that Christian morality is a mere fable of their enemies, invented to delude, ensnare, and enslave them, and which, while holding out to them the horrors of this slavery, binds them in their own chains, yet more galling. And now, concluding:

"As far as regards the church, its assistance will never be wanting, be the time or the occasion what it may, and it will intervene with the greater effect in proportion as its liberty of action is the more unfettered; let this be noted by those whose office it is to provide for the public welfare."

These words of solemn warning are addressed to those countries and those rulers who presume to fetter the freedom of the church, but in our own country she is absolutely free, and, therefore, happily, more powerful in her intervention in behalf of the weak and wretched multitude, and more efficient as a shield to the rich against the revolutionary and socialistic violence of turbulent secret societies, the great foes of peace and order.

One of the strongest papers of the Congress was read by Dr. August Kaiser, of Detroit, on "Immigration and Colonization," with special reference to German Catholic immigration. He said:

The Roman Catholic Church is a large family, a family not confined to one spot on the earth, nor to any single country, but embracing the whole surface of the globe. The Roman Catholic Church is not composed of a few individuals, is not made up of a single nation, but clasps all people of the earth with equal love to her maternal bosom. All the races of mankind, Caucasians and Mongolians, Ethiopians and Indians, she treats with equal and discriminating care. With the same hand she pours forth blessings upon every nation, upon every land. All languages of the earth are heard from her lips, but, above all, that loving language of the heart understood by all men. All her efforts tend to the one object, to make men Christians and to secure heirs of the kingdom of heaven.

Now there is no land on earth which puts so manifestly before us the truly Catholic character of the church as this land of the United States. All races are here represented, and the Church counts her children among them all. In all the principal languages prayers are blessed and fostered by the Catholic Church. Four nations especially have, since the discovery of America, gathered before the cross and the altar—the chivalrous Spaniard, the vivacious Frenchman, the Irishman, with his profound faith, and the cosmopolitan German. All, all have found in the land an asylum, and each one in his own way has contributed to the extension of the kingdom of God, to the development and strengthening of Catholic life and labor.

German Catholics, without exaggeration I may say it, have not been behindhand in this work of emulation. By their numbers alone they have always been a momentous element in our population, and already number the fourth part of the Catholic Church in the Union. Of almost 9,000 priests of this country, 2,700 are of German birth or descent. The influence of such a proportion must be felt throughout the land, must be felt in every domain of the life of the church. Already in family-life the German Catholic is characterized by his zealous and persistent endeavor to bring the principles and doctrines of his faith into his daily actions. He has the manly courage of his convictions, and endeavors to be in his daily life that which his principles require; and if, unfortunately, he ever comes to the point of not practicing his religion, then he ceases to profess himself a Catholic. The German Catholic distinguishes especially by his industry, economy, and by hastening to gain as soon as possible a home for himself. In his family rule Christian discipline and Christian spirit; the correlative obligations and duties imposed by the fourth commandment have not yet grown obsolete for him; conjugal fidelity is tenderly guarded and heaven is thanked for the blessings which it gives to the conjugal state. His olive branches grow up around him in the fear of God, and give earnest promise of becoming good Christians and upright, law-abiding citizens.

The German Catholic approaches the holy table at stated intervals; he is faithful in frequenting Divine worship, contributes joyfully and willingly to the support of his clergy, to the church, to the parochial school, the orphan asylum, and other institutions of charity; but, above all things, he is conscious of that most momentous of all obligations, to educate his children in sound Christian principles, and, if possible, to intrust them to none other than to the parochial school.

With a special zeal the German Catholics of our Union cherish the principle and practice of associations, so eminently manifested in the German Roman Catholic Central Verein. The Central Union embraces something like 500 branches of benevolent associations, with a membership of 50,000 in nearly all the States of the Union. The Central Union has paid out thousands upon thousands of dollars for charitable purposes, and thereby brought consolation and help to hundreds of afflicted homes.

The German-American secular and regular clergy are distinguished by the zeal which they display in their calling, by their exemplary lives, by their earnest and unceasing care for the young, and by untiring efforts to attain to a greater development of culture and knowledge, according to their state. Though the majority of these priests have crossed the Atlantic, yet every fibre of their nature has taken root in the land of their adoption, and by none are they surpassed in patriotic enthusiasm. Foreigners, it is true, but received with open arms by bishop and people, they have come hither with no other object in view than to labor as missionaries in the young church of this land, to work unceasingly for the salvation of immortal souls, sacrificing themselves in the painful service of young, still undeveloped communities. Their teaching and example have animated hundreds of young men to embrace the priestly state of life, so that at the very present moment more than 700 native clergymen of German descent are employed on our American missions. Bishops of highest merit have come forth from the ranks of this clergy, renowned for their zeal, immortal in their labors, labors which will be commemorated forever in the history of the United States.

Those sublime figures, to name but a few of our deceased prelates, those pillars of light, Archbishops Henni and Heiss, of Milwaukee; Bishops Junker and Baltes, of Alton; Luers and Dwenger, of Fort Wayne; Borgess, of Detroit; Melchers and Krautbauer, of Green Bay; Flasch, of La Crosse, and Neumann, of Philadelphia, whose beatification is pending in Rome; all these belong to us, are our kinsmen by blood and language.

Not inferior in merit to the German secular clergy of this country are their brethren of the religious orders. The first to enter this land (1832) were the Sons of St. Alphonsus Liguori, who gathered together their fellow-countrymen in the growing cities of the United States and developed their many-sided activity among them. Twelve years later they were followed by the Sons of St. Francis, from Tyrol, and in 1858 from Westphalia. In 1846 that zealous fisher of souls, Rev. Boniface Wimmer, of Bavaria, landed in this country to lead into our missionary territory the Order of St. Benedict, and to extend their teaching activity in every direction throughout the land. The Benedictines were followed by the Carmelites, Priests of the Precious Blood, Jesuits, Capuchins, Resurrectionists, Fathers of the Holy Cross, Passionists, all of whom set all their forces to work to extend the kingdom of God in this country and to give an impulse to true civilization.

The female orders also, which have been transplanted from Germany to America, have achieved great things, especially the poor Franciscan Sisters of Aix-la-Chapelle, by their charitable activity in the hospitals; the School Sisters of Notre Dame, of Milwaukee, originally from Bavaria, who, under the direction of Mother Caroline, lately deceased, that true Christian heroine, have rendered eminent services by their labors in the education of youth, and the Sisters of Christian Charity of Westphalia, who likewise have done great things in the same field of labor.

The Catholic Church is the home of all true education; her history for the last two thousand years proves that, no sooner has she firmly planted her foot in any land, than she immediately displayed her activity in this field which is so truly her own. Her vanguard—the religious orders— began here also without delay this work of hers. St. Vincent's in Pennsylvania—the name sounds bright and clear from ocean to ocean— was the most important nursery of higher education (for the Germans) for many a year. St. Meinrad's, Indiana; St. John's, Minnesota, with a number of local institutions, have added new lustre in the New World to the ancient and venerable name of the Order of St. Benedict. The Franciscans have had for many years excellent colleges in Cincinnati, Quincy, and Teutopolis, Ill.; the Capuchins at Calvary, Wis., and Herman, Penn.; the Fathers of the Holy Ghost at Pittsburg, the Jesuits in Buffalo and Cleveland; the Fathers of the Resurrection at Berlin, Ont., and St. Mary's, Ky.

The secular clergy are not behind their brethren of the religious orders. Their greatest, noblest, and most successful creation is the Salesianum, Milwaukee, which has sent forth hundreds of the ablest priests, and can boast of having admitted so far not a single Judas into the vineyard of the Lord.

The foregoing statements regarding the labors of German Catholics within the domain of the stars and stripes, are well calculated to prove that the German Catholics of America rank with all their co-religionists. I go a step further and maintain that they have acquired particular merit and deserve a special praise. The Germans are the only Catholics in this land, who, for years, have had a training school for teachers, a creation of that most deserving clergyman, Dr. Joseph Salzman, one of the founders of the Salesianum, near Milwaukee.

This Catholic Normal School at St. Francis has contributed much to relieve the pressing need of competent teachers, and it is at the same time the principal nursery of true ecclesiastical chants which has been most zealously cultivated by that distinguished musician and composer, Professor John B. Singenberger, and which from St. Francis is diffused more and more throughout the land. German Catholics alone in this Union can show a Catholic daily press, since besides some thirty excellent weekly papers they possess four thorough dailies (St. Louis, Philadelphia, Buffalo, Pittsburg), which energetically enter the lists for the interests of the Catholic Church and exercise great influence.

The greatest merit of German-American Catholics has been gained undoubtedly by their zeal for parochial schools, which they have erected at great sacrifice wherever it was possible, and for whose preservation and improvement they make every effort in their power. Wherever the cross was planted among the German Catholic immigrants, a school was erected near the church; nay, often, a school existed before the church. German Catholics were well acquainted with the principle: "Who possesses the youth is master of the future." They were convinced that the parochial school was the only sure bulwark against the fearful loss suffered by the church in this country. Freedom and independence permeate the air of our Republic so thoroughly that the rising generation are but too much inclined to extend these privileges to the domain of faith and morals. All Sunday schools are here impotent; that school alone, which is grounded on religious principles, in which all subjects of instruction are saturated with religion, can guard the tender germ of faith from the frost and wind of error, that it may become strong and capable of bidding defiance to all the storms of life, and of growing up to be a strong and vigorous tree.

German Catholics have given the example in the erection of parochial schools, and by their great success in this respect have led our co-religionists of other nationalities to follow in their footsteps. All Christian denominations in our land will have to imitate us if they wish to prevent Christianity from disappearing and infidelity from taking its place.

Ladies and gentlemen, such is, in concise terms, a faint image of the action and of the fulfilment of that mission of civilization intrusted by a wise Providence to the German Catholics of the United States. What I have said will surely suffice to convince this illustrious assembly that the German Catholics of this country stand on an equal footing with their brethren in faith of other nationalities, and have a right to claim their place as true children in the house of our mother and to be treated as such. Let us Catholics of this great and mighty Republic, a Republic so favorable to the free development of Catholicity, hold together irrespective of language and nationality, and, viribus unitis, struggle manfully for the preservation of our highest blessings, of the Holy Roman Catholic Faith which we have inherited from our forefathers, as well as for the rights which are solemnly guaranteed to us in the glorious Constitution of the United States! Let our war-cry be now and forever: "For God, for our Church, for liberty, and for our mighty Union, which gives happiness within the shadow of its lofty flag to all the nations of the earth."

Following is an abstract of Rev. Michael Callaghan's contribution to the symposium on "Immigration and Colonization."

When the eyes of the world are directed to the fitting celebration of the discovery of America by Columbus, it is appropriate that the Catholics of this great Republic in congress assembled, should discuss questions of serious importance, and it seems eminently in place to consider some of the causes that have led to this nation's growth and prosperity.

Apart from the liberty and patriotic spirit of our institutions there are no more potent factors in our country's greatness than immigration and colonization. True, the genius of Columbus opened a pathway across the Atlantic to this great continent, but what position would this country occupy to-day if there had not followed in his footsteps the thousands and tens of thousands of immigrants to people and develop its resources? Immigration and colonization are subjects capable of very extensive treatment. We might go back to the infant years of America and speak of the numerous adventurers who sought these shores, but these people left no impression on the country and need not be considered in reference to the building up of the Republic. It is better to begin at a time when the country had actually settled down to that internal development which has produced the America of to-day. Indeed, official statistics of immigration are not to be found further back than 1830, but from various sources we can arrive at a fair knowledge of the volume of immigration previous to that date, and also of the nationalities whence they came.

During the first century of the settlement of the country some few immigrants from Europe found their way into the New World, but scarcely as many in five years as now arrive in one day at the port of New York. Ireland and Germany were the principal countries which furnished immigration in the early days of the colonies. Under Dutch rule, from about 1725, some Germans were induced to immigrate to America by promise of land grants and other inducements. These people settled chiefly in the Mohawk Valley; others were induced to come by free or reduced passages, but these did not exceed over a few thousand. The English government did little or nothing to encourage European immigration. The first attempt was made about 1710, when 3,000 Swabians and Palatines, driven from their country by famine and religious persecution, threw themselves on the mercy and sympathy of the English government. England sent these people to New York, then a colony, presided over by Governor Hunter, who proposed to settle them along the Hudson River, where he intended to employ them in making naval stores, etc. This colonizing experiment failed, because the English government intended its proteges to become subjects and servants, while the immigrants wanted to be free and independent; hence a conflict, with victory on the side of the immigrants. After this, all those who came to the colonies had to do so on their own responsibility or by arrangements made by themselves.

An Irish colony was planted in the Carolinas in 1739 and an extensive tract of land was assigned it. In fact, it might be said that the Carolinas were settled almost exclusively by immigrants from the North of Ireland. Among those people were the fathers of Jackson, Calhoun, and Pickens. Ramsey, the historian of South Carolina, says, "Of all other countries none has furnished the province with so many inhabitants as Ireland. Scarcely a ship sailed from any of its ports to Charleston that was not crowded with men, women, and children." North Carolina received an Irish governor in James Moore, who headed the Revolution there in 1775. In Georgia, we find the Irish as far back as 1773, and at the first public meeting of the Sons of Liberty, held in Savannah, July 14, 1774, John Glenn was chairman, and among those present were S. Farley, J. Bryan, W. Gibbons, J. Winn, E. Butler, and a number of others bearing equally Irish names. The immigration to America during the years 1771, 1772, and 1773 from the North of Ireland exceeded all former precedents. Marmion's "History of the Maritime Ports of Ireland," page 333, states: "From Belfast there sailed during the three years mentioned thirty ships filled with immigrants; from Londonderry, thirty-six, and from Newry, twenty-two," and estimates the number of their passengers at over 25,000, "More than one Irishman," remarks the historian, "was naturalized in the forest, like Stark and Houston, and obeyed as chiefs. Of the number was the strange character known as 'Tiger' Roche, at one time the friend of Chesterfield, the idol of Dublin drawing-rooms, and at another time the leader of an Iroquois war party." Dougherty, from Donegal, we find as a leader with the Cherokee Indians in 1600. From Donegal also came Robert and Magdalen Pollock, with their six sons and two daughters, and settled in Maryland. The name was afterward abbreviated to Polk, and among the numerous descendants of this immigrant family from Donegal was President Polk. Major Caldwell, whose daughter was the mother of Vice-President Calhoun, also came from Donegal, while President Andrew Jackson, as all the world knows, "was born somewhere between Carrickfergus and the United States." Presidents James Monroe and James Buchanan also came from Irish stock.

Sir William Johnson was another remarkable Irishman who settled Johnstown, in the Mohawk Valley, in 1738. He had brought with him from Ireland, Lafferty, his lawyer; Flood, his gardener, and Daily, his physician. Twenty years later the Irish settled Manchester, N. H., and John Stark, who led 300 New Hampshire men, chiefly Irish, at the Battle of Bunker Hill, was born in Londonderry, Ireland, his family name being originally Starkey. We can, therefore, safely accept the testimony of Galloway, speaker of the House of Assembly of Pennsylvania, before a committee of the English Commons, June 16, 1779, who said that "the names and places of nativity having been taken down, he could state with precision that scarcely one-quarter of the men in the Revolutionary armies were natives of America, about one-half were Irish and the other fourth English and Scotch."

Curtis, the adopted son of Washington, speaking of the soldiers in the War of Independence, declares that, "Up to the coming of the French, Ireland had furnished in the ratio of about 100 to 1 to any other nation whatever. Then," he exclaims with enthusiasm, "honored be the old and good service of the sons of Erin in the War of Independence; let the shamrock be entwined with the laurels of the Revolution, and truth, and justice, guiding the pen of history, inscribe on the tablets of America's remembrance eternal gratitude to Irishmen!" We may also believe the declaration of Lord Mountjoy, in the English House of Lords, that "England lost America through Ireland." The testimony of Rev. Hugh Henry Breckenridge, a chaplain in Washington's army, is remarkable but no less valuable. In his political satire on "Modern Chivalry," published in Pittsburg in 1794, he apologizes for making the clown an Irishman, and gives his reason thus:

"The character of the English clown I do not well understand, nor could I imitate his manner of speaking; that of the Scotch I have tried and found it in my hands rather insipid; the American, as yet, has no character, so that I can not take one from my own country, which I would rather have done as the scene lies here. But the midland States of America and the Western parts in general, being half-Irish, the character of the Irish clown will not be misunderstood. This was much known among the immigrants or their descendants, so that it will not be thrown away."

The total population of the United States in 1870 was 38,500,000. Careful statisticians have found that at this date the joint product of the Irish colonial element and the subsequent Irish immigration, including that through Canada, was 14,325,000. The joint English product was 4,522,000, and the joint products of all other colonial elements and all subsequent immigration, including the colored population, was 19,653,000. Irish immigration since 1870, while not so proportionately heavy as it was previous to that date, had brought us over 1,300,000, and if we add these and their product to the product of the 14,325,000 people of Irish blood in the United States in 1870, it would be but a conservative statement to make that, of the 65,000,000 who form our population now, 20,000,000 of them have Irish blood in their veins.

At this point reference may be made to a private letter written last year by Vere Foster to the Immigration Commissioners at the port of New York, in which that gentleman states that he and his brother alone had in forty-four years enabled 22,000 young girls between the ages of sixteen and twenty-two years to go from Ireland to the United States.

This brief review of early Irish immigration and the benefits it has conferred upon the country is not given in any spirit of boastfulness, but simply to call attention to the fact that, until the strong current of German immigration began to set in, about 1840, nearly all the immigrants were Irish. From 1820 to 1830 Germany sent 6,761; during same period Ireland sent 50,724. This, as a matter of tardy justice to the Irish people, should be stated, because in the early days immigrants from Ireland were credited as coming from the United Kingdom, without specifying their particular nationality.

From a report prepared by the Bureau of Statistics at Washington, correct information as to immigration and nationality, subsequent to 1820, is obtainable. The total of immigrants arriving in the United States from the close of the Revolutionary War to June 30, 1892, was 16,750,000. Of these Germany supplied 4,748,440; Ireland, 3,952,247; and the other countries in lesser proportions. To the number officially credited to Ireland there should be three-quarters of a million added to make up for those who came here by way of Canada and who were recorded as from "British North American provinces." The excess of the German over the Irish immigration has been made up only of late years, and the fact should be borne in mind that it was the Irish in the earlier periods who so very materially aided in laying the foundations of our splendid Republic. While many of the Germans have remained in the Eastern States and become good, steady citizens, their greater number proceeded to the West and settled down on the fertile lands of Michigan, Wisconsin, and the Dakotas. The Irish have chiefly spread over the New England and Middle States. Of late years the Italian, Swedish, Austro-Hungarian, and Prussian immigration has grown very considerably. For example, the Italian immigration for the decade ending 1860 was only 9,231, while the decade extending from 1880 to 1890 registered 307,309. This proportion is likewise true of the other nations.

There is a common belief that in this immigration from the Continent of Europe there is a certain element injurious to the social institutions of the country. This has given excuse to some people, claiming to be the only true Americans, to raise a cry against immigration in general; but all intelligent people, unbiased by prejudice, agree that this cry is neither wise nor politic.

The present restrictive immigration laws, as now interpreted by the Treasury Department at Washington, *i.e.*, applied to cabin as well as steerage passengers, to protect us from the morally and physically undesirable, from the importation of paupers, criminals, and contract labor, are, if properly and fully enforced, fairly adequate to meet the necessities of the situation. I believe, however, that if the restrictions could be enforced on the other side of the Atlantic the results would be still better than we get now. The administration of the law would also be more humane. If prevented from embarking at an European port, the immigrant who had barely enough money to purchase a passage to America would thus be saved that sum, and also from the greater misfortune of chagrin, humiliation, and even despair, that seize him when turned away from our shores and sent back once more to his wretched lot.

The question of disposing of this crude mass of foreigners and absorbing them into our industrial, political, and social life is certainly a grave one. It is one in which all philanthropists, good citizens, and lovers of humanity should take a living interest. The question is, indeed, one as much for them as for legislatures, State or Federal; and this brings up the question of colonization as it presents itself to-day. The public press of New York of a recent date contained two very striking dispatches. One was from Denver, Col., telling how men were starving from hunger for want of employment, and were threatening depredations under the pressure of physical suffering from want of food and shelter. The other dispatch was from St. Paul, Minn., and told how difficult, even impossible, it was for the farmers of that State to procure hired labor to harvest their teeming crops. These dispatches, published side by side, on the same day, clearly indicate that it is not immigration, but peculiar social conditions that are to be dreaded. If the American laboring man, native or naturalized, could be taught that cultivating the soil is the most noble toil that a man can engage in, as by it he more closely than at any other work obeys the intentions of God, a mighty change for the better would be effected. If he could be brought to see that health and happiness, a quiet, peaceful, and long life—God's gifts to the tillers of the soil—are enjoyed in the retired rural communities where, free from nervous strain, mental worry, and the excessively laborious work of the business and professional man, the speculator, the mechanic, and the day laborer in the grinding cities, his life would be better and happier. The rural community affords a life that God intended for man; the city life is artificial, controlled by the ambitions of men. The farmer's increase comes by the beneficent laws of nature, even while he himself may rest in sleep. The toiler in the city must pay in brain and muscle for every mouthful of bread that keeps together soul and body in himself and family.

Colonization, to be successful, must have the spirit of humanity and philanthropy in it, as well as a view to financial returns to the men who supply the funds. When a colony is to be established, the utmost care should be taken that those placed in charge should be men suitable for the work, and who would not turn their management to aims of personal aggrandizement. Nor should the persons selected as members of the colony be taken indiscriminately and at random. Their character should be carefully judged and their capabilities for leading the industrious, sober, and honest lives that would be likely to make a colony successful, should be ascertained. Some time ago a reverend friend in a Western State wrote to me that there were excellent chances in a certain section of the West for young women to obtain large wages, steady employment, and, he added somewhat jocosely, alluring prospects of early and successful marriages. A newspaper man, by some means known only to journalistic enterprise, got hold of the letter and published it. It was copied all over the Eastern States, and a great number of applications came from young women offering to proceed at once to this Western paradise if their expenses for transportation were provided. In the whole shower of letters there were not twenty-five, judging from their contents, whose writers I would select for the work required. The girls were needed for general housework, but the applicants all wanted to be governesses, matrons, ladies' maids, music teachers, nurses, etc.—all very good in their places, but unsuitable for the positions to be filled in the modern Eden of our reverend friend.

In the same way a man may be capable of even excelling in certain departments of life, but may not have the requisites of a successful colonizer. Thus, much care should be exercised in selecting candidates.

Just ten years ago another Catholic Congress was assembled in the city of Chicago, at which were present many dignitaries of the Catholic Church and prominent laymen. The secretary of that Congress, William J. Onahan, who, by a happy coincidence, performs the same services to the present and more important Congress, called attention to the dangers and abuses which immigrants had to encounter on their entrance to America. Reports were frequent in the public press of wrongs, some of them irreparable, inflicted on immigrants landing at New York, notwithstanding the existence of the Castle Garden establishment. These reports clearly showed the necessity for a mission at Castle Garden to look after the spiritual and temporal welfare of the immigrants.

Some forty-six years ago a number of philanthropic and charitable men, aware of the sufferings and dangers to which the poor immigrants were exposed, organized a society called the State Board of Immigration. Its purpose was twofold, namely, to protect immigrants landing at the port of New York from those who sought to prey upon them, and also to care for the sick and helpless among them. The second object was to afford the several cities and counties of the State protection from the importation of paupers and criminals. In this year (1847) the Board of Commissioners of Immigration leased Castle Garden, which, up to that time, had been devoted to purposes of amusement. Its gates were thrown open to immigrants of every clime, and through them passed many men who subsequently became famous in history for many and great achievements. The immigrants here had a place of refuge where, while waiting for friends or employment to come, they were sheltered, not only from the designs of evil men, but from the biting frosts of the winter's night and the scorching rays of the midsummer's sun, and here also their hunger was appeased. Of course the accommodations were not comfortable, and often even inadequate, but the inmates were protected from robbery and assault. Even after arriving at Castle Garden and passing through the hands of the registration clerks, the immigrants were not safe. They went to the labor bureau to wait for employment or the arrival of friends to take them away. But where were they to go at night if no employer or friend turned up during the day? They had no alternative but to go with the first lodging-house keeper or runner who got hold of them. For anyone acquainted with life in a great city it is unnecessary to dwell on the dangers to which virtuous young girls and inexperienced young men were thus exposed. These dangers it would be impossible to exaggerate. Many a young woman was ruined for life, and many a young man had his whole career wrecked at the outset by the associations and circumstances among which they were thrown.

This was the condition of affairs, notwithstanding the efforts of the Castle Garden officials, when the Colonization Society had its attention attracted by Mr. Onahan to the evils prevailing. After discussion in the Congress, Bishop Ryan, of Buffalo, one of the members, was requested to lay before the late Cardinal McCloskey the opinion of the society that a bureau for the protection of immigrants should be established at Castle Garden. The cardinal warmly approved of the suggestion, and Rev. John Joseph Riordan, of happy memory, was selected for the work. June 1, 1884, Father Riordan regularly took his post at Castle Garden. He soon saw the necessity of a home where immigrant girls would remain until such time as they obtained employment, proceeded on their journey, or met their friends. A house was leased at 7 Broadway, and a temporary home established. The following year, 1885, the property at 7 State Street was purchased, and here the work has since been carried on. Since its establishment fully 40,000 young girls have experienced its protection and benefits. This building was constructed long ago, and was first occupied as a private mansion and afterward used for commercial business, and is consequently but poorly adapted for the purposes of the mission; but, as soon as funds can be raised, a new building will be erected more suitable for the work, and at the same time be a worthy memorial to the founder of the mission, Rev. John Joseph Riordan.

The mission, it may be stated, is American as well as Catholic, and extends its hospitality to all immigrant girls regardless of their religious beliefs. Non-Catholic young women are expressly informed that they are not obliged to attend the religious exercises given in the chapel of the home. The good resulting from the work done at the mission flows into American society, and will be felt in future generations. The mission should, therefore, be regarded as an American institution as well as a religious agency. Such a work needs no commendation here, and if it did, anything we could say would but feebly set forth its merits when compared with the eloquent words of Cardinal Gibbons when speaking about it on a recent occasion.

"The Mission of Our Lady of the Rosary," said his eminence, "has been doing a magnificent work in throwing a mantle of protection around these girls. And I am only too glad to lend my presence to any enterprise which is designed to help this noble work. These maidens, after escaping the perils of the sea and landing on our shores, become the prey of the landsharks that infest your city and seek to rob them of that which is more precious than life itself—their faith and the jewel of purity."

Martin F. Morris, of Washington, D. C., spoke at some length on "The Independence of the Holy See; Its Origin, and the Necessity for Its Continuance in the Cause of Civilization." He said:

On the morning of October 27, A. D. 312, two great armies confronted each other on the right bank of the River Tiber, about nine miles to the northeast of Rome. Not often before in its wonderful history had the din of battle come so close to the eternal city. Armies had often marched out from its gates to conquer. Armies had often marched back into its gates triumphant from the scene of distant wars. Now, for the first time since Breunus the Gaul, in the time of its infancy, had marched upon the capital, the fate of Rome and of the world was to be decided by the arbitrament of arms at the very walls of Rome itself.

Maxentius, a resolute soldier of fortune, led one of these two hosts, and his garrison held the city. At the head of the other army, which had come down from the North and had drawn its recruits mainly from Gaul and Britain, was one of those mighty men of destiny of whom the world has known but seven in all, who, as we read their history, impress us with the profound conviction of their ability to bear down all opposition and to reach the destiny assigned to them by heaven in spite of all obstacles.

Whether it be true or not that when upon that eventful morning Constantine the Great marshaled his legions for the fray his own imperial banner bore upon it the symbol of the cross and the legend "In hoc signo vinces," as some of the chroniclers tell us, certain it is that the result of this conflict was to disclose to the Roman world what the Roman world had scarcely suspected before—that it was no longer pagan, but Christian. For three centuries of merciless persecution Christianity had found a refuge in the catacombs; now it ascended the throne of the Cæsars. The transition perhaps was not as sudden as it seems to us to-day to have been. For, day by day during all these centuries, in spite of persecution, and even by reason of the persecution, Christianity had gained converts, not merely in the cottages of the lowly, but even in the palaces of the Cæsars themselves. The noblest names of Rome are found in the long roll of the Christian martyrology; and no doubt close observers of the course of events, if such observers existed at the time, may have anticipated the result. But, as frequently happens, the result came at last as the sequel of a sharp and bitter civil war; and when Maxentius, in his flight from the field of battle, was drowned in the Tiber, paganism went down with him, though it struggled desperately for a time against the overwhelming waters of the new civilization. The contest had not been in name a contest between paganism and Christianity. There had been no outward semblance, whatever, of a struggle between the rival forces then at work in the Roman Empire. Two rival contestants for the imperial throne had simply arrayed their forces against each other as similar contestants had often done before. But out of their struggle was evolved the triumph of Christianity and of the new civilization which Christianity represented.

It has always been a curious subject of historical inquiry and critical conjecture why Constantine the Great, as soon as he had secured the fruits of his victory and finally consolidated his power, removed the seat of government from the City of Rome to the City of Byzantium on the Thracian Bosphorus, ever since called from him by the name of Constantinople. But assuredly there was a purpose of profound statesmanship, as well as a providential dispensation to prepare Rome to become the religious capital of the world, while it ceased to be the center of political and governmental administration. It is not our purpose here to indulge in conjecture as to the political motives which may have induced Constantine to regard Byzantium as preferable to Rome for the capital of the empire. But the fact that this movement distinctly prepared the way for the conversion of Rome to be the ecclesiastical, instead of the political, capital of the world, without even the shadow of solicitation to that effect on the part of the Pope, is a circumstance that has not received from historians the consideration which it merits.

Cæsarean Rome was destined to become the Rome of the Pontiffs. Out of thirty-three popes who had sustained and guided the infant church during the three centuries of struggle and persecution, twenty-four had received the crown of martyrdom and had shed their blood for the faith. The ground which they had contributed so copiously to fertilize deserved to become their own.

We attach no credit, however, to the story of the grant of Rome by Constantine to the popes. In the nature of things neither Constantine or any of his successors could have dissociated the City of Romulus and of the Scipios from the mighty empire which it had established, and upon which it had impressed its name and its governmental institutions. But the removal of the seat of political authority from Rome to Byzantium naturally relegated Rome to the condition of local self-government, which it was always the policy of Roman administration to foster in all the cities of the great empire. By this removal Rome became practically a free city, with the power of the native senate restored to the management of all its local affairs, and with the superadded influence of the presence within it of the chief of the Christian religion to moderate its course of action and to protect it from the violence of external assault. Even when, under the sons of Theodosius, the Roman Empire was broken up into the Empire of the East and the Empire of the West, and Italy again became a center of political activity as the stronghold of the Western empire, it was not Rome, but first Milan and afterward Ravenna, that became the seat of imperial government. Either studiously and by design, or through an unconscious sense of the propriety of things, Rome was left to itself and to the popes. And when the empire fell, neither Visigoths, nor Ostrogoths, nor Lombards, nor Franks, nor Germans, ever interfered with this tacit arrangement. Never again was it sought by anyone to make Rome the seat of temporal government. The Ostrogothic capital was established at Verona; that of the Lombards at Pavia.

When the Roman Empire of the West was restored in name, and almost in fact, for Charlemagne by Pope Leo III., in A. D. 800, the restored sovereignty of the Cæsars was evidenced by the coronation of the Frankish monarch at Rome, and his successors in the dignity who claimed or bore the title of Kaiser of the holy Roman Empire were never regarded as fully entitled to the honor except as the consequence of a similar coronation by the hands of the holy Roman Pontiff in the City of Rome. And yet, never to any of them did it occur to attempt to transfer the seat of government from Aix-la-Chapelle, or Frankfort-on-the-Main, or Nuremburg, or Vienna, to its old location on the Palatine hill. The public sentiment of Europe would have been opposed to any such attempt. That public sentiment, silently, unconsciously, but for that reason all the more potently, had decreed that Rome should be a free city, free from the control of the great feudal monarchy, free from all external control of every kind.

And it is a singular fact that never, except upon rare occasions, did any of the feudal monarchies of Europe seek to interfere in the internal affairs of the City of Rome. Theoretically, the sovereign of the German Empire was required to go to Rome for his coronation, but with his coronation his functions within the eternal city were at an end. Henry IV. and Frederick Barbarosa sought to break through this rule of international and Christian law, and the public sentiment of Europe, stronger than even the arms of the great Countess Matilda or of Robert Guiscard, drove them both in disgrace from Rome. Within the walls of Rome the only power recognized by the public sentiment of Rome, was that of the Roman senate, the Roman people, and the Roman Pontiff. And down to the year 1870 this public sentiment was strong enough to preserve unimpaired the institutions that had thus been so quietly evolved and established. For we may unhesitatingly assert that the temporal power, as well as the spiritual authority, of the Roman pontiffs was the result of gradual evolution.

We presume that no one will pretend that the mass of dogma, and of doctrine, and of religious practice that now obtains among us was known in its fullness to the apostles or to their immediate successors. The germ of it all they undoubtedly had; but it was unnecessary, in the nature of things, that they should have had it in all the plentitude of its manifestations. The truth has been unfolded as occasion demanded, each subsequent declaration of it being the legitimate consequence of the original revelation.

So it was likewise with the temporal power. Who can assume to place his finger on the precise point of time when the Roman pontiffs became temporal rulers? We know when, and how, and by whom the monarchies of France and England and Germany were founded. We know when the Swiss Republic was born. We know the years whence Florence, Pisa, Genoa, and Venice severally became independent powers. The great landmarks of the world's history are the catastrophes out of which nations are born and dynasties reared. But who can say when the temporal power of the popes began?

We are told of a grant by Constantine the Great to which we have already referred; and we are told of a grant by Theodosius, and by Pepin, and by Charlemagne. But all these are undoubtedly apocryphal. We have more accurate knowledge of a grant by the great Countess Matilda of Tuscany; but the power of the popes had then been firmly established. And authentic history tells us, with circumstantial detail, how the feudal rulers of Urbino, Carrara, Bologna, and Benevento gave way to the milder sovereignty of the Roman pontiffs.

But neither to Constantine, nor to Theodosius, nor to Pepin, nor to Charlemagne, nor to the Countess Matilda is due the establishment of the temporal power of the popes. The silly imbecility of partisan bigotry has sometimes set down Pope Gregory VII., better known, perhaps, as Hildebrand of Sienna, as the founder of the temporal power of the papacy, and the latter end of the 11th century as the period of its establishment. But only the most intense bigotry or the most willful ignorance can be blind to the fact that Hildebrand of Sienna exercised no more power in Rome than his predecessors had done before him. History fails to disclose any change in his time in the government of the eternal city. The grant which was undoubtedly made by Matilda, of the Tuscan territory, subsequently known as the patrimony of St. Peter, enlarged the dominion of the popes, but it did not create or originate it. The Roman territory was no part of this grant, and in the Roman territory the power of the popes had already been established for several centuries.

In subordination, of course, to the divine ordination from which all power originates, to the will of the Roman people is immediately due the temporal power of the popes. To the spiritual chiefs, in whose honor, integrity and patriotism they had confidence, the Roman people deemed themselves justified in remitting, from time to time, the conduct of their temporal affairs. When Alaric the Visigoth, angered at the imbecility of the rulers of Ravenna, plundered the eternal city and looked from the Pintian hill over a scene of indiscriminate slaughter and carnage, it was Pope Innocent I. to whom the people turned in their despair, and who induced the fierce barbarian to withdraw. When, soon after, the terrible Atilla came down upon Italy with his savage Mongolian horde and spread desolation over the land, it was to the Pope again that the people turned, and it was Saint Leo and not a Roman general or an officer or army of the tottering empire that encountered the savage chief under the walls of Aquileia, turned him back from his purpose and saved Rome and Italy from the horror of Mongolian conquest. When Ostrogoths, and Lombards, and Saracens, and Normands, swarmed over the peninsula to ravage and plunder it was reserved to the popes to check their ravages and to mitigate the horrors of their invasion. Is it any wonder that the people of Rome remitted the temporal power in their State to those who alone could save them from destruction?

For a thousand years before it assumed definite shape, the temporal power of the popes in the city of Rome existed and was recognized by the tacit acknowledgment of the Christian world. Never before and never since in the history of the world has power been established so quietly and so greatly in accord with the wishes of the people over whom it was exercised. The power, in fact, was the gradual development of the people's will—so gradual, that, as we have said, no one can point to the actual time of its origin; for it had no such origin as other governments of the world have had.

It is very true, however, that, to the pontificate of Hildebrand of Sienna, or Pope Gregory VII., we are to refer the formal establishment of the temporal power of the popes, inasmuch as to that time we are to refer the culmination of the feudal system in Europe, and the first great victory of Christian civilization over it under the auspices of the Roman pontiffs. The contest between feudalism and civilization, beginning with the overthrow of the Roman Empire of the West, in A. D. 472, was a long and bitter one. It had lasted over a thousand years when the discovery of America enabled the world to insure the ultimate overthrow of the system. But the contest is not even yet entirely at an end. In that contest the feudal classes of Europe were banded against the people and the Christian Church. The Roman pontiffs were ever the most consistent opponents of feudalism; and it was the unceasing effort of the popes to restrain the rapacity of the "robber barons," and the arbitrary licentiousness of the feudal monarchs.

The feudal system was at its height when Hildebrand became Pope, in A. D. 1073. Henry IV. of the house of Franconia, an able and un-principled man, was then Emperor of Germany (A. D. 1056-1106), and as such the virtual head of the system. A violent contest broke out between the Pope and the Emperor. Henry sought to determine it by an appeal to the brute force of arms. He crossed the Alps, invaded Italy, and marched upon Rome with a view of deposing the Pope and procuring the election of a Pontiff more in accord with his wishes. Suddenly Matilda, Countess of Tuscany, appeared in arms against him and resisted his advance. Robert Guiscard hastened from Naples with his Normans to protect the City of Rome. Europe was aroused to a sense of danger. Rebellions broke out in Germany itself. Henry's army melted away. Matilda skilfully foiled all his movements, and the discomfited and baffled monarch at last was compelled to come to terms with the Pontiff. In their famous interview at the Castle of Canossa, in A. D. 1079, the independence of the Church from feudal restraint and the triumph of Christian civilization over feudal barbarism were definitely secured. And although feudalism survived for many a day, the result of that interview was to secure the church ever afterward from the encroachments of the Northern powers. It was further to insure that result that the Countess Matilda, either immediately afterward or at her death in 1115, donated to the popes the territory along the shores of the Mediterranean between the Tiber and the lake of Bolsona, known in subsequent times by the name of the patrimony of St. Peter.

Such was the origin of what is known as the temporal power of the popes. Assuredly no temporal power was ever more justly acquired; no temporal sovereignty ever had more just or more legitimate foundations. The free will of the Roman people and the public sentiment of Europe made of Rome what a similar sentiment, crystalizing itself in organic law, has made of the City of Washington and the District of Columbia for the purposes of our Federal Union. The government of the Union might, perhaps, have carried on successfully within the territorial limits of some one of the States of the Union, as indeed was done temporarily in the beginning, when the capital was located first at New York and afterwards at Philadelphia. But the better to secure the freedom of that government and its independent action, the founders of our constitutional system most wisely deemed it proper, and even necessary, to segregate the small territory of the District of Columbia, and to devote it for all time to that purpose. It was not their idea to create for the government which they established any imperial domain, but simply to insure its independence of action. By the divine ordination, and by the public sentiment of Europe acting in accordance therewith, Rome was intended to serve for the Christian world a purpose similar to that which the City of Washington serves for our Federal Union—as a place where all may meet on terms of equal freedom and independence.

The parallel may be even farther extended. We have said that it was not the intention of the founders of our Federal system to provide a large domain for our central government, although the powers of that government were to be co-extensive with the territorial limits of the Union, and its influence was to be co-extensive with the habitable globe. On the contrary, it was their express purpose to make that domain no larger than would be absolutely required to secure the independence of the government, and a small district, containing not more than 100 square miles of territory, was deemed amply sufficient for the purpose. The Christian Church was established as a power on earth independent of the nations, but to act upon all the nations, to pervade them with its influence, to weld them in the bonds of a common fraternity, but with a purpose and a sphere of action entirely distinct and separate from that of the nations. "Give unto Cæsar the things that are Cæsar's, and unto God the things that are God's," was the mandate of the Divine Founder of the church. And this mandate, as did our Federal constitution with the Union and States of the Union, established distinctly the co-ordination of the spiritual and the temporal power. The founder of Christianity no more contemplated the subjection of the temporal to the spiritual power, as in the Mohammedan system, than he did the subjection of the spiritual to the temporal power which it is the boast of Protestantism to have accomplished by a restoration of the infamous system of State religions, characteristic of the old pagan world, and which it was the mission of Christianity to destroy. By the separation and co-ordination of the spiritual and temporal powers the freedom of both were to be secured. And we may add that an alliance between the two was no more contemplated than the subjection of the one to the other.

Now, while it necessarily follows that the possession of temporal power as such by the church is not only not necessary to it, but is, in its nature, injurious to the purity of its existence; the possession of a locus for the free and independent exercise of its governmental functions is an entirely different matter. A place for a meeting of its councils outside of the territorial limits of any State or nation, and therefore, presumably free from the undue influence which would be natural within the limits of a State or nation—a place for the transaction of the executive business of the church—a place for the sessions of its general tribunals, for there is legislative, executive and judicial business to be transacted by the church as well as by the State, is just as much a necessity for the church as it is for the State, with this distinction, perhaps, that the exercise of temporal power is the primary purpose of the State, while to the church it is merely an incident, a convenient and proper incident to the exercise of its spiritual power, but yet never more than an incident.

The church may exist without the temporal power of the popes. It existed without it in the catacombs; it existed without it through all the ages of persecution. Popes may die in exile or in prison, as they have died. Godless conspirators against the cause of truth may raise again the banners of hell over the altars of religion, as they have frequently done in the past. They may slay the priest at the altar, scatter the worshipers and defile the sanctuary, and yet the spirit of religion will survive and the church will come forth again triumphant, as it came forth from the catacombs. Free or enslaved, in favor with princes or incurring their deadliest enmity, we have no apprehension for the church; her cause is the cause of God and it will survive. So many tyrants rage against the cause of human liberty; but the spirit of liberty can not be destroyed by tyrants. Assuredly it can not seriously be claimed that, because human liberty can survive the assaults of tyranny, therefore it should continue to be subject to them.

Is it any more reasonable to hold that because the church will undoubtedly survive persecution and the loss of its independence, therefore it ought to be subjected to persecution and deprived of the small allotment of temporal dominion that constitutes the guarantee of its freedom and independence?

Man is by nature entitled to be free; therefore is he entitled to free institutions. Man is entitled to freedom in his spiritual relations; therefore is the church, the organ of his religion, entitled to such measures of temporal authority as will secure its independence and its freedom of action. More than this there is not claimed for it; more than this it would not be wise for it to possess.

No dispassionate and impartial student of history can now fail to recognize the benefit that accrued to our civilization from the existence of the papacy. It was the papacy, and the papacy alone, that saved Europe from the grinding despotism of the feudal system. From the brigandage and licentiousness which that system was so well calculated to perpetuate, humanity found its only refuge in the power that was represented by the papacy. The independence of the papacy secured the independence of the church. And the ultimate triumph of all that the church represented and was to Europe—religion, morality, science, literature, female virtue, and the sanctity of the home. Recall for a moment the picture drawn by a great dramatist of our own age; it is a true picture. In the drama of Richelieu, by Edward Bulwer Lytton, when the famous French cardinal, driven from power, temporarily deprived of his honor, and shorn of all his authority by the loss of royal favor, was threatened with an assault upon the virtue of his favorite niece, what did he say and do; and what was the power that enabled him to hurl defiance on his enemies. Here are his words, that deserve to be immortal:

> Mark where she stand. Around her form
> I draw the awful circle of our solemn church;
> Let but a foot within that holy ground,
> And on thy head—yea, though it wore a crown—
> I launch the curse of Rome.

And the writer is true to the spirit of history when he makes the cardinal's enemies shrink from his denunciation more abjectly than they would have cowered before any manifestation of political authority.

During the Middle Ages, and even long after Protestantism had destroyed the spirit of Christian charity and the sentiment of the brotherhood of man in Europe, the Roman pontiffs were the arbiters of political quarrels and national controversies—not because they arrogated to themselves any temporal authority over the nations, as partisan bigotry has falsely asserted, but because on account of their spiritual character the Christian world looked to them as the most natural and the most impartial judges of national and international disputes, and the faith of the Christian world, in the rectitude of their decisions, has never been mistaken or misplaced. When were their decisions in this regard wrong?

A remarkable illustration is recalled by the history of the great event we are now commemorating. When the grand exploit of Columbus had opened up the Western World beyond the Atlantic to the daring adventure of Spain, and the contemporaneous maritime enterprise of Portugal threatened to occasion collisions between the two nations, Alexander VI., who then occupied the Papal chair, and to whose decision the matter had been referred for arbitration, decreed that the thirty-seventh meridian of longitude west of the straits of the Cape de Verde Islands should be the dividing line between the colonial empires of the two powers. There was no usurpation in this decision, as the malignant falsifiers of Edinburgh and Geneva would have us believe—no haughty arrogation of sovereignty over this newly-discovered world such as to justify the pontiffs in parceling it out between the two great maritime powers of the day. The action of the Pope was simply that of the judge or arbitrator to whom the controversy for the settlement of a disputed boundary had naturally been referred by those interested in its settlement. And strangely enough the two parties most nearly interested, Spain and Portugal, acquiesced in the decision of the Pontiff without a murmur of dissent. And it was not until long afterward, when the basest malignity of falsehood was never deemed too vile for the use of intolerant fanaticism and religious rancor, that one of the most beneficent acts of the Roman Pontiffs was characterized as an evidence of their usurpation of sovereign powers over the world.

As mediators of peace and arbitrators of international difficulties the popes of Rome have rendered services to the cause of human civilization, supposing for the moment that we can dissociate that term from religion, which no historical writer of the present day who has regard for the cause of truth can ignore. We think a period has been reached in the history of the world when arbitration between the nations may be substituted for the brutal agency of the sword as a more sensible and more satisfactory method for the determination of the quarrels and disputes that arise between the nations. More than once in late years we have had recourse as a nation to this method of settling our difficulties with other nations of the world; and the method has commended itself to the common sense of the age as eminently wise and just. In other words, by our sporadic efforts we are striving to return to the system of a more permanent character represented in past times by the Roman Pontiffs. Is it too much to hope that the time will come again when all the nations will agree by common consent to submit their controversies, which they are unable to settle amicably between themselves, to a supreme court of the world, presided over by the Roman Pontiffs? But in order that the Roman Pontiff may be free to act as such supreme arbitrator, in order that the Roman Pontiff may be free to act as the ordinary arbitrator of the affairs of our universal church throughout the nations, he must not be the subject of any power or nation himself. For such subjection would detract from his impartiality as well as from his independence. It is unjust to all of us throughout the world that the head of our religion should be under the suspicion even of being controlled, constrained or influenced by the temporal authority of any nation claiming political jurisdiction of his person or of his surroundings.

The writer of this paper is not an enemy to the sentiment of united Italy. On the contrary, he sympathizes most heartily, not only with the desire for freedom which is assumed to have been so large a factor in producing a united Italy, but with the general theory of a union, or at least of a confederation, of all the branches of cognate races so far as it may be feasible or practicable to fuse them into one nationality. But Rome was not necessary for the united Italy. Rome has become the capital of the world; we would not have it disgraced into becoming the capital of a petty European monarchy. Rome has not now, even if it ever had, any strategic, political, or commercial value as the capital of an Italian monarchy, or of an Italian republic, or of an Italian confederation of any kind. Italy would be as strong without it as with it; stronger, indeed, without it, because there would then no longer be the friction of the religious sentiment that must continue to struggle against the existing conditions, and that must necessarily succeed, sooner or later, in modifying those conditions. Rome should be a great free city, the great free city of the world, the holy city, and the religious capital of all the nations—not a mere competitor of London, or Berlin, or Vienna, but once again the city of the soul, as a noble poet has well named it, to which the " Orphans of the Heart" may ever turn as their home, and where the children of every nation under heaven may come and feel themselves at home. United Italy will make no real sacrifice of nationality by the restoration of Rome to the popes. The world will be the gainer by securing anew the independence of the Holy See.

Col. Robert M. Douglas, of Greensboro, N. C., read a paper on "Trade Combinations and Strikes," in which he said:

Trade combinations and strikes are twin children of an advancing civilization, in which the individual is becoming merged into the aggregate, not only as to his rights of property, but too often as to his manhood on the one hand and his conscience on the other. Trade combinations are of different kinds, varying with the objects of their formation and the character of the men organizing and controlling them; but throughout them all runs the essential object of obtaining by co-operation of efforts and resources what is beyond the power of the individual. Strikes, whatever may be their local causes and effects, and however perverted by unworthy leaders, must be finally regarded as the solemn protest of the individual against wrongs for which he feels the law presents no adequate remedy.

Trade combinations are almost invariably effected through incorporated companies, and this brings us to a consideration of the corporation laws of this country, which, in my opinion, through their unequal operation, are largely responsible for the unfortunate relations existing between labor and capital, with the resulting strikes.

What is a corporation? It is a fictitious person, created by law, possessing all the property rights of the individual, but lacking many of his limitations and enjoying greater privileges. Like an individual, it can buy and sell, take and hold, sue and be sued, and act as trustee, administrator, or guardian. Unlike an individual, it has neither conscience to appeal to, nor body to imprison. Its character is its soul, its capital stock is its life's blood. It enjoys peculiar privileges not given to individuals or firms. It has a fixed term of life, unaffected by the death of its members, and hence is not hampered by will or descent, dower, courtesy, or homestead. However great its capital or numerous its shareholders, it is not embarrassed by internal differences of opinion, for it has but one will, which is the will of the majority. Many corporations, like railroads, possess the power of condemnation, which is simply the practical exercise of the right of eminent domain, one of the highest privileges of the State.

Usually its shareholders have no personal liability beyond the amount subscribed; and by an ingenious process, based upon a fictitious purchase, subscriptions can be turned into paid-up stock upon the actual payment of a small percentage. The capitalization of railroad companies, that is, their issues of stock and bonds, rarely ever represent actual investments. A syndicate of stockholders of a projected railroad will, by appeals to the patriotism and self-interest of communities and individuals, obtain all the public and private subscriptions possible, and then organize a distinct corporation in the nature of a construction company. As officers of the railroad company, they will make a contract with themselves as the construction company to build the road for a fixed price per mile, generally amounting to the entire bonds and stocks of the road, including public and private subscriptions. These subscriptions, with the first mortgage bonds, usually build the road, leaving the entire second mortgage bonds and nearly all the stock as net profits.

These issues of stock and bonds, representing nothing but wind and water, of course contribute nothing to the productive capacity of the road, and yet they elect its officers, control its management, and absorb its profits. The mere payment of the interest on the bonds, without any dividend on the stock, would be an enormous profit to the builders. Six per cent on the par value of a bond becomes 100 per cent if the bond costs only six cents on the dollar, and over 1,000 per cent if it costs nothing.

If a corporation having 5,000 employes cut down their daily wages 5 cents—a reduction which none could afford to resist—it would be a net saving of $250 per day. It would mean on the one hand from $75,000 to $100,000 per year added to net profits of the corporation, and on the other 2,000,000 loaves of bread taken from the mouths of the suffering poor. Successive reductions complete the grinding process to the limit of human endurance. Is not this a dangerous experiment for the corporation to make or the State to permit?

Our civilization rests upon a surrender by the individual of a portion of his natural liberty in exchange for the protection of government, and he has a right to demand that the government shall use all powers necessary to his protection. Otherwise is he not relegated by the law of nature to his natural right of self-defense? If the State create an artificial person with powers greater than his own, with which he can not contend, has he not a right to demand that the State shall provide efficient means to prevent an abuse of the extraordinary powers it has given to its creature?

A corporation has no inherent rights, and if it receives from the State powers and privileges greater than an individual, it thereby assumes greater responsibilities, which neither it nor the State can ignore. This may require additional legislation, but as we have enlarged the common law in favor of the corporation, why not extend it for the protection of the individual? It contains the germs of all necessary remedies, not only for the abuse of corporate powers, but for many other existing evils.

At first, remedial legislation would necessarily be somewhat experimental; but experience would soon perfect it. All corporate privileges should be held at the will of the sovereign grantor. This is now the case with the present constitution of North Carolina and some other States. Of course the doctrine of "vested rights" will be invoked, and the Dartmouth College case cited, but it must be remembered that this case was decided on the ground that the college was an eleemosynary corporation. There is an essential difference between a charter granted merely to perpetuate the charitable purposes of a private founder and one conveying valuable franchises directly affecting the general public, and the abuse of which may vitally injure communities as well as individuals.

In any event, when remedial legislation is needed to correct great public wrongs, our legislators should always give the people the benefit of the doubt; and at least give the Supreme Court the opportunity of passing upon its constitutionality. If necessary the Constitution of the United States can be amended.

Each State should have a department or bureau of corporations, with visitorial powers, to which all corporations should report at stated times. This need not cost the State anything, as moderate fees would more than pay the expenses. The visitorial powers need not be exercised except upon complaint, and an appeal to the courts should be allowed. The majority of the States already have railroad, banking and insurance commissioners, and but a slight extension of their powers would be sufficient. There is no reason why large manufacturing corporations and transportation companies should be any more free from State supervision. Treat all alike and require from all a strict observance of the law. Trade combinations and strikes are not private affairs, concerning only employer and employed; but usually injuriously affect a large number of innocent people, and become public nuisances of the highest order. A nuisance is abatable, and an affray is punishable at the common law. In an affray, which is the voluntary fighting of two or more persons in a public place, both parties are guilty, no matter who began it. Why should it not be so with strikes, if the public peace be broken? I have no sympathy with the red-handed rioter; he should be promptly suppressed. But if the employer or his agent provokes a strike by oppression or unlawful combinations, why is he not equally guilty with the poor wretch whom he has driven to desperation?

Of course the government can not compel anyone to employ or work for a fixed price, but the strike or the lockout must be kept equally within the law. Whenever a strike occurs, especially one in any way affecting the general public, a prompt and thorough investigation should be made by the State authorities—not only into the acts committed, but also into the causes, remote as well as proximate. The resultant acts of the strikers are generally open and easily seen and punished, but the exciting acts of the employer are more secret and difficult of redress.

The investigations should extend not simply to overt acts, but to all causes of complaint, including the rate of wages; whether paid promptly, and in cash, or orders; the hours of labor, whether the employes live in houses belonging to the company, and, if so, whether the rental is fair, so as to determine whether, on the whole, the employes receive sufficient remuneration for their labor. Wages, apparently fair, can easily be largely reabsorbed by high rentals and store accounts, where the store and tenant houses belong to the company. The reasonableness of wages depends not only upon the labor of the employe, but also upon the resulting profit to the employer. This should include a fair return upon the original investment, the capital actually employed in carrying on the business, and the personal service of the owners. All these should be matters of official inquiry. The dividend declared upon the stock does not always show the actual profits, as large amounts may be carried to the surplus fund, expended in improvements, or paid to the principal owners in the shape of salaries.

It may be said that such inquiries are inquisitorial, but so is the cross-examination of any witness. Practically, all strikes occur with incorporated companies or large manufacturing establishments. We have seen that corporations would have no right to object, as they placed themselves under peculiar obligations to the state when they accepted their chartered rights. Private manufacturers are in no better position, as they derive peculiar benefits through the operation of our tariff laws. They should remember that the avowed purpose of all our protective legislation is to protect our laboring classes from competition with the pauper labor of Europe, and to enable our manufacturers to pay such wages as will permit their employes to support and educate their families in a manner befitting American citizens. I have always been in favor of a protective tariff, because I believed it protected the American aborer. In granting this protection to the manufacturer, the government should require him to show that he has shared its benefits with the humblest laborer from the sweat of whose brow he derives his profits.

One other danger inseparable from corporate bodies arises from their utter want of moral responsibility. Corporations are too often managed, not by their real owners, but by officers whose trained minds and consciences are devoted to the single purpose of producing the largest possible profits with a view to the largest possible salaries. There is no apparent reason why the right to apply for a writ of quo warranto should be reserved to the attorney-general alone, who too frequently owes his election to some powerful corporation.

But little can here be said about trade combinations in the nature of trusts Avowedly formed for the purpose of controlling prices by preventing competition or limiting production, they are essentially vicious in their nature, dangerous in their tendencies, and destructive in their results. The United States, as well as several of the States, have enacted laws against trusts and unlawful trade combinations, but so far apparently with little success, either owing to defects in the laws or lukewarmness in those charged with their execution. Even without such legislation, the old common law offences of forestalling, regrating, engrossing, and conspiracy would, if enforced, remedy many xisting evils.

In the taxing power the government possesses a most efficacious remedy for trade combinations. The right to tax is the power to destroy; and we have seen this power exercised with a vengeance on State bank issues and foreign imports.

This question of taxation brings us to another matter in which the poor man is placed at a disadvantage. It has been said that our churches are principally supported by the comparatively poor, and the same may be said of the government. The wealth of the rich consists largely in bonds and stocks and other convertible securities, which can be easily concealed without leaving any trace. That this can be done is self-evident; that it has been done has been recently shown in the most striking manner. A certain amount of revenue must be raised for the purposes of government; and when one species of property escapes taxation, the rate is necessarily increased upon what is taxed. What the locomotive fails to pay, must be levied upon the mule.

A laboring man can rarely escape taxation. He has no money or stocks or bonds to conceal. He can not evade the poll tax by hiding his own head, neither can he put his mule or cow in a safe-deposit vault and swear he does not own any. The poor farmer ploughing a brindled steer upon a barren hillside pays taxes upon his steer as well as upon his own head. He has fair cause for complaint if the railroad magnate rolling by in his private car shirks any part of the just burdens of government.

Another principle of taxation that operates very unequally is that which permits all debts to be deducted from solvent credits. That is, if a man owns $10,000 in notes or bonds; and owes $8,000, he returns only $2,000 for taxation. But if a man buys a house for $1,000, paying $200 cash and giving his note and mortgage for the remaining $800, he is compelled to pay taxes on the entire value of the place. His actual ownership extends only to the amount he has paid, and on that alone should he be required to pay taxes.

The best citizen on earth is the man who owns his home. Next to his wife and children, it is to him the dearest thing on earth, because it shelters them. He constantly improves and beautifies it, and becomes more and more identified with its every feature. He seeks to avoid and prevent every danger that may threaten it. He is never a rioter. The State should by every means in its power encourage a citizen to acquire a home as the surest pledge of his fidelity. Every little flower planted by the contented hand of a freeman is a stronger prop of a free government than a bayonet.

These few suggestions, the result of professional experience and earnest consideration, are submitted to you in the hope that, however crude and imperfect, they may contain a germ which, under the fostering care of an abler hand, may develop into some measure of public welfare. The dangers that threaten our country and its institutions are evident. The remedy is yet to be found; but its essential principle lies in a just recognition of the rights of all classes of our people. So make and enforce the laws that every one throughout this broad land shall feel and know that there is no one so rich and powerful as to be beyond the avenging arm of the law, and none so poor and humble as to be beneath its completest protection.

Rev. John R. Slattery, of St. Joseph's Seminary, Baltimore, Md., followed with an able paper on "The Negro Race; Its Condition, Present and Future." He said:

The religious condition of our eight millions of blacks gives food for anxious thought, and is fraught with lively interest to every citizen of this Republic. American Catholics may be said to have folded their arms for two and a half centuries, especially indeed since the war, and allowed their non-Catholic countrymen full swing in the religious training of the colored race. We did our share for them in other ways; we had more than a proportionate representation in the Union army which emancipated them, while we were in insignificant number on the opposite side. But as far as religion goes our efforts have been trivial. To appreciate how truly so, consider how few of the black race are Catholics—but one in fifty. And here is the first element in their religious condition; their actual numbers adhering to the various sects count up, all told, about four millions, while fully as many are without any religion at all.

Moreover, the peculiarity of their religious organizations is that they themselves do their whole religious work. They are the bishops, preachers, elders, deacons, and flock. Except a few Episcopal clergymen, all the ministers laboring among the blacks are of their own race. The white clergymen are found only in their universities, colleges, seminaries, and other higher schools; yet the African churches seem to move along smoothly enough.

As to their religious knowledge, it is no surprise to learn that very many of the negroes who profess religion are ignorant of the most fundamental truths of revelation. They have some idea of our Lord, a great reverence for His Holy Name, a notion of sin and of the Bible—the latter, however, more in a superstitious than a rational way. Baptism, in the eyes of a multitude of them, is all that is needed. No matter what sect may claim them, once baptized they are saved. "Once in grace never out of it;" or, to give another favorite saying of theirs: "The Blood of Jesus never burns." Now, as no soul is exempt from the necessity of learning the essential truths of God's revelation, it is a primary question as to whether or not these are acquired by the blacks through their church membership. Behold the drawback in the negro churches. They are taught the fundamental truths of the Christian religion but very imperfectly. Far too often their churches are mere hustings for political candidates, or are like social clubs; and their houses of worship are often used for nearly all kinds of gatherings.

At the same time the ignorance of religious truth among the negroes does not weaken the religious sentiment which is naturally strong in them, and which, strange as it seems, is often divorced from their sense of morality. In this matter, however, they are without anything worthy the name of guidance. Recently a leading preacher declared in the public press that two-thirds, if not three-fourths, of the colored preachers were immoral. "If the blind lead the blind, both shall fall into the ditch." It is impossible to say to what extent this laxity of morals is attributable to the frightful doctrine of the inadmissibility of grace, which is not theirs alone, but that of the many millions of Southern whites who profess the Calvinistic doctrine of justification. Their test of conversion, writes a Mrs. Rice in the *Christian Union*, is an abnormal paroxysmal experience, after which they have "got religion" and no sin is to be laid to their charge. This writer is also authority for the statement that even a murderer has been known to conduct a Sunday-school, with great apparent zeal and unction, for months after his undiscovered crime.

Unhappily the attitude of the whites towards the immoralities of the negroes works much harm in lowering the standard of morality in the poor people's eyes. A black person is not expected to be virtuous, and is looked upon with wonder if he or she happens to be so. It is related of an elderly colored woman, when urging a younger one to give up her bad ways, that the latter gave this scornful answer: "Huh! de white folks hires me, an' thinks as much o' me as dey does o' you." And even if the whites stopped here it would not be so bad. No race can throw the first stone at the negroes, for their hybrids belong to all races.

It can not be too much insisted upon that, as a rule, the whites give no edifying example to the blacks. Especially is this the case with many of those who have dealings with the negroes. Many employers, venders, traders, and agents are to blame for a downward moral drift in those poor people. Is our public sentiment, let me ask, calculated to engender noble aspirations in the negroes? Is the tone of the press such as would awaken in their hearts better thoughts? Do the corrupt practices so widespread in politics; the systematic adulterations in food, clothing, etc.; the frequent fraudulent failures—do such facts tend to elevate the negro race? We need not then be surprised at Fred. Douglass' question? "If the negro could be bottled up, who could or would bottle up the irrepressible white man?" Men are always ready to have a fling at the black man, who usually is more sinned against than sinning.

Who is responsible for the irreligion and immorality of the negro? The colored people did not intrude themselves upon us; they were brought here in chains, and held by a cruel slave code in the communities where they now are. Slavery, then, is the first cause; a negro was a chattel and counted as such. True, in good Christian families, which are too often the exception, the slaves were conscientiously looked after. But in the "negro quarters" it seldom happened that personal and family rights were or could be recognized or respected. Marriage, alas! was practically a union during the good pleasure of the master; nor were Catholic masters always found proof against the demands of poverty or cupidity when it was question of marital or parental rights among the slaves, even sacrificing their own offspring when of Ham's race. Nor in disposing of their slaves did they always consider whether the purchasers were Catholics or not.

The whole tendency of the slave code was in favor of the whites, who should be angels, indeed, not to abuse the practically limitless power by which the laws invested owners of slaves.

A concomitant to slavery was ignorance. In the earlier years of the Republic slaves were permitted to read and write; afterwards this was forbidden by severe laws. And we have heard former slaves tell how, when they were growing up, they would steal out at night with their spelling-book or reader hidden next the skin, in order to take reading lessons from some kind friend, although at the risk of a severe whipping if caught.

Nor, in this connection, should we forget the transition from slavery to freedom. Emancipation must have wrought a strange intoxication to the millions of slaves who had seen themselves ever surrounded by whites, who alone were respectable and who frequently idled away their entire lives. Emancipation, they thought, was to make the blacks like such whites. Wild dreams of ease and comfort must have flitted through their imaginations. Hence, to realize the stern condition which the daily life of duty and care entailed upon them must have produced among many of the emancipated very strange results.

We think that Protestantism may in part be held responsible for the present irreligious and immoral condition of the negroes. The widely-spread race prejudice, as powerful in the North as in the South, though shared by Catholics as well as by others, is truly a Protestant instinct. It is inhuman, un-Christlike, and unworthy even of our manhood, not to speak of our citizenship or our Christianity. For two and a half centuries our non-Catholic countrymen have had control of the negro in the South, and what is the result? They gave him in some measure their religion; they placed no restriction on their religious teaching or on their codes of morality; to-day the whites and blacks of the South profess common beliefs; yet in spite of all, we hear from the whites hardly a good word of the blacks. How marked a contrast is this to the influence of the Catholic Church!

From the baptism of Clovis, when the haughty Gaul despised the Goth fully as much as ever our Southern whites despised the blacks, to the crowning of Charlemagne as the common head of an undivided people, only the same period of time elapsed as that between the introduction of slavery into our territory and the present day. Yet it was long enough for the Catholic Church to blend the master and slave into one, and to make the new race the custodian of the ancient and the beginner of modern civilization. Nor was it different with Goths and Romans in Italy, with Normans and Saxons in Great Britain. Even in our day and in our own hemisphere, whatever misery afflicts Spanish America, the Catholic instinct of human equality has delivered it from race antagonisms. There is no negro problem in Catholic South America.

But when we look at our negro question from the missionary point of view, and ask, Is not the Catholic Church in America to be blamed for lack of zeal? I answer with an unhesitating Yes. After all, Protestantism has done something to Christianize the blacks; but we have done, I may say, nothing. They have made, and are making, great missionary efforts, pouring out money like water; but we have attempted almost nothing. In fact, it was announced a few years ago, at the Lake Mohonk conferences, that the various denominations had spent, since the war, on the negroes, thirty-five millions of dollars. Add to that immense sum the hundred and thirty higher institutions, with twenty-five thousand scholars, of whom one thousand are preparing for the Protestant ministry.

Imperfect as is this picture of the religious condition of the negro race and of its causes, it is enough, however, to give us a fair idea of the state of things. It tells us of from eight to nine millions of blacks, living in one section of our land, and that the most Protestant, just emerged from slavery; enjoying the franchise; learning how to read and write; two-thirds of them living on plantations, one and all being made to feel a frightful ostracism which descends so deep as to exclude them in some places from public conveyances; a people one-half of whom have no religion, and the other half are professing only a shade of sentimental belief.

Yet there is a cheerful view to be taken. However sadly situated this people may be, there are bright hopes in store for them. All drawbacks and discouragements notwithstanding, they have won the nation's respect. They are not rebels against public authority; they are law-abiding citizens. They love the worship of God; in their childish way they desire to love God; they long for and relish the supernatural; they willingly listen to the word of God; their hearts burn for the better gifts. They are hard working; patiently and forgivingly do they bear their wrongs. This is in marked contrast with their white neighbors, too many of whom have not a word of good to say for the black man, thus verifying the old paradox that we never forvive those whom we have wronged, much as we may pardon those who have injured us.

It is related of Michael Angelo that going along the streets of Rome he espied a rough, unhewn block of marble. "There is an angel hidden there," said he, pointing to the stone. Having had it brought to his studio, the immortal artist soon began to chip at it, and to hack at it, and to shape it, till finally there came forth from it the faultless angel in marble, which his prophetic eye had seen in it.

A similar block of marble is the negro; far harder to work upon than the Carrara lump of Michael Angelo, because the chisel must be applied to the human heart. And has the negro a human heart? Is he a man? Yes, thank God! he is a man, with all the affections and longings, all the faculties and qualities of human kind Behold, then, it is his manhood that is the first ground of our hope. Like the Roman poet Terence, who is himself supposed by some to have been a negro, since he was one of the slaves of Scipio Africanus, the black man may say: "Homo sum, et nihil humanum alienum a me puto." The negro's first claim upon us is our common humanity, and that means a close tie of brotherhood.

The future of the negro appears, therefore, to a missionary like myself to be hopeful. It rests primarily on the great truth that the human race is one. There is one Lord, one God, one Father of all. From this we rise to the supernatural destiny of our common humanity; one Jesus Christ, one church, one life of probation, one heaven, one hell. The negro has everything that makes a man, everything that makes a Christian. Holy Church teaches the same doctrine to blacks as to whites; furnishes the same sacramental channels of grace, baptizes the black infant, confirms the negro boy, administers Holy Communion to him, marries the black man and woman, ordains the black priest, gives him the same extreme unction as the white receives. As the negro passed out of slavery it was the Catholic Church which could say to him with the apostle, in his new relation: "For ye have not received the spirit of bondage again to fear, but ye have received the spirit of adoption whereby we cry, Abba! (Father)."—Romans viii. 15.

Her code of laws for the black is the same as for the white—no difference. Sunday mass, Friday abstinence, Lenten fast oblige the black man no more than the white. Yes, the human nature predestined to Christian grace, and so admirably recognized by the church, is the foundation of our hopes.

The negro's heart, like the white man's, is essentially good. Here we have a foothold. Grace we know builds upon nature and presupposes it. The civil law in its turn recognizes the manhood of the negro; who votes, or should legally vote, like a white man, is ruled by the same laws; bows to the same rulers in the general, state, and local governments; has before him, if delinquent (at least on the statute-book), the same legal process and sentence, the same jail and keepers as the white man. In antebellum days there were special enactments which made the negro a chattel. In our days all odious restrictions are disappearing before a juster and fairer recognition of his manhood.

The manhood of the negro race, moreover, is a truth of religion, and one which Leo XIII. has well insisted upon in his letter to the bishops of Brazil at the time of the emancipation of the slaves of that country. "It was sin," he writes, "which deserved the name of slavery; it was not natural. From the first sin came all evils, and specially this perversity, that there were men who, forgetful of the original brotherhood of the race, instead of seeking, as they should naturally have done, to promote mutual kindness and mutual respect, following their evil desires, began to think of other men as their inferiors, and to hold them as cattle born to the yoke." And the very argument which we hear so often in political agitation, and read so much in the public press, viz., that by nature the black man is inferior, Leo XIII. declares an outrage on our common humanity.

When in addition to the consideration of the negro's manhood we add the further reflection that the greater part of mankind were slaves at the coming of Christ, there is all the less reason to despise our black countrymen, and all the more hope for their future. Men go into ecstacies over the future of the white races; they love to recount their progress since the dawn of the Christian era. Let us remember to-day, however, how widespread slavery was in ancient days. We all are the offspring of races the vast majority of whom were legally or practically slaves. The negroes to-day are only taking their turn.

In the Roman Empire slaves were so numerous that Petronius in his "Satyrion" makes one of the players ask the servant how many infant slaves were born on his estates the preceding day, and is informed that thirty boys and forty girls were the increase of that day on that one estate. Roman patricians took a pride in having everything they needed made by their own slaves, thus destroying free labor, and with it, in the course of time, their own supremacy. These slaves were whites, and very many of them mechanics: carpenters, masons, shoemakers, millers, bakers, wool-combers, weavers, dyers, tailors, embroiderers, etc. Add to these carvers, mosaic workers, glaziers, painters, as well as three other grades corresponding to professions in our times, viz., architects, surgeons, and physicians.

As in Rome, so throughout the rest of the civilized world. White slavery flourished everywhere, and Canon Brownlow is the authority for the statement that serfdom has not as yet been legally abolished in England, although it has ceased to be a practical question since the War of the Roses — that is, for four centuries. In Italy a modified form of slavery existed to the end of the 17th century, in Spain till the first quarter of the 18th century, and only the revolution of 1789 blotted out French serfdom — all this in spite of the steadfast and aggressive efforts of Catholicity.

In Ireland, before St. Patrick came, a female slave, called "cumhal," was the unit of currency, thus showing how deeply rooted was slavery in ancient Irish institutions.

Although St. Patrick, once himself a slave, made great efforts towards emancipation, still slavery flourished in Ireland till St. Lawrence O'Toole moved, at a national synod, at Armagh, in 1170, to recognize the English invasion as a sign of divine anger against the Irish for their slave-holding. A peremptory admonition was thereupon sent out ordering the release of all English slaves in the land. Thenceforward it disappeared, till Cromwell sent thousands and tens of thousands of Irish men and women, boys and girls, as slaves into the West Indies.

In the life of St. Vincent de Paul we read that the thought of his foundling asylum originated at the sight of the place called La Cooche, where those unfortunates were sold to circus managers and the like. He himself for some years was a slave in Africa, and did not hesitate to escape at the first opportunity.

Since the discovery of America, however, the slavery that we have been familiar with is negro slavery. The color of the slave changed; and with it our memories seem comatosed. We forget the slavery of our ancestors. In modern times the negroes seem to have slipped into the shoes of the more ancient white slaves. There is nothing in the fact of slavery itself which will argue against the negroes, nor again will their color prove aught derogatory to their advancement. After, indeed, centuries of Christianity, the white races have not much to boast of. In the matter of religion they are much split up; in morals there is in our days a strange, sad laxity; in honesty the world is all but dominated by very loose and unjust principles. Of course there is progress — wonderful progress — yet not to such an extent as would belie the hopes of the negro's advance.

If, then, the negro may be called a man among men and an heir to all the glorious privileges of humanity, and also of Christianity, what, we may ask, are the means to be employed to place him in possession of his divine heritage? There is, I believe, one true means for his advancement, and that is the negro himself, guided and led by the Catholic Church. The first element in the elevation of the black race is the black man himself. To attempt anything for the blacks without making the black man himself the chief instrument for good, would be to attempt the play of "Hamlet" with the part of Hamlet left out.

His future demands the building up of his character, and this is best done by the mingled efforts of brotherly white men and worthy black men. His temperament, his passions and other inherent qualities, in great measure also his industrial and social environments, are beyond his control, and he needs the aid of the best men of his own race, but associated with and not divorced from the co-operation of the best of the white race. In the formation of his character, which is his weak spot, chief stress should be laid on moral training and education. External influences, controlled by noble men and women of both races, will count for more with him than with us. We can hardly appreciate how much the negro has to contend with while making his moral growth, for neither the antecedents nor surroundings of our black countrymen are calculated to draw out the noblest side of human nature. That personal encouragement to well-doing, to ambition to rise above degrading circumstances so necessary to all of us, so indispensably so to him, the black man rarely receives. Neither by nature nor by traditional training can the colored people, taken as a body, stand as yet upon the same footing of moral independence as their white brethren. The careful, patient, and Christian intervention of the whites, and the best of the blacks working together in using all the means demanded for the formation of manhood and womanhood is their right as well as their need in the present hour. They must be given the ample charity of Christ in their development, just as they have been given the full equality of citizenship. And in all this Catholics should lead the way. The influence of Catholics should be extended to foster and develop in the colored race those traits which tend to impart a sterling, self-reliant character.

Catholics may do very much. We are a large proportion, if not a majority, in many labor organizations. Let us welcome black working-men to every equality. We have very many influential Catholics in public life. Let them take sides in matters touching the blacks under the guidance of Catholic principles. There are about nine thousand priests in the land; let every priest exert an influence of sympathy in his personal dealings with the colored people of his vicinity. Perhaps there are twenty thousand religious teachers who, in their institutions, should receive negro boys and girls without discrimination. If Catholics, thus in possession of a vast power for moral elevation, give the right hand of fellowship to their black countrymen in all civil and personal relations, the work of converting them will be easy. Nor can we Catholics afford to ignore them or exclude them. For if we should do so, then the name "Catholic" would be a misnomer when applied to the American Church, and we should sink into the position of a sect. The negroes, as things stand, care nothing for the Catholic Church. Why should they? What has the Catholic Church done for them? But they would be the most ungrateful people earth ever bore if they should forget what our non-Catholic countrymen have done and are doing for them in every relation of life.

Turning again to ourselves, let every one of us in private life, whether laymen, priests, or religious, bear in mind that it is not enough to give a despised race their legal rights, but that Christian principle exacts a special regard for race susceptibilities. The Irish and Germans and Italians resent the terms, "Paddy," and "Dutchman." and "Dago," so let us cease to call the colored people "Niggers" and "Darkies," even in private conversation; and in every other way let us do unto the black people as we should wish to be done by were we blacks ourselves. Let us bear in mind that among whites of every kind there is an immense amount of partly Christian and partly natural tradition, which is weak among the blacks by no fault of their own. There is the home, the domestic fireside, the respect for Sunday, the sense of respectability, the weight of the responsibilities of life, the consciousness of duty, the love of honesty, which is regarded as true policy, the honor of the family name, the fear of disgrace, together with the aspirations for a share in the blessings and privileges which our country and civilization afford. And while very many of our white countrymen are not Catholics, and are even but nominal Christians, still these weighty influences wield a potent charm for good over their lives.

In regard to the negro race, however, these hardly exist; at best they may be found in isolated cases, though it is true that very encouraging signs of them are seen occasionally. Yet a vital part in the natural development of the negro will be secured by these elements, the sense of responsibility, the dignity as well as duty of labor, and, lastly, self-denial and thrift.

All these sit too lightly on the negroes. Care for the future they know not; and although they labor well enough, yet they lack thrift. Their cheerful dispositions lighten much of their sorrows; and their love for music also soothes full many an evil day and dismal night. A patient, suffering race are they, whose sorrows are sure to win for them the fulness of divine blessings. Poverty and lowliness were characteristics of the Messias; they are two marked traits in the negro race. They too are, as it were, "A leper, and as one stricken by God and afflicted." Surely, if fellow-suffering creates a bond of sympathy, our Lord and Saviour Jesus Christ must deeply sympathize with and love the negro race.

We have intimated that the Catholic Church has accomplished little for the conversion of the negroes. It is but just to add here what is really being done.

From the official report of the episcopal commission charged with the distribution of the annual collection for the negro missions, we learn that during the six years of its existence $220,220 have been distributed among negro missions, and as much more among Indians.

There are at present twenty-eight priests laboring among the negroes exclusively, who are in charge of thirty churches. Of course they do not include the many more in Maryland, Kentucky, Louisiana, Missouri, and elsewhere, whose churches are partly for whites and partly for blacks.

Since 1888, when the reports began to be published, the average number of adult converts yearly is about 670, while every year there were 4,500 children baptized. Moreover, twenty odd different orders of white women have charge of 108 schools, in which assemble 7,884 pupils. The orphanages and other institutions for colored children are growing. St. Benedict's Home, Rye, N. Y.; the Providence House of Mother Katherine Drexel, near Philadelphia; orphanages for boys, in Wilmington, Del., and Leavenworth, Kans.; one for girls, as also a foundling asylum, in Baltimore, Md., and two other orphan asylums in St. Louis, Mo., and New Orleans, La., are all doing good service for the homeless children of Ham, while the home for aged colored people in New Orleans, La., shelters the lingering days of its worthy inmates. The night-school and guild in Baltimore and the industrial school at Pine Bluff, Ark., are both paving the way towards teaching colored children a means of livelihood.

There are three orders of colored women, the Oblates of Baltimore, established in 1829; the Holy Family of New Orleans, dating from 1842, and the Sisters of St. Francis, started about five years ago by Bishop Becker, of Savannah. There are four sisterhoods exclusively devoted to the negroes: the Franciscans from England, who have houses in Baltimore, Richmond, Norfolk; the Sisters of the Holy Ghost in San Antonio, Texas; the Sisters of the Blessed Sacrament, Mother Katherine Drexel's Community, in Philadelphia; the Mission Helpers of Baltimore. These last-named are devoted to the home-life and training of negro women, visiting the jails, hospitals, and having sewing-schools even in private houses. In all about seventy Catholic sisters have consecrated, or will shortly consecrate, their lives before God's altar for the sake of the sin-laden and ignorant images of Christ in ebony setting.

Unhappily, however, none of our brotherhoods as yet have ever wielded a birch in a negro Catholic school.

The society to which I belong has missions in Maryland, Delaware, and Virginia. At our training school, the Epiphany Apostolic College, are upwards of sixty young men, of whom several are colored, studying the subjects necessary for their advance. At St. Joseph's Seminary, our mother-house in Baltimore, seventeen seminarians are being trained for the negro missions. These young men represent the whole country from Maine to Oregon, from the St. Lawrence to the Gulf of Mexico. This large number of aspirants for the negro missions is due to the generous co-operation of the bishops and clergy of our land, while their support is given us by the noble Catholic laity, who in very great numbers subscribe for our little annual—*The Colored Harvest.*

We may fitly close with the sentiment of St. Gregory the Great, when contrasting our Lord's conduct in refusing to go to the nobleman's dying son, although asked to do so, while unasked he went and healed the centurion's servant.

"He did not deem that the nobleman's son was worthy of His presence, but He refused not to help the centurion's servant. What is this but a rebuke to earthly pride, which maketh us to respect in men their honors and riches rather than that divine image wherein they are created? It was not so with our Redeemer, who would not go to the son of the nobleman, but was ready to come down for the centurion's servant, to show that to Him the things which are great among men are but of little moment, and the things which are little esteemed among men are not beneath His notice.

"Our pride, then, standeth rebuked—that pride which maketh us forget for the sake of one man that another man is a man at all. This pride, as we have said, looketh only at the surroundings of men, not at their nature, and seeth not that God is to be honored in a man because he is a man. Lo! how the Son of God will not go unto the nobleman's son, but is ready to go and heal the servant. Of myself I know that if any one's servant were to ask me to go to him, I have a sort of pride which would say to me, silently inside my heart: Go not; thou wilt lower thyself; the papal dignity would be lightly esteemed; thy exalted station will be degraded. Behold how He who came down from Heaven doth not deem it below Him to go to help a servant, and yet I, who am of the earth earthy, shrink from being trodden on."

"Prayer for America" is the subject of the following paper, which was prepared and read by Rev. F. G. Lentz, of Bement, Ill.:

Inspired by an all-knowing God, 400 years ago a man set out from a small port in Spain to find a new world. The consummation of his cherished desires was a most astonishing discovery, which has overshadowed all his weary years of waiting, and efforts to persuade a doubting generation of the truth of his predictions. His unbounded faith alone was great enough to overcome all obstacles, both by sea and land, and bring to a happy issue God's designs for the human race.

What Columbus attributed to special inspiration, many would have been glad to have claimed as the achievement of their own genius. But as a devout Catholic the discoverer of America would have held in abhorrence any attempt to deprive God of the honor due Him. But wherefore this special revelation? To the hour of his death Columbus claimed that God designed by him to make known a new world, that the faith might be spread and the Holy Name of Jesus be glorified. This he declared before the court of Spain; stated it in his prayer of thanksgiving for the great work accomplished by him, and dying charged that they, his children, should not fail to use a certain portion of the revenues derived from his wonderful discovery to propagate the faith. Glory to God, who took His faithful and suffering servant to Himself and left to us the extraordinary legacy of his discovery. The fruits of his laborings and sufferings we now enjoy; for not only was the settlement of a new continent made possible, but the establishment of the grandest and noblest government the world has ever seen, become practicable.

But man, every man has duties, not only to himself, but public duties which concern him and his fellow-man. Everyone leads a public as well as a private life. It is a natural instinct which makes us rejoice in our public joys and weep over our public sorrows. We have collective griefs and collective joys. It was not a vain thought that made Jeremiah weep over the destruction of Jerusalem. He forgot his own troubles in mourning over the downfall of his nation and the destruction of his countrymen; they were bone of his bone; they were sinew of his sinew, citizens of the same commonwealth, and a nation of his nationality, and whatever befell them happened to himself. This is an innate natural feeling in us all—love of our country and sorrow for our country's wrongs. We wish it well, and unless every spark of patriotism is dead within our bosoms we can have no pleasure but in its prosperity. It becomes us then to know its needs and to seek to effectuate them. Patriotism is born of religious life and we can not be true to heaven without embracing the divinity.

But right here comes in the question: What does our country most need in order to prosper and continue, aye, to propagate her glorious work till all the nations and people of the earth have learned from her to imitate her behests to humanity? What above all other things will enable her to proceed triumphantly on her career of not only giving the greatest blessings to her citizens, but teaching the human race the way thereto? What she needs above all things is the truth. "You shall know the truth and the truth shall make you free."—St. John viii., 32.

It was for this God inspired the discovery of America; it was for this Columbus labored and toiled for years amidst so many disappointments; it was for this so many missionaries sacrificed time and life; it was for that and this too that the persecuted of every race should find here a home and plenty; it is for this I appeal to you to endeavor to understand and do your part towards carrying out God's idea in revealing the American continent; and not to be an encumbrance, "a light hid under a bushel," that shall be removed because your candlestick leaves only darkness, where light should abound. If you have come into the inheritance, a larger freedom for truth, and greater worldly blessings, remember you are but stewards of God. All sacred writers teach us that we shall render to God according to our gifts. Our Lord shows us that the man with ten talents must account for more than he with only five. But woe to him who has not wisely used the talents intrusted to his care.

We have the truth; the faith that is in us must be made manifest. For this God opened up the New World; for this he enlarged our freedom, that we might make known the divine knowledge revealed to us. Unworthy nations have lost the great gift of faith because they knew not how to use the gratuity. Shall we, too, prove recreant to the trust? Shall we, too, hear one day the words, "Wicked and adulterous generation?" Matt. xvi., 1. God forbid!

We know that the whole law is founded on charity, love, not only for God, but our fellowmen. We do not, can not, love God if we do not love man, the image and likeness of the Divine Creator. No man can say he loves God and hates his fellowman. These two loves go hand in hand. "Love thy neighbor as thyself." But how can we say we love God if we do not aid our fellow-citizens to the truth? "Though I should speak with tongues of angels and men; though I have knowledge enough to fathom all mysteries, and faith enough to remove mountains; though I should give my goods to the poor, and my body to the flames, and have not charity, I am nothing. Everything else is useless to me." I. Cor. xiii., 7. "Silver and gold I have none," says St. Peter to the lame man, "but what I have I give thee. In the name of Jesus of Nazareth arise and walk." Acts iii., 6.

What have we to give this people? Above all things else, faith. What then, "Am I my brother's keeper?" In this matter we are. God brought about the discovery of this continent that His name might be made known and glorified; that we who have the faith are bound by every obligation to manifest it. It is a corporal work of mercy to instruct the ignorant, and God has declared that those who do so "shall shine as stars in the kingdom of heaven." And yet, my friends, how little has been done! Many a poor soul has gone through this world hungering for the faith that we might have brought to it, and we would not. We forget that faith is a divine gift. We do not seem to understand that these people have not the knowledge required to ask for it. "How shall they call upon Him whom they have not believed?" Rom. x. If they know not God they can not call upon Him. There never was yet a nation who came to the faith of their own volition; it must be brought to them, and the true Catholic has always been filled with the instinct to propagate the truth. It is only where this feeling does not exist that the faith makes no progress, even among Catholic people. "Why is the world covered with iniquities? Why are so many souls lost by the thou..

sands? Why is the earth made desolate? Because no one considereth in his heart." Jer. xii., 2. The lament of the prophet is applicable to our day and country. We may say, why do not these people come and learn the truth? My friends, if you and I had been raised under the same influence, surrounded by the same atmosphere, we would never have entered a Catholic Church. Don't blame them. Let us seek first to overcome our own indifference and then mark the result.

No people on the face of the earth were ever brought into the fold by the methods we have hitherto pursued. The apostles of all times have gone to the people and made known the message. The very word gospel means that—announcing the glad tidings. All may not indeed be apostles, but think you that while the apostles went forth to battle with error, the Christians of their day spent the time in idleness and indifference? While the army of the Lord is in the field battling for right and truth, have those of the household no duties? When the British sought to invade our country, and New Orleans was threatened, what did the Catholics do? They gathered 'round the tabernacle and incessantly besought the Lord of Hosts to protect the brave men in the field, and save their homes from rude invasion. When the Israelites of old were battling with the enemies of their race, did not the people come to the aid of Moses, praying upon the mountain top, until victory crowned their armies?

It may not be ours to apply the intellectual lance of argument, or expound the doctrine of the church, but it does become our duty to let the love of our heart rise in incessant prayer to the God of Light, that He may enlighten the darkness of their understanding, and make fruitful the work of apostolic men laboring to explain God's truths. Not only did the apostles pray, but the people also prayed, that the name of the Lord Jesus might be known and spread throughout all nations. St. Peter was praying when he received the call to go out to the centurion, Cornelius. St. Paul was praying when he beheld the vision inviting him to go to the Macedonians. But some say that non-Catholics do not wish to believe. I deny that these people desire to be unbelievers. They run hither and thither to everyone, saying: "Where is the Lord? Where is the Lord?" not knowing where the truth may be found. Their very earnestness teaches us that they have a desire to know the truth. Their conduct is vision enough for us if we only heed the warning. How many have not heard the cry, like Agrippa of old, "Thou almost persuadeth me." Convinced many of them are, but not persuaded, i. e., have not the grace of conversion. They know not how to ask. They still doubt, and "he who doubts is like the waves of the sea which come and go."—James i., 6.

And herein lies our work. We know the author of life and light and truth, and we know how to ask without doubting, and our prayers will be heard. We forget that those outside the church have neither the sacraments or the grace of a sinless person. We know and believe that he who is pure has more power than the sinner. Strong in our faith, we are capable of overcoming all obstacles and the Lord will hear our prayer. "Whatsoever you shall ask the Father with faith, you shall obtain."—Matthew xxi., 22.

Do not blame those who have not the faith; do not find fault with those who know not how to pray, or have little power because of unrepented souls; but rather let us reckon with ourselves and with the strength of giants, because of our belief, besiege the throne of grace, storm heaven with our humble petitions, and much shall be vouchsafed us because, in our burning charity for our brother, we "have loved much." We can convert this people, and make it one of the grandest missionary nations with which God has ever vouchsafed to bless the human race. With their enlightened freedom, a government founded on the natural rights of man, their large-heartedness, their generous impulses, their cleverness in surmounting all difficulties, they will lead all other peoples and nations in carrying the torch of enlightenment, preaching the truth, and bringing the blessing of God's holy word to others, and thus, by placing on Columbus' brow a diadem woven by the charity of his inheritors, they shall bring themselves into the ocean of infinite love, and for all eternity glow with the added luster of those to whom they have brought hope, peace, and heaven.

Surprise has often been expressed that the Irish race should cling to the faith, after so many tribulations. All that human ingenuity could do has been tried to dispossess them of the truth; yet no people have remained more faithful to the doctrine that was delivered to the saints. Fire and the sword, the rack and prison, exile and starvation, all in vain, have been used to extirpate faith. Well may they exclaim, "Where is the nation that has not heard our woes? All peoples have been a witness to our sufferings." Yet, glory be to God, they have ever been among the most exemplary and steadfast Christians the world has known. Why is it that when so many others have perished they never faltered? It can be explained only on one theory.

They have ever been the foremost missionary nation of the earth. From the day St. Kolumkill went to Iona, St. Call and his companions to the continent, to revive faith, to our own day, they have been scattered over the whole earth, everywhere bearing testimony of Jesus Christ crucified. Riches they had not, but of that which they had they freely gave to their fellow-beings, and the Lord God has preserved them a strong and vigorous people when others have perished. We look upon their woes, and, after the manner of the world, would commiserate the nation; we look to heaven and see them trooping within its portals triumphantly to enjoy an everlasting crown of bliss as a reward of their charity, piety, and zeal, in spreading the glad tidings of faith to all the nations of the earth. May those who are descendants of these people never waver in their energy, or forget their glorious lineage, but perpetuate the good work so gloriously undertaken by their forefathers.

If we have been "salted with fire," as the Lord says, the salt must not become unsavory. The penetrating fire of charity must ever burn brighter within our breasts until it becomes a consuming flame which shall warm all within its rays. It knows no failing; is not repulsed; will not desist from zealously loving God and its neighbor, but persevere until all are enwrapped in the bosom of the Infinite.

Difficulties will but stimulate us to greater exertion. Fear will leave us no rest until we have converted the nation, Christianized the people, and brought salvation to the country. The warning of the prophet, "Why are hearts made desolate? Why are souls lost by the thousands? Because no man considereth in his heart," should fill us with such a dread that we would gladly join heart and soul in the prayer already being offered up by the thousands of our brethren in the faith. Sacrifice and oblation we should offer. Our humble supplications we should pour forth at the throne of Divine Grace until we have won for our separated brethren that pearl without price, the in estimable favor of Divine Faith, that they who are not of the household may be brought into the fold, where "there shall be one fold and one Shepherd," the Lord Jesus Christ, reigning gloriously over all for time and eternity.

Frank J. Sheridan, delegate from the Diocese of Dubuque, Iowa, read an interesting paper suggesting plan and reasons for the establishment of an organization by the Catholic Columbian Congress to be known as the Catholic Association of the United States for the Promotion of Industrial Conciliation and Voluntary Arbitration. Mr. Sheridan said:

The Columbian Catholic Congress has been called into existence mainly for the purpose of discussing and putting into practical effect in the United States the encyclical of Pope Leo XIII. on the condition of labor. In that document the way is clearly pointed out for the solution of the labor problem and for improving the condition of the working people. The details are left for us to carry out.

The natural desire on the part of the wage-earner—to get as much for his labor as he can—and the like disposition on the part of the employer—to pay as little for it as possible—have brought about a series of conflicts, more or less violent and disastrous in their results, and reflecting severely on this age of progress, liberality and enlightened civilization.

The Department of Labor of the United States government, devoted to painstaking and searching investigation of industrial conditions in our own and foreign countries, and with which I have the honor to be connected, has made an elaborate report on the subject of strikes and lockouts. The figures presented therein throw startling light on the significance and magnitude of this system of industrial civil war. It shows that for the six years, from 1881 to 1886, there were strikes in 22,304 establishments in the United States, involving 1,323,203 employes, and that there were lockouts in 2,214 establishments, involving 170,747 employes, making a total of 1,493,950 persons directly affected.

The leading causes of the strikes were the question of wages and the question of hours; 9,439 or 42.30 per cent of the total number of strikes were for an increase of wages; 4,344 or 19.48 per cent of the total number were for reduction of hours; 1,734 or 7.77 per cent were against reduction of wages, and 1,692 or 7.59 per cent were for increase of wages and reduction of hours. From this we learn that the causes mentioned account for 77.16 per cent of all the strikes. The evils resulting are partially shown in the figures giving the losses to employers and employed. The loss to employes from these strikes and lockouts was: For strikes, $51,814,723; for lockouts, $8,157,717; a total of $59,972,440. The loss to employers for both strikes and lockouts was $34,163,814.

Quite 82 per cent. of the strikes were ordered by labor organizations, and 79 per cent. of the lockouts were ordered by combinations of managers. The figures show the immense loss in wages to the employes directly connected with the strikes. They prove that the workingmen lost nearly twice as much as the employers, while less able to bear it. We can trace more of the consequences in the records of the almshouses, the records of the houses of the Good Shepherd, the records of the police courts, the prisons, and the penitentiaries. Strange though it may seem, we can also trace it in the records of the divorce courts. The department of labor has given the number of divorces in our country for a period of twenty years, with minute detail as to cause and effect. An examination of this report shows that during periods of industrial depression, of which strikes and lockouts are but manifestations, divorces increased enormously, while in periods of prosperity there was an extraordinary decrease. I need hardly say that in divorce statistics Catholic families are not included.

It is not necessary to dwell further upon the distress caused by this system of righting alleged wrongs, In a convention of Catholic laymen, meeting for the express purpose of considering the condition of labor and to adopt plans for its improvement, the foremost topic must be how to put an end to the misery and crime attendant upon the settlement of labor troubles, and what can be done in the way of a peaceful solution in the adjustment of disputes. There are some who advocate governmental compulsory arbitration—the creation of a legal tribunal whose decisions would be final, and compelling the wage-worker to work for perhaps a less rate than he wishes to, or the employer to pay more than he can.

Compulsory arbitration is not arbitration at all. To arbitrate there must be two willing parties. A cut-and-dried board of arbitration, created by State legislation, and without the power of compelling obedience to its decisions, must be a failure. I might call the attention of the Congress to the fact that Cardinal Manning settled the great London strike by methods of conciliation and voluntary arbitration, and without appealing to the compulsory law of 1824. The great Cardinal had a more stubborn and less intelligent element to contend with, too, than we have here.

A more recent and gratifying result of voluntary arbitration, in another field, is that of the Bering Sea controversy. We agreed to submit the case. The arbitrators decided against us. We stand by the decision, and submit to the awards. And if we can induce American employers and workingmen to submit their cases in a like manner they also will stand by the decisions without any law of enforcement.

The highest American authority and compiler of an exhaustive report on the subject of "Arbitration"—the United States Commissioner of Labor—in the June (1893) *Forum* proves conclusively that compulsory arbitration is an impossible remedy, and would result in slavery for the workingmen and socialism at the point of the bayonet. He further asserts that "voluntary arbitration in industrial matters is one of the highest and broadest features of co-operation, and, at the same time, one of the simplest methods for restoring harmony where conflict is threatened or even where it exists."

This Congress must repudiate any policy which would make a slave of the working-man or establish State socialism at the point of the bayonet, while it also desires to settle this question by peaceable methods. The Catholic churches of the United States in the villages, towns, and cities are filled to the doors with wage-earners. They will readily listen to a method for the remedy of their grievances in accordance with the teachings of their religion. The influence of a grand Catholic organization, composed of wage-earners and employers, advocating brotherly co-operation and the reign of reason, instead of the passions, can not but tend to promote the happiness of all the people and the prosperity of our beloved country.

It is with the utmost confidence that the proposition is made to the Catholic Columbian Congress to organize the Catholic Association of the United States for the promotion of industrial conciliation and voluntary arbitration. This Congress is thoroughly representative of the Catholic laity of the United States. In its capacity it is fully competent to deal with all practical methods in a practical manner. The organization proposed is entirely practical, and comes within the scope of the work laid out for the Congress to accomplish.

I ask the delegates to carefully consider the plan proposed, and in connection therewith I submit the following extracts from Pope Leo's encyclical on the condition of labor, paragraphs 21 and 59:

"Mutual agreement results in pleasantness and good order; perpetual conflict necessarily produces confusion and outrage. Those Catholics are worthy of all praise, and there are not a few, who, understanding what the times require, have, by various enterprises and experiments, endeavored to better the condition of the working people without any sacrifice of principle. They have taken up the cause of the working man, and have striven to make both families and individuals better off; to infuse the spirit of justice into the mutual relations of employer and employed; to keep before the eyes of both classes the precepts of duty and the laws of the gospel—that gospel which, by inculcating self-restraint, keeps men within the bounds of moderation, and tends to establish harmony among the divergent interests and various classes which compose the State. It is with such ends in view that we see men of eminence meeting together for discussion, for the promotion of united action and for practical work."

It was with this in mind that the committee on organization, with Archbishop Feehan as chairman and W. J. Onahan as secretary, wrote the following in its official call and programme which is in your hands:

"The Congress must be prepared to propose practical reforms on the lines looked for at its hands. It will not suffice that it shall have been the medium and opportunity for the delivery of clever essays and eloquent addresses on the various themes. Much more is expected from it. Permanent and effective results and enduring benefits are looked for at its hands, as the outcome of this memorable assemblage of Catholic intelligence and Catholic earnestness."

I therefore beg to submit the proposed plan of organization and objects of the association.

NAME.—This organization shall be known as the Catholic Association of the United States for the Promotion of Industrial Conciliation and Voluntary Arbitration.

OBJECTS.—The objects of this association shall be the gradual abolition of strikes, lockouts, and boycots as remedies for the adjustment of the grievances arising between employers and wage-earners, and the substitution therefor of a policy of conciliation and arbitration, to be carried out in a wise and systematic manner. This system contemplates:

1. The removal of causes of discussion and the prevention of differences from becoming disputes.
2. The settlement of difficulties after a demand from either side has been made and before such demand has been resisted by urging the submission of such difficulties to arbitration.
3. The infusing of a spirit of justice into the mutual relations of employers and employed.

NATIONAL BOARD.—The aims of the association shall be carried out under the direction of a national board, which shall be composed of two laymen from each diocese in the United States, who shall be chosen in the first instance by the delegates of each diocese to the Catholic Columbian Congress at Chicago, and thereafter in such a manner as may be provided. The archbishops and bishops of the United States shall, ex-officio, be members of the national board.

The national board shall elect a president, secretary, and such other officers as may be necessary. It shall also enact such by-laws for the government of the association as it may deem proper.

SHALL ESTABLISH PARISH ORGANIZATIONS.—It shall bring all the weight of its influence and prestige to bear in the formation of subordinate local parish boards, and actively co-operating with the parish priests and the earnest, thoughtful, and influential wage-earners and employers of each congregation in the formation of such local boards, and thus create a grand national organization of Catholic men, intelligent of purpose, and, with influences permeating all classes of society, bring about an era of good will.

NOT AN OFFICIAL BOARD OF ARBITRATION.—While conciliation and the arbitration of labor difficulties are the ends aimed at by this association, it shall not, either as a local or a national body, constitute itself an official or semi-official board of arbitration. The very essence and successful workings of our policy lie in the voluntary selection of the arbitrators in each case, by the employers on the one hand and the employed on the other. The efforts of the association will be employed solely in bringing such a condition of affairs about.

I am not wedded to any one of the details of the proposed association. They can easily be amended and improved upon, but the organization itself is necessary. Unless all signs of the times fail, there will be immediate work for this association.

Let us open the conference doors through this board of arbitration, and keep them open until a perfect settlement is arrived at. With such an organization, and with such a man as Archbishop Ireland as its president, the working men of the United States will know that the Catholic Church is their friend. They would not listen in silence, as they do now in their labor unions and assemblies, to the voice of the anarchic continental socialist, who cleverly and with ability tells them that the church is their enemy and a hindrance to their liberty.

"Women of the Middle Ages" was the subject of an interesting paper by Anna T. Sadlier, of New York, N. Y. The substance of the paper follows:

Previous to the medieval era Christianity had raised womanhood from the slough of paganism. Already an astonished world had begun to cry out, "Ye gods of Greece, what women have these Christians!" During the middle ages, from the sixth to the middle of the 15th century, woman attained, as it were, her full growth under the ægis of the church, the church which serenely held sway over the mad chaotic world struggling into civilization. It would be an impossible task here to classify medieval woman by distinctions of race or epoch. Rather let us examine her condition, personal qualities, and the tone of society toward her on the broad lines of cloistered, royal, saintly, and learned women.

The nun played such a part in the drama of medieval life, as to raise woman to the climax of her power. The nun was a chief factor in procuring the emancipation of women and proclaiming her equality, in a Christian sense, with man, by giving her a separate, individual existence. Immured in her cloister, the nun exercised a protective influence over the wife and mother, and caused them to be reverenced on account of the possibilities of heroic virtue which she displayed. To the rudest warrior she was "a thing enskied and ensainted." In short, by her ideal of consecrated virginity, the church secured the elevation of woman.

"The protection and better education given to women in these early communities," says Mrs. Jameson, "the venerable and distinguished rank assigned to them, when as governesses of their order, they became in a manner dignitaries of the church, the introduction of their beautiful and saintly effigies, clothed with all the insignia of sanctity and authority, into the decoration of places of worship and books of devotion, did more, perhaps, for the general cause of womanhood, than all the boasted institutions of chivalry." Can the tremendous influence be overrated of such sanctuaries of learning as Whitby and Coldingham, Ely and Wimbourne, Barking and Folkestone, Hartpool and Hanbury, Roncerai and Chelles, Faremoutier and Brie, Luxeuil, and Les Andelys, Fontevrault and Longchamps, Gandersheim and Fulda, Cologne and Heidenheim.

Each an oasis in a barbaric land, redolent of spirituality, of asceticism, of refinement, and of culture. Sometimes particular inmates cast a luster on certain monasteries. As Hilda at Whitby, from her sanctuary, where it looked seaward on the cliffs, the abbess sent forth bishops, eminent ecclesiastics and apostolic women. For, after the custom of the times, she governed both men and women. Her influence, far reaching, extended over the surrounding country. Her exact discipline recalled primitive Christianity. She caused learning, like the palm tree, to grow and flourish. At Whitby, the Saxon, Milton Ceadon poured forth his inspired strain to Hilda, seated in state with disciples and counselors questioning him, with so keen a perspicacity, upon various points of his narrative.

Ebba of Coldingham, was scarcely inferior in learning and sanctity to the abbess of Whitby. Like her, she governed not only her dual monastery, but exercised for thirty years an important influence on the destinies of her country.

Walburga, or Walpurgis, a niece of Boniface, was speedily called from the cultured repose of Wimbourne into the Germanic field, where, with her nuns, she continued to cultivate letters, while she did much to civilize the people, besides presiding over the great school of Bischoffsheim and devoting her knowledge of medicine to the service of the poor. Her name, in course of time, became mingled with curious superstitions; for example, the Walpurgis night.

An attractive figure is that of the Abbess Lioba, or the beloved, with her learning, her knowledge of Scripture—she had committed the whole Bible to memory—her beauty, her humility, washing the feet of her nuns and serving them at table, her zeal, making her the valued auxiliary of Boniface, when she had passed from Wimbourne to Germany; her sweetness, her cheerfulness. "She was as admirable in her understanding as she was boundless in her charity," says her biographer, Ralph of Fulda.

The Anglo-Saxon cloisters were thronged with nuns of the blood royal, Ethelburga, the first royal widow to enter religion; Etheldreda, of the strange, romantic story; Elfleda, who aided Wilfred in his struggle to fix the Roman discipline upon the Celts; Earcontha, Domneva, Eanpleda, Ermenburga, Hereswida, Eadburga, Wereburga, Ermenilda and Sexburga were all nuns of royal birth—in one instance, three generations, grandmother, mother and daughter met in the cloister. Some were widows, some had, by permission, separated from their husbands, some had entered religion in early youth, being, in the forcible Saxon word, veritable "Godes-Brydes,"—"Brides of God."

To Heldilida and her nuns of Barking, Aldhelm dedicated his "Praise of Virginity." To the Abbess Cyndreda, he left his vestments when dying.

In Ireland, land of saints and scholars, where learning at the darkest periods found asylum, St. Bridget, of the royal house of Leinster, exercised much the same patriarchal sway over men and women as Hilda at Whitby. Many poetic legends cluster about that spot dedicated to virtue and learning, and for a thousand years after Bridget's death a lamp burned at her tomb. "That bright lamp which burned at Kildare's holy fane."

Hathmuda, daughter of Count Lindulph, "a lover of letters and student of scripture," restored at Gandersheim a school for Saxon ladies. It won celebrity through the acquirements of Hroswitha, "The White Rose of Gandersheim." She was second of the name, the first having been noted as a logician. She studied at the convent, besides grammar and the liberal arts, Greek and Latin and the philosophy of Aristotle, and wrote many works in prose and poetry. Of these the dramas after Terence met with instant recognition as models of pure diction and exquisite sentiment, also displaying a knowledge of dialectics and astronomy. Hroswitha's letters display a humility absolutely saint-like in one on whom the adulation of her contemporaries was lavished.

The author of "Christian Schools and Scholars," when remarking that the teachers of Hroswitha had preserved her modesty, her almost childlike naivete, and deep religious humility, adds: "And the same remark applies to the conventional schools in general." Better things were included in their scheme of education than a mere knowledge of the liberal arts, the wisdom, which is the beginning of discipline, and "unto which no defiled thing cometh."

St. Frideswida, flying from the importunities of a princely suitor, built at a certain spot a monastery, which in time, falling into the hands of canons regular, developed under the protection of Wolsey into Christ Church, Oxford. A second step toward the foundation of the university was made when Edith d'Oyley, who was not, however, a nun, built Osney Priory, at a spot indicated to her by the chattering of pies.

St. Croix Abbey at Poitiers, founded by Radegond, Queen of Clothaire I., received her into its silent life, after many useful years spent upon the throne, giving patronage to art and literature, laboring for the abolition of slavery, cultivating the society f the learned. She was the friend of Venantius Fortunatus, who composed the 'Vexilla Regis," on the translation of a relic of the true cross to her monastery. She possessed, as we read, "not only elegant letters, but profound erudition," and after her retirement to Poitiers, imparted those stories of knowledge to young girls of all classes whom she loved to collect around her.

Other high-born nuns, famous for their acquirements, were: Burgundofara, "la noble baronne de Bourgogne," abbess of Faremoutier; Adelaide, of Cologne; Hildegarde, of Bingen; Isabel, sister of St. Louis; Blanche, of France; Jane, of Navarre; Matilda, of Anjou.

The attainments of the nuns appear to have been, for the time, considerable. They studied philosophy and belles-lettres, the scriptures and the fathers. Their correspondence was kept up in Latin, and sprinkled with quotations, proving their acquaintance with the classics. Many of them knew Greek. They reached, in fine, the highest degree of culture then possible. Like their contemporaries, they were ignorant, no doubt, of much that we know. Probably they also knew much that would surprise our "sweet girl graduates," and knew it thoroughly and well. Many nuns were proficient as copyists, adorning manuscripts with gold and gems. They were accomplished needlewomen, skilled in rare tapestries and embroideries.

"Outside their communities, and mingling in the current of historical events, several of these vigorous women," says the chronicler, "have left their trace on the history of their country." The idea of spiritual assistance became so interwoven with the idea of nuns, as it has been remarked, that in many families a spectral nun was supposed to give warning of impending calamity.

"To early acquaintance with the cloister much that distinguished the character of women in the middle ages is due," remarks Digby; "even when education was not received there, visits were made to devout sisters. The maiden of the castle knew the sanctity and peace of cloistral life, and formed there her ideal of virtue." Symbols of a true democracy, the lowly mingled with the high-born in these communities, and often r se to commanding stations, though names and details concerning those of high rank were more carefully preserved by contemporary chroniclers.

Deaconesses were a recognised order in the church till the 9th century, as were also recluses, who inhabited caverns and mountains. Such was Rosalie of Palermo, whose name has remained in veneration through the centuries.

The queens of the middle ages are a numerous and important class. Among the Anglo-Saxons, who, in common with the other Teutonic races, assigned a lofty part to women, the queens possessed territorial rights and rights of jurisdiction, having separate courts and affixing their names to public documents. Like the nuns of their race, they were ardent as apostles. Thus the gentle Queen Bertha was saluted by Gregory as "a second Helena," who had given England to the faith, which she did, not only by protecting Augustine, but by converting Ethelbert, her husband. Her daughter, Ethelburga, brought Edwin and Northumbria to Christianity, as Achfleda converted Penda and the Mercians, and Ermenilda, with Egbert of Kent, aided in the spread of truth, and supported Wildfrid and Rome. Many of them were learned themselves, and the cause of learning in others, as Osburga, mother of Alfred, who inspired him with her own love of knowledge, and directed his studies.

Elsintha, his wife, and Etholfleda, his daughter, were of similar tastes. "Edith the Good," wife of Edward the Confessor, is quaintly called "a storehouse of liberal knowledge," and Ingulf, Abbot of Croyland, relates how, as a boy, she questioned him upon his studies, "readily changing from the quirks of logic, which she knew thoroughly well, she would entrap me," he says, "in the snares of argumentation."

The queens of the Norman period, beginning with the wife of the Conqueror, continued the high tradition of learning, sometimes of sanctity. For instance, the sisters and the two queens of Henry Beauclerc are mentioned as being accomplished scholars. "There is, perhaps, no more beautiful character recorded in history," says the Protestant Skene, in his Celtic Scotland, "than that of Margaret of Scotland. For purity of motives, for an earnest desire to benefit the people among whom her lot was cast, for a deep sense of religion and great personal piety, for the unselfish performance of whatever duty lay before her, and for entire self-abnegation, she is unsurpassed." This saintly queen labored with intelligence and a true understanding of the issues at stake to reform abuses in the contemporary church of Scotland and restored venerable Iona, fallen to ruins.

Another Margaret, a woman of a still more commanding intellect, but whose private life was far from irreproachable, united by her political sagacity and strength of will all the Scandinavian kingdoms under her sway. She was called "the Semiramis of the North."

The Frankish dynasty furnishes us with such lovable types of women as Clotilda, who obtained the somewhat dramatic conversion of her husband on the battlefield, and Bathildis, who labored for the abolition of slavery and the spread of learning, who founded and afterward became abbess of Chelles.

The life of Matilda, wife of Henry I. of Germany, reads like romance from the moment her royal lover beholds her, the pupil of Hereward convent, through the long years when they were "one in mind and heart, prompt to every good work," as through her regency and her widowhood, passed so holily. The following quaint account is given of her by a contemporary: "She ministered to the cock who announced the day to call up the faithful to serve Christ, nor did she forget the singing birds, for whom she scattered crumbs in the name of their Creator. She carried food to the poor and candles to oratories in her own chariot. In winter she caused great fires to be lighted and kept up all night, both in and out, so that everyone who wandered might have warmth and light."

Queen Elizabeth, of Portugal, who won by her unceasing efforts to promote peace the title of Pacis et Patriæ Mater and Sant Isabel de Pax, is only less interesting than that other Elizabeth, whose marriage to her beloved Landgrave Louis, her pathetic efforts to lead a saint's life at a court, the cruel persecutions she endured, and her widowhood, are so familiar to us. Of such a type was Hedwiga, of Poland, who married against her inclination to promote the peace of Christendom.

Bridget, Princess of Sweden, sanctified her husband, eight children, and edified a court before founding the Order of the Brigittines. Agnes of Bohemia, wife of Frederick II., Cunegonde of Bavaria, good Queen Maud of England, Hildegrade, Empress of Charlemagne; Agnes, wife of the German Henry III., so successful a regent, are among those who led a life of nun-like austerity upon thrones. Many medieval queens belonged to the Third Order of St. Francis.

Margaret of Anjou, by a series of splendid failures, strove to hold the scepter for a dynasty. Philippa of Hainault, was not only noted for learning, but for political wisdom. Blanche of Castile, the model of Christian mothers, was a patron of letters, and Blanche of Navarre deserved to be called "the mother of the poor." The life of Catherine Cornaro, Queen of Cyprus, reads like a romance. Theophania, the Greek princess, like Anna Commena, author of the Alexind, was an enthusiastic student. On her marriage she brought the brilliant literary atmosphere of Constantinople to the court of the Othos. Hedwiga of Bavaria, a Greek and Latin scholar, educated her nephew Burkhard, afterwards abbot. Anne of Brittany, the beloved, was "as skilled in Greek, Latin, and astronomy as any clerk in the kingdom."

The medieval households are, in the main, beautiful pictures of Catholic life. There, "at the fireside of the heart, feeding its flame," woman's true place, the mistress of the family shone. Wise, intelligent, loving and beloved, respecting and respected, she was troubled by no theories of female suffrage or equal rights or divided skirts. Her own rights, thanks to the church, were too secure; her duties too sacred. A helpful wife, a conscientious mother. "Happy the ages," cried Digby, "when men had holy mothers." She trained sons to fill high places and daughters to vigorous practical utility, and she gained the love of her servants. Every woman in those days was made acquainted with every detail of household duty. With high-born women the duties were simply wider and more onerous. She had to know medicine and surgery and church music and embroidery, as she was fitted to exercise the splendid hospitality of the times, with that exquisite courtesy to strangers, which was a rigid social law. But she had to sew and spin and cook and keep a time apart for reading. Spinning was a favorite occupation, by the way, of all classes of medieval women. Dante represents the women of Florence as spinning as "they listened to old tales of Troy, Fesole, and Rome."

Young women before marriage lived in much retirement. They never went forth unattended, and in public places usually wore white folds and black cloaks, such as are still worn by certain communities of nuns. Dress in general was, however, very much a matter of national or individual temperament. Sometimes medieval women are commended by contemporary writers for simplicity in dress, wearing "unornamental buskins and a plain robe of camlet or serge, with hood to match." Again they are reproached with a too great magnificence, reveling in clothes of gold and silver, embroidered with gold and gems. Sometimes among the Anglo-Saxons this love of finery infected even degenerate cloisters. Severe strictures were passed upon abbesses who appeared in scarlet or violet tunics and hoods edged with miniver, who curled their hair and arranged their veils as ornaments.

Charity toward the poor, the suffering, the afflicted was eminently characteristic of medieval women. Always munificent, their charity chose a thousand tender and delicate modes of manifesting itself, seeing even in the mendicant the person of Jesus Christ. Mary, the mother of God, was the first great cause of the elevation of women. Divinely fair and holy, ever present to the medieval mind, she taught man to reverence and woman to deserve reverence. She appeared upon the pennons of knights or in their war cries, particularly if the cause were holy. Upon her they framed their ideal. The maiden in the cloister, with her consecrated teacher, placed Mary's image in miniatures or illuminations. The lady of the castle, with her bondswoman, uttered the transcendent prayer: "Hail, full of grace." The wandering glee woman or the serf fresh from toil bent the knee at Mary's wayside shrine. Even the gypsies, in their midnight celebration of Christmas, joined with the generations in calling her blessed.

Everywhere that ideal, divinely human, before which all mere earthly perfection fades. Therefore any summary of the woman of the middle ages must be faulty, even as a matter of philosophical or ethical inquiry, which ignores the omnipresent and almost omnipotent influence of Mary, mother of God.

Under the head of "Guilds and Fraternal Benefit Societies," J. P. Lauth, of Chicago, Ill., read a paper on "Their Insurance Feature Preferable to Pension Funds." He said, in substance:

I shall undertake in the brief time at my disposal to deal in a general way with one or two phases of the much-vexed labor question, such as, first, the old guilds and recently organized labor societies; and, second, why their insurance feature is preferable to a pension fund for workmen. It may be in order to say, by way of introduction, a few words touching the dignity of labor and the attitude toward it of the church:

Cardinal Manning said: "Labor is capital in the truest sense. The strength and skill that are in a man are as much his own as his life-blood; and that skill and strength which he has as his personal property no man may control." And, according to Adam Smith, "The property which every man has in his own labor, as it is the original foundation of all other property, so it is the most sacred and inviolable." Labor is the exercise of the best powers of man. As Herbert Spencer says: "All observing instruments, all weights and measures, scales, micrometers, thermometers, barometers, etc., are artificial extensions of the senses; and all levers, screws, hammers, wedges, wheels, lathes; etc., are artificial extensions of the limbs." And how, then, since it is so potential an agency, and so much more enterprising when free than when controlled, can it be consistently sought to have the law apply to and control its operations? The answer is, that it is sought simply to have the law define its rights within the scope of reasonable freedom, so that they may not be invaded to its detriment by unscrupulous and designing persons. It should be made possible for workmen to collect their wages with less difficulty. They should be enabled to recover damages in case of personal injury through the employer's wrong without weary years of delay and heavy expense. In fact, in many respects the law could and should serve them more efficiently than it does.

I need not hesitate to state that the church has always been well disposed toward labor. She interposed in behalf of the villeins of the feudal period at all proper times, and finally succeeded in bringing about their emancipation. She favored the guilds during the middle ages, and steadily sought to promote their welfare. She opposed slavery in every form and shape from the beginning, and does so still. To her the condition of the working population has always been a subject of special solicitude. The great labor encyclical of Leo XIII. affords ample proof as to the attitude of the church in this respect. It expresses sympathy with labor and the legitimate aspirations of toilers throughout the world. It points out the reciprocal duties of labor and capital. It urges the necessity of ameliorating the condition of poorly-paid and neglected workers. It acknowledges the right of laborers to combine in fraternal societies and unions, with a view to securing remunerative wages and protecting their interests. It asserts that it is the right of the State, if not its duty, to interfere in behalf of shorter hours, better sanitary conditions, and the prevention of female and child labor in exhausting employments. It contends that the standard of labor should not be that of mere subsistence, but such as may facilitate the acquirement of property, provide for the feebleness of old age, and the diminished earning capacity resulting from accident, afford opportunity for moral and intellectual improvement, and give the means of cultivating the physical powers, together with time for necessary recreation. That, surely, is a most enlightened view to take of the labor question. The most enthusiastic advocate of the rights of the working people could not reasonably ask for more.

The church says, in the language of the gospel, that "the laborer is worthy of his hire." But at the same time she informs him that he has reciprocal duties, in that he must faithfully seek to promote the interests of his employer and exercise reasonable diligence in the performance of his work. If a man will not work, neither let him eat." (Thess. iii, 10.) In short, he should be a true laborer as defined by the great bard of Avon in "As You Like It:" "I am a true laborer. I earn that I eat, get that I wear, owe no man hate, envy no man's happiness, glad of other men's good, content with my harm."

I shall now refer more particulary to the guilds, so notable and important in their relations to labor during the middle ages. Fraternal societies, composed of artisans, existed in Greece and Rome at an early period. They became incorporated under the last of the Cæsars. The church recognized and favored them, and they became the Christian guilds. In 364 Valentinian I. confirmed the privileges granted by the preceding emperors. In succeeding centuries all persons who were members of a particular trade in a city or locality became united in a guild, which had the right to regulate the production and sale of the things made by such trade. A person was not permitted to work at a trade unless he had become a member of the guild controlling it, and one of the primary conditions of membership was to have served as an apprentice for a designated number of years. The apprentice was bound out to a master, of whose family he became, for a time, a member. His moral education and technical training were committed to the master. He was required to learn to make the tools of his trade, as well as to do its work. Only one or two apprentices could be taught at a time. When the young man had served the requisite number of years, he became a journeyman or hired workman.

A stainless reputation was necessary to membership in the guild. Known immorality or dishonesty was a sufficient ground for expulsion. The guild settled the hours of work and the rate of wages. In certain lines of handicraft, workmen were accustomed to travel from town to town in order to see the different processes of carrying on their trades. When the savings of a workman were sufficient to enable him to pay the prescribed fees and his technical skill was proved by the making of what was called a masterpiece, he rose to the third and highest stage of the industrial order and became himself a master. But he remained subject to the control of the guild which, in conjunction with the local authorities, regulated the hours of labor, the ecclesiastical holidays, etc.

The guild acted also as a court of arbitration for the settlement of controversies between the master and his workmen. It restricted the number of workmen that a master might employ. This removed from him the temptation of seeking to get rich by their labor. Thus, too, the number of masters was kept comparatively large, and every industrious apprentice could hope to become one in time and attain to the highest grade in the industrial ranks.

The guild carefully guarded against the sale of goods adulterated, or ill-made, or of short weight or measure. It discharged the duties, also, of a benefit society and popular bank. It aided sick members and took care of the families of those deceased. It had a corporate fund, or regularly collected subscriptions or dues from the members, and was thus in a position to make advances to such of their number as were in difficulty, to support the aged, and to maintain the widows and orphans of members deceased. Each guild had a patron saint whose festival it specially celebrated. For example, St. Joseph was the patron saint of carpenters, while St. Crispin represented shoemakers and workers in leather. Religious exercises and the giving of alms were recommended and fostered. Production was so arranged as to keep all employed. About the time of the reformation, the religious element of the guilds became subordinated to the more worldly aims and selfish interests of the members, and thereafter they declined and finally disappeared, although within recent years an effort has been made to revive them.

Referring now to more recent times. We know, historically, of only one labor organization as having had an existence in this country prior to the Revolutionary War, and that was the Calkers' Club of Boston. The word caucus is said to be a corruption of it in our political nomenclature. In 1792 a trades' union of shoemakers existed in Philadelphia. The earliest strikes, of which we have record, took place in the same city in the years 1798 and 1805. Two or three years later, there was an extensive strike in New York. However, it is only within the past twenty-five years that labor organizations have made anything like substantial headway in this country. They comprise now over two-thirds of all our artisans and workmen. The individual trades are, generally speaking, well organized, and seek, so far as practicable without the active exercise of the religious principle, to follow in the footsteps of the old guilds. The efforts heretofore made, however, to band them together in unity of purpose and active co-operation in respect to matters effecting them jointly, or as a whole, have not been specially successful.

In Great Britain labor fraternities, or trades unions, came into being with the growth of factories and the destruction of domestic hand industries. The organization of these unions was prohibited by law and so remained until 1824. They began in secrecy, and their maintenance often depended upon the exercise of force and violence. However, little by little, they won toleration and recognition. In 1875 they had become so powerful as to secure public approval. The working people of France, Germany, Austria, Italy, Belgium, and the Continent generally, have also organized labor fraternities or trades unions. The spirit of the French Revolution, toned down to a kind of a weak socialism, seems to pervade a large number of them. However, they have won successes.

In 1883, the French Premier made arrangements with the land bank of France for advances of 20,000,000 francs to build 13,000 dwellings for artisans in the environs of Paris, the government guaranteeing payment. The houses were sold to workmen under agreement that payment should be made in twenty annual installments of less than the ordinary rental of the poorest city quarters. The work of erecting them was begun in a period of financial stringency, and thus thousands of artisans who could not afford to be idle were kept employed. Moreover, the city of Paris borrowed 50,000,000 francs for the erection in like manner of model tenement-houses, designed for rent to persons not able to pay more than 150 or 300 francs a year. The tenants are relieved in part from taxation while occupying these tenements.

The German insurance bill of 1887 provides that all workmen who pass the age of 70 years, or become completely and permanently incapacitated for work, shall have a pension. The bill affects only workmen, apprentices, servants, and administrative employes having a yearly pay of not more than 2,000 marks. Premiums on the insurance must have been paid for thirty years, or for five years where it is claimed on the ground of disability. A third of the premium is paid by the insured, another third by the employer, while the other third comes from the imperial treasury. The pension rate in the case of old age is 120 marks a year, while it varies from that amount to 250 marks when given for disability. Women, under like circumstances, are entitled to only two-thirds of what men receive. The pension system of Germany includes civil officials and even teachers. The greatest burdens that the working classes of Germany have now to bear consist in heavy taxes and service in the army. The generality of the pension system and the great size of the army necessitate the imposition upon the labor of the country of an extraordinary burden of taxation. And yet, strange to say, there seems to be no special opposition to the pension policy, which has a firm foothold in the country.

The fraternities of workmen in Belgium have been a source of much concern to the government, yet numerous salutary laws have been enacted at their instance. For example, wages must be paid in cash; two-fifths of salaries not exceeding 1,200 francs are exempt from execution for debts; councils of industry have been established to reconcile differences between employers and employes; debts contracted in liquor houses can not be recovered, and those who sell liquor to intoxicated persons, as well as the intoxicated persons themselves, are liable to fine and imprisonment.

The influence of labor fraternities, properly conducted, has been salutary. They have contributed to secure higher wages, bring about shorter hours, remove middlemen or sub-contractors, and support members when out of work. They resemble the guilds in acting as benefit societies and insuring members against accident, sickness, and old age. Moreover, they expend large sums in a direction foreign to the solicitude of the guilds, and that is in providing for unemployed members. All who were able and willing to work had plenty to do in the time of the guilds.

I need hardly apologize for referring so often to the guilds, for every person interested in the growth of our modern fraternities of workmen may study them with advantage. Such study in connection with the perusal of the late encyclical of our Holy Father on the subject of labor can not fail to arouse something like a fitting appreciation of the great and constant interest of the church in the welfare of the working people. The church favored the guilds, and the guilds were powerful and prosperous while they hearkened to and obeyed her. In the same spirit she favors to-day our fraternal organizations of workmen. She favors them, not as revolutionary bodies, not as materialistic agencies, not as societies banded together for purposes so mean, selfish, or unworthy as to make secrecy seem necessary. On the contrary, she favors them as a means of enabling workmen to secure and maintain their rights; to advance their common interests by means of the educational agencies available; to be guided by the same ethics and rules of morals collectively that individually they acknowledge; to be good citizens and obedient to the laws, and to be directed by the light of faith in Him who wrought with His own hands and gave His life for others.

These societies are beneficial in a high degree when honestly, intelligently, and properly managed and directed. The members are mutually benefited and the interests of the entire community advanced. The place of meeting becomes a school in the most practical sense. Men thus brought together become a great force for the accomplishment of good. They combine almost spontaneously to defend right against wrong in contests involving that issue. Viewed in that light, our labor societies deserve the support and co-operation of all good citizens without reference to vocation, position, or station. The old guilds had such support, employers, merchants, public officials and clergymen co-operating with them, and no one can deny that they contributed to promote the common good, maintain the public tranquility and restrict to narrowest limits the evidences of poverty and mendicancy.

The insurance feature of these societies is deserving of unqualified commendation. It is essential to their prosperity, if not their very existence. It aims at realizing in a secure and comparatively easy way some of the chief ends for which we live and labor. It provides for sick and needy members. It is by their bedside in illness and their grave in death. It alleviates their last suffering by the assurance that want shall be averted from those near and dear to them. It stimulates the courage of the widow and orphans. It affords them the means of battling successfully against the adversities of the world. It enables the careful and provident mother to maintain, educate and rear her children as good Christians and useful members of society. It bespeaks a continued interest of the members of the fraternity or union in the family of their deceased associate, and an effort to procure suitable employment for the children.

A workman acting by himself and for himself frequently forgets, till too late, the important duty of making provision for his helpless family. His example teaches selfishness, improvidence and vicious habits to his children. In their poverty and bitter need they are prompted each to look out for himself. The tie to the family center is broken. They lose sight of one another, and their fortune is as varying as their environments. Again, the mother's death may be hastened through the weight of her sorrow and the consciousness of her helplessness. Then the last hope is gone. No one is left to guide them in the way of religion, in the path of morality, in the instruction of the schools. Look around you in this great city—aye, even in the State and country! Trace to their origin vice and intemperance, indifference to religion or even actual apostacy. Do they not, as a rule, lead you up to a condition of things such in the main as I have described? How many children might be saved to the church and morality, to the school and usefulness, if provision were made for them before the death of the father—if they could continue to live under the family roof-tree.

Men are differently constituted. It may as well be admitted that a great many of our working people seem to lack the power to save. There can be no doubt, I submit, that every man of that class would derive advantage from joining a fraternal benefit association. In it he would meet the best element of working men—men who read and think, men who enjoy a sense of manly independence in the consciousness that neither in sickness nor death need they or their families fear the poorhouse or soul withering consequences of abject poverty. Membership in it would teach him to be practical, industrious, economical and attentive to the probable wants of the future. It would make him self-respecting and manly. It would encourage him to strive to provide a home for his family, and to surround himself with the comforts of life, if not the luxuries. It would bring him into closer relationship with his associates of the brotherhood than he would otherwise be. He would become interested in their welfare and they in his. They would advance mutually their common weal. Their interest in his welfare would make him a greater power in the community than ever he was before or could be without their co-operation. In short, he would become a steadier man and better citizen.

The insurance feature of such societies is, in my opinion, far preferable to the German policy of pensioning workmen. We know that in this country there is a formidable feeling of opposition to anything like a civil pension list. Moreover, we may well believe that no man of becoming pride would wish to be a beneficiary of the government on a civil pension list in the face of that feeling. His pension dole would be regarded simply as a gratuity or charitable offering to aid him in keeping out of the poorhouse. It would not tend to stimulate to honorable enterprise either him or his children; but it would tend to make him a mere creature of the government or an automaton, so to speak, which might be moved at its will this way or that. In fact, it might become dangerous to the liberties of the country to have so great a power subject to the caprice of any administration or political party.

In the fraternal society a member gives a legal consideration for what he or his family is to receive. It is honorable for him to receive it, for it proves him to have been industrious and frugal, intelligent and far-seeing. It provides means to rear and educate the children, and his example is a salutary inspiration to them. They are kept together and work with and for one another until grown. They live long enough under the same roof-tree to know and share the beautiful love distinguishing the relations existing between parents and children, and brothers and sisters. Such children are proud of their parents and proud to remember and do what their parents taught them. They are true to one another, and seek to be guided by the inspirations and hallowed memories of their youthful companionship.

Fortunately, in this glorious country of ours—a country formally placed under the standard of the cross by the great discoverer, whose achievement we commemorate this year—labor is to-day freer to act and stronger in union than ever it was before, and the influence of our fraternal benefit societies has not been without avail in contributing so to make it. But its freedom may become license and its strength dissipated and lost in outbreaks of lawlessness, unless it acknowledges and seeks to be guided by sound moral principles, such as the church prescribed for the guilds. To these principles our fraternal benefit associations have sought to conform so far as practicable under existing conditions. Let them be strengthened, for they tend to secure unity, impart confidence and increase the power of labor. Let them be established far and wide, and, like the guilds of old, they will satisfactorily settle the hours of, and remuneration for, toil. Acting in line with the sound principles prescribed by the church, as indicated in the recent labor encyclical of Pope Leo XIII., it would be within their power, as of old, to provide steady employment at fair wages for workmen, teach them to become "true laborers," and solve the many serious problems presented by the labor question.

"Life Insurance and Pension Funds for Wage Workers," was the title of an organization paper read by E. M. Sharon, of Davenport, Iowa. The contents of the paper were as follows:

Christianity applied to the labor problem illumines it and furnishes new rules for its solution. The encyclical of Leo XIII. is the most comprehensive and enlightening declaration of the rights of labor ever enunciated. The ruler of the spiritual world becomes the philanthropic statesman of the age and applies the treasured wisdom of the church of Christ to devising means to better the condition of the wage worker. He brushes aside the sophistries of capitalists and economists, and recognizes no conditions which limit the rights guaranteed him and due from every industrial system. In his Christian philosophy, the rise and fall of stocks, the ups and downs of markets, human tariffs, over or under-production, the exigencies of states, create no just excuse for depriving the laborer of the means of providing a reasonable frugal support for himself and family. The wage-worker himself can make no contract which attains less than this. He gives the reason.

Man, no matter what his position beyond the things personal to himself, is a member of society, the head of a family, the head of a society, one of the societies whose aggregation makes up the State. To injure him injures that society, injures the State. His relation to his fellowman, to the church, imposes other duties than those which he owes to the mere bodily wants of himself and dependents. Society must protect itself, must continue itself, must enforce the foundation factors of its own propagation and prosperity.

Here arises the necessity of "life insurance and pension funds for wage workers." Without them the position of the most fortunate laborer is insecure. He is able to give no assurance that he will continue to provide for himself and his family; that he will maintain his position in society and perform the duties which society exacts from him, instead of becoming a burden upon it.

Were it not for sickness, for body maiming accidents and unprovided old age, assurance would be useless. If old age alone took from man his earning capacity, if through all the years of his manhood, he continued to support his family, rearing a generation to take its place, full-fledged, in life's field of labor, if filial duty supported his faltering steps to the grave, insurance and pensions would not have a necessary place in man's economy, nor an advocate before this Congress.

But even in this favored land, liability to accident besets the wage-worker round about, follows his every step through life. The railroads alone, last year, killed 2,451 of their employes, and maimed and injured 22,390. It is claimed that accidents in mine and factory, and outside of them, in the United States, annually destroy the earning capacity of workmen to the amount of $150,000,000. This vast amount is destroyed and taken from the productive labor and wealth of the nation. These injuries entail sickness, loss of time and wages, lasting disability and death. They come when the domestic sky is brightest; they come to the home where are wife and lisping, helpless children.

These conditions demand decisive, comprehensive remedies. Let us see what has been done to allay the blasting effects of industrial injuries. The trades unions have within the past decade taken up the matter of sick, disability and mortality benefits, and are doing a splendid work for their members, through their own unaided efforts. The industrial insurance associations are furnishing a large amount of insurance in small sums. The fraternal and benevolent mutual assessment societies are doing a good work at a small cost. A beneficial class of work is done by voluntary action of manufacturers, railroad managers and other employers of labor. But this is not enough. These systems do not comprise the insurance of one-twentieth of the real wage-workers of the country.

In striking contrast to this condition, under the German compulsory system of insurance, sixty-four trades unions report an insured membership of five millions, and there are other insured employes to the number of eight and one-half millions. Germany, with less than fifty million inhabitants, has adopted an insurance and pension system that includes in one branch over thirteen and one-half millions of her people. This is purely an accident insurance. There are sick and invalidism and old age insurance associations which complement this system, and make it, in the results accomplished, the most perfect ever devised.

We do not take kindly to compulsory measures in this country. We are apt to conjure up the ghost of governmental paternalism; sumptuary laws are but to be so named to be condemned. But in practice the State provides unquestioned that the relatives of a poor person shall contribute to its support and the summary processes of the courts are invoked to enforce the mandates of the State. The State compels obedience to sanitary rules and regulations before the dire results of their violation manifests itself in disease and death. The State already supervises railroads and public carriers, has a voice in their every contract, fixes the limits of compensation for freight and passenger carriage, regulates the appliances of cars and engines, locates their stations and compels reports of every transaction. This governmental interference has been deemed necessary for the protection of the natural rights of individuals and the well-being of the society of which they form a part. It might exercise its paternal care for the benefit of wageworkers also without transcending its legitimate and proper powers.

It is comparatively easy to state what we want, what any system must provide. Every man, woman, and child, employed for wages, should receive free medical attendance and, at least, half wages during disability, from any cause, whether connected with his or her employment or not, and, in case of death, funeral benefits and a pension equal to half-wages to wife and children or other dependents during the continuance of such dependency. Only the grossest negligence, willful conduct, or dissipation should deprive of these benefits. When disabling injury or death comes to a household, it is not justice, it is not Christianity, it is not social economy, before despairing wife and helpless babies, to weigh with over-nicety the degrees of negligence of master and servant; to inquire how far each contributed to death or disability; nor to enter upon that usual learned discussion of latent and patent defects in destructive machinery, or whether the danger was so obvious that the workman should have given up the means of earning a livelihood for himself and family, or was justified in believing that the master had performed his duty. Nor does society care. It sees the destruction of a member, useful and valuable. It sees the destruction of its earning capacity, a contributing, paying member of itself transformed into a dependent burden, another self-supporting family for which it must become responsible.

Abolish the distinction between principal and vice-principal, employe and co-employe, independent employment and privity of contract, abolish everything that stands between the injured, disabled, or destroyed husband, father, or son, and the recompense that would have been his had the injury not occurred. Abolish all distinctions which have allowed the industrial world to unload its burdens on the social world. Provide that for the wage-worker, his wife and children and parents, provision has been made, and that neither want nor want's temptation shall ever come to him or his.

Whence shall come the millions to provide these benefits and pensions? They should come from the industries that the wage-workers build up, from the billions of wealth that their labor produces. Industrial interests can be adjusted to such changed conditions.

There are two sources from which to draw the funds necessary to support a system accomplishing the necessary results. These are the wage fund and that part of the cost of production or of operation known as the employer's liability expense. To pay insurance and pensions from these sources would obviate the objection that such a system would unduly derange or increase the cost of production in mining, manufacturing, and farming, and of operation for public carriers. It is advisable to make this concession in inaugurating a new system, although every sentiment of justice and humanity demands that the industries of the country ought to bear the burden of supporting the victim whose brawn and sweat and blood create its wealth and insure its prosperity, and the sooner our industries adjust themselves to such a liability the better it will be for our general prosperity and our claim of being a Christian nation. The people of this country, as consumers, are willing to have such charge added to the cost of the products which they consume.

The law, the common and statute law of this country, does impose some obligation on the employer of labor, when it is shown that the relation of master and servant exists. That law, while assuming that the servant "hires out," and gets paid, with reference to the usual dangers and hazards of his occupation, graciously holds the employer liable if he negligently increases these hazards and dangers. The employer's liability, in case of injury to his employe, is measured by the expense of getting a release from the injured or proving successfully to a court, and sometimes to a jury, that he did not increase the usual hazards of the employment, or if he did, that the employe ought to have seen it. It takes years to prove this or to have it disproved, and in the meantime the injured employe, weary of enforced idleness, in despair, too often has gone to the poorhouse or to his grave.

How much this liability costs in lawyers' fees and court costs and enforced or voluntary payments, is not wholly a matter of conjecture. The railroads reporting to the Iowa railroad commissioners in 1892, with a pay roll, exclusive of general officers and telegraphers, of $30,000,000, reported disbursements on account of injuries to persons, of $1,190,000 and legal expenses, exclusive of salaried solicitors and attorneys, of $590,000. It will be conceded that the incidental expense of employes acting as witnesses, adjusters, engineers, general solicitors and attorneys and their assistants, would offset all legal expenses not connected with claims for damages for personal injuries.

The way to ascertain the expense of the liability of manufacturers, builders, mine owners, municipal and private corporations, and other employers of labor, is to inquire what is paid to others for assuming this liability. Employers are very generally carrying liability insurance. For this a premium is paid equal on the average of about 1 per cent. of the wages paid the employes whose wages are insured against. Five of the companies doing business in Iowa last year reported premium receipts of over $7,763,000.

Upon what principle of economy is this vast amount of money paid, under proper regulations, directly to those who are injured? From the standpoint of social economy, employers pay nothing or too little in many cases and too much in some others. Legal technicalities defeat worthy claims, and juries, when they get an opportunity, allow excessive amounts in special cases. The amount paid ought to be a matter of equitable adjustment with little or no expense to either party. The first step toward the establishment of a correct system of life insurance and pension funds should be to abolish actions against railroad companies for personal injuries to employes.

Let a fund be created under the supervision of the insurance department of the State. Require the management of each railroad company to pay into such fund a fixed percentage of the wages paid to each employe in its service, such percentage to be fixed from time to time by the railroad commissioners. The assessments should be paid directly to some officer of the State or to a board created under legal authority, by the companies interested. Let that fund be large enough to pay compensatory, monthly pensions to every employe injured in the service of a railroad, and to the dependent relatives of those killed. Let the State recover for the benefit of the pension fund, penalties for gross negligence producing injuries or death, and similar penalties by way of deduction from benefits, against employes for gross carelessness, contributing to injuries. These penalties, coupled with suitable requirements of safety appliances and conditions, to be enforced with the sole object of lessening accidents and injuries in the operation of railroads. Depositories for this fund could be established by the insurance or railroad commissioners, under requirements and safeguards guaranteeing its absolute safety and material increase from the income of the surplus that should be carried over from year to year to meet long time pensions for the permanently disabled or heirs of deceased members, or it might be controlled and invested by the State as the permanent school funds are now managed. The amount necessary to compensate the results of accidents should be paid wholly by the railroads as a consideration of their release from all other liability to their employes. Liability for damage to others than employes should remain as now until such time as our people generally are brought within the protection of some general insurance system. For sick and old age insurance the employe should be required to pay a fixed percentage of wages monthly into a special or the general insurance fund. This would be for the special protection of those making payments and their dependents, with equitable provisions for changing from one employment to another, with preserved rights and the withdrawal of a certain percentage of the amount paid, on gaining a competence, or, for other allowed causes, leaving the protected class.

Commencing with the railroads, let the State do for the wage-workers what it has done, what the general government has done, for shippers, for property, in the regulation and supervision of State and inter-State traffic—pay attention to the death of an engineer, or fireman, or brakeman, equal to that paid to a discrimination of a few dollars in a freight bill.

Commence with the railroads—the State has already asserted its right to dictate to them and to supervise their operation. It has the machinery necessary to carry the system into effect already provided and in operation. The railroad commissioners could look after the details of fixing the amount of assessments to be paid by each company, and the amount of damage or pensions to be paid injured employes. The insurance department could look after the funds, see to their care and absolute safety, and the investment of the surplus. Any system would be more or less experimental, but all matters could be adjusted by experience from time to time. The supervision and assistance of the State would reduce to a minimum the expense of transacting the large business of the system.

The association would extend itself. The supervising authority could fix the terms, based upon the experience of each industry, upon which the employes in any trade or industry could be brought within its protection. It would only be necessary to change the employers' liability laws, making each responsible for injuries to persons, without regard to the laws as to fellow-servants, or to other causes not connected with the voluntary acts of the employe, to make it to the interest of every employer of labor to seek admission to the general insurance system. It would be cheaper than paying a premium to liability insurance companies, which collect premiums 100 per cent larger than all the losses they pay; cheaper for all, by reason of the large general average as applied to all accidents, than paying their own probable liability even under the present law. Those engaged in dangerous employment would join the association to lessen their liability in less dangerous employments, because the percentage of payments would be small. The greater benefits to their employes, their greater satisfaction and contentment, would make it the part of wisdom and self-interest to join the association.

Such a system would equalize the cost of production. Each employer in the same industry would pay the same percentage according to amount of production for liability for injuries to persons. The liberal employer and the industrial Shylock would both stand on the same footing as to cost of labor. Nor would such a system destroy the usefulness of beneficial trades unions. They will still have their proper work to do. The State which will first take up this matter of securing under wise provisions insurance against accidents and sickness the wage-workers within its limits, will be doing a greater work, building a more worthy monument than has been erected to philanthropic Christian government since the great Lincoln emancipated a race and removed the last shackle of legal slavery from the limbs of human labor.

Rev. Joseph L. Andreis, pastor of St. Luke's Church, Baltimore, Md., read an essay on "Italian Immigration and Colonization," in which he urged his ideas as follows:

The problems specified in the programme as coming before this Congress for consideration and solution are most important, but not essentially local, for they are the subject of actual, deep study for economists and churchmen in Europe as well as here. The one which towers above all others in importance—being new to past history, affecting this country only, and calling for prompt and unequivocal solution—is that of immigration. With the large number of new immigrants pouring almost weekly into these United States, there is an immense wave of stormy elements coming along with hem, composed of heterogeneous tongues, manners, habits, national prejudices, errors of mind, malice of heart, indifference to religion, and infidelity. A large number of these immigrants are Catholics. Hence the church in America must meet them as they are, take care of them, and labor to make them what they should be. Among them are hundreds of thousands of Italians. The writer of this essay on "Italian Immigration and Colonization" has considered it from its social, moral, and religious standpoints, and taken the liberty of suggesting the means of effecting the amelioration of Italian immigrants, socially, morally, and religiously.

As effects are accounted for by their relative causes, so the Italian immigration to the United States is explained by the causes of emigration. What can they be? A craving to see and enjoy this immense Western hemisphere, discovered by the Italian Christopher Columbus, and named after another Italian, Americus Vespucci? No; for the Italians are accustomed to national—nay, world-wide glories. Italy, itself, is too charming a country to be exchanged for any other, even this America of liberty and plenty—Italy, the garden of Europe. The Italians know this, and are loth to leave it. But why have they emigrated, and still do emigrate, in such great numbers? Is not Italy's soil fertile and rich in all sorts of produce? So it is; but with all that, the large masses of Italians suffer from great distress and poverty. What is the cause of it? "Inimicus homo hoc fecit "—" An enemy has done this."

In their great sagacity, the sovereign pontiffs, Gregory XVI. and Pious IX. sounded the alarm of warning to the Italians, and did all in their power to thwart his coming. Time has fully justified the warnings of the aforesaid pontiffs, and particularly proved that the enemy was, and is, the cosmopolitan sect of Freemasonry; for, spurning the liberal concessions made to his people by Pious IX. it aimed at undermining the principle of authority, un-Christianizing the masses, and reducing them to poverty by its own aggrandizement and enrichment. In fact, no sooner did it begin to wield power than the enemy, with a stroke of the pen, suppressed the religious orders, devoured their estates, together with the patrimonies of the poor; and when all that great wealth was gone, begun to feed himself upon the people through the levying of enormous taxes. These are so exorbitant that the small-scale farmers are unable to pay them, and, in consequence, are by the ruthless law expropriated of their lands by the inexorable tax-gatherer. Meantime, the cost of house-rent and the necessaries of life have increased and the wages of mechanics decreased.

Not content with having robbed the people of means of subsistence, the enemy forcibly takes all the able-bodied young men and enrolls them in his immense army. Crushed by forced poverty, and dismayed by the threatening danger of losing their lives or limbs in a more or less proximate European war, they turn their eyes westward and, with heavy hearts, resolve to come to our shores in quest of what they have a right to in their mother country, but which is denied them.

To urge the timid to consummate their resolve to emigrate, Italian sharpers, both here and in Italy, are engaged in the profligate business of making false representations to them of the abundance of work to be found in this country, the easy way of securing employment and earning high wages. These sharpers, or padroni, commence with robbing them of their little savings, through the ostensible formality of a contract by which they promise to take them to the place of work and secure employment for them. Through the medium of bankers located in the principal seaport cities of this country, the padroni or their agents advance the money to those laborers who have none to pay their passage, with the proviso of being reimbursed and receiving a heavy percentage from their earnings after having arrived and been put to work.

The results of these infamous transactions has been that thousands of poor Italians have been cajoled to emigrate hither to work for months and months without any compensation, except scanty meals and bad lodging. Finding thousands duped and oppressed, and unable to obtain redress, many have lost their health and died brokenhearted; while a large number of others, penniless, ragged, and fasting, have tramped hundreds of miles on foot to reach the steamer and work their way back to their native country. Great as the evil of the slave traffic in Africa is, the injustice and cruelty inflicted upon the Italian immigrants in this country at the hands of padroni and bankers associated with them is by far a greater evil, which this Congress should endeavor to remove. To this end two means are hereby respectfully suggested: One is to forcibly represent the aforesaid great grievance to our national government and urge it to take proper action in regard to it; the other is to appeal to either our Most Holy Father, or to the Central Catholic Union in Rome for the adoption of such methods as will, without failure, convey the much-needed warnings to all Italians who contemplate emigration.

The census bulletins published by the United States Government through the Department of the Interior, Washington, give the following table of Italian immigration to this country:

Increase from 1850 to 1860	6,783
Increase from 1860 to 1870	6,639
Increase from 1870 to 1880	27,073
Increase from 1880 to 1890	138,350
Total	178,845
In 1890	62,969
In 1891	69,297
In 1892	30,086
April 30, 1893	26,422
Total	188,774

Italian immigrants love to work, and, as a rule, are law-abiding. This is proved by the statistics of prisoners and paupers published February 9, 1893, by the Census Bureau at Washington. The official report shows that out of the total number of 55,296 foreign-born paupers in the alms-houses of the United States, 290 only are Italians, and out of the total number of 31,861 foreign-born prisoners but 1,124 are Italians. A large percentage of the latter owe their penalty to having taken the law into their own hands by punishing unprovoked insults, or resisting inhuman treatment from their employers, or trying to obtain by violence the hard-earned wages they were denied.

A serious charge is often made against a portion of Italians in our large cities. It is that they live huddled up in slums and tenement-houses. The charge is substantially correct, but its worst features can be amended. The complained-of places are only for transient immigrants, until employment can be found. The causes of their selecting objectionable quarters are: First, because they can be rented cheaply; second, because they find in them people akin to their own tongue, manners, and habits. In order to do away with the best part of the nuisance arising from the aforesaid slums and tenement-houses, two things are necessary: One, to have a large number of small houses at low rent, and the other to prevail on the civil authorities to refuse the license to open a saloon in them—nay, even in proximity to them.

Though Italians are generally temperate, still the saloon at their door is an open avenue to immoralities of various sorts, especially where the access to the home is by the saloon entrance.

To form the right estimate of the morality of the Italian colony it is necessary to be well acquainted with the moral atmosphere existing in Italy. In her is found a dualism, namely, two factors: one for good, the other for evil. The former consists in the fact that nearly every inch of Italian soil is saturated with martyrs' blood, or made famous by the lives of great saints; that from the beginning of Christianity Italy has been blessed in having in her very heart the chair of St. Peter—the beacon of divine light to the whole world—the center of unity for all churches. By being born and reared in Italy the Italians must naturally be Christians, and therefore good. They would undoubtedly be so were it not for the other factor, namely, the rampant Freemasonry, which for the past forty-five years has been hard at work to un-Christianize the nation. When we take into account all the agencies used to poison the minds and corrupt the hearts of the people, it is not to be wondered at if a large portion of Italian immigrants show indifference in the practice of religion. They are Catholic at heart; but, to avoid ridicule, they have habitually desisted from the exterior profession of their faith.

Realizing that in this country they are laboring under various disadvantages, such as the total absence of their native customs on the one hand and the existence of new ones on the other, the use of a language they do not know and apprehend to be too difficult to learn, the finding of Protestant churches, the sight of many people professing no faith, the poor Italian immigrants feel out of their sphere—a fact which shows that this North America is the least suitable land for them.

The old aphorism, "Like parent, like child," applied to the children of Italian immigrants, is only partially correct, whether they be considered under the social or moral standpoint. Considered socially, they soon learn the English language—breathe the American spirit—and acquire American manners. In consequence, they yearn to raise themselves above their parents' standing, and a good many even Americanize their surnames so as to pass for genuine Americans, with the view to paving their way to success. It is clear from this that their minds and hearts are centered in this country, and that they never dream of leaving it for Italy. But, alas! Not much good can be said of all of them as to their moral condition.

Nearly one-half of all the children are allowed to grow up ignorant of religion, or do not profess it at all. The consequence of this is that a good many turn Protestants, or marry before Protestant preachers, and rear their offspring either in none or other religion than Catholic. We have then in this country about half a million of Italians, some of whom are ignorant of the Christian doctrine; most of them do not live up to it, and nearly one-half of their children are permitted, by either ignorant or neglectful parents, to grow up to manhood and womanhood in utter ignorance of the truths and precepts of that divine faith which was and is infused into their souls through the sacrament of baptism.

Meanwhile the various agencies of the powers of darkness are active in preventing their intellect from seeing the true light and their will from complying with the divine law. Such being their abnormal and frightful condition, the question suggests itself: What is to be done? They are all Catholic, and, while in these United States, form a portion of the sheepfold of Jesus Christ, to be guarded against the wolves by the divinely-appointed shepherds, fed upon the pastures of Christian instruction and worship, and watered with the sacraments. They are Catholic, and hence members of the mystical body of Christ, the church.

Therefore, the American Catholic laity must regard them as such; the American priesthood must love and care for them as such; the American Episcopate must see to their spiritual welfare just as much, nay, even more than all the other members of the Catholic church living in this country. Since, then, the fact is that these Italian Catholics, both adult and young, are here, the question is: How is religion to be brought to them? The episcopate in these United States is fully equal to devising the means to attain that object.

If religion is to reach the people, it must be through the medium of the language spoken by them. Now, the majority of adult Italian immigrants speak Italian only; that language must be the medium, therefore, whereby religion is to be conveyed to them. Who are the laborers to be? They ought to be priests affiliated to the same religious order, such as the Salesians, whose founder was the late saintly Don Bosco, of universally cherished memory. By having the Salesians in the principal cities of this country we would secure most zealous missionaries for the Italians, a college with efficient proffessors to impart all the desired branches, excellent educators of young men and great factors for developing ecclesiastical vocations.

But the objection may be here advanced: How are these religious to teach Christian doctrine if this is to be taught in the English language, which is spoken by the children of Italian immigrants? The answer is this: For a while lay teachers would have to give religious instruction. The English-speaking laity should be called upon and made use of in this great work of Christian charity, not only as teachers of catechism, but also as animators of Christian piety with the grown people.

Among the laity of every parish there are sufficient intelligent and practical Catholics. Their power for good should no longer be allowed to remain inoperative.

All admit that "exampla trahunt," but we must also admit that a good word said well, and in season, is often what makes surrender to the already felt force of good example. It is not too much to insist upon the efficiency of properly organized conferences of St. Vincent de Paul for the above mentioned object, as through them we would see the realizaton of the "fortier" and "sauveur" of the servants who, complying with their Master's bidding, went out into the streets and lanes of the city and brought into the supper-room the poor and the feeble, and the blind and the lame. Even if children of Italian immigrants went to no school, or all went to public schools, they can all be reached through the exertion of the priest, especially if ordered by the good Catholic laity, and, above all, by the members of the Conference of St. Vincent de Paul.

The Italians have always been taught to look up to priests as the divinely commissioned teachers of religion, and believe that Christ's injunction, "Go and teach all things whatsoever I have commanded you," was not made to the people for the priests, but to the priests for the people. But what is the situation of the Italians now in this country? Their teachers of religion are not to be found, for more than half of them are "like sheep that have no shepherd." Are they to remain so? The Lord forbids it. Can we, while the principles of perversion are daily doing their deadly work, be justified in delaying the provision of the priests that are laborers in the sense of the gospel? Application for them should be made at once, for there is great danger in delaying it. This is all the more true because the number of Italian immigrants is increasing every week by hundreds.

The day when, with oneness of spirit and direction (as the Salesians), the priests will be brought here in sufficient numbers to take charge of the Italians scattered about our cities and country-places, with the American laity to lend them assistance, both adults and their children will receive the necessary dispensation of religion. By the attaining of this longed-for result those whom God has placed to rule His church in this country, and the Catholic laymen aiding them, will have successfully solved the difficult problem of the religious amelioration of the Italian immigrants, and will have thereby rendered a signal service to our great commonwealth, by helping it to solve its vexed problem of immigration in general, socially, morally and economically. In pursuance of the constitution of our Republic, the civil powers welcome all the well-meaning comers to our shores, favor their temporal prosperity and protect their lives, rights and property. The Church of Christ cannot be less generous in the spiritual order. She must follow her Divine Founder, who came upon earth to "seek and save that which was lost;" therefore, she must in this country welcome all Catholic immigrants, provide for their spiritual wants and care for the salvation of their souls.

In giving expression to the foregoing statements and considerations, the writer of this essay feels that he is only voicing the sentiments of this vast assembly, and that all the members composing it will be of one mind and heart in reckoning among the laurels achieved through their combined efforts, that of securing the religious amelioration of the Italians who are enjoying with us the fruitful land discovered by their co-national Christopher Columbus, for the true freedom and prosperity of man, and for the exaltation of the glory of God!

This Congress with its deliberations will pass to history; posterity will know of its worth, as the tree is known by its fruit, and pronounce its judgment,. This judgment will be Catholic!

"Pauperism; The Cause and the Remedy," was the subject of the paper prepared and read by M. J. Elder, of New Orleans, La. Folllowing are the contents of the paper:

Without having read any of the other papers on this subject; without any knowledge of the contents of a single one of them, I nevertheless feel morally certain of six salient points wherein we all agree.

We agree in naming, as five leading causes of pauperism: First, intemperance; second, idleness; third, sickness; fourth, general incompetence; and fifth, lack of work. A sixth point on which, without previous arrangement, we all perfectly agree, is that this evil of pauperism is too vast, too limitless, to be tinkered with; that dole of alms will never remedy it, and that all existing measures have proved inadequate.

But outside these six points, I fear we differ radically, for, after referring to those five causes of pauperism, I must go on to explain that I regard them, potent though they be, as mere effects of another cause—a great, remote, and terrible cause, whose ceaseless operating will continue to produce inevitable pauperism, despite our most strenuous efforts against the five immediate causes which we so plainly see. Therefore, right here we separate, and going our widely divergent ways, I am left alone to travel unaccompanied this woeful line of the remote and real, and primal cause of pauperism.

But I am not without great support from current literature, from the secular press, and from the Protestant periodicals. Quoting but a very small part of the references I have at hand, I give the following: The *Illustrated American* of July 15th, this year, says—

"Our census of 1890 shows a decrease in 455 agricultural counties in New England, New York, Illinois, Indiana, Kentucky, Ohio, Tennessee, Michigan, and other States. The tendency to abandon the fields and to flock to the city is marked and significant. It is foolish to believe the exodus due to the opening up of Western lands. The real cause is that the sturdy farmer lad, educated in the public schools, leaves the hard, physical labors of the soil to seek lighter work and greater prosperity in the cities. There is danger in this."

Joseph Kirkland, writing of the Chicago poor, says: "The overwhelming tendency of modern life is toward cities. Everything done to alleviate the condition of the poor in great cities works in the direction of bringing more into them; and no argument or persuasion prevails to get them out again. * * * They would rather starve in a crowd than grow fat in quietude, especially if the 'crowd' is sprinkled with aromatic 'charity.'"—[*From Scribner's Magazine, July, 1892.*

General Booth, in his "Darkest England," says: "The deterioration of population in large towns is one of the most undisputed facts of social economics. The country is the breeding ground of healthy citizens. But for the constant influx of countrydom, cockneydom would long ere this have perished. But, unfortunately, the country is being depopulated. The towns are being gorged with undigested and indigestible masses of labor. The race from the country to the city has been the cause of much of the distress we have to battle with."

The Earl of Roseberry says: "I am always haunted by the awfulness of London; by the great appalling effect of these millions. Sixty years ago Cobbett called it a wen. If it was a wen then, what is it now? A tumor, an elephantiasis, sucking into its gorged system half the life and the blood and the bone of the rural districts."

Paolo Mantegazza, in his Testa, says: "Did not the country send to our cities a continuous tribute of robust members, they would be depopulated in less than a century. How few are able to say: 'My grandfather was born in this, my city.' No one is able to say it of his own great-grandfather. The cities are machines that destroy and consume what the fields produce; are hot-houses where men and women produce precious flowers and fruit, but at loss of life; are great millstones where all the human energies raise themselves to the heat of a continuous excitement."

Thus the consensus of opinion, gathered from most competent sources, gives this as the greatest cause of pauperism.

My own opinion, however, though similar, is modified. I believe the great cause of pauperism to be indeed the urban tendency, but only when coupled with all lack of rural tendency. For I claim that the urban tendency is not necessarily evil, but that the lack of a rural tendency is necessarily and wholly evil.

The country is a nation's lungs. The city is its heart. It is well that the fresh blood flow from the lungs to the heart. But it is ill, indeed, for the heart to return no blood to the lungs. This is the trouble from which our nation is suffering.

The blood from our country lungs flows into the heart of the city fast enough—too fast, perhaps; but there it stays, and congests, and stagnates, and we suffer from elephantiasis, from fatty degeneration of the heart, and from a thousand other ills, and no amount of doctoring will cure us, unless it promote the free flow of blood again, and its due return to our country lungs. My explanation of this deplorable condition is as follows:

The chief reason that rural populations are pouring too rapidly into towns is because rural interests the world over are (and have been for generations) neglected. Indifference and even injustice are shown to the farm and the farmer by education, by government, by legislation, by the press, and even by religion, aye, by charity itself. This explanation will develop later on.

The second phase of the trouble—the lack of rural tendency—is also because of the injustice and contempt shown the farmer and, further, because individuality is a necessary element for success in rural life, and individuality is exactly that element which urban life destroys. It is in the very nature of things that it depresses energy and individuality.

See how small and stunted are the trees that have been planted too close together.

Then look at the vigorous growth, the spreading branches, the noble height of the tree that stands alone on a plain. The typical urban has a horror of rural life, a dread disgust of it. He will tell you this is because "country life is too lonesome, too uninteresting, too slow; country work doesn't pay," etc.

But the real reason—all unsuspected though it be by him—lies in his own instinct. His instinct tells him he is too weak to cope with the invigorating vicissitudes of rural life; tells him he is too small mentally and physically to battle with the large difficulties in the way of rural success. Gregariousness has stunted him. His posterity will be more and more stunted, until they reach the dwarfed and helpless level of pauperism.

Now for the remedy. (Rather singular to speak of "hopelessness" in one breath and of "remedy" in the next; but explanation will come in due time.) The causes themselves suggest the remedy. True, we can do little toward getting justice for the farmer from government or legislation, from public education or the press. But we can do a great deal toward getting justice and attention from the Catholic press and the Catholic pulpit, from Catholic education, and, strongest of all, Catholic charity.

At the outset we must acknowledge specifically that the efforts of all these have availed but little; nay, that in many, many cases, they but promote the very evils they aim to abolish. Let us establish soup houses without number, night refuges plentiful; self-improvement clubs for young working women; mutual benefit societies for young men; insurance companies on solid basis; Keeley institutes; asylums numerous, vast, splendidly equipped; hospitals handsomely endowed; schools on modern plans, even industrial and polytechnic schools; free kindergartens; day creches for poor mothers; gratuitous loan funds; fresh air funds; labor unions, and no end of homes (!), protectorates, reformatories,etc. Let us keep these numberless charities in full swing, and still will pauperism and distress go on almost unabated. Why? Because we do not lay the ax to the root. Nay, we actually fertilize that root. Our charities encourage the undesirable traits of dependence and and gregariousness—traits that inevitably lead along the downward grade to pauperism.

And so we must change our methods. * * * * It seems almost superfluous to instance the object lessons of the World's Fair. They are so plain, so clear. Can anyone who runs fail to read the object lessons of the the Irish village? There is the sort of charity we should emulate. Those philanthropists did not lose their time and money trying to remedy city pauperism. They sought to cure country poverty, and they succeeded. There is the vital difference between the poverty of the city and that of the country. City poverty is constitutional; country poverty but accidental. City poverty is chronic; country poverty acute. The former incurable, the latter easily preventable.

The philanthropist of the Irish village taught butter-making and other rural industries, with such success that the formerly poverty-stricken neighborhood is now become quite prosperous. I have yet to hear of one urban district raised from pauperism to prosperity by any amount of charities.

Another object lesson is in the Louisiana exhibit. Look at our peasant women at their weaving. Look at evidences of their Acadian home-love and content in the homemade looms, home-made chairs, tables, lamp-stands, prie-dieus, etc. Throughout all our rural settlements of Catholic Acadians in Louisiana there is no chronic pauperism. And yet, bear it well in mind, these people have not enjoyed the advantages (!) of free kindergartens, nor polytechnic schools, nor free libraries, nor free clinics, nor free-lunch houses, nor free anything. Only one in fifteen knows how to read and write. And, nevertheless, Rev. Father W. J.Kennely, S. J., rector, who resided among them for years, says of these same illiterate "Cajians:"

"The Father's work in Grand Coteau and its environs has not been in vain. It is what I would call a model parish. I can say the same of the other parishes, and I may add of the whole country. The faith is alive; religion is respected and generally practiced; the priests are looked up to and obeyed. The people may be thriftless, but they are not ungrateful, they are not given to drunkenness and other crimes. They support their priests and pay their taxes when they can."

Now, how many city pastors can speak this of the poor of their parishes? Think of the hoodlums and toughs, the sports and ward politicians, the drunkards and loafers, who abound in Catholic urban parishes among the poorer districts, and see if any pastor can say of them: "The faith is alive; religion generally practiced; priests looked up to and obeyed. The people are not given to drunkenness," etc. Our rural "Cajians" are given the same reputation, but with more enthusiasm, by Catherine Cole, a Protestant; George W. Cable, a bitter anti-Catholic, and by many other writers for Protestant literature. They are described as frugal, content, virtuous, sober, famous for hospitality, gentleness, neighborliness, superb health, and large families. They are a standing testimony of what rural life can do for our Catholic poor. Similar testimony is given by travelers regarding Catholic peasantry everywhere, Europe, Ireland, Canada, Central America and South America.

Now, let our philanthropists study this idea in connection with the five immediate causes of pauperism.

1. Intemperance. All authorities agree in declaring that drunkenness does not prevail among Catholic rurals to anything like the same extent as among urbans. This is especially true of grape-raising and wine-making countries. Indeed, were I asked to name that practical measure most efficacious in the cause of temperance, I would vehemently exclaim, "Vineyards!"

And yet, of all the total abstinence societies and other temperance workers, whether Protestant or Catholic, I have yet to hear of one that gives any attention to that most practical and promising of remedies. Here in Louisiana alone our experimental station has demonstrated that 120 varieties of grapes can be successfully raised. And yet I can pretty safely estimate that there are not a half-dozen vineyards managed by Catholics in this entire State. Here is a method whereby hundreds of Catholic young men and young women, hundreds of Catholic families, could be earning an honest livelihood, doing effective service in the temperance cause, benefitting themselves and their posterity, and using a most efficacious means of preventing pauperism. Still our charitable societies do not lift a finger in this direction.

2. Idleness. This, too, is a vice demonstrated to be far less prevalent among the rural poor than among the urban poor. Religion having a firmer hold upon Catholic peasantry than upon our city poor, idleness and kindred vices are more easily combated among the former than among the latter. Take France for instance. Authorities state that among the city paupers, an appalling proportion is utterly vicious and incorrigible; whereas, the peasantry retain much of their old time faith and virtue. Why such facts are not acted upon by our charitable organizations is a mystery I cannot penetrate. I delight to recall that when the great Ozanam had organized the conference of St. Vincent de Paul, the very first charity he performed under its auspices was to separate from a drunken father the mother and children, and send them "happy as larks," the chronicle says, back to their peasant home in Brittany.

Also I delight to instance the penal settlement of Cayenne in French Guiana. "So far as reformation of criminals is concerned, the benevolent results of this colonial experiment are said to have surpassed all expectations. * * * A great majority of the female prisoners are given small farms, as a reward for good conduct during imprisonment. They marry other ex-convicts, and generally prove exemplary wives and mothers."

3. Ill-health. It is needless to dwell on this. Everybody knows that the "farmer lad" and "the country girl" are terms for sturdy strength and blooming health. And every philanthropist knows that the ill-health of the city poor is one of the most disheartening phases of poverty. But all this knowledge seems to be a dead letter. We keep on providing big hospitals and infirmaries, free clinics and dispensaries, homes for curables and incurables; and not one man in a thousand ever gives or wills a dollar toward the country cure; nay, not the country cure, but better far, the country prevention. No wonder pauperism continues to be the running sore it is.

4. General incompetency. To me this sad heritage of the city poor seems even worse than the preceding ones. From long dwelling in devitalized atmosphere, from long laboring at deadening work, from long-continued gregariousness, the urban poor so lose their grit and individuality as to become helplessly machine-like and stupid. This is what makes me qualify pauperism as hopeless. We might as well seek to raise the dead from their graves as to raise paupers from their pauperism. No, we cannot cure pauperism any more than we can cure death. But we can, and most positively should, prevent it. Hear what Charles J. O'Malley says in this connection:

"Would it interest you to learn, I wonder, that I live in the midst of a wide, open country on a large farm, and have few associates. * * * This is the great agricultural county of Kentucky, is fully two-thirds Catholic, and *here* the members of our faith are remarkable for their enterprise, sobriety, and industry. We are the largest landholders and every way superior to the common, inert idlers found in Southern cities."

There is the living testimony of a living writer? No pauperism, no hopeless incompetency, but instead "enterprise, sobriety, industry."

5. Lack of work. This to me is the astonishing phase. Looking both at the

boundless possibilities of our agricultural regions, and at the extensive and sincere efforts of our charitable organizations, I am amazed that the latter do not find in the former a solution of this part of the problem. Objectors will say this is all very fine on paper, but it won't work elsewhere. True. I acknowledge it. There is Ruskin, for instance. How complete was the failure of his rustic paradise! There is General Booth. He has not succeeded. There was the Brook Farm experiment, and many others similar to it. All failures. And still I reiterate any arguments.

Why? Because I believe and know that that which, outside the Catholic Church, is impossible, becomes, within her pale, the possible.

Whenever a great need cries out for relief it is the Catholic Church which answers, All other powers have proved unequal to the terrible need of remedying, or, rather, preventing, pauperism. Now, the time is ripe for the superhuman power of the Catholic Church to assert itself once more. And if no lay charity be organized among us whose members will actually and literally take the lead in this rural movement, then I am persuaded that a new order will arise in the church whose consecrated sons and daughters shall be pledged to spend themselves in life-long effort toward checking this urban tendency and promoting a rural tendency. In my ecstatic rejoicing over the mere prospect of such an era, I feel like saying: "When will be the beginning of the millennium?"

Those heaven-guided souls, instead of concentrating all their efforts on rural interests, will devote them solely to rural interests, especially in education. Whereas now, alas, is there one educated Catholic young man in a thousand who can run a farm, or manage a plantation, or start a vineyard, or boss a ranch, or do anything that is virile, strong, productive, and becoming a manful Catholic? Is there one in ten thousand who can offer country work and country wages to the workless and wageless thousands of our cities?

Only one more catechetical venture and I will end. What are we doing for our country poor? Nothing. What are we doing for the city poor? Everything. What is the natural and inevitable consequence? The answer to this query I leave to those who are capable of putting together two thoughts and of arriving thereby at a third.

Elizabeth A. Cronyn, of Buffalo, N. Y., read the following paper on "Alumnæ Associations in Convent Schools:"

Alumnæ associations in Catholic schools are novelties. The first one was organized twelve or thirteen years ago in the Grey Nuns' Academy of the Holy Angels, Buffalo. Its formation was suggested, remotely, by a wish to emulate the usefulness of similar societies in Catholic colleges for men, and stimulated by local needs as well as by the example of achievement in graduates' associations attached to local secular schools. It was, however, from its inception more comprehensive in scope than either of these. Shortly after, a like association was formed at Nazareth Convent, Rochester, under the Sisters of St. Joseph, and within three years the movement has extended, it is said, to many of the older academies.

As understood by those who have followed the progress of one, the purpose of an alumnæ association in a convent school is both educational and social. As an educational force its object is, first, to band together graduates of the school for more advanced study and for general self-improvement along the lines of their previous training. Earlier these growing minds are taught to realize something of their possibilities, habits of study are formed, taste is cultivated, and character developed; but our average graduate who is very young when she leaves the security of convent halls, can scarcely have more than peered into that book of knowledge which educators say must be so thoroughly conned—a book at times so diversely interpreted to Catholic and non-Catholic readers. Commentators do not agree, but meanwhile it is important that the law and the prophets of what is called secular as well as of sacred learning be expounded with safety to those who are seeking it. Daily observation shows us that young women, no less than young men, need to be fortified against the assaults of a prevailing and most pernicious literature and of so-called science—science "run wild, like a planet broken loose from its celestial system." "The punishment of licentious writers," says the Abbe Roux, "is that no one will read them or confess to having read them." Alas! that is no longer true.

In convent, far more than in other private schools, young girls of widely differing fortunes find themselves classmates. School days ended, they go their several ways, but whether in the world of fashion or at a teacher's desk, in domestic or professional life, the talk of and love, more or less sincere, of education, of culture, seem part of the very atmosphere they breathe. All sorts of theories and every species of "fad" have their apostles. Lecturers in hall and drawing-room—text-books in the schools—if not aggressively hostile to the church, are effectively so by their persistent ignoring of what it has done and is doing in all departments of education. Young Catholics must study history with, and receive a standard of beauty and truth in literature from, their own qualified teachers, or they are going to take both from the lips and pens of the incapable and misleading. If they think they cannot find at home the pleasure and profit they are seeking, they will go abroad for them. A realization of these facts originated and developed our reading-circle movement.

The alumnæ association is a reading circle—and something more. At its weekly fortnightly, or monthly meetings a plan of study is followed. Original papers are prepared or readings given bearing upon the subject under consideration. Books of reference are indicated on a printed study card, and are almost exclusively by Catholic authors, for the reason that in such an association everything is to be studied from the Catholic point of view. The other side is sufficiently in evidence always and every where. When means permit, an alumnæ association provides itself with a code of postgraduate lectures, or detached lectures upon various subjects determined by the year's study or by special circumstances.

When the convent has a suitable hall, and these lectures can be enjoyed also by the community and advanced classes, another phase of such an association's usefulness is presented. Regular meetings are held always at the convent. Officers are elected annually; but of one which I have in mind the president, happily, is never changed.

Self-improvement, as it may be striven for in an alumnæ association, is by no means limited to intellectual culture. There is something for the heart to do, and it is natural to suppose that a society whose members are all well known to one another may be an excellent medium for the distribution of activities.

For example, a certain one furnished the nucleus of what has become a most flourishing tabernacle society. It has also committees which labor for the diffusion of good literature, and, in particular, provide wholesome reading for penal institutions within reach. Others help the nuns in their prison and hospital work. Others, again, busy themselves in behalf of the mission of Mary Immaculate and for the Indian Missions, here. These works do not cripple or supplant, but supplement parish sodalities and charitable societies. Thus, it will be seen, an alumnæ association affords several channels through which its members' energies are directed, according to their individual sympathies and capacity.

Its second object as an educational force is to advance the interests of the school of which it is part. This can be done in many ways. It is not common to find our convent schools blessed with over-abundant means. As in most Catholic institutions, their growth to that much of prosperity marked outwardly by fine buildings, and well-equipped classrooms has been slow and only possible—under Providence—to the utter self-abnegation and marvelous executive ability of those who manage them.

If I tell you how one body of alumnæ has contrived to measurably hasten that growth in the case of its own alma matter, it may suggest to others greater possibilities in similar directions, when community rules permit, and the good nuns think it expedient to accept such assistance.

The association mentioned arranges to give its lectures and a certain number of musical recitals every year in the convent hall, always during school session and immediately after class hours. Thus teachers and pupils are free to profit by them. Aside from their educational advantage to all immediately concerned, these literary and artistic gatherings serve to popularize the school, raise it in the estimation even of its patrons, and attract many who otherwise would be at no pains to enter or inquire into the workings of Catholic institutions. Lectures have been delivered before this school and its alumnæ association by some of the ablest and most distinguished Catholics in America. The musicals being given rather for instruction than diversion, programmes are kept to the highest standard, and are usually interpreted by professional musicians.

The school itself is forced to no outlay for these, as all expenses are borne by the association. An annual membership fee, occasional self-imposed taxes, voluntary contributions, and a few tickets sold to outsiders, friends of members, are the sources of revenue. This association also adds a number of books every year to the school library, offers annually two prizes, and in various ways seeks to improve, if may be, and to multiply the resources of its academy. What one can, many may do, secure that in so acting they minister to noblest needs, and repay a small part of the devotion which Catholic educators have lavished upon the youth of our country. An alumnæ association should be a corporate act of gratitude. Who can be aware of this century's activities—hearing what in the name of education is claimed for women, and seeing what in the name of enlightenment is often done by women—and not thank God for that deep-laid, broad-built, tried system of Catholic training which crushes no individuality, represses no legitimate aspiration, and sets no narrow bounds to "woman's sphere," but holds the sex ever lovingly attached to the truth that its most respected, best rewarded, most arduous, most womanly, most heavenly work is in the home! What Catholic daughter having any experience of life is not grateful to the parental wisdom which gave her the blessings of a convent education, and having a heart is not anxious to widen the circle of that uplifting influence?

As already stated, the pupils of a convent school are more variously conditioned than those of any other, this holding true in the graduates' society as in the class-room, though as years roll on positions may be reversed. Whatever their domestic environment, at school all have had about the same advantages. There sit side by side in perfect equality, affection, and amiable rivalry the heiress of a millionaire and the young girl whose parents at great sacrifices have done their utmost in giving her a convent education. One looks forward to foreign travel, pleasure, perhaps a brilliant marriage, as the sequel of graduation; the other says with Viola—

> I am all the daughters of my father's house
> And all the brothers too—

and when school days are ended must take upon herself the duties of breadwinner. They both kneel at the same altar. Shall the accident of wealth keep them utter strangers to each other in after-life?

In a company of twelve graduates four find themselves, by virtue of inheritance, in the ranks of the so-called "privileged classes," four are at home in that happy middle state for which Ozanam prayed, and four go out into the busy, selfish world to earn their bread as best they may. Naturally, their respective duties—which we assume they perform cheerfully and well, whether poor, rich, or "comfortable"—forbid frequent intercourse. Who sees much of her friends in this crowded, careworn age? The parish sodality, or charitable society, does not always bring them together, even occasionally, since their parishes may lie at the extremes of a great city. . . . Is there not, then, some ground to which a community of tastes and some special endeavor may draw them? Can they not enjoy together a book, a lecture, music, art as when they were school girls—and be the better for it?

Have not those who retain their love of all beautiful things, with little means to gratify it, something to say to their fortune-blessed associates? And have these not something to do for the less favored ones? Where can it better be said and done than in the well-ordered work of an alumnæ association. There can arise no suspicion of offensive patronage on the one hand or fear of wounded self-respect on the other. All are friends; all contribute alike to a common fund; it is an intellectual mutual benefit society; all know they are aiding the cause of Christian education; all are under the leadership of some dear nun who has been friend and teacher to them—and, it may be to their mothers for long years.

The rich woman here has her opportunity of quietly making it possible for the association to hear some noted lecturer or great artist, and meet men and women whose names and work are world-famous. We are all hero worshipers and like to come face to face with our heroes.

Why should not the ideal conditions of an alumnæ association extend themselves? Women legislate for that small bit of society which is called par-excellence society—that little world that men speak of as "the great world." Their will is law therein. Shall we not see the mistress of a magnificent home, the leader of a salon, ruled by the principles that govern our entirely possible and wholly desirable alumnæ association—and inviting her guests—not for what they have or wear, nor for the quarter they live in, but for what they are? Then should we behold an ideal aristocracy—an aristocracy of faith and brains! Or, rather, let us say a democracy of faith and intellect. And "democracy in a right sense," says a recent writer, "is Catholicity."

Do I claim that our alumnæ associations in convent schools are going to change the face of the earth? No, but they can be a powerful factor in the adjusting of many social difficulties which now exist.

Walter George Smith, of Philadelphia, Pa., spoke on "Civil Government and the Catholic Citizen." He said:

Although the wonderful growth of the Catholic Church in the United States in numbers, in wealth, and in influence, has extended a knowledge of its moral and political influence far wider and deeper than a few generations ago seemed possible, the thought must have come home repeatedly to every thinking member of its fold that on certain vital points a large element in the community still look upon it as an organization to be distrusted, no matter how pure may be the character, how useful the lives of its members. How often does the Catholic layman, whose daily life is passed among friends, whose training from childhood has been such as to keep from them a true knowledge of what Catholicism means, finds himself called upon to meet and perhaps struggle with a feeling expressed in language or in manner that places him outside of the mass of the community that looks upon him as governed by a code of morality, personal and political, different from his neighbor's, and irreconcilable with a true allegiance to the State. The reason of this phenomenon is not hard to trace. For generations the English-speaking world has been taught, directly and indirectly, by literature and by tradition, by precept and by assumption, that the theology of the Church of Rome and the tendencies resulting from it are contrary to the political and social ideals most generally accepted among civilized people. The present age is marked, perhaps, by a greater and more extended refinement than any that has preceded it, since the records of history have been preserved, and with softening of manners has come a softening of prejudices, so that we do not have to complain often of unkind or bigoted utterances in opposition of our faith. Nay! We are very often praised for the general morality that prevails among our co-religionists; but certain it is that in the minds of a very large proportion of the American people the fact that a man is a Catholic marks him in some sense as peculiar, while if he were known as a member of any one of the non-Catholic Christian denominations, his religious views would not for a moment arrest attention.

The consequence of such a condition is to put upon every Catholic a responsibility, proportioned to the position he holds in the community, of defining, always by the practical habit of his life, and sometimes by the verbal exposition of his views, the dogma of the religious mother whose son he is. I do not understand that it is a Catholic's duty always and under all circumstances to attempt by argument to win proselytes to his faith, but that he should show so far as in him lies the guiding influence of his life to be in accordance with true reason, and, therefore, not opposed to what the common assent of all men shows to be right, would seem to be apparent.

I have made these observations preliminary to a brief study of the duty of the Catholic citizen in relation to the State.

It is on this point, if we may accept their expressions as sincere, that the only real alarm is felt by those who are earnestly struggling against the extension of the power of the church, whether in Europe or America. Could they be satisfied that the development of Catholic thought would have no effect upon political government, or would have no effect contrary to that which their own teaching inculcates, there would be no attacks, open or covert, upon the venerable church of St. Peter by any save those who find in the unrestrained gratification of every tendency of human nature, the ideal towards which human progress should tend.

Can we say, then, in a broad sense, that the Catholic Church does not desire to have any influence upon the State? That she looks upon it with indifference, careless as to its methods, and blind to its imperfections? Should we answer thus, we should be forthwith confronted by many an historical incident from the days when the venerable pontiff met the barbarian conqueror at Mantua and by his intercession saved Italy from invasion, or at the gates of Rome mitigated the horrors of pillage through the centuries to our own times, when the illustrious occupant of the Vatican utters his protest against the spoliation of the papal dominions. No, the church does desire to influence human government; it does watch empires, kingdoms, republics, or whatever be the form such corporations may take, with anxious eyes, but the influence she seeks to exert is through the individual members of the government, requiring of them to administer their trusts in accordance with the eternal rules of right and justice for the benefit of the community whose interests they are called upon to protect. In opposition to the theory of modern political writers, who have contended that government had its origin in sources purely human, and is founded on compact originally entered into between the governors and the governed. Catholic theologians have held that such compacts were not voluntarily entered into by the people themselves, but were imposed by the law of nature, which means that they came from God. This doctrine bears the necessary consequence of denying State absolution. As is pointed out by Brownson (American Republic, p. 79) the ancient Republics recognized rights of the State and rights of the citizen, "but no rights of man, held independently of society and not derived from God through the State. The recognition of these rights by modern society is due to Christianity;" and he proceeds to illustrate by reference to the fact that the Roman Empire was converted to Christianity in defiance of State authority, and this event "infused into modern society the doctrine that every individual, even the lowest and meanest, has rights which the State neither confers nor can abrogate" (Ibid, p. 80). These are rights which the Creator has given to all endowed with reason and free will, and all acts of the State which contravene them are violences and not laws, as St. Augustin has pointed out (Ibid, p. 89). But in the proper sphere of action the State, whatever be its form, is an institution derived from God, through the force of natural law, and is entitled to the allegiance of its citizens, through whom its power is conferred, and to whom it is accountable for any abuse.

"The church and the State, as corporations or external governing bodies, are indeed separate in their spheres, and the church does not absorb the State, nor does the State the church, but both are from God, and both work to the same ends, and when each is rightly understood there is no antithesis or antagonism between them. Men serve God in serving the State as directly as in serving the church. He who dies on the battlefield fighting for his country ranks with him who dies at the stake for his faith. Civic virtues are themselves religious virtues, or at least virtues without which there are no religious virtues, since no man who loves not his brother does or can love God." (Ibid. pp. 127-128.)

The State, then, does not proceed from the church, nor the church from the State. The State is a necessary consequence of the law of nature imposed by God, requiring for their very existence that all men shall live in communities of some sort and find its rights to be in "the just consent of the governed." When it imposes regulations contrary to the natural law it is acting outside of its sphere, but within its sphere it is entitled to the obedience of all its inhabitants. The church has proceeded directly from God, was founded by Himself; it takes cognizance of and approves of the existence of the State as it approves of all institutions founded upon the will of its Divine Head. But as to the form of government the church has no dogma. In the language of Balmes, "the Roman Pontiff acknowledges equally as his son the Catholic seated upon the bench of an American assembly and the most humble subject of the most powerful monarch. The Catholic religion is too prudent to descend upon any such ground. Emanating from heaven itself, she diffuses herself, like the light of the sun over all things and enlightens and strengthens all, and is never obscured or tarnished. Her object is to conduct man to heaven by furnishing him in his passage with great assistance and consolation on earth. She ceases not to point out to him eternal truths; she gives him in all his affairs salutary counsels, but the moment we come to mere details she has no obligations to impose, no duty to enjoin. She impresses upon his mind her sacred maxims of morality, admonishing him never to depart from them. Like a tender mother speaking to her son, she says to him: "Provided you depart not from my instructions, do what you consider most prudent (Protestantism and Catholicity Compound, p. 357.)

As has been said by Cardinal Gibbons: "Our Holy Father, Leo. XIII., in his luminous encyclical on the constitution of Christian states declares that the church is not committed to any particular form of civil government—she adapts herself to all. She leaves all with the sacred leaven of the gospel * * * in the congenial atmosphere of liberty; she blossoms as the rose." (Quoted by F. Hacker—" The Church and the Age," p. 101.)

Such being the doctrine of the church upon civil government, why should there be any doubt or distrust of American Catholics in the minds of their fellow-citizens? So long as the theory of our republican constitution is carried into practical operation there can be no clashing between the duties owed by the Catholic citizen to his Church and to his State. The cry that he is bound by allegiance to a foreign government because he recognizes the Pope as the visible head of his church is unfair and confusing. Whatever be the practice (and the records of American Catholics in all the relations of civic life will at least bear comparison with those of other religionists), his theory in no wise differs from that of men who, in all ages of the world, have felt it right to recognize that there exists a law transcending any that may emanate from human government. It is the same theory which (as has been said) gave Christianity to the Roman Empire, and the assertion of which did much to awaken the conscience of this modern Republic to the evils of African slavery. And when it is understood, this theory will be opposed by none save those philosophers who find in the theories which had their fruition in the French revolution, and have been developed by constant logical processes into the wild isms of certain of the socialists and anarchists of to-day.

If I am right in this exposition of the doctrine of the church (and it needs only to examine the luminous writings of its ablest champions and the authoritative definitions of its Pontiff to show its correctness in theory, while the appeal to history, if requiring more discrimination, is hardly less convincing), no Catholic need be confused in his efforts to perform his duty to the State. The present age, as far as we can know, presents problems for solution more difficult than any that have preceded it, more difficult because history affords no precedents by which men may act upon them. Evils of social life have become so obvious and so dangerous that the best thought of all people is concentrated upon their consideration. Men of undoubted sincerity and of heroic courage, deceived by their own ardor and generous impulses and without guidance from spiritual authority, have not hesitated to advocate theories of relief that involve the complete revolution of that order which has been accepted as second only to revelation. While the church teaches and has taught that the right of private ownership of property, while not directly of divine ordinance, is yet essential to the well-ordered happiness of mankind, the so-called philosophers of the revolution advocate its unconditional abolition; while the church maintains the doctrines of personal liberty and individualism, the tendency of the revolution is to absorb the individual in the State. The revolution bases its arguments upon the assumption of a social contract and the perfect ability, if not the perfection of human nature *per se*; the church looks upon government as a mediate ordinance of God, arising from the constitution of man, and human nature as imperfect, tainted with sin. The revolution insists that the popular will, and the popular alone, is the supreme fount of justice."

The church maintains "that justice is anterior to all experience, wholly independent of the volition of any man or number of men, eternal, immutable, absolutely binding upon the race, as upon the totality of existence." (Lily, p. 53). A century of revolution. How widely these lines diverge, it requires no imagination to picture. The doctrines of the revolution, while professing to advocate liberty, equality, and fraternity, have resulted, wherever they have obtained sway, in tyranny, in class legislation, and bitter strife; and developed as they have been by many, have led and are leading to a subversion of social order that directs the human races back to barbarism. What then is the duty of the Catholic citizen in all countries, but especially in these United States, where the obligations of a free government intensify his responsibility? Is he to shut his eyes to the admittedly existing evils? Or is he to turn them doggedly backward to the ages of faith, and warming his imagination by the contemplation of the glorious relics and traditions of days long gone, when the church was recognized by all civilized peoples as the mother of progress and truth, refuse to recognize the facts of every-day existence. To do this is to grant the truth of the sneer of the atheist and agnostic that the church is the opponent of progress, and can live only in this peculiar athmosphere of medievalism. No, there must be a sturdy recognition of the dangers of modern society—dangers that have arisen because men have thrown off the yoke of subjection to the law under which they were born; and the remedy must be sought in unceasing efforts to re-establish among men the true standard of living. Can any men doubt that if the rich felt universally with a conviction, deep and sincere, the teaching of the church that they were but stewards of the fortunes God has given them, they would no longer be looked upon as a class separated by a wide barrier from their poorer brethren? Can any man doubt that if there pervaded all ranks of employers the feeling that their workmen should share in proportion their prosperity, there would be fewer strikes and disagreements, and the spectre of conflict unceasing between capitalist and laborer would fade from our horizon. Did the laborer in his sufferings look beyond this life to the glories of immortality, could he cherish in his heart hatred and envy of this employer?

Here is the disease in our social conditions. The teachings of Christian morality in large portions of the community have been undermined, and in their stead there is naught but the tendencies of our fallen nature to appeal to as the standard of right. Of what avail are theories the most beautiful, plans of political or economical government the most ingenious, based upon a false assumption of the intrinsic excellence of our natures. The pagan civilization was saved from ruin by Christianity. Christianity has taught mankind that in lessons of self-control and unselfishness of the individual alone can the miseries of life be lightened, and to Christianity must men turn in these modern days when dangers not less serious than those that encompassed the ancient world press upon them. The church in all ages has been the most democratic of all organizations; the church alone has taught the true theory of the fraternity and equality of all men before God, and to her precepts must mankind look for the foundation of their measures of relief from present dangers. Under her ægis tyranny, whether of the individual or of the class, whether of the plutocrat or of the proletariat; can not exist. As in days of old she resisted the wrath of despotic kings or checked the cruelty of powerful nobles, so in these modern days she interposes her commands between the antagonistic classes into which society has been so rapidly drifting. She teaches that all men are children of a common father, and that the command to love one another must be the keynote of their conduct toward each other. This is all. Let royalist, aristocrat, or democrat plead for the excellence of his plan of human government. She looks not at the details, but at the principles that underlie them, and she tests them all by the standard of her founder's law.

To be true to the teaching of his church and false to the republic is impossible for the American Catholic, and in the spread of the morality, political and economical, of which he is the exponent, lies the solution of the problems of modern life.

Rev. Dr. William Barry, of Dorchester, England, wrote upon the "Duties of Capital" as follows:

In discussing this great and momentous issue, which threatens in the modern world to absorb every other, a Catholic assembly must take its stand upon Catholic and Christian principles. Now Pope Leo XIII. (whom God preserve) has told us in the plainest language that it is labor which has created wealth, and hence that capital, which is merely wealth stored up, is due to labor for its production, preservation, and increase. He argues again and again that the fruits of toil should in justice belong to the toiler; that morality and not mere expediency ought to be the rule of the market, and that men have no warrant for ceasing to be Christians because they are handling goods on the largest scale or dealing with stocks and shares even in Wall Street.

But he goes on to say that when he looks out over the world, he sees the old Mammon of unrighteousness flourishing under new names. Usury, which was held by the church of the middle ages to be a crime against God and man, is by no means extinct; on the contrary, it has widened its borders and multiplied its victories. The system which in our text books of political economy is termed capitalism has, according to the Pope, "thrown into the hands of a few the control of labor and of the world-commerce, so that a small number of opulent and amazingly rich individuals have laid a yoke almost equal to that of slavery upon the infinite multitude of the proletarians." That is to say, of workmen who possess no capital.

These things are sadly exemplified in the monarchies of Europe, but experience proves that their baleful influence has made itself felt in the United States also. The disastrous consequences of capitalism without check or limit do not follow upon any one form of government. They are an immense evil which is growing while we speak. And if on the American continent man is destined to begin a happier century than the nineteenth, it will only come to pass when for the injustice and misery of the present confused and desolating system there is brought in a code of business morals to which the Lord Jesus Christ can give His blessing.

The end or purpose of wealth is not simply the production of more wealth nor is it the selfish enjoyment even of those who produce it. Man is a moral and religious being, and the industries which exhaust so large a part of his time, thought, and labor, should be carried out under the law which is supreme in conscience. To make, or increase, or distribute wealth is a social function. It is so because man was intended to live in society, because society does in fact acknowledge and secure his individual rights, and because no one of his single, unaided efforts could store up the accumulated resources to which these "few rich people" are indebted for their leisure and luxury. It is not the "silver king," who has dug out his own mine; neither is it the "railroad king," by whose hands or intellect the railroad has been created. When we allow the utmost to any one man as worker, manufacturer, superintendent, or all three together, it should still be clear to us that the social element in what he produces can never be done away. He enters into the labors of his fellow-men, and they have accordingly their claims upon him, which both justice and charity forbid him to pass over without recompense. If, then, capital, by which I mean private property yielding a revenue, is to exist in a Christian commonwealth, it must fulfill its duties to the public. For it is a trust given to the individual upon condition of his exercising the social function which corresponds to it as a Christian ought. And where custom has failed to enforce this view of things, law has every right to interfere. Those who are suffered by the enactments of the State to control the means of production and distribution must be looked upon as in a true sense ministers of the State; subject to its oversight; answerable for their dealings with what they never did and never could create by their own exertion; and not, as many suppose, irresponsible, absolute, and utterly independent "owners" of all the land, water, mines, minerals, and machinery which by legal process they may have acquired.

Leo XIII. defines it to be a sin against justice when one man appropriates, whether in the shape of profit, or of tax, or of interest, the fruits of another man's industry without rendering him an equal return. He does not say that the return must be directly economical. But certainly he does mean that there ought to be an adequate return of some sort. The rich man, therefore, whose riches are nothing else than the surplus fruits of his fellows' toil, is bound, first, to render a just human wage to the toiler, and second, so to employ this "wealth" which has been put into his hands as, on the whole, to make the condition of those who toil more advantageous to them than if private capital did not exist.

In other words, private capital is an expedient, like constitutional government or manhood suffrage, by which the great ends of society are meant to be furthered. If it does this, it is justified; if it does not, how can it endure? The resources of civilization are earned by one set of men, and disposed of by another. I will not call that an iniquitous arrangement. But it stands to reason that those who distribute are bound to do so for the good of the social organization which they do, in fact, govern. The ministering class of capitalists, supposing they minister, deserve fair wages. But those wages are most unfair which can not be paid except at the cost of a permanent nucleus of misery and demoralization, such as the capitals of Europe have long contained within them, and some of the American cities may now see growing up in their midst

Therefore, as "the end of all commerce" is not "individual gain," so it is righteousness, and not anarchic revolution, which insists on teaching capitalists their duties toward the organism which supports them. Let us reckon up some of these duties.

Negatively, capitalists have no right to interfere with the workingmen's right to combine in trades unions; and hence they cannot fairly require their workmen to give up belonging to such associations, nor can they make it the condition of a just contract.

Again they have no right to take advantage of the distress of human beings by beating down the just price of labor; to do so is usury and has been condemned times out of number by the Catholic authorities.

Nor must they lay upon their workmen inhuman tasks, whether as regards the length, quality or conditions of labor. And the whole legislation of factory acts, inspection and the protection of women and children is in its idea as truly economic as it is Christian, and capitalists ought not to complain of it. Further, the lowest fair wage is one which, although varying according to country, sex and time of life, will enable the worker to fulfill the ordinary duties of humanity, to keep God's law and to provide against sickness and old age.

It is the bounden duty of capitalists to allow their workpeople the Sunday rest.

Corporations are as much under these obligations and bound to fulfill them as individuals.

Workpeople can not justly contract themselves out of these and similar rights. And every agreement to disregard them is so far null and void.

Again, it is elementary good sense, as well as law, that lying, cheating, misrepresentation, when they enter into the substance of a contract, make it of no effect. And that a thief can not prescribe or plead lapse of time as legalizing his theft. And that he who has stolen, whether from the public or from private citizens, is bound to restore. And that the greater the robbery the greater the sin. And that even a State is capable of robbing its citizens collectively, as when it surrenders without a proper equivalent rights of way, or public lands, or the common right of market—and, in general, when it creates or suffers to grow up unchecked monopolies which take an undue share of the products of labor, and which violate the economic freedom of others. To make thieves restore their ill-gotten goods, to put down "rings and corners," to keep intact the right of "eminent domain," to safeguard the health, morals, and religious freedom of its citizens, are duties incumbent on the State, especially when the majority of the people seem to be at the mercy of private capitalists. Nor can it be objected that these things constitute an "intolerable interference with the rights of property," for property never has any right to do wrong. And, on the whole, weighing impartially the evidence which has accumulated from all sides regarding modern commerce and business, I would suggest as a meditation for many capitalists these words of St. Paul: "Let him that stole steal no more, but rather let him labor, working with his hands the thing which is good, that he may have to give to him that needeth."

All this means, then, the imperative necessity of a constitution for capital. Religion furnishes the ideal, morality the grounds, and law and custom the methods upon which this mighty task is to be achieved. To make democracy a real thing is all one with limiting, defining, and Christianizing the powers of those who wield at present according to their good pleasure the material resources gathered by the thought, labor and perseverance of millions upon millions. Individual ownership, when divorced from its social functions, is the parent of all those barbarians who have now become a menace to civilization from within. No spasmodic attempts at private benevolence, no driblets of "ransom" doled out from superfluous millions, no universities called after reigning monopolists, will do the work which society has neglected. The organization of industry means the supremacy of the Christian law in store, factory, market, and exchange. When individuals make their large bequests in the shape of libraries, picture-galleries, parks, or music-halls, they confess that indefinite accumulation of wealth in private hands requires some public apology.

Now, all we who have accepted the principle of democratic institutions believe that an absolute monarch is in politics a mistake, an anachronism, a lapse into a less civilized past which we are glad we have left behind. In like manner, and by reasoning no less demonstrative, it may be shown that an absolute monarch in economics is nothing less than the survival of tyranny under a new form. Democracy and unlimited capitalism are simply irreconcilable; they will ever be enemies, one of the other. When the American continent is fully peopled, the handful who are enormously rich will of necessity create and perpetuate a multitude of proletarians sunk into degrading and shameful poverty—serfs with manhood suffrage—with an acknowledged right to vote and a more doubtful right to eat. If capitalists do not become servants of the commonwealth they will be its masters.

What, then, should the people do in this day of their political supremacy? Two things, I answer. They should insist, by custom and legislation, on making the contract between capitalist and workingman a just human bargain, on the lines so plainly drawn out by Leo XIII. in his encyclical.

And they should defend, by every fair means at their disposal, the rights of public property, which is, in fact, their property, not permitting it to be sold, or squandered, or stolen away, under pretense that the individual who is going to get rich by appropriating it has acquired a legal claim upon that which in such absolute fashion never could legally be made over to him.

If all this amounts to no less than reforming your legislatures, then, in God's name, set about reforming them, root and branch. And if a mandate to your executive is required, shall it never be forthcoming? Is not the responsibility of a free citizen something which he neither can nor ought to give to another? Your political freedom should bring with it economic justice. There is little meaning else in that declaration of independence which is written upon American hearts.

At all events, let not those who uphold democracy imagine that capitalism without religious or moral obligations to society at large is but the proper expression of its principles, or that State interference with it is against the constitution. Just because all citizens have an inalienable right to life, liberty, and the pursuit of happiness, it is undemocratic, un-American and un-Christian, that a few should be millionaires without duties, and that the millions should become a proletariat deprived of decent leisure, home affections, Sunday rest, and the possibility of serving God religiously; or be doomed, in spite of their utmost efforts, to see old age coming upon them with no refuge but charity or the workhouse.

Our hope is that the Christian democracy of America will, by peaceful and appropriate legislation, put an end to these things which have lasted too long. It seems to me, in an especial way, the duty of Christian teachers, be they laymen or ecclesiastics, to hasten that wished-for consummation, and to show that the gospel in which they believe is indeed a law of liberty, the condition of the highest form of government and as fraternal as it is just.

Dr. Charles A. Wingerter, of Wheeling, W. Va., read an interesting paper on "Public and Private Charities." He said:

It is fitting that a Catholic Congress should take up the consideration of the great problem of practical charity, for charity is the heart of the new dispensation whose hold upon the world of men a Catholic Congress is designed to strengthen. It is especially fitting that this problem should be of interest to an American Catholic Congress, for poverty tends to be especially dangerous in a republic, and inequality in social condition, in the possession of power, in the distribution of wealth, though, perhaps, it will ever exist, is most out of place in a land like ours, whose greatest boast before the nations is that it would have all men equals. It is meet and just, then, that we, as American Catholics, face fairly and squarely this question of public and private charities, and how they shall be made more beneficial and effective.

There should be no need of enforcing upon Catholics the duty of charity. Time was when it was a new doctrine that we are bound to love and work good to all men, even to our enemies. That time is past. The blessed doctrine of the Saviour is now a platitude, a commonplace. The danger is that familiarity with it may lead us to indifference. It is therefore wise that on occasions like this we should remind ourselves of the doctrine and duty of charity; that we should put ourselves anew into right adjustment with it, and make right adjustment between it and the tendency surrounding us.

It is common knowledge that the distinguishing characteristic of the century is a fine impatience to be doing good. Altruism is the shibboleth of the hour. Philanthropy is the banner of the times. What the Germans well name the "Zeitgeist," the spirit of the age, may be described as a two-fold desire: First, the desire to systemize all things which is embodied in the modern scientific spirit; and secondly, that material good things shall be distributed among all men. Of this latter desire are born communism and socialism, under whatever mask they hide. Add to these two desires but one thing, the spirit of the church, which is identical with the spirit of Christ, her spouse, and there will be evolved therefrom a motive power and a means of surely making public and private charities more effective and beneficial.

The spirit of the church must come first, however. An edifice cannot outstand its foundations. Charity and philanthropy, if they are to be lasting, must not be reared on the shifting sands of a false philosophy. Man is a creature of motives. His conduct will not outlive the motives that inspire it. Before all else, then, he must have a great and lasting motive for his charity. There has been evolved during the century a philosophy, called by its followers a religion, which inspires much of the philanthropy of the day, though the philanthropists themselves do not always perceive it. This philosophy, the positivism of Comte, teaches the worship of humanity and can urge charity to the poor for no higher motive than this, that poverty is directly degrading to the poor and thus indirectly degrading to humanity. Therefore poverty must be abolished. Positivism is a husk of glamour round a heart of weakness. Humanity in the abstract is too vague a deity for human hearts to worship, and philanthropy done in so unreal a spirit and for so untangible an end is surely doomed to death. A new life, which is the old life of the ages of faith, must be infused into modern philanthropy if it is to be saved from going down to death with dying positivism. Therefore the necessity of crying aloud from the housetops to all the passers-by the sweet doctrines of Christian charity. Therefore the fitness that from this Congress should go forth an earnest reminder of those doctrines and the duties flowing from them.

The poor are God's chosen ones—beati pauperes. Nay, they are His representatives. He was one of them when on earth, and He left as one of our precious legacies the assurance that what we do for the least of them is done even to Himself. Such is the first great truth that serves as a part of the corner-stone of Christian charity. The second is no less known to us, for the New Testament but rehearses the truth of the old dispensation when it bids us be ever mindful that we are only stewards set over part of the riches of this world. "The silver is Mine and the gold is Mine, saith the Lord of Hosts." We are but the almoners of His bounty, and shall be called to give an account of our stewardship. Thus far all is clear enough. God demands from us part at least of the increase of the substance He has given us. He has left us His representatives on earth to receive it—His poor and the Ministers of His Gospel. Now, how can we make this duty tangible? Surely we have not been left without a standard to gauge our faithfulness to the duty of returning to God His portion.

One of the greatest difficulties in the way of practical charity work will have been overcome when we have all learned to set aside a definite portion of our income for the poor. The amount given in charity is too often measured by the transient feelings and circumstances of the hour when call is made upon us; and we too often allow the poor to suffer because of the follies and extravagances which have eaten up the portion that should be reserved for the luxury of charity. What we waste foolishly must not be made amends for from the portion of God and His poor, but from our own portion.

But, it will be asked, how much does God demand from us? At least one-tenth. Some will not conceive their duty so narrowly and will be generous, giving more than one-tenth, but the sad truth is that many give less and some nothing. The whole Christian world does not give to God more than one-third of the one-tenth due. If any among us find ourselves startled, as some of us may, at the thought of parting with one-tenth of our incomes, thinking it too much, be assured we have not really believed the teaching of God's church during the vanished centuries and to-day, for that teaching is plain beyond all dispute. We must not allow the luxuries which we love to win us from the mindfulness of the dangers and responsibilities of wealth; to seduce us from our duty on the specious plea that "charity begins at home." Direct duty to God is before all else, and even before ourselves and families may profit from our income God's part must be laid aside and kept sacredly for Him. And if there be any here who are so weak in faith as not to trust God in this matter without His express promise that they shall not lose by obeying Him, even they must not think to escape. The Omnipotent has given His word that the paradoxical shall become truth. "Some distribute their own goods and grow richer; others take away what is not their own and are always in want." Pro. xi., 24. "Honor the Lord with thy substance and with the first of all thy fruits, and thy barns shall be filled with abundance and thy presses shall run over with wine." Pro. iii., 9-10. It is even to our worldly, material interest to fulfil the law in this matter. If we take God into partnership with us in our worldly business (I speak in all respect and humanly) He has promised that He will prosper us. "Try Me in this," saith the Lord. If we obey His ordinance and tithe our income for the propagation of the faith and the relief of His poor, He will open for us the flood-gates of heaven and pour us forth a blessing even to abundance. Observe how expressly He promises material blessings, wealth, and honor, and power, and prosperity, so that all nations shall call us blessed. And we know that the God of Truth can not become a liar and a breaker of promises. And by way of parenthesis, I should say that I believe one of the secrets of the proverbial great material prosperity of the Jewish people throughout the world is to be found in the fact that nearly all, either through custom or conviction, tithe their incomes for the benefit of their poor even to this day.

The German mind is eminently a scientific mind, and to the Germans we owe a system of charity work which is theoretically perfect, and if it be not absolutely without all flaw in practice, the reason is that the faults of our frail human nature enter into every work done by human agents, I wish to call your earnest attention to this system, for it is the best answer of which I know to the question that forms the title of this paper. How shall public and private charities be made more effective and beneficial? Let us first, however, duly emphasize the truth that there should be method in our giving. The necessity for organized charity is especially evident in the towns and the cities. In hamlets and villages, where every man and his real wants and deserts are known of his neighbors, the spirit of neighborly helpfulness suffices to bring relief to the distress of the worthy poor. There is here little danger of hurtful giving. But where, as in larger centers of population, the helped are always to some extent strangers to the helpers, and where the needy, who still retain some part of their self-dependence, must be sought out if they are to be helped, gifts are often bestowed on the unworthy, while deserving unfortunates are left in distress. The newspapers have too often recorded the story of a starving family found too late. And perhaps over the way the thriftless and the lazy, who do not shrink from making full parade of their wants, and by long practice are become adepts in the parading, are riotously abusing the charity that would have relieved the worthy victims of poverty and saved them to life and to life's hopes and efforts.

This is no fancy picture I am suggesting. Such miscarriages are as common as they are shameful, and are due to a lack of organized charity, They are to be laid at the door of indiscriminate giving. Indiscriminate giving is hurtful whenever it puts a premium on deception; and it does no good when it serves us a cloak to hide the fact that the givers give less than their share. Most often these results are its only fruit.

As I have already said, Germany has offered, in what is now universally known as the Elberfeld system of charity organization, a model that we would do well to follow, for it seems as nearly perfect a practical system as human brains can devise, I sincerely regret that a hurried outline of this plan is all that I can venture upon here if I would not have you turn from me as from a guest who has outstayed his welcome.

First of all, it is an outdoor system, in contra-distinction to the poorhouse system. Our present method of public charity is an inherited tradition that finds full force in the English poor law. Our public charity may be described very briefly; we pay our taxes and support a poorhouse and then rid ourselves of any further responsibility in the matter. The self-acting poorhouse test is our ultimatum. If a person is not willing to go to the city or county poorhouse we assume that he does not need or deserve public help. It needs no second thought to see how false a test this is, as we apply it. Could we not more truthfully say: A man who, rather than vegetate in an almshouse, prefers to stay in the struggle of life and to make another effort to overcome defeat is the man most deserving of aid? The soul of the German system is a desire to help the laggards in the march of life to a more effectual struggle. Where the English system lets him who has fallen by the wayside lie to rot in soul and body, the German system offers him a helping hand.

One of our most earnest strivers in the cause of practical scientific charity work has described so well the difference between the English and the German methods that I make bold to quote his words. Professor F. G. Peabody says:

"These two systems start from opposite points of view and proceed on opposite principles. The English test of poverty is the willingness of the pauper to go to the poorhouse; the German test is that of personal and continual investigation of each case. The English plan, roughly speaking, is for the town to do as little for the poor outside of its institutions as is safe for the community; the German plan is to do as much as is safe. English citizens are accustomed to let the poor law ruin itself; German citizens are trained to be its agents. Thus the one plan, completely carried out, would be wholly official and mechanical; the other would be wholly personal and human. The one is defensive of the community; the other is educative of the community. The one opposes outdoor relief; the other consists almost wholly of outdoor relief. The one frees citizens at large from obligation to the poor, except through taxation; the other calls on citizens at large to serve the poor as a part of their duty to society. We stand for the present between these two principles. On one hand the official work of our cities is done for the most part under the English tradition. On the other hand, our private charity is guided more and more by the Elberfeld model. Which way are we likely to move? Which tradition is likely to prevail?"

I have spoken of the German system as new, meaning that it is new to America. It is not new in the sense of being an untried theory. It was introduced in Elberfeld in 1853, since which time it has won its way by sheer force of worth and effective practicability, until it is to-day actively in operation in more than thirty-five German towns and cities, such as Barmen (1862), Bremen (1878), Dresden (1880), Leipzig (1881), Frankfurt (1883), Berlin (1884), Stuttgart (1886), Hamburg (1891). The main features of the Elberfeld system which distinguish it from private charity work in this country most approaching it in spirit and method are two: First, the distribution of work by spaces instead of cases; and secondly, the institution of a thoroughly maintained charity clearing-house or central office. This central office is, moreover, like a bridge uniting public and private work, enabling them to be mutually helpful, saving for each a vast deal of labor and time and money.

Now to explain a little in detail. An ample corps of the best members of the community are selected by the public authorities to act as visitors. In Germany the municipal system is universally compulsory, but to read the list of the visitors is to find names which make the list a roll of honor. The whole city is divided into small squares, a certain number of which are aggregated into a ward conference. To each of these squares is detailed a visitor, generally one living in the near neighborhood. It is his duty to know if there are any families within his district absolutely in need of immediate relief, and he is empowered to furnish such temporary relief until his ward conference, which meets every week, shall take the matter up. Whenever more than five families needing help are found in any square, it is redivided and a new worker put on. These visitors report to the ward conference, which relieves temporary wants and in turn refers important questions to the central committee. This central committee represents the different interests involved in charity work, is elected for short terms and is responsible to the people. At its head is a responsible, directing superintendent who, like the president of a bank or railroad, holds his position for a long service—in fact during efficiency, and is thus enabled to work effectively and skillfully as manager of the central office or clearing-house, where the records of all cases of need and help are kept. An instance will show how admirably public and private charities, by means of this central office, are enabled to work in harmony and to mutual advantage, and with economy of work and means.

A case of temporary need arises and is reported to a private society, which relieves temporarily but invariably reports to the central office. Here the history of the case is promptly referred to. The records permit immediate answers to the following questions: What is the petitioner's reputation on the record? Has he received help from the city? From any other relief society? From any local benefit society? From any trades union? Are there any convictions or bad reports against him in the police offices? Has he answered truthfully the questions of the visitor? The answers to these and such like questions enable the private society to decide if the case be appropriate to its sphere. If so the case is accepted; if not it is referred back to the central office and from there to the proper channel of relief. Thus the assignment of cases to the appropriate charity becomes easy; the duplication of relief to designing impostors is made practically impossible and the labor of investigation is done once for all.

Such is the system in outline. Now let us rehearse briefly some of the more salient advantages that commend it. Best of all, it makes thorough work possible. We all know that with the present method of assigning workers to cases instead of to small districts it often happens that cases just as necessitous on the same street are overlooked. The same unfortunate thing occurs where visitors have a large district to oversee—a whole ward, for instance. Nor is this surprising. Thorough work is practically impossible with our present methods. We must have a new method if we are to work effectively. There might be suggested to your minds as an objection to the German method that difficulty in finding visitors enough would render it impracticable. This objection disappears with a second thought. The present difficulty to find charity workers arises from the magnitude and indefinite character of the work. Any one who has had any experience in charity work will confirm me on this point. Men will say: "See here, I don't care to undertake the work you propose because it may grow to such proportions that my time and business will not permit me to attend to it properly. I am willing to help, but what I do must be definite. I will give a specified sum of money every week or month, because I know then to what I am binding myself."

Suppose, however, that we should say to such men: "Will you, under printed instructions, take upon yourself to supervise Market Street from Twenty-Fifth to Twenty-Sixth streets on condition that if you find more than four families needing continuous help your district will be subdivided?" Few would be found to refuse and there would be no difficulty in finding visitors for all the small squares. Many men who are now willing, perhaps anxious, to take up practical poor relief are deterred by present methods, and would enlist themselves in the ranks of helpers when the work is specified and definitely fixed by rule.

With the new system, as has been said, the labor of investigation is done once for all. This point is important, because the unworthy poor, knowing that they are sure of temporary relief during investigation, shrewdly use this knowledge where there is no clearing-house such as I am describing. They apply in turn to all the charitable associations and, since under present methods the investigation in each case is to be repeated, they are encouraged to postpone all effort at self-help until they have made the tour of all the relief societies. Where the Elberfeld system is in practice no encouragement is given to those who make a profession of abusing charity.

In this system, then, we have not only organized and personal work but uplifting and educative work, inasmuch as it encourages self-help, self-respect, self-dependence. In every appeal for help the reputation of the petitioner and the condition of his home must be described by the visitor. It is to the advantage of the applicant to be described as moral, upright, neat, and thrifty. He is not tempted to make his personal condition and surrounding filthy and degraded. Rather is he encouraged to be clean in character, person, and home, for he thus increases his chances of substantial help. If charity is to be truly effective it must restore, where need be, and at all events preserve physical, moral, and mental health and vigor among the needy. To take to them money or food or fuel is not enough. We must take to them knowledge and a stronger will; we must infuse into them a life which is so virile and robust as to throw off poverty as a healthy body throws off disease; nay, rather a life which impels and helps them to raise themselves out of the atmosphere and surroundings which poverty needs to thrive in. To borrow an illustrative example from the science of medicine, the wise physician would not be content to administer anti-malarial medicines to the dwellers in a swamp. He would also encourage them to rise up from their miasmatic surroundings and find higher ground, to flee from the cause of their distemper. In like manner, we must not be content simply to tide the poor over a week of hunger if they will be as hungry in a week to come. To be satisfied simply with giving relief to present distress is, in many cases, simply to make assured the recurrence of such distress. We must take to the needy strength to make efforts in their own behalf. We must fortify them for a more effectual struggle.

But I must end, though I have been able to give only the roughest outline of this admirable German system and its main developments. I would like especially to speak of the tramp-colonies and the child-colonies. The aim of these colonies is but a particular application of the general principle of the German system—that is, thorough charity work—the carrying of individual cases to recovery. The tramp-colonies serve as breathing spots for the struggling traveler on life's journey, and the child-colonies strive to save the children. When, as unfortunately happens sometimes, men and women have pursued evil courses so long that they can no longer be roused to hate the causes of poverty, which are discouragement, vice, and unfitting surroundings, the one thing urgent is to save the children. But, these features are refinements of the system and therefore forbidden a place in such a limited paper as this, which must now come to an end. I will be more than content if, by calling your attention to the system, I can bring you to interest yourselves in a study of it. Admiration will do the rest.

Now to rehearse briefly the ideas which I would that we could all carry home with us to serve as seeds of earnest practical efforts to make public and private charities both effective for the relief of the poor and beneficial to ourselves as well as to them.

1. All charity work must be done along the line of moral considerations if it is to be lasting, and therefore we must strengthen the moral forces. We have a duty to the poor and should appreciate it fully. We have not appreciated it fully if we have not realized the grounds on which that duty rests. We have not appreciated it fully unless we recognize its tangibleness, unless we learn to remember always that a certain portion of our income is owed as a debt of honor to the Master and to the poor, His pensioners.

2. After these two lessons have been well learned and put into practice, there must be personal sacrifice of time and service to the cause of our less fortunate brethren.

3. Our work must be organized, discriminating, with no waste of time or labor or money.

4. It must be humane, done in the spirit of fraternal sympathy. A Good Samaritan is wanted and not a charity machine.

5. It must be educative, elevating the helpers and the helped.

6. It must be continuous. Every individual case must be carried to recovery. We must keep fast hold of our stumbling brother's hand until we have helped him to the ground where he can advance alone. In a word, our charity must be thorough and it will be effective.

I have almost done. My spirit sinks within me when I think how jejune and hurried and unsatisfactory is all that I have written, and how overwhelmingly vast, how almost inexhaustible is the subject that inspires the treatise. I can only hope that my effort has not been altogether vain. My pen and lips are young and inexperienced, but my heart is full. If I can but persuade you to take with you as my charity offering one tithe of the earnestness with which I put these few thoughts before you, your own Christian nobleness of heart and love of duty will enable you to far outstrip in deeds the thoughts suggested in this paper. Let each one of us go home resolved that charity shall no longer be the vague, unknowable angel she has been in the past. Let us realize that if hitherto she has walked lame and halting it is because we have by our indifference thrown stumbling-blocks in the way she has so eagerly but hopelessly pursued; because we have mockingly bid her God-speed on her bright errand of mercy, and yet have taken her hand only to serve as a drag-chain to hinder her advance, if indeed we have even offered to her that semblance of help. Henceforth all shall be different. Henceforth we shall know charity for what she is—the fairest handmaid of religion. When we leave this hall let every man go resolved to do something tangible and practical for the cause of charity before the next Congress meets. Consider a moment how much will have been done for the cause of rational charity work if, as a result of this meeting, every man here present resolves here and now sacredly to put apart for the betterment of the poor that portion of his income which belongs to them by right; and if in only one out of every ten of the cities represented here there shall have been established, by the time of the next Congress, a charity clearing-house or a system of working that will cover the ground, making it impossible for those cities to be shamed by some suddenly discovered case of harrowing and long-standing distress. And, however humbly a man may have done his part in feeding the hungry, in giving drink to the thirsty, in clothing the naked, in healing the sick, and in consoling the sorrowing, if only he has done it earnestly, on the Book of Life will be written of him as is written of his Elder Brother, Christ, pertransivit benefaciendo—"He went on His way doing good." And when time and life have worried him like a spent hound, and he is laid to rest, he liveth still, for "to live in hearts we leave behind is not to die."

Thomas F. Ring, of Boston, Mass., in his paper "Public and Private Charities; How Can They Be Made More Effective and Beneficial—a Catholic Layman's Experience," said in substance:

It was my fortune to have been introduced by a good priest to the Society of St. Vincent de Paul, in Boston, in 1863. I have remained in its ranks up to the present time. In this best of training schools for a layman, I have seen much of charity as dispensed by Catholic and Protestant organizations. When the opportunity of taking part in public charities presented itself I felt it to be my duty as a citizen to do my share for the good of the unfortunate of all classes in the community, and gave nine years of unpaid service to the Overseers of the Poor, as the contribution of one whose modest financial means have never permitted him to do much good except through personal services.

An excellent opportunity to visit and closely study the various public institutions of the city of Boston, was given me last year. In this series of visits, I had in mind two objects, first, the public good, and, second, the interests of the Catholic inmates. The immediate cause that gave this chance of seeing the inside workings of the public institutions was the frequent complaints appearing in the newspapers regarding the management of the different houses by the Commissioners of Public Institutions.

Outbreaks in the prisons, magnified into riots; reports of overcrowding in the lunatic asylum, and lack of proper care or sufficient attendance; neglect and disorder in the almshouse; the entire lack of any serious attempt to improve the boys sent for reformation; a confusion and absence of any valuable results from the method of carrying on the truant school. A well-qualified lawyer, two physicians of high local repute, one business man, a lady who has been years secretary of a State board, another lady member of the Overseers of the Poor, and one excellent woman, a quiet but efficient worker in Catholic charities, made up the committee to visit the institutes. When the final report of the committee was made public the whole press of the city declared the document to be one of lasting value, and, coming from a source that could not be accused of having any political bias, was entitled to receive the confidence of the people. The calm, temperate tone of the document, the plain intent to be perfectly fair while being perfectly fearless, giving the commissioners full credit for all the good points revealed by the inquiry, still pointing the way to many improvements in the general methods in management, certainly gave great weight to the recommendations of the committee.

What was the immediate result? The appropriation of $327,000 for the purchase of land and the erection of a first-class modern hospital for the insane. Four hundred new cells for the House of Industry. The closing of the truant school on the island when the new parental school, authorized to be built, shall be completed. Within a few months an incident led to the passing of a city ordinance authorizing the mayor to appoint a visiting committee of five, two of whom to be women, to inspect the public institutions and to report at the end of the year, or at any time, to the mayor as to the condition of the institutions and their recommendations in relation to the same. The committee, during their term last year, visited many of the lunatic asylums, prisons, and almshouses in the State, and consulted with officials and individuals who had knowledge of the broad question of the care of the defective, delinquent, and dependent classes, as they are termed. In the course of this widened search careful note was taken of the number of Catholic inmates by the two Catholic members of the committee.

Beginning with the city institutions, we found that three-quarters of all the poor and the prisoners were of the Catholic faith. In the Reformatory for Boys and the Boys' Truant School the proportion holds practically the same. In the State institutions one-half of the children are Catholics. The city institutions are attended by priests and every reasonable opportunity is given by the commissioners to the inmates to avail themselves of the religious ministrations. The policy of the city and State is to retain children within the institutions for only the shortest term, then to place them at board in families at the public cost, or to bind them out to learn some trade or calling until eighteen years of age, without payment of board. Here, then, in our commonwealth were 2,000 Catholic children, nearly all in Protestant families, or likely to be in them within a year. The Catholics usually have so many of their own to care for that one must generally look elsewhere for the childless home waiting for the homeless child. Here is a fearful annual loss to the church. Is it only in Massachusetts such a loss can be found?

The policy of the St. Vincent de Paul Society in Boston, in the domain of private charities, has been to join hands at once with our Protestant fellow-citizens in any work where it felt it could be of any use to Catholic poor children. "Don't meddle with the faith of the Catholic child and we will go any length with you" is what we have said from the start. We have found our Protestant fellow-citizens, as a rule, well disposed, and, without surrendering our Catholic faith, we can work side by side with them for the good of the community of which we are a part. Our danger does not lie so much in the antagonism of our Protestant neighbors as in the apathy of our Catholic selves. Now, I will venture to say, no Catholic child in Boston need drift out of Catholic hands if the facts can be placed in our possession in time. Protestant societies inform us of Catholic children; we turn over all Protestant children to Protestant societies. We are in the field to protect our own and have our hands full.

If I were asked to say in one word how the public and private charities of the country can be made more beneficial and useful, I should select the word "co-operation." Co-operation, frankly and cordially, with all our fellow-citizens for the common good of the community. A Catholic citizen is bound, under command of God, to yield faithful obedience to lawfully constituted civil authority. When the State arrogates to itself the power that belongs to heaven and attempts to seat itself in the throne of God, He is justified in repudiating the usurped authority. The care of the sick, the demented, the destitute child, and feeble age, is part of the duty of the whole community, and every citizen who can help should not at need, refuse or withhold his aid. In addition to his duty as a good citizen he has another duty as a Catholic: To watch with tender care over the poor who are of the household of the faith; to work hand in hand with all who labor for the temporal and spiritual good of the little ones of Christ; to give himself, which is worth more than mere giving of money. Let him hold constantly in his mind the warning of St. James, "Faith without works is dead." Let his faith be a living faith, full of good works for his country, full of good works for God.

SIXTH DAY.

On Saturday, September 9th, the proceedings of this memorable gathering came to an end, with the most fervid enthusiasm, in the presence of a vast concourse of the clergy and laity. Following are the adopted

RESOLUTIONS OF THE CONGRESS.

The Columbian Catholic Congress of the United States, assembled in Chicago, in the year of grace, one thousand eight hundred and ninety-three, with feelings of profound gratitude to Almighty God for the manifold blessings which have been vouchsafed to the Church in the United States and to the whole American people, and which blessings in the material order have found their compendious expression in the marvelous Exposition of the World's Fair held to commemorate the four hundredth anniversary of the discovery of this continent by the great Catholic navigator, Christopher Columbus, conforming to the custom of such occasions adopt the following resolutions:

1. We reaffirm the resolutions of the Catholic Congress held in Baltimore, Nov. 11 and 12, A. D. 1889.

2. We declare our devoted loyalty and unaltered attachment to our Holy Father, Pope Leo XIII., and we thank him for sending us a special representative, and we enthusiastically hail his Apostolic Delegate as the hostage of his love for America and a pledge of his paternal solicitude for our country and its institutions. It is the sense of this Congress that the Vicar of Christ must enjoy absolute independence and autonomy in the exercise of that sublime mission, to which, in the providence of God, he has been called as the head of the Church for the welfare of religion and humanity.

3. We congratulate our Hierarchy on the wondrous growth and development of the Church throughout the United States, the results, under God, of the united wisdom and unselfish devotion of those true shepherds of the Christian flock, and we pledge to our bishops and priests our unfaltering devotion and fidelity.

4. While the signs of the times are hopeful and encouraging, and material prosperity is more widely diffused than in any previous age, we should be willfully blind should we fail to recognize the existence of dangers to the Church and to society requiring a most earnest consideration. Among the most obvious of these dangers is the growing discontent among those who earn their living by manual labor. A spirit of antagonism has been steadily growing between the employer and the employed that has led in many instances to deplorable results.

The remedies suggested vary from the extreme of anarchical revolution to different types of state socialism. These remedies, by whatever names they may be called, with whatever zeal and sincerity they are urged, must fail wherever they clash with the principles of truth and justice. We accept as the sense of this Congress, and urge upon the consideration of all men, whatever be their religious views or worldly occupations, the Encyclical of our Holy Father Leo XIII., on the "Condition of Labor," dated May 15, A. D. 1891. In the spirit of his luminous exposition of this subject, we declare that no remedies can meet with our approval save those which recognize the right of private ownership of property and human liberty. Capital can not do without labor, nor labor without capital. Through the recognition of this interdependence and under the Christian law of love and by mutual forbearance and agreement must come the relief, for which all good men should earnestly strive.

5. We strongly indorse the principles of conciliation and arbitration as an appropriate remedy for the settlement of disagreements between employer and employed, to the end that strikes and lockouts may be avoided; and we recommend the appointment by this Congress of a committee to consider and devise some suitable method of carrying into operation a system of arbitration.

6. We suggest to our clergy and laity as a means of applying the true principles of Christian morality to the social problems that have now attained such importance the formation of societies, or the use of already existing societies of Catholic men, for the diffusion of sound literature and the education of their minds on economic subjects, thus counteracting the pernicious efforts of erroneous teachings; and we especially recommend the letters of our Holy Father, particularly those on "Political Power," "Human Liberty," and "The Christian Constitution of the State." The condition of great numbers of our Catholic working girls and women in large towns and cities is such as to expose them to serious temptations and dangers, and we urge, as a meritorious work of charity as well as of justice, the formation of Catholic societies for their assistance, encouragement, and protection. We advocate also the continued extension of Catholic life insurance, beneficial, and fraternal societies. The work that such associations have already accomplished warrants the belief that they are founded upon true principles.

7. One of the great causes of misery and immorality is the indiscriminate massing of people in cities and large towns and their consequent crowding into tenement houses, where the children are, from their infancy, exposed to every bad example and corrupting influence. This evil has drawn the attention of legislators in foreign countries. We believe it wise charity to help the poor to help themselves, and therefore advise the adoption of appropriate measures to encourage and assist families to settle in agricultural districts. As indicated by the Holy Father, the true policy is to induce as many as possible to become owners of the land.

8. In discharging the great duty of Christian charity the Catholic laity can and should do much by personal service to supplement the admirable work of the religious orders devoted to charity, and we urge them to join or otherwise encourage the conferences of the Saint Vincent de Paul and kindred organizations for rendering systematic aid to the needy. And we would recall to the minds of all people the time-honored Catholic practice of setting apart from their incomes a proportionate sum for charity.

9. An obvious evil to which may be traced a very large proportion of the sorrows that afflict the people is the vice of intemperance. While we believe that the individual should be guided in this matter by the dictates of right conscience, we cannot too strongly commend every legitimate effort to impress upon our fellowmen the dangers arising not only from the abuse, but too often from the use, of intoxicating drink. To this end we approve and most heartily commend the temperance and total abstinence societies already formed in many parishes, and we advise their multiplication and extension. We favor the enactment of appropriate legislation to restrict and regulate the sale of intoxicating liquors, and emphasizing the admonition of the last Plenary Council of Baltimore, we urge Catholics everywhere to get out and keep out of the saloon business.

10. To the members of our secular clergy, religious orders, and laity who are devoting their lives to the noble work of educating the Indian and negro races, we extend our hearty sympathy and offer our co-operation. We congratulate them on the consoling success thus far attending their labors, and wish them Godspeed.

11. As the preservation of our national existence, the constitution under which we live, and all our rights and liberties as citizens depend upon the intelligence, virtue, and morality of our people, we must continue to use our best efforts to increase and strengthen our parochial schools and Catholic colleges, and to bring all our educational institutions to the highest standard of excellence. It is the sense of this Congress, therefore, that Catholic education should be steadfastly upheld, according to the decrees of the Council of Baltimore and the decisions of the Holy See thereon. In the elevating and directing influence of Christian higher education in particular we recognize the most potent agency for the wise solution of the great social problems now facing mankind. We recognize the signal wisdom of our Holy Father, Leo XIII., and of the American hierarchy in founding an institution of highest Christian learning in our national capital. And with confidence in their wisdom so to direct it that it shall be fully adequate to the needs of our age and our country, we cordially pledge to them our active

co-operation in making it one of the chief glories of the Catholic Church and of the American Republic. We appeal to our fellow-citizens of all religious denominations to teach the rising generation to love, honor, and fear our common Creator, and to instill into their hearts sound principles of morality, without which our glorious political liberty can not continue. Profoundly appreciating the love for education shown by the Sovereign Pontiff and our bishops, we repeat what has been said in this Congress—that "it is only the school bell and the church bell which can prolong the echo of the liberty bell."

12. We desire to encourage the Catholic Summer School of America, recently established on Lake Champlain, as a means of promoting education on university extension lines, and we also commend the forming of Catholic reading circles as an aid to the summer school, and an adjunct to higher education in general.

13. We recognize in the Catholic Truth Society of America one of the results of the first American Catholic Congress of Baltimore, and, believing it to be admirably adapted to the needs of the times, we earnestly recommend it to the Catholic laity as offering them an excellent means of co-operating with Holy Church in her glorious work of disseminating Catholic truth.

14. As immoral literature is one of the chief agencies in this country and in Europe for the ruin of faith and morality, we recommend a union of Catholics and non-Catholics for the suppression of this evil, whether in the form of bad books, sensational newspapers, or obscene pictorial representations.

15. We have no sympathy with any effort made to secularize the Sunday. We urge upon our fellow-citizens to join in every effort to preserve that day as sacred, in accordance with the precepts and traditions of the Church.

16. We heartily approve of the principle of arbitration in the settlement of the international disputes. We rejoice in the happy results that have already attended the application of this ancient principle of our holy mother, the Church, and we earnestly hope that it may be extended and that thereby the evils of war between nations may be gradually lessened and finally prevented.

Finally, as true and loyal citizens, we declare our love and veneration for our glorious Republic, and we emphatically deny that any antagonism can exist between our duty to our Church and our duty to the state. In the language of the Apostolic Delegate, let our watchword be, "Forward! in one hand the Gospel of Christ and in the other the Constitution of the United States." Let us keep on in the path of virtue and religion, that the blessings of our national liberties, born of the stern energy and morality of our forefathers, may be preserved for all time as a sacred heritage.

On rising to deliver the closing address, Cardinal Gibbons was received with the utmost enthusiasm. He saluted the chairman, archbishops, and prelates on the platform, and said:

THE CARDINAL'S CLOSING ADDRESS.

Ladies and Gentlemen: Owing to the condition of my health, which is not very strong to-day, and the brief notice that I received to address you this morning, my remarks will be necessarily very short, but I assure you they will come from the depth of my heart. When I had the honor to address you on last Monday morning, at the opening of this Catholic Congress, I expressed the fond anticipation that the prayer of hope that was offered up then would be crowned to-day by a thanksgiving full of gratitude to God and of joy and jubilation. My fondest anticipations have been more than realized. This Congress has been a great success. The eyes of the civilized world, as you all know, have been directed during those days toward what is called the White City of Chicago, and I may also add that the ears of the Catholic world have been attentive to the voice that has proceeded from this hall of Congress; and the voice that came forth from this hall has uttered no uncertain sound. There has been no confusion, no conflict, no dissension; but there has been peace and concord and unanimity from beginning to end.

The voice of the Congress has succeeded in dissipating prejudices and in removing many misunderstandings in regard to the teachings and practices of the Church of God. First of all, as was right to do, the voice issuing from this hall has proclaimed the necessity of honoring and glorifying God. It has been a voice in behalf of God and of religion. Next to religion our love for our country should be predominant, and therefore we have recently heard a resolution offered and adopted attesting the love and affection which we have for our country and for our political institutions. This Congress has also proclaimed the necessity of good government, and it has told us that there can be no good government without law and order, that there can be no law without authority, there can be no authority without justice, there can be no justice without religion, there can be no religion without God.

I need not say that the voice of this Congress has also gone forth in vindication of the rights of labor and also of its obligations. We have spoken in the cause of humanity and the cause of the toiling masses, and we have been told that every honest labor in this country is honorable. Ever since Jesus Christ, our Savior, worked in a carpenter shop at Nazareth he has shed a halo around the workshop, and he has made labor honorable.

This Congress has also spoken both during its sessions and by its resolutions in the cause of Christian education. It has spoken of the importance and the great necessity of Catholic education. At the same time let it not be understood that whilst we are advocating Catholic education we are oppposed to secular education. The whole history of the Church speaks the contrary. There can be no conflict between secular and religious knowledge. Religious and secular knowledge, like Mary and Martha, are sisters, because they are the children of the same God. Secular knowledge, like Martha, is busy about the things of this world, while religious knowledge, like Mary, is found kneeling at the feet of her Lord.

But above all, ladies and gentlemen, the voice of this Congress has spoken out clearly and fully in vindication of the holy Catholic Church; it has removed many prejudices and misunderstandings. This Congress helped to tear off the mask that the enemies of the Church would put upon her fair visage. This Congress has torn those repulsive garments with which her enemies would clothe her, and has presented her to us in all her heavenly beauty, bright as the sun, fair as the moon, with the beauty of heaven shining upon her countenance. This Congress has well shown that the Catholic Church, properly understood, is the light of the world and the refuge of suffering humanity. You have a white city here. The white city of Chicago has seen passing through it men from various countries, many of whom are assembled here now. But may I not say the Catholic Church is pre-eminently the White City? She has within her streets men of all nations and tribes and peoples and tongues, and we who are assembled here together to-day may exclaim in the language of Holy Writ: "Thou hast redeemed us, O Lord God, to go out to every tribe and nation and people and tongue." Yes, ladies and gentlemen, this Congress will result in bringing more love and admiration to the Church. Men will look at her now and admire her, and admiring her they will love her, and loving her they will embrace her. With the blessing of God, many who were before strangers to our Faith will come forward and embrace her in the view of the light that has been shed upon her here. In the language of Augustine, they will say: "Too late have I known thee, O beauty, ever ancient and ever new, too late have I loved thee."

And now, though I have been somewhat anticipated, I deem it a sacred duty to invite you to join with me in offering the thanks of this congress and of this vast assembly to all who have participated in making it so grand a success. First of all let us give our thanks, after God, to our Holy Father, Leo XIII, who, in his letter addressed to me recently, manifested, as he has on many previous occasions, his love for our religious institutions and his admiration and love for the political institutions of America. I beg also to ask you to return thanks to the Most Reverend Archbishop of Chicago, who has done so much to make this Congress successful and who was always ready, when called upon, to give his counsel and advice to the secretary of the Congress. I beg also in a special manner to return thanks in your name to the distinguished chairman, Judge O'Brien. He has shown you in the Congress his judicial wisdom—I will not say his judicial firmness, because firmness was hardly required here. The conspicuous position which he occupies in the great City of New York, and the reputation which he has well merited for judicial wisdom and knowledge have been more than sustained by his conduct in the City of Chicago. May I also beg leave to return thanks to the gentlemen and to the ladies who have prepared with so much care and ability the papers that were read before the Congress. Those papers have not only reflected credit on themselves, but honor to the Church of God. They deserve our thanks.

And last, though not least, I beg leave to thank one man in particular, without whose labors this Congress would not have been a success. I refer to one who has labored in season and out of season in organizing the Congress, who has done, I might say, the greatest share in bringing it to a successful issue. I refer to W. J. Onahan, secretary of the committee on organization. In conclusion I humbly propose that, after thanking from our hearts our Holy Father for the encouragement he has given us, this vast audience manifest its appreciation of what has been done by pouring forth its thanks to the Most Reverend Archbishop of Chicago, to the distinguished chairman and secretary, and that you will express your appreciation by a rising vote.

In addition to the general resolutions given above, the Congress adopted the following special Peace Memorial, which was sent to the rulers of all nations. The memorial was printed in twenty-five different languages, and was an invitation to the rulers of all lands to settle the controversies between nations by means of arbitration. The transcript in English to the President of the United States reads as follows:

THE CATHOLIC CHURCH WISHES YOU GRACE, MERCY, AND PEACE! We, in co-operation with other Christian bodies, humbly memorialize you, as the guardian of your people, in behalf of peaceful arbitration as a means of settling questions that arise between nations. The spectacle that is presented of Christian nations facing each other with heavy armaments, ready upon provocation to go to war and settle their differences by bloodshed or conquests, is, to say the least, a blot upon the fair name of Christians. We can not contemplate without the deepest sorrow the horrors of war, involving the reckless sacrifice of human life that should be held sacred; bitter distress in many households, the destruction of valuable property, the hindering of education and religion and a general demoralizing of the people.

Moreover, the maintaining of a heavy war force, though war be averted, withdraws multitudes from their homes and the useful pursuits of peace and imposes a heavy tax upon the people for its support. And, further, let it be borne in mind that wars do not settle causes of disputes between nations on principles of right and justice, but upon the barbaric principle of the triumph of the strongest.

We are encouraged to urge this cause upon your consideration by the fact that much has already been accomplished: as, for example, by the Arbitration of Geneva, in the Alabama case and by the deliberations of the American conference at Washington not to mention other important cases. It will be a happy day for the world when all international disputes find peaceful solutions, and this we earnestly seek.

As to the method of accomplishing this end we make no suggestions, but leave that to your superior intelligence and wisdom in matters of state policy.

We invoke upon ruler and people the richest blessings of the Prince of Peace.

Similar messages were sent to Queen Victoria, the Emperor of Germany, the President of the French Republic, the Czar of Russia, King of Belgium, Humbert of Italy, Queen of the Netherlands, King Christian of Denmark, King Oscar of Norway; the regent of Spain, Maria Christina; Don Carlos I. of Portugal, and to the rulers of all the South American and Central American republics. The beautiful incident may well close these volumes of "The Columbian Jubilee." It is typical of the spirit of peace and charity toward all mankind which has pervaded the Catholic Church in America from the beginning.

Brother Maurelian, on behalf of all Catholic Educators, greeting Monsignor Satolli, special delegate to represent Pope Leo XIII, at the opening of the World's Columbian Exposition.

MONSIGNOR O'CONNELL.   ARCHBISHOP SATOLLI.   BROTHER MAURELIAN.

PART II.

CATHOLIC EDUCATION DAY

WORLD'S COLUMBIAN EXPOSITION.

Chicago, 1893.

BY

BROTHER MAURELIAN F. S. C.,
Secretary and Manager.

TO

RIGHT REVEREND J. L. SPALDING, D. D.,
Bishop of Peoria and
President Catholic Educational Exhibit,

World's Fair, 1893.

Letter from His Holiness Pope Leo XIII.

TO

Right Rev. J. L. Spalding, D. D.,

Bishop of Peoria and President Catholic Educational Exhibit,
World's Columbian Exposition, Chicago, 1893.

LEO P. P. XIII.

(ENGLISH TRANSLATION.)

VENERABLE BROTHER:

Health and Apostolic Benediction. We recognize with pleasure from your letter dated the 20th of May, that a not insignificant part of the vast collection of all kinds of things which will be exhibited in Chicago, the coming year, will consist of the resources which Catholics will bring together and by which the exhibition will be the richer; we also recognize the fact that the heads of all Catholic Institutions devoted to the instruction of the young have been urged to do their share by the exhortation of our Venerable Brothers the Archbishops of the United States.

Although there is in the united voice of the authority of the forementioned Archbishops, and that so far it is evident to us that all to whom this exhortation is directed will carry out their desire, nevertheless, we are unwilling, that our commendation should be wanting to this noble idea and undertaking. In short, we rightly understand that the affair tends to this: that the efforts of those who devote themselves to the education of the young, may be increased, and that greater aids and appliances may be at their service, so that they may acquit themselves of their duty in the best possible manner.

Moreover, this undertaking will tend to show that the Catholic Church is not to be satisfied with the lack of culture or with the obscurity of ignorance; but that mindful of its being built by the Divine Wisdom, it bestows care everywhere in general, and prefers especially what is most perfect in those things which relate to the proper communication of knowledge. Wherefore for you Venerable Brother, who have chiefly undertaken the care of this project, and likewise for those by whose aid you may be strengthened to attain more fully the proposed end we, in a special manner, invoke the most abundant helps of the Divine favor.

Finally we most lovingly implore for you the guidance of the Divine Goodness, and impart to all zealous co-operators the Apostolic Benediction.

Given at Rome at St. Peter's, the 20th day of July in the year 1892, of our Pontificate the Fifteenth.

    (Signed)   LEO P. P. XIII.
To our venerable Brother
       JOHN L. SPALDING,
            Bishop of Peoria.

Catholic Education Day.

WORLD'S COLUMBIAN EXPOSITION,
CHICAGO, 1893.

Most Rev. P. A. FEEHAN, D. D. Archbishop of Chicago, Presiding.
Rt. Rev. J. L. SPALDING, D. D., President Catholic Educational Exhibit, Director of Ceremonies.

ORDER OF EXERCISES.

AMERICAN REPUBLIC MARCH—(Thiele),   -   -   Brand's Cincinnati Band.
WORDS OF WELCOME,   -   -   -   -   His Grace. Archbishop Feehan.
THE CATHOLIC VIEW OF EDUCATION,
    Most Rev. John Hennessy, D. D., Archbishop of Dubuque.
ORGAN SOLO—Tema Con Variazioni (Moszowski),   -   -   Harrison Wilde.
VOCATION OF THE CHRISTIAN EDUCATOR,
    Most Rev. P. J. Ryan, D. D., Archbishop of Philadelphia.
WHAT CATHOLICS HAVE DONE FOR EDUCATION IN THE UNITED STATES,
    Hon. Morgan J. O'Brien, New York State Supreme Court.
ORGAN SOLO—OVERTURE—"Guillaume Tell" (Rossini),   -   Harrison Wilde.
PATRIOTISM—A Sequence of Catholic Education,
    Hon. Thomas J. Gargan, Boston, Mass.
HYMN, TE DEUM (Holy God We Praise Thy Name), Organ Accompaniment.
FINALE—American Airs (Catlin),   -   -   -   Brand's Cincinnati Band.

At the conclusion of the American Republic March by Brand's Cincinnati Band, ARCHBISHOP FEEHAN, delivered the address of welcome. He spoke as follows:

ARCHBISHOP FEEHAN'S ADDRESS.

We are assembled to-day, ladies and gentlemen, in a very noble cause. We are come together as Catholics, and as good citizens also. We are assembled as Catholics, deeply and earnestly interested in that great cause—and I may say one of the greatest of causes,—that of the Catholic education of youth. And because we are interested in the matter of education in its great, grand, true sense, therefore we are also assembled as good citizens of the Republic; because we believe most thoroughly that the more perfect education of the young in every true sense, the more perfect will be the order of citizenship in this great country.

As we know that the stream coming from the mountain bears with it its own purity and freshness, so this great intellectual training and education of the young, coming from the first fountain and the purest of all knowledge—that fountain of Religion—we believe must give to the young its own freshness, its own holiness, its own beauty, its own completion and finish.

Within a few months there has arisen here this wonderful exhibition of man's enterprise and genius. Men come from every clime to see it, not only with pleasure, but with wonder. And when we look around and see these wonderful material things, indicating the material progress of the world up to the time of our era, we are pleased, also, to understand and to know that there are signs and proofs of a higher development and of a nobler work than that merely material one, and that is, that during this great Exposition there are so many proofs given of the intellectual, the moral and the religious welfare, and, I may say, progress of man. It is a great advantage to enjoy these improvements of modern times, and yet we know that men might be highly cultivated and highly civilized even without these, as they have been in the past. We know that Plato and Aristotle and St. Thomas never saw a steamer—they knew nothing of the great wonders of electricity, and yet they were highly civilized and cultivated.

Amongst the wonderful things to be seen here that tend to the higher things of man—to the higher development and the higher cultivation and civilization, I may mention, with great and supreme pleasure, that great exhibition of our Catholic schools, of the methods and the systems employed throughout this broad land by the Catholic Church in the education of the young. There could be no higher or greater object lesson than this. We, who have witnessed—have diligently examined—the Catholic exhibition from every part of the country, have acknowledged its excellence. And whoever earnestly and impartially examines even a little of this proof of the methods of the training and education of Catholic youth; from little children to the highest finish of our schools and colleges—whoever does this earnestly, can never again say, and should not permit it to be said in our generation, that Catholic schools and Catholic education are inferior to any other to be found in the whole country.

Those wonderful works of this strange city; those great proofs of talent and genius, that have formed the delight and the pleasure of all who have visited this great Exposition—this will soon pass away: in a few brief months there will be none of them here. They will all pass from man's sight, it is probable, before the snows fall upon the ground here. But we know that everything that this great Exposition has brought forward and developed, and that it represents, will not pass away; that the higher things concerning the welfare and the benefit of man will not be covered up by the snows of winter, and that they will not disappear. There are many things connected with this wonderful Exposition that will live, not only for our time, but for the generations that are coming after. And amongst the things that will not perish, that will certainly live, not only for our time but for those that come after us, will be the lessons and the results of this grand exhibition of the teachings and the methods of Catholic schools. They will give a development to Catholic education. This exhibition will give encouragement to those who devote themselves to Catholic education. Catholic education will acquire from them new springs of wealth, a new force and new development, to increase and spread over the whole land; and we look forward to the time coming when this wonderful system of the education of our schools will be everywhere, and we know that the effects will be holy, beautiful, beneficent; it will make men wiser and better than they would be without it; that it will make them good citizens and strong and conservative men; that its influence will be for good and for the highest order—that it will be like the beneficent effects of those dews that God sends to make the earth fruitful.

It is in order to emphasize this great work of the Catholic exhibit, and to emphasize, also, this great system of Catholic teaching and training, that those so much interested thought well of having what they call Catholic Education Day, and then notified distinguished men and orators, some of them from distant parts of the country, to come to speak to you, to say a word of encouragement and advice to all the people—to all of us, and, in an especial manner, must I not say, to all those who have made this a possibility, amongst us, and they who have made this a possibility amongst us are the members of these great teaching communities that are doing this wonderful work throughout the land everywhere of Catholic education.

In connection with our interests as regards this great Fair, it will not, I am sure, be considered out of place for me, as representative of the Catholic interests of this great city, to express our thanks to the managers of the Exposition—to the gentlemen connected with it with whom we have had occasion to come directly in contact. All who are interested in the great work of the exhibit of Catholic education have experienced, I believe—I am sure—at every time, the greatest kindness and the greatest courtesy from the gentlemen connected not only with educational matters, but with all the business of this wonderful Exposition. And, therefore, I take the liberty to-day, in the name of our people of our section, to say this word of thanks and gratitude to all these gentlemen.

You will have the pleasure of hearing eloquent voices, who will speak to you a good deal better than I can, though they cannot be more interested than I in the great cause of Catholic education.

Director General Davis by reason of his many engagements was unable to be present, and Dr. Selim H. Peabody, Chief of the Department of Liberal Arts, responding to the words of welcome, said:

DR. SELIM H. PEABODY'S ADDRESS.

No one will regret more than I that the distinguished gentleman who stands at the head of this Exposition as the Director-General cannot be present this morning, to accept the thanks which the Archbishop has so courtly presented to him and to his colleagues, and to express to you his gratification at this large audience on this auspicious day.

The Exposition, which celebrates the coming of Columbus over the water and the discovery of this continent, would not be complete in its recognition, in its preparation, in any of its results, if it should forget the auspices under which Columbus came to America. We remember that, in 1492, the last of the Moors passed away from Granada, and Spain became one kingdom. The last, the long, contest between the Cross and the Crescent culminated in the victory of the Cross in Spain and the monarchs, who then were united in one family, governing one kingdom, earned the title, which they have ever since worn, The Most Catholic Majesty of Spain.

Now, Queen Isabella, when she sent Columbus across the waves that he might discover a new continent, or a new way to an old one, remembered that this continent would be peopled with men and women having souls, and she cared for what she understood to be the welfare of these souls, by sending with Columbus the representatives of the Catholic Church, which she so loved. I might say, further, that no body of people counting themselves Christians has so fully responded to that great commission, "Go ye into all the world and preach the gospel to every creature," as this body represented before me today. And so we find the paths of the missionaries who went out without force of arms behind them, to open the way before them to other nations; we see them treading their course across these prairies and teaching Indians the way of life. So, while we learn of LaSalle, we remember also Father Hennepin and Pierre Marquette. So I say that this Exposition could not do otherwise than recognize the force, the underlying power, the great results which have been brought to America by the Catholic teachers, carrying with them the Cross and the symbols of the Catholic faith. It is not necessary for you to attempt to make any specific ecclesiastical exhibit, other than such grand exhibits as you bring on a day like this, when you bring your own highest dignitaries—when you bring those who represent your orders of men and women, and when you bring representatives of your people—bring all those orders who reverence your symbols, who hold your faith—those are your exhibits.

But I should speak more directly of the Catholic Educational exhibit. It has been my fortune to look after that in some directions; to see that it had a position and a suitable one, and I have observed the great skill, the wisdom, the patience, the care, the consideration, which have been exhibited by all of those who have had charge of gathering this exhibit, of putting it in place, and of keeping it before this great American people. You have done admirably in all these respects. I think of the hundreds and thousands of fingers which have been employed all over this land in the preparatition of this exhibit. I think of the hundreds and thousands of fingers and of minds and teachers who have cared for the general educational exhibit. My friends, I believe we have the most wonderful, as we have the most extensive, educational exhibit which this world has ever seen. I expect that its influence upon all phases of education will be stimulating, will be encouraging, will be developing, and that your portion of it, as the other portions of it, will receive the rewards which naturally follow from the labors presented in such an exhibit. We rejoice in all its beauty and in all its completeness, in all the great excellence that it exhibits. It will not be necessary for me to enter into detail here. Most of you have seen it; others, who have not seen it, will take the opportunity to-day to look through it carefully and see what it presents.

I must then, Your Grace, thank you, in the name of the Director-General, for the kind expressions which you have stated for him and for his colleagues, and express my belief that all which you have said in regard to this educational exhibit will be found to come true in the fruitions which are to follow.

Archbishop Feehan, in introducing the Most Rev. John Hennessy, D. D., Archbishop of Dubuque, said:

I have the honor, ladies and gentlemen, of introducing to you Archbishop Hennessy, of Dubuque, who will now address you.

ARCHBISHOP HENNESSY'S ADDRESS.

The Catholic view of education can be obtained from the consideration of certain points of Catholic teaching bearing upon the subject, as well as from the practice of the Church in her schools for children.

To obtain a clear and correct idea of education, it is necessary to consider who is to be educated, his condition, his destiny, the means and aids provided to attain it, and the obstacles in the way, if any. God and man and their relations to one another must be considered, also the dignity of man, his fall, and that of the angels, and the effects of both on him, the mysteries of the Incarnation and Atonement, the institution of the Church and its purpose, her mission, her prerogatives and possessions, and the result of her labors. All these are so closely related to the question of education that without a thorough consideration of them the subject itself cannot be understood, nor its importance and difficulty duly appreciated.

God made all things for man and man for Himself. He made him in His own image and likeness. He created him in grace, the masterpiece of omnipotence. Everything else He made by a word in an apparently careless manner, man by the joint effort of the three divine persons after consultation over their work. In creation made up of spirit and matter, substances by their nature far removed one from the other, man is the bond between them and also the link in the chain of beings by which

STATUE OF ARCHBISHOP FEEHAN IN CARRARA MARBLE, GIFT OF THE CLERGY OF CHICAGO, ON EXHIBITION AT CATHOLIC EDUCATION EXHIBIT AT WORLD'S FAIR.

GOD DRAWS ALL THINGS TO HIMSELF

and holds them together in the mystery of the Incarnation. In the Church he is a new creature. A member of the mystic body of Christ, the temple of the Holy Ghost, a sharer of the divine nature, an adopted son of God, a brother and co-heir of Jesus Christ. His nature in the persons of our Lord and His blessed Mother occupies the highest place in heaven next to God. The education of such a one should be, as indeed it is, exceedingly important. Man is not as he came from God's hands. He is fallen by his own fault. Oh, what a fall! Who will measure its depth and the ruin it effected. The terrible sentence of two-fold death, death of soul and death of body, pronounced by God on man, such a sentence as human ears never heard, and the mode of reparation adopted by Him, throw a lurid light on the terrible wreck. God might have forgiven the outrage, He might have accepted any reparation and reinstated man. He did not do so: He demanded full satisfaction and that of man, the offender. Hence the need of a man who could make an infinite atonement and thus satisfy the most rigorous exactions of Divine justice. After God's Son had descended to the depths of our degradation and by a sort of annihilation of self become one of us, a sigh, a tear, a prayer, a wish of His would have satisfied justice, yet was His life demanded to mark the anger of God and the enormity of the outrage. Thus did sin take the life of God incarnate, as it had attempted to do from the beginning, but attempted in vain till he put on a body. God annihilated himself, as it were, to come in contact with our humanity that He might seize it with both His hands to lift it, God dead in the effort to reinstate it, serves to show, if anything can show us, the depths of our degradation and misery in His eyes. Add to this the wicked work of the fallen angels. Their name is legion; they are of all the choirs of the hierarchy; they are intelligent,

CUNNING, DECEPTIVE, TIRELESS AND UBIQUITOUS.

They hate God with all the intense malignity of their depraved condition, and this hate, impotent against Him, is turned on man in all its fury, to thwart and defeat, as far as in them lies, the reparation in him of God's image and likeness. "The devil goeth about like a roaring lion, seeking whom he may devour," says St. Peter, and St. Paul says our wrestling is not with flesh and blood, but with principalities and powers. Thus revelation teaches us the spirit and mission of the rebel angels, whilst the records of history and daily experience attest aloud their ruinous success. By order of the Holy Father, every morning after Mass the priest prays to St. Michael to defend us in the day of battle, to be our safeguard against the wickedness and snares of the devil, and by the power of God to thrust down to hell the wicked spirits that seek the ruin of souls. To repair the ruin of our nature, to help us defeat the machinations of the evil one, to guide homewards men of good will, God instituted His Church and enriched her with His merits. The work assigned her and faithfully performed by her is eminently that of education.

To educate is to draw out and develop the latent or feeble powers of a given subject in relation to its end. Man belongs to God and was made to enjoy His society forever. Soul and body he should tend towards his destiny. In his soul there are various faculties, namely memory, imagination, intellect, free will, also appetites. The soul and all these powers should live and work for God. They have a beginning, a growth, a development. To aid this growth, to advance it and direct it to its proper end, this is education. Any action on the soul or on any of its powers or faculties that has not this aim is not education, but the reverse.

EDUCATION BUILDS UP AND TENDS TO PERFECTION,

it never obstructs or pulls down. "Education," says Webster in his dictionary. "is properly to draw forth, and implies not so much the communication of knowledge as the discipline of the intellect, the establishment of the principles and the regulation of the heart. Instruction is that part of education which furnishes the mind with knowledge." An integral education," says Johnson in his cyclopedia, "must include at least five branches,—physical, moral, intellectual, æsthetic and religious. The tendency," he says, "is to remove all purely religious teachings from all institutions of public instruction, leaving it to the family and the Church. Hence the great development of the Sunday School." Education, according to both, embraces a religious element. "To furnish the mind with knowledge is but a part of education," says Webster, who seems to lay stress on the principles that regulate the heart.

The education of man made for God must in all its detail be on the line of his destiny; the education of a supernatural being must be in that order, and therefore religious; the education of an immortal being must in all its powers and faculties have an influence reaching away beyond the limits of time and must therefore be religious; the education of a soul made in the image and likeness of God must tend to draw out, define and perfect that image, and therefore be eminently religious. To speak of educating or set about educating a man in this or that science, in these or those branches usually taught in our schools with a view only to his comfort here for a few—a very few—years, and make no other provision for his welfare, is to betray a stupid, a shameful ignorance of who he is and what he is; it is to deny practically the immortality of the soul and the supernatural order; and to treat him as an animal. This is sheer materialism. From the contagion of such a view of education and its consequences may God preserve the country.

EDUCATION IS TWOFOLD, RELIGIOUS AND SECULAR,

it fits man at once for this life and for that which is to come. The religious is the dominant, the essential element in education, it is its soul. The two elements, which, like soul and body, are one, can and should mutually aid each other. The religious element ennobles, elevates, purifies, inspires, directs the secular or scientific element, and the secular furnishes it in turn with basis for greater growth. They should not be divorced, and cannot be without detriment to both. God and nature, with whom they are busy, cannot be separated. As the separation of soul and body means death and dissolution, so the separation or divorce of religion and science will inevitably result in the corruption of the latter.

The nature of the child to be educated is fallen. The sad consequences of the fall are traceable in body in soul, in all the sources of one, in all the faculties of the other. The intellect is dark, the will weak, imagination defiled, the memory leaky, treacherous, the lower appetites insubordinate. The soul is a feeble government in a state of anarchy. Human nature is like the man who fell among robbers on his way to Jericho, stripped, wounded, crippled. It is the theater of all the woes that lead up to death.

The intellect made for truth is the hospitable home of errors of all kinds and the will which should be at one with that of God is the very womb of vice. Errors of all kinds cover the whole field of human nature, ever active, ever spreading, ever growing with amazing rapidity. Vice is behind and before and all around them eating its way like a cancer, spreading contagion and corruption on all sides. These evils are

LIKE A DELUGE WHOSE FOUNTAINS CANNOT BE CLOSED.

Evil spirits without number foster and propagate these curses incessantly with all their might and all their venom. Human nature is like a field overgrown with thorns and thistles of the rankest growth, and these spirits are the enemy who never cease night or day to sow it with cockle.

There is an alliance between the evil one and men. There is a triple alliance between the world, the flesh and the devil. No such alliance has ever crushed the earth or polluted with its abombinations the historic page. It is an alliance strong as hell, everlasting, aggressive, irrepressible; death, desolation and ruin track its course. It is not, I know, popular to expose it, brand it and raise a warning voice against it. The world and the flesh cannot bear it, will not bear it, and they have some influence. They regard it rude, retrogressive, shocking and offensive to the refined. It is, I know, the fashion to pass it over, keep it in the background and though dealing death around like a masked battery, to wink at it and call attention to more pleasing subjects such as history, science, philosophy, social, economical and political questions, but I know also that this fashion is pernicious and fatal and responsible for many scandals that thwart the true progress of our race, our age and country.

Before making light of this alliance pause, reflect, look around you. God's Son died for the human race to raise, sanctify, deify it. He left the race of men His merits for that purpose. He instituted the Church to teach the nations the whole Gospel which he has pledged himself to ever preserve on her lips in its purity and integrity. He has opened fountains in her

FOR THE HEALING OF THE NATIONS.

He has perpetuated the sacrifice that redeemed the world. The Church is His body, she is the dwelling place of the Holy Ghost. He is here below, the embodiment of omnipotence and mercy, to raise man, guide him and help him on his way, and yet, though she has worked in the name of God, with the aid of God, and the riches of His mercy throughout the world for nearly 1900 years, she has not succeeded in bringing one-sixth of the human race under her direct influence, while the other five-sixths stand outside her pale with the enemy in an attitude of independence and unbelief. And of the one-sixth who are hers and bear her name, how many are there who have their own views and their own ways, and though of the fold pay little attention to the voice of the Shepherd. Again, God has become the teacher of mankind to unite all intellects in faith in His teaching, he has turned torrents of grace on human wills and hearts to unite them to the will and heart of God. He has exhausted, as it were, omnipotence to unite men in mind and heart. All men belong to Him, their bodies are His, their souls are His, their intellects and their wills are His. They should be one with Him and in Him. He is Father of all, His family should be one and wholly under His authority. Now go, attend the congress of religions, see there the children of God divided, distracted; listen to the vagaries about God and man, which they call doctrines, the babel of tongues and the conflict of thoughts. See the temple not built with hands in which God should be adored and served, in ruins, ruins which were under the eyes of Christ, as he wept and sobbed and stammered on the slope of Mount Olivet, and as you turn away in sadness reflecting on what they might and should have been, as you turn away from ruins that may never be repaired, certainly not by congresses, think lightly if you can of the triple alliance and keep it out of the discussion of the question of education. But do what you will the triple alliance and education cannot be kept apart. They are in the field in conflict and will so continue

TILL THE DAY DIES OUT AND THE FIGHT IS OVER.

The work of education is an effort to make a man under the light and by the aid of Heaven according to the model furnished, but the alliance is always in the way, bent on the work of ruin. The soul, like the body, has its infancy and manhood, so have it faculties. To nurse these faculties, to promote their growth and strength, to stimulate their activity and direct them on their course homewards, this is to educate. All education must be on that line. It must build up, not tear down; or advance, not obstruct. The two leading faculties of the soul are the intellect and the will, both of which suffer not a little from concupiscence. The intellect is the basis of the human edifice whose architect is God; it is the seat of knowledge, natural and supernatural. It is to it God and man and nature speak. The lamp of the soul, its light must be steady; the guide of the soul, its course must be true. It must not be in doubt or hesitancy about the way. It needs certainty, stability, firmness; it needs something solid to rest on, a rock foundation. It needs faith, it needs a creed, it needs authority. The strength of the intellect does not consist in the extent or variety of its knowledge. It is somewhat like a tree. The strength of a tree lies not in the size of its trunk and branches, the abundance and freshness of its foliage. All these it may have, be apparently strong and beautiful to behold, yet fall before the first shock of the storm. It consists rather in the strength of its roots, in the depths to which they have struck down and out into the soil that nourishes them, in their ability to suck in and elaborate the juices that become the life blood of the tree and distribute it all over under the light and heat of heaven. So the vigor of the intellect is not in its knowledge of the arts and sciences, in the cramming of the schools which, like undigested food or excessive flesh, is injurious and debilitating, but in the grasp with which it seizes and the tenacity with which it holds

THE GREAT PRINCIPLES THAT UNDERLIE IT,

that reveal to it its origin and destiny, furnish it life and health and growth, and in its power to assimilate the nutriment received and make new drafts for every emergency. The intellect is the seat of faith, and the active recipient of its object, the Gospel. It needs faith and revelation for its appointed work. Baptism imparts new life to the soul, it makes a new creature. This life surging from the heart of Christ fills the whole soul. As the soul is everywhere in the body, this new life is everywhere in the soul. It is in the intellect, where it deposits the germ of faith and preserves it. This germ has a growth, an office and a chequered history, somewhat governed by time and circumstances. God demands of man the acceptance of His word under pain of incurring His displeasure. "Without faith it is impossible to please God." His word is the Gospel addressed to reason. The intellect enlivened by faith can receive it and meet the demand. By reason of this demand and for other reasons, the intellect has a right to the Gospel, a right from God, a right to it in its integrity and purity. Else why has God by a miracle of omnipotence so preserved it, and commanded an imperishable Church to propose it? What are our high seminaries and universities and our world-renowned professors and our long and extra courses of theology for if not to give us men who will teach it fully, clearly, acceptably? By this teaching faith grows, and with it the intellect. As through the eye of the body in the light of the sun, moon and stars, the intellect looks out on the heavens and the earth, by day and by night, admiring their beauty, and their purpose, and reading the lessons they unceasingly teach, so through the eye of faith, and the light of the Gospel, brighter than that of ten thousand suns, it looks out on a new creation, grandest of all, God's own kingdom, with its suns and moons and stars revolving in their orbits, the triune God, the Incarnation, the Atonement, Jacob's ladder, the couriers from earth to heaven, the Church, the body of Christ and abode of the Holy Spirit, and all the forces which set it in love, transfigure it into a pillar of fire for the guidance of the human race, and shower manna in abundance all over the desert. To make the intellect, animated by faith, a lamp on the road to heaven, to light it up with religion, and science, the divine and human, to harmonize these forces and urge them forward on their course, this is

EXHIBIT OF BISHOP'S MEMORIAL HALL, ETC.,
NOTRE DAME UNIVERSITY, NOTRE DAME, IND.

THE WORK OF EDUCATION VIEWED FROM THE STANDPOINT OF CATHOLICS.

From the intellect let us pass to the will. The intellect is its guide. A good will follows the light of reason. The will is the great faculty of the soul; it is the queen of all the rest; it is, so to speak, the powerhouse of the soul, where the electric forces that move the others are generated; it is free, it is responsible for its acts, it is the seat of virtue and of vice. It brought death into the world and all our woes, and gave God's Son a body in the womb of a Virgin. More than any other faculty it marks the difference between man and man. It makes saint and sinner, martyr and apostate; it sinks to the pit and elevates above the stars. At the great assize the human family will be divided into two sections, never more to meet, set as far apart as hell is from heaven. That division takes place here, though we cannot define its limits, and it is the will of man that makes it. Strength of the will does not lie in independence, obstinacy, tenacity of purpose, despotic force, self-assertion. No; it lies rather in humility, obedience, love, respect, reverence, rectitude, purity. A strong will loves God, obeys Him, respects His authority and every authority that emanates from His; that is, every well-founded authority. It respects and venerates what is pure and holy, and reverences the great and good of every age and clime who served God in their day, blessed their kind and left to posterity the bright example of their virtues. Peter, before the High Priest, when commanded not to speak at all in the name of Jesus, answering: "If it be just in the sight of God to hear you rather than God, judge ye. For we cannot but speak the things which we have seen and heard," furnishes an instance of strength of will. The martyr in the arena, commanded by Cæsar, or in his name, to renounce Christianity and sacrifice to the gods, in the midst of all the terrors of that place of torture, answering "No"—

IN THE VERY TEETH OF TYRANNY,

and in spite of bribes and threats and torments, persevering in that answer till the victorious spirit flies home to God to enjoy freedom forevermore, is an example of strength of will, of love, of liberty and of God, which only religion could produce. To promote, foster and invigorate this spirit by all the resources available therefor, is within the province, and is the work of Christian education. The will is the home of the affections. It is the seat of that Divine gift, love, which keeps the affections turned on God and on the neighbor for God's sake. It is the furnace of that heavenly fire, which, fanned by faith and fed by all the forces of religion, shoots upward to Him who enkindled it, and gaining new strength in His embrace sweeps down and out over land and water, clasping in its bright red arms friends and enemies without distinction, every child of Adam from him who sits in the chair of Peter sending blessings to the nations, to the savage in the jungle voraciously feeding on quivering Christian flesh. Such a faculty needs care, supreme care. Will-culture is preeminently the great work of education. Bright intellects in myriads have gone down to hell, a good will never.

Opposed to the legitimate growth of intellect and will, stand the appetites of the lower nature. By clouding the one and warping the other, they aim to control the soul. To repel these assaults, put down rebellion, faith and love stir up and strengthen conscience, a tribunal set up by God to judge of right and wrong, before which the pleadings of passion are disregarded and the suggestion of the wicked one swiftly condemned. Anarchy thus repressed, and order maintained, the soul speeds on her way rejoicing.

THE FORMATION OF A VIGOROUS CONSCIENCE IS OF THE ESSENCE OF EDUCATION.

Where is this religious education to be given, and by whom? At home by the parents, in church by the priest, in school by the teacher, and all three should aid, and it will be a case of joy if their united efforts prove successful. They who, for obvious reasons, are opposed to religious instruction in the school and dare not deny the duty of giving it to children somewhere, say the proper places for it are the home and the church. This is a miserable subterfuge, an imaginary expedient to get rid of a difficulty by disregarding a duty. Religious education is not given at home, nor will it be, for the excellent reason that parents as a rule (there is question here for a general provision) have neither time nor inclination nor ability to give it. The bulk of the people are neither rich or learned. Fancy a poor man, laborer or mechanic, with little if any learning, tired after a hard day's work, taking up the catechism in the evening late when the chores are over to give instruction to his boy of twelve or fourteen, who is about to pass from the ward to the high school. Where is the boy at that hour? Who will find him, bring him home and hold him during this imaginary farce? Go call the man of leisure and some pretensions to letters who has not been to confession for years, neglects Mass on Sundays, eats meat on Fridays and fast days, from his cups and cards and other amusements to teach religion to his children. What mockery! When you consider the necessity, and the difficulty and the magnitude of the work of preparing a youth for duties of manhood, to say that it may be done at home by the fathers and the mothers of the masses is an insult to reason, it is cruel trifling.

Well, surely, the church is the proper place for religious instruction, and the priest is the proper person to give it. This seems plausible, but is it a provision that will prove adequate and satisfactory? Let us see. When is the instruction to be given? Not on a week day, for the children are at school or at work. Sunday is the only day on which it can be given, and between the end of High Mass and Vespers the only time.

THE SUNDAY SERMON IS NOT ADAPTED TO THE CAPACITY OF SCHOOL CHILDREN.

They do not profit by it, for it is beyond their comprehension, and when there is mention of children attending schools from which religion is excluded if they happen to hear it, it is not too much to say that as a rule they care little about it. What of the catechetical instruction in the afternoon before vespers? Very many priests, pastors of congregations, have no assistance. Indeed, it may be said the average pastor has no one to assist him. In the Diocese of Dubuque there are nearly two hundred priests doing missionary work, and of these not more than six outside the city are assistants. It is quite likely that the same is true to some extent of many, if not most other dioceses. The bulk of the congregation of one of these pastors lies in the country within a radius of six or more miles of the town or village in which he resides. On Saturday evenings the priest hears confessions, he does the same on Sunday morning before and after first Mass, he says two Masses, sings one, preaches a sermon, baptizes whatever children are presented, and when all this work is over, about 1 o'clock or later, if he have not a headache or a fever or both after the long fast and labor of the morning, you can readily realize that he is not in a favorable mood to take up catachetical instructions. Be that as it may, he cannot have the children. The country children go home after Mass with their parents to escape a long fast and a long walk in the afternoon, only a few children from the town and its immediate vicinity can be had for catechism. The fact is, as a rule, and it is facts, not theories, we must consider, that children who depend on the priest for religious instruction go without it, and many of them otherwise intelligent and talented will not know enough catechism to memory at the ages of fourteen, sixteen and eighteen to secure them a ticket for Confirmation. The priest who is liked well enough by his congregations says he cannot have the children for instruction on week days nor on Sunday except a small fraction as already stated. Be this as it may, the fact stands and is indisputable that the children of the people as a body are not instructed in their religion by their pastors.

As to the Sunday school conducted by young ladies and gentlemen, it is not worth speaking of. A moment's reflection will suffice to realize of how little value it is. As a provision for a great work it is simply ridiculous. The best if not the only good thing done there is to hear a memory lesson, but the memory is not the intellect, nor the intellect the soul, and

IT IS THE SOUL WITH ALL ITS FACULTIES THAT IS TO BE EDUCATED.

If children of school age, say from seven to fourteen, or from eight to sixteen years, are to receive a religious education to which they have a Divine right on many heads, the school is the place in which to give it. To prepare Christian youth for all the duties of Christian manhood, to case them in a Christian mould and fashion them after the model furnished by religion, to make another Christ out of human nature in its present state, is a work so great, so noble and withal so difficult that to essay it with a fair prospect of success, time, talent and favorable opportunity are needed. All these the teacher has or is supposed to have. He has ability, else why should the parents and the Church present to him the child and delegate to him their God-given authority. After some study of his pupil he is supposed to know him, his talents, his temper, disposition, habits, the strong and weak points of his nature. He is supposed to consider well his supernatural life and destiny, the faculties of the soul, the germs of the virtues, especially the theological, and the dangers that beset them, all the treasures of the Church, how to prepare for them and communicate them so as to prove productive. His is not the task to carve the image of a man out of the marble or put his likeness on canvas as sculptors and painters do, but to build up out of poor human nature a living, breathing, speaking, active image of God's Son made man. For this work, more difficult far than that of Eden, the riches of heaven and the forces of omnipotence are at his service, and, under God, the chief agent in this greatest work, in the accomplishment of this prodigious feat is the Christian teacher in the Christian school.

OF THE MODEL BEFORE HIM THE TEACHER HIMSELF SHOULD BE AS FAR AS POSSIBLE A FAULTLESS COPY.

He has time for the work, not one day in the week or rather one poor hour, but five days in every week and six hours of every day for seven, eight, or ten years as the case may be. I say six hours of every day he is making a religious impression all the time. Whatever he teaches regarding man or nature has a religious aspect and a religious influence. In teaching history and science he is teaching religion indirectly. The world without God is not a fact, it is a fiction. As He is everywhere, the healthy eye, the Christian eye sees Him everywhere, and thus every lesson taught by a Christian and studied by a Christian furnishes its contribution to the formation of a man.

He has opportunities that are golden. He has youths to work on. Youth is the springtime of life, the season of sowing and planting. The soil is at its best. Youth is innocent, pure, loving, confiding, respectful docile, most susceptible of virtuous impressions. The teacher can mould the soul of youth as he pleases, it is like wax in his hands. He can fill it with admiration of the works of God, of His Church, of saints, heroes and all the models of true greatness furnished by history. From admiration imitation is but a step. If he does not form Christian character, who will? If in five days of every week and six hours a day for seven, eight, or nine years such a man with his ability, opportunity, and many advantages will not prepare youth for manhood, who will? Will you take the work out of his hands and give it over to parents, laborers, brick-layers, carpenters, plasterers, painters, etc., etc., and to many, many fathers who can only make a flying visit to their little families once a week or once a month, or to the average priest who says, and says truly that he cannot get the children for instruction?

THIS FORM OF INSANITY SEEMS TO PREVAIL.

Remove religious education from the school and you do away with it altogether. To refer it to the home and the church and the Sunday-school is a mock provision that will deceive only those who are willing to be deceived. Banish religion from the school and you leave the intellect of the pupil without the knowledge of God, his heart without the love of God, his will without motive or desire to obey or serve God. Banish religion from the school and you leave the supernatural or Divine life of the soul received in baptism—the only true life, the only life that is crowned with glory—without the nutriment and the care that every kind of life needs. You leave the germ of faith and love which should grow up and acquire strength in intellect and will in a comatose condition; you leave the soul without moral or religious principles, and therefore without conscience. Heaven and hell and purgatory and judgment are but names—words, that are used after the prevailing fashion. Meanwhile, give the best secular education you can. Fit a youth as best you may for what is called success in life, for a career of prosperity. Teach him history, and the sciences and the arts, social and political economy, natural and mental philosophy, etc., etc. Sharpen the intellect, enrich the imagination, cram the memory, and what do you do but give light and strength and cunning, strong mental powers, to a man without faith, or love, or conscience. That is like giving tools to a burglar, or fire-arms to a footpad. You prepare the way for accomplishments which when discovered are sometimes sent for a time for safe keeping to state's prison. With the growth of the body that shoots up like a plant, and the growth of the soul in secular knowledge, the animal propensities gain strength daily. Freed from all control they grow apace. What is true of one child is true of all. They have the same nature and are similarly circumstanced. These appetites are stimulated by association, fomented by the surroundings and fed by the five senses. The sensational novel, the columns of scandal in the daily papers, which are devoured with avidity, the low theater, street scenes, indecent pictures, and the ways of the world, do their work in contributing to their growth. They crave indulgence, the same desire is on all sides. Why should they not be gratified, the ways of the world followed, its pleasures enjoyed?

THE EVIL ONE IS NEITHER IDLE NOR IGNORANT.

His suggestions succeed. Every indulgence is as oil on the flames which blaze more fiercely. Demands for pleasure are more strong and frequent; repeated acts become a habit, and habit, like that of intemperance, is a tyrant that holds its victim in the toils. Thus the youth of eighteen or twenty, a graduate with honor of some high school or college, but at the same time the slave of bad habits, without faith or love or conscience passes out into the world, into the garish day of public life, associating with the multitudes who are struggling or striving for the good things of this life, with scant respect for the Decalogue, to complete his education among them and become a man of the age.

Is this to be the type of the coming man, the father and head of the Christian family, the proud citizen of the great Republic? Is it on such as he we base our hopes of our country's future, its prosperity, its progress, its civilization? Progress and civilization, which are the outcome of great virtues, never were and never will be the product of such factors.

Lecturers subversive of religion and morality, of the foundation of society, because they deny or question the existence of God, which forty years ago, if heard accidentally, would have been hissed and hooted with virtuous indignation by an honest, Christian community, are now listened to with pleasure and received with thunders of applause by tens of thousands all over the land. Crimes are committed to-day that excite no surprise, so common are they, which in times within our recollection would have so shocked the public that some good people would begin to think that Antichrist was let loose and the end of the world was at hand. Witness the mania for suicide as the climax of great crime, the silly reasons for its commission sometimes, the startling methods of self-destruction and their horrid originality. Public morality does not seem to be improving, nor, due regard being had to varying population, does crime seem to be decreasing. And yet within the time before mentioned, schools, high and low, have been multiplied by the hundreds, they cover the land and billions of money have been expended on their support. Everything that can be thought of,

SAVE THE ONE THING NECESSARY,

is done to improve them. Themselves and the system on which they are conducted, are lauded to the stars by press and pulpit, and a certain class of speakers and writers point to them with pride as the bulwark of the commonwealth. What is the matter with public opinion? How explain facts that stare us in the face? A good tree does not produce bad fruit. Let people say what they will or act as they may, education without religion, that is without God, is not a good tree, it is a body without a soul, a corpse.

Even in the department of secular or scientific studies it is defective. How can you study nature properly, if you put out of it nature's God, or the lives of men, if you make no account of Him? Though God was never absent from man whose biography if history, not even for a moment, though God was always with the race of men, with the individual, the family, the community, though the philosophy of history is the tracing of the action of God in society shaping and directing its course without detriment to free will—though God's Son on the cross redeeming the human race is the central figure in history, Jesus Christ yesterday and to-day and forever, the very soul and life of it as He is of humanity, though all the lines of this history of the nations in the hands of God and under the guidance of His providence tend toward Golgotha like the radii of a circle to the center, or the lines of steel on which the multitudes from east and west, and north and south travel to Chicago, yet, notwithstanding all this, there is not a word about God and his Christ in all the lessons and lectures on history. Is this the way to teach history? Not a word about God in science. Though all creatures are the work of His hands, though nature's laws are His and nature's forces are His, though His finger is on every atom of matter in the universe, His blessing on every seed, His power and providence manifest in every blade of grass and in every ear of corn, yet is His name never mentioned in the discussion of the sciences that treat of plans and planets. But enough. Education without religion is not a good tree, on what side soever you view it it is found wanting.

THE EDUCATION OF A CHRISTIAN,

a child of God, a brother and coheir of Christ should be religious. Such education if given at all in any proper sense of the word must, save in very exceptional cases, be given in the school, during the years of schooling and by the most competent teachers that can be had. In this education the family, the Church and the State have the deepest interest. Who will respect or obey cordially authority in Church or State or family, if he know not or care not for the authority of God from which it emanates. "There is no power but from God" and without such respect and obedience what becomes of the foundation and super-structure of the social edifice? Where there is a common interest there should be united action. Instead of wasting time on useless, irritating discussion, parents, priests and rulers should consider their duty to God, to their little ones, to themselves and to society, and do it promptly and manfully by uniting in giving to the youth of the nation that truly religious education to which they have a right from God. If any one, fond of flimsy objections should say or think that the study of religion in schools retards progress in other studies, let him go over to the Exposition grounds and examine for himself the Catholic Educational Exhibit. Growth in the body of Christ is in light, not in darkness.

After Mr. Harrison Wilde had rendered Moszowski's Tema con Veriazioni upon the organ, the Most Rev. P. J. Ryan, D. D., Archbishop of Philadelphia, was presented by Archbishop Feehan, in the following language :

It gives me great pleasure of introducing to you Archbishop Ryan, of Philadelphia.

ARCHBISHOP RYAN'S ADDRESS:
THE VOCATION OF THE CHRISTIAN EDUCATOR.

To form an adequate estimate of the exalted vocation of the Christian Educator we must bear in mind that he who is called to this position must be all that the secular educator should be, in knowlege and aptitude to convey it to others, and must, in addition to all this, be qualified for the far higher education of the human soul in the knowledge of God and of itself, and in the preparation of man for his eternal destiny. The vocations of the religious and secular educators have much in common. Both are destined to dispell ignorance, to enlighten and enlarge the human mind, so that it may contemplate truth more perfectly, to refine and elevate our love of the True, the Beautiful and the Good. These two educators are thus far united in vocation and in mission. They ascend the mountain of God together, for all knowledge, whether religious or scientific, is holy, for God is master in the temporal as in the spiritual order—God of the starry firmament as well as of the sanctuary. Behold then these two lovers of truth ascending the mountain together. At a certain point marked by a cross on the wayside, the secular teacher stops and says "Thus far may I go, but no farther. I must return to bring pupils to this point and here part with them." "Do not go back, but give me thy hand," says the religious educator. "To these summits above us, bathed in celestial light, let us ascend and see what greater and newer things our God has made, and let us hear his voice speaking to us." Education to be perfect must consider man in his entirety, must call out the heart power as well as the intellect power, and educate the great religious element within as real as either and partaking of both. We must not omit the great fundamental principles of our existence, why we were made, for what object we are placed in this world, what is our future. The very philosophy of our being, the principle which determines the value of all other knowledge, cannot be ignored in a thorough education. The great infinite Being who placed us on earth and our relations to him ; the source of all knowledge and all good, must find the supreme place in education.

His existence and attributes are so mingled with all knowledge that to separate them and lay them aside for a distinct study, as we would arithmetic or geography, is an impossibility. If we exclude religion from education we must, of course, exclude the consideration of God. Who is the being thus excluded, and what are his relations to human knowledge? Cardinal Newman, in a passage of surpassing eloquence, speaking on this subject in one of his university lectures, thus describes the Being whom the secularist would exclude:

"To Him must be ascribed the rich endowments of the intellect, the irradiation of genius, the imagination of the poet, the sagacity of the politician, the wisdom (as Socrates calls it) which now rears and decorates the temple, now manifests itself in proverb and parable. The old saws of nations, the majestic precepts of philosophy, the luminous maxims of law, the oracles of individual wisdom, the traditionary rules of truth, justice and religion, even though embedded in corruption or alloyed with the pride of the world, betoken His original agency and His long-suffering presence. Even where there is habitual rebellion against Him of profound, far-spreading social depravity, still the undercurrent, or the heroic outburst of natural virtue, as well as the yearnings of the heart after that which it has not, and its presentiment of its true remedies, are to be ascribed to the author of all good. Anticipations or reminiscences of His glory haunt the mind of the self-sufficient sage and of the Pagan devotee; His writing is upon the wall, whether of the Indian fane or of the porticoes of Greece. . . . . He speaks amid the incantations of Balaam, raises Samuel's spirit in the witches' cavern, prophesies of the Messiah by the tongue of the sybil, forces Python to recognize His ministers, and baptizes by the hand of the misbeliever. He is with the heathen dramatist in his denunciations of injustice and tyranny and auguries of divine vengeance upon crime. Even upon the unseemly legends of a popular mythology He casts His shadow, and is dimly discerned in the ode of the epic, as in troubled water or fantastic dreams. All that is good, all that is true, all that is beautiful, all that is beneficent, be it great or small, be it perfect or fragmentary, natural as well as supernatural, moral as well as material, comes from Him."

Behold, then, how the Christian educator rounds and perfects education by teaching man what may be learned of the great Infinite Educator, who planted at once and developes all that is great and good in our nature, and replies to the soul's questionings concerning man, his origin and destiny.

It is also the vocation of the Christian educator, by the great truths which he teaches, to restrain human passion, and thus by acting on the heart of man to clarify his intellect and make him at once the best scholar and the best citizen. There is more intimate connection between head and heart than the generality of men imagine. The unrestrained passions of the heart send up mists from its valleys that rest on the headlands. Men cannot see truth through the prejudices which passion generates. It is the sacred office of religion to dispel these mists. Hence we find the great pagan philosopher, Pythagoras, bringing his pupils away from the world and its distractions, and in chastity, mortification and prayer to the gods, communicating the great truths of philosophy. This, though an extreme measure, inculcates a great truth—the influence of the state of the heart on the intellect. "What has piety to do with learning?" men may ask. "Some of the most learned men have been anything but saints. The fact that they are not bound down by the trammels of religion makes them freer to soar into the regions of speculation and theory, and no monkish chronicles or unscientific Bibles can call them back." But, as I have said, this freedom from the just restraint of the passions does darken the soul by prejudice. It is false to say that the most learned men have been those who ignored religion. Did Plato, Socrates and Pythagoras, did Cicero and Pliny and Seneca, did Augustine and Thomas

Aquinas and Lord Bacon and Copernicus and hundreds of others whose names stand so high in the history of intellectual progress, ignore the influence, the truth, the beauty and the goodness of religion? If others there were who were great without religion, what might they have been under its influence? And it is false to say that the intellectual liberty, or rather license of speculation unrestrained by any influence, is conducive to truth, just as it is false to say that liberty unrestrained by any command—divine or human—is truest liberty.

Who has speculated more boldly than St. Thomas Aquinas? Who has presented more powerfully the objections of infidelity and error? The men who held such opinions were unable to express and urge them as this intellectual giant could do for them. Why? Because, free from the darkness of prejudice, he could see the amount of truth mixed with their errors, and then, being absolutely certain of the truth of religion, he knew with the same certainty that there could be nothing to contradict in the region of science and true philosophy. The last man of earth to fear the progress of scientific and philosophic investigation is the Catholic, and the better Catholic he is and the more thoroughly instructed, the more fearless he should be. All truth is one, and from God. He cannot speak one thing in nature and reason, and another in revelation. If, therefore, I am absolutely certain of my religious truths, I am as absolutely fearless of scientific truth. But if I have only opinions, more or less vague, on religious subjects, I may fear that some day scientists may discover something to undermine them. The same is true of opinions in the natural order, and if I have an opinion that the moon is inhabited, I should not wonder if science proved the contrary; but I have no fear that science is about to prove that two and two are not four, for of this I am certain.

Now, I think it can be safely asserted that no class of religionists are more certain of the truths they profess and teach than Christian, Catholic educators. I am not here inquiring into the grounds for the certitude, but simply stating the fact. Hence, such educators must be the last to fear scientific revelations.

Another and most important part of the vocation of the Christian Educator is that of teaching the great, restraining doctrines of our religion which help to form the law-abiding citizen as well as the good Christian. One of the many delusions of the age is that education of itself is enough to form the moral man, by elevating and refining our tastes, giving wholesome thought-food to the intellect, thereby excluding what is coarse and vicious, and filling the heart and imagination with pure and beautiful ideals. No doubt all these things help, but they are far from being sufficient. Education will refine even vice itself, but perhaps it is more fatal in its refined than in its gross, repulsive condition.

No secular education can strike at the root of evil as religion does. "Quarry the granite rock with razors or moor the vessel with a thread of silk, then may you hope, with such keen and delicate instruments as human knowledge and human reason to contend against these giants, the passion and the pride of man," says Cardinal Newman. Experience confirms what the great Cardinal asserts. Greece and Rome in the days of their highest culture were vicious to the core—elegantly vicious, if you please, but supremely vicious.

"Whatever may be conceded to the influence of refined education on minds of peculiar structure," says George Washington in his inaugural address, "reason and experience both forbid us to expect that national morality can prevail in exclusion of religious principles." No, ladies and gentlemen, morality requires sacrifice, sacrifice requires a motive, and religion alone can furnish adequate motives for all kinds of temperaments. Religion must furnish motives stronger than those that move to sin in order that a man may rationally decide for the right against the wrong, for the pure against the impure. Hence religion must not be mere sentimentalism or probability. It must be founded in our rational nature and appeal with irresistible force to a power within us stronger than passion. Its truths must be clear and convincing, and man must be educated in them. This is the office, supreme and all-important to the interests of the individual, the family and human society, of the Christian Educator. Of course, I shall be told that this is not properly the office of the mere educator. The parent and the priest can alone enter the sanctuary gates of the heart; and the home and the Sunday-school are the places for Christian education. I say, ladies and gentlemen, that these are sacred and appropriate schools, but I say that experience clearly proves that they are not sufficient, that when you take from the great body of parents three classes—those who have not the time, those who have not the ability, and those who with time and ability, have not the inclination, very few will be left to attend to the vital duty of religious education. The Sunday-school held once a week is wholly insufficient and very precarious. No child could learn arithmetic or grammar by one weekly lesson, and yet the all-important subject on which time and eternity depend is supposed to be left to this precarious mode of teaching. Are chastity and honesty and obedience to law less important than arithmetic and grammar?

But it may be still further urged, let us by all means have the Christian Educator, or rather, to render the title less sectarian, the Moral Instructor—the man who, rising above all sectarianism, teaches only the great moral principles upon which all men agree, who, eliminating dogmas, confines himself to morals alone. This vague general talk has done great harm to morality. I have shown that dogmas of religion, absolutely certain and well inculcated, are essential to give motive to self-sacrifice, and hence to morality. As well expect the flower and fruit without the stem or root as expect morality without the doctrines that give it motive and power. In unsectarian moral education the teacher is supposed to avoid touching on any doctrine which might clash with the faith of his pupils or with that of their parents. Let me suppose, for illustration, a congress of these youths taking your places in this hall. They are sharp nineteenth, nearly twentieth century young people combining Yankee acuteness with Chicago push. I, a quiet non-sectarian moral instructor from placid Pennsylvania and friendly Philadelphia, appear before them, giving them permission to object to anything like sectarianism, which may perhaps, unconsciously appear in my moral instruction, and to ask questions in explanation. I begin my address. "My dear young friends, fully impressed with the fact that I must avoid in my discourse any doctrine which may clash with the convictions of you or your parents, I shall, first of all, treat of a subject on which Pagans, Jews and Christians of all denominations entirely agree. I mean the voice within us that tells us that some things are right and some things wrong. This is the voice of conscience, which is the voice of God. "But," interrupts a smart young pupil amongst my auditors, "Who is God? What is God? Is He a person or only an invisible power, as my father thinks, and conscience, is it not the memory of perhaps a punishment received for doing wrong, as we see in the lower animals when they have been chastised and afterwards act as if conscious of guilt when they do something for which they had been chastised? Have animals consciences, sir?"

"I perceive," says the moral instructor, "that we have some atheists here; now, I come to instruct American Christian youth. Let the atheists, if such there be, retire. They require special treatment, and alone. Now, my dear Christian young men, I shall speak to you in a non-sectarian manner." "Christian young men," cries out a pale, intellectual young man, "my father is a taxpayer and a Hebrew, and he does not believe, of course, in Christianity. He thinks Christ at the very best, to have been an enthusiast, who fancied himself to be the Son of God. If this instruction is to be non-sectarian and intended for all taxpayers, it cannot be Christian." "Well, young gentlemen," says the bewildered non-sectarian teacher, "I see the point, but this is a Christian country, and as I cannot be with Christ and Annas and Caiphas at the same time, let the Jewish boys leave; they also require special treatment. Now, thank Heaven, I have young American Christian boys to teach, boys who honor Christ as the Son of God." "Hold!" says a voice with a strong New England ring, "If by Son of God you mean that He was God, equal to His Father, the Great Almighty, I object, for my parents and I are Unitarians, from Boston, and I did not expect to have sectarian teaching inculcated in a purely non-sectarian school." Another crowd is dispersed, and the moral instructor, not yet entirely demoralized, proceeds with his lecture. "As I told you, conscience declares that some things are right and some things wrong, and that we shall be rewarded for doing the right and punished for the wrong.

Some believe that the punishment of a really bad man will be eternal, but as I am to be non-sectarian, I will not enter on that subject. "But, sir," interrupts a youth in the crowd, "it's a mighty important subject to know something about." "Well, replies the instructor, "suppose we say the punishment is eternal." "Then," says the pupil, "that is sectarian doctrine, for my father is a Universalist preacher and thinks and teaches that the doctrine is monstrous and contrary to all that we know of God's mercy." "Well, then, suppose we say the punishment is just temporal and just proportioned to the crime, and after this temporary hell God will receive the soul into heaven." "Temporary hell," cries out one in the audience, "I declare that most sectarian doctrine, for a temporary hell where souls suffer for some time before they enter heaven sounds mighty like what Roman Catholics call purgatory." By this time the poor moral instructor begins to feel something like the pains of purgatory, with a fear that he may get farther south, if these youngsters so torment him. I might, ladies and gentlemen, continue this examination until the hall of the moral instructor would become vacant, as some one would be found to object to every dogmatic utterance of his. In vain will he cry out, "Why, young men, the very Pagans believed in God and his providence and future rewards and punishments. Can I not teach this much? "Yes, sir," some one answered, "if you propose to make us young Pagans. But the world is progressing. Dogmatism, which, as some one has happily said, is only puppyism fully matured, has had its day, and we must think for ourselves and act out our own nature as we please."

Now, ladies and gentlemen, what is to become of a generation thus unrestrained by the great religious element within, and the great God above them? With a mother's instinct, the Catholic Church, who knows the human heart, who has been looking into it for nearly two thousand years, sees and feels the danger, and makes every sacrifice to avert it. Hence she offers her religious orders of teaching men and women in every part of the world, who in poverty and chastity and obedience give themselves to teach not only the intellect, but the heart, and thus save humanity from its own fierce passions. She appreciates the sublime vocation of the Christian educator. If it be noble for the painter or the sculptor to reproduce on canvas or in marble some great work of God, what of him who fashions the young soul, and impresses more vividly on it the very image of God, who points out the glories of the starry worlds above us, and fears not to soar higher to the God of these worlds of light? The Christian educator who, in teaching the history of humanity and its civilization, points to the great central Figure of both—the glory of our humanity and the founder of our civilization—Jesus Christ. He fears not the charge of sectarianism when speaking of Him, his Lord and his God. He hangs the image of Him Crucified on the wall of the school-room, and points to it as the symbol of "the wisdom of God and the power of God."

Look at that gentle, consecrated virgin, the Sister-teacher, with her young pupils around her. She speaks to them of the truths of human science, teaches them most diligently what is necessary to be known to fit them for their position in life, and then, as her heart glows and her eye brightens and her voice is tremulous with emotion, she speaks of Him whom she loves, to whom and to whose little ones she has given her young heart and bright intellect. She speaks of love and loyalty towards Him—of purity, of mastery of the passions. She is herself the living sermon which must leave its indelible impress on the hearts of her pupils. The Catholic Church, with a maternal instinct for the preservation of the spiritual life of her children, knows no sacrifice too great to be made for their religious instruction. You behold the result. Thousands of school-houses surmounted by the cross, and second only in importance to our churches, are seen throughout the land. Many religious orders of men and women are devoted to the same work. You behold at this Columbian Exposition some of the visible results of this remarkable self-sacrifice for the cause of education. You see how charity can do more than gold.

Therefore, ladies and gentlemen, to sum up what I have said to you; because the vocation of the Christian educator is to the human intellect and includes all that is glorious in the vocation of the purely secular teacher, because in addition to all this it has a mission to the human heart, to the great religious element in man, to man in his entirety, because it elevates him at once to the plane of the supernatural, and by restraining passion, makes him the best individual and the best citizen; because it clarifies and strengthens conscience, which in a country like ours, where external control is so gentle, should act as a strong internal ruler; because unsectarian generalities and mere sentiment can never affect the passions so as to really master them, and only the truths taught by the Christian educator can effect this; therefore, am I not safe in concluding that the vocation of the Christian educator in this free land, and in this progressive nineteenth century, is one of supreme importance to the individual, to the nation, and to humanity?

The band then rendered a medley of American airs by Catlin.

Archbishop Feehan, in introducing Hon. Morgan J. O'Brien, said:

I now have the pleasure of introducing the Hon. Morgan J. O'Brien, of the Supreme Court of New York, who will speak to you upon "What Catholics have done for Education in the United States."

ADDRESS OF HON. MORGAN J. O'BRIEN, SUPREME COURT, NEW YORK STATE.

WHAT CATHOLICS HAVE DONE FOR EDUCATION IN THE UNITED STATES.

Among the manifestations of God's creative power in this world man occupies the first place, not alone that he is the greatest and highest, but principally because of his moral nature and ultimate destiny.

This idea of his position and destiny is the characteristic distinction between his status under a Pagan and under a Christian civilization. Under the former, where the State was everything and the individual nothing, man had no rights which the State need respect.

The Christian idea of individual responsibility and glorious destiny has not only fixed the relative rights of a citizen toward his government, but has covered our land with asylums for the sick and aged, infirm and decrepit, which were unheard of under a Pagan civilization.

The progress made in the march of civilization is in nothing more marked than in the recognition of individual rights and duties. Man's past and present reads like a book on astronomy. Once astronomy considered the stars as mere fixed points of light, placed in space and without relation to other heavenly bodies; now it studies them, determines their size, movements, and the revolution of their planets. Astronomy now knows that each star has its relative place, performs its particular functions under given laws, gives out its light to illumine earth and space and aids in producing that life and beauty which make up the harmony of ten thousand worlds.

So since the Pagan times when death was thought to be annihilation, we know that man's use and function is to be witness of the glory of that God, who is the creator of these stars and numberless worlds, and to advance that glory by his reasonable obedience and resultant happiness.

In determining, therefore, the benefits of any system, either of religion or education, it must be judged not alone by its effects or results upon man in his connection with what transpires about him here, but also by its influence upon his ultimate destiny.

This dual relation to time and eternity, though susceptible, in the abstract, of separate treatment and consideration, cannot, in the concrete, be dissevered, any more than can the body and soul.

Man's rights and duties, whether considered as an individual, as a member of the family, or that greater society known as the State, cannot be correctly determined without bearing this fact constantly in mind. What changes this wrought in men's lives, what transformations effected in nations, is most strikingly shown by contrasting Pagan and Christian civilization. The problem of life, the mystery of death, unknown to Pagan people, and the source of perplexity to the greatest sages and philosophers were solved, and are now in the possession of the poorest and most illiterate in Christendom. No longer left to the caprice of passion, this knowledge elevated man's dignity and position, and no longer left to journey from the cradle to the grave in doubt and uncertainty, he became infused with new blood, inspired with new hopes, and stood firmer, erect on God's footstool, with eyes ever fixed on his eternal home.

It would be both interesting and instructive to trace the influence that this knowledge of his dual relation to the here and the hereafter exerted upon man's condition and action, crystallizing in that Christian civilization which is now the heritage of all. It would exceed, however, the object, scope and expected limits of this paper, which will deal with it so far only as may be essential to answer the question presented for our consideration, viz.: What have the Catholics done for education in the United States?

There can be no question of more vital importance to the American people than this: How are children, who, within a few years are to be trusted with the responsibility of citizenship, and the destinies of the nation to be educated? The growth, development and prosperity of the State depends on the intelligence of the people.

Educational institutions may be divided into primary and secondary; the former embraces public, parochial and similar schools, devoted to elementary education, while secondary institutions comprise colleges and universities. Leaving out of view the religious feature, which we will discuss hereafter, and contrasting, from a secular standpoint, Catholic colleges and universities with other denominational or non-sectarian colleges, so-called, we are forcibly struck with how favorable, taking the past, is the comparison. Without means, without subsidies, without rich or influential friends, amidst trials and tribulations that would have excused failure, they have grown, flourished and multiplied, until to-day, we possess colleges and universities where every ambition for the most advanced higher education can be satisfied. The abundant money and resources of other colleges is equalized by the superiority, as a rule, of the faculty of Catholic colleges.

But when we come to consider our parochial as compared to the public schools, then the results are remarkable. That the public schools, in their appointments, in their completeness and in their system and methods of instruction, are superior, must be conceded. But it should be remembered, that though the parochial school dates back forty years, it has only been within the past twenty years that Catholics have been in a position to devote to their advancement either time, money or effort. Yet the statistics show that there are between 700,000 and 800,000 in our parochial as against seven to eight millions in the public schools. In addition, there are many orphanages, children's homes and similar institutions, whose inmates receive a Catholic elementary training. So that, if we take the number of children of school age, it will be found, taking our entire population, that the per centage, as between Catholic and public schools, is greater in favor of Catholic.

When we remember that this involves the double burden of building and maintaining our own schools, besides contributing, in the way of taxation, to public instruction, the result is not only extraordinary, but is evidence of a deep-seated and sincere belief in the necessity of Catholic Schools and Catholic Education.

We could continue our comparison and show that the education thus provided, regarded solely as secular education, equips the pupil with as good a mental training and intellectual equipment to contend for a successful position in life, as that furnished by other schools, public or private. But no idea of comparison, antagonism or competition, or even ambition to provide a better secular education, induced the establishment of the various Catholic schools, colleges and universities throughout our country. We recognize the necessity and utility of public schools and public instruction. These are essential for the safety and permanence of our country, needful to make intelligent citizens, and, for those who are indifferent or opposed to religion and education going hand in hand, or are opposed to religion, or who are indifferent to both the education and religion, and would neglect, were it not for the State, the obligation imposed upon them as parents to properly educate their children, as well as those who, with means, ability and disposition, are able to provide a thorough religious training otherwise, the public schools are highly necessary and beneficial. It is, therefore, a mistake to assert that Catholics are opposed to public schools. Gladly would we avail ourselves of their great advantages, willingly would we lay down the burden of maintaining separate schools, if this could be done without the sacrifice of principle. If conducted after the plan of the National School System of Ireland, or upon the denominational plan of Canada, which permits religious training, then could we conscientiously give up our own schools. We recognize their necessity, efficiency and usefulness for classes, some of which have been, and others which might be, enumerated, but they do not come up to the requirements of what, in a Catholic view, is essential to a true and sound education. Not the mind alone, but the heart, and the whole man, must be trained, because we accept alone as the true definition that given by Webster, according to whom to educate is "to instil into the mind principles of art, science, morals, religion and behavior." "To educate in the arts is important, in religion indispensable." As said Our Holy Father, "He who, in the education of youth, neglects the will, and concentrates all his energies on the culture of the intellect, succeeds in turning education into a dangerous weapon in the hands of the wicked. It is the reasoning of the intellect that sometimes joins with the evil propensities of the will, and gives them a power which baffles all resistance."

It is, therefore, in the language of Cardinal Manning, that we insist: "that a Christian child has a right to a Christian education, and a Catholic child to a Catholic education." There is nothing new in this definition of education, which has not only been consistently maintained by Catholics under every form of government, but has received the sanction and endorsement of some of the most eminent Protestant writers and thinkers who have spoken of the dangers attending education without religion.

Although we have, considering the difficulties, obstacles and lack of means, just cause for pride in the number of our schools, colleges and universities, providing as they do, for fully eight hundred thousand pupils, with well equipped and disciplined teachers and professors, who have sent forth young men who have successfully battled in every walk and profession of life for the world's highest honors, it is not in any or all of these that we find our chief pride and glory, or on which we rest our just claim to the gratitude of our fellow-countrymen in what we have done for education.

Though we had for lack of means, been powerless to accomplish what has been achieved, nevertheless, the principle which has stimulated us to spend millions of dollars, to sacrifice the life and ambition of thousands of our Catholic teachers, to assume the burden of a double taxation would carry us on, stimulate us with the zeal and courage to carry to a successful issue a work that must redound in the greatest benefits to the individual and the permanent welfare of our country. It has never been questioned but that the safety of a Republic rests upon the virtue of its citizens, just as monarchies are sustained by strong central governments, supported by large standing armies, and in which the governing principle is force. The world knows but two principles of government, one the power of the sword, sustained by the hand that wields it, the other the power of law, sustained by a virtuous and intelligent public opinion. "Or, differently expressed, there is the principle of force and the principle of love."

Whilst intelligence, therefore, is a necessity, and tends to promote virtue and eradicate vice, besides qualifying a man for citizenship, it still remains true that virtue is essentially based on religion. There may be individuals peculiarly endowed, who may be exceptions, but it can be truly stated, as a rule, that intelligence may make a brilliant, but can never make a virtuous people. As well may we expect a tree torn up by the roots, and thrown on the wayside to grow and blossom, as to expect that virtue, separated from religion, can survive. The ages and nations that produced a Plato, an Aristotle and a Cicero were noted for the intelligence, not alone of a few, but of the entire people. But what of their virtue? No picture brush could paint, or pen describe, could ever color the frightful moral condition of Greece and Rome, the two greatest and most intelligent nations of antiquity. The history of those nations, as well as the study of all the civilizations known to man, bear striking testimony to that oft quoted, but profound expression of Washington, the Father of our Country, who, in his farewell address, said: "Whatever may be conceded to the influence of refined education on minds of peculiar structure, reason and experience both forbid us to expect that national morality can prevail in exclusion of religious principle,"

And our own beloved Cardinal Gibbons, in his admirable book, "Our Christian Heritage," justifies the summary that "every philosopher and statesman who has discussed the subject of human governments has acknowledged that there can be no stable society without justice, no justice without morality, no morality without religion, no religion without God." And in this place I cannot forbear quoting from the same eminent author his eloquent description of religion and its salutary and far-reaching influences: "Religion is anterior to society and more enduring than governments, it is the focus of all social virtues, the basis of public morals, the most powerful instrument in the hands of legislators, it is stronger than self-interest, more awe-inspiring than civil threats, more universal than honor, more active than love of country—the surest guarantee that rulers can have of the fidelity of their subjects, and that subjects can have of the justice of their rulers; it is the curb of the mighty, the defense of the weak, the consolation of the afflicted, the covenant of God with man, and, in the language of Homer, it is "the golden chain which suspends the earth from the throne of the eternal."

Religion, however, it may be asserted, is the proper theme for the church or home, but has no place in the school. That churches and the teaching of Christian homes do much to foster and promote religion must be conceded, but, generally speaking, churches are more potent in maintaining religious convictions already formed than successful in the inculcation of religion in children. Hence their greater utility for adults than for children. The benefits of a Sunday-School or of home training cannot be over-estimated, but what impracticable difficulties are there in the way of their ever being so arranged as to produce the desired results, for the great mass of our children, either because of the small time devoted each week in the Sunday School or the limited number that ever receive a thorough religious training at home.

That churches, Sunday-schools and home influence have not been as far-reaching as demanded by the religious wants of the people or nation, may be conclusively shown by dwelling for a moment on the past and present religious condition of our country. Those who founded our colonies, as well as our Revolutionary forefathers, were religious men. Physically rugged and hardy, they were imbued with strong religious convictions that influenced their every act. They came over a trackless ocean, and cut a way through impenetrable forests, and through their religion, intelligence and courage, established society and government and laws, and, after finally throwing off a foreign yoke, laid deep the foundations of a constitutional republic that is seemingly destined to be the foremost nation of the world. Are we acting up to the spirit, the principles, the traditions of the past? Are we advancing or retrograding? To assert that, having advanced morally to a certain point, we can then remain stationary, is to utter an absurdity, for a nation can no more remain morally passive than can a man; he is bound to go on and upward or to go on and downward.

That, in material prosperity, we have made giant strides is apparent. Our towns, cities and states have increased and multiplied. Men have amassed wealth running into the millions and hundreds of millions. Our corporations are striding a continent, but are we not equally accursed by incipient pauperism and discontent, do we not know that thousands are deprived of the very necessaries of life, deprived of the benefits of education, religion and civilization, deprived of the very blessings which our Constitution guarantees, and which God seemingly intended for every man, woman and child in our land?

Has not agnosticism, materialism, infidelity and other forms of irreligion been as rapidly augmented as our national prosperity? Has not polygamy, under the form of Mormonism, or lax divorce laws, alarmingly increased? Have we the same spirit of public or private virtue that prevailed in the early days of the Republic? Have not immorality, gambling, intemperance, breaches of private and public trust, become prevalent among our citizens?

The fact, therefore, stands prominently forth that virtue has decreased in proportion to the destruction of the religious sentiment among our people, and it requires no prophet to tell what must be the inevitable end if some check to the rapid inroad of irreligion be not found. Kingdoms, empires and republics, some of which in territorial aggrandizement were larger than our own, some obtaining an intellectual supremacy which yet commands the admiration of the world, have, at times, glistened along the past only to be extinguished and to fade as atterly as the vivid glories of the sunset. Shall our country, whose glory and prosperity are linked with every fibre of our hearts, whose foundations were laid so deep and strong, which through the heroism and patriotism of our fathers has given to the world a government so adjusted as to satisfy the highest and noblest demands of social and civil life, is this, through our indifference or folly, to repeat the history of nations which have fallen to rise no more? We believe that more of man's destiny has been committed to our country than to any other nation in Christendom.

But we know that nations, like men, may live to the fullness of their time, or perish prematurely for want of guidance or through internal disorders. Viewing, therefore, the causes which threaten our national existence, most if not all of which are directly traceable to moral decadence among our people, may we not profitably inquire into the remedy for these evils? That these have grown and increased, in spite of the influence of churches, and the possibility of children being given a religious training at home, is evident from the present social conditions.

That they could not be so alarmingly increased, augmented or prevalent, were our people as virtuous now as in the past, we think equally demonstrable. It is conceivable that even a highly educated and intelligent people may be both corrupt and immoral, as shown in the history of Greece and Rome, but it is a contradiction in terms to assert that any people with deep-seated religious convictions, based on Christ's teachings, can ever be any but a virtuous people. Catholics regard, therefore, the proper religious training of their children as essential, not only for moral perfection in the individual and in the family, but equally necessary to the formation of virtuous and patriotic citizens. Catholics regard the teachings of religion as of paramount importance to the individual and the State, and, to that end, have earnestly and conscientiously labored to adopt the most effective means of securing it.

We rightly view youth as the seed-time of life. If the ground is then tilled and watered and sown with good seed the perennial flowers of religion and virtue will bloom in the summer's sun, and their sweetness and perfume continue until winter's snow shall linger and be dissolved in the lap of an eternal spring.

Experience, human nature, the necessity of first, as lasting impressions, all teach that the seat of all that is good and bad, the source of virtue as well as vice—the human heart—shall receive the same continuous, devoted and consistent training as the human mind. The error of delaying this work, or having it imperfectly done, is fraught with such terrible consequences to the individual, the family and the State, that Catholics regard religious as superior in its claims to mere mental training. If we would, therefore, ask what have Catholics done for education, we would answer, though we might point with pride to the number and character of our schools, colleges and universities, that we have joined in holy wedlock religion and education in conformity to the eternal decrees and fitness of things; that we have produced teachers who have consecrated their lives to the work of the Divine Master, laboring to lift not only our minds but our hearts, who have struggled to emancipate us from the encroachments of a debasing materialism, who daily teach us there is something in life higher, better and more important than commerce and wealth, than poetry, eloquence and song, that spiritual life which holds us responsible for what we may do while here and accountable at last to the final Judge.

In our schools, therefore, there is taught all that is taught in others and something more. They teach not only the geography of this, but of the world beyond.

How important and beneficial such an education is, both to the in-

1st. Annunciation Academy and Colored Industrial Institute, Pine Bluff, Arkansas.
2d. Carved Altar by Students, Josephinum College, Columbus, Ohio.
3d. Exhibit Schools Sisters of Notre Dame, Milwaukee, Baltimore, Quincy, Etc.

dividual and the State, I have endeavored imperfectly to outline. The underlying principle that distinguishes Catholic education is equally important to every other Christian denomination.

All professing Christians, be they Catholic or not, value the inestimable blessings conferred by religion in developing the men who hewed out of impenetrable forests a country, a government and a Constitution that is the envy of the world, and which, in its integrity, if preserved, assures not only to the present but to ages unborn the divine rights of civil and religious liberty. Our great achievements, our phenomenal growth, our long list of illustrious heroes, were the result of the religious spirit abiding in our people, and which found expression "in an admirable public conscience, rich in maxims of sublime morality, in laws of justice and equity, in sentiments of honor and dignity, in a profound respect for man and all that belongs to him, in a tendency to improve the condition of the many, to protect the weak and succor the unfortunate, in the indelible stamp which it has affixed on all our laws and all our institutions, and which has given us a civilization superior to that of all other civilizations, ancient or modern."

The weakening of this spirit, which we believe has occurred, is a national calamity, and the evils that must inevitably follow, if not already apparent, is due to the original vigor and strength as it existed, and which, thus far, it has been impossible to wholly obscure or destroy.

If religion, then, was the fruitful product of so much good, what other remedy so effective can be suggested for renewing the original energy of the nation? And, in what manner can this be more effectually accomplished than by properly training our youth? Feeling, as we do, that time and the sense of justice that ever abides in the American people will, sooner or later, bear testimony to the sincerity and value of the principle for which Catholics contend, we will patiently bear our present burdens, subject ourselves to the misrepresentation of those who will not understand us, and continue to uphold the principle that we shall not sacrifice the moral to the mental well being of our youth.

This idea, or principle, which we believe will finally meet with the assent and approval of all thoughtful and right minded men, is the Catholic contribution to education. This does not, let us repeat, place itself in antagonism to our public schools, nor does it, in any way, include the right of the State to teach religion. The latter would, to that extent, be a union of Church and State, to which in this country, where religious freedom is guaranteed, we, as American Catholics, are unalterably opposed.

The objection that this principle is opposed to the State is an old one, and was answered by Christ himself, when, in the Temple, he took the Roman coin, and enunciated the cardinal and guiding principle of civic rights and duties, by requiring tribute to Cæsar "of things that are Cæsar's and to God the things that are God's."

That some will be found who, opposed to all religion, will not regard our contribution to education as valuable we know, but for those who believe in Christianity, be they Catholic or Protestant, no logical reason can be suggested why they should oppose the principle for which we contend.

When we find arranged against Christianity all the forces of irreligion—forces most powerful and unrelenting—having a single bond of union, hostility to religion, should the time of Christians be taken up in bitter strife among themselves, instead of directing their strength against the common enemy? What a striking parallel in our present attitude and that so graphically described by Scott in his "Talisman" of the spirit that filled the allied Christian princess before the walls of Jerusalem.

After years of preparation, after months of long and dreary marches, after suffering and untold hardships, with ranks already decimated by the assaults of the enemy, they stood before the city of their God, which they had sworn should be wrested from the Saracen's hands. Instead of marching on the city, which the rank and file were anxious to do, they spent the time in vainly discussing as to who among them was, by right of precedence, entitled to lead the Christian hosts. After days thus spent by Richard the lion hearted, Philip of France, and Leopold of Austria, in useless wrangling, the debate was happily terminated by their uniting in a sentiment which we now adopt as our own, and which led the Christian hosts to victory: "In the face of our common enemy, let our quarrels be those of the past—to-day let each lead his own, and hereafter let him take precedence who shall carry furthest into the ranks of the enemy the Banner of the Cross."

The Hon. Thomas J. Gargan, of Boston, Mass., was introduced by Archbishop Feehan in the following words:

The Hon. Thomas J. Gargan, of Boston, will now address you, ladies and gentlemen, on "Patriotism—a Sequence of Catholic Education."

ADDRESS OF THOMAS J. GARGAN, OF BOSTON, MASS., AT CHICAGO, SEPTEMBER 2, 1893.

Subject: Catholicity and Patriotism.

I have been invited to speak to you on "Catholicity and Patriotism," and what more appropriate time than this to speak, when we are celebrating the four hundredth anniversary of the great Catholic discoverer who made this Republic possible, and in this city, where the courage of our Catholic fellow citizens, acting as peace officers during the anarchistic disturbances, was put to its supremest test to uphold and maintain the doctrine of the founders of our constitution, "That this should be a government of laws and not of men." Catholicity and patriotism seem to me synonymous terms. What do we mean by Catholic? We mean universal, whole, liberal, not narrow minded. What is the end and aim of Catholicity? The happiness and eternal welfare of mankind. What is Patriotism? Love of country. The passion which aims to serve one's country. What is the end and aim, then, of patriotism? The prosperity and welfare of one's country. It is true, the end of Catholicity is the welfare of all mankind, while patriotism is defined to be the welfare of one's country; yet they are not inconsistent, for Catholicity teaches that we are to "Render unto Cæsar the things that are Cæsar's, and unto God the things that are God's." In other words, we owe our duty and allegiance in all temporal matters, to properly instituted, authorized and organized government. We, as Catholics and citizens of the United States, yield, in our love and devotion to the country and its institutions, to no other organization or body of men; and we may be pardoned if at this time we indulge somewhat in retrospection.

De Toqueville, in his Democracy of America, and Bryce in his American Commonwealth, agree that the government of the United States had its origin in the New England town meeting, where exists to-day the best form of Democratic government; yet the idea of the town meeting came from Catholic Normandy, where it was the custom from the earliest history of the church after the last mass on Sunday, when the congregation was dismissed, to assemble on the common or green in front of the church and discuss the questions of new roads, and to fix the local rates and taxes, and to debate all matters appertaining to the material welfare of the people of the parish. The Normans, after the conquest, established this same custom in England, and the Plymouth and Massachusetts Bay colonists brought over this idea to America. And thus we have in this Catholic custom the germ of our whole system of Democratic government, the foundation stone on which our Union is builded.

Need I recall to you the early history of our country, or the events which led up to the American Revolution and the Declaration of Independence? We cannot forget that Magna Charta, won from King John, of England, was the precursor, of that declaration, and that the great charter of England was won by the Catholic Archbishop Langton, who on the field of Runnymede administered the oath by which the barons and two thousand knights, esquires, and followers bound themselves "to conquer or die in defence of their liberties." The same liberties which were afterwards proclaimed and set forth in the immortal declaration and the bill of rights. That the subject should be secure in his person, liberty, and property; that he should not be deprived of either without due process of law; that the courts should no longer follow the person of the king, but be held in some certain place confirmed to all cities and towns, the enjoyment of their ancient liberties according to the terms of their charters and reaffirmed the rights of trial by jury. Thus, five hundred and fifty years before the Declaration of American Independence the spirit of catholicity, as expressed by Archbishop Langton, compelled King John to grant larger liberties to the people of England. The great charter was the dawn, the Declaration of Independence the full noon of liberty's day. In the events preceding the birth of the United States, the Catholics of the colonies were true patriots mindful of the teachings of catholicity. Catholic Maryland, the first of the colonies to grant civil and religious liberty to all settlers, gave aid and comfort to Massachusetts in her agitation against taxation without representation, and early in the struggle, Father John Carroll, afterwards bishop of Baltimore, went on a diplomatic mission to Canada to secure aid of the French colonists, a mission which would have been successful in adding Canada to our Union if it were not for some New England Burchards of those days. In one of the colonial congresses, prior to the Declaration of Independence, much was said about the doctrine of the divine rights of kings, when a Catholic patriot arose and said: "What about the divine rights of the people," and anybody who reads carefully the proceedings of the congresses and conventions must be struck with the wisdom of the utterances and the catholic spirit of the men who framed this government of ours. A government which Lord Brougham said: "Was the wisest and best government ever devised by the ingenuity of men."

The framers of our government were not mere theorists and experimenters. They were men who had thought seriously and soundly upon the great problems before them. They were men not unfamiliar with the teachings of the early Catholic philosophers and doctors, for when they proclaimed the doctrine that all government rests upon the consent of the governed, they had to sustain such authorities as Saint Thomas Aquinas, the great doctor, who says "that the ruler has not the power of making law except in as much as he bears the power of the multitude." And Sir Thomas More, in spite of King Henry VIII., maintained that the King held his crown by Parliamentary title, and Suarez taught "Whenever civil power is found in one man or legitimate prince by ordinary right it came from the people and community, either proximately or remotely; it cannot be otherwise possessed so as to be just," and Bellarmine says: "Divine right gave the power to no particular man; it, therefore, gave the power to the multitude." Is there a Catholic who can read without a patriotic thrill the original document of the Declaration of Independence? While venerating the memory of all who did and dared so much that this government of ours, founded upon manhood, suffrage, might exist, we recall with affection the memory of Charles Carroll, who affixed "of Carrollton" to his signature in that instrument that there might be no mistake as to his identity and that he might bear the full consequences of his act, believing that if death were to be the penalty for his devotion to a righteous cause, "The fittest place for man to die is where he dies for man."

It would be invidious in me to single out names to show the patriotism of Catholics during those seven eventful years of toil and battle for the independence of our country. Washington bore testimony in his letter to his Catholic fellow-countrymen to their bravery and fidelity to the American cause, and to erase the names and deeds of Catholics from the history of our struggle to become a nation, would be to erase from the annals of our country's history some of its brightest pages. During all this critical period, after the peace of Versailles and preceding the formation of the Federal Constitutions, the patriotism of the Catholics of the United States was conspicuous. Nor was it less so during the war of 1812, where notably our victories upon the sea placed us in the front rank of naval powers. Nor could there have been a more complete answer to the slanders against Catholics as patriots than was afforded in the war against Mexico, a so-called Catholic nation—a war that was in many of the States an unpopular war; yet the Catholics followed the flag of their country on every battlefield, from Reseca de la Palma to the City of Mexico, and, while there are many Catholic names worthy of mention, I recall only the name of General Shields, conspicuous for bravery and gallantry not only in Mexico, but in our late war, a Catholic patriot, the hero of two wars and one who has had the distinguished honor of having served the United States as Senator from three States in the Union.

Faithful in three great struggles for the maintenance of their country's honors, where should we expect to find the Catholics of the United States in that great conflict which threatened the destruction of the Union? Perhaps if the framers of the Declaration of Independence had not omitted that clause in the Declaration intending the abolition of the slave trade, civil war might have been averted; a clause which Mr. Jefferson said was struck out in compliance to South Carolina and Georgia, and not without tenderness to some of our northern brethren, who, although they had very few slaves themselves, were very considerable carriers of them to others; yet, when that conflict came, much as it was deplored, while many recognized that the logic and the law and the constitution leaned in the direction of the legal existence of slavery, the logic and the law went down before the appeal to humanity; and when one of the States of the Union committed that supreme act of folly, firing on the flag of our country, the uprising of the people of the North was almost universal; Catholic and non-Catholic forgot all differences of politics and creed in the common danger that threatened us. The Puritan and the Catholic marched shoulder to shoulder; and on every battlefield of the late war where battle was fought or blood was shed, the Catholic soldiers fought, and bled, and died, with a courage and heroism not surpassed by any others; and they have bequeathed a rich legacy of patriotism to posterity, and have left memories and traditions to their children and children's children, with which history will indissolubly bind them to the soil forever; and the names of such brave Catholic soldiers as Sheridan, Rosecranz, Shields, Mulligan, and Corcoran, will be remembered so long as men love and are ready to die for the flag of their country; and so long as will spring in human hearts a responsive throb at the rehearsal of brave deeds, their fame will be secure in the United States of America. Not only on the field of battle, but in the councils of the country did Catholics furnish abundant evidence of patriotism. The clergy and the laity vied with each other, and the late Mr. Seward, our Secretary of State, under Mr. Lincoln, told me, a few years before his death, that no greater service was rendered by any one man for his country than had been rendered by the late Archbishop of New York, on his diplomatic mission to France in the early days of the rebellion; a patriotic service for which this country would always be grateful, and which could never be repaid.

Nor will the American people forget the piety and devotion of the Catholic priests, the chaplains in the field, who shared in the dangers and hardships of the camp and the battlefield, administering, under the hottest fire of battle, the last consolation of religion to the dying. No march was too long, no cold too severe, no sun too hot. to deter these soldiers of the cross, and they have added a new lustre to the name of Catholics. Nor should we be unmindful of those noble women of the Catholic sisterhoods, "Angels of Mercy," as the soldiers of all creeds and of no creed call them; who in the field and in the hospitals soothed and comforted the sick and wounded and whispered words of hope and comfort to the dying soldier, actuated by that same spirit of love which inspired the divine mother at the foot of the cross of her son, where, nearly two thousand years ago, for the eternal instruction of the generations, the human law nailed the divine. With such examples and such evidence before us that Catholicity and patriotism in this country have walked together hand in hand, what is our duty as Catholics and patriots in our day and generation? We may not live in times when our services are called for on the battlefield, yet we must remember, that every privilege that we enjoy has been obtained by battle of some kind. What are the dangers that confront this Republic? Can a government founded upon manhood suffrage be maintained if the voters are not educated, and know nothing of the origin and early history of our government? Can it be maintained if in the system of education the youth receives no moral training? Will it live if men of education and property stand aloof, and by their silence and inaction allow ignorance and corruption to dominate?

To quote Jeremy Taylor "I cannot but think as Aristotle (liber 6) did of Thales and Anaxagoras that they may be learned but not wise, or, wise but not prudent when they are ignorant of such things as are profitable to them. For suppose they know the wonders of nature, and the subtleties of metaphysics and operations mathematical, yet they cannot be prudent to spend themselves wholly on unprofitable and ineffective contemplation." Are there not grave questions affecting the future of our Country requiring the active participation of Catholics and Patriots? Is there no menace and danger to our form of government in the concentration of population in the great cities of the Union? Are we not creating the causes or do some of them already exist that produced the French Revolution? I am not a pessimist; I am willing to trust the common people who saved this Union in the dark days from 1861 to 1865. Corruption has not vitiated the masses; it has to some extent poisoned our legislative bodies; we ought therefore as Catholics and Patriots to begin our reforms there; carefully scrutinize all expenditures of the public moneys; watch the actions of corporations, who by their very organizations are grasping and desirous of controlling municipal bodies and legislatures. We know that much of the discontent and unrest has arisen in our Country since the advent of great corporations. While the people have been benefited by cheap and rapid transit, and many articles have been made cheaper by the co-operation of capital; yet since the displacement of the individual employer, the individual laborer has been correspondingly depressed and degraded; under individual employers there was a personal sympathy with the employe; this has been lost under the corporation system. The man feels that he is looked upon as a mere piece of machinery, of no use except to earn dividends for stockholders, who live in cities, towns, and even countries far distant from his own, and in many instances endeavor to escape their fair share of taxation and place the burden on the working man.

In the last thirty years have we not looked on in silence and indifference when corporations have succeeded in inducing legislatures to grant them power to increase their capital without adding any value to their original plant; have we not permitted the creation of fictitious indebtedness, and upon these fictitious values the masses of the people have been called upon to pay interest in the increased cost of all the necessaries of life? Is there not cause for the present condition of our country deeper than the depression of silver, requiring the thoughtful consideration of every patriot? Patriotic duty demands that we should visit all persons found guilty of dishonesty in public office with the severest penalties, and render them incapable of holding positions of public trust. Let the quality of our condemnation be not strained, but be visited on him that gives as well as on him that takes the bribe. Ours is the age of thought. We are living at the end of the nineteenth century, when every appeal to the enlightened conscience of the people receives thoughtful consideration. I have yet to meet with an intelligent and thoughtful non-Catholic American citizen, who has read the Encyclical letter of Our Holy Father, Leo XIII., on the Labor question, who has not expressed his unqualified approval of its spirit and sentiments, and has not hesitated to say that a Catholic who followed the advice and teachings could not be anything but a patriot and a good American citizen.

We observe, then, that the Catholic cause progressess and the world moves. As Catholics and patriots it is our duty to keep step with the march of the age. We must jealously guard our institutions and the principles of our government. Let us remember that the chief provisions of our constitution are absolute freedom of religion, the right of the citizen to keep and bear arms, compensation for private property taken for public uses, trial by jury according to the common law, and that all powers not delegated by the United States nor prohibited by the constitution to the States are reserved to the States respectively or to the people thereof. Catholicity and patriotism command us to maintain and uphold these principles. Catholicity, which declares that all men are equal in the sight of God, will not refuse to acknowledge that all citizens are equal in the eyes of the law. Let us not forget that self-government politically depends upon self-government personally. Law has not an atom of strength unless public opinion endorses it. We must do our share to arouse that proper public spirit necessary to insure the perpetuity of our institutions. "I have an ambition," said Lord Chatham; "it is the ambition of delivering to my posterity those rights of freedom which I have inherited from my ancestors." Such an ambition should be ours. We can never pay the debt to the generations that have preceded us, but the generations to come will hold us responsible for the sacred trust delegated to our keeping. May the generations to come be able to say truthfully of us, as we now say of those who preceded us in their day and generation, they deserved well of their country and their God.

The Rt. Rev. J. L Spalding, D. D., Bishop of Peoria and President Catholic Educational Exhibit then addressed the audience as follows:

It is not my intention to make an address. After the discourses which you have heard, anything I might say would be superfluous.

I wish, however, as having had the privilege of taking an active part in bringing about the succes of the Catholic exhibit in the Columbian Exposition, to say that, though its success is due, of course, to the prelates who first set the enterprise afoot, and to the orders who so gladly availed themselves of the opportunity to bring their work, as far as such a thing can be done, before the great American public,—I wish to say that its success, nevertheless, is due to Brother Maurelian more than to any other man. And it is for the purpose of saying this, more than for any other reason, that I have presumed to present myself before this audience.

I will say that I am persuaded that our Catholic educational system is great proof of the vitality of our religion here in the United States, more than anything else we have done or are doing. The sacrifices we make, and the success with which we meet, in giving to nearly a million of Catholic children, an education which is at once intellectual, moral, physical, and religious, proves the living force of our faith. We do that at the sacrifice of money; we do it because the people—the multitude of Catholics are in sympathy with us.

It is the fashion to talk as though bishops and priests exercised an almost omnipotence over the people. I tell you where a mighty achievement, such as the Catholic educational system of the United States, exists, it does not exist through the power of the priesthood alone; it exists because the great heart of the people beats God-ward. The people stand back of us. The hundreds of thousands of young women, who go forth from happy homes, turning away from worldly love and domestic bliss, go, believing that it is a God-like thing to rear children for Heaven, even as it is a holy thing to bring them forth to be citizens and patriots here on earth.

This system of ours is an opportunity of our religious life. What does "America" mean? It means boundless opportunities. That is the only meaning I have for America. If it be better than any other land, it is because here is a fuller opportunity to bring forth whatever makes man God-like—what makes him intelligent, moral, religious, praying, true, loving, beautiful and fair—opportunity. That is America.

Freedom is but an opportunity to make one's self a man or a woman. Wealth is but opportunity for larger life. Physical strength is but opportunity to to bring out the spirit of man, which is like God.

Here (holding in right hand a cablegram) the wires have flashed across the ocean the glad tidings that Home Rule has passed.

What, in the name of God, is Home Rule but opportunity for Ireland and Irishmen to come out before the world and free themselves?

But I am not going to make a speech.

I wish to have the privilege of introducing to this audience Mrs. Isabella Beecher Hooker, who is to greet you in the name of the Lady Managers of the World's Fair.

MRS. ISABELLA HOOKER'S ADDRESS.

Holy fathers—beloved sisters—of the Holy Mother Church: I greet you first in my own name, because I come of a family that believes in freedom—in the right of speech, in the right of thought, and in that deep love for religion and morality for which this mother church is found throughout the centuries. If our Board of Lady Managers were in session I am sure they would have, in a body, officially, welcomed you to the gates of this beautiful White City.

Mrs. Hooker concluded her remarks with the following lines:

> "I think when I read that sweet story of old,
>   How Jesus came among men;
> How he took little children as lambs to his fold,
>   I wish I had been with Him then.
>
> "I wish that His hands had been placed on my head;
>   That His arms had been thrown around me;
> That I might have seen His kind looks when He said:
>   'Let the little ones come unto Me.'
>
> "But still to His footstool in prayer I may go,
>   And ask for a share of His love;
> For if I thus earnestly seek Him below,
>   I shall see Him and hear Him above.

34 CATHOLIC EDUCATION DAY.

PROTEST AGAINST EXHIBITING INDECENT PICTURES.

During the fall of 1892, some daily papers published illustrations and descriptions of certain sensational and objectionable paintings, and stated that they were to be exhibited at the World's Columbian Exposition.

The subject called for the following article from the pen of Right Reverend J. L. Spalding, D. D., Bishop of Peoria, and was published in the "Sunday Post," Chicago, January 1, 1893:

Pure Morals at World's Fair.

This is true liberty, when free-born men,
Having to advise the public, may speak free;
Which he who can, and will, deserves high praise;
Who neither can, nor will, may hold his peace;
What can be juster in a state than this?

—EURIPIDES.

Ours is the busiest of all ages and we are the busiest people of the age. As a result, the wealth of the world is now greater than ever before, and we are rapidly becoming the richest nation in the world. What ends do our diligence and our money serve? They seem to enable us to become more diligent and to get more money. We are made the slaves of business and toil, and our wealth stifles the nobler faculties, shutting us out from the true intelligence and from the gentle usages which make life pleasant and sweet. In the midst of national prosperity there is an increasing dearth of men and women who are exalted by knowledge and virtue, who stand forth conspicuously as the intellectual and moral leaders whose speech and example enlarge and refine the life of the multitude. The feverish and absorbing pursuit of money, while it has established a great and growing inequality of possession, seems to make the rich and the poor equal in hardness, in narrowness in discontent and unintelligence. Our schools, which have helped to make us shrewd, and keen-witted, have failed to give us faith in high ideals or a sense for beauty or a love of culture.

Our material progress is a marvel to all men; our efforts to develop a nation of nobler, purer, more enlightened human beings than have ever existed elsewhere have been disappointing. This, however, is our mission, if we have a mission, and it is encouraging to know that the best among us feel this to be so. Hence, when they turn

SCENES FROM THE LIFE OF COLUMBUS FROM HISTORIC PAINTINGS EXHIBITED AT WORLD'S FAIR.

their thoughts to a national enterprise, such as the Chicago Columbian Exposition, they are less concerned to know what its effect upon trade and manufacture will be than what will be its religious, moral and intellectual influence.

Considered from a financial point of view, it will stimulate what does not need stimulation, but it will not help to solve any social problem growing out of inequalities in the distribution of wealth. If it is to lead to good results it must exercise an intellectual and moral influence on the millions by whom it will be visited. Returning to their homes, scattered throughout the land, they should carry with them new and fresh thoughts, deeper impulses to high and pure life. The gathering of vast multitudes in a great city inevitably leads to immorality of various kinds. What is unavoidable we accept without protest, but we have the right to demand that the municipal authorities of Chicago provide for the bodily health and well-being of its visitors by employing whatever means hygiene and sanitation may suggest; and still more that they remove, as far as possible, all temptation to wrong-doing. During the Fair the city should be cleaner than it ever has been, and its moral atmosphere should be purer. It will be crowded with the human beasts of prey who make a living by pandering to man's greed and sensual passions, and hence the laws of decency and order should be enforced with more than ordinary vigilance and severity. The amusements offered to the public outside the Exposition grounds should be of an elevating character, and the exhibition of the bodies of women in a condition more suggestive and more degrading than that of nudity, should be forbidden. Steps should also be taken to put a stop to the disgusting disfigurement of the city through the posting of indecent pictures, which tend to destroy both taste and morality. In this exposition Chicago will be taken, first of all, as a type of western life and civilization, and she must have a care that those who have persuaded themselves that the West is coarse, vulgar and material, shall not be confirmed in this opinion.

Chicago is the metropolis of a progressive, powerful and aspiring people, and there should be found nothing in it to remind us of the border town or mining camp, whose chief institutions are the saloon, the gambling hell and the brothel. As to the exposition itself, the directors and managers have repeatedly assured the public that it is to have an educational value; that its influence will be for good, both morally and intellectually. If this is to be made true, they must refuse to be guided by French standards, in the art exhibit at least, and in the character of amusements they offer visitors. The Paris exposition of 1889, in these two matters, certainly was a source of corruption. Many of the paintings were fit to be hung only in a temple of Venus, and the lascivious dances which were performed every day in the Rue de Caire and in the theater on the grounds could be tolerated only among a people given over to the worship of the goddess Lubricity. Art ceases to be art when it becomes cynical and profligate, when it appeals to sensual instinct, and not to the soul. To permit the paintings of a certain French school to be shown in the exposition buildings would be an insult to every pure woman. Nothing should be found there before which a true man may not stand without blushing by the side of his mother or sister. The great weight of enlightened opinion favors the opening of the exposition on Sundays, but if the laborers, with their wives and daughters, are to be invited to inspect paintings and dances which one would not think it possible to find outside of the low haunts of debauchery, then no one who has at heart the welfare of his fellowmen, his country's good, can desire that the gates of the exposition be kept open Sunday or any other day.

Would not the efforts to induce Congress to take the Sunday clause from its souvenir money grant be more likely to prove effective if the assurance were given by the managers that the Exposition shall in no way whatever be made to subserve the interests of the great goddess, Lubricity? The motive of the Fair directors in wishing to open the gates of Jackson Park on Sundays, has, of course, nothing to do with the lawfulness and propriety of such a proceeding. If it is right to visit the Fair on any day it is right to visit it on Sunday; and if the American people are once persuaded that whatever is objectionable to the moral sense will be kept away they will not insist on closing the Exposition against the toiling masses on the only day of the week on which they have leisure. The manifest indifference of some of the members of the board of the education exhibit has awakened the suspicion in a great many minds that the whole business will be conducted in a petty shop-keeping spirit, without regard to its intellectual and moral influence. The attractions of the Columbian Exposition will surely be great enough without such pitiful adjuncts as dance halls and obscene pictures.

Let the religious and enlightened minds of the country turn their attention to this matter; let them insist that the Exposition shall be such that it will be altogether good for man, woman and child to see it, and then there will be no sufficient reason why it should not be visited on any and all days. Those who observe, easily perceive that the danger which threatens our national life more than any other, is not drunkenness, but sexual immorality. Renan, uttering the thought of the whole French infidel school, has said that nature cares nothing for chastity, thereby implying that it is more or less a matter of indifference. Matthew Arnold says, in reply, that whatever nature may or may not care for, human nature cares for chastity, and that the worship of the great goddess Lubricity is against human nature—it is ruin. "For this," he continues, "is the test of its being against human nature, that for human societies it is ruin."

Impurity is not the only vice, but more than any other vice it stunts and mars what is high and harmonious in man; it robs the mind of noble thoughts, the heart of sweet love; it leads to hardness and insolence, to dishonesty and brutality; it feeds the beast in man and starves his soul. When a people hearken to false prophets, proclaiming that chastity is of no importance, it is lost beyond recovery. What its representatives are ready to do when opportunity is given we may learn from the disgusting disclosures of the Panama Canal scandal. It were idle to deny that the worship of the impure goddess threatens to bring calamities upon us. Who can read the advertisements in some of our most widely circulated newspapers, who can look upon the bill-boards of our cities, reeking with vulgarity and obscenity, who can watch the proceedings of the divorce courts, who can stroll through the streets at night without being made aware that the sense of chastity is dying or dead? To add to the danger the reformers and zealots, shutting their eyes to this cankerlike and all-pervading evil, sit complacently astride some prohibition of the Sabbath hobby-horse, predicting woe if a glass of wine is sold or the gates are open on Sunday.

If the Columbian Exposition is to be a blessing and not a curse, its managers must see that it is kept pure and clean from even the suspicion of pandering to the worship of the goddess Lubricity. If it leave us less moral, less chaste; if it lead us deeper into what Huxley calls the rank and steaming valleys of sense, then, though it should bring us billions of money, there will be hopeless loss.

[signature]

The repeated announcement that improper paintings were to be exhibited, caused the following form of protest to be circulated for signatures:

SOLEMN PROTEST.

Against Exhibiting Indecent Pictures at the World's Fair, Chicago, 1893. This Protest, with Signatures, to be Presented to the Art Committee in Chicago, March 1, 1893.

CHICAGO, ILL., February, 19, 1893.

To the Officers and Members National Commission, Executive Committee, Council of Administration and Art Committee, World's Columbian Exposition, 1893:

Free from the mercenary motives that may prompt interested persons, and actuated by a desire to keep our moral atmosphere as untainted and fresh as possible, we are impelled, for the sake of all that has moral worth in our national existence, and in the name of Religion and her daughters, Art and Piety, to enter SOLEMN PROTEST against the proposed exhibition at the World's Fair of the nude and lewdly suggestive subjects that have been made the theme for the brush and chisel of talented men, who have thus prostituted the gifts to which high Heaven has made them heir.

COLUMBIAN LIBRARY OF CATHOLIC AUTHORS.

An appeal was made to Catholic authors and publishers to contribute to the establishment of a complete library of Catholic authors in print in the English language.

The time was too limited to complete the collection. About three thousand volumes were contributed. Eight hundred and fifty-five authors whose names are known are represented in this library. Of three hundred and thirty-nine volumes the names of authors or translators are unknown.

The Jesuit Fathers of London, Rev. H. J. Coleridge and Rev. John Morris, sent 128 volumes of which the Jesuit Fathers are authors.

There are in the collection a number of French, Latin, German, Spanish, and Italian books. There are 225 autograph letters from authors and publishers, the result of correspondence concerning the Columbian Library. Many of the volumes were contributed by authors. The following publishers deserve credit for generously contributing their publications.

J. S. Hyland & Co., Chicago, Ill.; Appleton & Co., New York City; Art and Book Co., London, Eng.; Benziger Bros., New York and Chicago; Brown & Nolan, Dublin, Ireland; Catholic Publication Society, New York; W. J. Cahill, London, Eng.; Robert Clark & Co., Cincinnati, Ohio; F. De Richmont, Watertown, N. Y.; P. F. Fletcher, London, Eng.; M. H. Gill & Son, Dublin, Ire.; I. J. Griffin, Philadelphia, Pa.; St. Anselm's Society, London, Eng.; Burns & Oates, London, Eng.; Blackwood & Sons, London, Eng.; Denis Lane, London, Eng.; Straker & Sons, Whitefriars, Eng.; John Hodges, London, Eng.; P. F. Cunningham & Sons, Philadelphia, Pa.; McMillin & Co., New York and London; Catholic Truth Society, St. Paul, Minn.; Catholic Truth Society, London, Eng.; Patrick Fox, St. Louis, Mo.; Harper & Sons, New York; Hoffmann Bros., Milwaukee, Wis.; B. Herder, St. Louis, Mo.; W. H. Allan & Co., London, Eng.; Kegan Paul, Trench, Trubner & Co.; H. L. Kilner & Co., Philadelphia, Pa.; Lee & Shepherd, Boston, Mass.; McGrath & Sons, Philadelphia, Pa.; J. B. McDevitt, Dublin, Ireland; McClurg & Co., Chicago, Ill.; Frank P. Murphy, Baltimore, Md.; David Nutt, London, Eng.; P. O'Shea, New York.; Rev. John E. O'Brien, Cambridge, Mass.; F. Pustet & Co., New York.; Porter & Coates, Philadelphia, Pa.; Sealy, Byrnes & Walker, London, Eng.; D. & J. Sadlier, New York; Sullivan Bros., Dublin, Ireland; C. L. Webster & Co., New York, and Fredrick Warne & Co., London, Eng.

The following magazines were sent in sets or parts of sets:

"St. Joseph's Advocate," "Georgetown College Journal," "Records of the American Catholic Historical Society," "Quarterly Bulletin of the American Catholic Historical Society," "Researches of the American Catholic Historical Society," "Der Armen Seelen Freund," "Messenger of the Sacred Heart," "Pilgrim of Our Lady of Lourdes," "The Dublin Review," "St. Joseph's," "The Marygold," "The Rosary," "St. Franziskus Bote," "Poor Soul's Advocate," "The Month," "Annals of Our Lady of the Sacred Heart," "The Little Bee," "Ave Maria," "Notre Dame Scholastic," "Sacred Heart Review," "Annals of St. Joseph," "Catholic Reading Circle Review," "The Owl," "Catholic Youth's Magazine," "Catholic Family Annual."

The Columbian Library of Catholic Authors has been placed with the "Catholic Historical Collections of America," at Notre Dame, Ind., and will form part of the "Catholic Reference Library of America." The original idea of a complete collection of Catholic Authors will thus be carried out, as there are already in this Reference Library of Notre Dame thousands of rare volumes of which copies could not be secured during the brief period of the World's Columbian Exposition, Chicago, 1893.

APPRECIATION OF EXHIBITS.

The kind words of appreciation received from the World's Fair Officials, Educators, Foreign Commissioners, the Press and Visitors, is a source of gratification and of encouragement to the Projectors, Managers, Patrons and Pupils of all our Catholic schools.

Letter from Director-General Geo. R. Davis, Commissioner.

WORLD'S COLUMBIAN EXPOSITION.
OFFICE OF THE
DIRECTOR-GENERAL OF THE EXPOSITION.
504 Rand-McNally Building.

CHICAGO, ILL., U. S. A., April 17, 1894.

BROTHER MAURELIAN,
Secretary and Manager Catholic Educational Exhibit,
World's Columbian Exposition.

DEAR SIR:

I have the honor of acknowledging the receipt of a copy of the catalogue of the Catholic Educational Exhibit, which you were kind enough to send me, and beg leave to compliment you on the complete and attractive form in which it has been issued.

I embrace this occasion to also express my appreciation of your most satisfactory management of the affairs of the Catholic Educational Exhibit in its dealings with the Exposition. Considering the extent of interests involved, it has been conducted with noteworthy smoothness and order—thanks to your own excellent judgment and executive ability, and the wisdom and experience of the distinguished Catholics throughout the world, who lent their powerful influence and aid.

Occupying about one-sixth of the entire space set apart for educational purposes, in the department of Liberal Arts, and embracing subjects in range from the kindergarten to the university, the exhibit constituted a complete representation of the Catholic educational institutions of the country, and also contained much that was interesting from abroad. It has been seen by hundreds of thousands of visitors from abroad, and may be regarded as one of the marked successes of the exposition.

The efforts put forth to secure this result were in the highest degree gratifying to the management. Indeed, the flattering interest evinced toward the entire exposition by His Holiness in Rome, has been the cause for great congratulation, and the favorable disposition of the Vatican, manifested in various ways, has been regarded as an important factor in furthering our own efforts and contributing to the general success of the undertaking.

Wishing you a long life of continued usefulness and successful achievement, I have the honor to remain, with great respect, Yours very truly,

GEO. R. DAVIS, Director-General.

Letter from Right Reverend J. L. Spalding, D. D., Bishop of Peoria, and President of the Catholic Educational Exhibit, to Brother Maurelian, Secretary and Manager.

MY DEAR BROTHER MAURELIAN: Your final report, made to me, as President of the Catholic Educational Exhibit, at the World's Columbian Exposition, is evidence of the intelligence and earnestness with which this enterprise has been undertaken and brought to end. Of your zeal and unflagging interest in the work, the success of which depended, in so large a measure upon you, I need not speak. To have done well is enough, is more than praise. The ends for which the Exhibit was made have been attained. It was made possible by the generous co-operation of those who are engaged or interested in Catholic Education, in whatever part of the country, and had it done nothing more than show how united these willing workers are, the gain would not be small. In presenting the results of their labors to the world, in so far as this is possible in an Exposition, they proved their confidence in the worth of what they are doing and their desire to submit its value to the test of enlightened criticism. Not to know our educational work, our system and methods, is henceforth inexcusable. No one now, who respects himself, will affirm that our parish schools are inferior to the public schools, or that our teachers in appealing to the heart, the conscience and the imagination, lose sight of the importance of quickening and training the mental faculties. In the Catholic Directory for 1894, 768,498 pupils are reported as attending our parochial schools, and the number is rapidly increasing. When we consider that our school system is a work of conscience, which involves a very large expenditure of money and labor, it may be held to be, from a moral standpoint, the most important fact in our national life. For various reasons it is worthy the attention of enlightened and patriotic minds. It is the only elementary education in the United States which holds to the traditional belief that the morals of a people can be rightly nourished and sustained only by religious faith. Whether a purely secular system of education will not prove fatal to religious faith is as yet a matter of doubt, it being in no way doubtful that the basis of popular government is popular virtue. What Catholics then are thus doing deserves consideration, though it be looked at as an experiment or as a survival of what is destined soon to pass away. Indeed, the best people in America, if the case be presented simply as it is here presented feel an interest akin to sympathy in Catholic schools: and our position is really altogether plain and simple. We believe that religion is an essential element of human life, and therefore of human education, and we establish and maintain schools in which we strive to put this belief into practice.

We do this as a matter of conscience, and without ulterior views. In this country, at least, Catholics claim and exercise a large freedom of opinion, and hence we are not surprised to find among them, men who have plans and schemes for the overcoming of whatever difficulties; but the church is not responsible for their views and does not commit itself to them. If here and there a compromise has been proposed with the purpose of getting support from the public moneys, or agitation for a system of denominational schools has been recommended, this has been done by individuals, who have never succeeded in gaining a numerous following. The Church has contented itself with urging the establishment and support of parish schools. Double taxation for education is, of course, a grievance; but the Catholics of the United States believe in free schools for all, and since the religious condition of the country is such that denominationalism could not be introduced into the State schools, without risk of ruin, they are willing to bear the burthen of a double school tax; and, with few exceptions, they have no desire to introduce this question into politics. What they have been doing with constantly increasing success, they are content to continue to do—to build and maintain their own schools.

Among the good results springing from the Catholic Exhibit, not the least, is the impression we have received of the extent and efficiency of our parish school system. We thence derive new zeal and confidence. The revelation of what we have done becomes a promise and a prophecy of what we shall do. We feel the work is great enough and holy enough to command our best efforts. We resolve to concentrate them upon the upbuilding of a system of more effective religious education, persuaded, that we thus most surely promote the interests both of the Church and the State. This is our task, and anything that might divert us from fulfilling it, is to be put aside as evil. We love our religion and our country well enough to be glad to make sacrifices for both.

Another result of the Exhibit is a better acquaintance of Catholic teachers with one another, and with the various methods of our schools. The bringing together the work of the different orders and of numberless individuals has been an objective lesson of real value. Our labor and expense would not have been in vain had we done nothing else than give to the members of our religious-teaching orders a unique opportunity to study the work of the Catholic Schools. Nothing in the World's Fair appeared to me more beautiful or more inspiring than the groups of Catholic sisters, to be seen at all times, in the booths of the Exhibit, wholly intent upon learning whatever there was to be learned. From that little space a spirit of enthusiasm, a desire for excellence, has been carried throughout the land, into the schoolrooms of a thousand cities and towns. Many a one who, in some remote village, felt lonely and half discouraged in what seemed to be unavailing work, became conscious of belonging to a great army of men and women who bring strength to souls and light to minds. The whole country, in fact, is indebted to us; for the zealous and energetic efforts of the managers of the Catholic Exhibit had not a little to do with the appropriation of the large sums of money and the allotment of the great space, devoted to educational matters, at the Columbian Exposition. Your report, my dear Brother, is a fitting memorial of a noble and fruitful work. Affectionately and sincerely yours,

PEORIA, July 19, 1894.   President of the Catholic Educational Exhibit.

CATHOLIC EDUCATION DAY.

All then rose and sang the Te Deum (Holy God, We Praise Thy Name), to an organ accompaniment by Mr. Harrison Wilde, after which the audience adjourned to visit the Catholic Educational Exhibit in the southeast gallery of the Manufactures and Liberal Arts Building.

On the stage were the following prelates, clergy and persons:

Mt. Rev. P. A. Feehan, Chicago.
Mt. Rev. P. J. Ryan, Philadelphia.
Mt. Rev. J. J. Hennessy, Dubuque.
Mt. Rev. F. J. Katzer, Milwaukee.
Rt. Rev. J. Lancaster Spalding, Bishop of Peoria and President Catholic Educational Exhibit.
Rt. Rev. M. J. Burke, St. Joseph, Mo.
Rt. Rev. J. Janssens, Belleville, Ill.
Rt. Rev. Silas Chatard, Vincennes.
Rt. Rev. Thos. Heslin, Natchez. Miss.
Rt. Rev. C. B. Maes, Covington, Ky.
Rev. Canon Bruchesi, Commissioner for the Province of Quebec, Catholic Educational Exhibit.
Rev. Father McGuire, Chicago, rector St. James' school.
Rev. Brother Maurelian, F. S. C., Secretary and Manager Catholic Educational Exhibit.
Rev. Bro. Paulian, F. S. C., president Christian Brothers' College, St. Louis, Mo.
Rev. Bro. Emery, F. S. C., Assistant Provincial Christian Brothers.
Rev. Bro. Felix, F. S. C., Vice-President Christian Brothers' College, St. Louis, Mo.
Rev. P. J. Muldoon, Chancellor of the archdiocese of Chicago.
Ex-Gov. Hoyt, of the Bureau of Awards.
Dr. S. H. Peabody, chief of Liberal Arts.
Hon. Morgan J. O'Brien, New York.
Hon. Thomas Gargan, Boston.
Hon. Jno. Hyde, Chicago.
Prof. J. E. Edwards, Notre Dame University.
John D. Crimmins, New York.
Rev. Andrew Morrissy, Pres. Notre Dame University, Notre Dame, Ind.
Gen. John Eaton.
Mrs. Isabella Beecher Hooker and Mrs. Mulligan, of the Board of Lady Managers.

A very large number of the Reverend Clergy, Brothers of Teaching Orders, and about 900 members of the various sisterhoods were in the Auditorium.

An effort was made to secure the names of all of the Reverend clergy present. The following names were obtained:

Rev. F. X. Antill, C. M., Chicago, Ill.
Rev. B. Baldi, O. S., Chicago, Ill.
Bro. Baldwin, F. S. C., Chicago, Ill.
Rev. J. A. Balthasard, Quebec, Can.
Rev. F. J. Barry.
Rev. M. E. Begley, Boston, Mass,
Rev. Alphonsus Bergeur, O. S. F. Quincy, Ill.
Rev. A. L. Bergeron, Chicago, Ill.
Rev. Alfred Belanger, C. S. V. Chicago, Ill.
Bro. Bernard Leimkuhler, Dayton, O.
Rev. Mariames Beyerle, O. S. B. Decatur, Ala.
Rev. P. J. McDonney.
Rev. C. A. McEvoy, O. S. B.
Rev. S. P. McDowell, Chicago, Ill.
Rev. Thos. McLaughlin, Whitehall, N. Y.
Rev. P. A. McLaughlin, Chicago, Ill.
Rev. Thos. McMillan, New Yor' N. Y.
Rev. D. J. McNamee, Aurora, Ill.
Rev. C. Mahe, Lake Providence, La.
Rev. Bede, Maler, O. S. B., St. Meinrad's Abbey, Ind.
Rev. Thos. F. Mangan, Joliet, Ill.
Bro. Max, Chicago, Ill.
Rev. M. Meagher.

Rev. P. L. Biermann, Chicago, Ill.
Rev. B. Biermann, Newport, Ky.
Rev. Francis Bobal, Chicago, Ill.
Rev. G. Boll, Crete, Neb.
Rev. J. B. Bourassa, Pullman, Ill.
Rev. J. A. M. Brosseau, Montreal, Can.
Rev. P. R. Bulfin, Chicago, Ill.
Rev. P. F. Burke, Philadelphia, Pa.
Rev. Edm. Byrnes.
Bro. Calixtus, F. S. C.
Rev. T. F. Galligan, Chicago, Ill.
Rev. Louis A. Campbell, Austin, Ill.
Rev. J. J. Carroll, Chicago, Ill.
Rev. J. P. Carroll, Dubuque, Ia.
Rev. J. J. Cassidy, Brooklyn, Ia.
Rev. J. F. Clancy, Woodstock, Ill.
Rev. P. A. Clancy.
Rev. N. Chartieu, Canada.
Rev. J. Chundelak, Omaha, Neb.
Rev. P. P. Cooney, C. S. C. Notre Dame, Ind.
Rev. M. J. Corbett, S. J., Chicago.
Rev. R. Coyle, Jamestown, N. Y.
Rev. M. T. Crane, Avoca, Pa.
Rev. H. Crevier, O. S., Chicago, Ill.
Rev. John H. Crowe,
Rev. Delisle, Quebec.
Rev. Dr. DeParadis, Coal City, Ill.
Rev. J. J. Denison, Chicago, Ill.
Rev. Jno. Dogherty, Norfolk, Va.
Bro. Domuan, F, S. C.
Rev. M. J. Dorney, Chicago, Ill.
Rev. N. Dreher, Chicago, Ill.
Rev. Thos. Drum, A. D.M., Mullinga, Ireland.
Rev. E. J. Dunn, Chicago, Ill.
Rev. J. F. Durin, W. De Pere, Wis.
Rev. C. J. Eckert, Chester, Ill.
Bro. Edward, F. S. C.
Rev. Jno. Egan, Belwood, Ill,
Bro. Fidelian, F. S. C., Chicago, Ill.
Rt. Rev. Mgr. Fetu, Quebec, Can.
Rev. Jno. S. Finn, Chicago, Ill.
Rev. Bro. Fink, Chicago, Ill.
Rev. P. Fischer, Chicago, Ill.
Rev. C. P. Foster, Joliet, Ill.
Rev. J. E. Foucher, C. S. V. Quebec, Can.
Rev. Cyrille Fournier, C. S. V.
Rev. T. J. A. Freeman, S. J., New York.
Rev. J. Friolo.
Rev. Jas. A. Gallagher, Clinton, Ia.
Rev. J. B. Galvin, Boston, Mass.
Rev. G. C. Gamache, Detroit, Mich.
Rev. J. Gernest, Southbridge.
Rev. Geo. Geigler, D. D. West Burlington, Iowa.
Rev. Jos. Glenon, Hyde Park.
Rev. Bro. Geo Meyer, S. M., Dayton O.
Rev. Jos. Molitor, Chicago, Ill.
Rev. N. J. Mooney, Chicago, Ill.
Rev. P. C. Moormann, Chicago, Ill.
Rev. E. M. Nattini, Council Bluffs, Ia.
Rev. Maximilian Neumann, O. S. F., Chicago, Ill.
Rev. P. Prokop Neuzil, O. S. B.
Rev. M. Nevin.
Louis E. Newell, S. J., Chicago, Ill.
Rev. Pius Niermann, O. S. F., Chicago, Ill.
Rev. P. Nolte, O. S. F., Chicago, Ill.
Rev. J. Van den Noort, Putnam, Conn.
Rev. A. Numicki, South Chicago, Ill.
Rev. M. J. O'Dwyer.
Rev. T. F. O'Gara, Wilmington.
Rev. Thos. O'Neil, S. J.
Rev. A. O'Neill, S. J., Chicago, Ill.
Rev. Jos. H. O'Niell, Philadelphia, Pa.
Rev. Denis T. O'Sullivan, Woodstock, Md.
Rev. M. O'Sullivan, Chicago, Ill.
Rev. W. J. Peil, Manitowoc, Wis.
Rev. H. Picherit, Vicksburg, Miss.
Bro. Pius, F. S. C., Chicago, Ill.
Rev. F. S. Plante, Minneapolis, Minn.
Rev. V. E. Richmond.
Rev. M. J. Regan, C. S. C.
Rev. P. H. Riley, Cambridgeport, Mass.
Rev. D. J. Riordan, Chicago, Ill.
Rev. E. V. Rivard, C. S. S., Bourbannais, Ill.
Rev. Ant. Rossbach, Cassville, Wis.
Rev. A. Rousseau.
Rev. Jos. Ruesing, West Point, Neb.
Rev. F. J. Saxer, Chicago, Ill.
Rev. J. M. Schafer, Chicago, Ill.
Rev. A. P. H. Schacken, Patterson, N. J.
Bro. Bernard Schub, Chicago, Ill.
Rev. Benj. Schmittdiel, Monroe, Mich.
Rev. Thos. Scully, Boston, Mass.
Rev. Jos. Selinger, D. D.
Rev. Jas. Sheil.
Rev. T. E. Shields, St. Paul, Minn.
Rev. A. Snigurski, Chicago, Ill.
Rev. J. R. Slatterly. Baltimore, Md.
Rev. E. M. Smith, Chicago, Ill.
Rev. Anthony B.Stuber,Cleveland,O.
Rev. J. J. Sullivan, California.
Rev. A. J. Thiele.
Rev. D. A. Tighe, Chicago.

Rev. J. J. Gormully, Renovo, Pa.
Rev. F. E. Hannigan, New York.
Rev. J. A. Hamel.
Rev. Wm. Hein, O. S. B. Chicago, Ill.
Bro. Geo. Heintz.
Rev. G. D. Heldmann, Chicago, Ill.
Bro. Henry, S. M. Chicago, Ill.
Rev. W. S. Hennessy, Chicago, Ill.
Rev. N. J. Hitchcock, Chicago, Ill.
Rev. M. J. Hoban, Scranton, Pa.
Rev. J. E. Hogan, Harvard, Ill.
Rev. P. N. Jaegar O. S. B.
Rev. Alex. Jacovits, Greek Priest, Streator, Ill.
Bro. John, S. M.
Bro Joseph, F. S. C.
Bro. Julius, F. S. C.
Bro. Justinian, Chicago, Ill.
Bro. Albert Kaiser, Chicago, Ill.
Bro. John Kautz.
Rev. H. B. Kelley, Marengo, Ill.
Rev. Chas. S. Kemper, Nat'l Military Home, Ohio.
Rev. John F. Kemper, Adair, Ia.
Rev. W. Kockuik, O. S B. Chicago, Ill.
Bro. Chas. Koetzner, Chicago, Ill.
Bro. Jos. A Kress, Chicago, Ill.
Rev. A. La Chance.
Rev. D. I. Lanslot, O. S. B. Pawhuska, O. T.
Rev. D. J. Larkin, Dayton, Tenn,
Bro. Jos. Lattner, Chicago, Ill.
Rev. Bro. Leo, F. S. C., Feehanville, Ill.
Rev. J. S. La Sage, Brighton Park, Ill.
Rev. M. J. Lochemes, St. Francis, Wis.
Rev. M. Tatu, Quebec, Can.
Rev. August Tolton, Chicago, Ill.
Rev. B. Torka, O. S. F., Harbor Springs, Mich.
Rev. F. J. Van Antwerp, Detroit, Mich.
Rev. H. G. Van Pelt., Chicago, Ill.
Rev. E. J, Vattermann, Ft. Sheridan, Ill., (U. S. Army).
Rev. Dominic Wagner, St. Joseph, Mo.
Rev. John A. Waldron, Dayton, O.
Rev. J. T. Walsh, Stanford, Conn.
Bro. Mart. Werheburg, Chicago, Ill.
Bro. Willebrord, O. S. B., Muscogee, Ind. Ty.
Rev. J. H. O'Neil, Philadelphia.
Rev. J. B. Galvin, Boston.
Rev. J. Chundelak, Omaha, Neb.
Rev. J. P. Carroll, Dubuque, Ia.
Rev. J. A. Balshsard, Quebec, Can.
Rev. J. E, Foucher, Quebec, Can.
Rev. V. Chartier, Quebec, Can.
Rev. John T. Walsh, Stamford, Conn.
Rev. D. F. Dunn, Depere, Wis.
Bro. Abban, F. S. C.
Bro. Adjutor, F. S. C., Chicago.
Bro. Adjutor, F. S. C., New York.
Bro. Ambrose, F. S. C., Chicago.
Bro. Andrew, F. S, C., Chicago.
Bro. August, Chicago.
Bro. Quintinian, New York.
Rev. J. McCarthy.
Rev. Canon McCarthy, Ottawa, Can.
Rev. C. McCarthy, Cahvicireen, Ireland.
Rev. R. F. Sylvester, O. S. F., Superior, Wis.

The train conveying His Eminence Cardinal Gibbons, Bishop Phelan, of Pittsburgh, and other distinguished prelates, arrived too late to enable them to attend the exercises, very much to their regret.

Very many letters were received, explaining that previous engagements would prevent their arriving in Chicago in time for the exercises, and expressing regret at being unable to attend. Among those whose letters are on file are the following:

Mt. Rev. P. W. Riordan, D.D., archbishop of San Francisco.
Mt. Rev. J. B. Saltpointe, D.D., archbishop of Santa Fe, N. M.
Rt. Rev. Henry Joseph Richter, D.D., bishop of Grand Rapids.
Rt. Rev. Wm. Geo. McCloskey, D.D., bishop of Louisville.
Rt. Rev. Denis M. Bradley, D.D., bishop of Manchester.
Rt. Rev. John Phelan, D.D., bishop of Pittsburg.
Rt. Rev. Stephen Vincent Ryan, C.M., D.D., bishop of Buffalo.
Rt. Rev. J. O'Sullivan, D.D., bishop of Mobile.
Rt. Rev. James Augustine Healy, D.D., bishop of Portland.
Rt. Rev. Ignatius Frederick Horstman, D.D., bishop of Cleveland.

Mt. Rev. John Joseph Williams, D.D., archbishop of Boston.
Mt. Rev. Francis Janssens, D.D., archbishop of New Orleans.
Rt. Rev. John J. Kain, D.D., coadjutor archbishop of St. Louis.
Mt. Rev. Michael A. Corrigan, D.D., archbishop of New York.
Rt. Rev. Henry Cosgrove, D.D., bishop of Davenport.
Rt. Rev. Theophile Meerschaer, D.D., vicar apostolic of Indian Ty.
Rt. Rev. Henry Gabriel, D.D., bishop of Ogdensburg, N. Y.
Rt. Rev. Joseph Rademacher, D.D., bishop of Nashville.
Rt. Rev. M. F. Burke, D.D., bishop of St. Joseph.
Rt. Rev. Richard Scannell, D.D., bishop of Omaha.
Rt. Rev. James Ryan, D.D., bishop of Alton.
Bro. Justin, New York.
Rt. Rev. Thos. D. Beaven, D.D., bishop of Springfield.

From Canada:
Cardinal Tachereau, archbishop of Quebec.
Mt. Rev. L. M. Begin, archishop of Cyrene.
Mt. Rev. C. E. Fabre, archbishop of Montreal.
Mt. Rev. J. T. Duhamel, archbishop of Ottawa.
Rt. Rev. L. C. Morean, bishop of Hyacinthe.
Rt. Rev. Max Decelle, bishop of Druzipora.
Rt. Rev. A. A. Bloris, bishop of St. Germain de Rimouski.
Rt. Rev. L. F. Laflache, bishop of Three Rivers.
Hon. L. P. Petterer, secy. Province of Quebec.
Mgr. E. U. Archambault, Montreal.
Abbe Roulian, Quebec.

Vicar-General F. Bourgeault, Montreal, and other Rev. Clergy sent letters of regret, that they were unable to attend and of expressed assurance of full sympathy with the great cause of Catholic education.

Many prelates and clergy called at the Catholic Educational Exhibit and expressed regret that they had not been able to attend.

PRESS NOTICES.

EDUCATION DAY AND THE CONGRESS.

THE NEW WORLD this week devotes a large amount of its space to reports of the two great Catholic events of this and last week, Catholic Education day and the Catholic Columbian Congress. We regret that we cannot devote more space to them than is at our disposal. Catholic Education Day was celebrated on last Saturday, and the Catholic Congress opened on Monday of this week. There has already been one Catholic Congress in the United States—the present one is the second. But Catholic Education Day was never before celebrated in the United States—nor in any other country. It would be impossible this year but for the existence of the Catholic Educational Exhibit, and this exhibit would be impossible but for the World's Fair. No one can tell when a World's Fair will again be held in the United States, but Catholic Congresses may be held as often as our Catholic people determine to have them.

This will explain the priority and preference we give to the report of Catholic Education Day in this issue of THE NEW WORLD. But another and stronger reason justified us, which is this: Catholic Education Day was the celebration of the success—may we not say triumph?—of Catholic education in the United States. It was the celebration of the triumph of our Catholic schools, and by our Catholic schools we mean every one of our Catholic educational institutions, from the kindergarten to the university. It is by our Catholic schools, Catholic congresses are made possible. Without our Catholic schools there could not be a Catholic congress in the United States. Our people would be so uneducated, so ignorant, that they could not conceive of a Catholic congress, or they would be so indifferent to the needs of the Church in our country, so de-Catholicized, let us say, that they would never think of holding a Catholic congress.

The Catholic Congress that is now in session in Chicago is the result, the consequence, the fruit of Catholic education. The men who conceived it and the men who are now directing it, as well as those who compose it, are men who, all of them are imbued with the spirit of Catholic education; and many, if not most of them, received in Catholic parochial schools, colleges and universities the talents, the abilities and the spiritual force which they display in this great Catholic Congress.

We devote to reports of the Catholic Congress as much space as possible this week, and we hope to devote to it much more next week. But we make the statement candidly, that, notwithstanding its great importance, we would exclude every line of it from our columns this week, were it necessary to do so in order to make room for the report of Catholic Education Day. The proceedings of last Saturday within the grounds of the World's Columbian Exposition, in the presence of more than eight thousand of the Catholic *elite* of the United States, was the greatest, the most imposing and impressive manifestation of the love of American Catholics for education that this country has ever seen. And besides this, it was a declaration, in the presence and hearing of our non-Catholic fellow-citizens, that the Catholics of the United States demand Christian education, and that, regardless of cost to them, they will have no other education, except when forced by circumstances of direct necessity.

What stores of strength and spirits the teachers of our Catholic schools took home with them from Festival Hall last Saturday cannot be measured, even by themselves. How the hearts of the pastors must have been cheered, and how their determination to do more and more for the Christian education of our children must have been strengthened by the glorious manifestation they witnessed of the determination of the Catholic laity of the United States to be loyal to the principle of religion in education!—*Editorial New World, Chicago.*

An Authoritative Expression.

The Parliament of Religions was prefaced yesterday with Catholic Education Day. The hierarchy of the Roman Catholic Church presided in Festival Hall over an imposing scene, the audience comprising large numbers of the teaching communities, men and women, of that church, assembled in public and in common with the laity for, undoubtedly, the first time in the long history of the creed to which they belong. The speakers were Archbishop Feehan, of Chicago; Archbishop Hennessy, of Dubuque; Archbishop Ryan, of Philadelphia; Bishop Spalding, of Peoria, and two eminent laymen, Morgan J. O'Brien, of the Supreme Court of New York, and a gallant soldier and polished advocate of Boston, Thomas J. Gargan.

It will not be contended that the concurrent speech of these hierarchs and laymen is lacking in any note to make it absolutely authoritative on the attitude of their Church on any questions in which Americans or the times are concerned. It was inevitable that the occasion should voice the determination of the hierarchy on the school question; and, judging by the enthusiasm and applause of the audience, the laity are in indivisible accord with their leaders. There was but one strain directed toward the public schools of the country—one of kindness; and only one concerning the parochial schools of the Catholic communion—that of invincible resolution to maintain them in their present complete detachment.

There was frank affirmance of indefinite content to pay the double taxation now borne; but by neither reserve nor intimation was it indicated that any portion of State money would ever be sought to help perpetuate the separate school system. All the speeches and the music were rife with ardent devotion to American institutions.

The oratory, as might have been expected, was characterized by breadth of learning and embellished with the graces of culture.

—*Editorial Chicago Herald, September* 3, 1893.

At the conclusion of the formal ceremony an invitation will be extended to all present to go to the exhibit in the Manufactures Bulding. It is located in the east gallery and takes up half of the entire section on the west side of the great floor. Here Brother Maruelian and a committee appointed for the purpose will receive the visitors and take them through the display, explaining the various methods of instruction and school work exhibited. The specimens of work done by the children to be seen in this department are worthy of particular notice. If the visitors manage to get through the exhibit in the half day that is left them after the ceremony they will have done better than any one has yet been able to do and they will secure a fund of information that will give them food for thought for a long time to come. Plans are being made for the entertainment of the educators and churchmen on the grounds in the evening, and it is probable many of them will remain for the night attractions on the grounds. —*Chicago Evening Post, Sept. 1, 1893.*

No more notable gathering of the priesthood ever faced a speaker than that which Archbishop Feehan saw when he arose to greet the audience at nine o'clock. Festival Hall was crowded with Catholic clergy and laymen, and in the center were several hundred sweet-faced sisters of charity.—*Chicago Herald.*

Speaking of Bishop Spalding's remarks the Chicago *Herald* writes: As the Bishop thundered forth these impassioned sentences the mighty audience rose to its feet and cheered to the echo. The speaker checked himself as the demonstration began, and when the applause died away he declared that he had not intended to make a speech, and abruptly retired to his seat. The remarks and the demonstration they elicited were a fitting climax to a memorable day.

Archbishop Corrigan in referring to the Catholic Educational Exhibit said: What do we find in that educational exhibit? I trust you have all made a special business to examine the magnificent display of our schools and academies in the World's Fair. That exhibit speaks volumes of itself for the self-sacrifice and enthusiastic devotion of the teachers of our Catholic faith, of our sisters, of our brothers, who have toiled day after day to accomplish such results, and all this without State aid, in the midst of many difficulties, sowing in tears that they might reap in joy. The results speak for themselves. [Cheers.] St. John, in one of his homilies, said: "Great, indeed, is the power of the painter, wonderful the profession of the sculptor, of those who make the picture canvas breathe, and the marble instilled with the glow of life; and yet nobler far is he who, from unformed materials, fashions and models the soul to lineaments of virtue." And this is what is being done all our country over by our teachers. [Applause.]—*Chicago Herald.*

The Catholic Educational Exhibit in the Liberal Arts Building is very extensive. The drawing from casts and the plaster bas-relief work in many of the booths are excellent. The example of illuminated text work shown in the California section, the work of the pupils and teachers of the Convent of the Sacred Heart, is exquisite, and excels any work of the same character exhibited in the Columbian Exposition. The system of map drawing continues to be taught in all Catholic schools; the specimens displayed are well drawn and colored with pretty effect. The profile maps, the work of young children, are most interesting. The lingerie from the various convents is undoubtedly the best at the Fair.—*Art Critic in Chicago Herald.*

CATHOLIC EDUCATION DAY.

The committee charged with the arrangements of Catholic Education Day, in connection with the Columbian Exposition, which is fixed for September 2, could hardly have chosen two more qualified speakers for the subjects they are to present, than Abp. Ryan, who is to speak on "The Vocation of the Christian Educator," and Abp. Hennessy, whose theme is "The Catholic View of Education."

Both of these distinguished divines have a national, aye, more than a national reputation for eloquence; and what is more to the purpose, both have proven themselves staunch friends of Catholic education and parochial schools. The pages of the current *American Catholic Quarterly* bear testimony, in addition to the many previous similar evidences he has given of the high regard in which the Philadelphia prelate holds the Catholic school and the Catholic teacher; and what better proof of Archbishop Hennessy's qualifications to present the Catholic view of education can be asked than is contained in the simple fact that since he assumed charge of the Dubuque diocese its parochial schools have increased in number from two to one hundred!

The committee in charge of this Catholic Education Day have also done well in providing for addresses which shall show how the Catholic idea of education has benefitted and is still benefitting this country, by imparting to so large an element of the rising generation moral as well as intellectual instruction, and by imbuing them with a patriotic love of their land and its noble institutions. Such addresses cannot fail to remove many of the prejudices with which a certain class of non-Catholics regard the parochial schools, and to effectively silence the slanderous statements sedulously circulated about those institutions by the A. P. A. calumniators.—*Catholic Columbian, Sept. 2, '93.*

CONCLUSION.

In conclusion, I wish to express heartfelt thanks for the generous aid and co-operation by which I have been enabled to carry out the difficult work assigned me.

To you, my very dear Bishop, I am profoundly grateful for your kind, prudent, and wise direction in all matters relating to the Catholic Educational Exhibits.

I also offer sincere thanks to the Most Reverend and Right Reverend Prelates, the Reverend Clergy, the Religious Teaching Orders, the Officials of the World's Columbian Exposition and National Commission, the Laity, the Press, and all the Catholic Institutions of Learning who have in any way contributed to the success of the Exhibits.

I have always regarded it a very high privilege to serve the cause of Christian education.

Asking your blessing, I remain,
Very sincerely and gratefully,

Brother Maurelian

Secretary and Manager, Catholic Educational Exhibit.

VOL. I.
INDEX CATHOLIC CONGRESS.

PAGE.

Imprimatur, Archbishop Feehan	
Preface, Rev. P. J. Muldoon	1
Letters of Indorsements	5
List of Bishops, etc.	5
Hon. C. C. Bonney's Letter	6
Contents—Catholic Congresses	7
Contents—Education Day	8
Opening of the Catholic Congresses	9
Sermon of Welcome by Chancellor Muldoon	10
Inauguration of Proceedings by Hon. W. J. Onahan, Sec.	13
Address of Welcome by Archbishop Feehan	13
Official Welcome, Hon. C. C. Bonney	14
Cardinal Gibbons' Address	15
Pope Leo's Greeting and Blessing	17
Temporary Organization of the Congress	17
Chairman O'Brien's Address	17
Archbishop Redwood's Address	19
Cardinal Vaughan's Message	20
Dr. R. A. Clarke's Address	21
Miss Mary J. Onahan's Address	28
Mr. E. H. Gan's Address	33
Archbishop P. J. Ryan's Address	39
List of Committees	41
Bishop Watterson's Address	42
Mgr. Satolli's Address	44
"Labor and Capital"—Hon. E. O. Browne	46
"Labor Problem"—Hon. John Gibbons' Address	52
"Catholic Missionary Work"—Rev. Walter Elliott, C. S. P.	55
"Discovery of the New World"—Geo. Parsons Lathrop	61
Archbishop Corrigan's Address	66
Archbishop Corrigan's Thanks	67
"Woman's Work in Religious Communities"—F. M. Euselas	69
"The Catholic Church and Charity"—Archbishop Ireland	74
"The Church and the Republic"—Rev. Patrick Cronin	75
"The Drink Evil"—Rev. James M. Cleary	76
Bishop Burke's Address	78
"Woman's Work in Art," Eliza Allen Starr	79
"Woman and Mammon"—Mrs. Rose Hawthorne Lathrop	83
"Woman in Literature"—Miss Eleanor C. Donnelly	83
"The Work of St. Vincent de Paul"—Jos. A. Kernan	88
"The Indian in This Republic"—Bishop McGolrick	91
"Catholic Higher Education"—Bishop Keane	95
"Catholic Educational Exhibit"—Brother Ambrose	99
"Catholic Organization"—H. L. Spannhorst	101
"The Needs of Catholic Colleges"—Dr. Maurice Francis Egan	103
"The Catholic Summer School"—Katharine E. Conway	106
"Catholic High Schools"—Rev. Jno. T. Murphy, C. S. S.	111
"Young Men's Societies"—Warren E. Mosher	114

INDEX CONTINUED.

	PAGE
"Workingmen's Organizations"—Rev. Francis J. Maguire	117
"Our Catholic School System"—Brother Azarias	120
"Future of the Negro Race"—Chas. H. Butler	122
"Catholic Truth Society of America"—Wm. F. Markoe	125
"Public and Private Charities"—Richard R. Elliott	127
"Pauperism"—Thos. Dwight	130
"Pope Leo XIII. on Labor"—H. C. Semple	134
"Immigration and Colonization"—Dr. Augustus Kaiser	138
Rev. M. Callaghan on Immigration	140
"Independence of the Holy See"—Martin F. Morris	144
"Trade Combinations and Strikes"—Robert M. Douglas	150
"The Negro Race"—Rev. Jno. R. Slattery	153
"Prayer for America"—Rev. F. G. Lentz	159
"Catholic Association of the United States"—Frank J. Sheridan	162
"Women of the Middle Ages"—Anna T. Sadlier	164
"The Insurance Feature Preferable to Pension Funds"—J. P. Lauth	168
"Life Insurance and Pension Fund for Wage-Workers"—E. M. Sharon	172
"Italian Immigration and Colonization"—Rev. Jos. L. Andreis	176
"Pauperism; the Cause and the Remedy"—M. J. Elder	179
"Alumnæ Associations in Convent Schools"—Elizabeth A. Cronyn	183
"Civil Government and the Catholic Citizen"—Walter Geo. Smith	185
"Duties of Capital"—Rev. Dr. Wm. Barry	189
"Public and Private Charities"—Dr. Chas. A. Wingerton	191
"Public and Private Charities"—Thos. F. Ring	196
Resolutions of the Congress	198
Cardinal Gibbons' Closing Address	202

VOL. II.
INDEX CATHOLIC EDUCATION DAY.

Title Page	1
Letter from Pope Leo XIII	2
Catholic Education—Order of Exercises	3
Archbishop Feehan's Address	3
Dr. Selim H. Peabody's Address	5
Archbishop Hennessy's Address	6
Archbishop Ryan's Address	16
Hon. Morgan J. O'Brien's Address	21
"Catholicity and Patriotism"—Hon. Thos. J. Gargan	28
Bishop Spalding's Address	32
Mrs. Elizabeth Hooker's Address	33
Bishop Spalding's Plea for Pure Morals at World's Fair	34
Bishop Spalding's Protest Against Exhibiting Indecent Pictures	37
Columbian Library of Catholic Authors	38
Appreciation of Exhibits	39
Letter from Director-General Geo. R. Davis	39
Letter from Rt. Rev. J. L. Spalding	40
Visitors on Catholic Education Day	42
Press Notes on Education Day	45
An Authoritative Expression	46
Letter Expressing Thanks by Brother Maurelian	47

www.ingramcontent.com/pod-product-compliance
Lightning Source LLC
Chambersburg PA
CBHW031343230426
43670CB00006B/422